FOXTROTIUS MAXIMUS

Other FoxTrot Books by Bill Amend

FoxTrot
Pass the Loot
Black Bart Says Draw
Eight Yards, Down and Out
Bury My Heart at Fun-Fun Mountain
Say Hello to Cactus Flats
May the Force Be with Us, Please
Take Us to Your Mall
The Return of the Lone Iguana
At Least This Place Sells T-shirts
Come Closer, Roger, There's a Mosquito on Your Nose
Welcome to Jasorassic Park
I'm Flying, Jack . . . I Mean, Roger
Think iFruity
Death by Field Trip
Encyclopedias Brown and White
His Code Name Was The Fox
Your Momma Thinks Square Roots Are Vegetables
Who's Up for Some Bonding?
Am I a Mutant or What!

Anthologies

FoxTrot: The Works
FoxTrot *en masse*
Enormously FoxTrot
Wildly FoxTrot
FoxTrot Beyond a Doubt
Camp FoxTrot
Assorted FoxTrot
FoxTrot: Assembled with Care

FOXTROTIUS MAXIMUS

BY
BILL AMEND

**Andrews McMeel
Publishing**

Kansas City

04 05 06 07 08 BAM 10 9 8 7 6 5 4 3 2 1

ISBN: 0-7407-4661-8

Library of Congress Control Number: 2004105599

──────── **ATTENTION: SCHOOLS AND BUSINESSES** ────────

Andrews McMeel books are available at quantity discounts with bulk purchase for educational, business, or sales promotional use. For information, please write to: Special Sales Department, Andrews McMeel Publishing, 4520 Main Street, Kansas City, Missouri 64111.

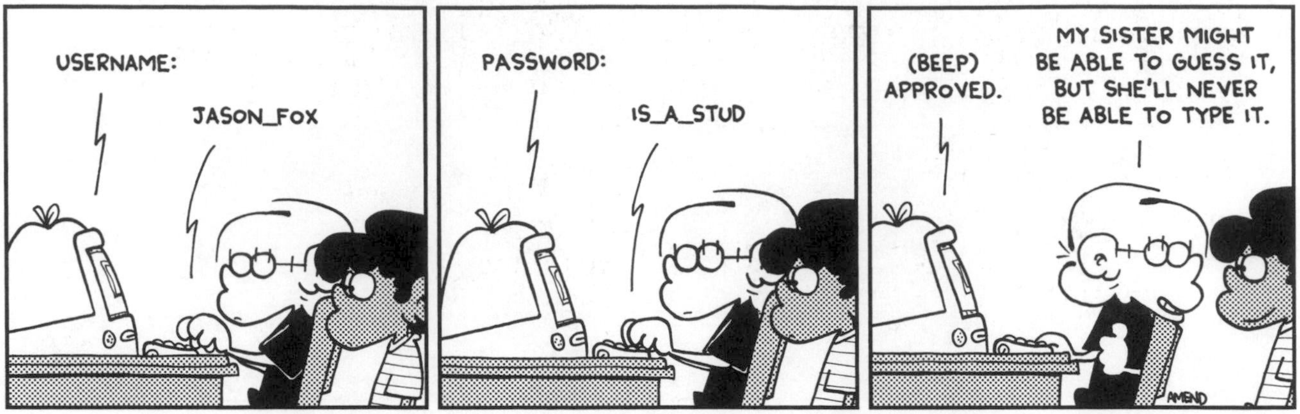
USERNAME:
JASON_FOX
PASSWORD:
IS_A_STUD
(BEEP) APPROVED.
MY SISTER MIGHT BE ABLE TO GUESS IT, BUT SHE'LL NEVER BE ABLE TO TYPE IT.
AMEND

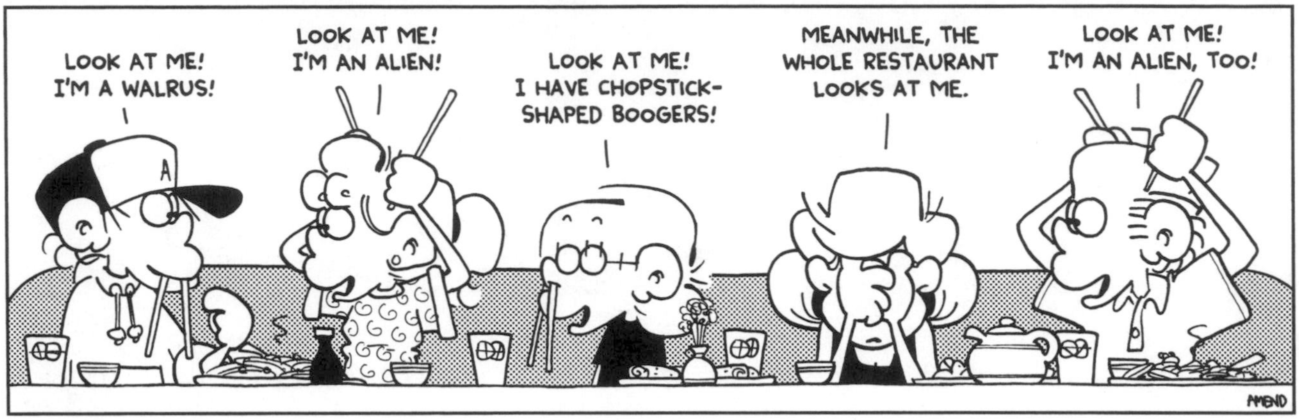
LOOK AT ME! I'M A WALRUS!
LOOK AT ME! I'M AN ALIEN!
LOOK AT ME! I HAVE CHOPSTICK-SHAPED BOOGERS!
MEANWHILE, THE WHOLE RESTAURANT LOOKS AT ME.
LOOK AT ME! I'M AN ALIEN, TOO!
AMEND

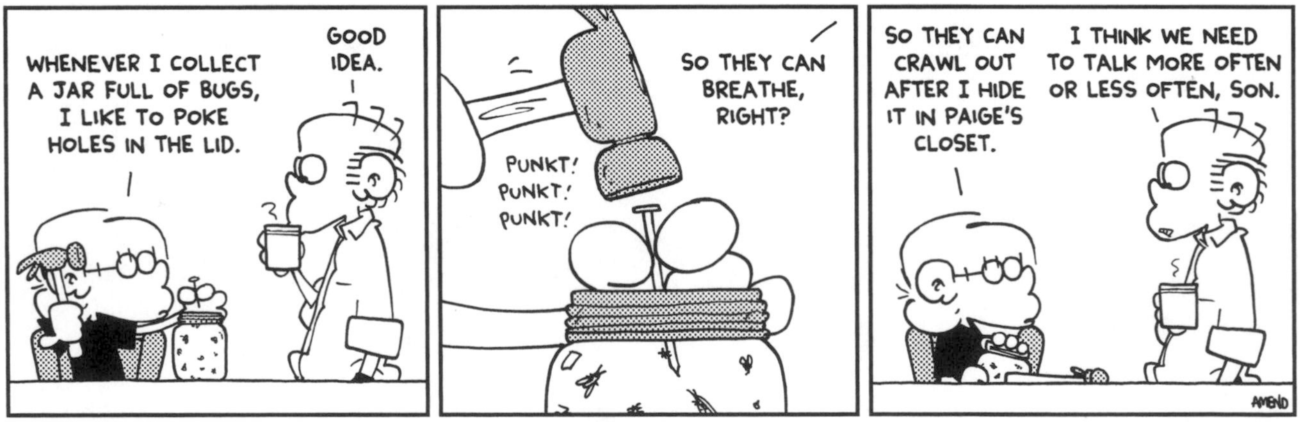
WHENEVER I COLLECT A JAR FULL OF BUGS, I LIKE TO POKE HOLES IN THE LID.
GOOD IDEA.
PUNKT! PUNKT! PUNKT!
SO THEY CAN BREATHE, RIGHT?
SO THEY CAN CRAWL OUT AFTER I HIDE IT IN PAIGE'S CLOSET.
I THINK WE NEED TO TALK MORE OFTEN OR LESS OFTEN, SON.
AMEND

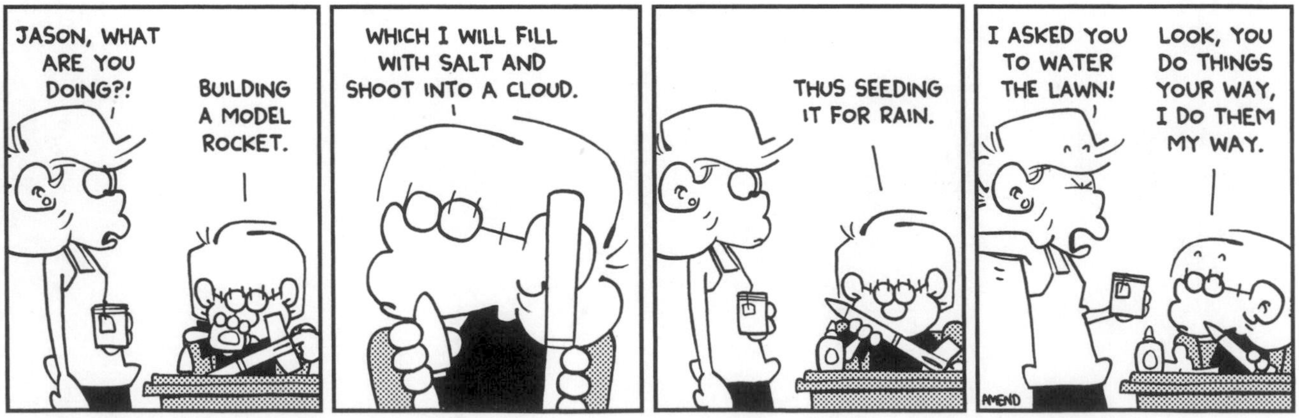
JASON, WHAT ARE YOU DOING?!
BUILDING A MODEL ROCKET.
WHICH I WILL FILL WITH SALT AND SHOOT INTO A CLOUD.
THUS SEEDING IT FOR RAIN.
I ASKED YOU TO WATER THE LAWN!
LOOK, YOU DO THINGS YOUR WAY, I DO THEM MY WAY.
AMEND

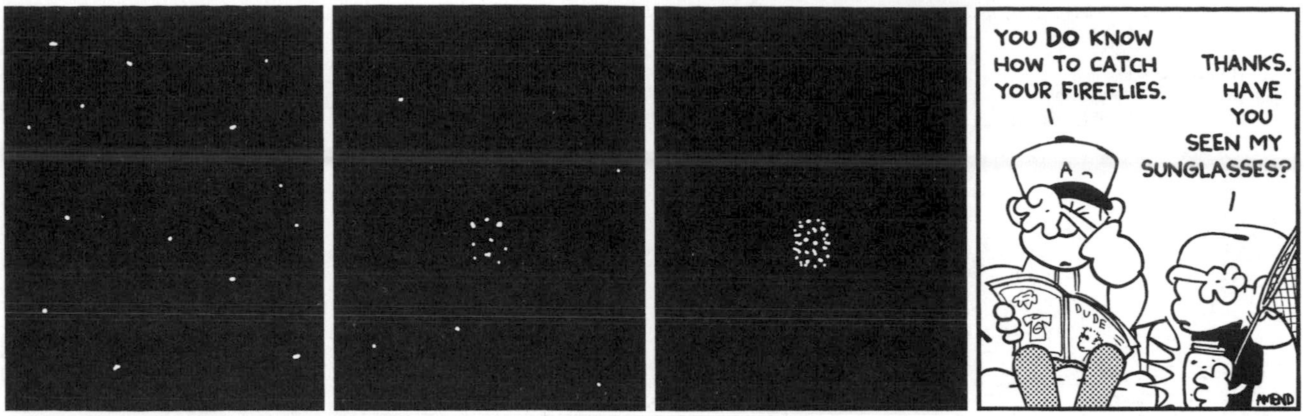
YOU **DO** KNOW HOW TO CATCH YOUR FIREFLIES.
THANKS. HAVE YOU SEEN MY SUNGLASSES?
DUDE
AMEND

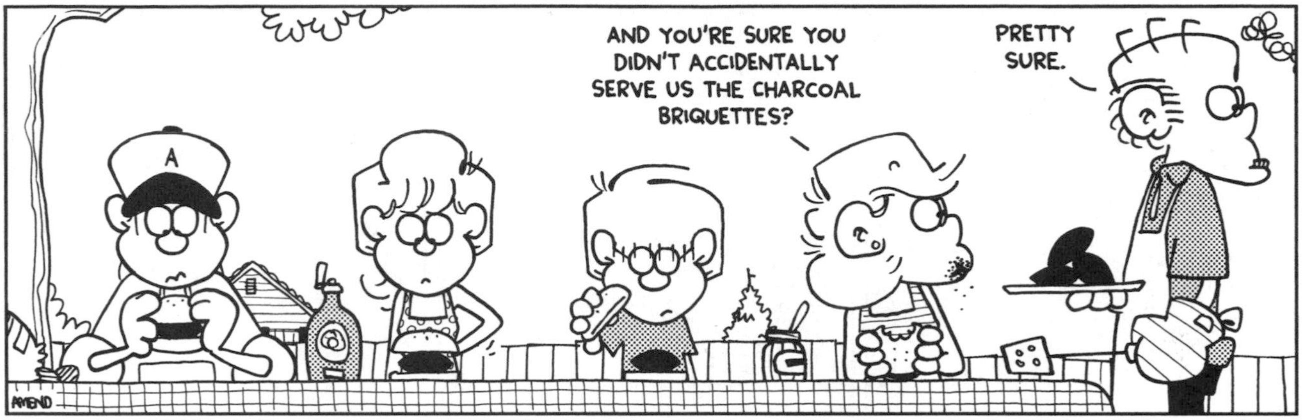
AND YOU'RE SURE YOU DIDN'T ACCIDENTALLY SERVE US THE CHARCOAL BRIQUETTES?
PRETTY SURE.
AMEND

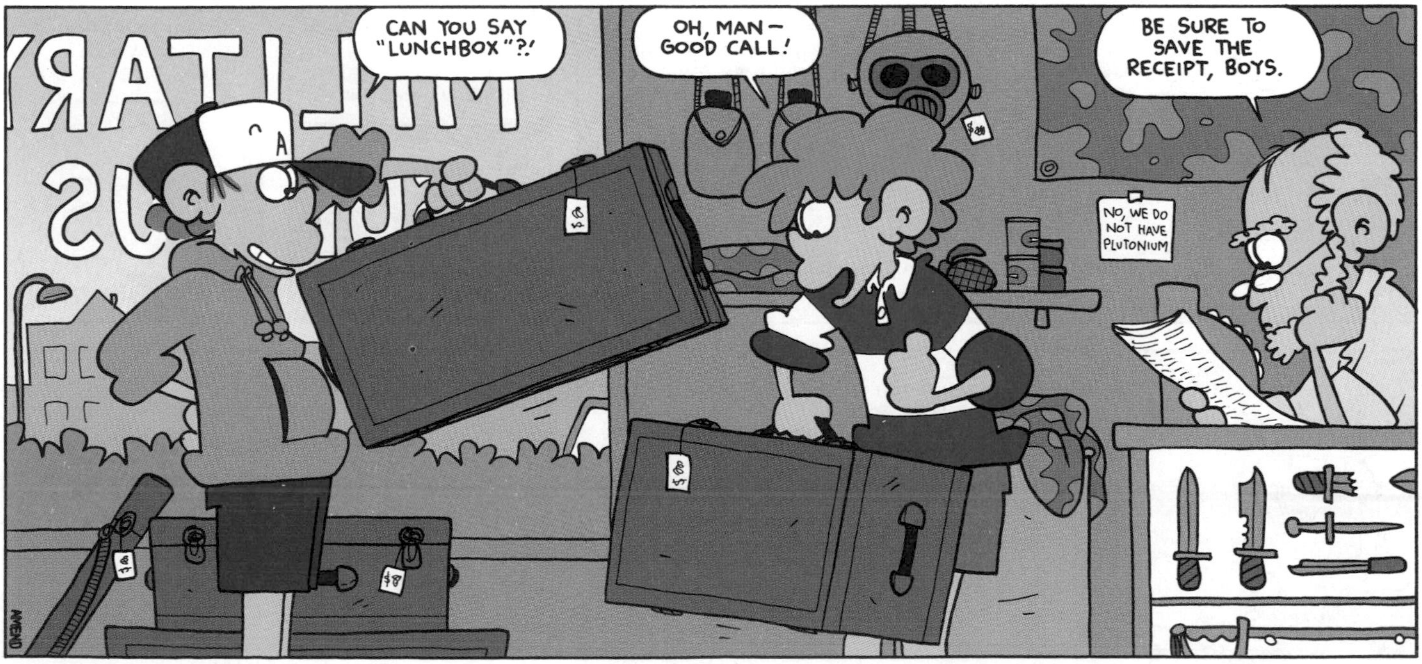
CAN YOU SAY "LUNCHBOX"?!
OH, MAN— GOOD CALL!
BE SURE TO SAVE THE RECEIPT, BOYS.
NO, WE DO NOT HAVE PLUTONIUM
AMEND

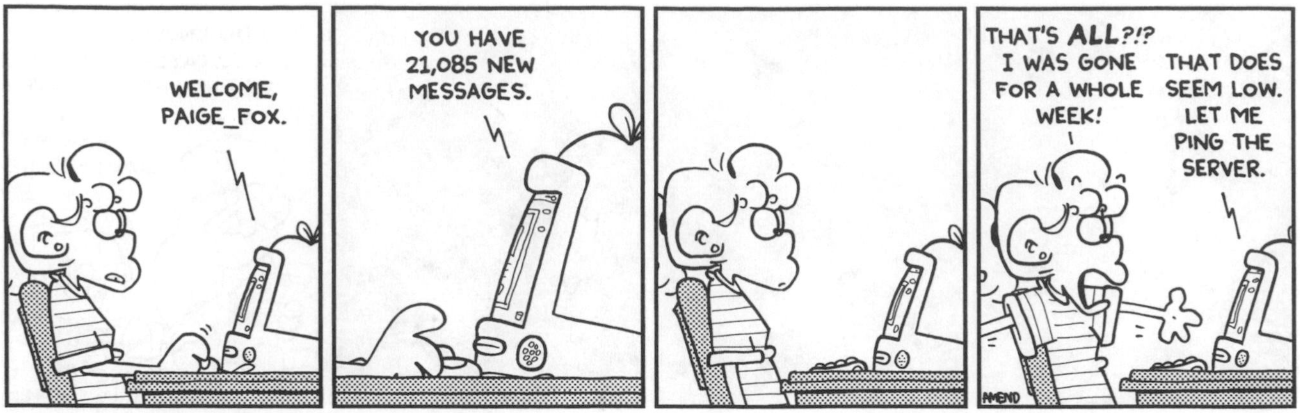
WELCOME, PAIGE_FOX.
YOU HAVE 21,085 NEW MESSAGES.
THAT'S **ALL**?!? I WAS GONE FOR A WHOLE WEEK!
THAT DOES SEEM LOW. LET ME PING THE SERVER.
AMEND

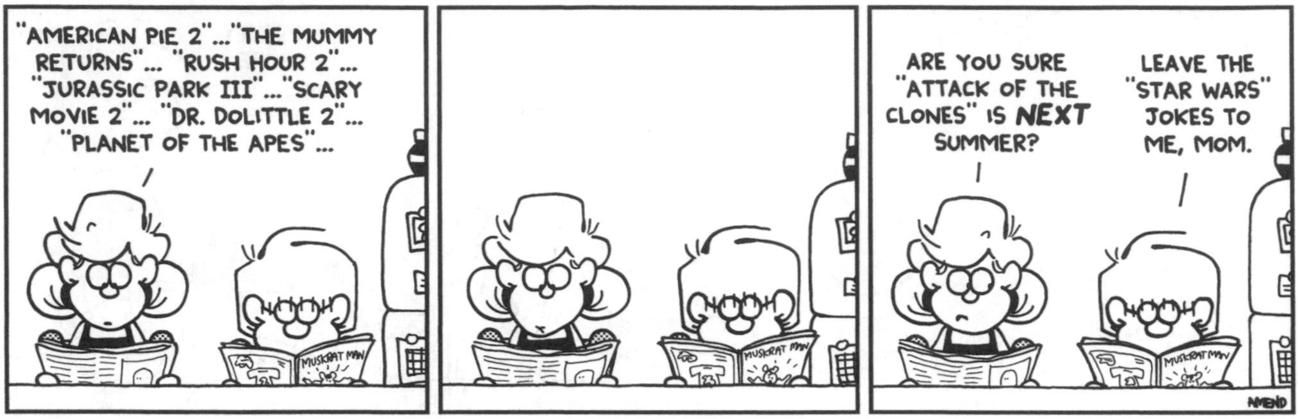
"AMERICAN PIE 2"..."THE MUMMY RETURNS"... "RUSH HOUR 2"... "JURASSIC PARK III"..."SCARY MOVIE 2"... "DR. DOLITTLE 2"... "PLANET OF THE APES"...
ARE YOU SURE "ATTACK OF THE CLONES" IS **NEXT** SUMMER?
LEAVE THE "STAR WARS" JOKES TO ME, MOM.
AMEND

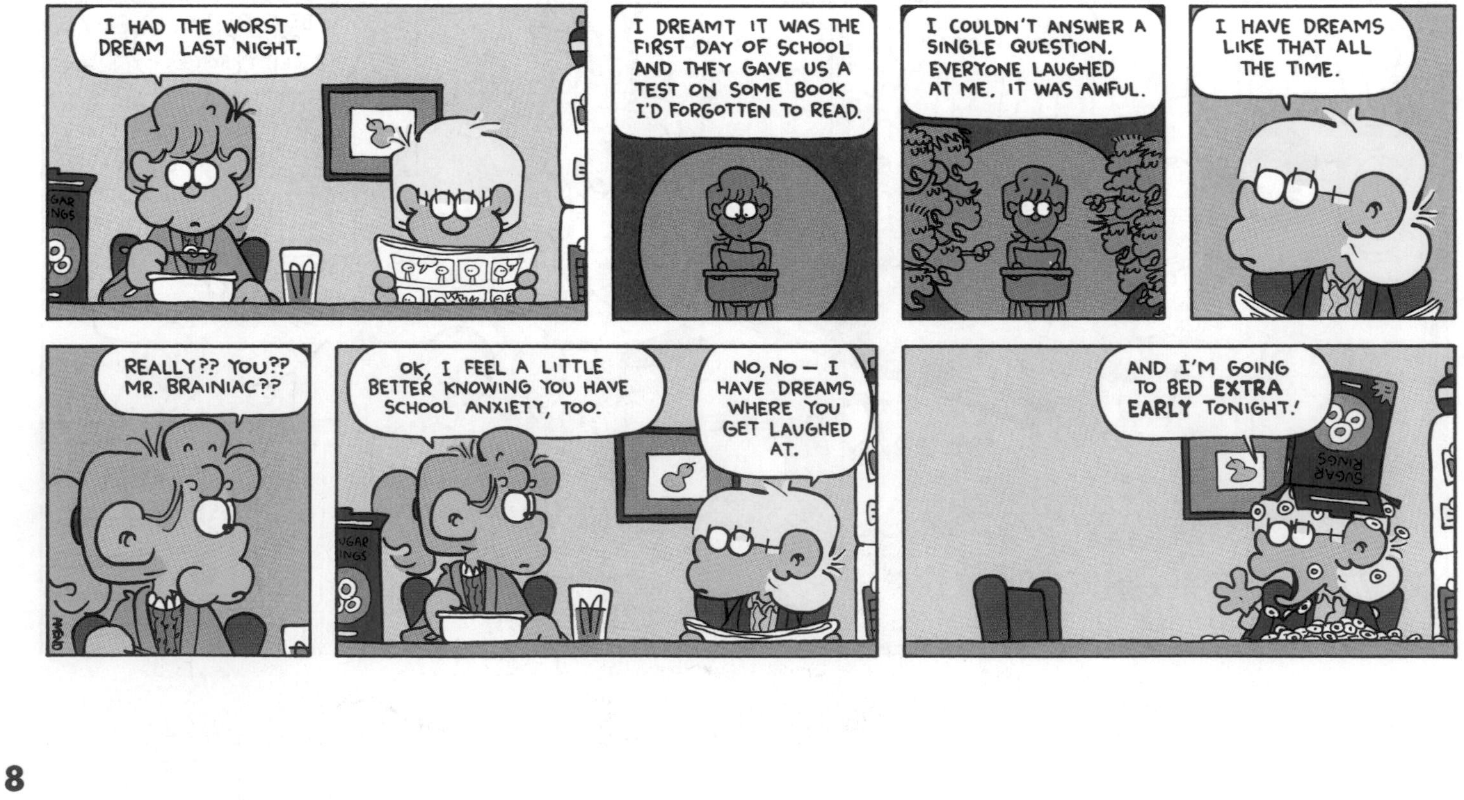
I HAD THE WORST DREAM LAST NIGHT.
I DREAMT IT WAS THE FIRST DAY OF SCHOOL AND THEY GAVE US A TEST ON SOME BOOK I'D FORGOTTEN TO READ.
I COULDN'T ANSWER A SINGLE QUESTION. EVERYONE LAUGHED AT ME. IT WAS AWFUL.
I HAVE DREAMS LIKE THAT ALL THE TIME.
REALLY?? YOU?? MR. BRAINIAC??
OK, I FEEL A LITTLE BETTER KNOWING YOU HAVE SCHOOL ANXIETY, TOO.
NO, NO — I HAVE DREAMS WHERE YOU GET LAUGHED AT.
AND I'M GOING TO BED **EXTRA EARLY** TONIGHT!
SUGAR RINGS
AMEND

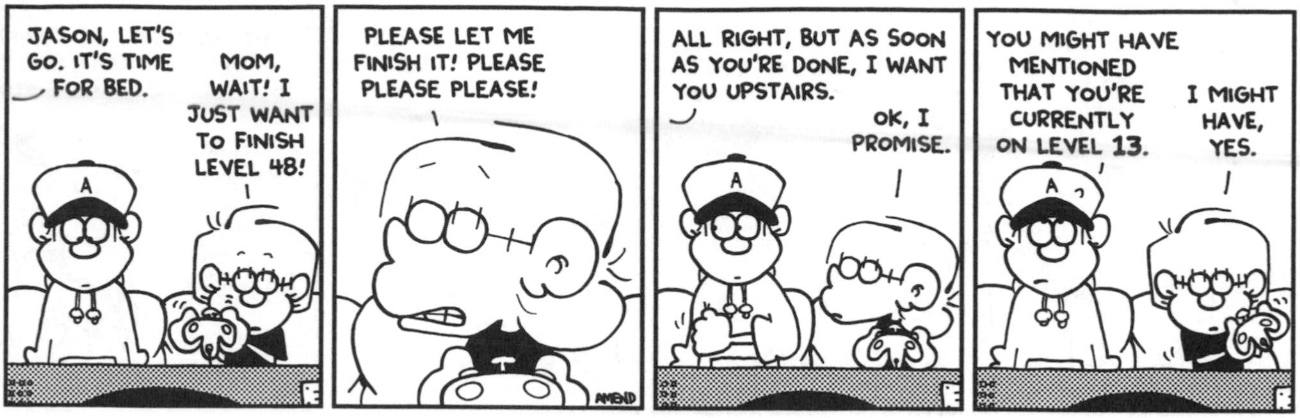
JASON, LET'S GO. IT'S TIME FOR BED.
MOM, WAIT! I JUST WANT TO FINISH LEVEL 48!
PLEASE LET ME FINISH IT! PLEASE PLEASE PLEASE!
AMEND
ALL RIGHT, BUT AS SOON AS YOU'RE DONE, I WANT YOU UPSTAIRS.
OK, I PROMISE.
YOU MIGHT HAVE MENTIONED THAT YOU'RE CURRENTLY ON LEVEL 13.
I MIGHT HAVE, YES.

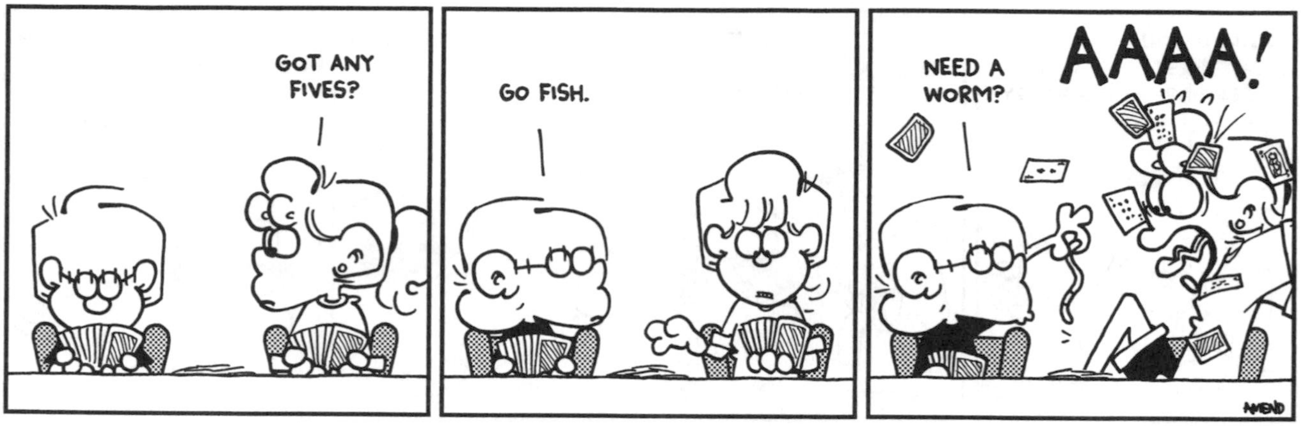
GOT ANY FIVES?
GO FISH.
NEED A WORM?
AAAA!
AMEND

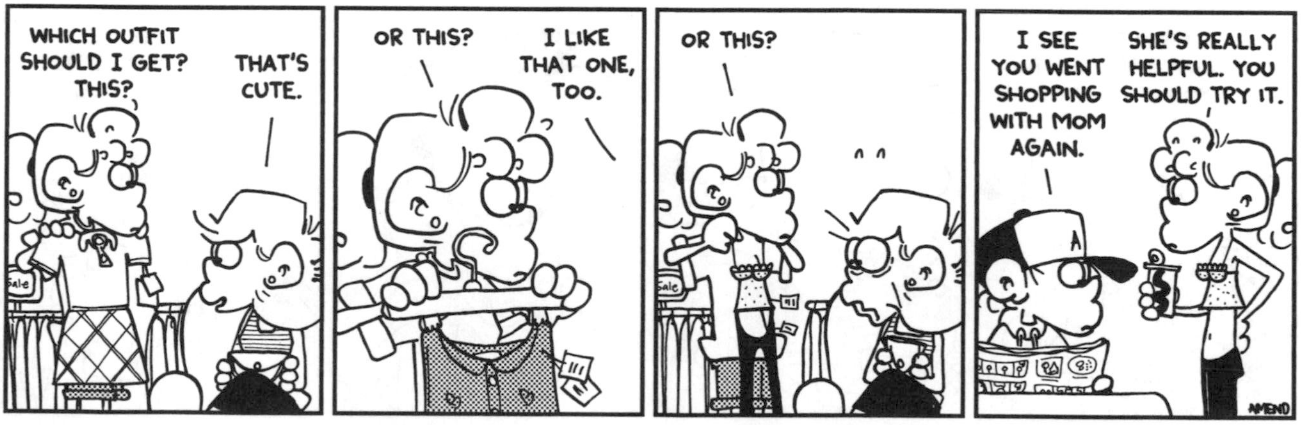
WHICH OUTFIT SHOULD I GET? THIS?
THAT'S CUTE.
OR THIS?
I LIKE THAT ONE, TOO.
OR THIS?
I SEE YOU WENT SHOPPING WITH MOM AGAIN.
SHE'S REALLY HELPFUL. YOU SHOULD TRY IT.
AMEND

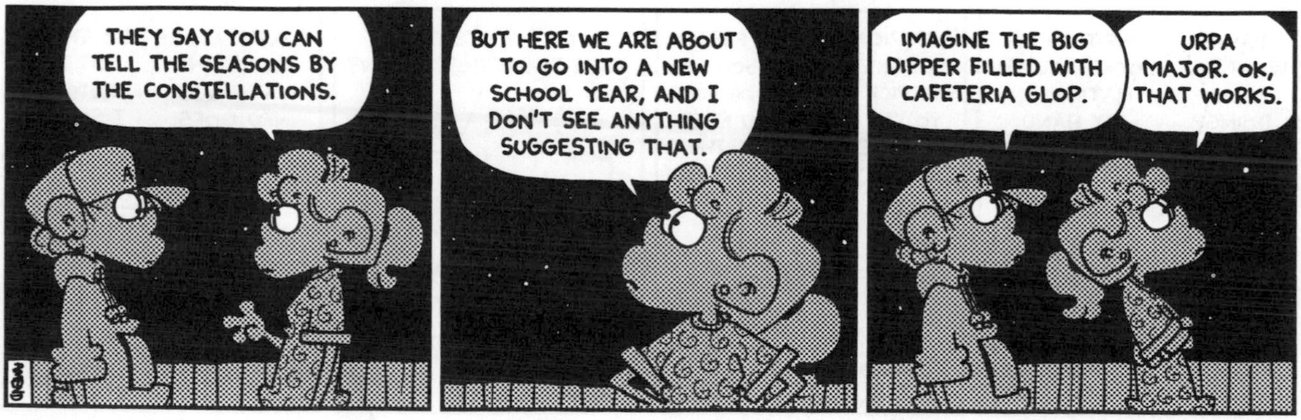
THEY SAY YOU CAN TELL THE SEASONS BY THE CONSTELLATIONS.
BUT HERE WE ARE ABOUT TO GO INTO A NEW SCHOOL YEAR, AND I DON'T SEE ANYTHING SUGGESTING THAT.
IMAGINE THE BIG DIPPER FILLED WITH CAFETERIA GLOP.
URPA MAJOR. OK, THAT WORKS.

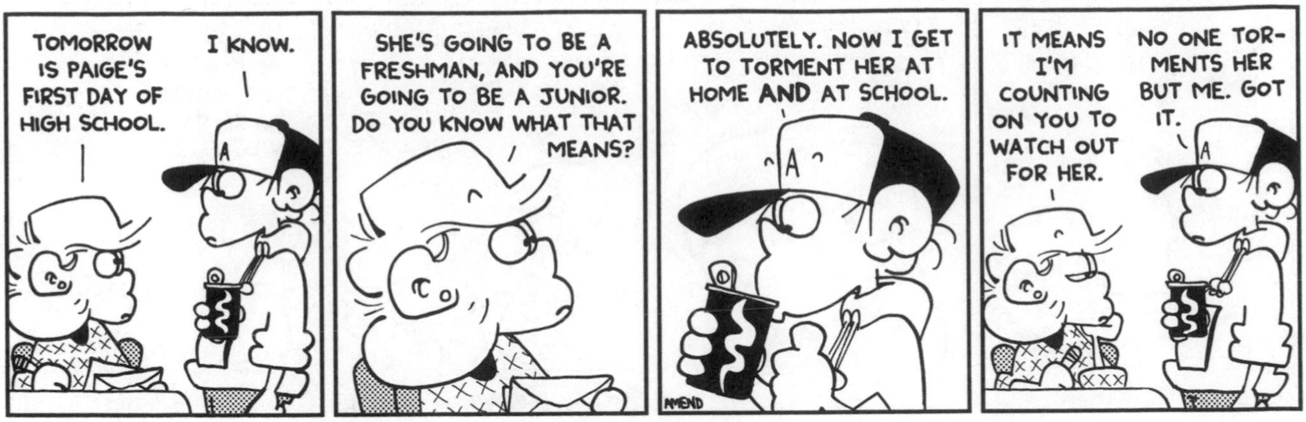
TOMORROW IS PAIGE'S FIRST DAY OF HIGH SCHOOL.
I KNOW.
SHE'S GOING TO BE A FRESHMAN, AND YOU'RE GOING TO BE A JUNIOR. DO YOU KNOW WHAT THAT MEANS?
ABSOLUTELY. NOW I GET TO TORMENT HER AT HOME AND AT SCHOOL.
AMEND
IT MEANS I'M COUNTING ON YOU TO WATCH OUT FOR HER.
NO ONE TORMENTS HER BUT ME. GOT IT.

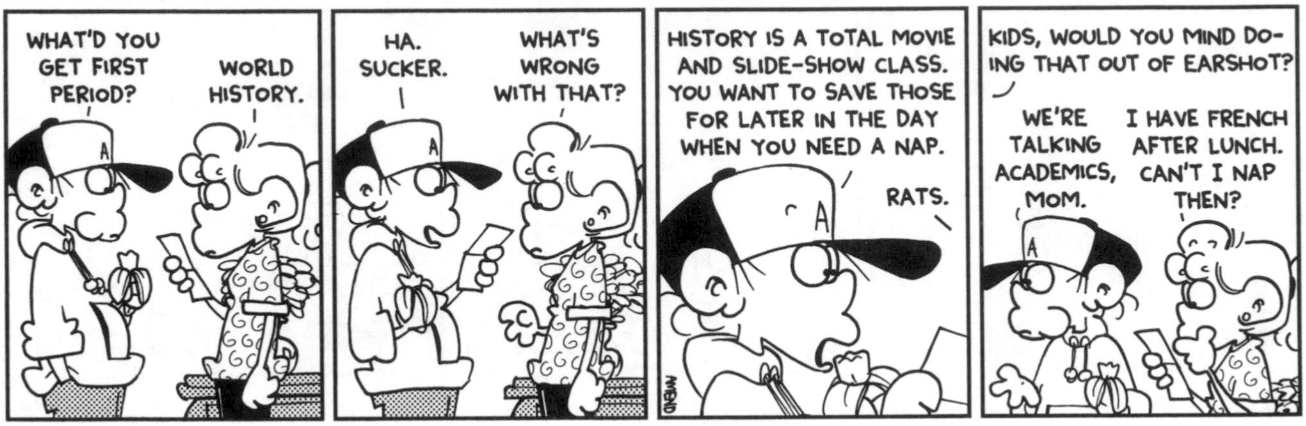
WHAT'D YOU GET FIRST PERIOD?
WORLD HISTORY.
HA. SUCKER.
WHAT'S WRONG WITH THAT?
HISTORY IS A TOTAL MOVIE AND SLIDE-SHOW CLASS. YOU WANT TO SAVE THOSE FOR LATER IN THE DAY WHEN YOU NEED A NAP.
RATS.
AMEND
KIDS, WOULD YOU MIND DOING THAT OUT OF EARSHOT?
WE'RE TALKING ACADEMICS, MOM.
I HAVE FRENCH AFTER LUNCH. CAN'T I NAP THEN?

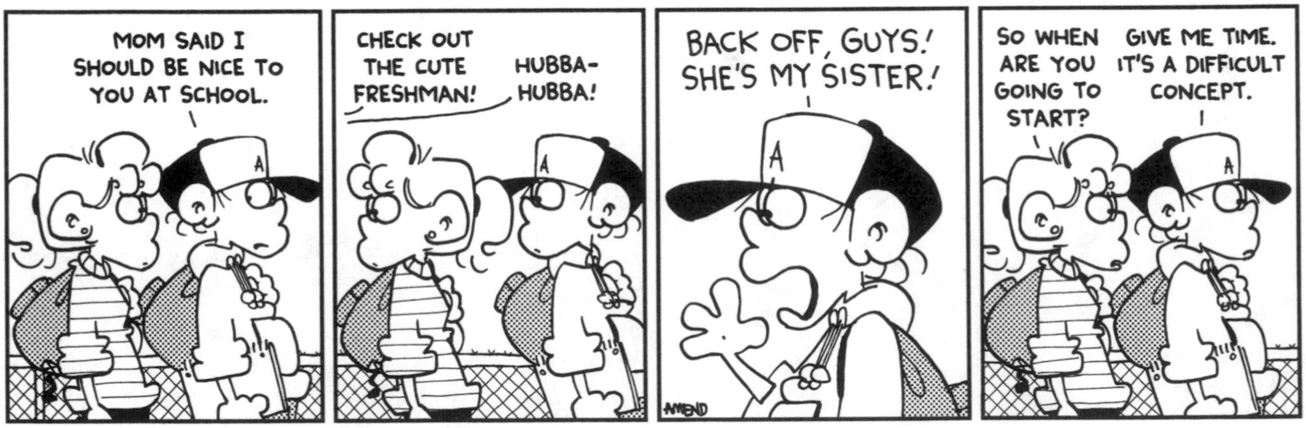
MOM SAID I SHOULD BE NICE TO YOU AT SCHOOL.
CHECK OUT THE CUTE FRESHMAN!
HUBBA-HUBBA!
BACK OFF, GUYS! SHE'S MY SISTER!
AMEND
SO WHEN ARE YOU GOING TO START?
GIVE ME TIME. IT'S A DIFFICULT CONCEPT.

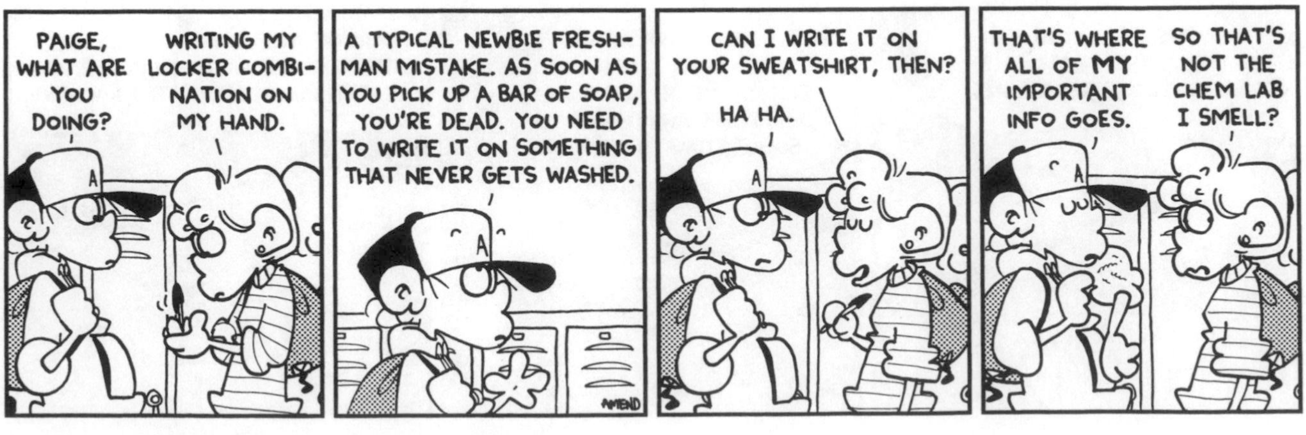
PAIGE, WHAT ARE YOU DOING?
WRITING MY LOCKER COMBINATION ON MY HAND.
A TYPICAL NEWBIE FRESHMAN MISTAKE. AS SOON AS YOU PICK UP A BAR OF SOAP, YOU'RE DEAD. YOU NEED TO WRITE IT ON SOMETHING THAT NEVER GETS WASHED.
AMEND
CAN I WRITE IT ON YOUR SWEATSHIRT, THEN?
HA HA.
THAT'S WHERE ALL OF MY IMPORTANT INFO GOES.
SO THAT'S NOT THE CHEM LAB I SMELL?

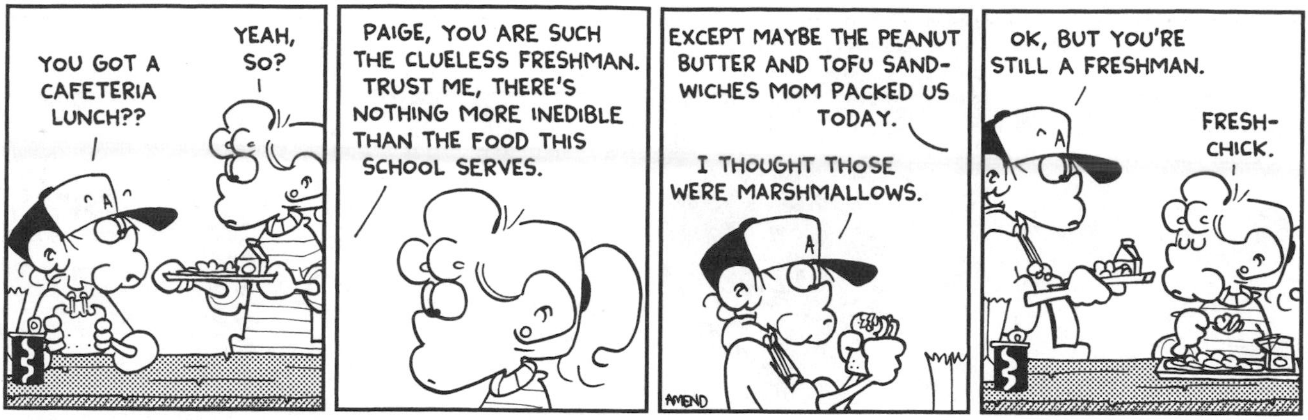
YOU GOT A CAFETERIA LUNCH??
YEAH, SO?
PAIGE, YOU ARE SUCH THE CLUELESS FRESHMAN. TRUST ME, THERE'S NOTHING MORE INEDIBLE THAN THE FOOD THIS SCHOOL SERVES.
EXCEPT MAYBE THE PEANUT BUTTER AND TOFU SANDWICHES MOM PACKED US TODAY.
I THOUGHT THOSE WERE MARSHMALLOWS.
OK, BUT YOU'RE STILL A FRESHMAN.
FRESH-CHICK.
AMEND

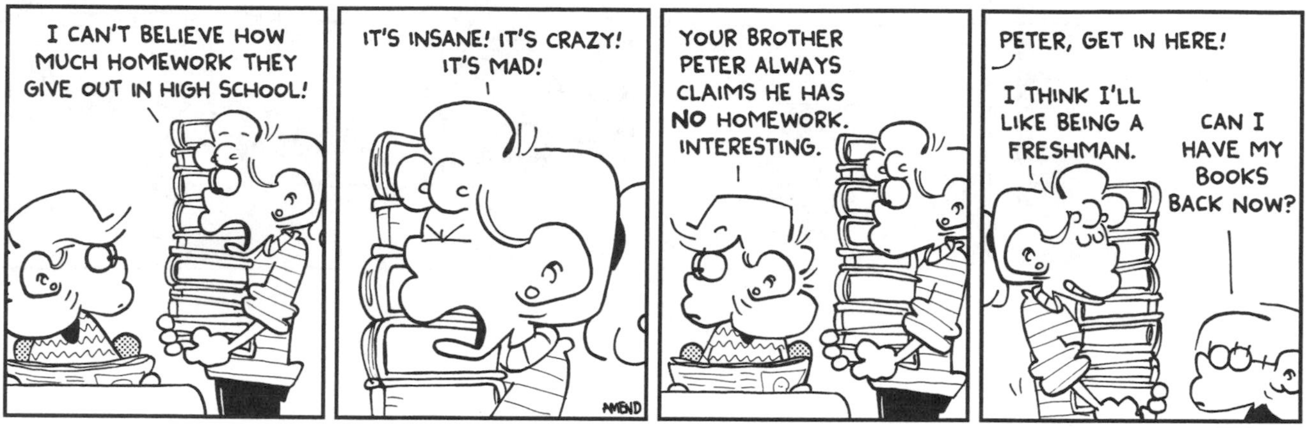
I CAN'T BELIEVE HOW MUCH HOMEWORK THEY GIVE OUT IN HIGH SCHOOL!
IT'S INSANE! IT'S CRAZY! IT'S MAD!
YOUR BROTHER PETER ALWAYS CLAIMS HE HAS NO HOMEWORK. INTERESTING.
PETER, GET IN HERE!
I THINK I'LL LIKE BEING A FRESHMAN.
CAN I HAVE MY BOOKS BACK NOW?
AMEND

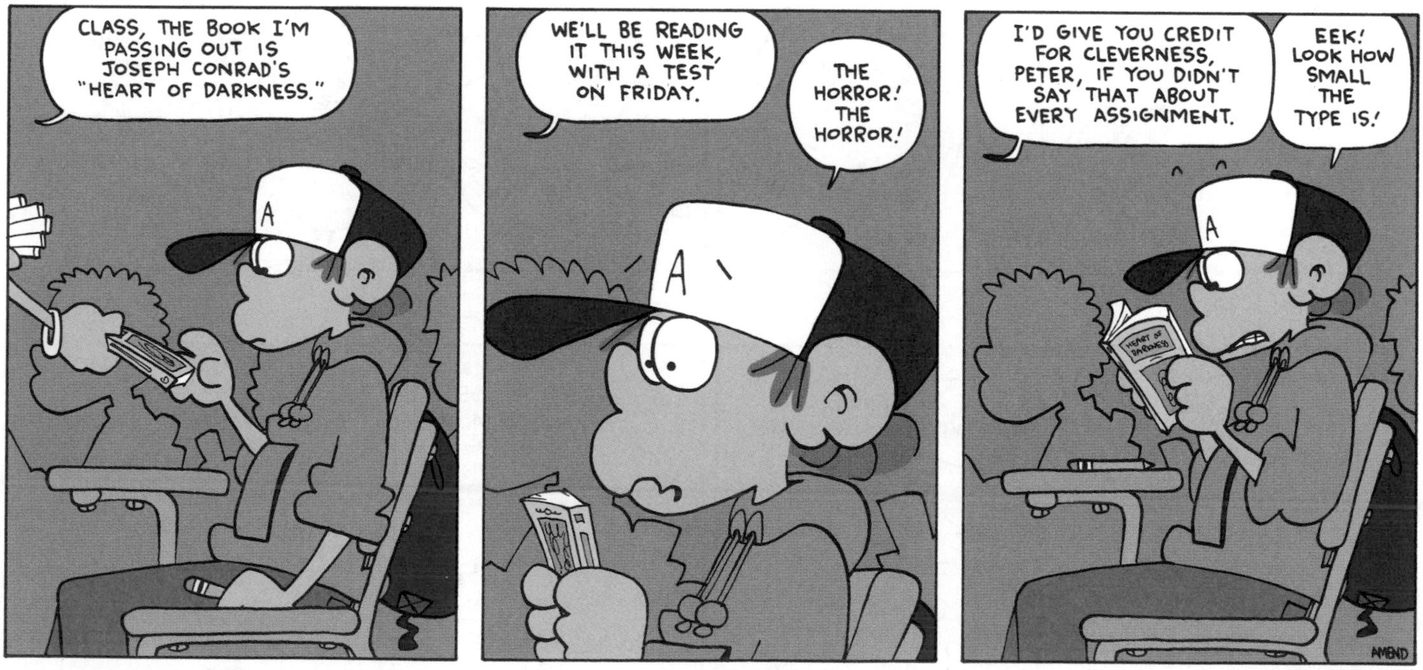
CLASS, THE BOOK I'M PASSING OUT IS JOSEPH CONRAD'S "HEART OF DARKNESS."
WE'LL BE READING IT THIS WEEK, WITH A TEST ON FRIDAY.
THE HORROR! THE HORROR!
I'D GIVE YOU CREDIT FOR CLEVERNESS, PETER, IF YOU DIDN'T SAY THAT ABOUT EVERY ASSIGNMENT.
EEK! LOOK HOW SMALL THE TYPE IS!
AMEND

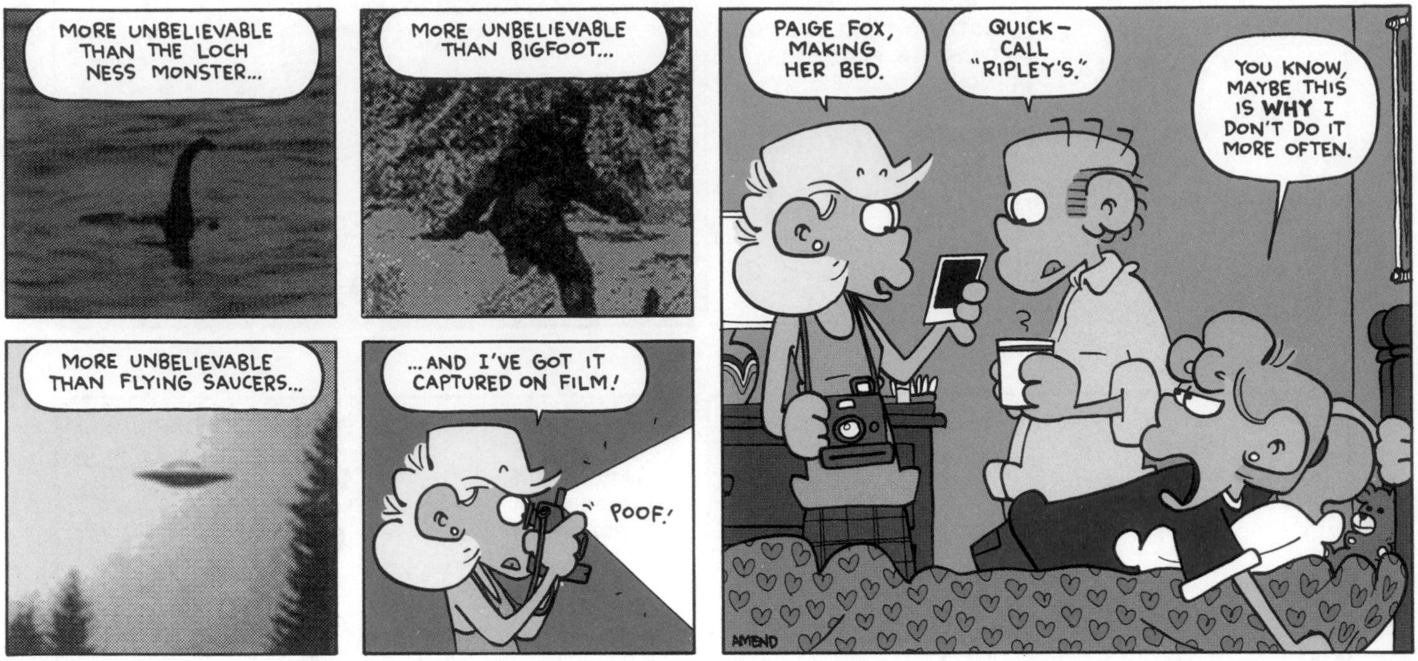
MORE UNBELIEVABLE THAN THE LOCH NESS MONSTER...
MORE UNBELIEVABLE THAN BIGFOOT...
MORE UNBELIEVABLE THAN FLYING SAUCERS...
...AND I'VE GOT IT CAPTURED ON FILM!
POOF!
PAIGE FOX, MAKING HER BED.
QUICK– CALL "RIPLEY'S."
YOU KNOW, MAYBE THIS IS **WHY** I DON'T DO IT MORE OFTEN.
AMEND

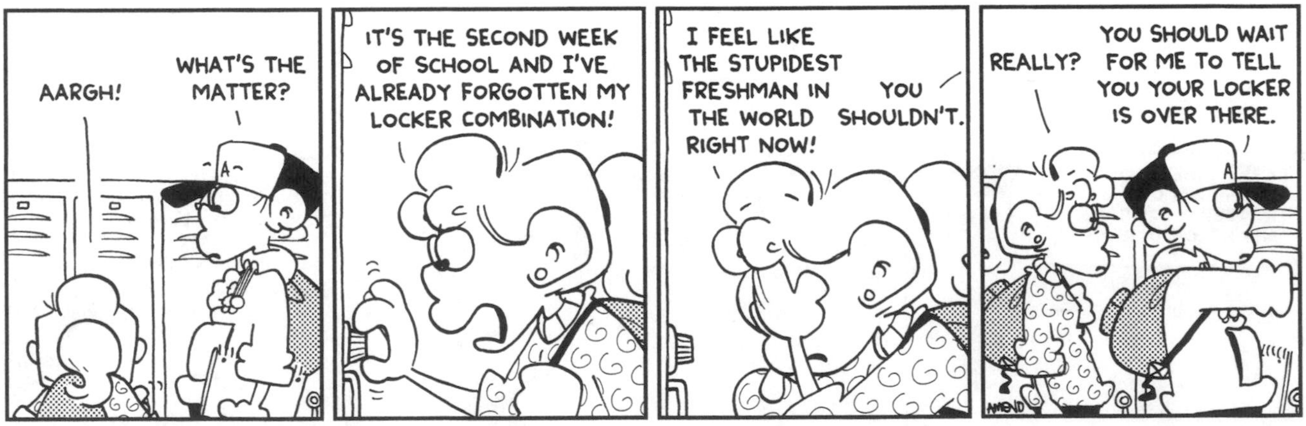
AARGH!
WHAT'S THE MATTER?
IT'S THE SECOND WEEK OF SCHOOL AND I'VE ALREADY FORGOTTEN MY LOCKER COMBINATION!
I FEEL LIKE THE STUPIDEST FRESHMAN IN THE WORLD RIGHT NOW!
YOU SHOULDN'T.
REALLY?
YOU SHOULD WAIT FOR ME TO TELL YOU YOUR LOCKER IS OVER THERE.
AMEND

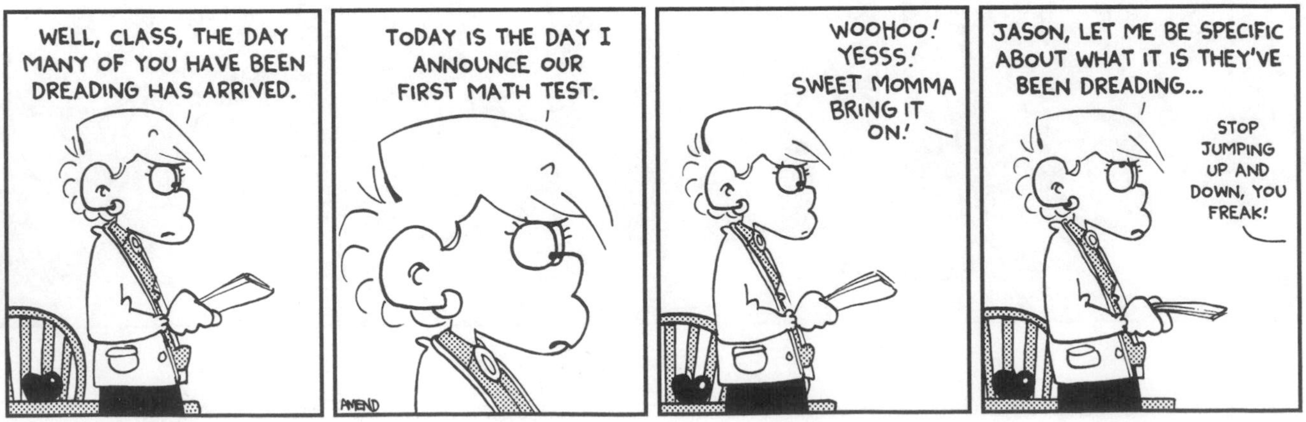
WELL, CLASS, THE DAY MANY OF YOU HAVE BEEN DREADING HAS ARRIVED.
TODAY IS THE DAY I ANNOUNCE OUR FIRST MATH TEST.
WOOHOO! YESSS! SWEET MOMMA BRING IT ON!
JASON, LET ME BE SPECIFIC ABOUT WHAT IT IS THEY'VE BEEN DREADING...
STOP JUMPING UP AND DOWN, YOU FREAK!
AMEND

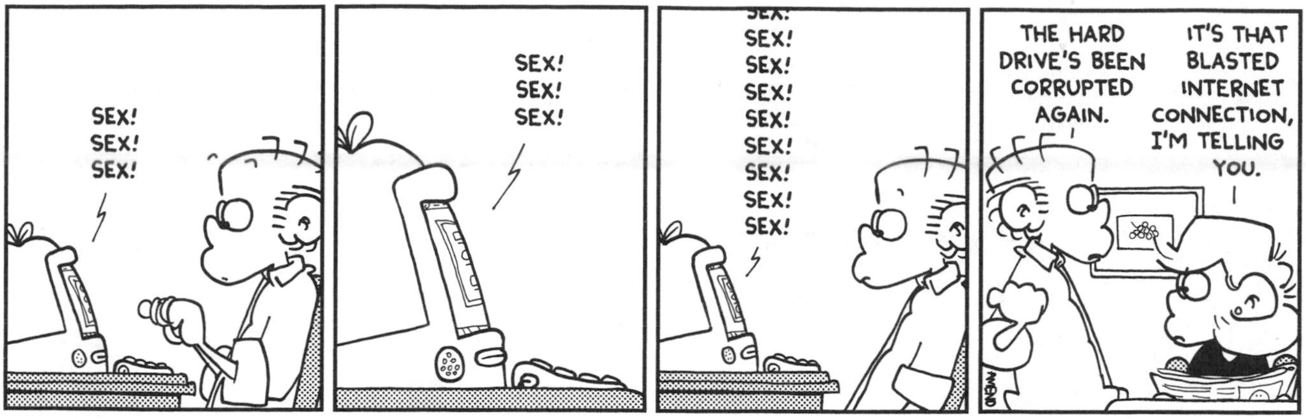
SEX!
SEX!
SEX!
SEX!
SEX!
SEX!
SEX!
SEX!
SEX!
SEX!
SEX!
SEX!
SEX!
SEX!
THE HARD DRIVE'S BEEN CORRUPTED AGAIN.
IT'S THAT BLASTED INTERNET CONNECTION, I'M TELLING YOU.
AMEND

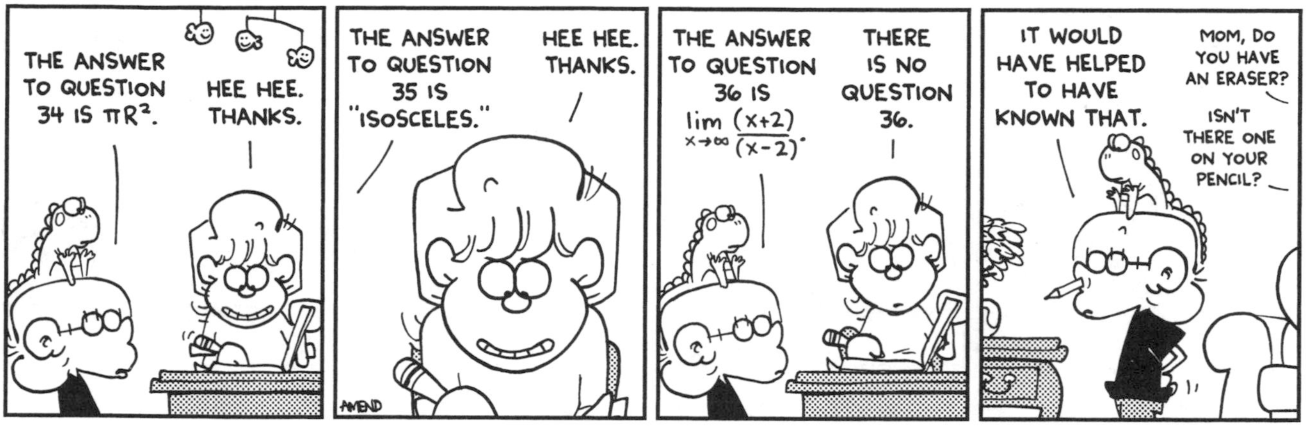
THE ANSWER TO QUESTION 34 IS πR^2.
HEE HEE. THANKS.
THE ANSWER TO QUESTION 35 IS "ISOSCELES."
HEE HEE. THANKS.
AMEND
THE ANSWER TO QUESTION 36 IS $\lim_{x \to \infty} \frac{(x+2)}{(x-2)}$.
THERE IS NO QUESTION 36.
IT WOULD HAVE HELPED TO HAVE KNOWN THAT.
MOM, DO YOU HAVE AN ERASER?
ISN'T THERE ONE ON YOUR PENCIL?

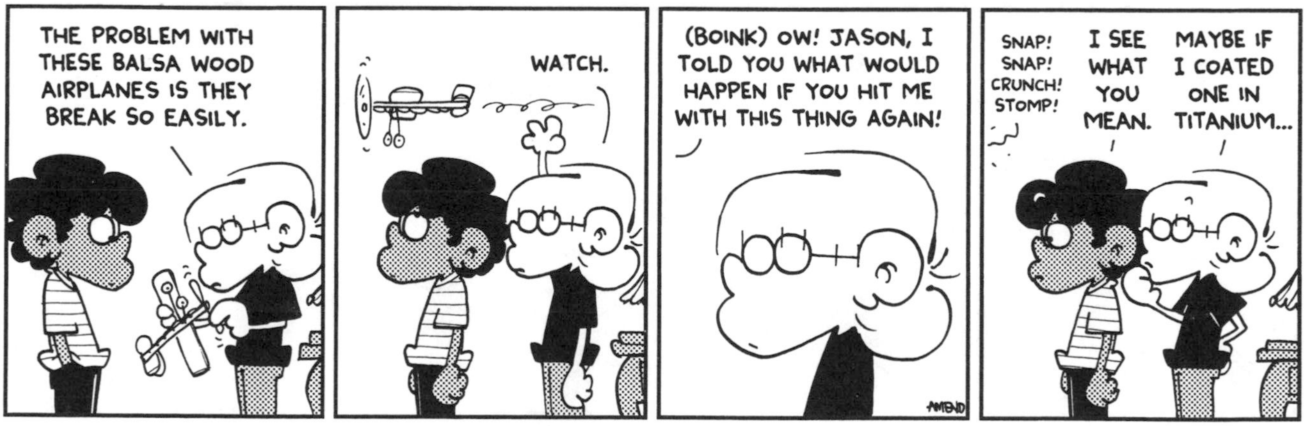
THE PROBLEM WITH THESE BALSA WOOD AIRPLANES IS THEY BREAK SO EASILY.
WATCH.
(BOINK) OW! JASON, I TOLD YOU WHAT WOULD HAPPEN IF YOU HIT ME WITH THIS THING AGAIN!
AMEND
SNAP! SNAP! CRUNCH! STOMP!
I SEE WHAT YOU MEAN.
MAYBE IF I COATED ONE IN TITANIUM...

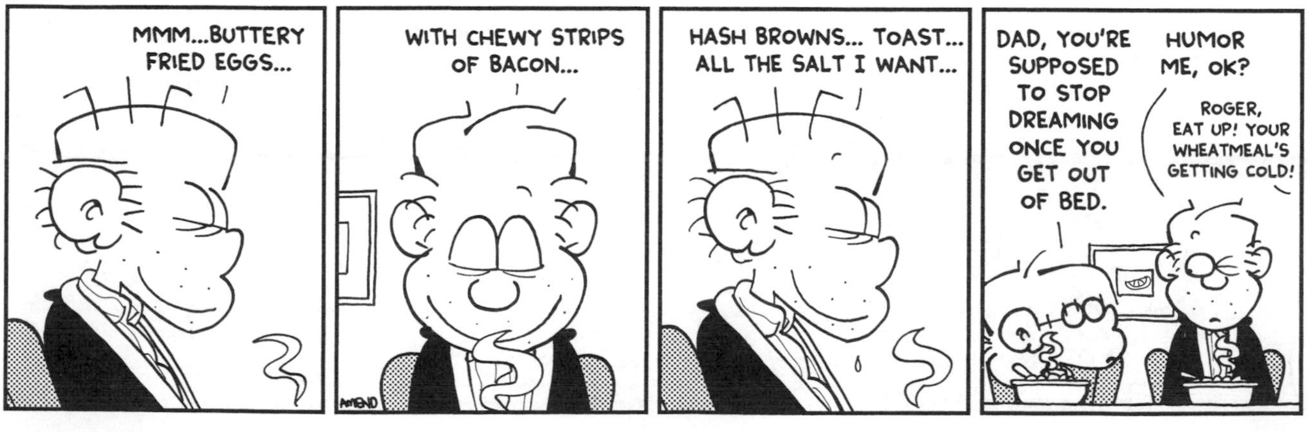
MMM...BUTTERY FRIED EGGS...
WITH CHEWY STRIPS OF BACON...
AMEND
HASH BROWNS... TOAST... ALL THE SALT I WANT...
DAD, YOU'RE SUPPOSED TO STOP DREAMING ONCE YOU GET OUT OF BED.
HUMOR ME, OK?
ROGER, EAT UP! YOUR WHEATMEAL'S GETTING COLD!

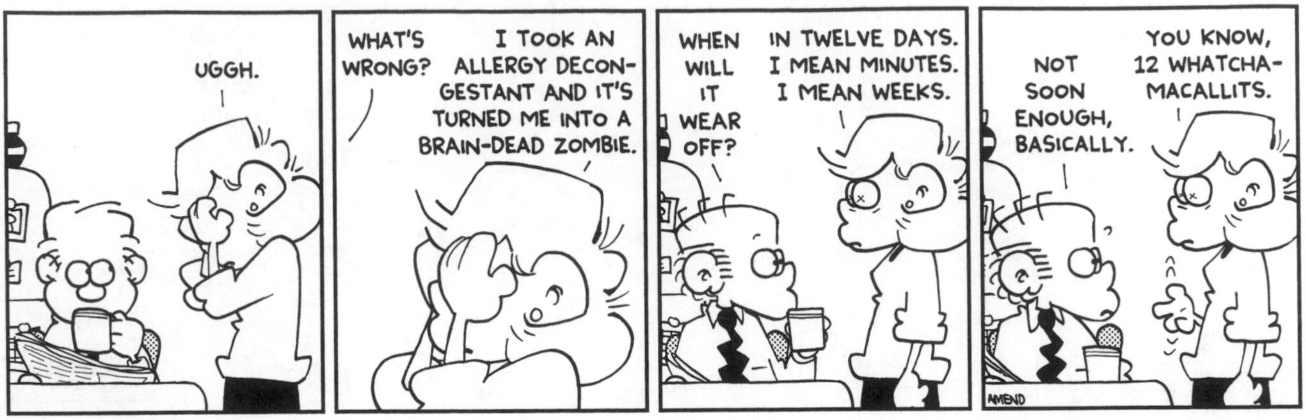
UGGH.
WHAT'S WRONG?
I TOOK AN ALLERGY DECONGESTANT AND IT'S TURNED ME INTO A BRAIN-DEAD ZOMBIE.
WHEN WILL IT WEAR OFF?
IN TWELVE DAYS. I MEAN MINUTES. I MEAN WEEKS.
NOT SOON ENOUGH, BASICALLY.
YOU KNOW, 12 WHATCHAMACALLITS.
AMEND

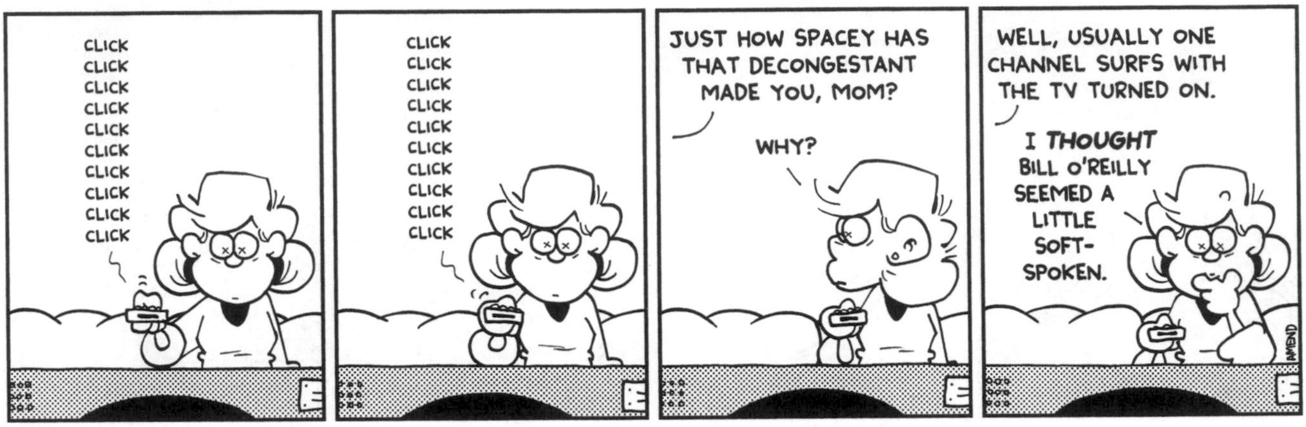
CLICK CLICK CLICK CLICK CLICK CLICK CLICK CLICK CLICK CLICK
CLICK CLICK CLICK CLICK CLICK CLICK CLICK CLICK CLICK CLICK
JUST HOW SPACEY HAS THAT DECONGESTANT MADE YOU, MOM?
WHY?
WELL, USUALLY ONE CHANNEL SURFS WITH THE TV TURNED ON.
I *THOUGHT* BILL O'REILLY SEEMED A LITTLE SOFT-SPOKEN.
AMEND

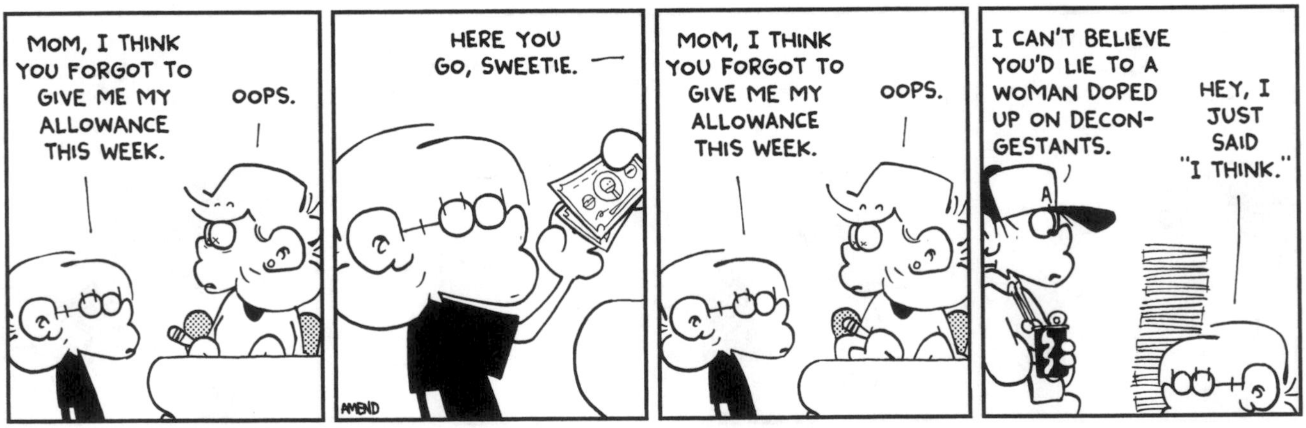
MOM, I THINK YOU FORGOT TO GIVE ME MY ALLOWANCE THIS WEEK.
OOPS.
HERE YOU GO, SWEETIE.
AMEND
MOM, I THINK YOU FORGOT TO GIVE ME MY ALLOWANCE THIS WEEK.
OOPS.
I CAN'T BELIEVE YOU'D LIE TO A WOMAN DOPED UP ON DECONGESTANTS.
HEY, I JUST SAID "I THINK."

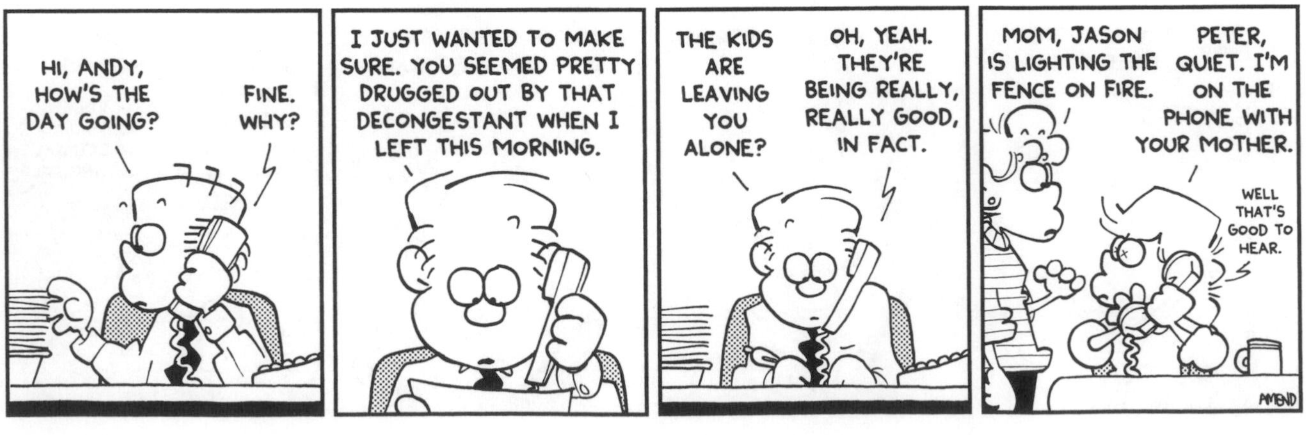
HI, ANDY, HOW'S THE DAY GOING?
FINE. WHY?
I JUST WANTED TO MAKE SURE. YOU SEEMED PRETTY DRUGGED OUT BY THAT DECONGESTANT WHEN I LEFT THIS MORNING.
THE KIDS ARE LEAVING YOU ALONE?
OH, YEAH. THEY'RE BEING REALLY, REALLY GOOD, IN FACT.
MOM, JASON IS LIGHTING THE FENCE ON FIRE.
PETER, QUIET. I'M ON THE PHONE WITH YOUR MOTHER.
WELL THAT'S GOOD TO HEAR.
AMEND

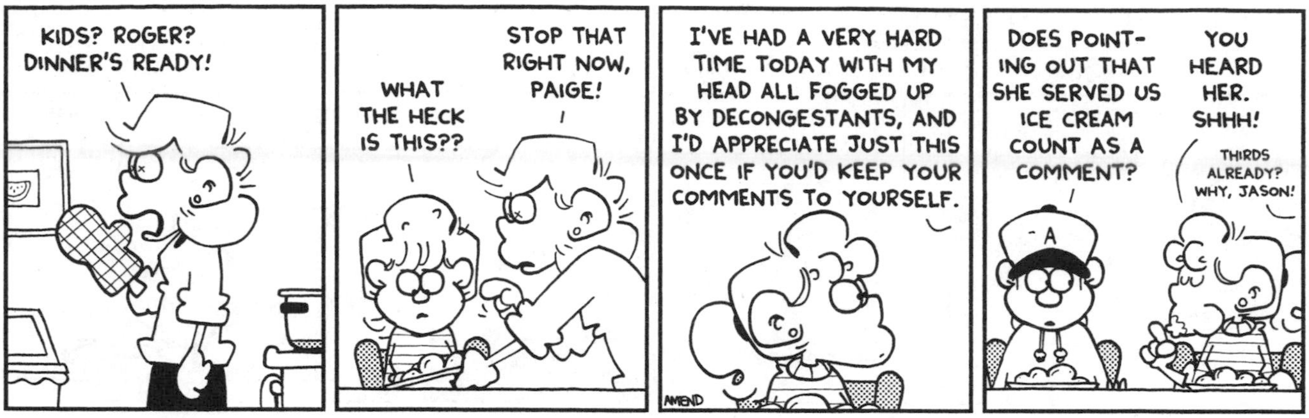
KIDS? ROGER? DINNER'S READY!
WHAT THE HECK IS THIS??
STOP THAT RIGHT NOW, PAIGE!
I'VE HAD A VERY HARD TIME TODAY WITH MY HEAD ALL FOGGED UP BY DECONGESTANTS, AND I'D APPRECIATE JUST THIS ONCE IF YOU'D KEEP YOUR COMMENTS TO YOURSELF.
AMEND
DOES POINTING OUT THAT SHE SERVED US ICE CREAM COUNT AS A COMMENT?
YOU HEARD HER. SHHH!
THIRDS ALREADY? WHY, JASON!

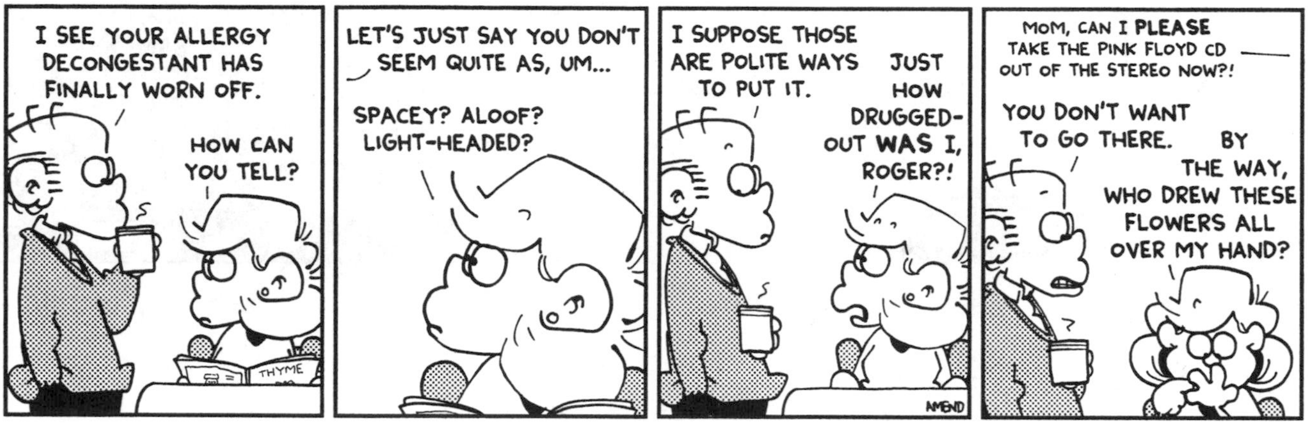
I SEE YOUR ALLERGY DECONGESTANT HAS FINALLY WORN OFF.
HOW CAN YOU TELL?
THYME
LET'S JUST SAY YOU DON'T SEEM QUITE AS, UM...
SPACEY? ALOOF? LIGHT-HEADED?
I SUPPOSE THOSE ARE POLITE WAYS TO PUT IT.
JUST HOW DRUGGED-OUT WAS I, ROGER?!
AMEND
MOM, CAN I PLEASE TAKE THE PINK FLOYD CD OUT OF THE STEREO NOW?!
YOU DON'T WANT TO GO THERE.
BY THE WAY, WHO DREW THESE FLOWERS ALL OVER MY HAND?

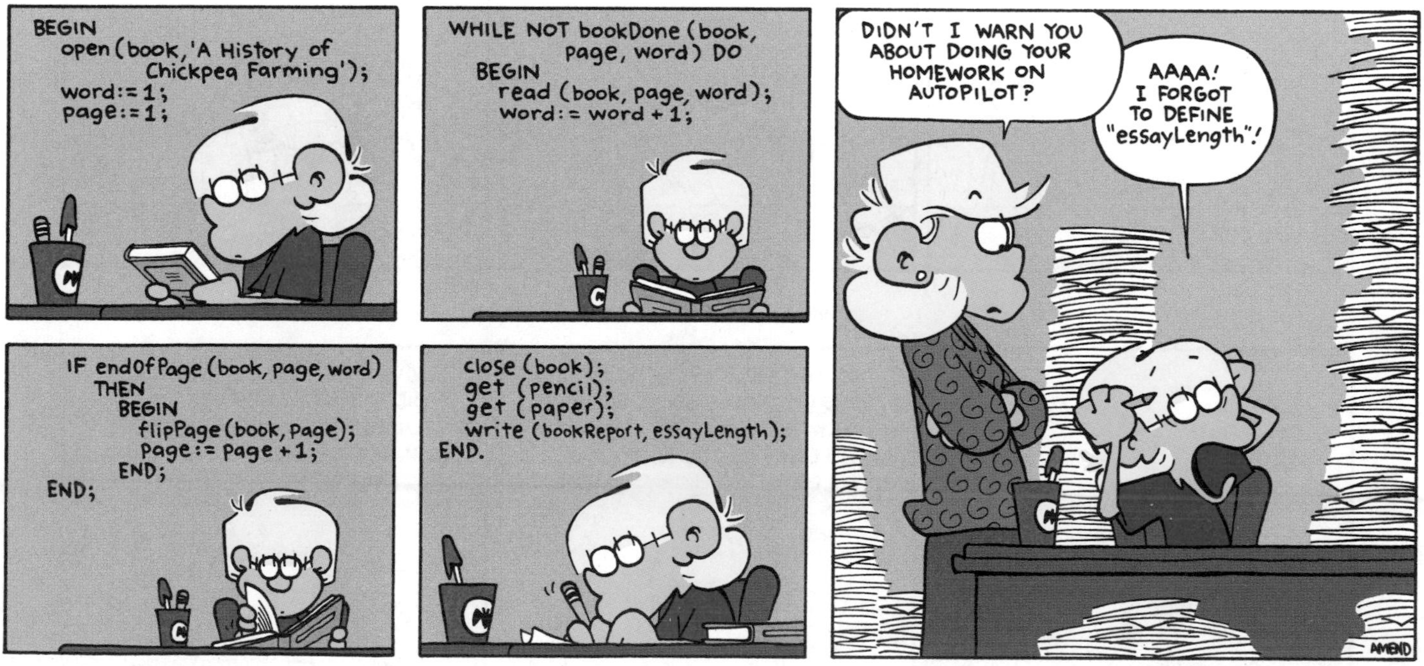
BEGIN
open(book,'A History of Chickpea Farming');
word:=1;
page:=1;
WHILE NOT bookDone(book, page, word) DO
BEGIN
read(book, page, word);
word:= word + 1;
IF endOfPage(book, page, word)
THEN
BEGIN
flipPage(book, page);
page:= page + 1;
END;
END;
close(book);
get(pencil);
get(paper);
write(bookReport, essayLength);
END.
DIDN'T I WARN YOU ABOUT DOING YOUR HOMEWORK ON AUTOPILOT?
AAAA! I FORGOT TO DEFINE "essayLength"!
AMEND

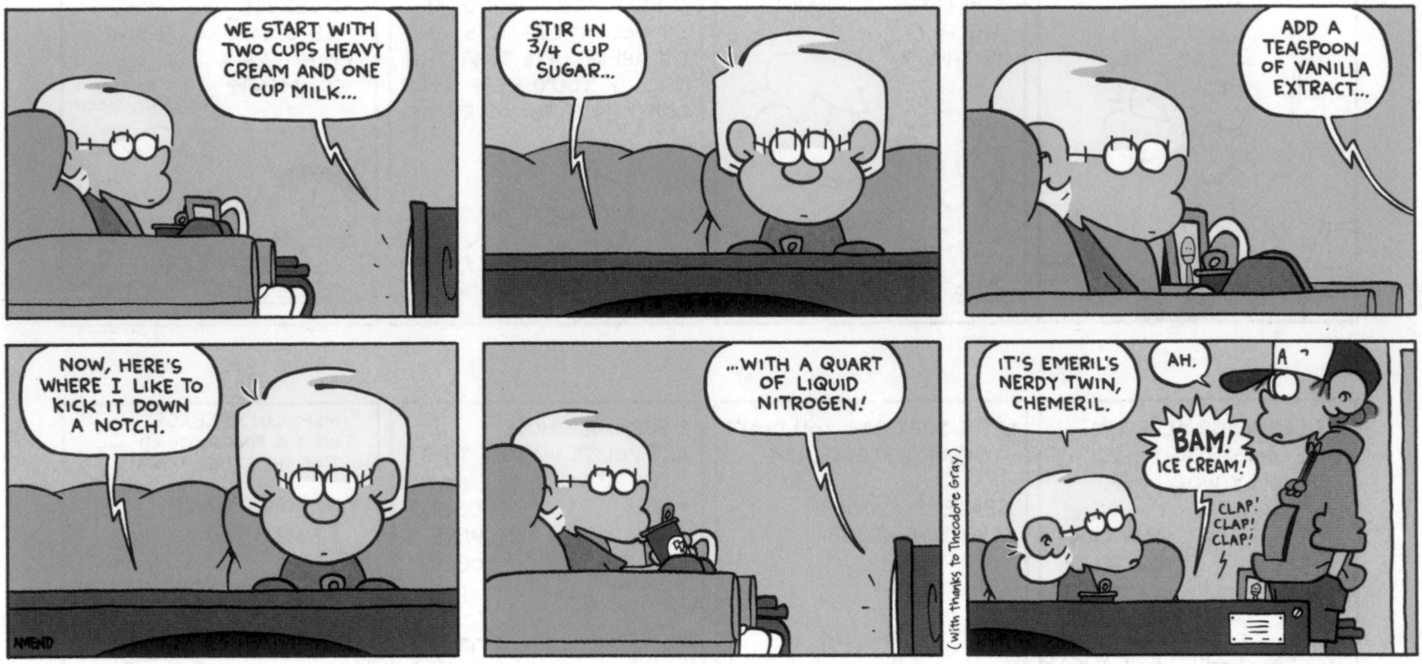
WE START WITH TWO CUPS HEAVY CREAM AND ONE CUP MILK...
STIR IN 3/4 CUP SUGAR...
ADD A TEASPOON OF VANILLA EXTRACT...
NOW, HERE'S WHERE I LIKE TO KICK IT DOWN A NOTCH.
...WITH A QUART OF LIQUID NITROGEN!
IT'S EMERIL'S NERDY TWIN, CHEMERIL.
AH.
BAM! ICE CREAM!
CLAP! CLAP! CLAP!
(With thanks to Theodore Gray)
AMEND

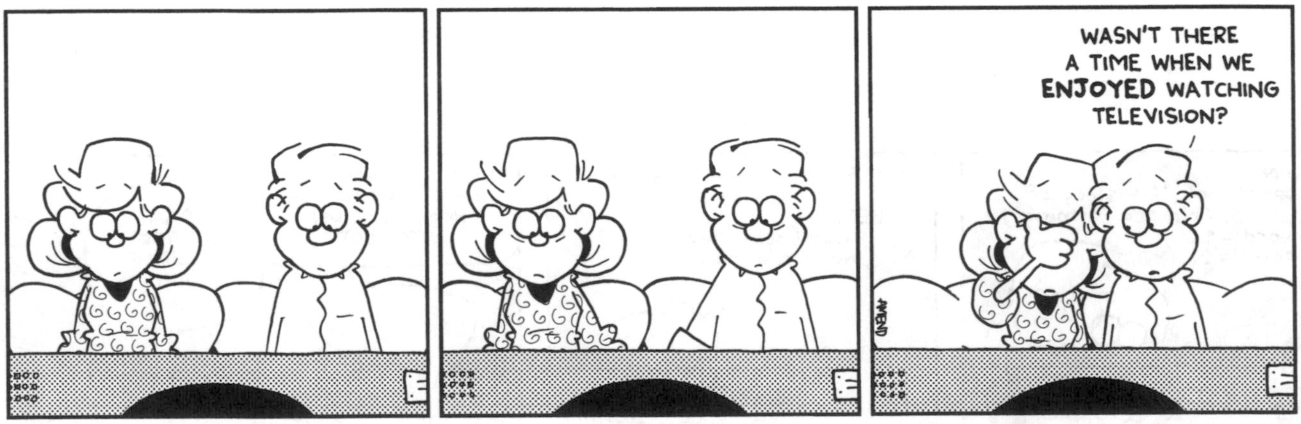
WASN'T THERE A TIME WHEN WE **ENJOYED** WATCHING TELEVISION?
AMEND

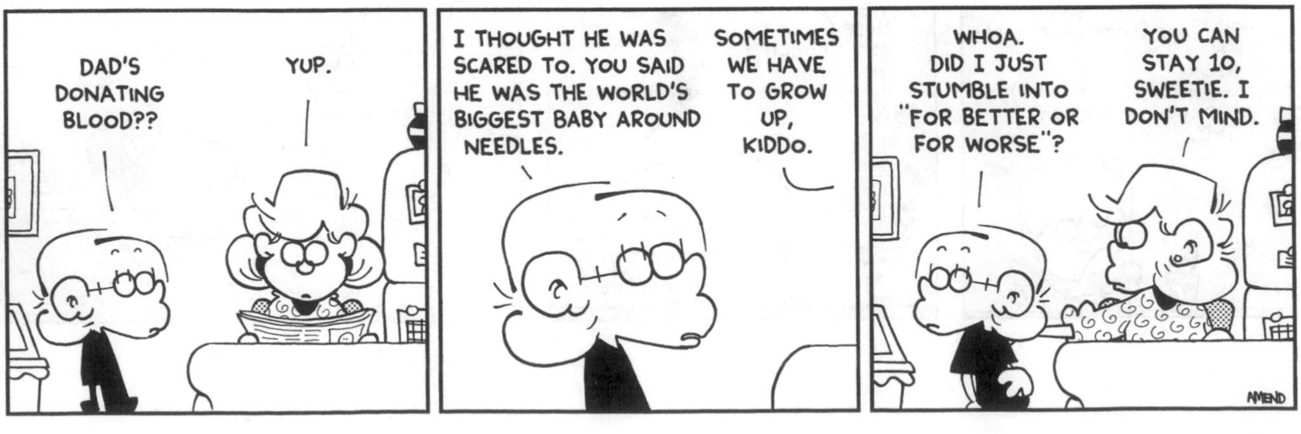
DAD'S DONATING BLOOD??
YUP.
I THOUGHT HE WAS SCARED TO. YOU SAID HE WAS THE WORLD'S BIGGEST BABY AROUND NEEDLES.
SOMETIMES WE HAVE TO GROW UP, KIDDO.
WHOA. DID I JUST STUMBLE INTO "FOR BETTER OR FOR WORSE"?
YOU CAN STAY 10, SWEETIE. I DON'T MIND.
AMEND

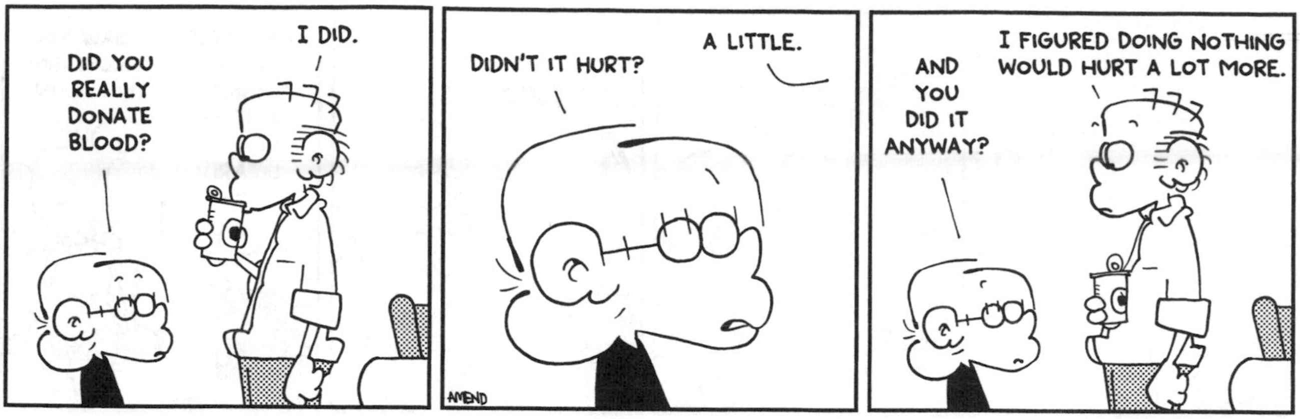
DID YOU REALLY DONATE BLOOD?
I DID.
DIDN'T IT HURT?
A LITTLE.
AMEND
AND YOU DID IT ANYWAY?
I FIGURED DOING NOTHING WOULD HURT A LOT MORE.

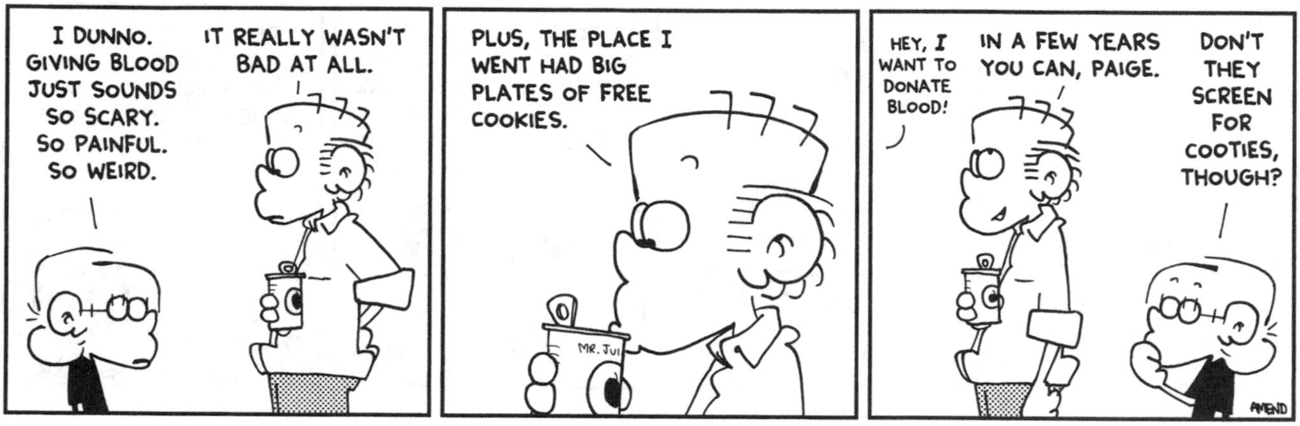
I DUNNO. GIVING BLOOD JUST SOUNDS SO SCARY. SO PAINFUL. SO WEIRD.
IT REALLY WASN'T BAD AT ALL.
PLUS, THE PLACE I WENT HAD BIG PLATES OF FREE COOKIES.
HEY, I WANT TO DONATE BLOOD!
IN A FEW YEARS YOU CAN, PAIGE.
DON'T THEY SCREEN FOR COOTIES, THOUGH?
AMEND

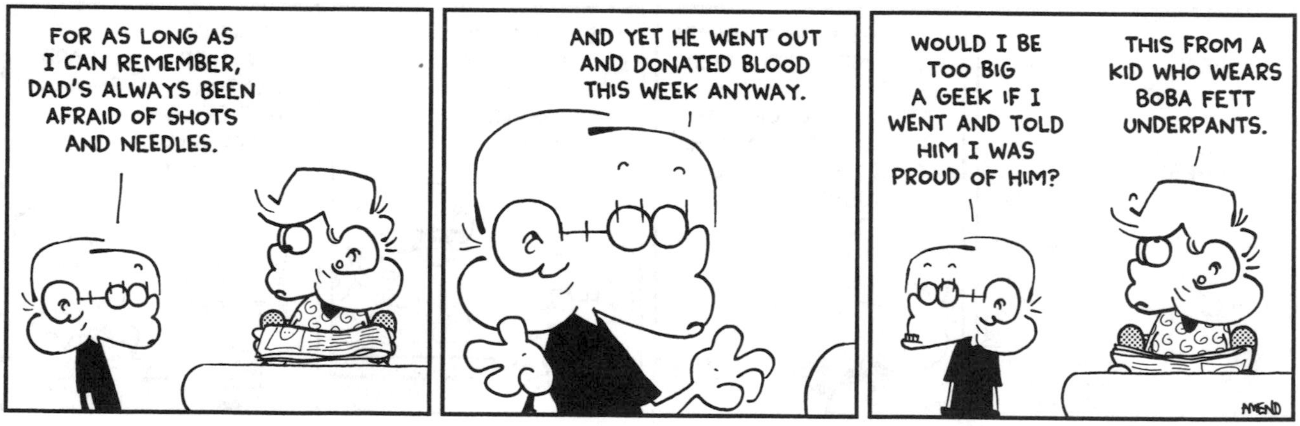
FOR AS LONG AS I CAN REMEMBER, DAD'S ALWAYS BEEN AFRAID OF SHOTS AND NEEDLES.
AND YET HE WENT OUT AND DONATED BLOOD THIS WEEK ANYWAY.
WOULD I BE TOO BIG A GEEK IF I WENT AND TOLD HIM I WAS PROUD OF HIM?
THIS FROM A KID WHO WEARS BOBA FETT UNDERPANTS.
AMEND

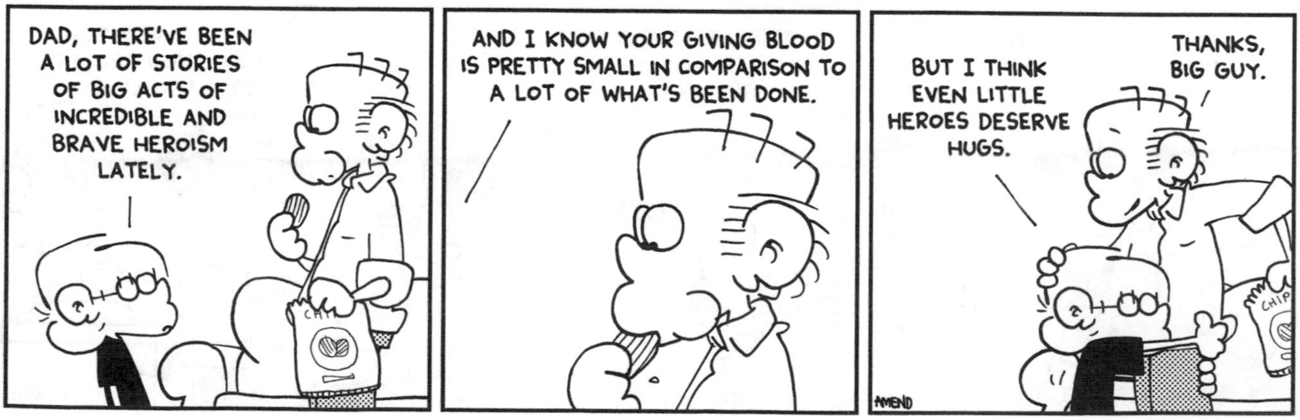
DAD, THERE'VE BEEN A LOT OF STORIES OF BIG ACTS OF INCREDIBLE AND BRAVE HEROISM LATELY.
AND I KNOW YOUR GIVING BLOOD IS PRETTY SMALL IN COMPARISON TO A LOT OF WHAT'S BEEN DONE.
BUT I THINK EVEN LITTLE HEROES DESERVE HUGS.
THANKS, BIG GUY.
AMEND

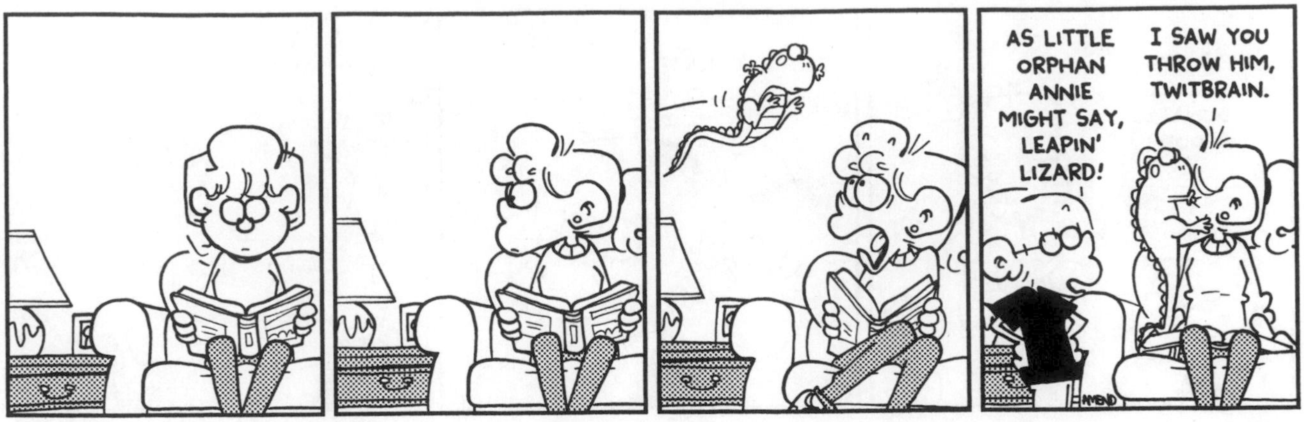
AS LITTLE ORPHAN ANNIE MIGHT SAY, LEAPIN' LIZARD!
I SAW YOU THROW HIM, TWITBRAIN.
AMEND

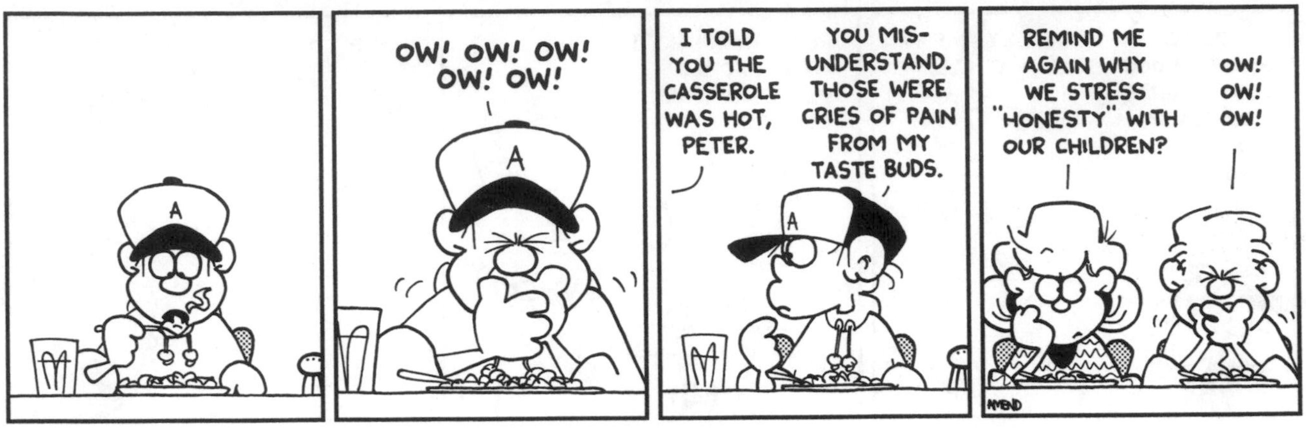
OW! OW! OW! OW! OW!
I TOLD YOU THE CASSEROLE WAS HOT, PETER.
YOU MIS-UNDERSTAND. THOSE WERE CRIES OF PAIN FROM MY TASTE BUDS.
REMIND ME AGAIN WHY WE STRESS "HONESTY" WITH OUR CHILDREN?
OW! OW! OW!
AMEND

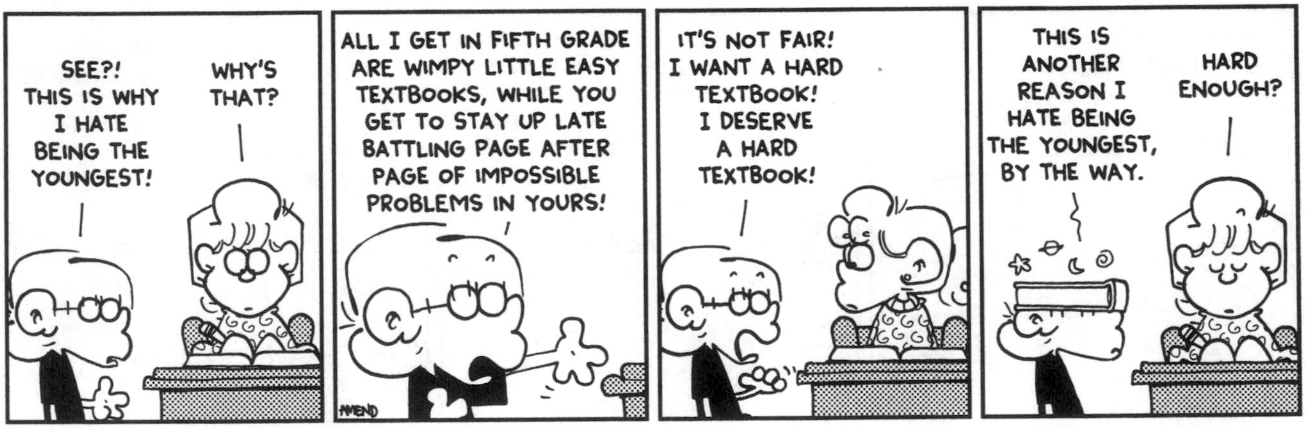
SEE?! THIS IS WHY I HATE BEING THE YOUNGEST!
WHY'S THAT?
ALL I GET IN FIFTH GRADE ARE WIMPY LITTLE EASY TEXTBOOKS, WHILE YOU GET TO STAY UP LATE BATTLING PAGE AFTER PAGE OF IMPOSSIBLE PROBLEMS IN YOURS!
AMEND
IT'S NOT FAIR! I WANT A HARD TEXTBOOK! I DESERVE A HARD TEXTBOOK!
THIS IS ANOTHER REASON I HATE BEING THE YOUNGEST, BY THE WAY.
HARD ENOUGH?

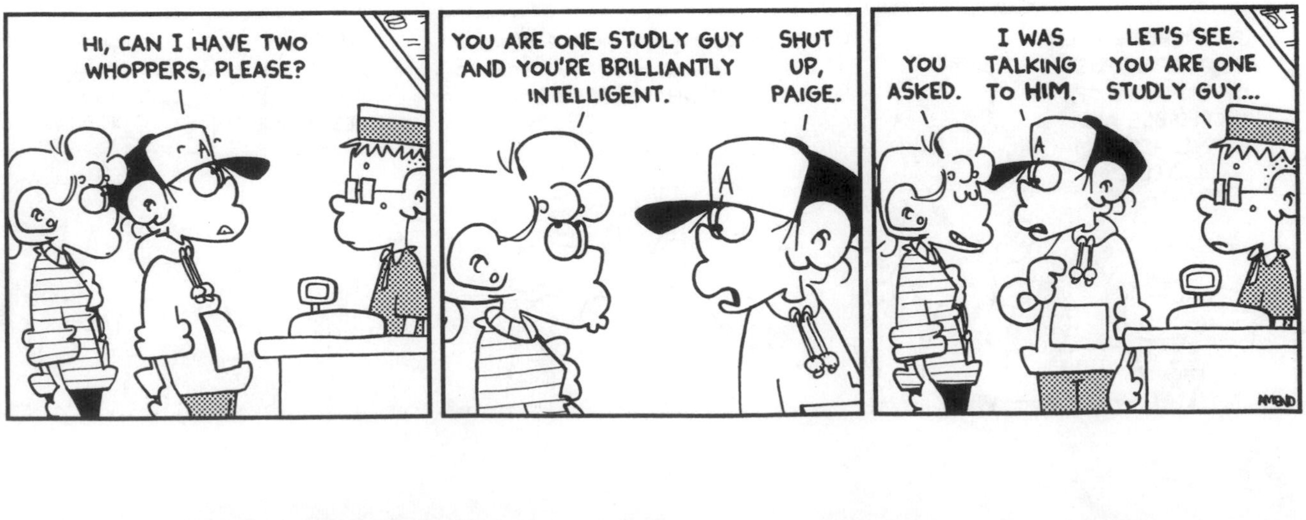
HI, CAN I HAVE TWO WHOPPERS, PLEASE?
YOU ARE ONE STUDLY GUY AND YOU'RE BRILLIANTLY INTELLIGENT.
SHUT UP, PAIGE.
YOU ASKED.
I WAS TALKING TO HIM.
LET'S SEE. YOU ARE ONE STUDLY GUY...
AMEND

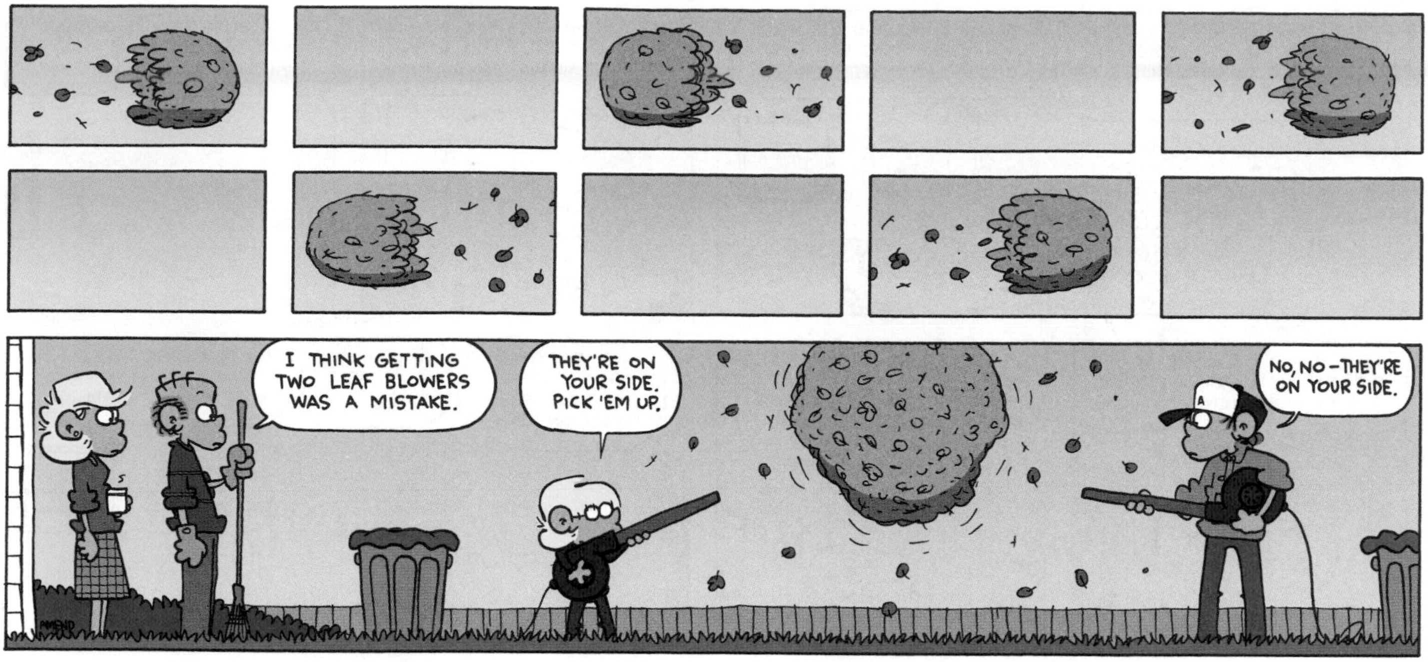
I THINK GETTING TWO LEAF BLOWERS WAS A MISTAKE.
THEY'RE ON YOUR SIDE. PICK 'EM UP.
NO, NO—THEY'RE ON YOUR SIDE.
AMEND

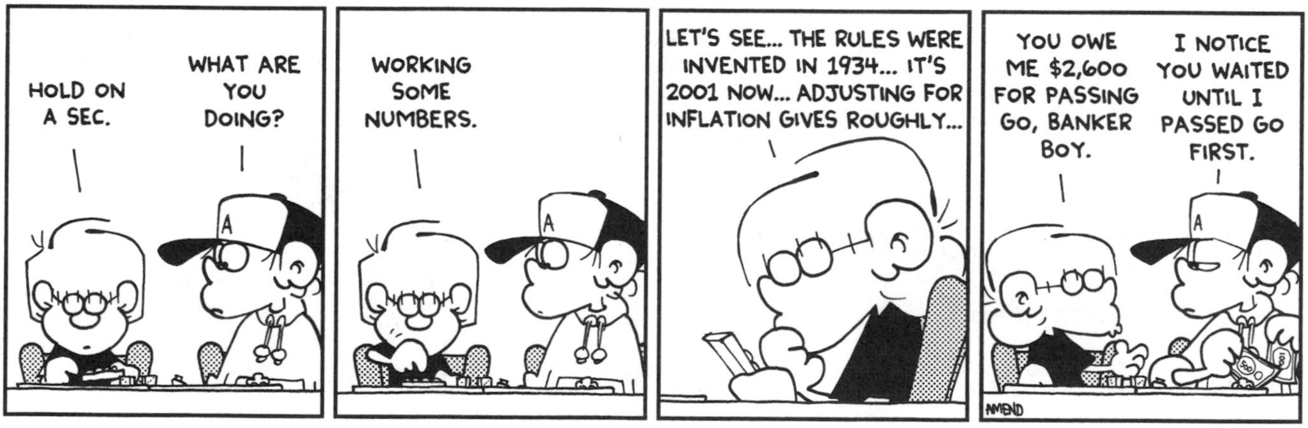
HOLD ON A SEC.
WHAT ARE YOU DOING?
WORKING SOME NUMBERS.
LET'S SEE... THE RULES WERE INVENTED IN 1934... IT'S 2001 NOW... ADJUSTING FOR INFLATION GIVES ROUGHLY...
YOU OWE ME $2,600 FOR PASSING GO, BANKER BOY.
I NOTICE YOU WAITED UNTIL I PASSED GO FIRST.
AMEND

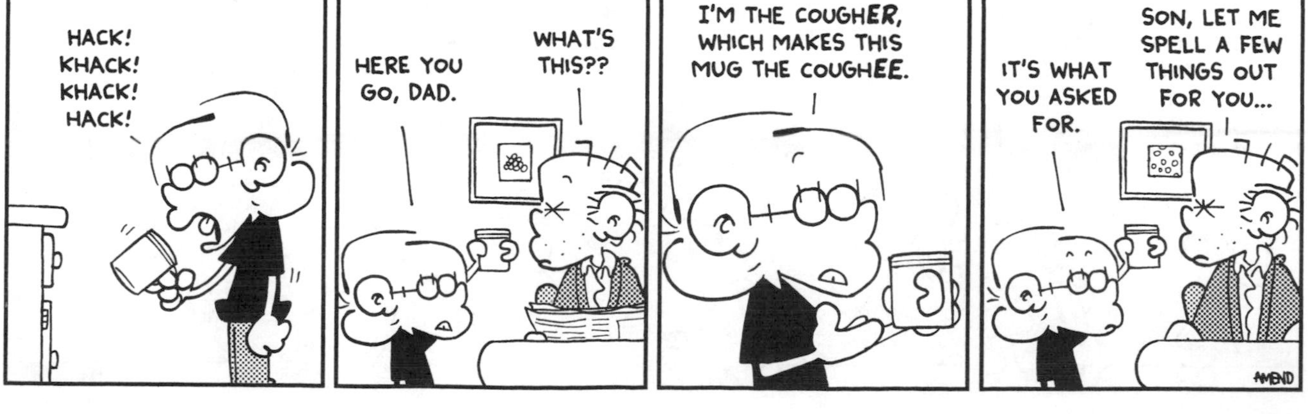
HACK! KHACK! KHACK! HACK!
HERE YOU GO, DAD.
WHAT'S THIS??
I'M THE COUGHER, WHICH MAKES THIS MUG THE COUGHEE.
IT'S WHAT YOU ASKED FOR.
SON, LET ME SPELL A FEW THINGS OUT FOR YOU...
AMEND

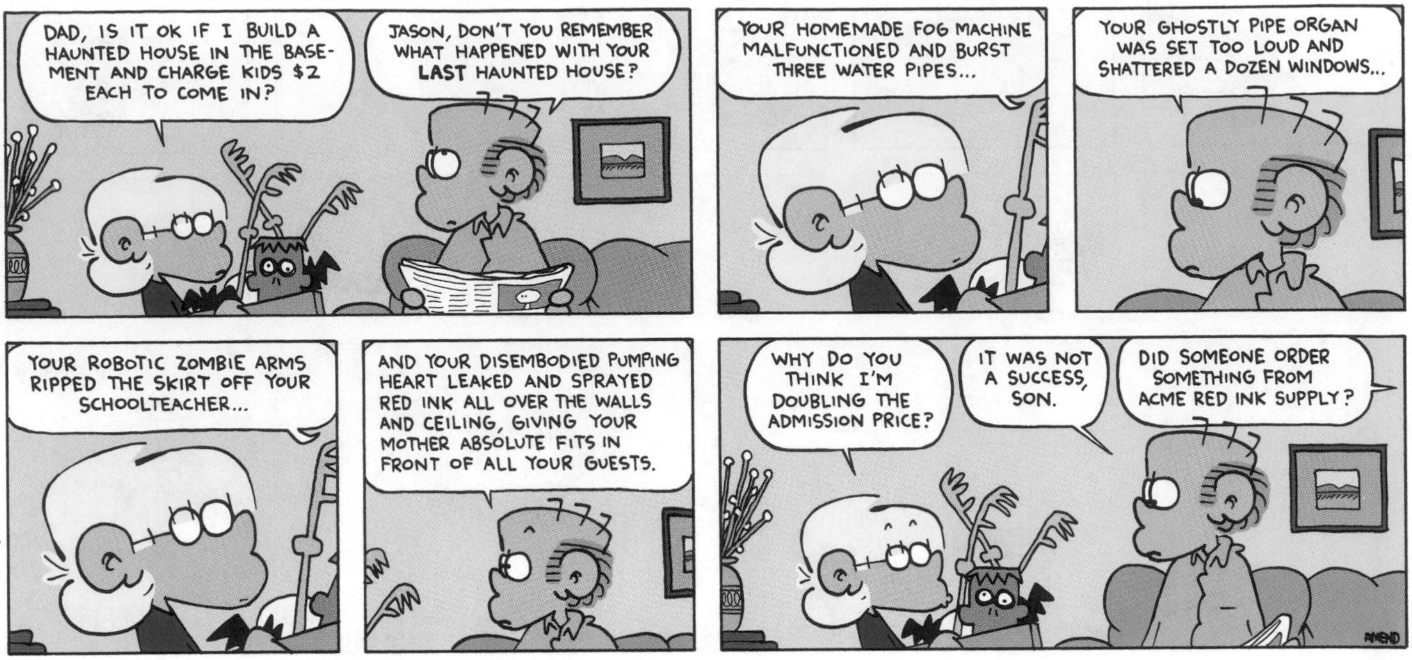
DAD, IS IT OK IF I BUILD A HAUNTED HOUSE IN THE BASEMENT AND CHARGE KIDS $2 EACH TO COME IN?
JASON, DON'T YOU REMEMBER WHAT HAPPENED WITH YOUR LAST HAUNTED HOUSE?
YOUR HOMEMADE FOG MACHINE MALFUNCTIONED AND BURST THREE WATER PIPES...
YOUR GHOSTLY PIPE ORGAN WAS SET TOO LOUD AND SHATTERED A DOZEN WINDOWS...
YOUR ROBOTIC ZOMBIE ARMS RIPPED THE SKIRT OFF YOUR SCHOOLTEACHER...
AND YOUR DISEMBODIED PUMPING HEART LEAKED AND SPRAYED RED INK ALL OVER THE WALLS AND CEILING, GIVING YOUR MOTHER ABSOLUTE FITS IN FRONT OF ALL YOUR GUESTS.
WHY DO YOU THINK I'M DOUBLING THE ADMISSION PRICE?
IT WAS NOT A SUCCESS, SON.
DID SOMEONE ORDER SOMETHING FROM ACME RED INK SUPPLY?
AMEND

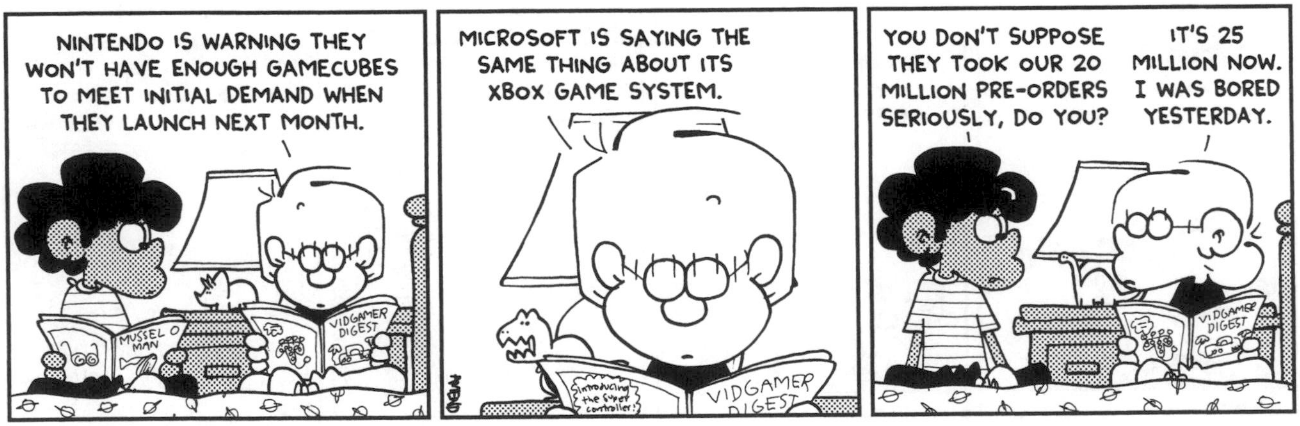
NINTENDO IS WARNING THEY WON'T HAVE ENOUGH GAMECUBES TO MEET INITIAL DEMAND WHEN THEY LAUNCH NEXT MONTH.
MUSSEL O MAN
VIDGAMER DIGEST
MICROSOFT IS SAYING THE SAME THING ABOUT ITS XBOX GAME SYSTEM.
VIDGAMER DIGEST
YOU DON'T SUPPOSE THEY TOOK OUR 20 MILLION PRE-ORDERS SERIOUSLY, DO YOU?
IT'S 25 MILLION NOW. I WAS BORED YESTERDAY.
VIDGAMER DIGEST

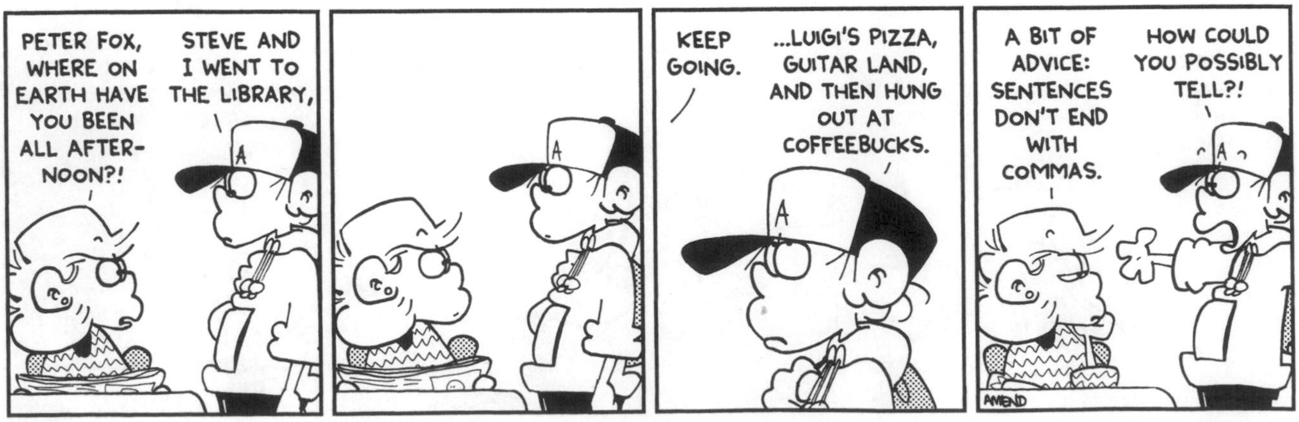
PETER FOX, WHERE ON EARTH HAVE YOU BEEN ALL AFTERNOON?!
STEVE AND I WENT TO THE LIBRARY,
KEEP GOING.
...LUIGI'S PIZZA, GUITAR LAND, AND THEN HUNG OUT AT COFFEEBUCKS.
A BIT OF ADVICE: SENTENCES DON'T END WITH COMMAS.
HOW COULD YOU POSSIBLY TELL?!
AMEND

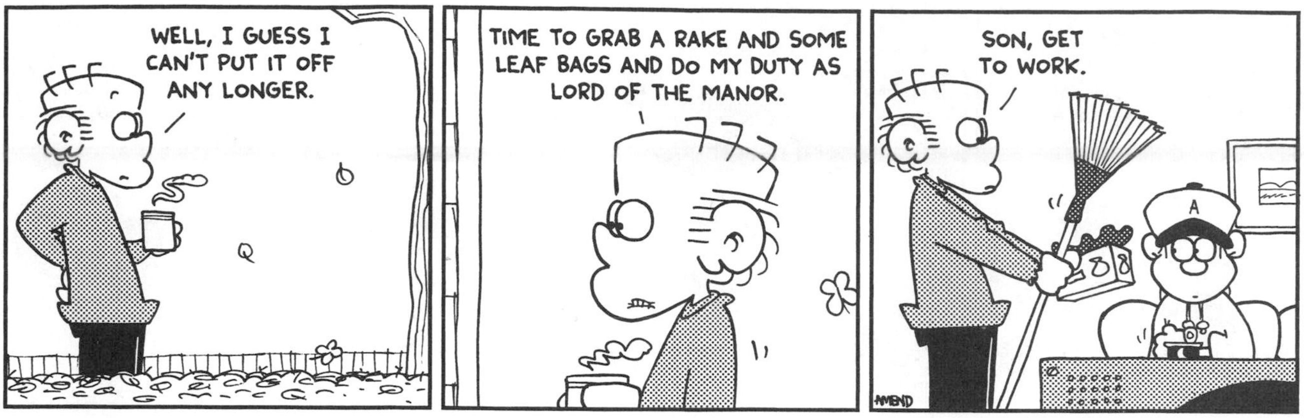
WELL, I GUESS I CAN'T PUT IT OFF ANY LONGER.
TIME TO GRAB A RAKE AND SOME LEAF BAGS AND DO MY DUTY AS LORD OF THE MANOR.
SON, GET TO WORK.

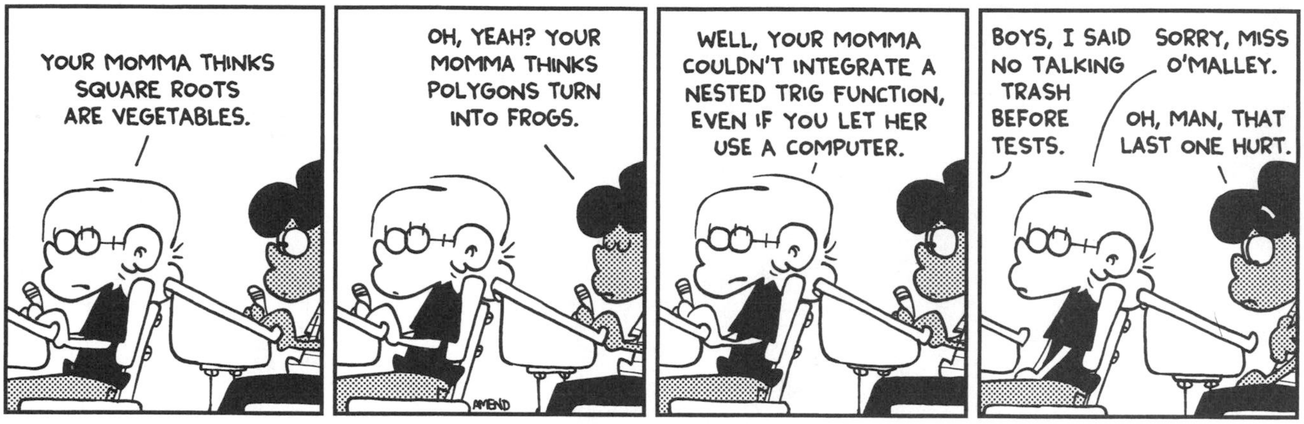
YOUR MOMMA THINKS SQUARE ROOTS ARE VEGETABLES.
OH, YEAH? YOUR MOMMA THINKS POLYGONS TURN INTO FROGS.
WELL, YOUR MOMMA COULDN'T INTEGRATE A NESTED TRIG FUNCTION, EVEN IF YOU LET HER USE A COMPUTER.
BOYS, I SAID NO TALKING TRASH BEFORE TESTS.
SORRY, MISS O'MALLEY.
OH, MAN, THAT LAST ONE HURT.

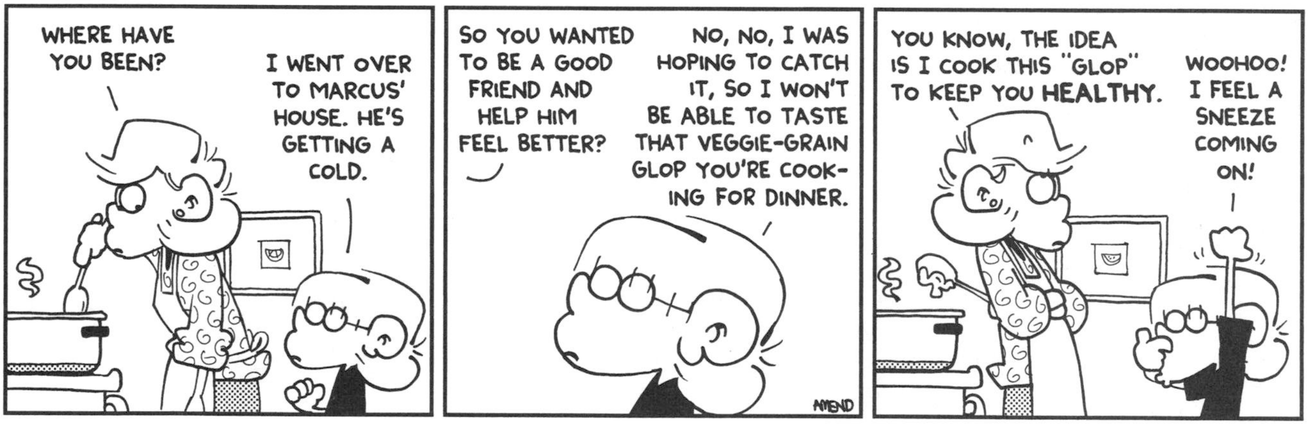
WHERE HAVE YOU BEEN?
I WENT OVER TO MARCUS' HOUSE. HE'S GETTING A COLD.
SO YOU WANTED TO BE A GOOD FRIEND AND HELP HIM FEEL BETTER?
NO, NO, I WAS HOPING TO CATCH IT, SO I WON'T BE ABLE TO TASTE THAT VEGGIE-GRAIN GLOP YOU'RE COOKING FOR DINNER.
YOU KNOW, THE IDEA IS I COOK THIS "GLOP" TO KEEP YOU HEALTHY.
WOOHOO! I FEEL A SNEEZE COMING ON!

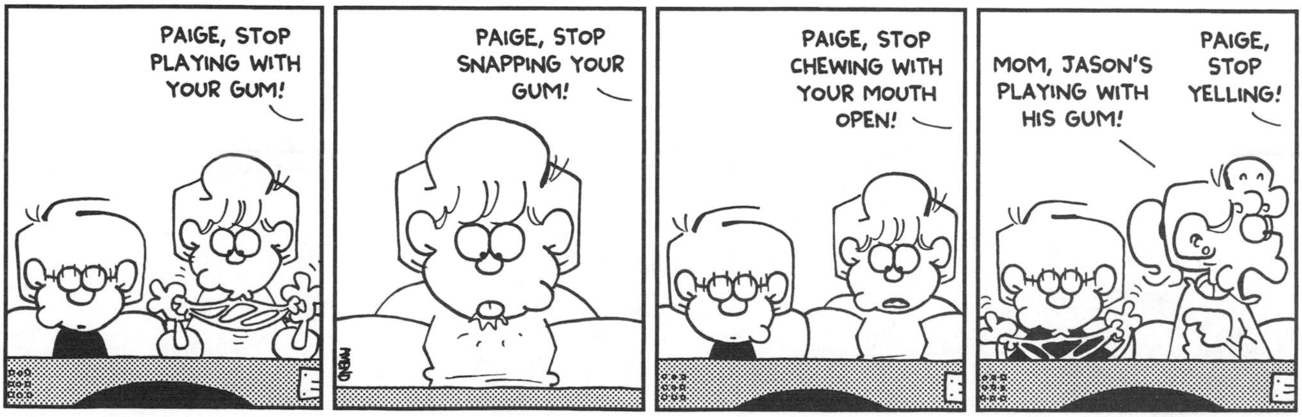
PAIGE, STOP PLAYING WITH YOUR GUM!
PAIGE, STOP SNAPPING YOUR GUM!
PAIGE, STOP CHEWING WITH YOUR MOUTH OPEN!
MOM, JASON'S PLAYING WITH HIS GUM!
PAIGE, STOP YELLING!

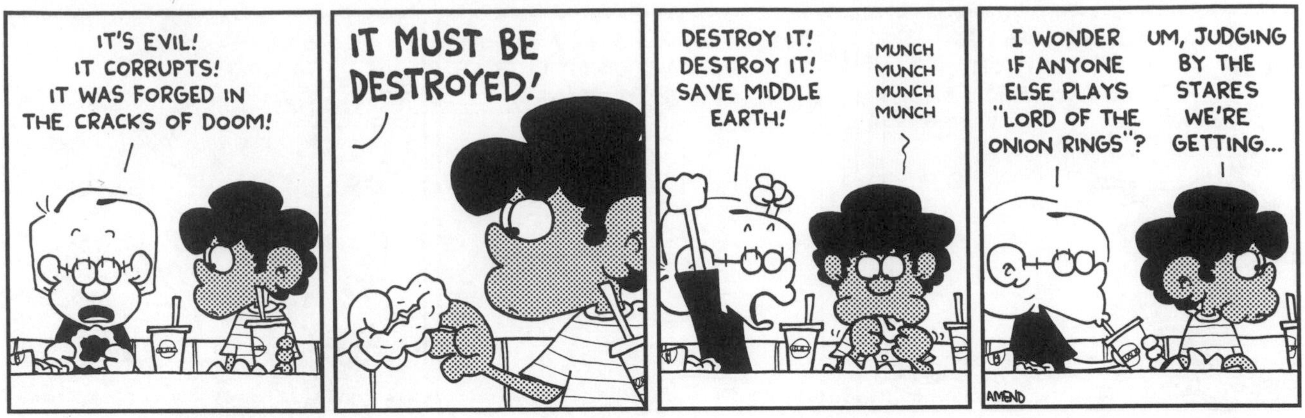
IT'S EVIL! IT CORRUPTS! IT WAS FORGED IN THE CRACKS OF DOOM!
IT MUST BE DESTROYED!
DESTROY IT! DESTROY IT! SAVE MIDDLE EARTH!
MUNCH MUNCH MUNCH MUNCH
I WONDER IF ANYONE ELSE PLAYS "LORD OF THE ONION RINGS"?
UM, JUDGING BY THE STARES WE'RE GETTING...
AMEND

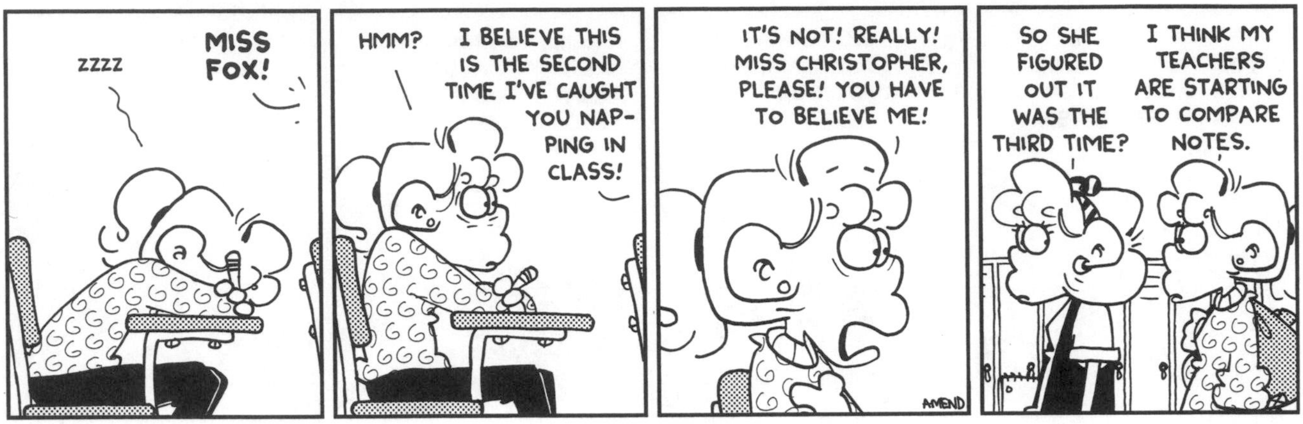
ZZZZ
MISS FOX!
HMM?
I BELIEVE THIS IS THE SECOND TIME I'VE CAUGHT YOU NAPPING IN CLASS!
IT'S NOT! REALLY! MISS CHRISTOPHER, PLEASE! YOU HAVE TO BELIEVE ME!
AMEND
SO SHE FIGURED OUT IT WAS THE THIRD TIME?
I THINK MY TEACHERS ARE STARTING TO COMPARE NOTES.

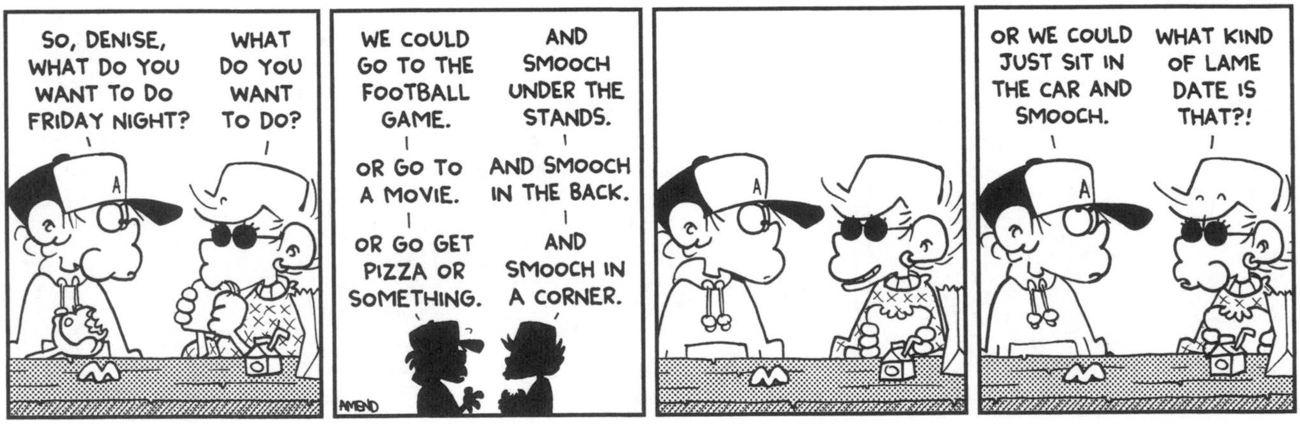
SO, DENISE, WHAT DO YOU WANT TO DO FRIDAY NIGHT?
WHAT DO YOU WANT TO DO?
WE COULD GO TO THE FOOTBALL GAME.
AND SMOOCH UNDER THE STANDS.
OR GO TO A MOVIE.
AND SMOOCH IN THE BACK.
OR GO GET PIZZA OR SOMETHING.
AND SMOOCH IN A CORNER.
AMEND
OR WE COULD JUST SIT IN THE CAR AND SMOOCH.
WHAT KIND OF LAME DATE IS THAT?!

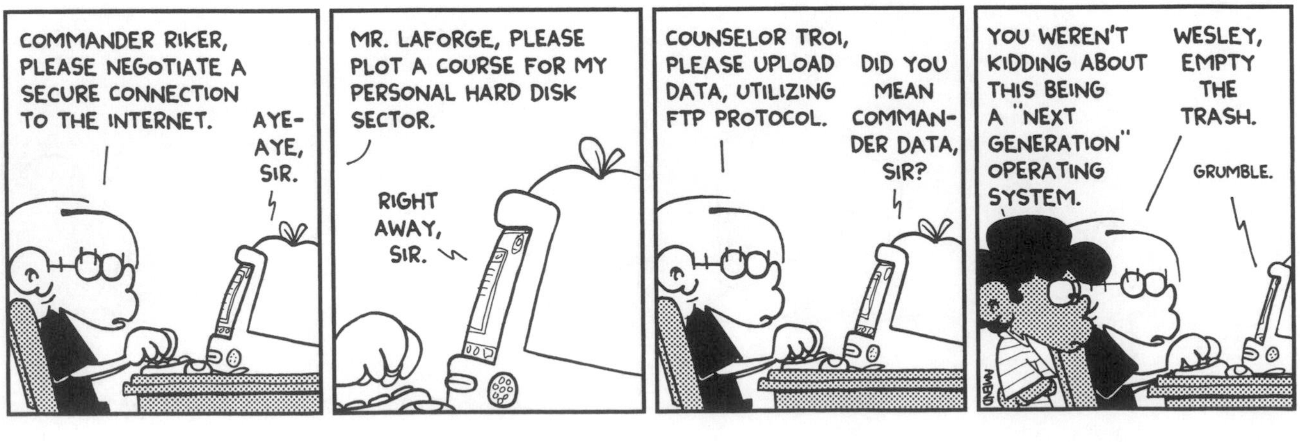
COMMANDER RIKER, PLEASE NEGOTIATE A SECURE CONNECTION TO THE INTERNET.
AYE-AYE, SIR.
MR. LAFORGE, PLEASE PLOT A COURSE FOR MY PERSONAL HARD DISK SECTOR.
RIGHT AWAY, SIR.
COUNSELOR TROI, PLEASE UPLOAD DATA, UTILIZING FTP PROTOCOL.
DID YOU MEAN COMMANDER DATA, SIR?
YOU WEREN'T KIDDING ABOUT THIS BEING A "NEXT GENERATION" OPERATING SYSTEM.
WESLEY, EMPTY THE TRASH.
GRUMBLE.
AMEND

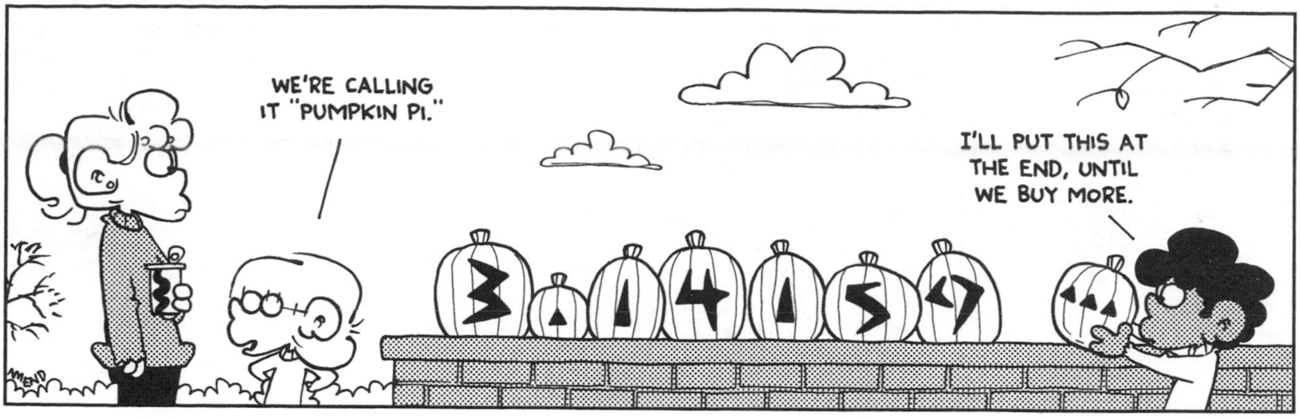
WE'RE CALLING IT "PUMPKIN PI."
I'LL PUT THIS AT THE END, UNTIL WE BUY MORE.
AMEND

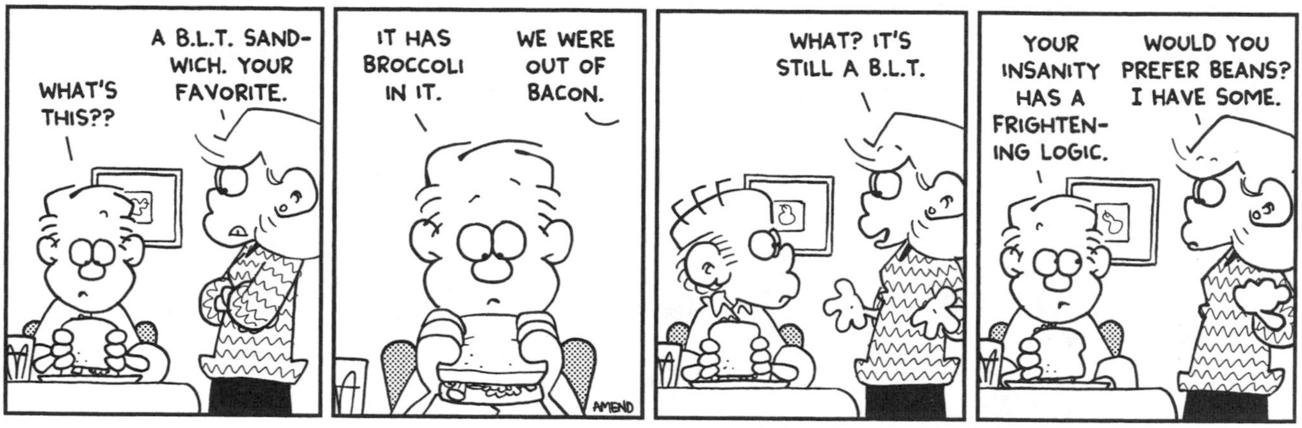
WHAT'S THIS??
A B.L.T. SAND-WICH. YOUR FAVORITE.
IT HAS BROCCOLI IN IT.
WE WERE OUT OF BACON.
WHAT? IT'S STILL A B.L.T.
YOUR INSANITY HAS A FRIGHTEN-ING LOGIC.
WOULD YOU PREFER BEANS? I HAVE SOME.
AMEND

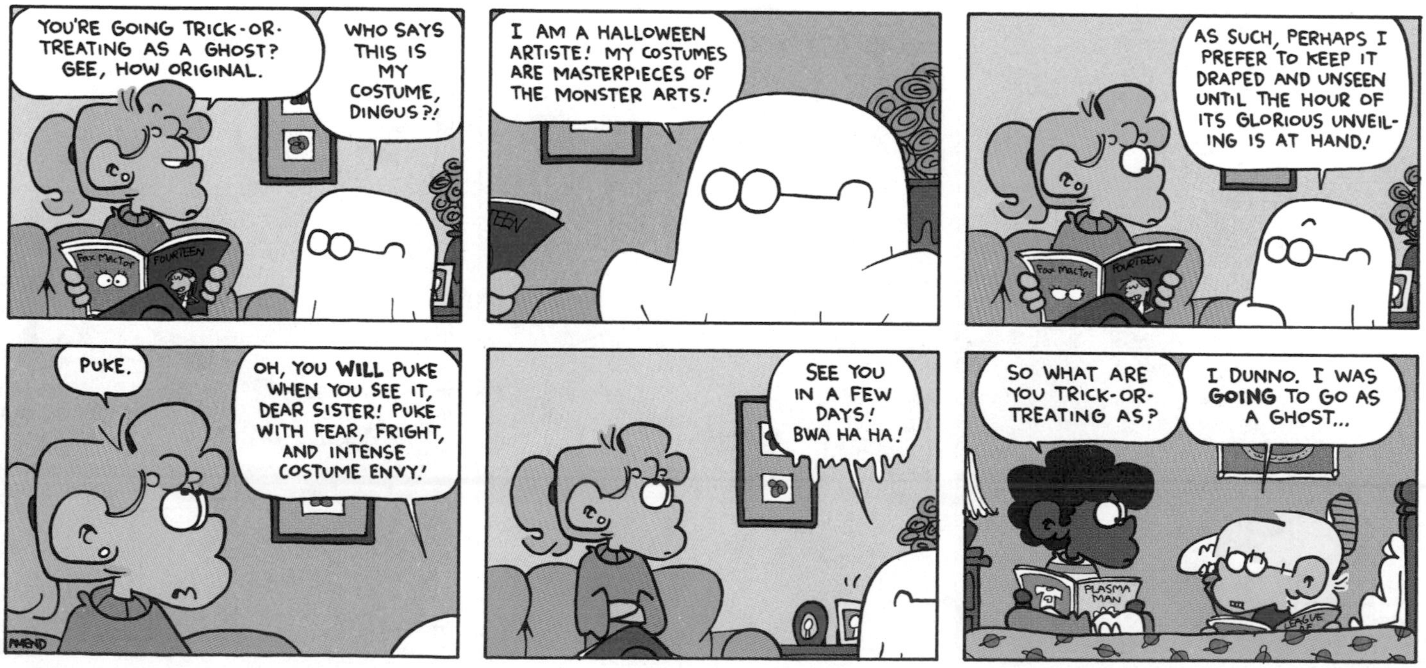
YOU'RE GOING TRICK-OR-TREATING AS A GHOST? GEE, HOW ORIGINAL.
WHO SAYS THIS IS MY COSTUME, DINGUS?!
I AM A HALLOWEEN ARTISTE! MY COSTUMES ARE MASTERPIECES OF THE MONSTER ARTS!
AS SUCH, PERHAPS I PREFER TO KEEP IT DRAPED AND UNSEEN UNTIL THE HOUR OF ITS GLORIOUS UNVEIL-ING IS AT HAND!
PUKE.
OH, YOU **WILL** PUKE WHEN YOU SEE IT, DEAR SISTER! PUKE WITH FEAR, FRIGHT, AND INTENSE COSTUME ENVY!
SEE YOU IN A FEW DAYS! BWA HA HA!
SO WHAT ARE YOU TRICK-OR-TREATING AS?
I DUNNO. I WAS **GOING** TO GO AS A GHOST...
AMEND

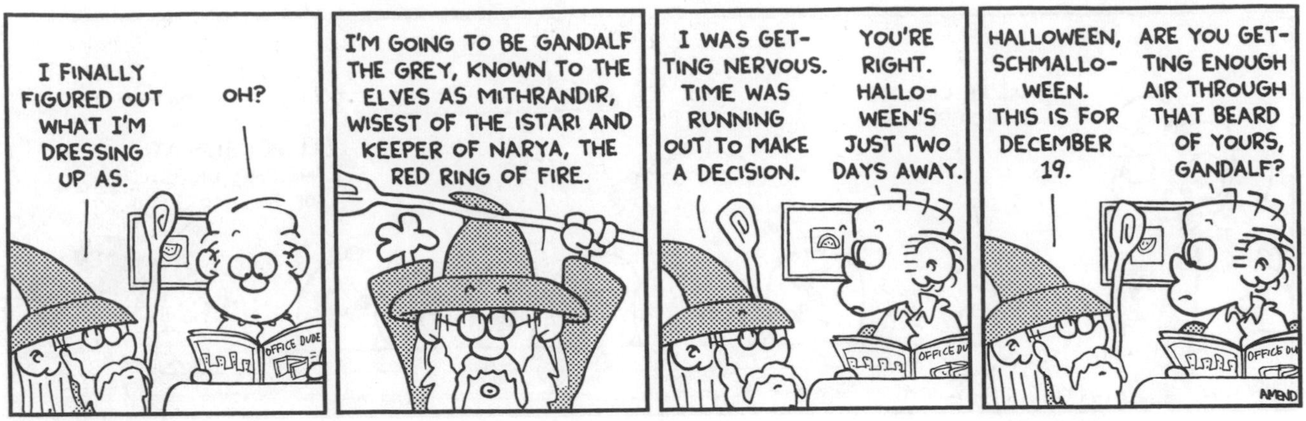
I FINALLY FIGURED OUT WHAT I'M DRESSING UP AS.
OH?
I'M GOING TO BE GANDALF THE GREY, KNOWN TO THE ELVES AS MITHRANDIR, WISEST OF THE ISTARI AND KEEPER OF NARYA, THE RED RING OF FIRE.
I WAS GETTING NERVOUS. TIME WAS RUNNING OUT TO MAKE A DECISION.
YOU'RE RIGHT. HALLOWEEN'S JUST TWO DAYS AWAY.
HALLOWEEN, SCHMALLOWEEN. THIS IS FOR DECEMBER 19.
ARE YOU GETTING ENOUGH AIR THROUGH THAT BEARD OF YOURS, GANDALF?
OFFICE DUDE
AMEND

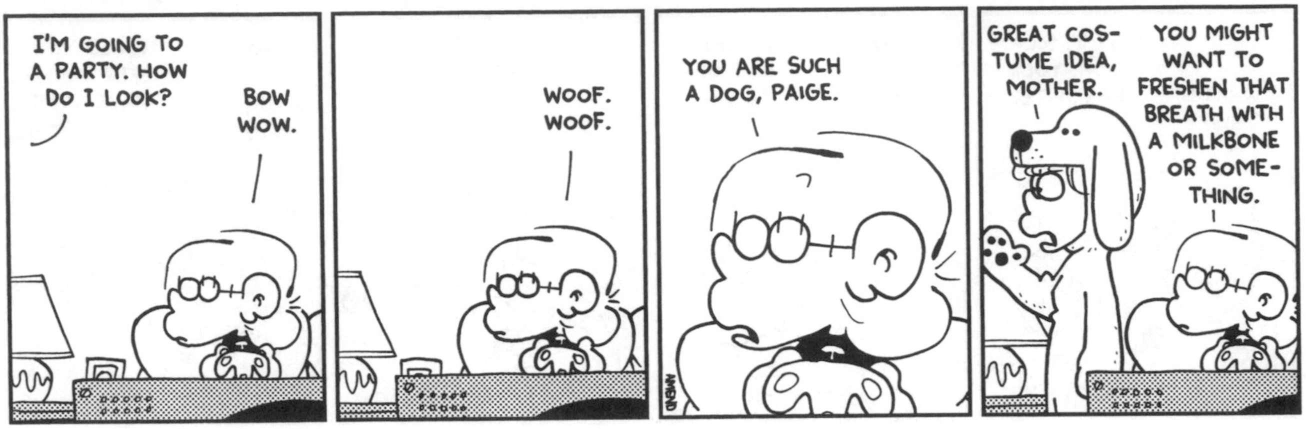
I'M GOING TO A PARTY. HOW DO I LOOK?
BOW WOW.
WOOF. WOOF.
YOU ARE SUCH A DOG, PAIGE.
GREAT COSTUME IDEA, MOTHER.
YOU MIGHT WANT TO FRESHEN THAT BREATH WITH A MILKBONE OR SOMETHING.
AMEND

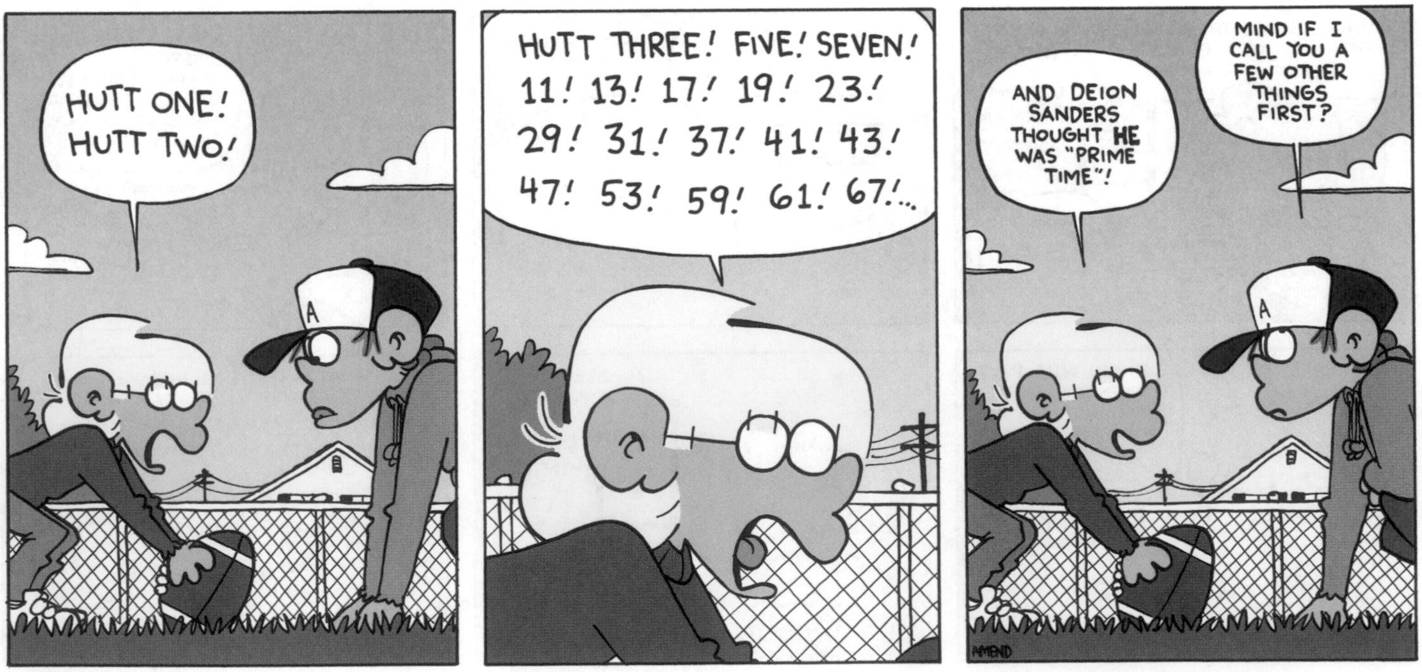
HUTT ONE! HUTT TWO!
HUTT THREE! FIVE! SEVEN! 11! 13! 17! 19! 23! 29! 31! 37! 41! 43! 47! 53! 59! 61! 67!...
AND DEION SANDERS THOUGHT HE WAS "PRIME TIME"!
MIND IF I CALL YOU A FEW OTHER THINGS FIRST?
AMEND

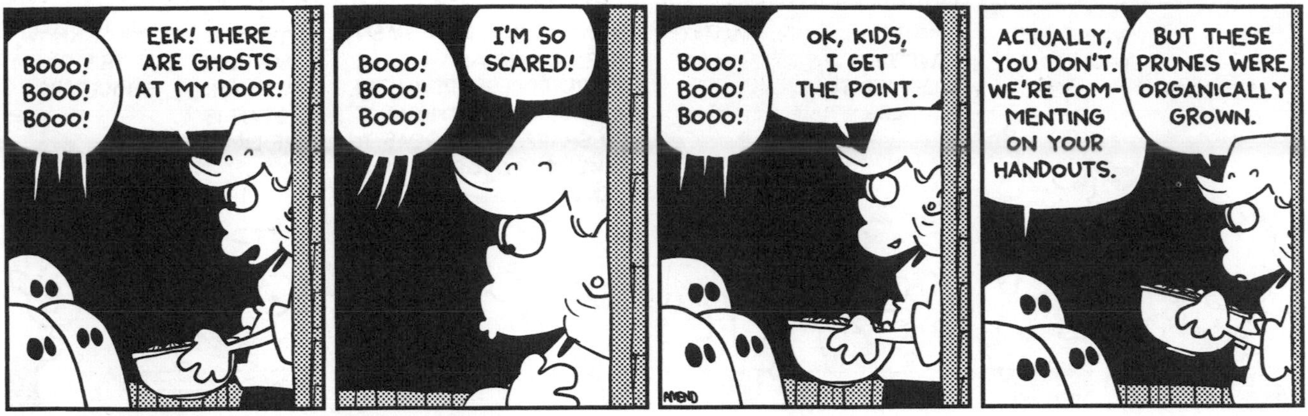
BOOO! BOOO! BOOO!
EEK! THERE ARE GHOSTS AT MY DOOR!
BOOO! BOOO! BOOO!
I'M SO SCARED!
BOOO! BOOO! BOOO!
OK, KIDS, I GET THE POINT.
ACTUALLY, YOU DON'T. WE'RE COM-MENTING ON YOUR HANDOUTS.
BUT THESE PRUNES WERE ORGANICALLY GROWN.
AMEND

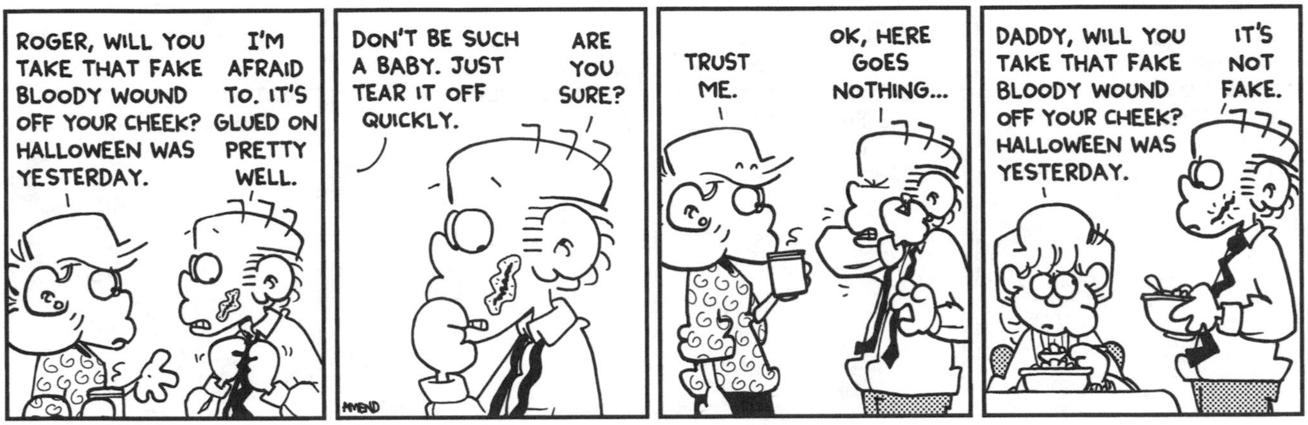
ROGER, WILL YOU TAKE THAT FAKE BLOODY WOUND OFF YOUR CHEEK? HALLOWEEN WAS YESTERDAY.
I'M AFRAID TO. IT'S GLUED ON PRETTY WELL.
DON'T BE SUCH A BABY. JUST TEAR IT OFF QUICKLY.
ARE YOU SURE?
TRUST ME.
OK, HERE GOES NOTHING...
DADDY, WILL YOU TAKE THAT FAKE BLOODY WOUND OFF YOUR CHEEK? HALLOWEEN WAS YESTERDAY.
IT'S NOT FAKE.
AMEND

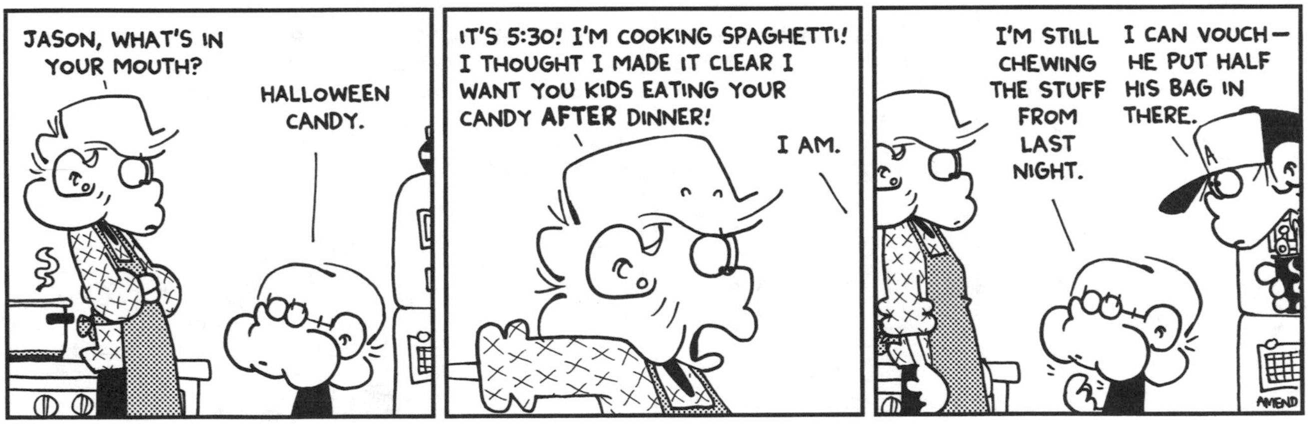
JASON, WHAT'S IN YOUR MOUTH?
HALLOWEEN CANDY.
IT'S 5:30! I'M COOKING SPAGHETTI! I THOUGHT I MADE IT CLEAR I WANT YOU KIDS EATING YOUR CANDY AFTER DINNER!
I AM.
I'M STILL CHEWING THE STUFF FROM LAST NIGHT.
I CAN VOUCH— HE PUT HALF HIS BAG IN THERE.
AMEND

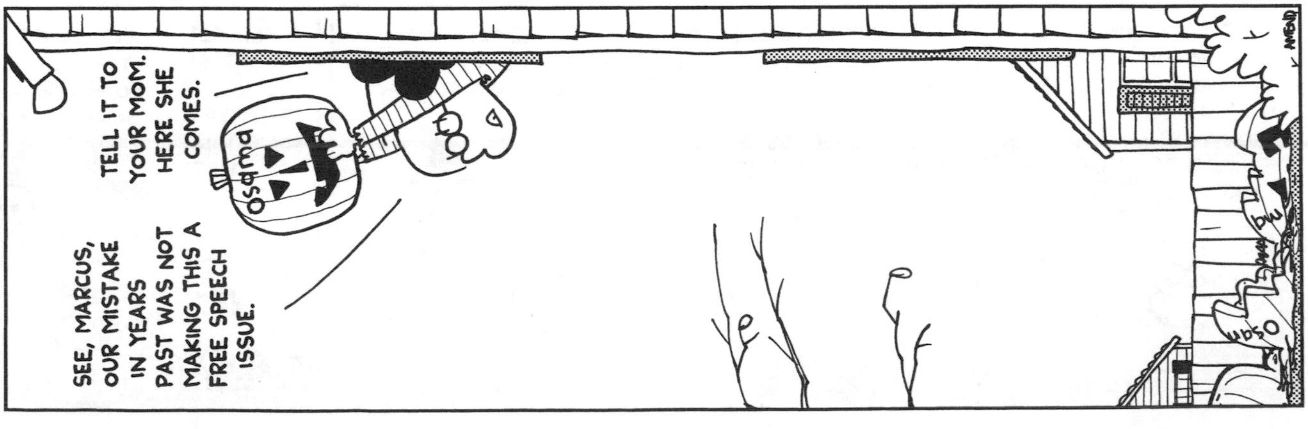
SEE, MARCUS, OUR MISTAKE IN YEARS PAST WAS NOT MAKING THIS A FREE SPEECH ISSUE.
TELL IT TO YOUR MOM. HERE SHE COMES.
osama
AMEND

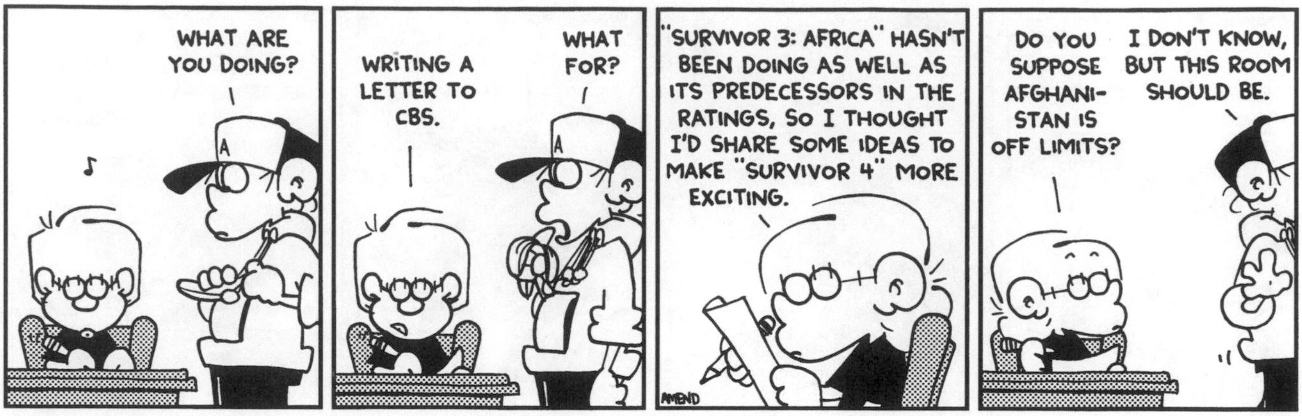
WHAT ARE YOU DOING?
WRITING A LETTER TO CBS.
WHAT FOR?
"SURVIVOR 3: AFRICA" HASN'T BEEN DOING AS WELL AS ITS PREDECESSORS IN THE RATINGS, SO I THOUGHT I'D SHARE SOME IDEAS TO MAKE "SURVIVOR 4" MORE EXCITING.
AMEND
DO YOU SUPPOSE AFGHANI-STAN IS OFF LIMITS?
I DON'T KNOW, BUT THIS ROOM SHOULD BE.

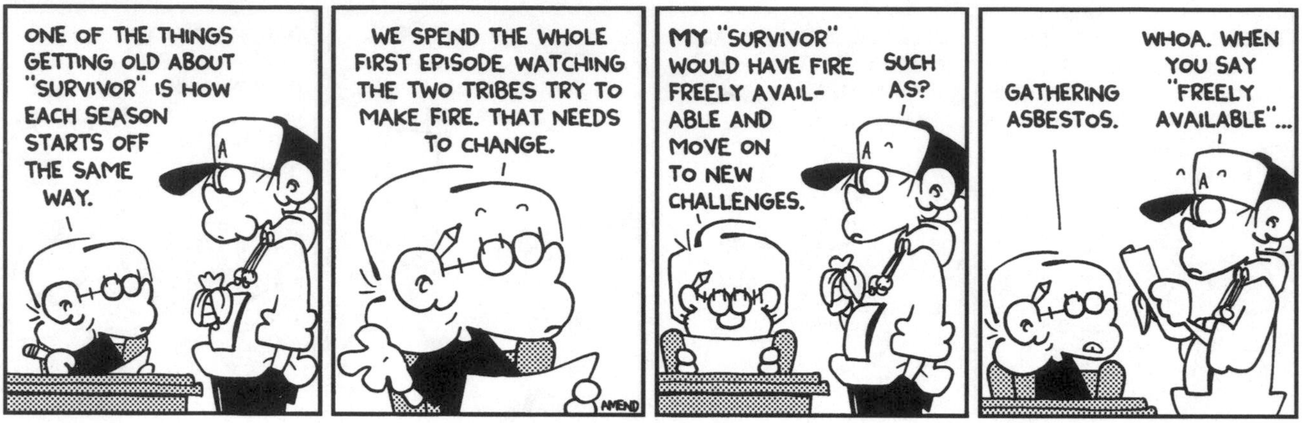
ONE OF THE THINGS GETTING OLD ABOUT "SURVIVOR" IS HOW EACH SEASON STARTS OFF THE SAME WAY.
WE SPEND THE WHOLE FIRST EPISODE WATCHING THE TWO TRIBES TRY TO MAKE FIRE. THAT NEEDS TO CHANGE.
AMEND
MY "SURVIVOR" WOULD HAVE FIRE FREELY AVAIL-ABLE AND MOVE ON TO NEW CHALLENGES.
SUCH AS?
GATHERING ASBESTOS.
WHOA. WHEN YOU SAY "FREELY AVAILABLE"...

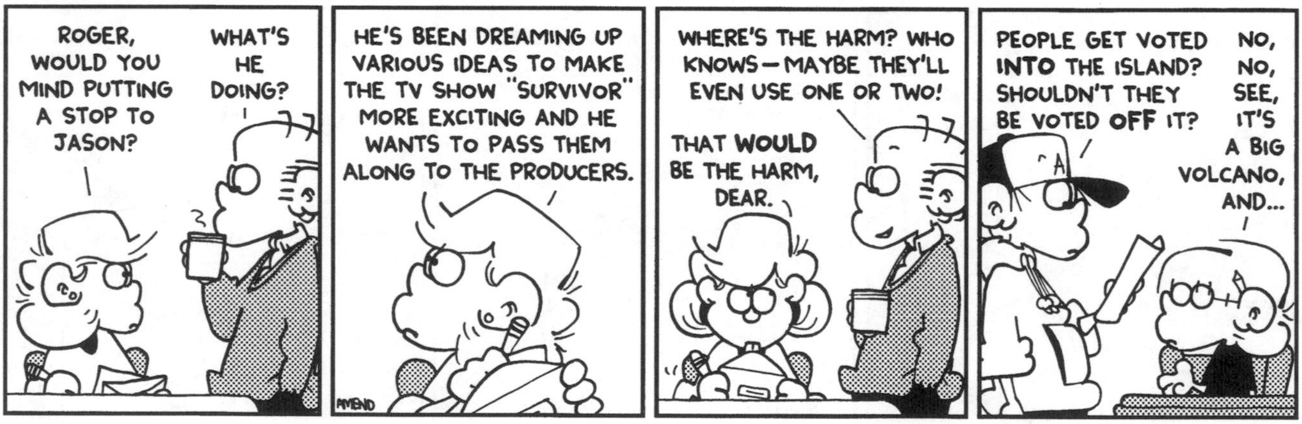
ROGER, WOULD YOU MIND PUTTING A STOP TO JASON?
WHAT'S HE DOING?
HE'S BEEN DREAMING UP VARIOUS IDEAS TO MAKE THE TV SHOW "SURVIVOR" MORE EXCITING AND HE WANTS TO PASS THEM ALONG TO THE PRODUCERS.
AMEND
WHERE'S THE HARM? WHO KNOWS—MAYBE THEY'LL EVEN USE ONE OR TWO!
THAT WOULD BE THE HARM, DEAR.
PEOPLE GET VOTED INTO THE ISLAND? SHOULDN'T THEY BE VOTED OFF IT?
NO, NO, SEE, IT'S A BIG VOLCANO, AND...

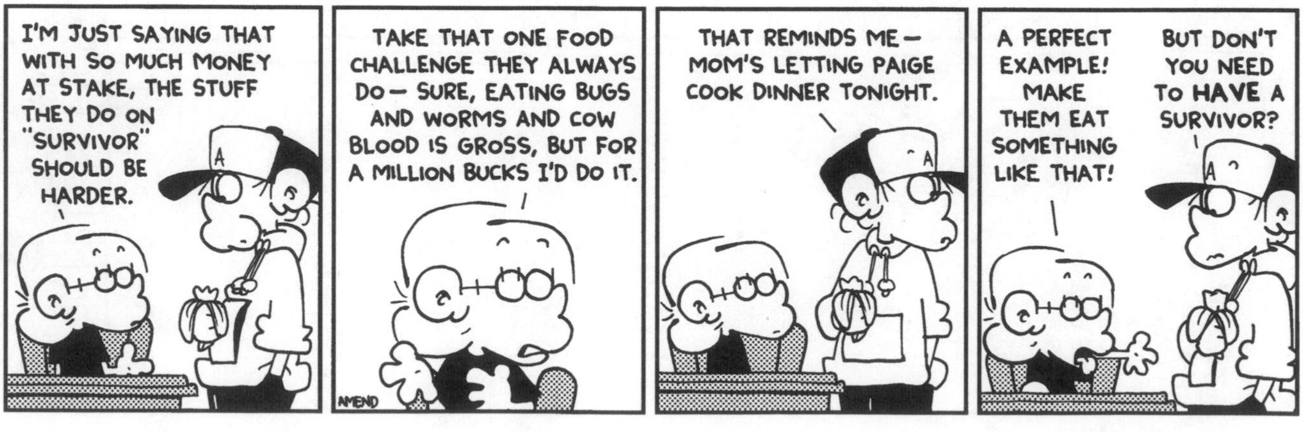
I'M JUST SAYING THAT WITH SO MUCH MONEY AT STAKE, THE STUFF THEY DO ON "SURVIVOR" SHOULD BE HARDER.
TAKE THAT ONE FOOD CHALLENGE THEY ALWAYS DO— SURE, EATING BUGS AND WORMS AND COW BLOOD IS GROSS, BUT FOR A MILLION BUCKS I'D DO IT.
AMEND
THAT REMINDS ME— MOM'S LETTING PAIGE COOK DINNER TONIGHT.
A PERFECT EXAMPLE! MAKE THEM EAT SOMETHING LIKE THAT!
BUT DON'T YOU NEED TO HAVE A SURVIVOR?

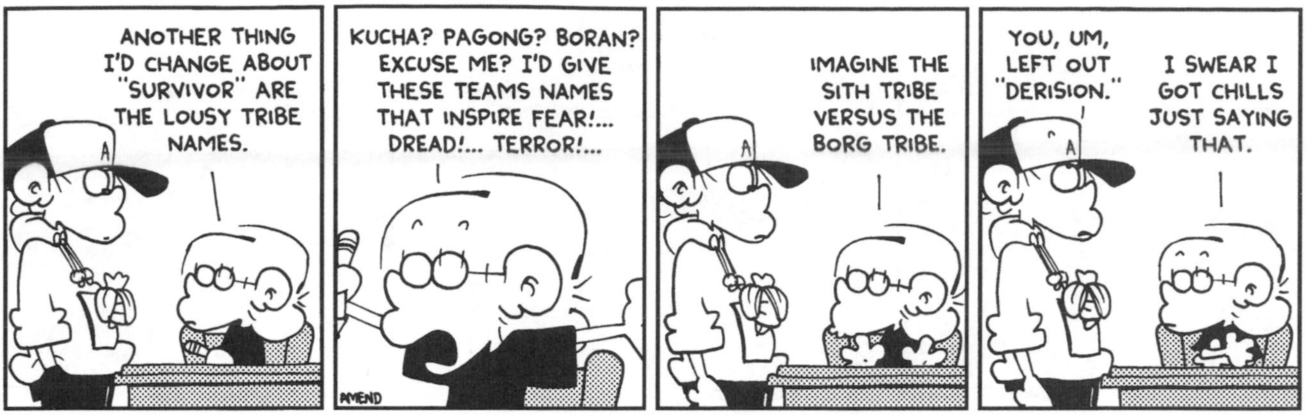
ANOTHER THING I'D CHANGE ABOUT "SURVIVOR" ARE THE LOUSY TRIBE NAMES.
KUCHA? PAGONG? BORAN? EXCUSE ME? I'D GIVE THESE TEAMS NAMES THAT INSPIRE FEAR!... DREAD!... TERROR!...
AMEND
IMAGINE THE SITH TRIBE VERSUS THE BORG TRIBE.
YOU, UM, LEFT OUT "DERISION."
I SWEAR I GOT CHILLS JUST SAYING THAT.

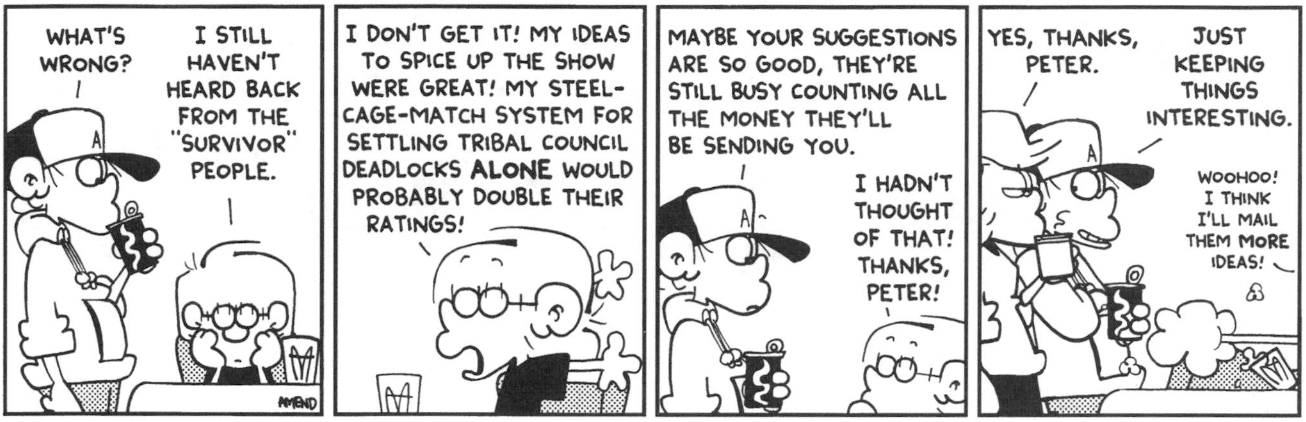
WHAT'S WRONG?
I STILL HAVEN'T HEARD BACK FROM THE "SURVIVOR" PEOPLE.
AMEND
I DON'T GET IT! MY IDEAS TO SPICE UP THE SHOW WERE GREAT! MY STEEL-CAGE-MATCH SYSTEM FOR SETTLING TRIBAL COUNCIL DEADLOCKS ALONE WOULD PROBABLY DOUBLE THEIR RATINGS!
MAYBE YOUR SUGGESTIONS ARE SO GOOD, THEY'RE STILL BUSY COUNTING ALL THE MONEY THEY'LL BE SENDING YOU.
I HADN'T THOUGHT OF THAT! THANKS, PETER!
YES, THANKS, PETER.
JUST KEEPING THINGS INTERESTING.
WOOHOO! I THINK I'LL MAIL THEM MORE IDEAS!

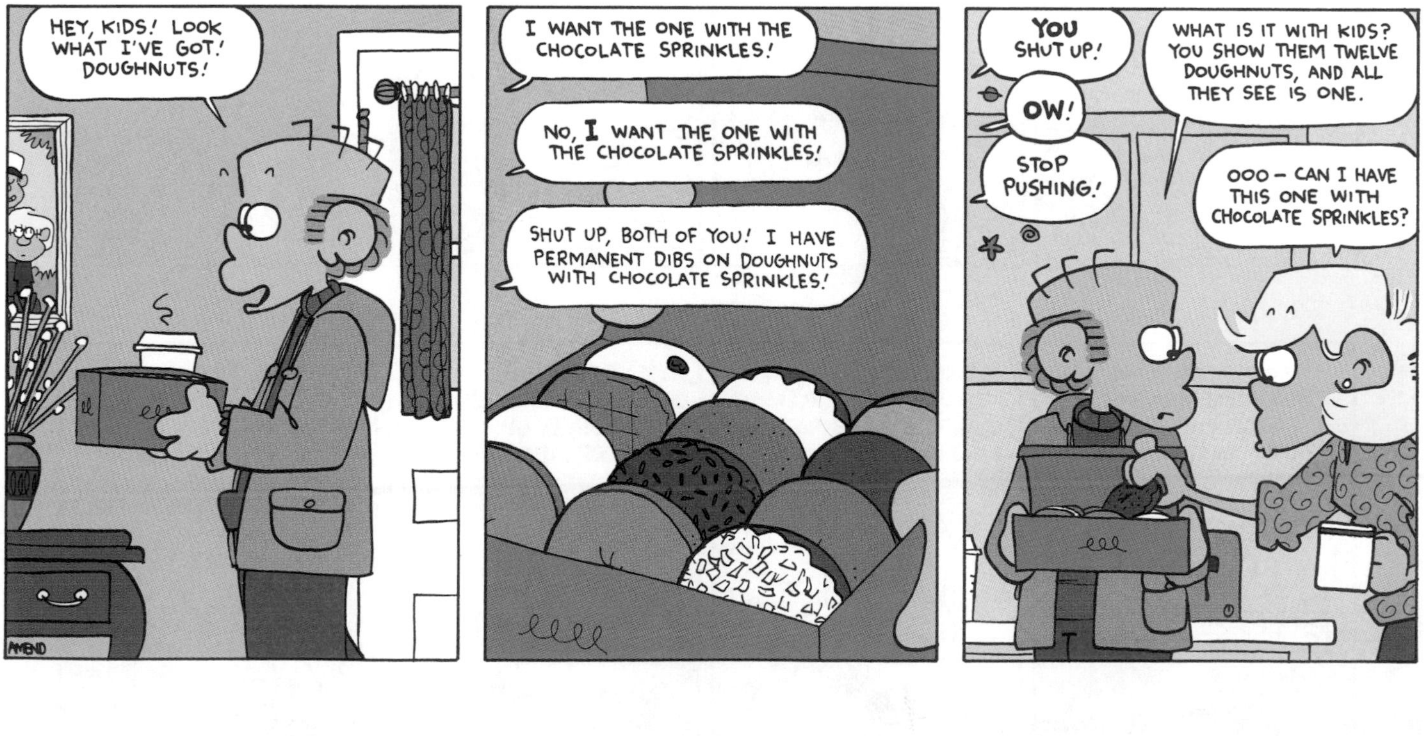
HEY, KIDS! LOOK WHAT I'VE GOT! DOUGHNUTS!
AMEND
I WANT THE ONE WITH THE CHOCOLATE SPRINKLES!
NO, I WANT THE ONE WITH THE CHOCOLATE SPRINKLES!
SHUT UP, BOTH OF YOU! I HAVE PERMANENT DIBS ON DOUGHNUTS WITH CHOCOLATE SPRINKLES!
YOU SHUT UP!
OW!
STOP PUSHING!
WHAT IS IT WITH KIDS? YOU SHOW THEM TWELVE DOUGHNUTS, AND ALL THEY SEE IS ONE.
OOO – CAN I HAVE THIS ONE WITH CHOCOLATE SPRINKLES?

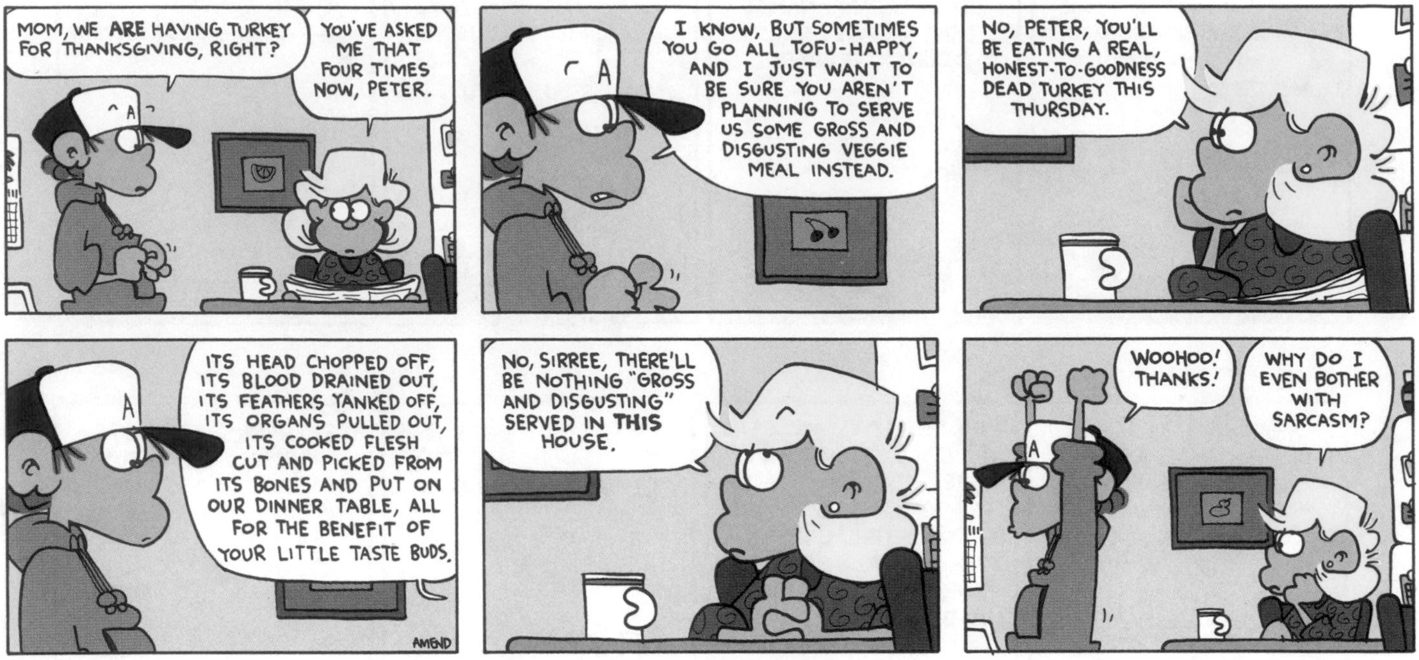
MOM, WE **ARE** HAVING TURKEY FOR THANKSGIVING, RIGHT?
YOU'VE ASKED ME THAT FOUR TIMES NOW, PETER.
I KNOW, BUT SOMETIMES YOU GO ALL TOFU-HAPPY, AND I JUST WANT TO BE SURE YOU AREN'T PLANNING TO SERVE US SOME GROSS AND DISGUSTING VEGGIE MEAL INSTEAD.
NO, PETER, YOU'LL BE EATING A REAL, HONEST-TO-GOODNESS DEAD TURKEY THIS THURSDAY.
ITS HEAD CHOPPED OFF, ITS BLOOD DRAINED OUT, ITS FEATHERS YANKED OFF, ITS ORGANS PULLED OUT, ITS COOKED FLESH CUT AND PICKED FROM ITS BONES AND PUT ON OUR DINNER TABLE, ALL FOR THE BENEFIT OF YOUR LITTLE TASTE BUDS.
AMEND
NO, SIRREE, THERE'LL BE NOTHING "GROSS AND DISGUSTING" SERVED IN **THIS** HOUSE.
WOOHOO! THANKS!
WHY DO I EVEN BOTHER WITH SARCASM?

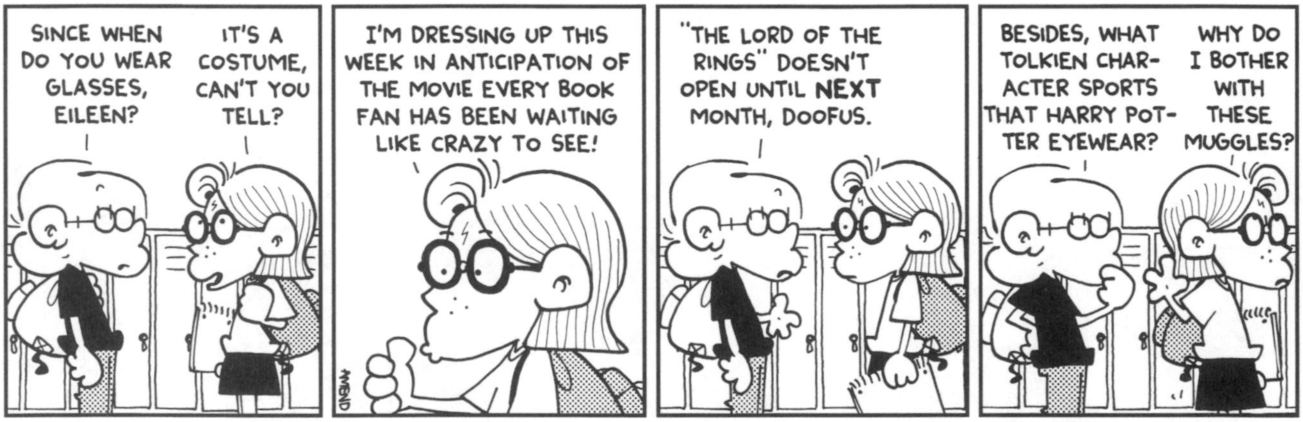
SINCE WHEN DO YOU WEAR GLASSES, EILEEN?
IT'S A COSTUME, CAN'T YOU TELL?
I'M DRESSING UP THIS WEEK IN ANTICIPATION OF THE MOVIE EVERY BOOK FAN HAS BEEN WAITING LIKE CRAZY TO SEE!
AMEND
"THE LORD OF THE RINGS" DOESN'T OPEN UNTIL **NEXT** MONTH, DOOFUS.
BESIDES, WHAT TOLKIEN CHARACTER SPORTS THAT HARRY POTTER EYEWEAR?
WHY DO I BOTHER WITH THESE MUGGLES?

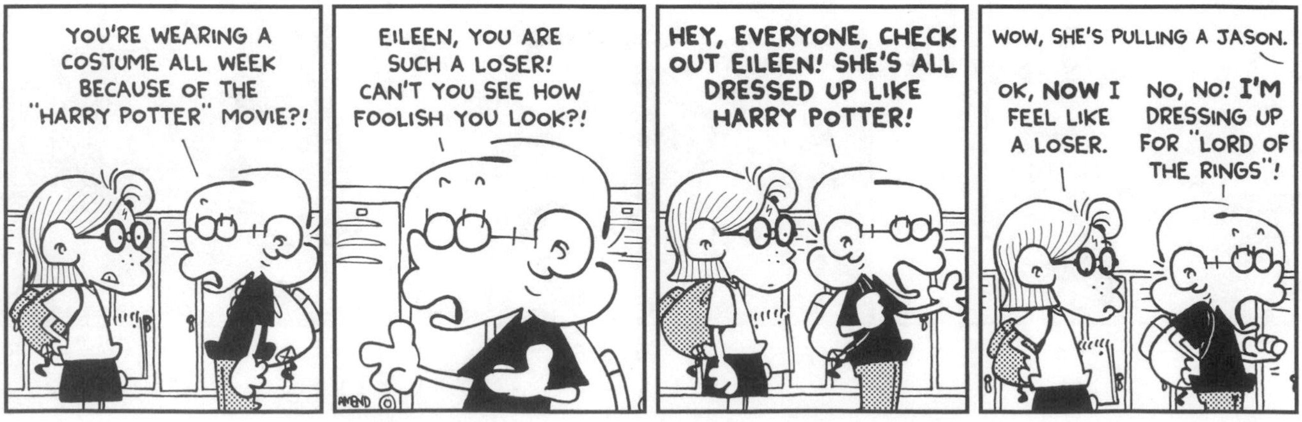
YOU'RE WEARING A COSTUME ALL WEEK BECAUSE OF THE "HARRY POTTER" MOVIE?!
EILEEN, YOU ARE SUCH A LOSER! CAN'T YOU SEE HOW FOOLISH YOU LOOK?!
AMEND ©
HEY, EVERYONE, CHECK OUT EILEEN! SHE'S ALL DRESSED UP LIKE HARRY POTTER!
WOW, SHE'S PULLING A JASON.
OK, **NOW** I FEEL LIKE A LOSER.
NO, NO! **I'M** DRESSING UP FOR "LORD OF THE RINGS"!

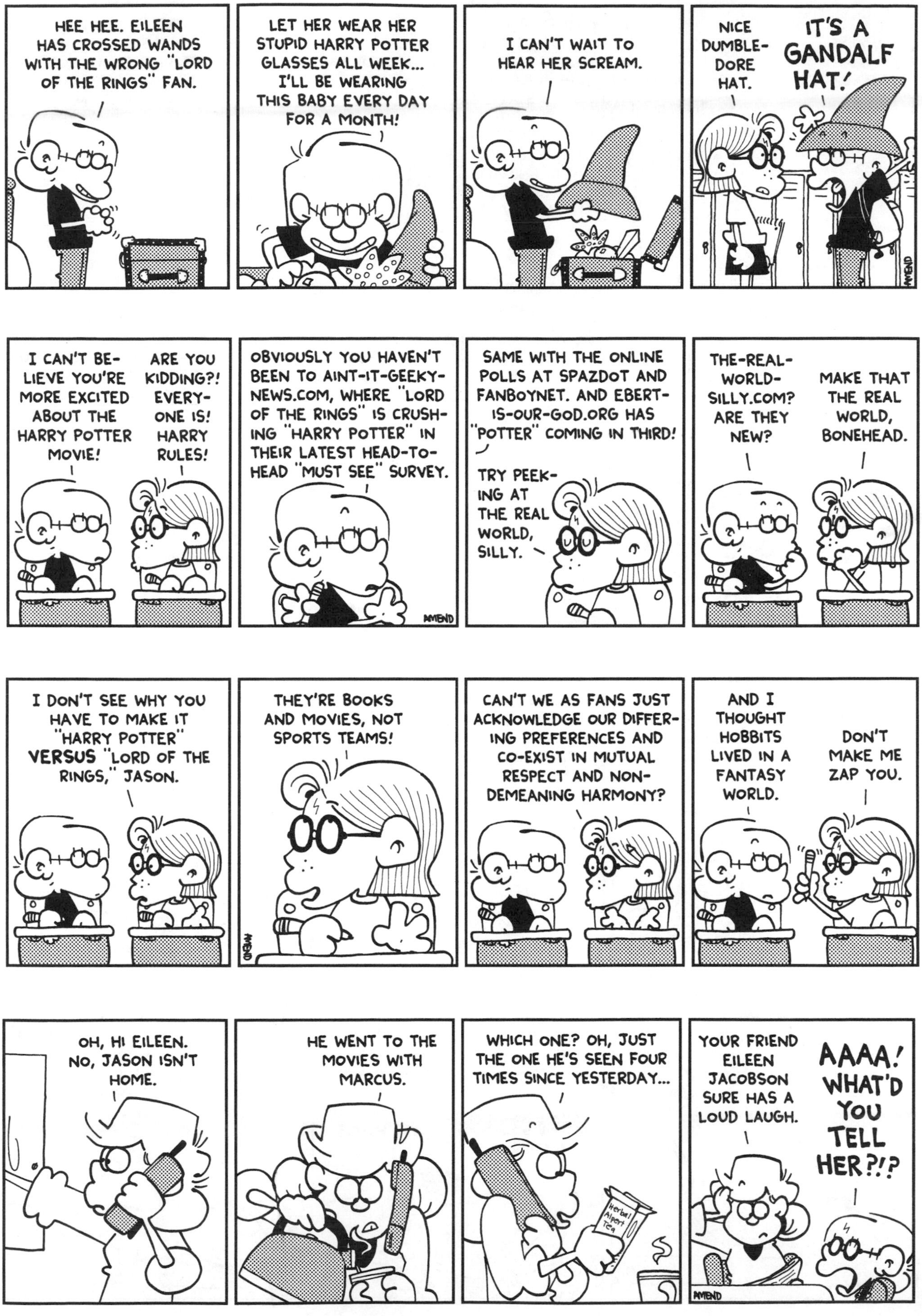
HEE HEE. EILEEN HAS CROSSED WANDS WITH THE WRONG "LORD OF THE RINGS" FAN.
LET HER WEAR HER STUPID HARRY POTTER GLASSES ALL WEEK... I'LL BE WEARING THIS BABY EVERY DAY FOR A MONTH!
I CAN'T WAIT TO HEAR HER SCREAM.
NICE DUMBLE-DORE HAT.
IT'S A GANDALF HAT!
AMEND
I CAN'T BE-LIEVE YOU'RE MORE EXCITED ABOUT THE HARRY POTTER MOVIE!
ARE YOU KIDDING?! EVERY-ONE IS! HARRY RULES!
OBVIOUSLY YOU HAVEN'T BEEN TO AINT-IT-GEEKY-NEWS.COM, WHERE "LORD OF THE RINGS" IS CRUSH-ING "HARRY POTTER" IN THEIR LATEST HEAD-TO-HEAD "MUST SEE" SURVEY.
AMEND
SAME WITH THE ONLINE POLLS AT SPAZDOT AND FANBOYNET. AND EBERT-IS-OUR-GOD.ORG HAS "POTTER" COMING IN THIRD!
TRY PEEK-ING AT THE REAL WORLD, SILLY.
THE-REAL-WORLD-SILLY.COM? ARE THEY NEW?
MAKE THAT THE REAL WORLD, BONEHEAD.
I DON'T SEE WHY YOU HAVE TO MAKE IT "HARRY POTTER" VERSUS "LORD OF THE RINGS," JASON.
THEY'RE BOOKS AND MOVIES, NOT SPORTS TEAMS!
AMEND
CAN'T WE AS FANS JUST ACKNOWLEDGE OUR DIFFER-ING PREFERENCES AND CO-EXIST IN MUTUAL RESPECT AND NON-DEMEANING HARMONY?
AND I THOUGHT HOBBITS LIVED IN A FANTASY WORLD.
DON'T MAKE ME ZAP YOU.
OH, HI EILEEN. NO, JASON ISN'T HOME.
HE WENT TO THE MOVIES WITH MARCUS.
WHICH ONE? OH, JUST THE ONE HE'S SEEN FOUR TIMES SINCE YESTERDAY...
Herbal Alport Tea
YOUR FRIEND EILEEN JACOBSON SURE HAS A LOUD LAUGH.
AAAA! WHAT'D YOU TELL HER?!?
AMEND

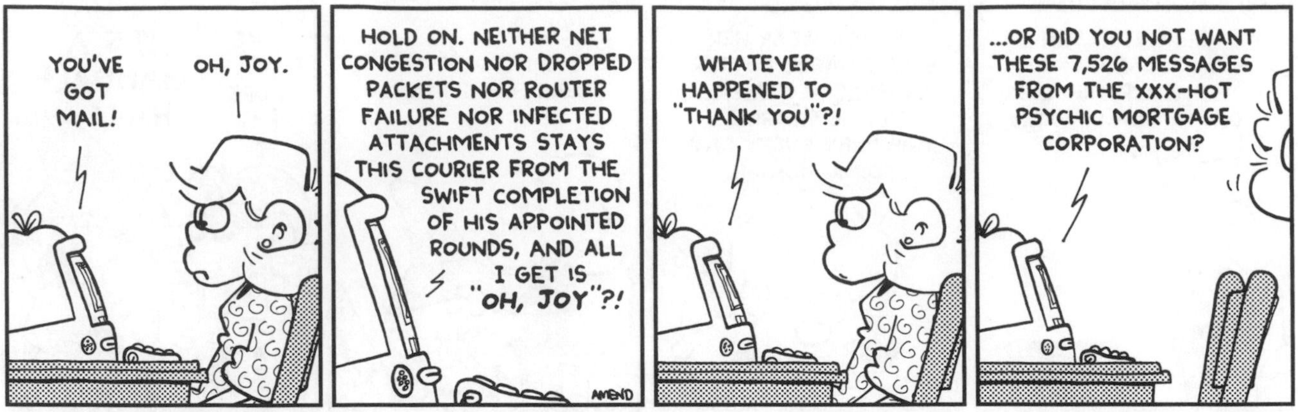
YOU'VE GOT MAIL!
OH, JOY.
HOLD ON. NEITHER NET CONGESTION NOR DROPPED PACKETS NOR ROUTER FAILURE NOR INFECTED ATTACHMENTS STAYS THIS COURIER FROM THE SWIFT COMPLETION OF HIS APPOINTED ROUNDS, AND ALL I GET IS "OH, JOY"?!
AMEND
WHATEVER HAPPENED TO "THANK YOU"?!
...OR DID YOU NOT WANT THESE 7,526 MESSAGES FROM THE XXX-HOT PSYCHIC MORTGAGE CORPORATION?

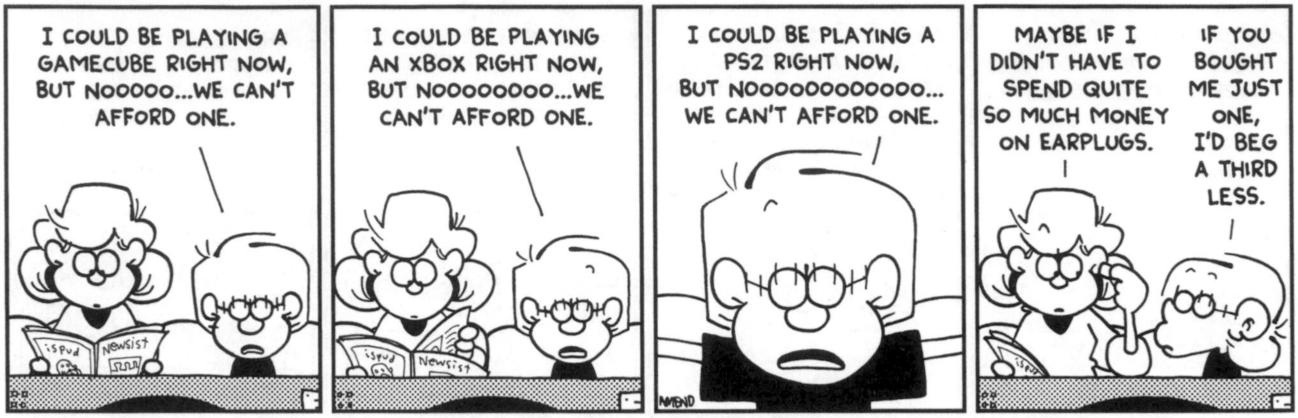
I COULD BE PLAYING A GAMECUBE RIGHT NOW, BUT NOOOOO...WE CAN'T AFFORD ONE.
I COULD BE PLAYING AN XBOX RIGHT NOW, BUT NOOOOOOOO...WE CAN'T AFFORD ONE.
I COULD BE PLAYING A PS2 RIGHT NOW, BUT NOOOOOOOOOOOO... WE CAN'T AFFORD ONE.
AMEND
MAYBE IF I DIDN'T HAVE TO SPEND QUITE SO MUCH MONEY ON EARPLUGS.
IF YOU BOUGHT ME JUST ONE, I'D BEG A THIRD LESS.

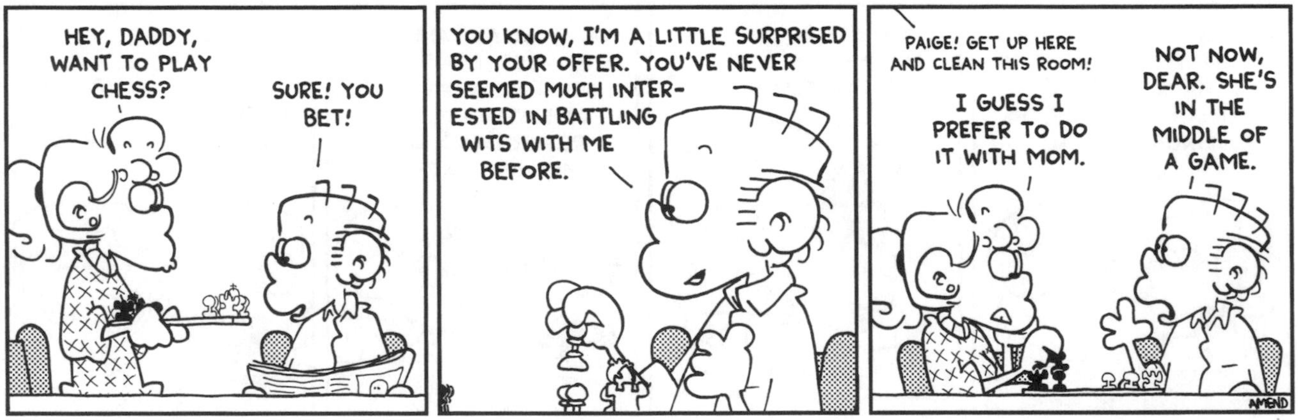
HEY, DADDY, WANT TO PLAY CHESS?
SURE! YOU BET!
YOU KNOW, I'M A LITTLE SURPRISED BY YOUR OFFER. YOU'VE NEVER SEEMED MUCH INTER-ESTED IN BATTLING WITS WITH ME BEFORE.
PAIGE! GET UP HERE AND CLEAN THIS ROOM!
I GUESS I PREFER TO DO IT WITH MOM.
NOT NOW, DEAR. SHE'S IN THE MIDDLE OF A GAME.
AMEND

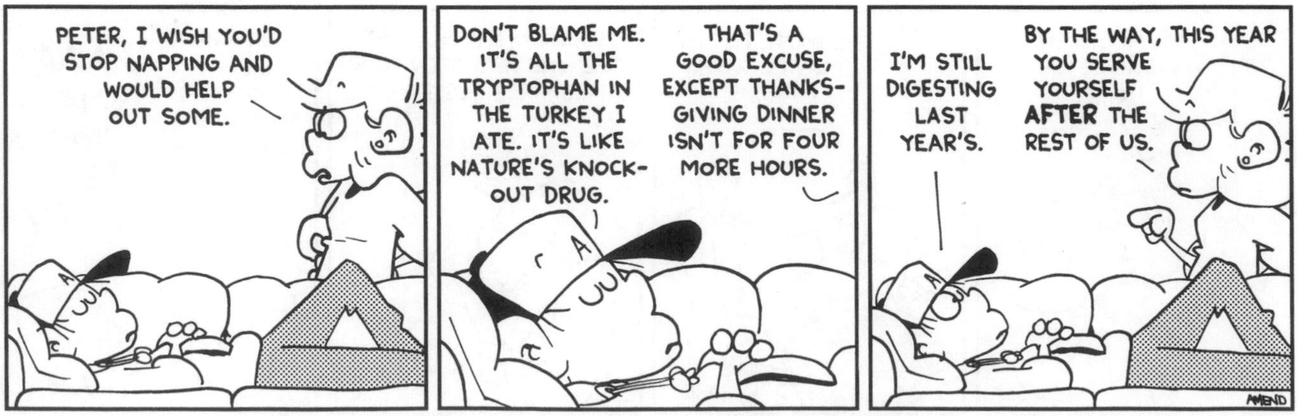
PETER, I WISH YOU'D STOP NAPPING AND WOULD HELP OUT SOME.
DON'T BLAME ME. IT'S ALL THE TRYPTOPHAN IN THE TURKEY I ATE. IT'S LIKE NATURE'S KNOCK-OUT DRUG.
THAT'S A GOOD EXCUSE, EXCEPT THANKS-GIVING DINNER ISN'T FOR FOUR MORE HOURS.
I'M STILL DIGESTING LAST YEAR'S.
BY THE WAY, THIS YEAR YOU SERVE YOURSELF AFTER THE REST OF US.
AMEND

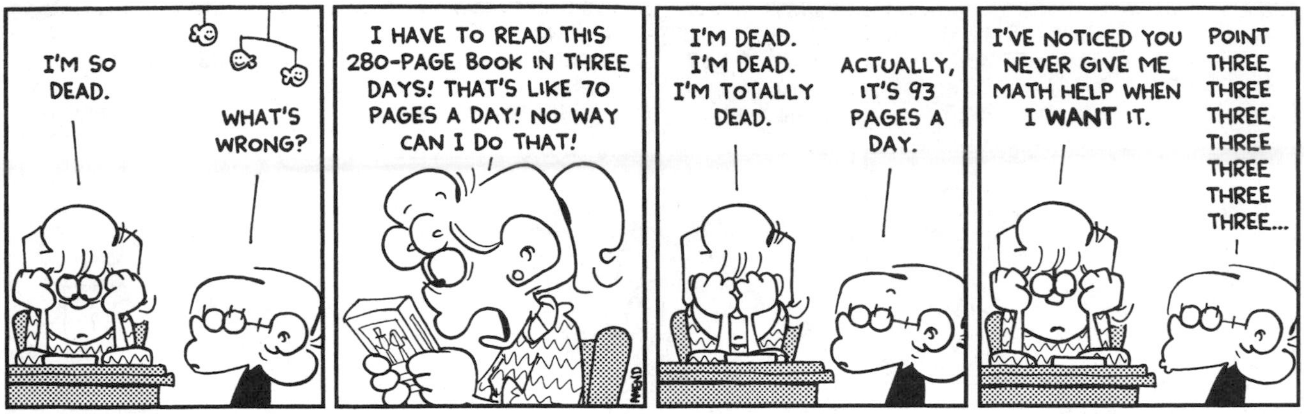
I'M SO DEAD.
WHAT'S WRONG?
I HAVE TO READ THIS 280-PAGE BOOK IN THREE DAYS! THAT'S LIKE 70 PAGES A DAY! NO WAY CAN I DO THAT!
I'M DEAD. I'M DEAD. I'M TOTALLY DEAD.
ACTUALLY, IT'S 93 PAGES A DAY.
I'VE NOTICED YOU NEVER GIVE ME MATH HELP WHEN I **WANT** IT.
POINT THREE THREE THREE THREE THREE THREE THREE...
AMEND

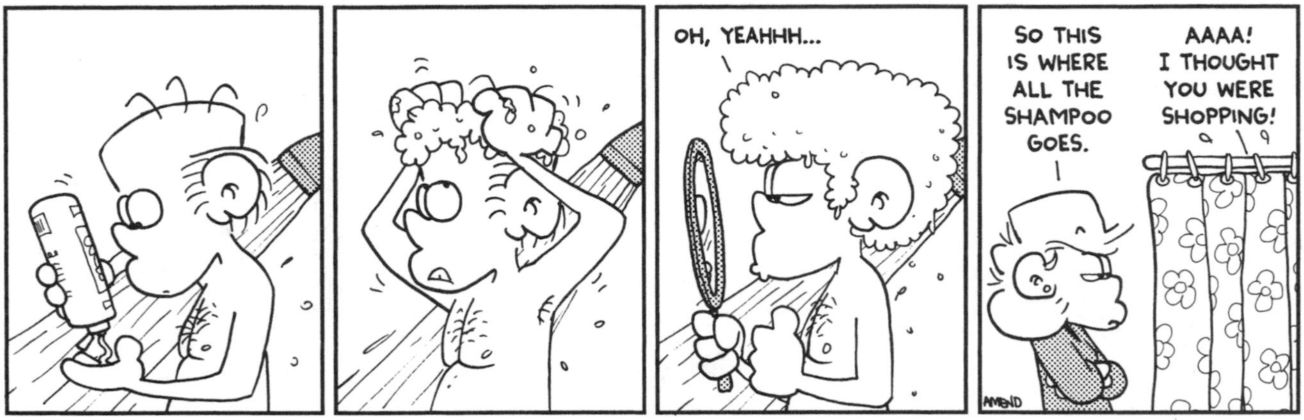
OH, YEAHHH...
SO THIS IS WHERE ALL THE SHAMPOO GOES.
AAAA! I THOUGHT YOU WERE SHOPPING!
AMEND

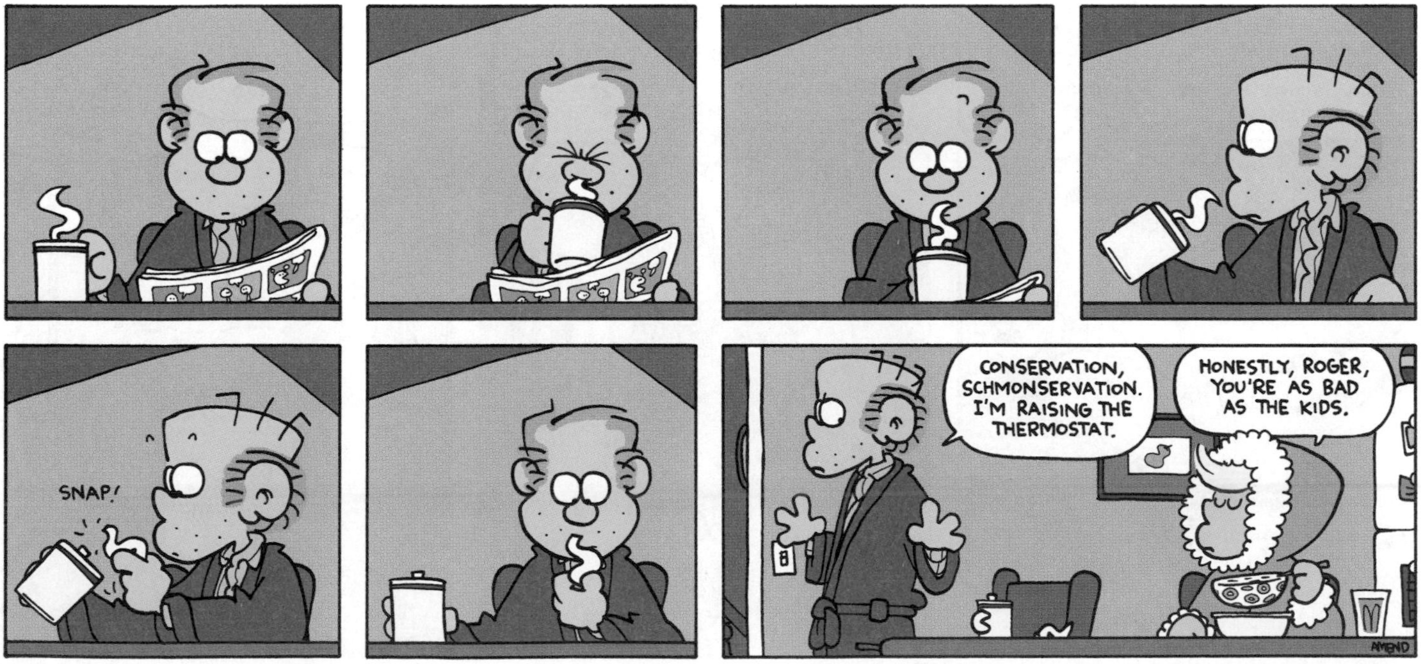
SNAP!
CONSERVATION, SCHMONSERVATION. I'M RAISING THE THERMOSTAT.
HONESTLY, ROGER, YOU'RE AS BAD AS THE KIDS.
AMEND

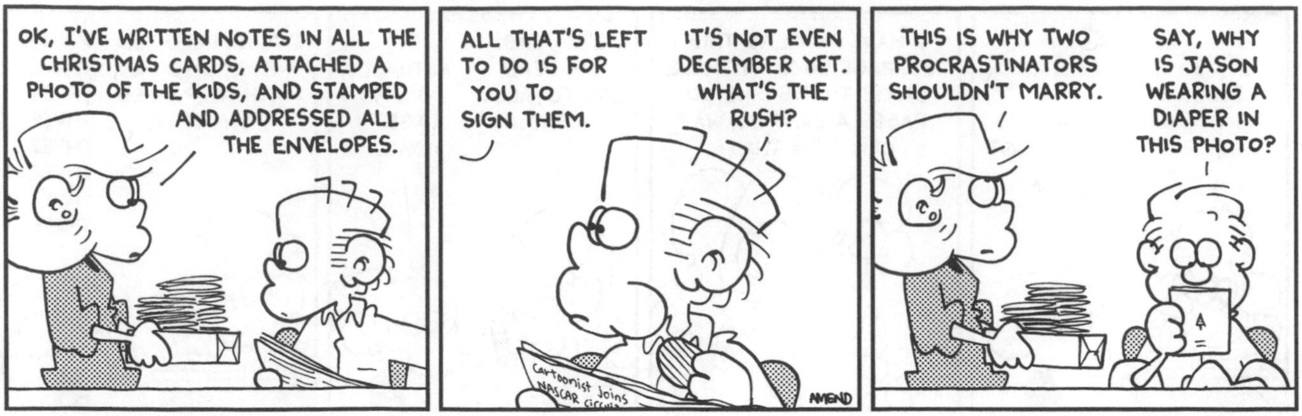
OK, I'VE WRITTEN NOTES IN ALL THE CHRISTMAS CARDS, ATTACHED A PHOTO OF THE KIDS, AND STAMPED AND ADDRESSED ALL THE ENVELOPES.
ALL THAT'S LEFT TO DO IS FOR YOU TO SIGN THEM.
IT'S NOT EVEN DECEMBER YET. WHAT'S THE RUSH?
THIS IS WHY TWO PROCRASTINATORS SHOULDN'T MARRY.
SAY, WHY IS JASON WEARING A DIAPER IN THIS PHOTO?

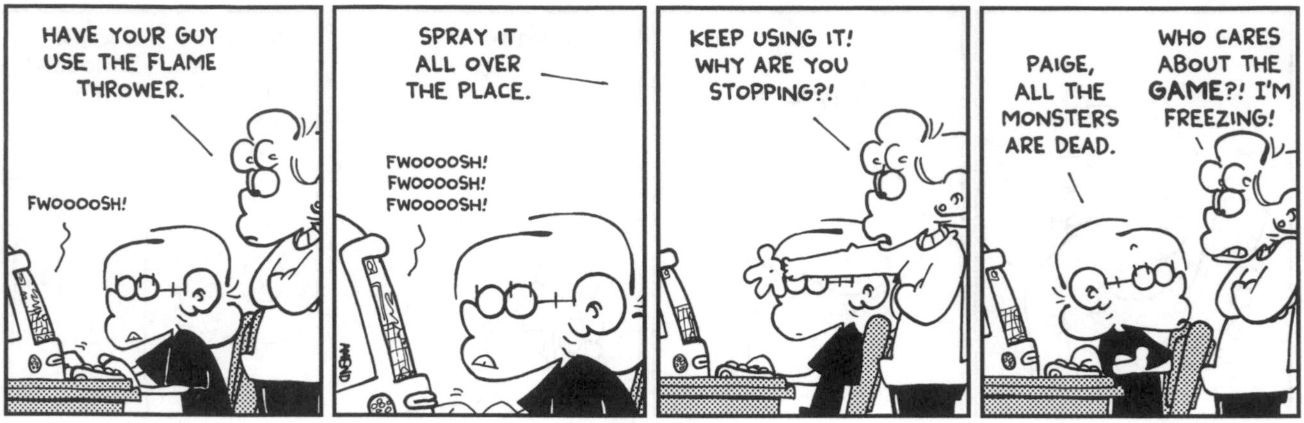
HAVE YOUR GUY USE THE FLAME THROWER.
FWOOOOSH!
SPRAY IT ALL OVER THE PLACE.
FWOOOOSH! FWOOOOSH! FWOOOOSH!
KEEP USING IT! WHY ARE YOU STOPPING?!
PAIGE, ALL THE MONSTERS ARE DEAD.
WHO CARES ABOUT THE GAME?! I'M FREEZING!

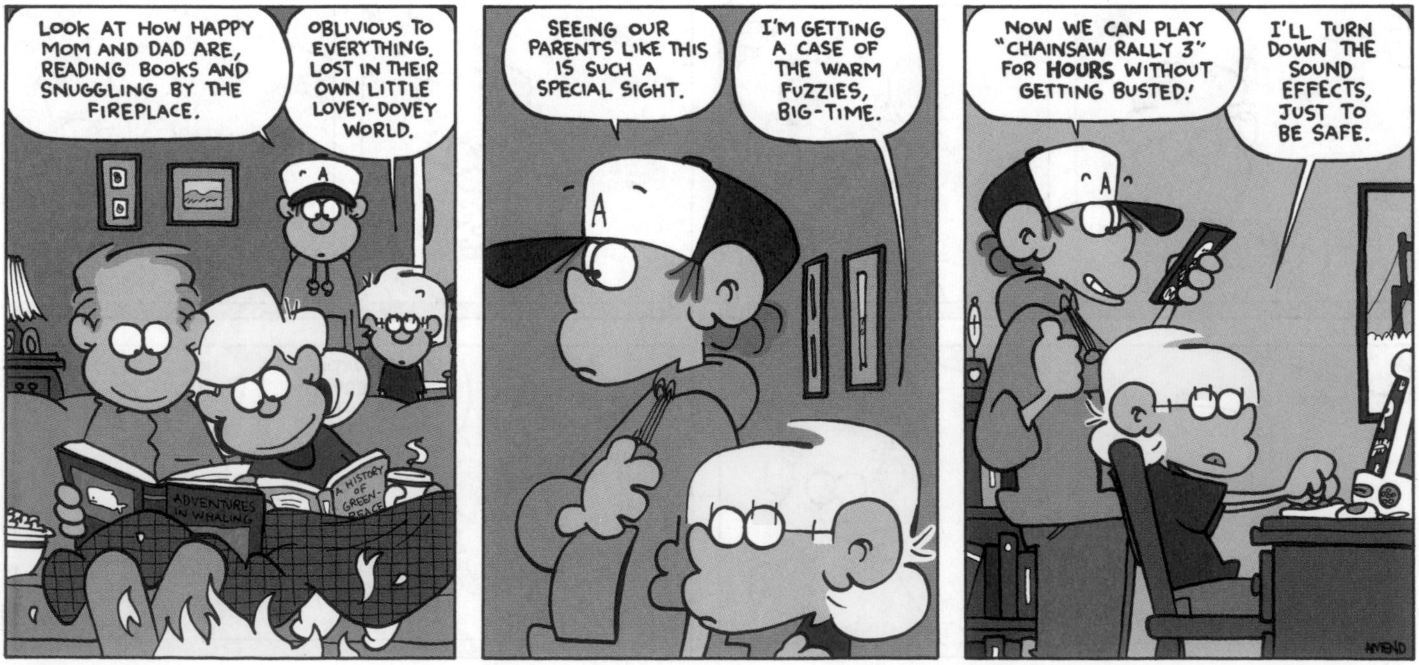
LOOK AT HOW HAPPY MOM AND DAD ARE, READING BOOKS AND SNUGGLING BY THE FIREPLACE.
OBLIVIOUS TO EVERYTHING. LOST IN THEIR OWN LITTLE LOVEY-DOVEY WORLD.
ADVENTURES IN WHALING
A HISTORY OF GREEN-PEACE
SEEING OUR PARENTS LIKE THIS IS SUCH A SPECIAL SIGHT.
I'M GETTING A CASE OF THE WARM FUZZIES, BIG-TIME.
NOW WE CAN PLAY "CHAINSAW RALLY 3" FOR HOURS WITHOUT GETTING BUSTED!
I'LL TURN DOWN THE SOUND EFFECTS, JUST TO BE SAFE.

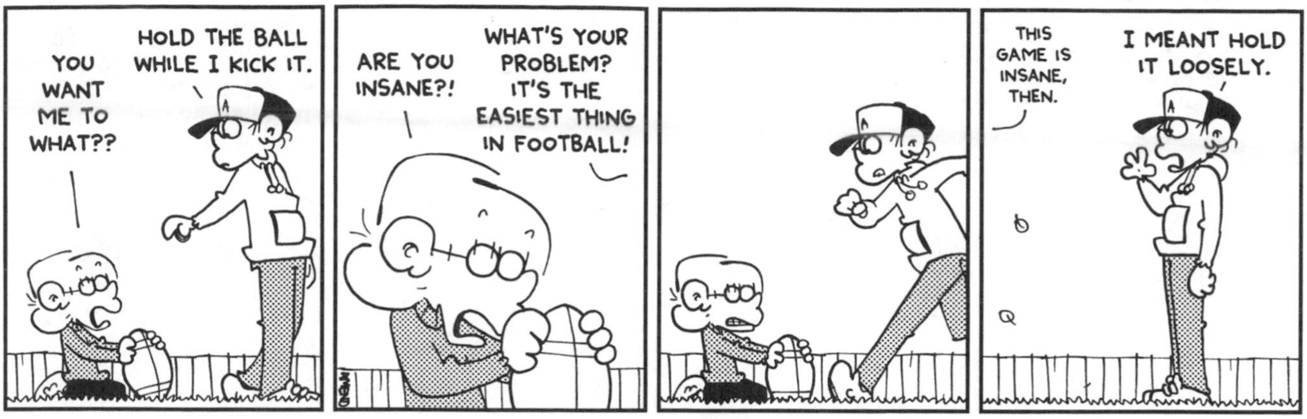
YOU WANT ME TO WHAT??
HOLD THE BALL WHILE I KICK IT.
ARE YOU INSANE?!
WHAT'S YOUR PROBLEM? IT'S THE EASIEST THING IN FOOTBALL!
THIS GAME IS INSANE, THEN.
I MEANT HOLD IT LOOSELY.

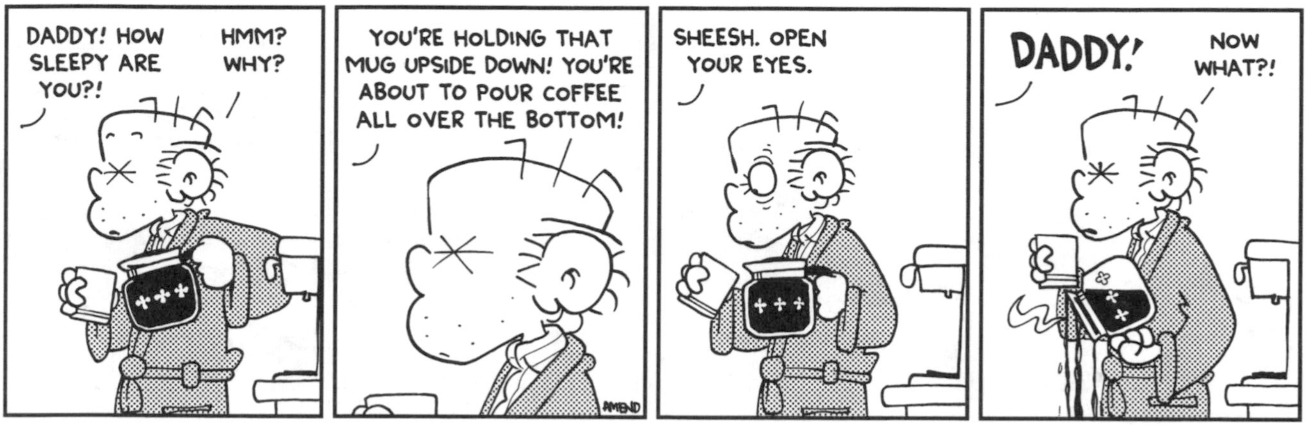
DADDY! HOW SLEEPY ARE YOU?!
HMM? WHY?
YOU'RE HOLDING THAT MUG UPSIDE DOWN! YOU'RE ABOUT TO POUR COFFEE ALL OVER THE BOTTOM!
AMEND
SHEESH. OPEN YOUR EYES.
DADDY!
NOW WHAT?!

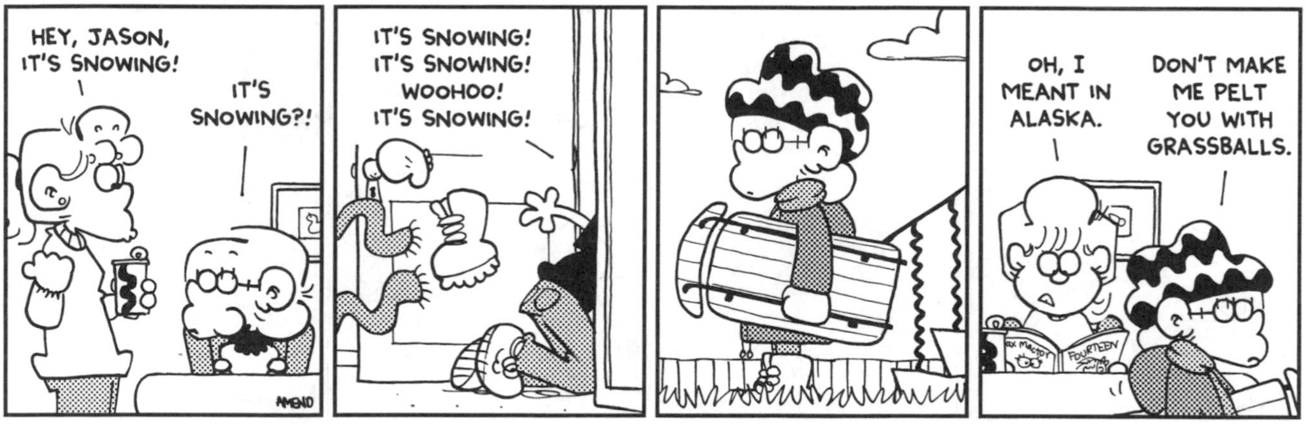
HEY, JASON, IT'S SNOWING!
IT'S SNOWING?!
AMEND
IT'S SNOWING! IT'S SNOWING! WOOHOO! IT'S SNOWING!
OH, I MEANT IN ALASKA.
DON'T MAKE ME PELT YOU WITH GRASSBALLS.

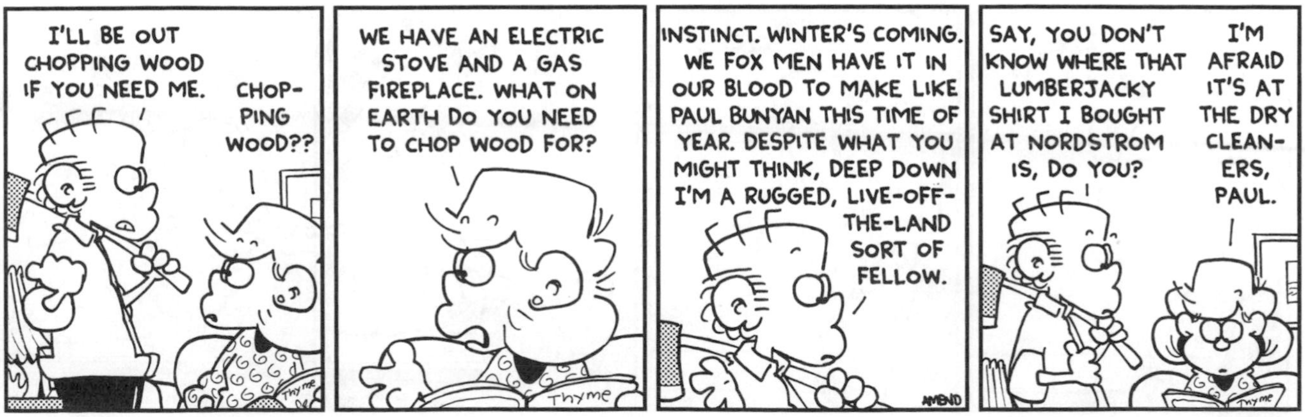
I'LL BE OUT CHOPPING WOOD IF YOU NEED ME.
CHOP-PING WOOD??
WE HAVE AN ELECTRIC STOVE AND A GAS FIREPLACE. WHAT ON EARTH DO YOU NEED TO CHOP WOOD FOR?
INSTINCT. WINTER'S COMING. WE FOX MEN HAVE IT IN OUR BLOOD TO MAKE LIKE PAUL BUNYAN THIS TIME OF YEAR. DESPITE WHAT YOU MIGHT THINK, DEEP DOWN I'M A RUGGED, LIVE-OFF-THE-LAND SORT OF FELLOW.
AMEND
SAY, YOU DON'T KNOW WHERE THAT LUMBERJACKY SHIRT I BOUGHT AT NORDSTROM IS, DO YOU?
I'M AFRAID IT'S AT THE DRY CLEAN-ERS, PAUL.

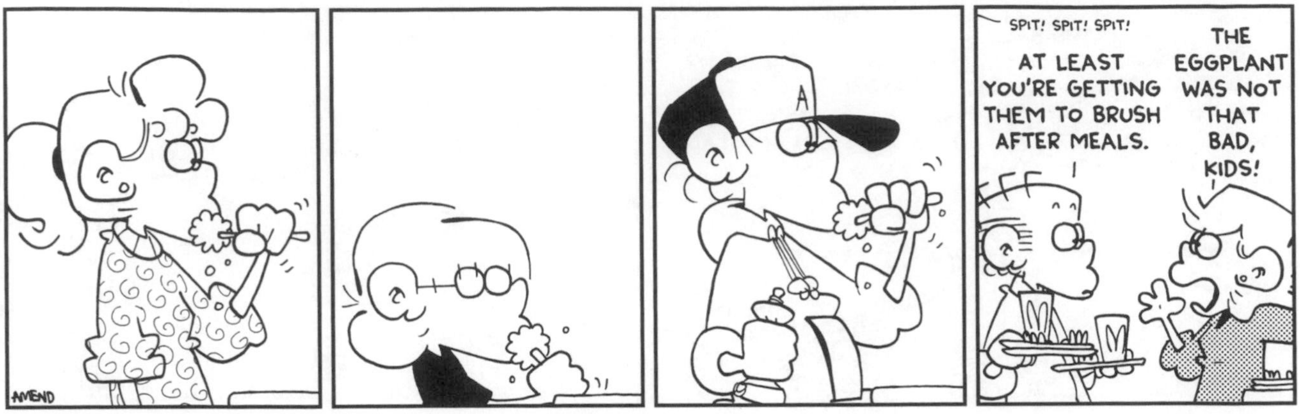
SPIT! SPIT! SPIT!
AT LEAST YOU'RE GETTING THEM TO BRUSH AFTER MEALS.
THE EGGPLANT WAS NOT THAT BAD, KIDS!

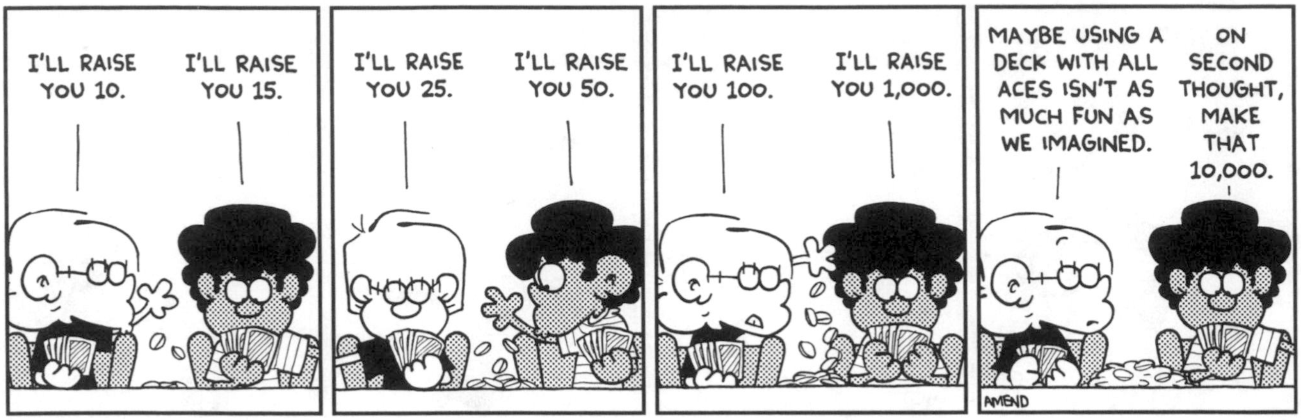
I'LL RAISE YOU 10.
I'LL RAISE YOU 15.
I'LL RAISE YOU 25.
I'LL RAISE YOU 50.
I'LL RAISE YOU 100.
I'LL RAISE YOU 1,000.
MAYBE USING A DECK WITH ALL ACES ISN'T AS MUCH FUN AS WE IMAGINED.
ON SECOND THOUGHT, MAKE THAT 10,000.

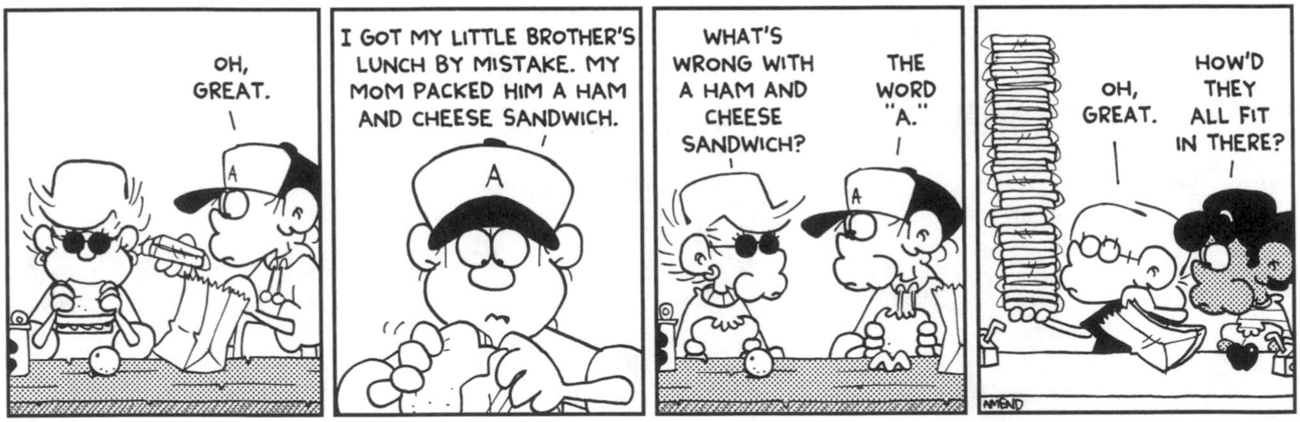
OH, GREAT.
I GOT MY LITTLE BROTHER'S LUNCH BY MISTAKE. MY MOM PACKED HIM A HAM AND CHEESE SANDWICH.
WHAT'S WRONG WITH A HAM AND CHEESE SANDWICH?
THE WORD "A."
OH, GREAT.
HOW'D THEY ALL FIT IN THERE?

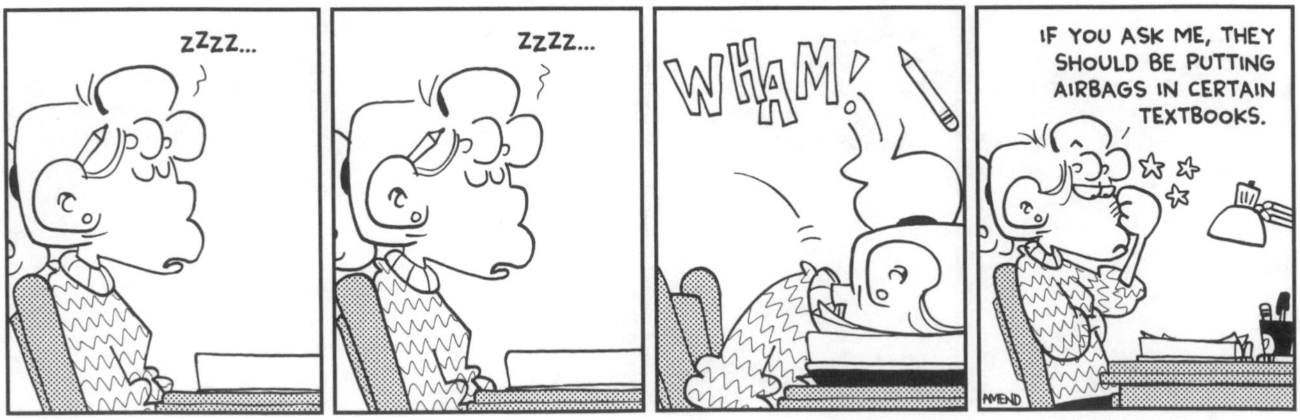
ZZZZ...
ZZZZ...
WHAM!
IF YOU ASK ME, THEY SHOULD BE PUTTING AIRBAGS IN CERTAIN TEXTBOOKS.

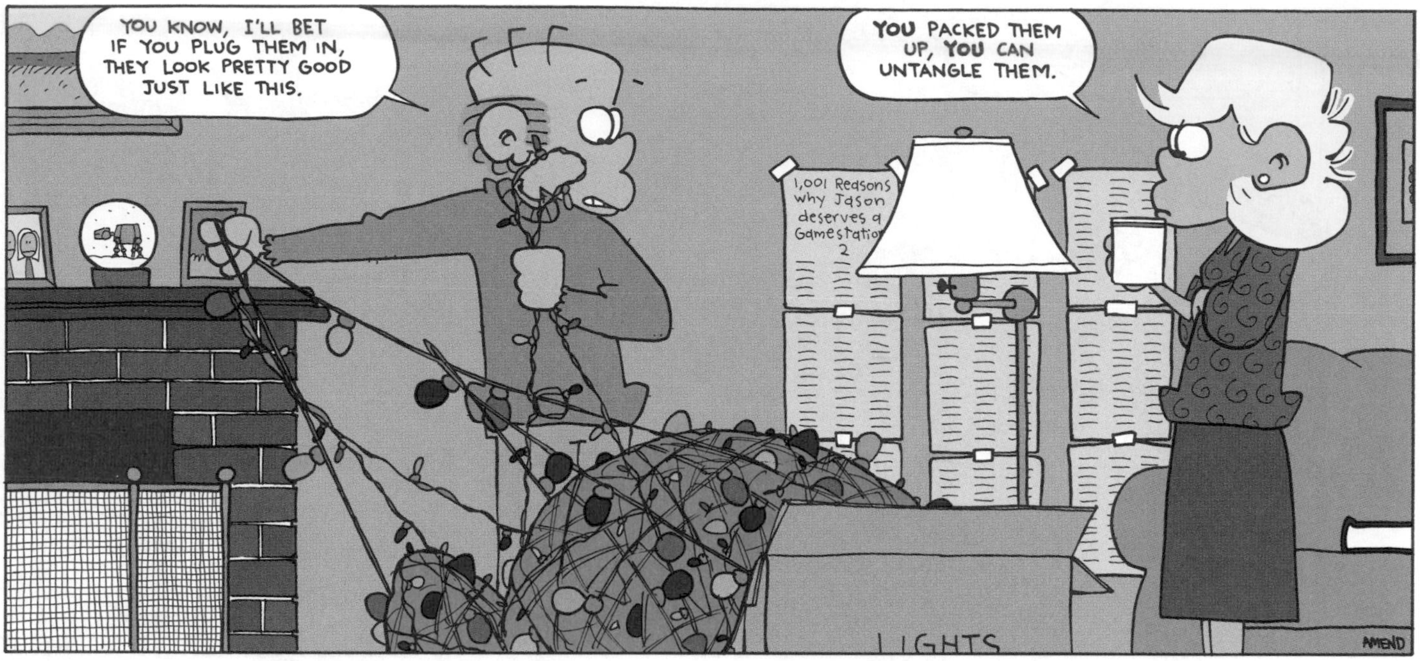
YOU KNOW, I'LL BET IF YOU PLUG THEM IN, THEY LOOK PRETTY GOOD JUST LIKE THIS.
YOU PACKED THEM UP, YOU CAN UNTANGLE THEM.
1,001 Reasons why Jason deserves a Gamestation 2
LIGHTS
AMEND

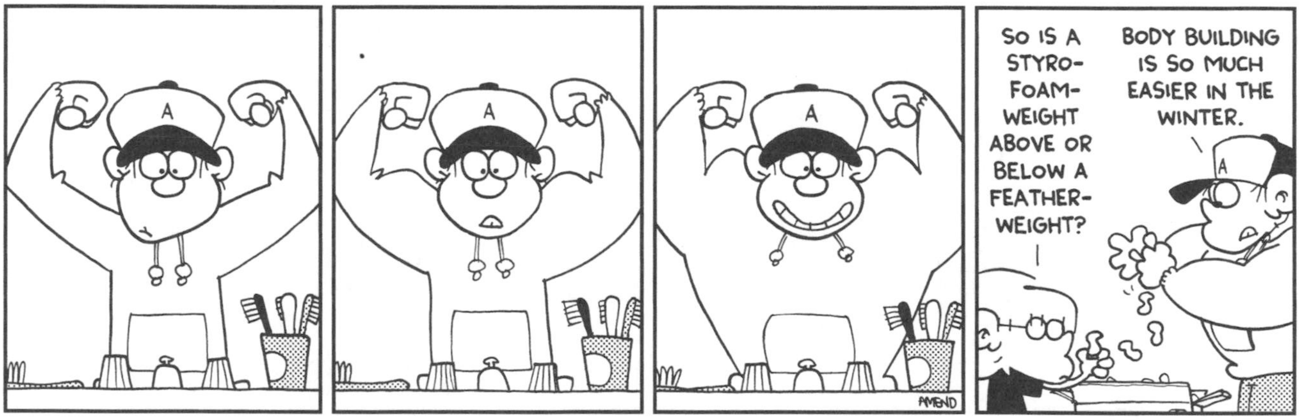
A
AMEND
BODY BUILDING IS SO MUCH EASIER IN THE WINTER.
SO IS A STYRO-FOAM-WEIGHT ABOVE OR BELOW A FEATHER-WEIGHT?

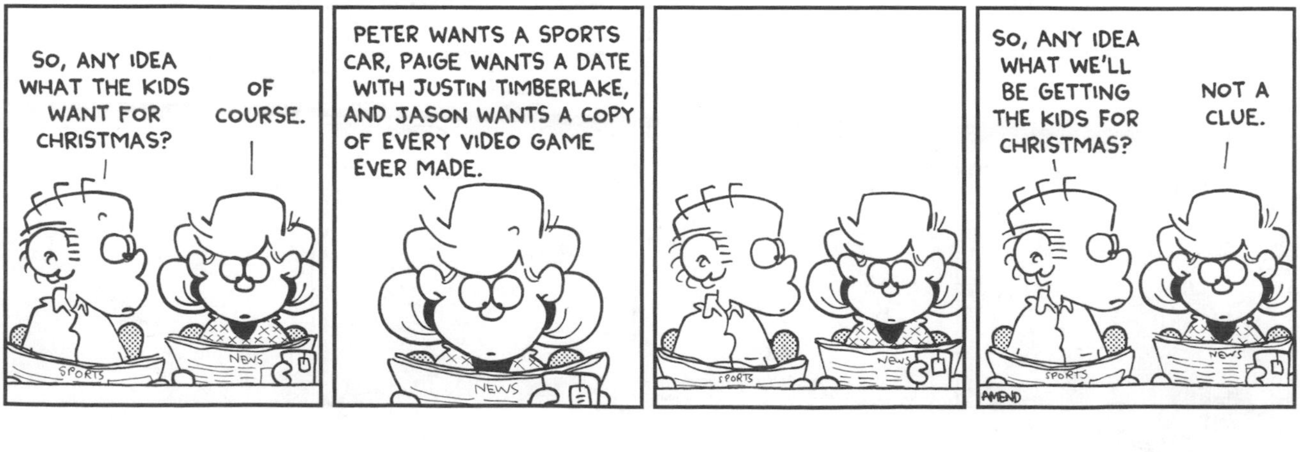
SO, ANY IDEA WHAT THE KIDS WANT FOR CHRISTMAS?
OF COURSE.
SPORTS
NEWS
PETER WANTS A SPORTS CAR, PAIGE WANTS A DATE WITH JUSTIN TIMBERLAKE, AND JASON WANTS A COPY OF EVERY VIDEO GAME EVER MADE.
SO, ANY IDEA WHAT WE'LL BE GETTING THE KIDS FOR CHRISTMAS?
NOT A CLUE.
AMEND

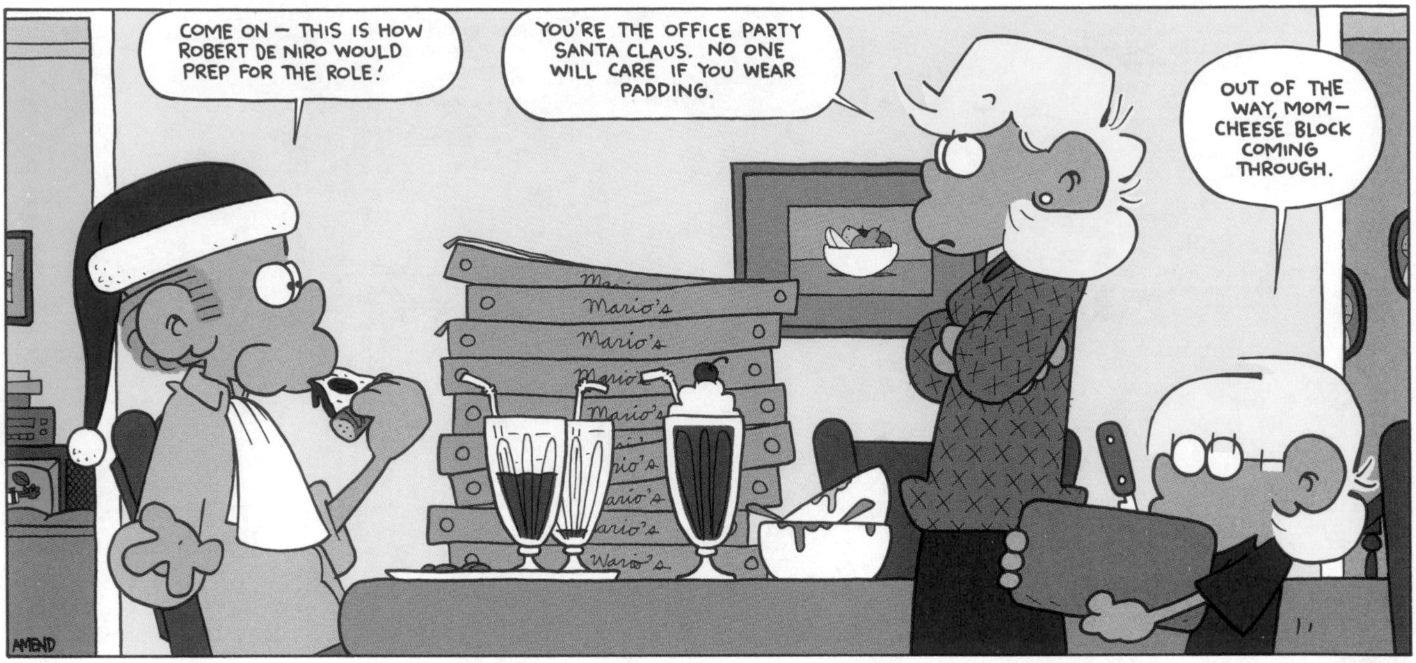
COME ON — THIS IS HOW ROBERT DE NIRO WOULD PREP FOR THE ROLE!
YOU'RE THE OFFICE PARTY SANTA CLAUS. NO ONE WILL CARE IF YOU WEAR PADDING.
OUT OF THE WAY, MOM— CHEESE BLOCK COMING THROUGH.
Mario's
AMEND

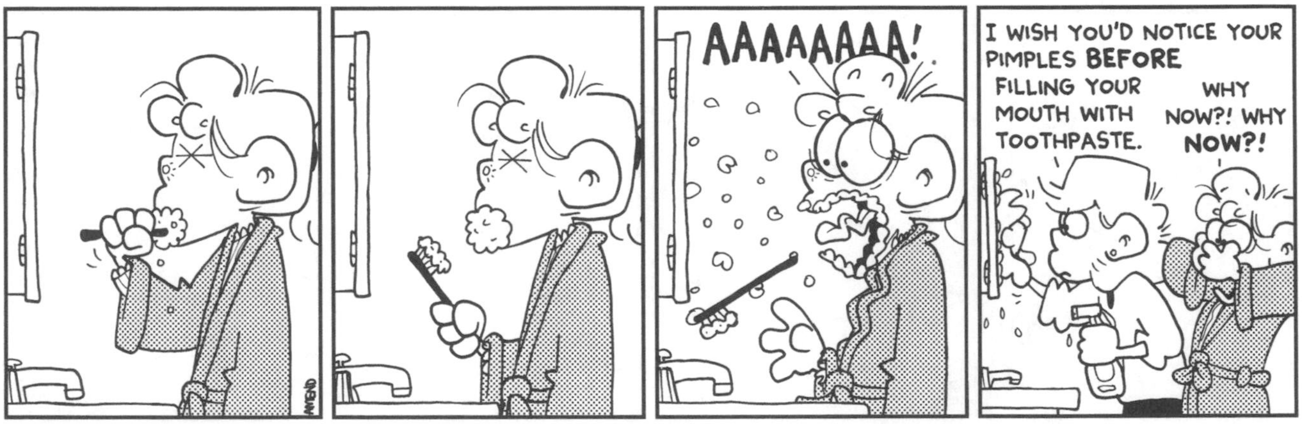
AAAAAAAA!
I WISH YOU'D NOTICE YOUR PIMPLES BEFORE FILLING YOUR MOUTH WITH TOOTHPASTE.
WHY NOW?! WHY NOW?!
AMEND

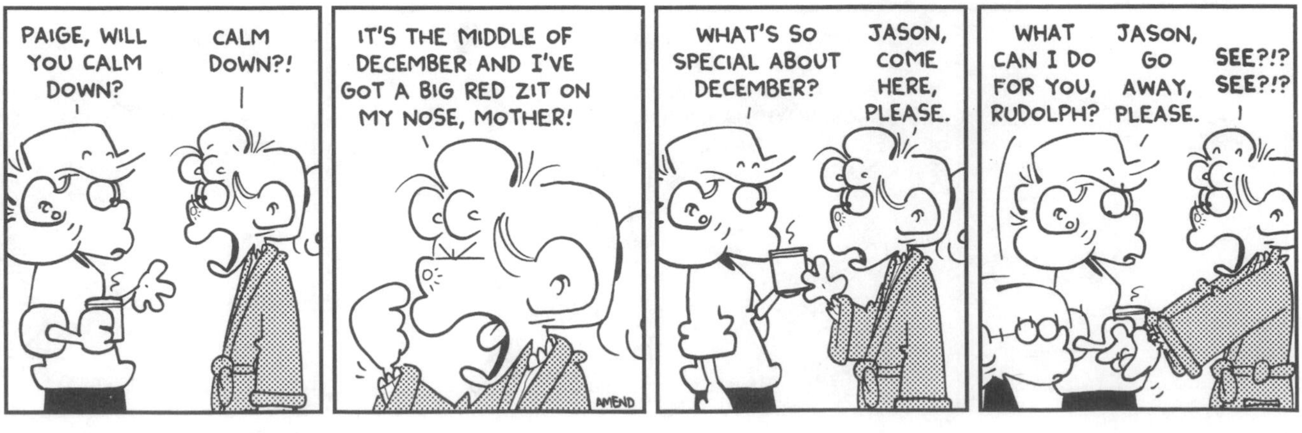
PAIGE, WILL YOU CALM DOWN?
CALM DOWN?!
IT'S THE MIDDLE OF DECEMBER AND I'VE GOT A BIG RED ZIT ON MY NOSE, MOTHER!
WHAT'S SO SPECIAL ABOUT DECEMBER?
JASON, COME HERE, PLEASE.
WHAT CAN I DO FOR YOU, RUDOLPH?
JASON, GO AWAY, PLEASE.
SEE?!? SEE?!?
AMEND

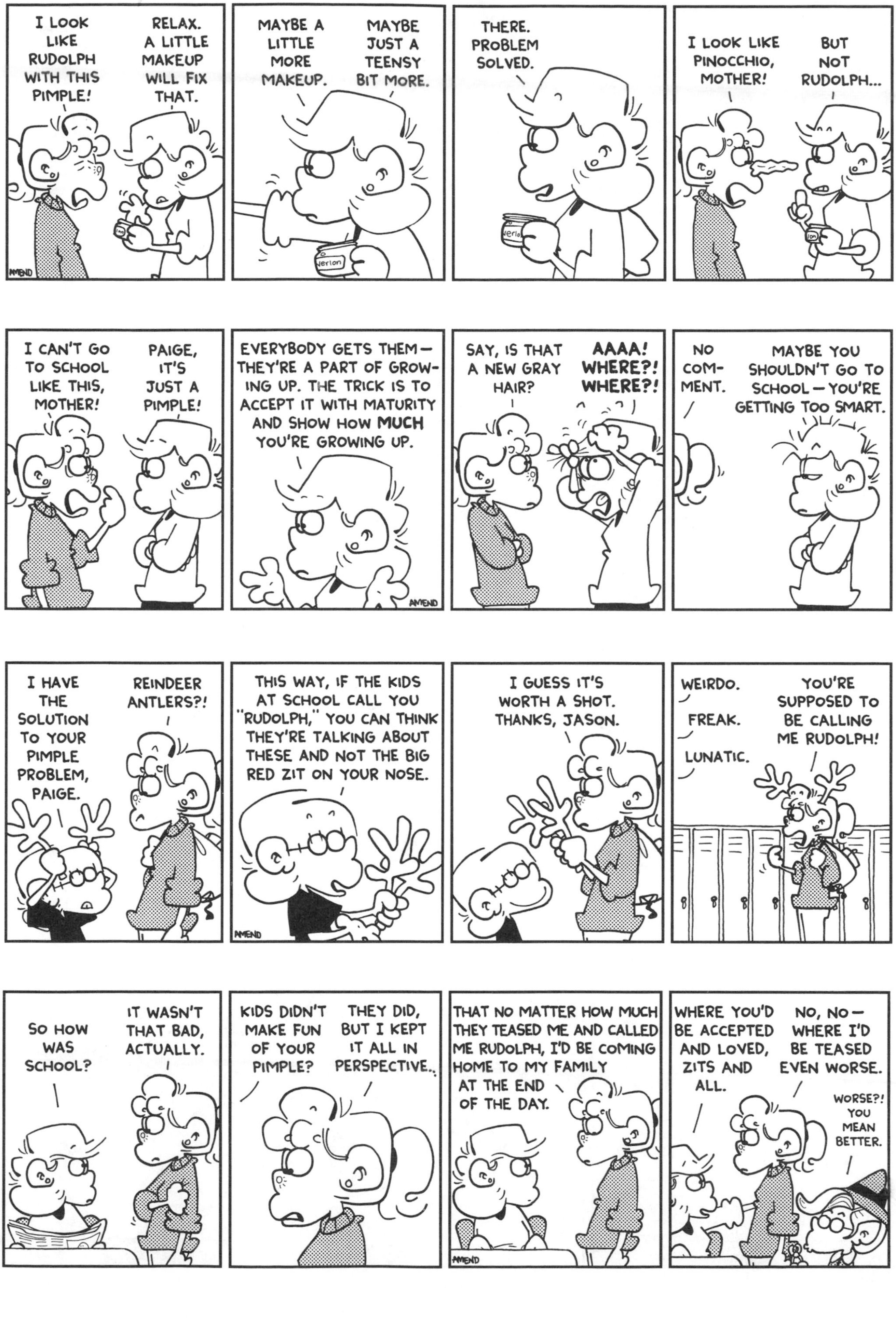
I LOOK LIKE RUDOLPH WITH THIS PIMPLE!
RELAX. A LITTLE MAKEUP WILL FIX THAT.
MAYBE A LITTLE MORE MAKEUP.
MAYBE JUST A TEENSY BIT MORE.
THERE. PROBLEM SOLVED.
I LOOK LIKE PINOCCHIO, MOTHER!
BUT NOT RUDOLPH...
I CAN'T GO TO SCHOOL LIKE THIS, MOTHER!
PAIGE, IT'S JUST A PIMPLE!
EVERYBODY GETS THEM— THEY'RE A PART OF GROWING UP. THE TRICK IS TO ACCEPT IT WITH MATURITY AND SHOW HOW **MUCH** YOU'RE GROWING UP.
SAY, IS THAT A NEW GRAY HAIR?
AAAA! WHERE?! WHERE?!
NO COMMENT.
MAYBE YOU SHOULDN'T GO TO SCHOOL—YOU'RE GETTING TOO SMART.
I HAVE THE SOLUTION TO YOUR PIMPLE PROBLEM, PAIGE.
REINDEER ANTLERS?!
THIS WAY, IF THE KIDS AT SCHOOL CALL YOU "RUDOLPH," YOU CAN THINK THEY'RE TALKING ABOUT THESE AND NOT THE BIG RED ZIT ON YOUR NOSE.
I GUESS IT'S WORTH A SHOT. THANKS, JASON.
WEIRDO.
FREAK.
LUNATIC.
YOU'RE SUPPOSED TO BE CALLING ME RUDOLPH!
SO HOW WAS SCHOOL?
IT WASN'T THAT BAD, ACTUALLY.
KIDS DIDN'T MAKE FUN OF YOUR PIMPLE?
THEY DID, BUT I KEPT IT ALL IN PERSPECTIVE...
THAT NO MATTER HOW MUCH THEY TEASED ME AND CALLED ME RUDOLPH, I'D BE COMING HOME TO MY FAMILY AT THE END OF THE DAY.
WHERE YOU'D BE ACCEPTED AND LOVED, ZITS AND ALL.
NO, NO— WHERE I'D BE TEASED EVEN WORSE.
WORSE?! YOU MEAN BETTER.

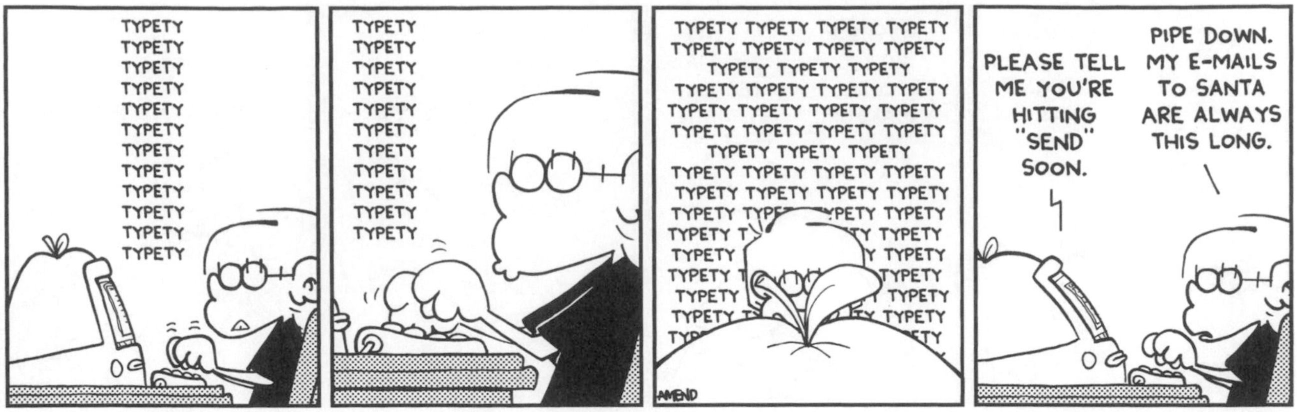

TYPETY TYPETY TYPETY TYPETY TYPETY TYPETY TYPETY TYPETY TYPETY TYPETY TYPETY TYPETY
TYPETY TYPETY TYPETY TYPETY TYPETY TYPETY TYPETY TYPETY TYPETY TYPETY TYPETY
TYPETY TYPETY TYPETY TYPETY
TYPETY TYPETY TYPETY TYPETY
TYPETY TYPETY TYPETY
TYPETY TYPETY TYPETY TYPETY
TYPETY TYPETY TYPETY TYPETY
TYPETY TYPETY TYPETY TYPETY
TYPETY TYPETY TYPETY
TYPETY TYPETY TYPETY TYPETY
TYPETY TYPETY TYPETY TYPETY
AMEND
PLEASE TELL ME YOU'RE HITTING "SEND" SOON.
PIPE DOWN. MY E-MAILS TO SANTA ARE ALWAYS THIS LONG.

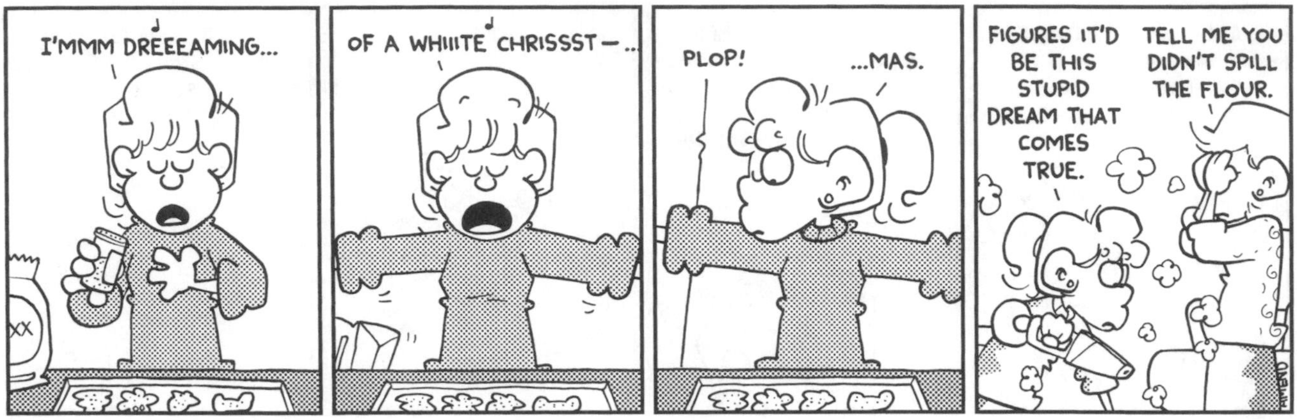

I'MMM DREEEAMING...
OF A WHIIITE CHRISSST—...
PLOP!
...MAS.
FIGURES IT'D BE THIS STUPID DREAM THAT COMES TRUE.
TELL ME YOU DIDN'T SPILL THE FLOUR.
AMEND

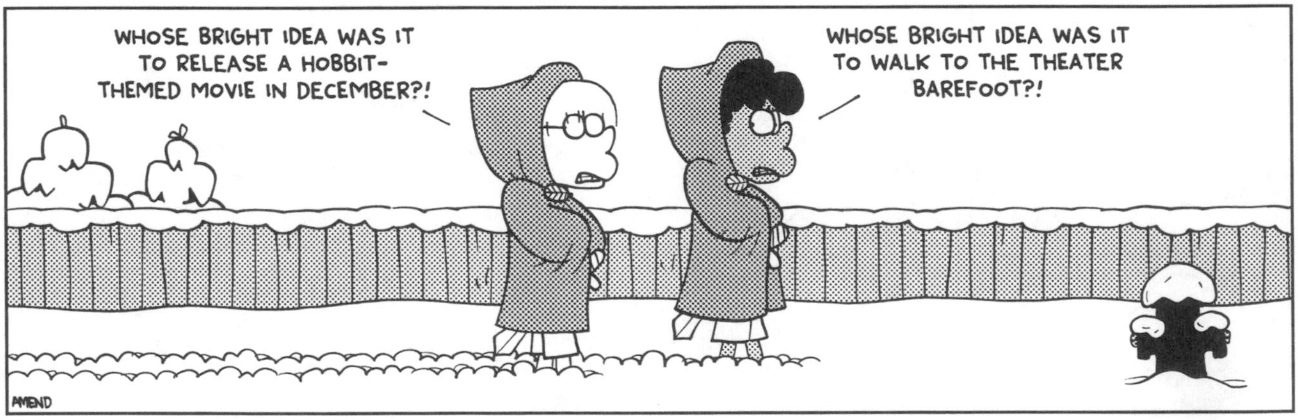

WHOSE BRIGHT IDEA WAS IT TO RELEASE A HOBBIT-THEMED MOVIE IN DECEMBER?!
WHOSE BRIGHT IDEA WAS IT TO WALK TO THE THEATER BAREFOOT?!
AMEND

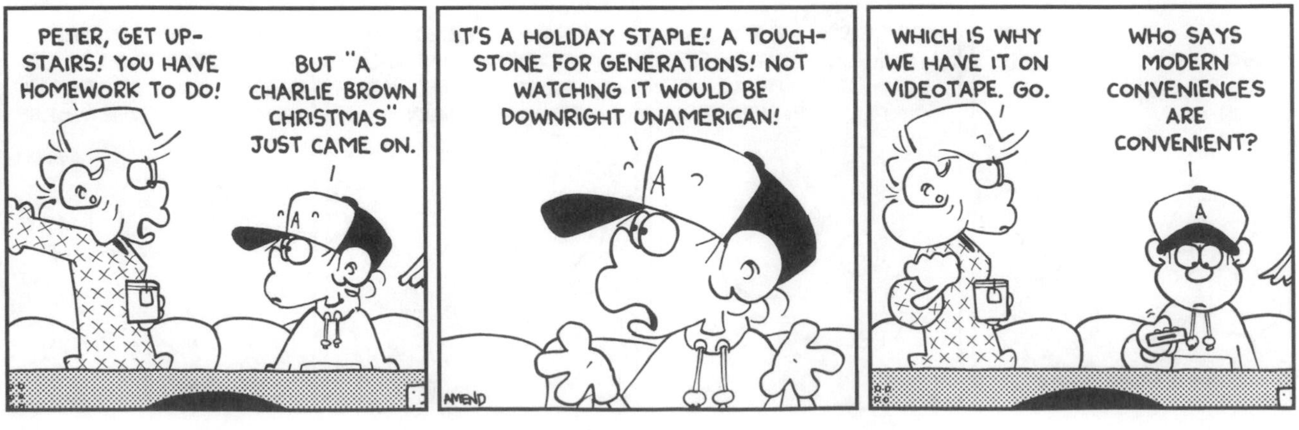

PETER, GET UP-STAIRS! YOU HAVE HOMEWORK TO DO!
BUT "A CHARLIE BROWN CHRISTMAS" JUST CAME ON.
IT'S A HOLIDAY STAPLE! A TOUCH-STONE FOR GENERATIONS! NOT WATCHING IT WOULD BE DOWNRIGHT UNAMERICAN!
AMEND
WHICH IS WHY WE HAVE IT ON VIDEOTAPE. GO.
WHO SAYS MODERN CONVENIENCES ARE CONVENIENT?

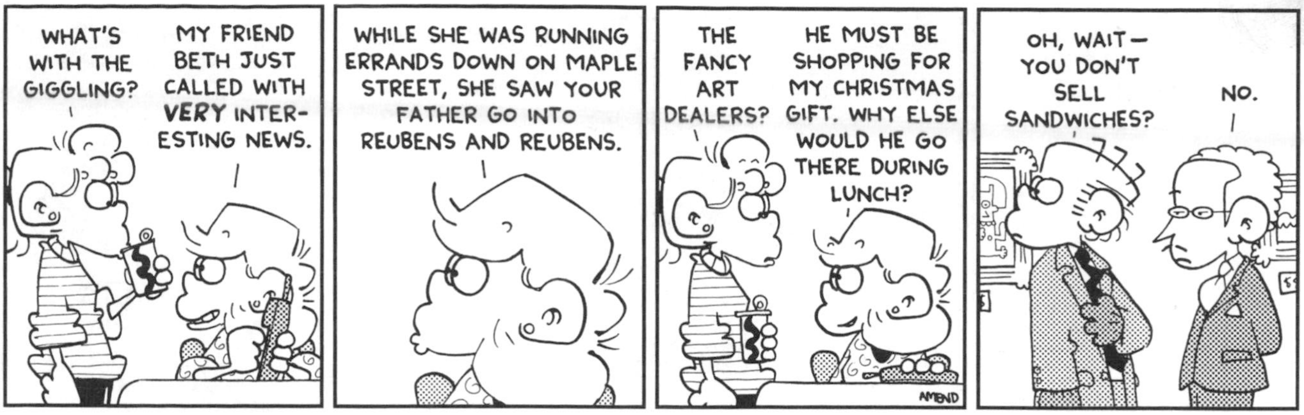
WHAT'S WITH THE GIGGLING?
MY FRIEND BETH JUST CALLED WITH **VERY** INTERESTING NEWS.
WHILE SHE WAS RUNNING ERRANDS DOWN ON MAPLE STREET, SHE SAW YOUR FATHER GO INTO REUBENS AND REUBENS.
THE FANCY ART DEALERS?
HE MUST BE SHOPPING FOR MY CHRISTMAS GIFT. WHY ELSE WOULD HE GO THERE DURING LUNCH?
OH, WAIT— YOU DON'T SELL SANDWICHES?
NO.
AMEND

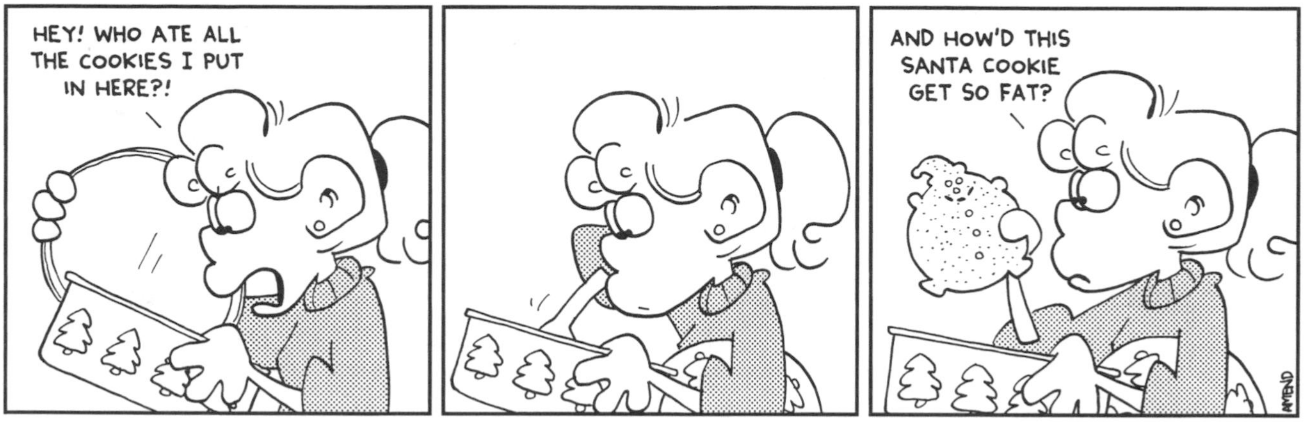
HEY! WHO ATE ALL THE COOKIES I PUT IN HERE?!
AND HOW'D THIS SANTA COOKIE GET SO FAT?
AMEND

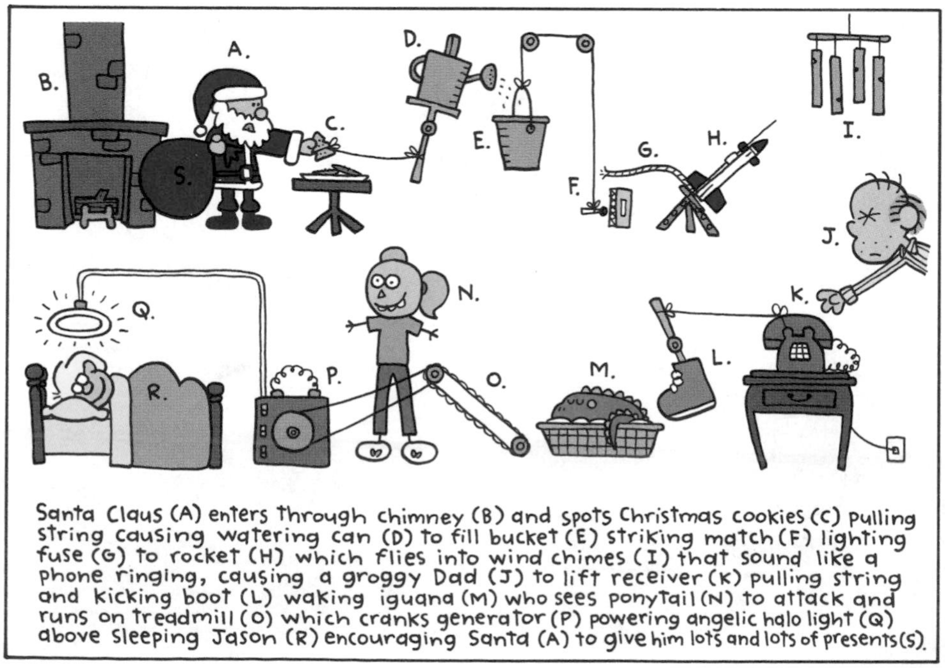
A.
B.
C.
D.
E.
F.
G.
H.
I.
J.
K.
L.
M.
N.
O.
P.
Q.
R.
S.
Santa Claus (A) enters through chimney (B) and spots Christmas cookies (C) pulling string causing watering can (D) to fill bucket (E) striking match (F) lighting fuse (G) to rocket (H) which flies into wind chimes (I) that sound like a phone ringing, causing a groggy Dad (J) to lift receiver (K) pulling string and kicking boot (L) waking iguana (M) who sees ponytail (N) to attack and runs on treadmill (O) which cranks generator (P) powering angelic halo light (Q) above sleeping Jason (R) encouraging Santa (A) to give him lots and lots of presents (S).

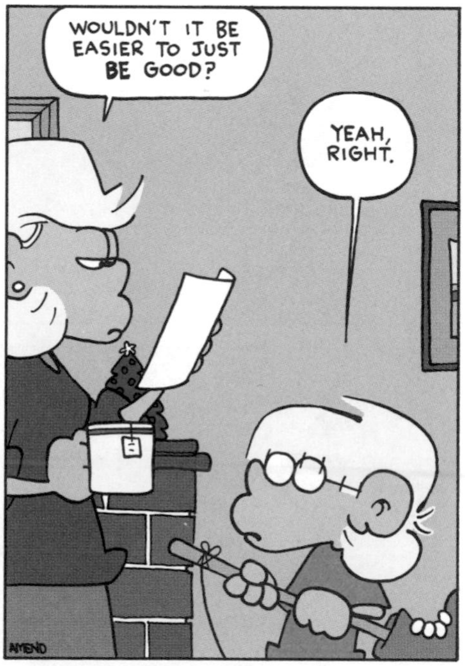
WOULDN'T IT BE EASIER TO JUST **BE** GOOD?
YEAH, RIGHT.
AMEND

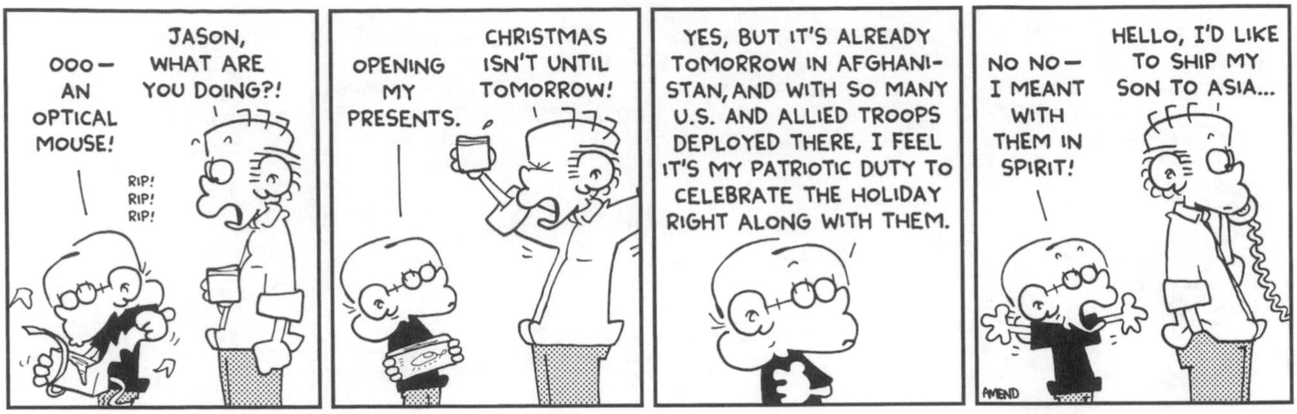
JASON, WHAT ARE YOU DOING?!
OOO— AN OPTICAL MOUSE!
RIP! RIP! RIP!
CHRISTMAS ISN'T UNTIL TOMORROW!
OPENING MY PRESENTS.
YES, BUT IT'S ALREADY TOMORROW IN AFGHANISTAN, AND WITH SO MANY U.S. AND ALLIED TROOPS DEPLOYED THERE, I FEEL IT'S MY PATRIOTIC DUTY TO CELEBRATE THE HOLIDAY RIGHT ALONG WITH THEM.
HELLO, I'D LIKE TO SHIP MY SON TO ASIA...
NO NO— I MEANT WITH THEM IN SPIRIT!

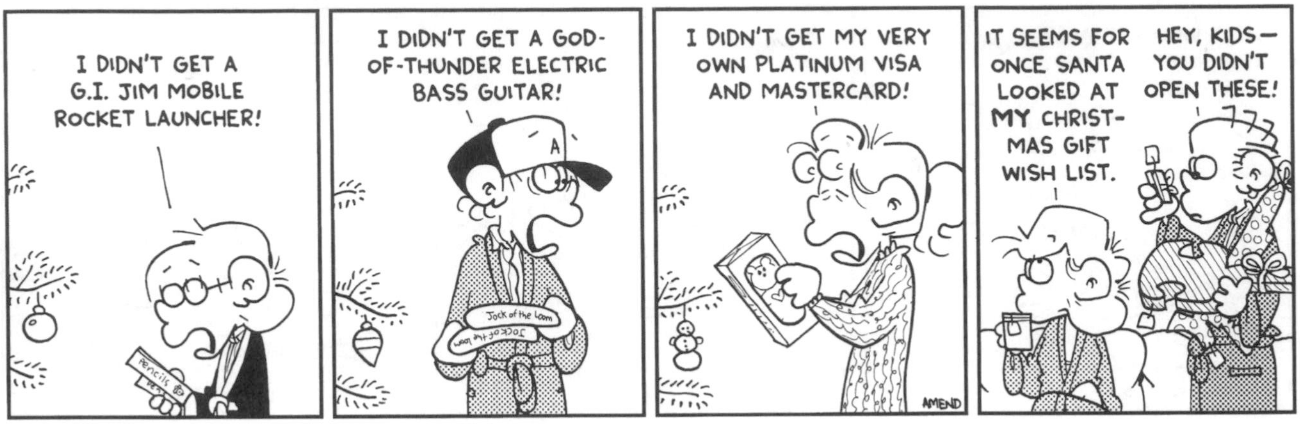
I DIDN'T GET A G.I. JIM MOBILE ROCKET LAUNCHER!
I DIDN'T GET A GOD-OF-THUNDER ELECTRIC BASS GUITAR!
Jock of the Loom
I DIDN'T GET MY VERY OWN PLATINUM VISA AND MASTERCARD!
IT SEEMS FOR ONCE SANTA LOOKED AT MY CHRISTMAS GIFT WISH LIST.
HEY, KIDS— YOU DIDN'T OPEN THESE!

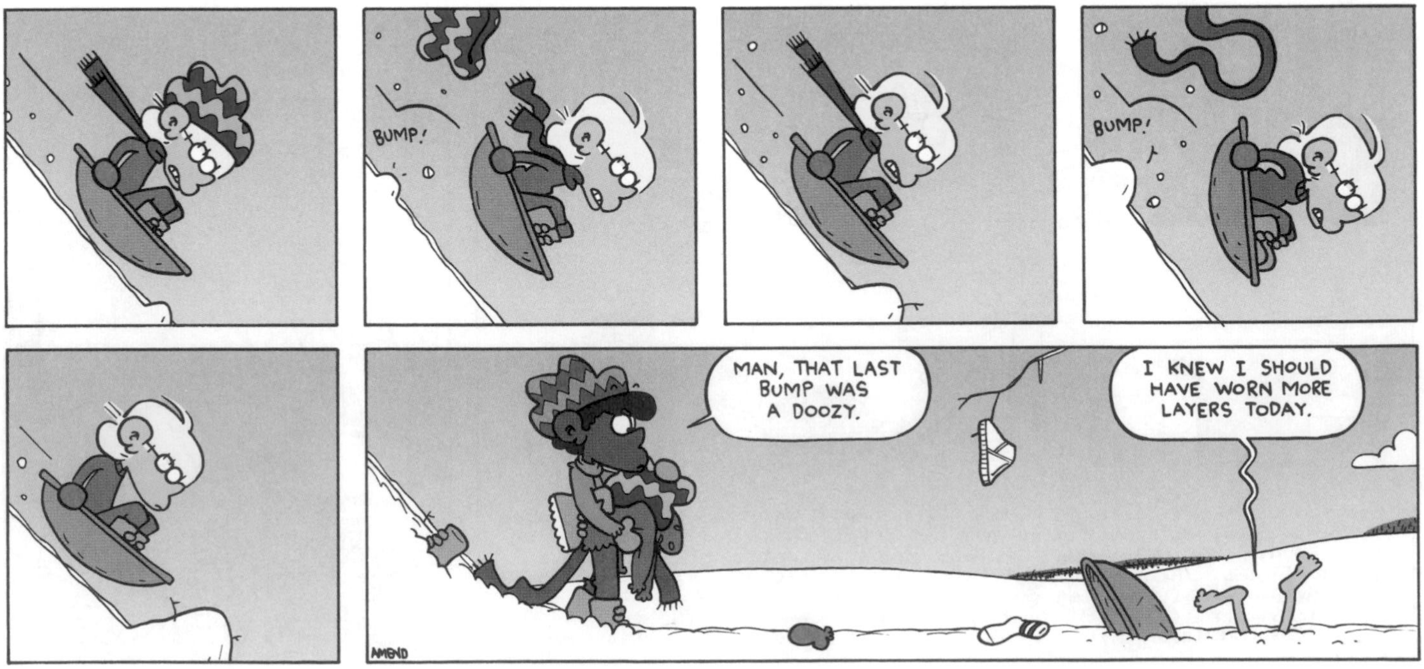
BUMP!
BUMP!
MAN, THAT LAST BUMP WAS A DOOZY.
I KNEW I SHOULD HAVE WORN MORE LAYERS TODAY.

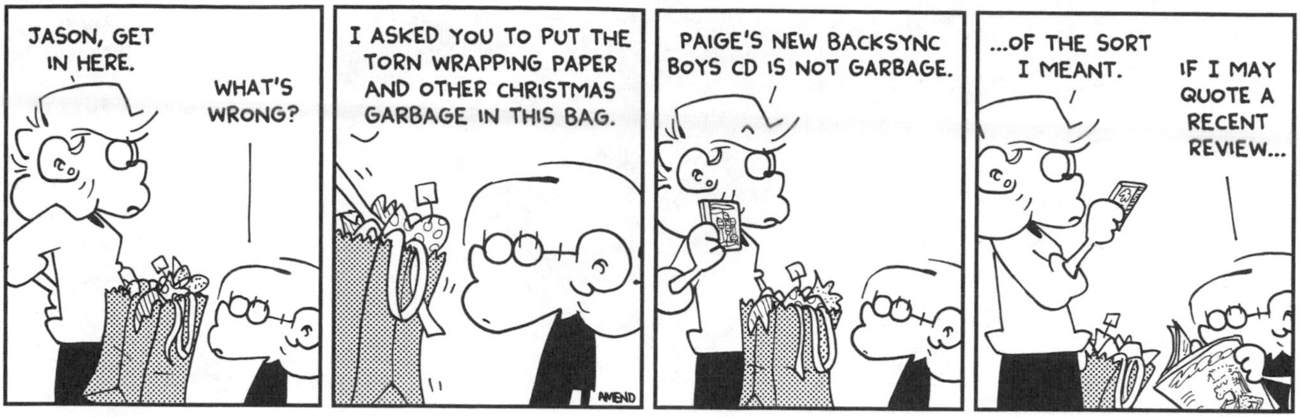
JASON, GET IN HERE.
WHAT'S WRONG?
I ASKED YOU TO PUT THE TORN WRAPPING PAPER AND OTHER CHRISTMAS GARBAGE IN THIS BAG.
PAIGE'S NEW BACKSYNC BOYS CD IS NOT GARBAGE.
...OF THE SORT I MEANT.
IF I MAY QUOTE A RECENT REVIEW...
AMEND

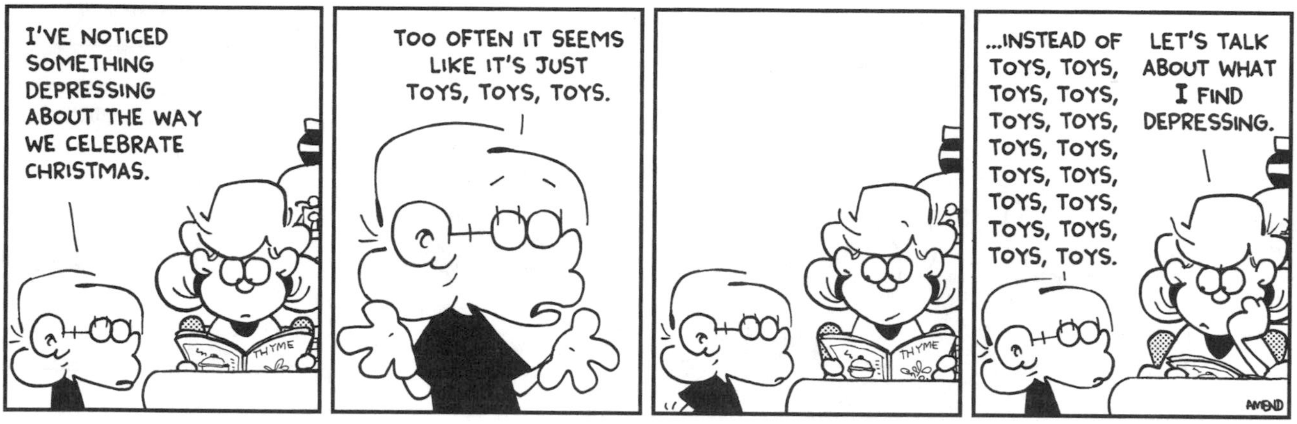
I'VE NOTICED SOMETHING DEPRESSING ABOUT THE WAY WE CELEBRATE CHRISTMAS.
THYME
TOO OFTEN IT SEEMS LIKE IT'S JUST TOYS, TOYS, TOYS.
THYME
...INSTEAD OF TOYS, TOYS, TOYS, TOYS, TOYS, TOYS, TOYS, TOYS, TOYS, TOYS, TOYS, TOYS, TOYS, TOYS, TOYS, TOYS.
LET'S TALK ABOUT WHAT I FIND DEPRESSING.
AMEND

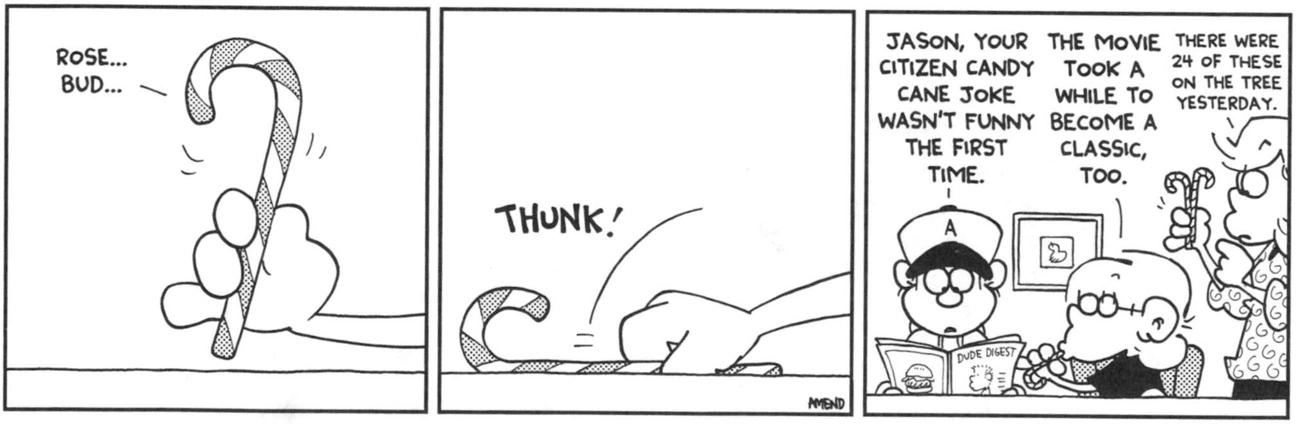
ROSE... BUD...
THUNK!
AMEND
JASON, YOUR CITIZEN CANDY CANE JOKE WASN'T FUNNY THE FIRST TIME.
THE MOVIE TOOK A WHILE TO BECOME A CLASSIC, TOO.
THERE WERE 24 OF THESE ON THE TREE YESTERDAY.
A
DUDE DIGEST

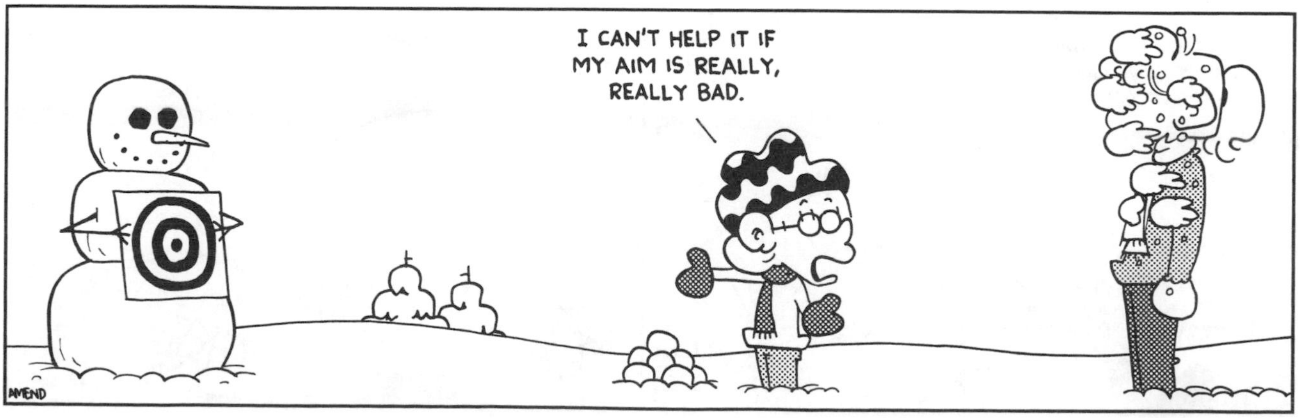
I CAN'T HELP IT IF MY AIM IS REALLY, REALLY BAD.
AMEND

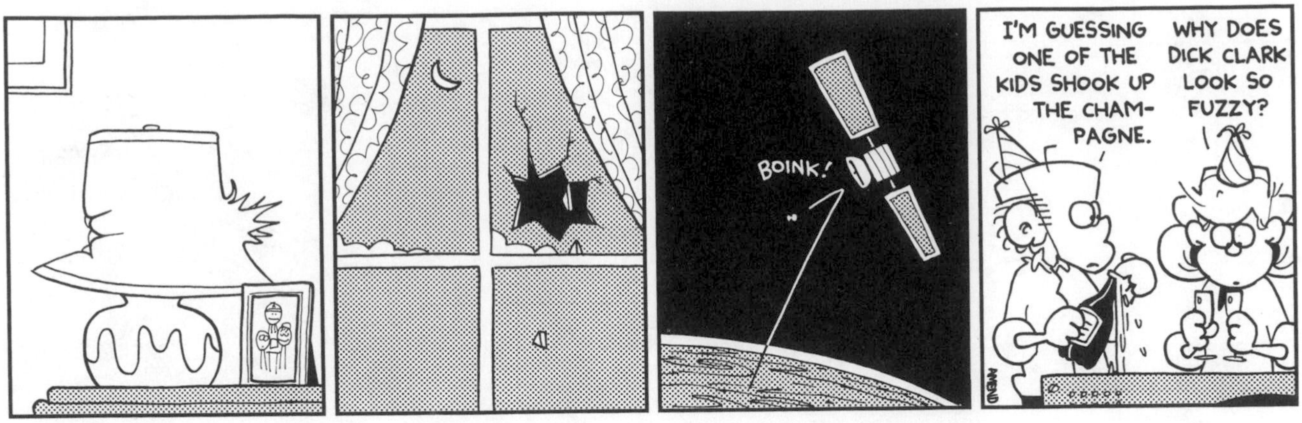
BOINK!
I'M GUESSING ONE OF THE KIDS SHOOK UP THE CHAMPAGNE.
WHY DOES DICK CLARK LOOK SO FUZZY?

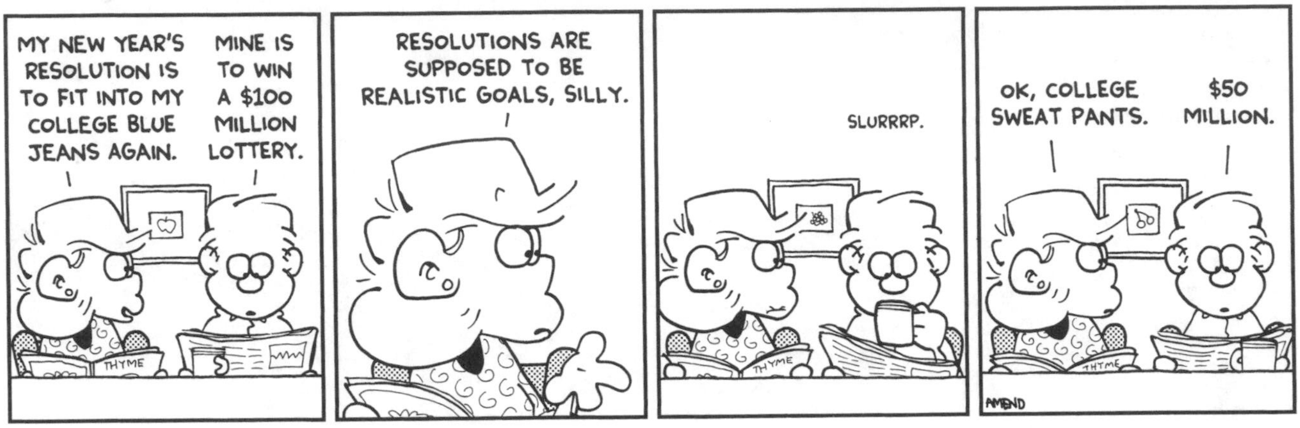
MY NEW YEAR'S RESOLUTION IS TO FIT INTO MY COLLEGE BLUE JEANS AGAIN.
MINE IS TO WIN A $100 MILLION LOTTERY.
RESOLUTIONS ARE SUPPOSED TO BE REALISTIC GOALS, SILLY.
SLURRRP.
OK, COLLEGE SWEAT PANTS.
$50 MILLION.

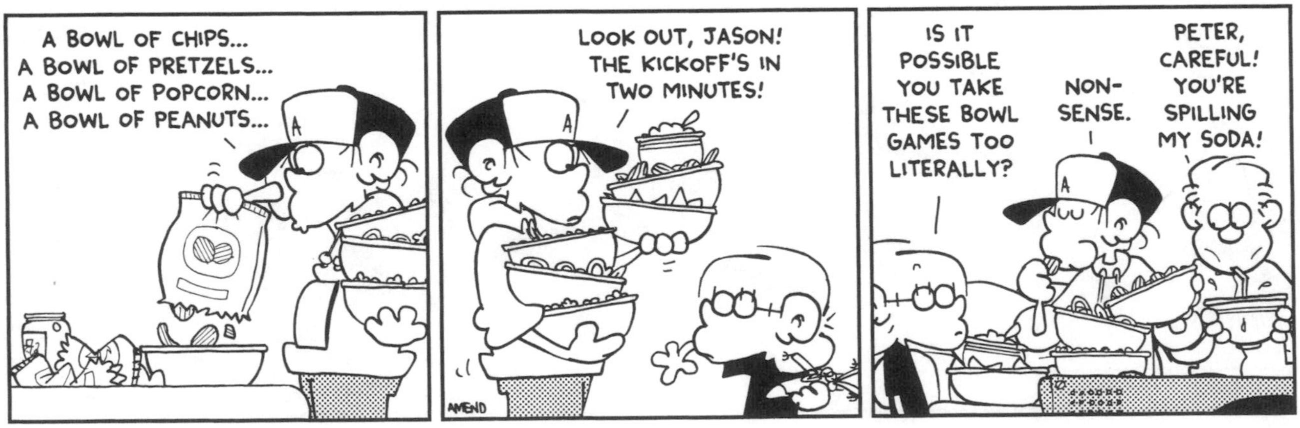
A BOWL OF CHIPS... A BOWL OF PRETZELS... A BOWL OF POPCORN... A BOWL OF PEANUTS...
LOOK OUT, JASON! THE KICKOFF'S IN TWO MINUTES!
IS IT POSSIBLE YOU TAKE THESE BOWL GAMES TOO LITERALLY?
NONSENSE.
PETER, CAREFUL! YOU'RE SPILLING MY SODA!

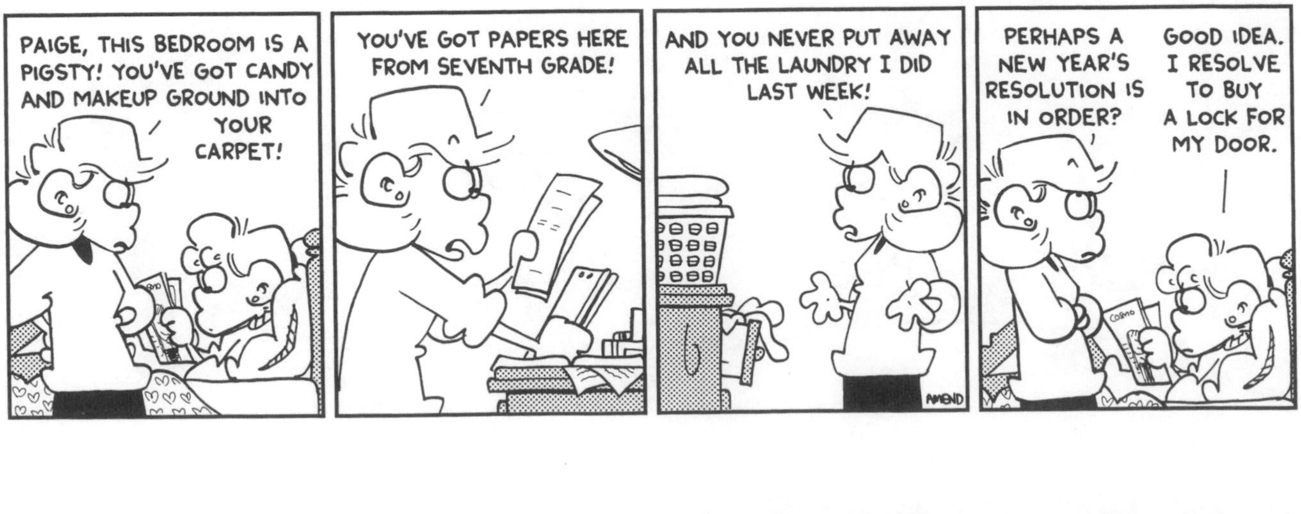
PAIGE, THIS BEDROOM IS A PIGSTY! YOU'VE GOT CANDY AND MAKEUP GROUND INTO YOUR CARPET!
YOU'VE GOT PAPERS HERE FROM SEVENTH GRADE!
AND YOU NEVER PUT AWAY ALL THE LAUNDRY I DID LAST WEEK!
PERHAPS A NEW YEAR'S RESOLUTION IS IN ORDER?
GOOD IDEA. I RESOLVE TO BUY A LOCK FOR MY DOOR.

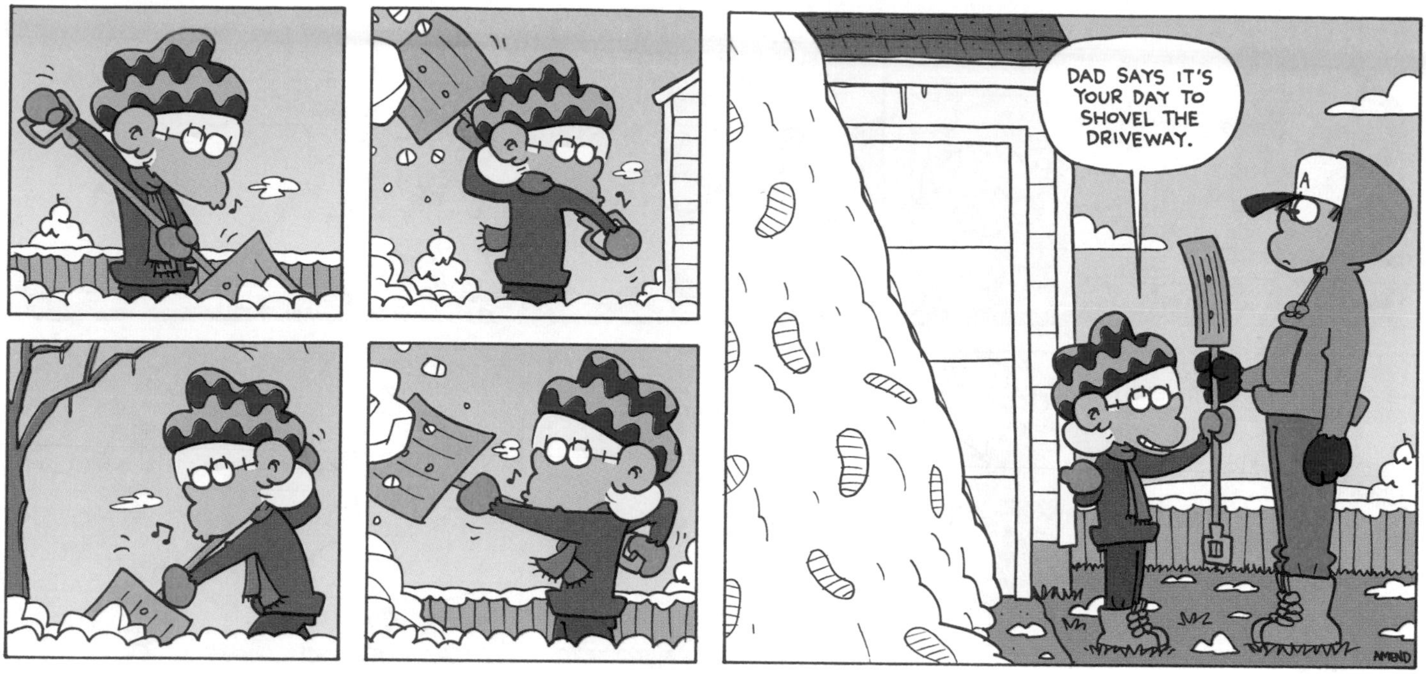
DAD SAYS IT'S YOUR DAY TO SHOVEL THE DRIVEWAY.
AMEND

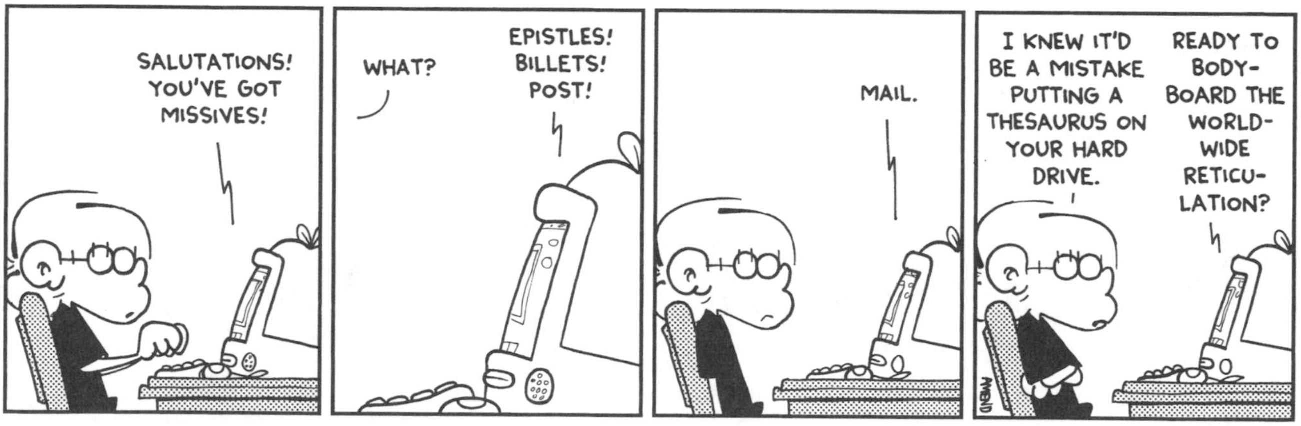
SALUTATIONS! YOU'VE GOT MISSIVES!
WHAT?
EPISTLES! BILLETS! POST!
MAIL.
I KNEW IT'D BE A MISTAKE PUTTING A THESAURUS ON YOUR HARD DRIVE.
READY TO BODY-BOARD THE WORLD-WIDE RETICU-LATION?
AMEND

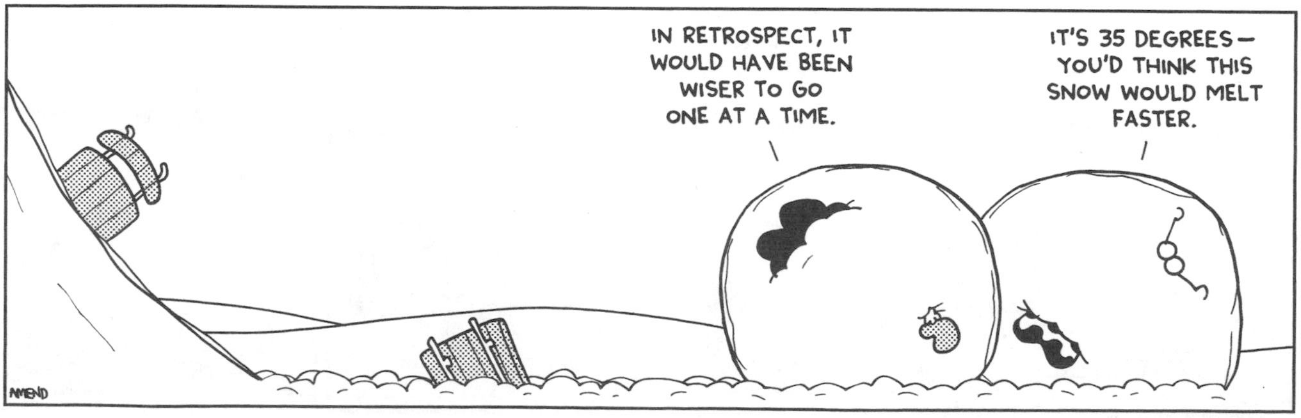
IN RETROSPECT, IT WOULD HAVE BEEN WISER TO GO ONE AT A TIME.
IT'S 35 DEGREES— YOU'D THINK THIS SNOW WOULD MELT FASTER.
AMEND

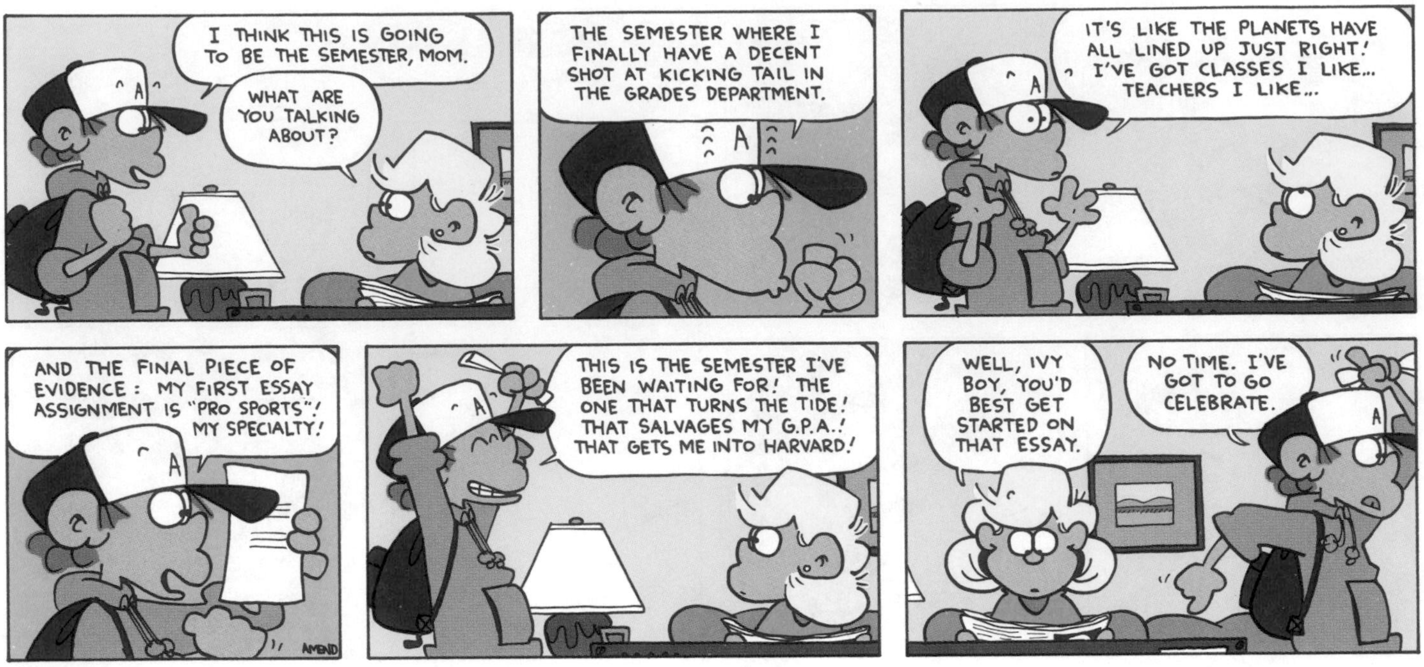
I THINK THIS IS GOING TO BE THE SEMESTER, MOM.
WHAT ARE YOU TALKING ABOUT?
THE SEMESTER WHERE I FINALLY HAVE A DECENT SHOT AT KICKING TAIL IN THE GRADES DEPARTMENT.
IT'S LIKE THE PLANETS HAVE ALL LINED UP JUST RIGHT! I'VE GOT CLASSES I LIKE... TEACHERS I LIKE...
AND THE FINAL PIECE OF EVIDENCE: MY FIRST ESSAY ASSIGNMENT IS "PRO SPORTS"! MY SPECIALTY!
THIS IS THE SEMESTER I'VE BEEN WAITING FOR! THE ONE THAT TURNS THE TIDE! THAT SALVAGES MY G.P.A.! THAT GETS ME INTO HARVARD!
WELL, IVY BOY, YOU'D BEST GET STARTED ON THAT ESSAY.
NO TIME. I'VE GOT TO GO CELEBRATE.
AMEND

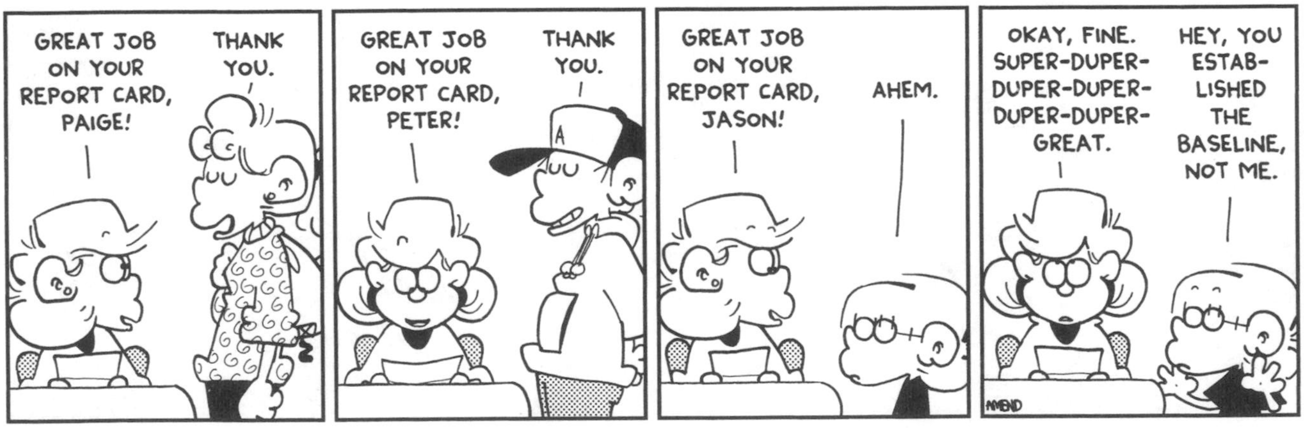
GREAT JOB ON YOUR REPORT CARD, PAIGE!
THANK YOU.
GREAT JOB ON YOUR REPORT CARD, PETER!
THANK YOU.
GREAT JOB ON YOUR REPORT CARD, JASON!
AHEM.
OKAY, FINE. SUPER-DUPER-DUPER-DUPER-DUPER-DUPER-GREAT.
HEY, YOU ESTABLISHED THE BASELINE, NOT ME.
AMEND

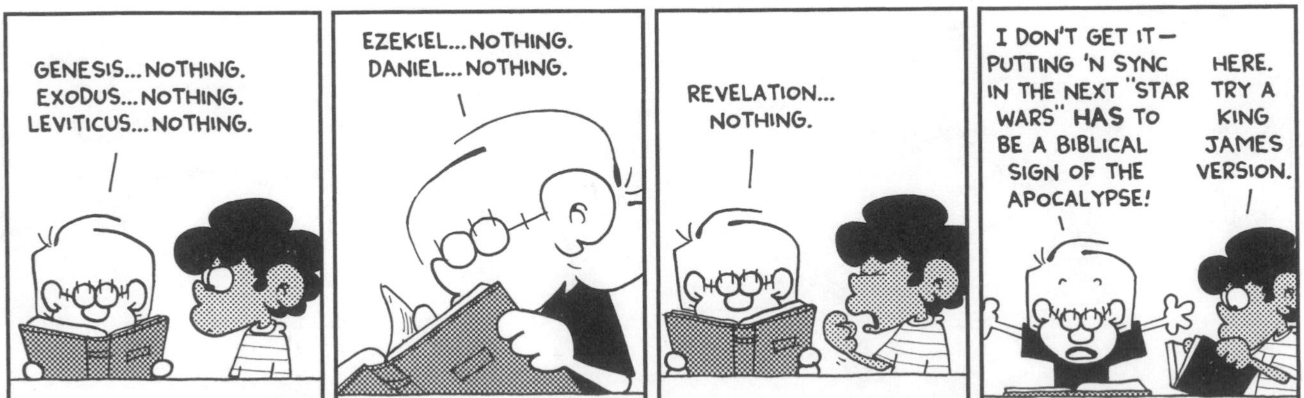
GENESIS... NOTHING. EXODUS... NOTHING. LEVITICUS... NOTHING.
EZEKIEL... NOTHING. DANIEL... NOTHING.
REVELATION... NOTHING.
I DON'T GET IT— PUTTING 'N SYNC IN THE NEXT "STAR WARS" HAS TO BE A BIBLICAL SIGN OF THE APOCALYPSE!
HERE. TRY A KING JAMES VERSION.
AMEND

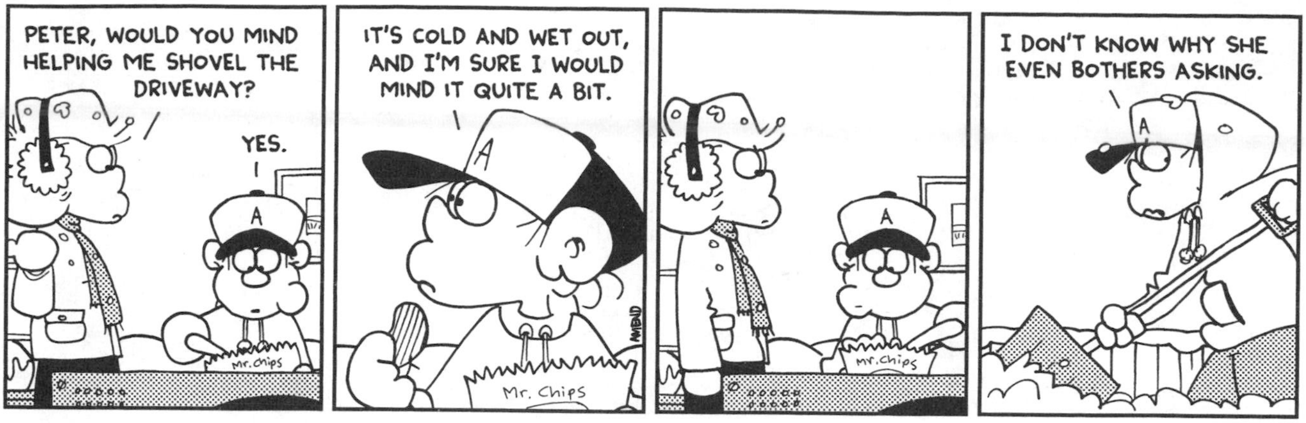
PETER, WOULD YOU MIND HELPING ME SHOVEL THE DRIVEWAY?
YES.
IT'S COLD AND WET OUT, AND I'M SURE I WOULD MIND IT QUITE A BIT.
Mr. Chips
I DON'T KNOW WHY SHE EVEN BOTHERS ASKING.
AMEND

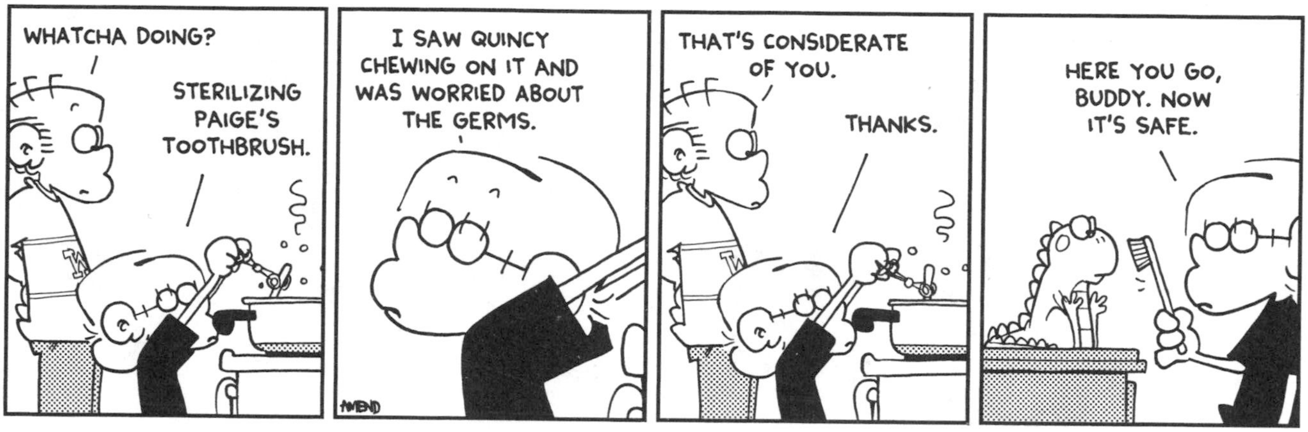
WHATCHA DOING?
STERILIZING PAIGE'S TOOTHBRUSH.
I SAW QUINCY CHEWING ON IT AND WAS WORRIED ABOUT THE GERMS.
THAT'S CONSIDERATE OF YOU.
THANKS.
HERE YOU GO, BUDDY. NOW IT'S SAFE.
AMEND

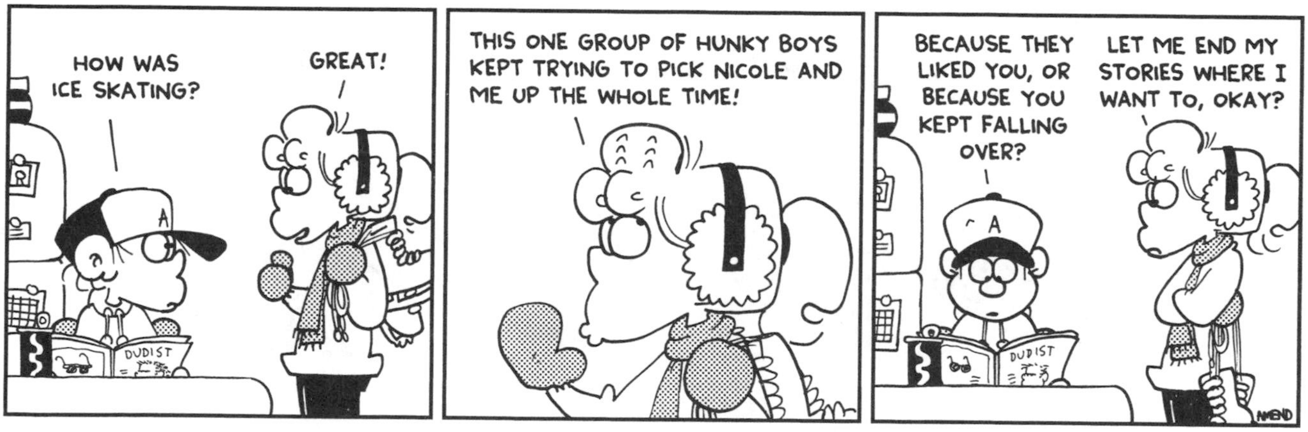
HOW WAS ICE SKATING?
GREAT!
DUDIST
THIS ONE GROUP OF HUNKY BOYS KEPT TRYING TO PICK NICOLE AND ME UP THE WHOLE TIME!
BECAUSE THEY LIKED YOU, OR BECAUSE YOU KEPT FALLING OVER?
LET ME END MY STORIES WHERE I WANT TO, OKAY?
AMEND

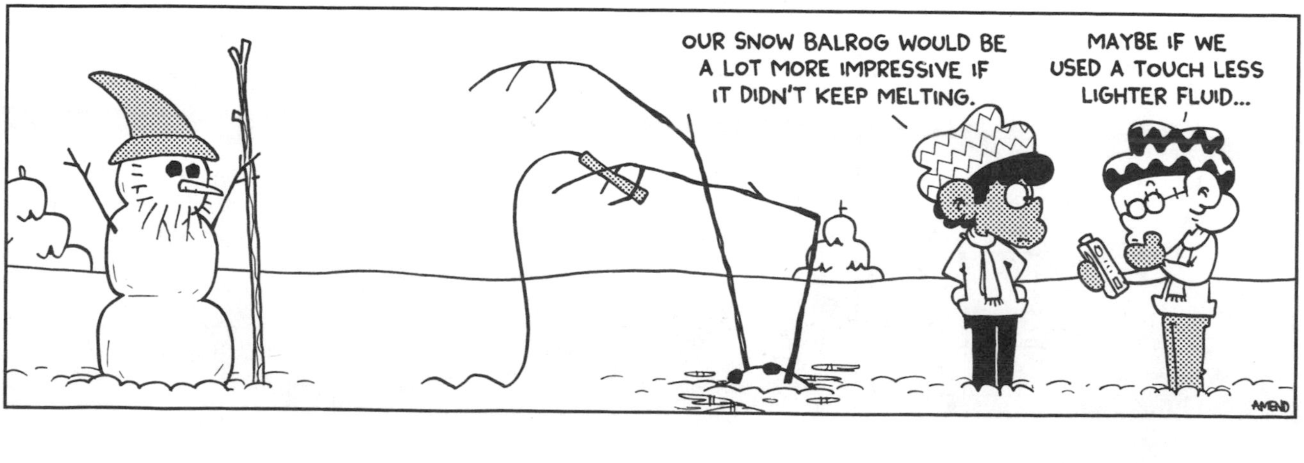
OUR SNOW BALROG WOULD BE A LOT MORE IMPRESSIVE IF IT DIDN'T KEEP MELTING.
MAYBE IF WE USED A TOUCH LESS LIGHTER FLUID...
AMEND

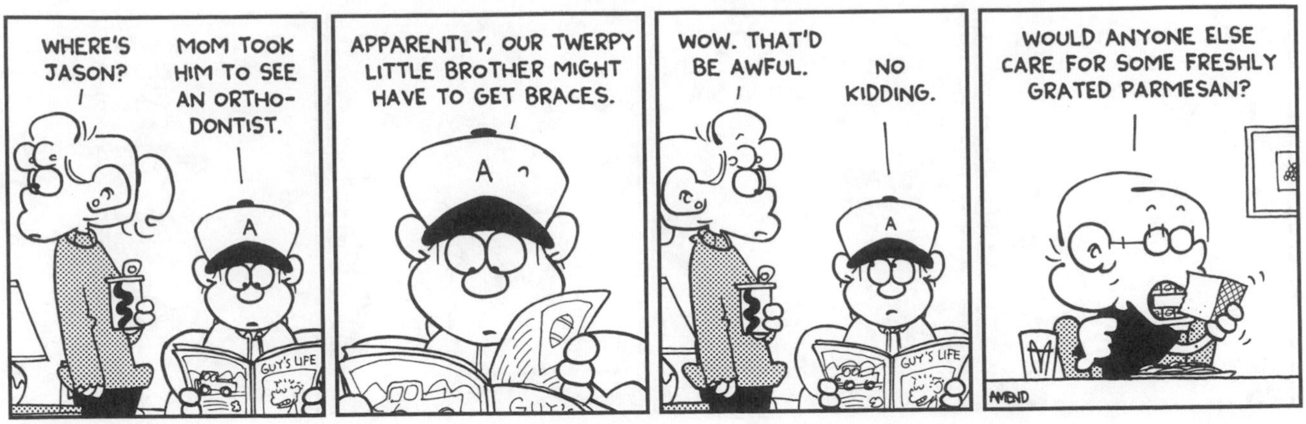
WHERE'S JASON?
MOM TOOK HIM TO SEE AN ORTHODONTIST.
APPARENTLY, OUR TWERPY LITTLE BROTHER MIGHT HAVE TO GET BRACES.
WOW. THAT'D BE AWFUL.
NO KIDDING.
WOULD ANYONE ELSE CARE FOR SOME FRESHLY GRATED PARMESAN?

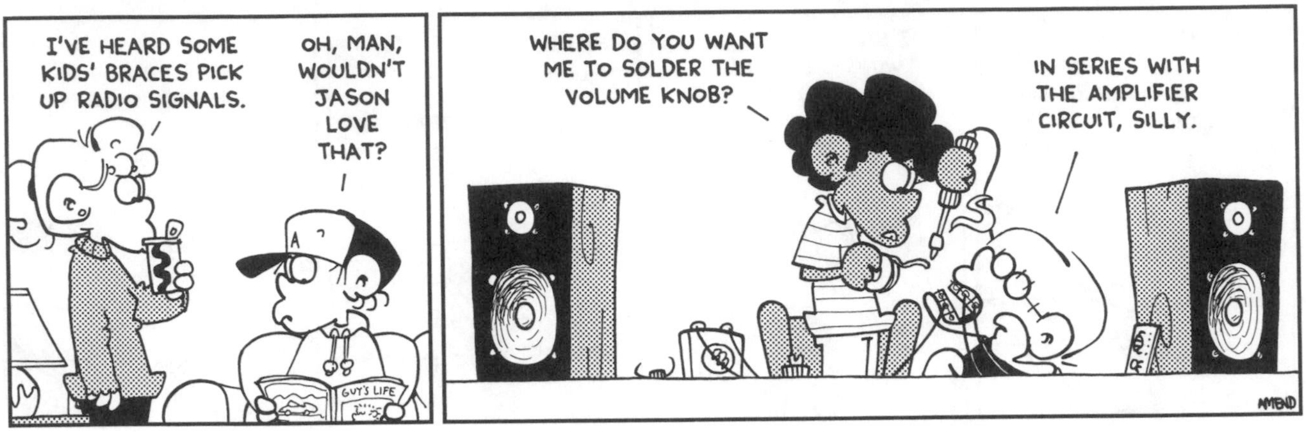
I'VE HEARD SOME KIDS' BRACES PICK UP RADIO SIGNALS.
OH, MAN, WOULDN'T JASON LOVE THAT?
WHERE DO YOU WANT ME TO SOLDER THE VOLUME KNOB?
IN SERIES WITH THE AMPLIFIER CIRCUIT, SILLY.

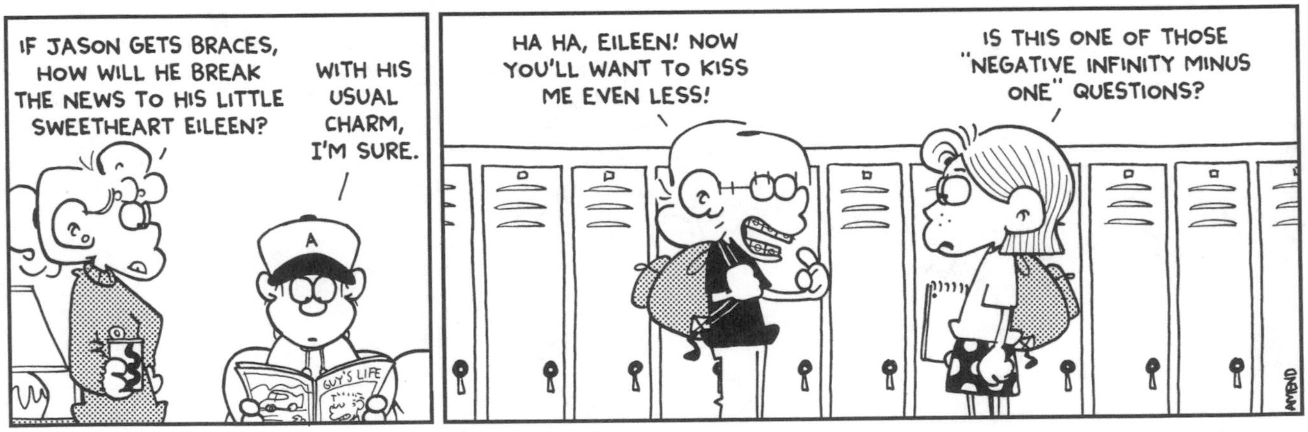
IF JASON GETS BRACES, HOW WILL HE BREAK THE NEWS TO HIS LITTLE SWEETHEART EILEEN?
WITH HIS USUAL CHARM, I'M SURE.
HA HA, EILEEN! NOW YOU'LL WANT TO KISS ME EVEN LESS!
IS THIS ONE OF THOSE "NEGATIVE INFINITY MINUS ONE" QUESTIONS?

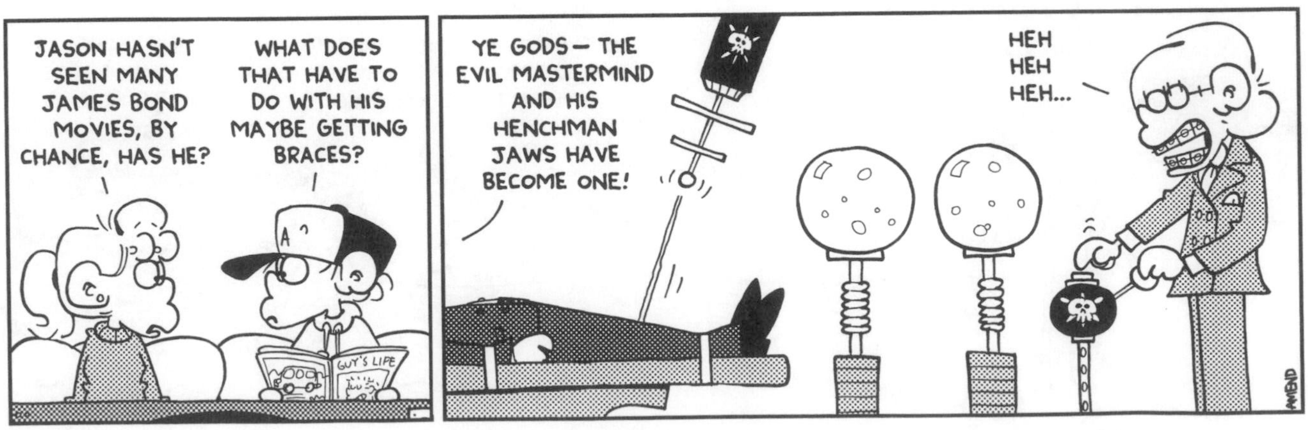
JASON HASN'T SEEN MANY JAMES BOND MOVIES, BY CHANCE, HAS HE?
WHAT DOES THAT HAVE TO DO WITH HIS MAYBE GETTING BRACES?
YE GODS — THE EVIL MASTERMIND AND HIS HENCHMAN JAWS HAVE BECOME ONE!
HEH HEH HEH...

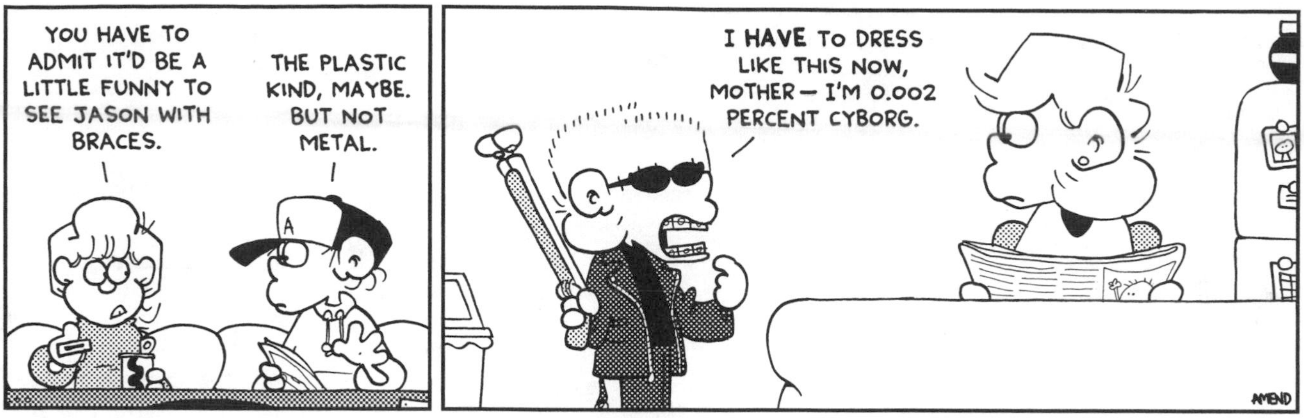
YOU HAVE TO ADMIT IT'D BE A LITTLE FUNNY TO SEE JASON WITH BRACES.
THE PLASTIC KIND, MAYBE. BUT NOT METAL.
I **HAVE** TO DRESS LIKE THIS NOW, MOTHER — I'M 0.002 PERCENT CYBORG.
AMEND

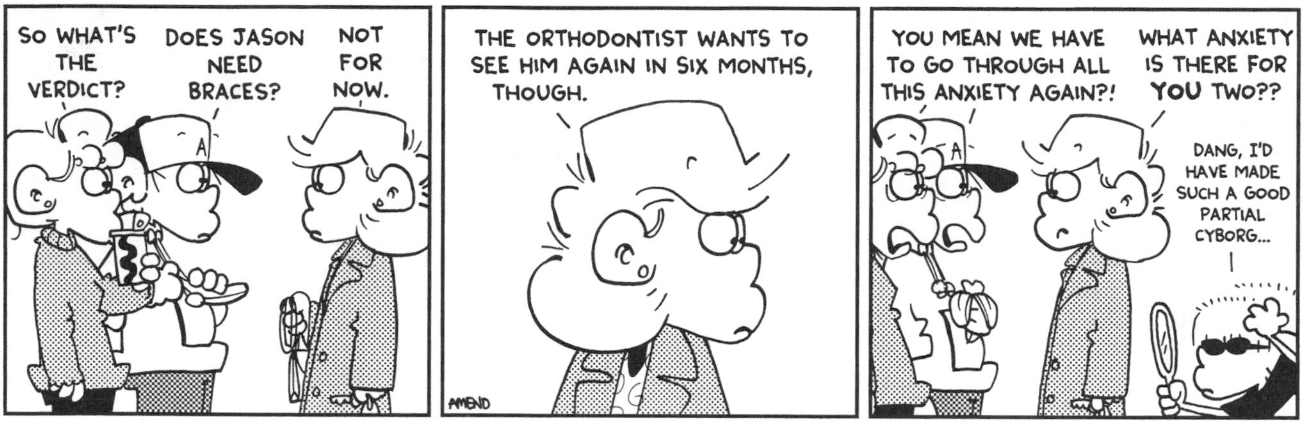
SO WHAT'S THE VERDICT?
DOES JASON NEED BRACES?
NOT FOR NOW.
THE ORTHODONTIST WANTS TO SEE HIM AGAIN IN SIX MONTHS, THOUGH.
AMEND
YOU MEAN WE HAVE TO GO THROUGH ALL THIS ANXIETY AGAIN?!
WHAT ANXIETY IS THERE FOR **YOU** TWO??
DANG, I'D HAVE MADE SUCH A GOOD PARTIAL CYBORG...

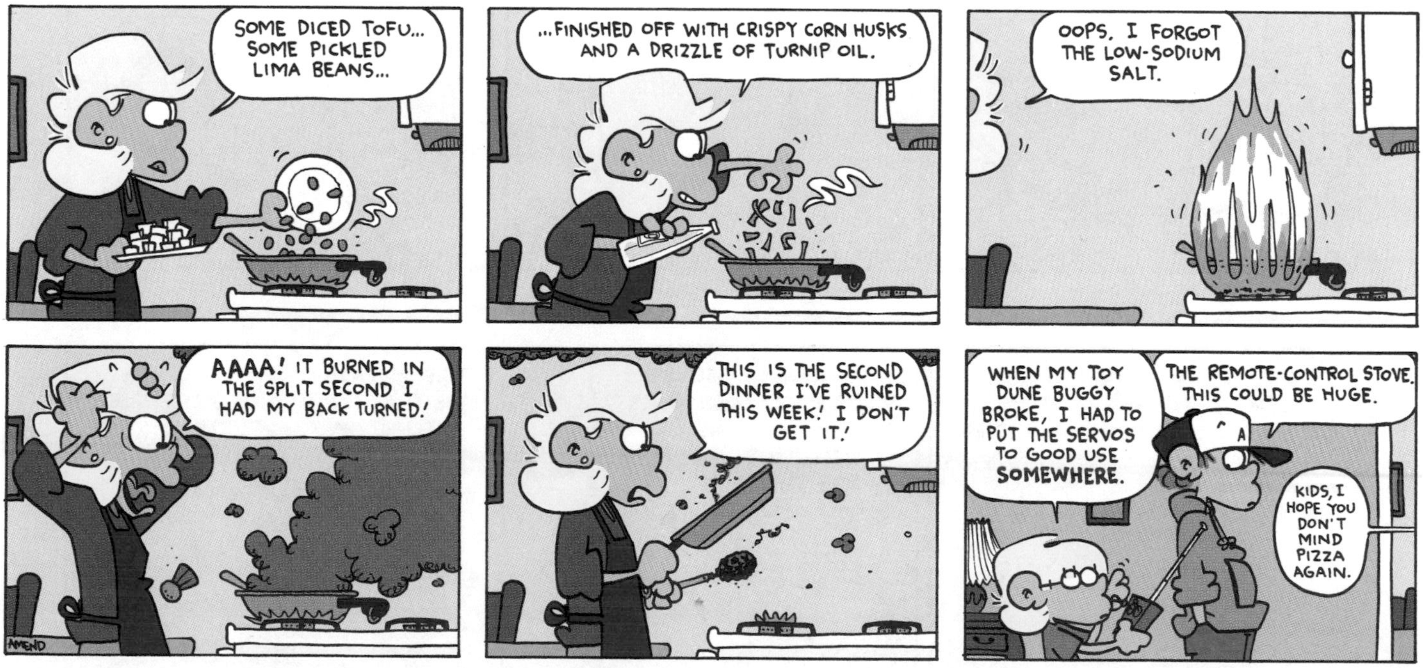
SOME DICED TOFU... SOME PICKLED LIMA BEANS...
...FINISHED OFF WITH CRISPY CORN HUSKS AND A DRIZZLE OF TURNIP OIL.
OOPS. I FORGOT THE LOW-SODIUM SALT.
AAAA! IT BURNED IN THE SPLIT SECOND I HAD MY BACK TURNED!
AMEND
THIS IS THE SECOND DINNER I'VE RUINED THIS WEEK! I DON'T GET IT!
WHEN MY TOY DUNE BUGGY BROKE, I HAD TO PUT THE SERVOS TO GOOD USE **SOMEWHERE**.
THE REMOTE-CONTROL STOVE. THIS COULD BE HUGE.
KIDS, I HOPE YOU DON'T MIND PIZZA AGAIN.

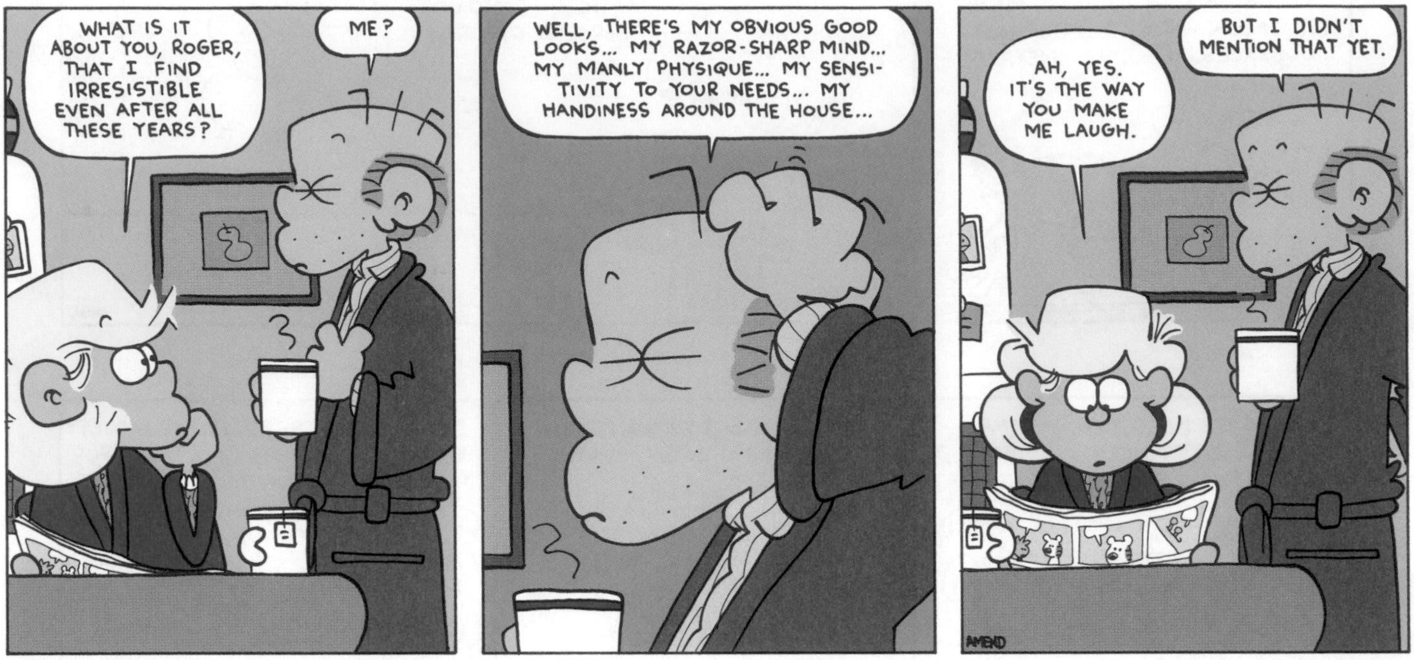
WHAT IS IT ABOUT YOU, ROGER, THAT I FIND IRRESISTIBLE EVEN AFTER ALL THESE YEARS?
ME?
WELL, THERE'S MY OBVIOUS GOOD LOOKS... MY RAZOR-SHARP MIND... MY MANLY PHYSIQUE... MY SENSITIVITY TO YOUR NEEDS... MY HANDINESS AROUND THE HOUSE...
AH, YES. IT'S THE WAY YOU MAKE ME LAUGH.
BUT I DIDN'T MENTION THAT YET.
AMEND

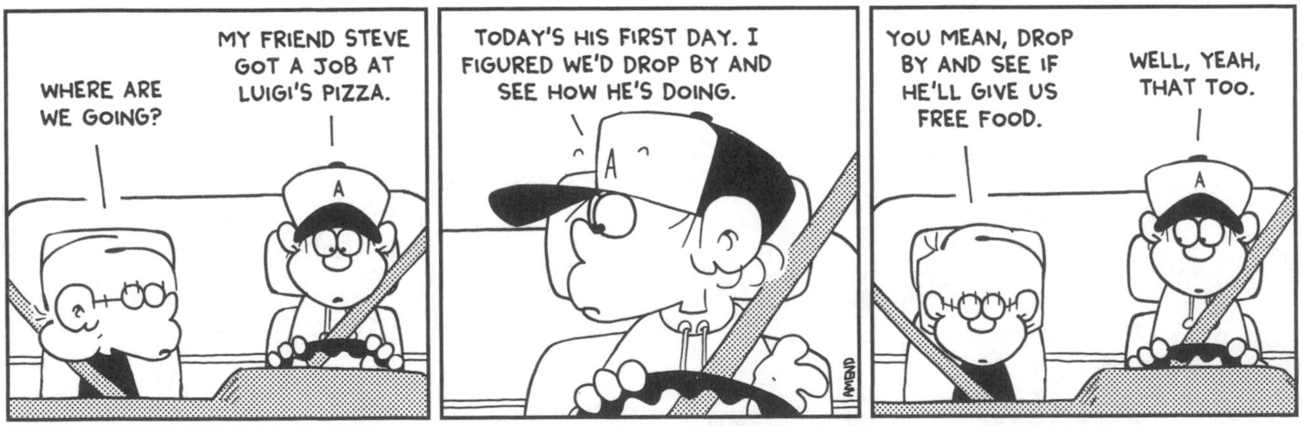
WHERE ARE WE GOING?
MY FRIEND STEVE GOT A JOB AT LUIGI'S PIZZA.
TODAY'S HIS FIRST DAY. I FIGURED WE'D DROP BY AND SEE HOW HE'S DOING.
AMEND
YOU MEAN, DROP BY AND SEE IF HE'LL GIVE US FREE FOOD.
WELL, YEAH, THAT TOO.

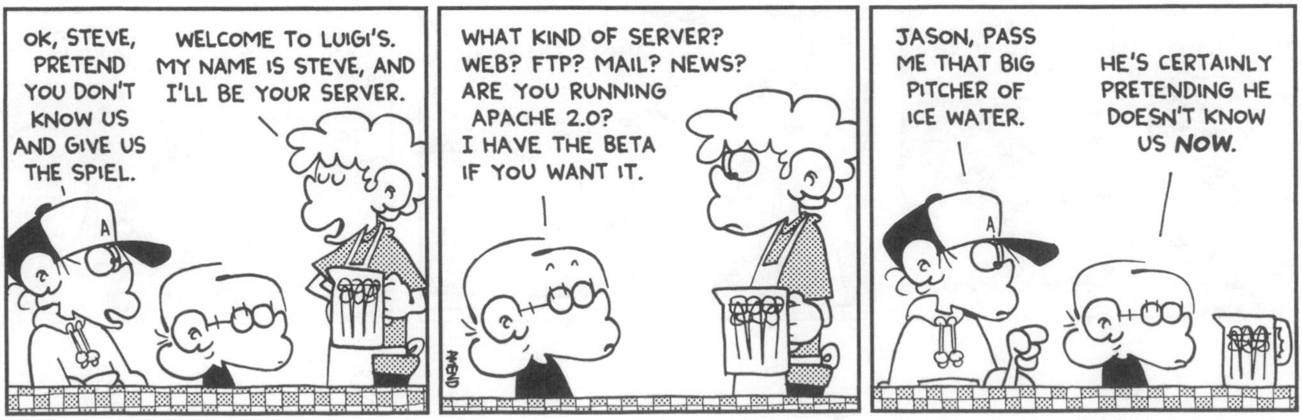
OK, STEVE, PRETEND YOU DON'T KNOW US AND GIVE US THE SPIEL.
WELCOME TO LUIGI'S. MY NAME IS STEVE, AND I'LL BE YOUR SERVER.
WHAT KIND OF SERVER? WEB? FTP? MAIL? NEWS? ARE YOU RUNNING APACHE 2.0? I HAVE THE BETA IF YOU WANT IT.
AMEND
JASON, PASS ME THAT BIG PITCHER OF ICE WATER.
HE'S CERTAINLY PRETENDING HE DOESN'T KNOW US NOW.

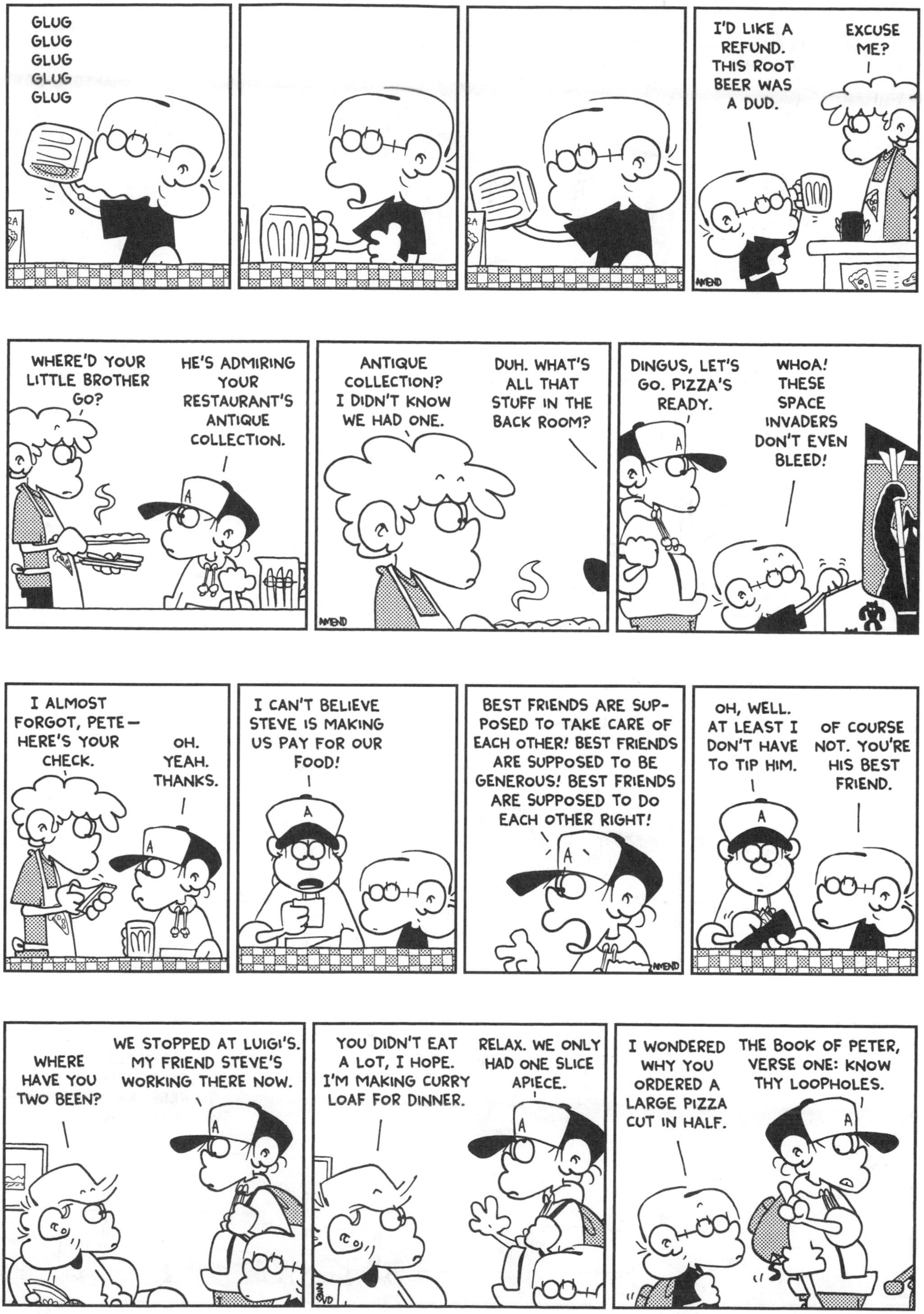

GLUG GLUG GLUG GLUG GLUG
I'D LIKE A REFUND. THIS ROOT BEER WAS A DUD.
EXCUSE ME?
AMEND
WHERE'D YOUR LITTLE BROTHER GO?
HE'S ADMIRING YOUR RESTAURANT'S ANTIQUE COLLECTION.
ANTIQUE COLLECTION? I DIDN'T KNOW WE HAD ONE.
DUH. WHAT'S ALL THAT STUFF IN THE BACK ROOM?
AMEND
DINGUS, LET'S GO. PIZZA'S READY.
WHOA! THESE SPACE INVADERS DON'T EVEN BLEED!
I ALMOST FORGOT, PETE— HERE'S YOUR CHECK.
OH. YEAH. THANKS.
I CAN'T BELIEVE STEVE IS MAKING US PAY FOR OUR FOOD!
BEST FRIENDS ARE SUPPOSED TO TAKE CARE OF EACH OTHER! BEST FRIENDS ARE SUPPOSED TO BE GENEROUS! BEST FRIENDS ARE SUPPOSED TO DO EACH OTHER RIGHT!
AMEND
OH, WELL. AT LEAST I DON'T HAVE TO TIP HIM.
OF COURSE NOT. YOU'RE HIS BEST FRIEND.
WHERE HAVE YOU TWO BEEN?
WE STOPPED AT LUIGI'S. MY FRIEND STEVE'S WORKING THERE NOW.
YOU DIDN'T EAT A LOT, I HOPE. I'M MAKING CURRY LOAF FOR DINNER.
RELAX. WE ONLY HAD ONE SLICE APIECE.
AMEND
I WONDERED WHY YOU ORDERED A LARGE PIZZA CUT IN HALF.
THE BOOK OF PETER, VERSE ONE: KNOW THY LOOPHOLES.

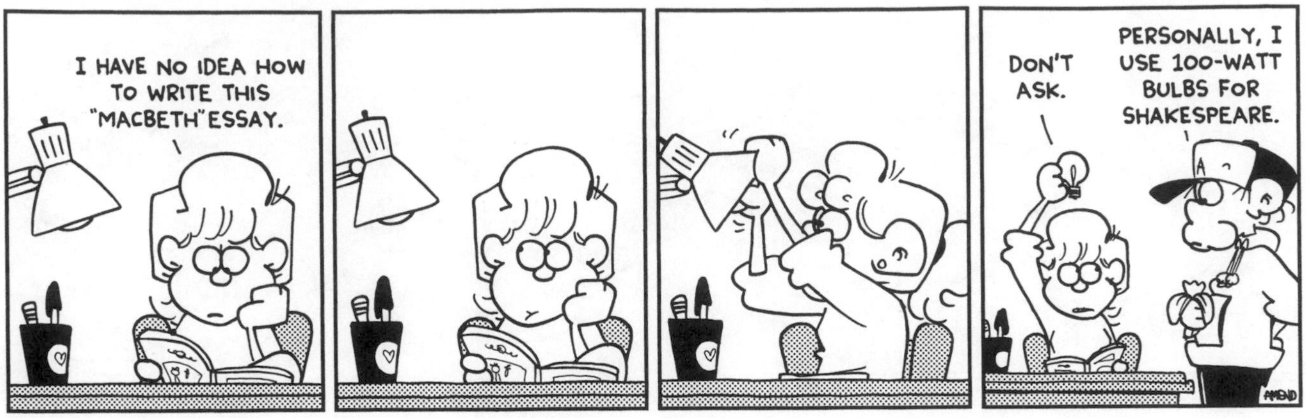
I HAVE NO IDEA HOW TO WRITE THIS "MACBETH" ESSAY.
DON'T ASK.
PERSONALLY, I USE 100-WATT BULBS FOR SHAKESPEARE.

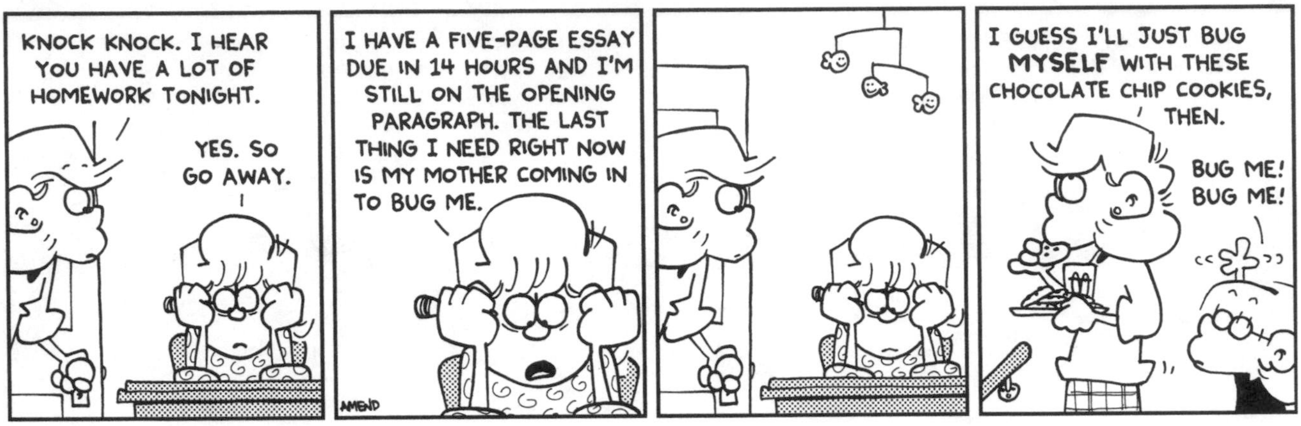
KNOCK KNOCK. I HEAR YOU HAVE A LOT OF HOMEWORK TONIGHT.
YES. SO GO AWAY.
I HAVE A FIVE-PAGE ESSAY DUE IN 14 HOURS AND I'M STILL ON THE OPENING PARAGRAPH. THE LAST THING I NEED RIGHT NOW IS MY MOTHER COMING IN TO BUG ME.
I GUESS I'LL JUST BUG **MYSELF** WITH THESE CHOCOLATE CHIP COOKIES, THEN.
BUG ME! BUG ME!

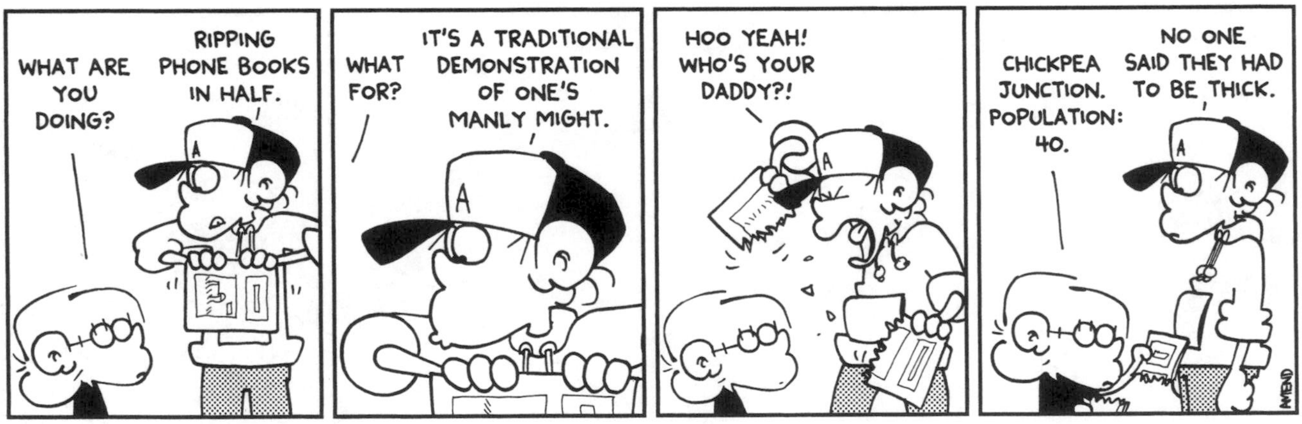
WHAT ARE YOU DOING?
RIPPING PHONE BOOKS IN HALF.
WHAT FOR?
IT'S A TRADITIONAL DEMONSTRATION OF ONE'S MANLY MIGHT.
HOO YEAH! WHO'S YOUR DADDY?!
CHICKPEA JUNCTION. POPULATION: 40.
NO ONE SAID THEY HAD TO BE THICK.

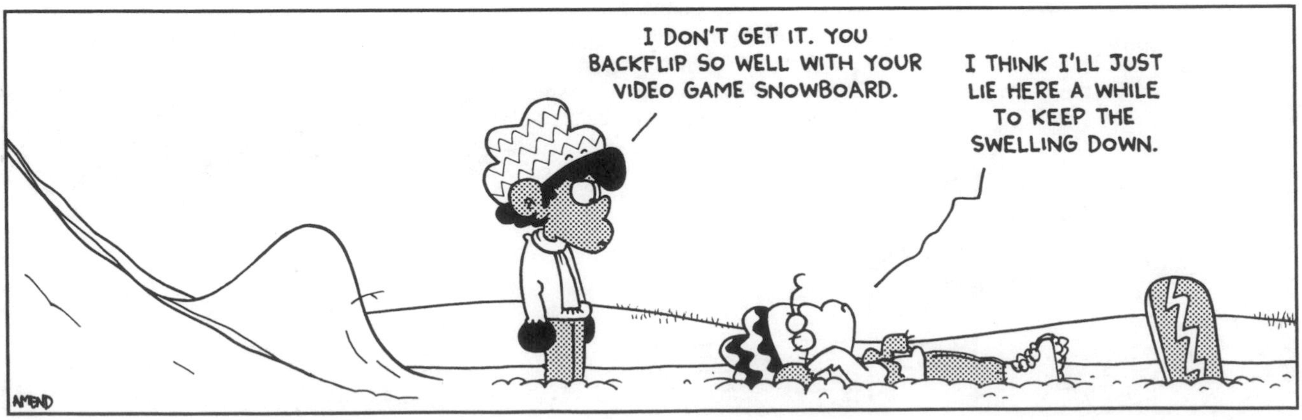
I DON'T GET IT. YOU BACKFLIP SO WELL WITH YOUR VIDEO GAME SNOWBOARD.
I THINK I'LL JUST LIE HERE A WHILE TO KEEP THE SWELLING DOWN.

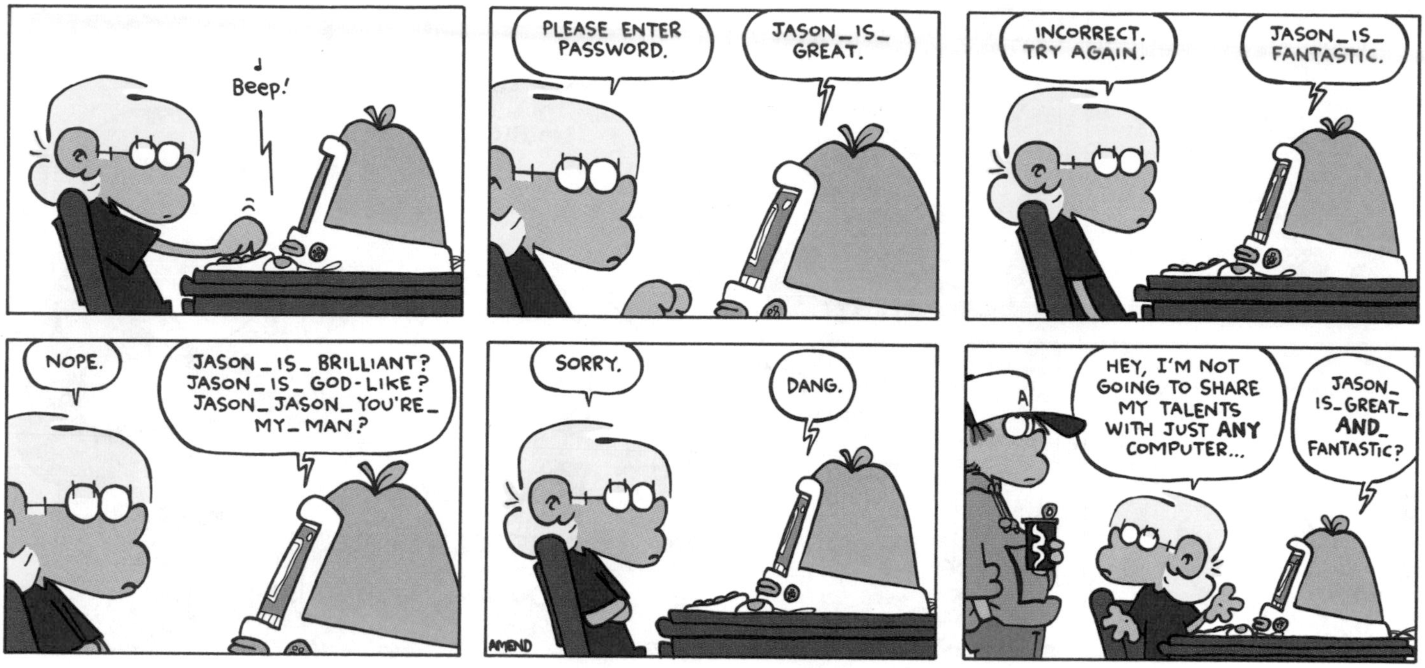
Beep!
PLEASE ENTER PASSWORD.
JASON_IS_GREAT.
INCORRECT. TRY AGAIN.
JASON_IS_FANTASTIC.
NOPE.
JASON_IS_BRILLIANT? JASON_IS_GOD-LIKE? JASON_JASON_YOU'RE_MY_MAN?
SORRY.
DANG.
AMEND
HEY, I'M NOT GOING TO SHARE MY TALENTS WITH JUST ANY COMPUTER...
JASON_IS_GREAT_AND_FANTASTIC?

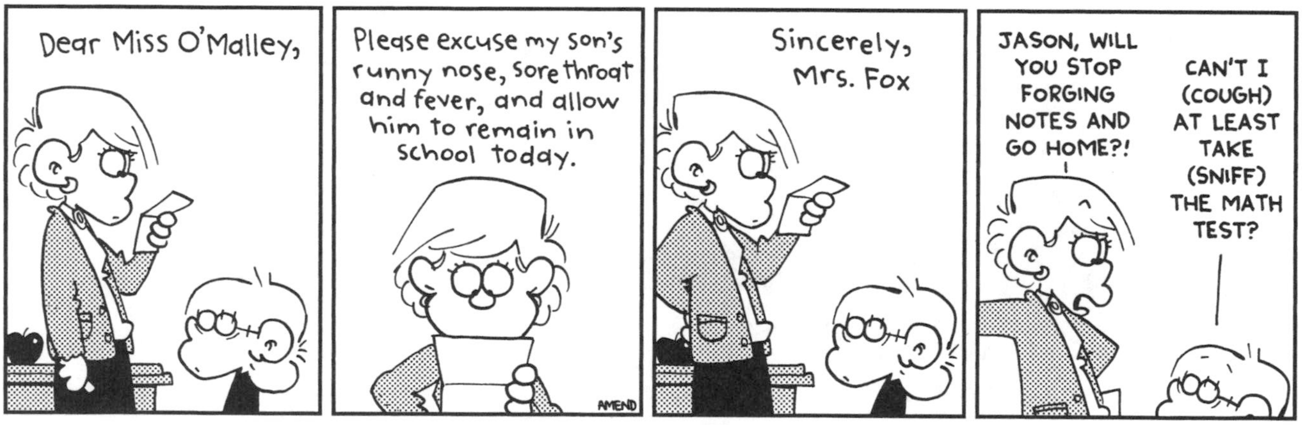
Dear Miss O'Malley,
Please excuse my son's runny nose, sore throat and fever, and allow him to remain in school today.
AMEND
Sincerely, Mrs. Fox
JASON, WILL YOU STOP FORGING NOTES AND GO HOME?!
CAN'T I (COUGH) AT LEAST TAKE (SNIFF) THE MATH TEST?

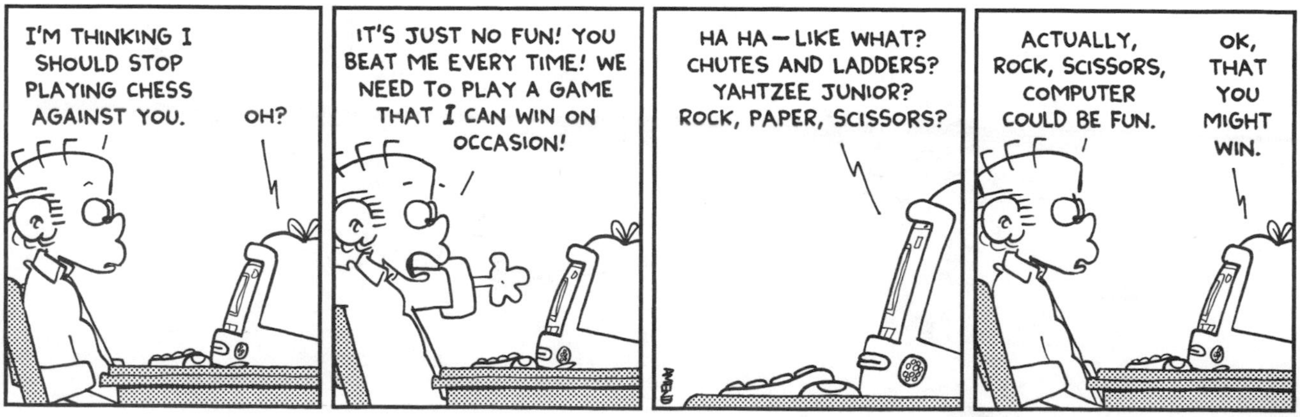
I'M THINKING I SHOULD STOP PLAYING CHESS AGAINST YOU.
OH?
IT'S JUST NO FUN! YOU BEAT ME EVERY TIME! WE NEED TO PLAY A GAME THAT I CAN WIN ON OCCASION!
HA HA—LIKE WHAT? CHUTES AND LADDERS? YAHTZEE JUNIOR? ROCK, PAPER, SCISSORS?
AMEND
ACTUALLY, ROCK, SCISSORS, COMPUTER COULD BE FUN.
OK, THAT YOU MIGHT WIN.

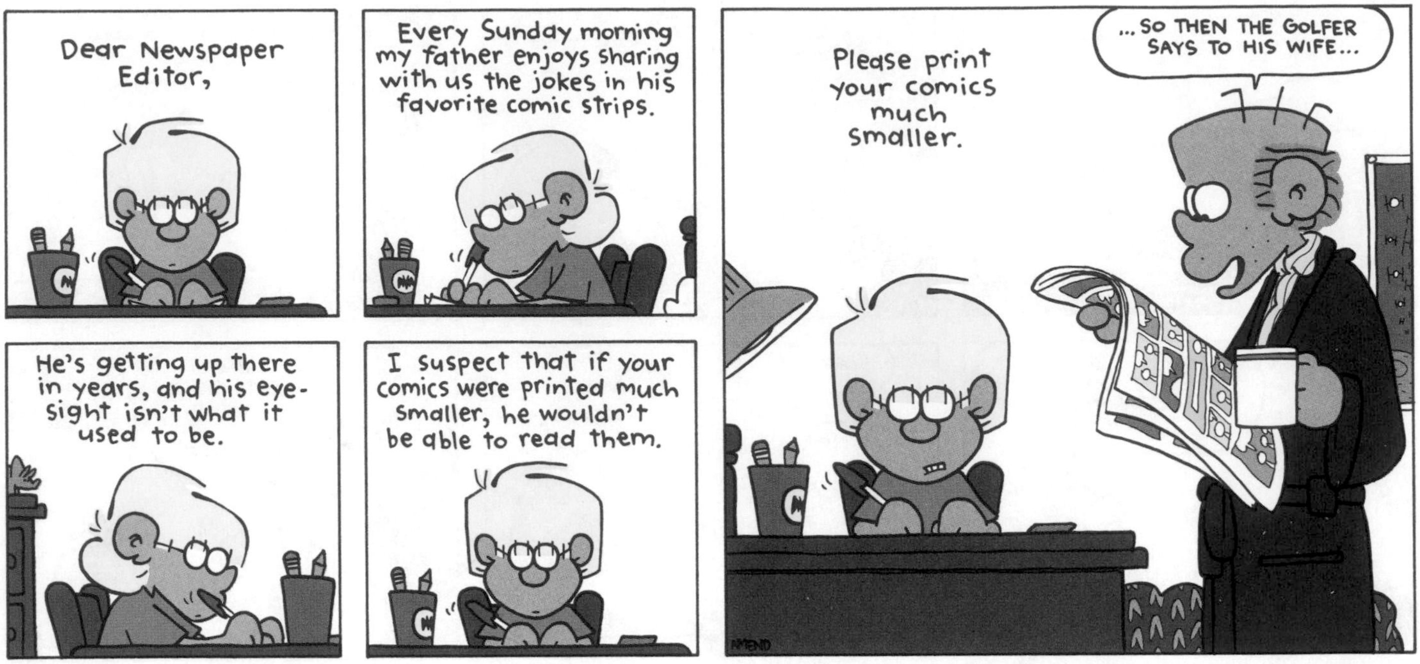
Dear Newspaper Editor,
Every Sunday morning my father enjoys sharing with us the jokes in his favorite comic strips.
He's getting up there in years, and his eye-sight isn't what it used to be.
I suspect that if your comics were printed much smaller, he wouldn't be able to read them.
Please print your comics much smaller.
...SO THEN THE GOLFER SAYS TO HIS WIFE...
AMEND

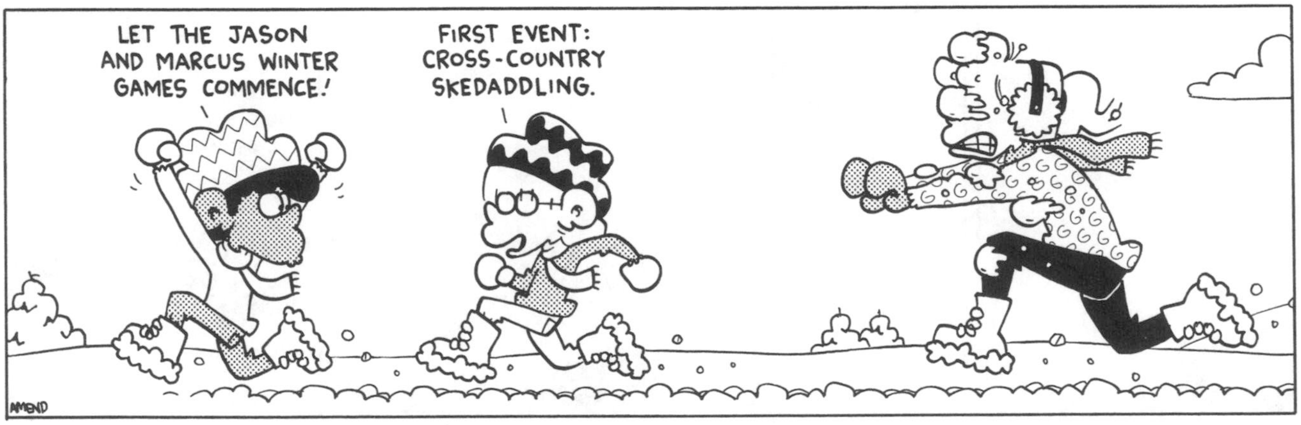
LET THE JASON AND MARCUS WINTER GAMES COMMENCE!
FIRST EVENT: CROSS-COUNTRY SKEDADDLING.
AMEND

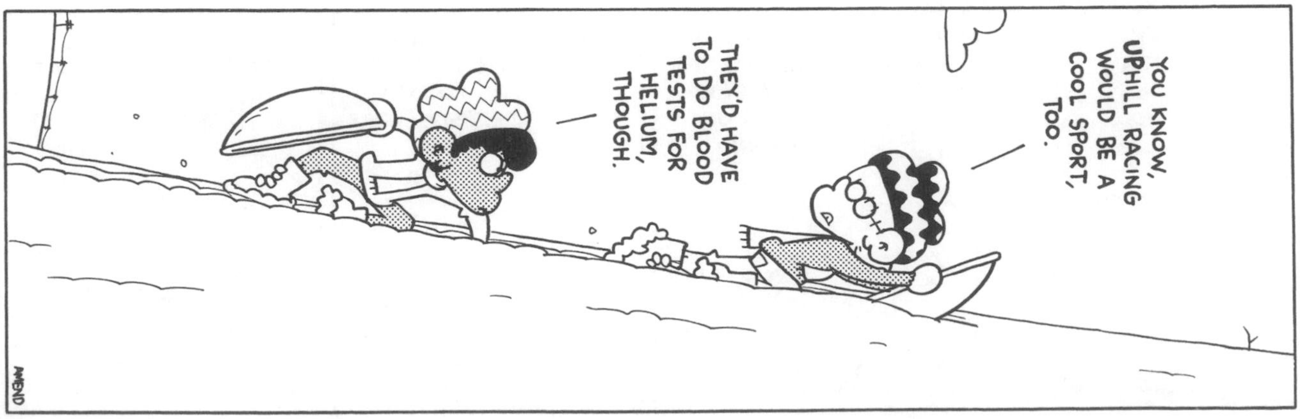
YOU KNOW, UPHILL RACING WOULD BE A COOL SPORT, TOO.
THEY'D HAVE TO DO BLOOD TESTS FOR HELIUM, THOUGH.
AMEND

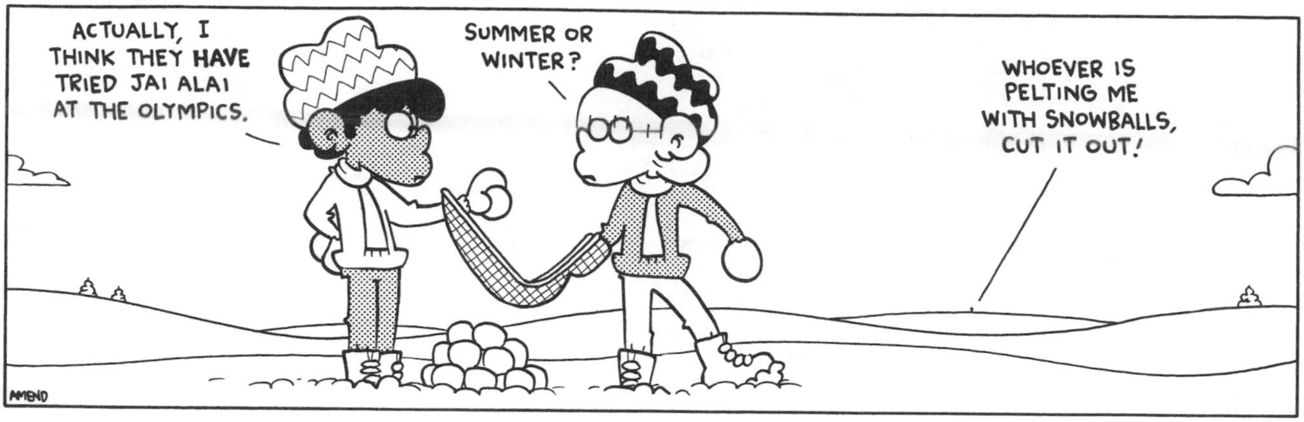
ACTUALLY, I THINK THEY HAVE TRIED JAI ALAI AT THE OLYMPICS.
SUMMER OR WINTER?
WHOEVER IS PELTING ME WITH SNOWBALLS, CUT IT OUT!
AMEND

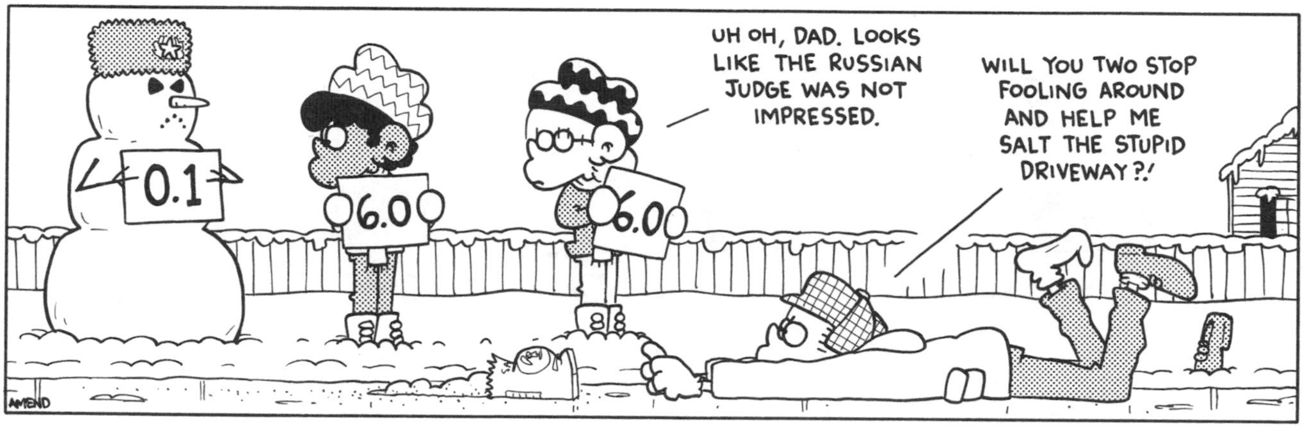
0.1
6.0
6.0
UH OH, DAD. LOOKS LIKE THE RUSSIAN JUDGE WAS NOT IMPRESSED.
WILL YOU TWO STOP FOOLING AROUND AND HELP ME SALT THE STUPID DRIVEWAY?!
AMEND

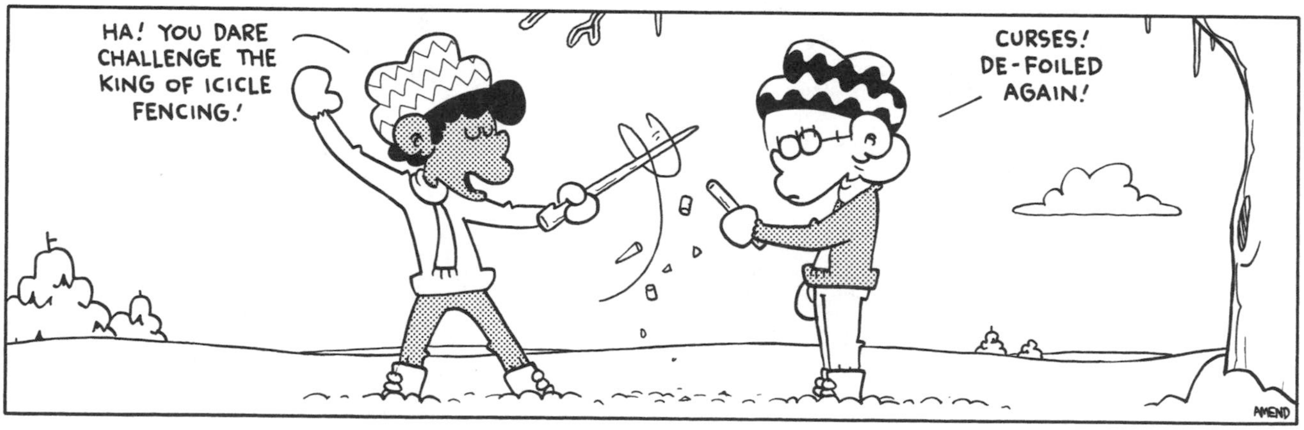
HA! YOU DARE CHALLENGE THE KING OF ICICLE FENCING!
CURSES! DE-FOILED AGAIN!
AMEND

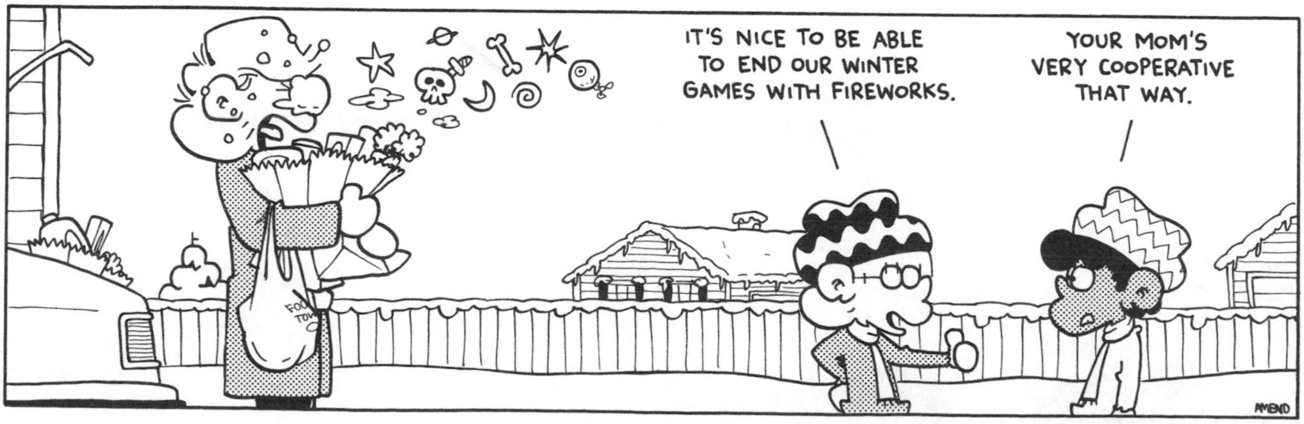
IT'S NICE TO BE ABLE TO END OUR WINTER GAMES WITH FIREWORKS.
YOUR MOM'S VERY COOPERATIVE THAT WAY.
AMEND

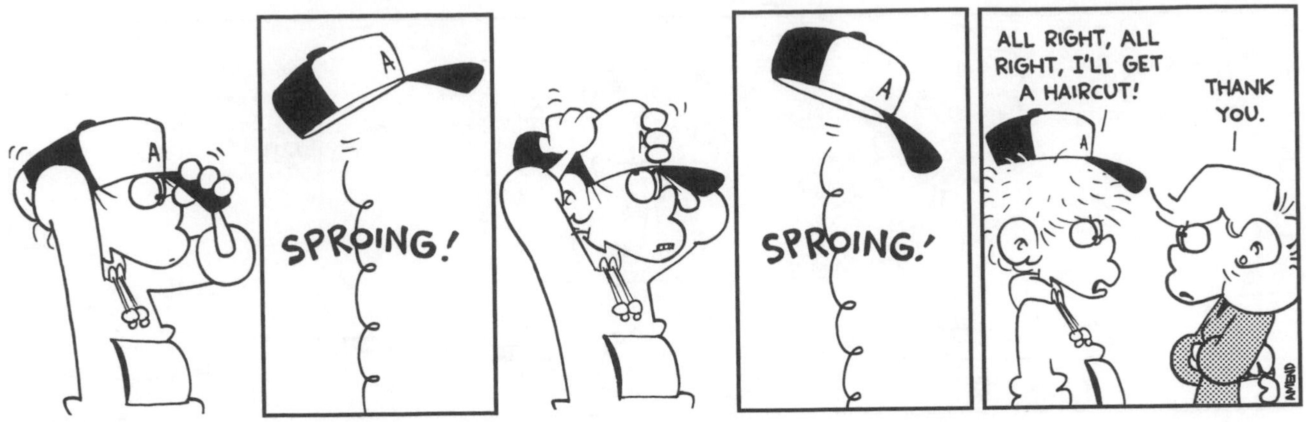
SPROING!
SPROING!
ALL RIGHT, ALL RIGHT, I'LL GET A HAIRCUT!
THANK YOU.
AMEND

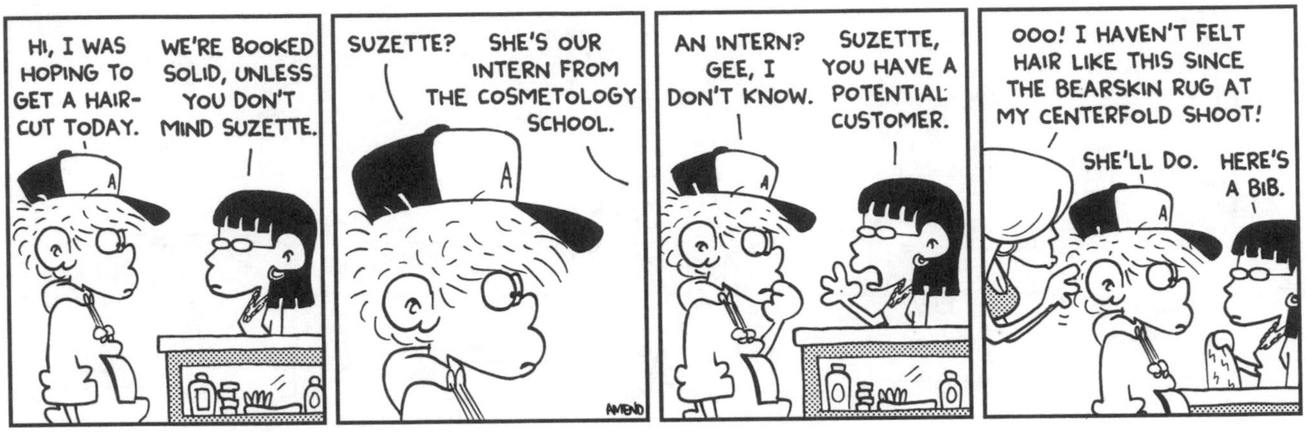
HI, I WAS HOPING TO GET A HAIR-CUT TODAY.
WE'RE BOOKED SOLID, UNLESS YOU DON'T MIND SUZETTE.
SUZETTE?
SHE'S OUR INTERN FROM THE COSMETOLOGY SCHOOL.
AN INTERN? GEE, I DON'T KNOW.
SUZETTE, YOU HAVE A POTENTIAL CUSTOMER.
OOO! I HAVEN'T FELT HAIR LIKE THIS SINCE THE BEARSKIN RUG AT MY CENTERFOLD SHOOT!
SHE'LL DO.
HERE'S A BIB.
AMEND

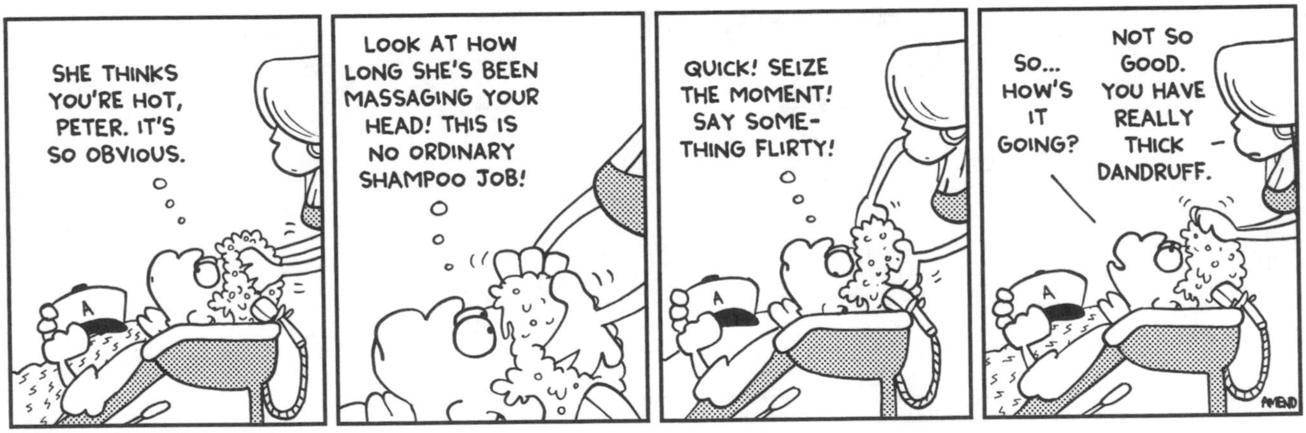
SHE THINKS YOU'RE HOT, PETER. IT'S SO OBVIOUS.
LOOK AT HOW LONG SHE'S BEEN MASSAGING YOUR HEAD! THIS IS NO ORDINARY SHAMPOO JOB!
QUICK! SEIZE THE MOMENT! SAY SOME-THING FLIRTY!
SO... HOW'S IT GOING?
NOT SO GOOD. YOU HAVE REALLY THICK DANDRUFF.
AMEND

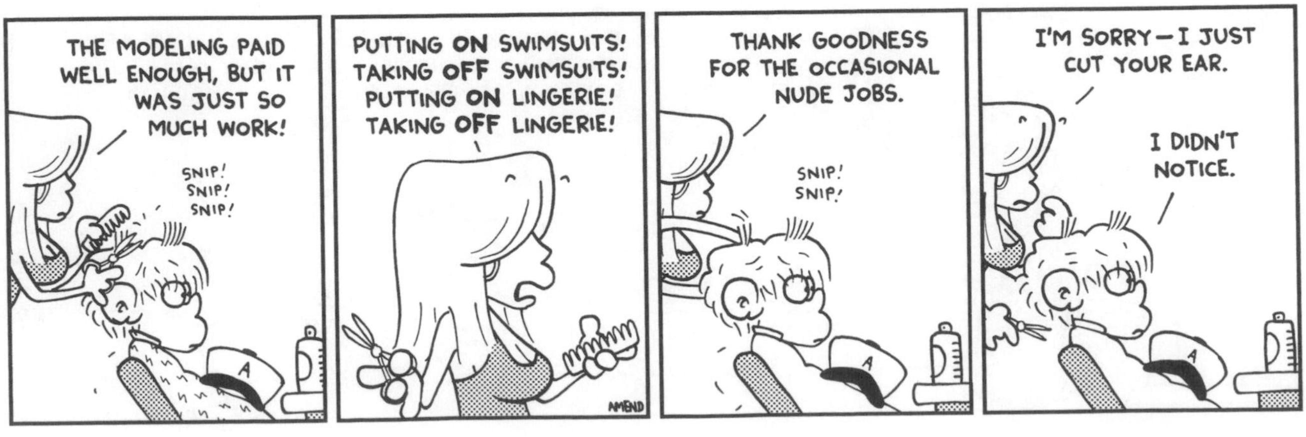
THE MODELING PAID WELL ENOUGH, BUT IT WAS JUST SO MUCH WORK!
SNIP! SNIP! SNIP!
PUTTING ON SWIMSUITS! TAKING OFF SWIMSUITS! PUTTING ON LINGERIE! TAKING OFF LINGERIE!
THANK GOODNESS FOR THE OCCASIONAL NUDE JOBS.
SNIP! SNIP!
I'M SORRY—I JUST CUT YOUR EAR.
I DIDN'T NOTICE.
AMEND

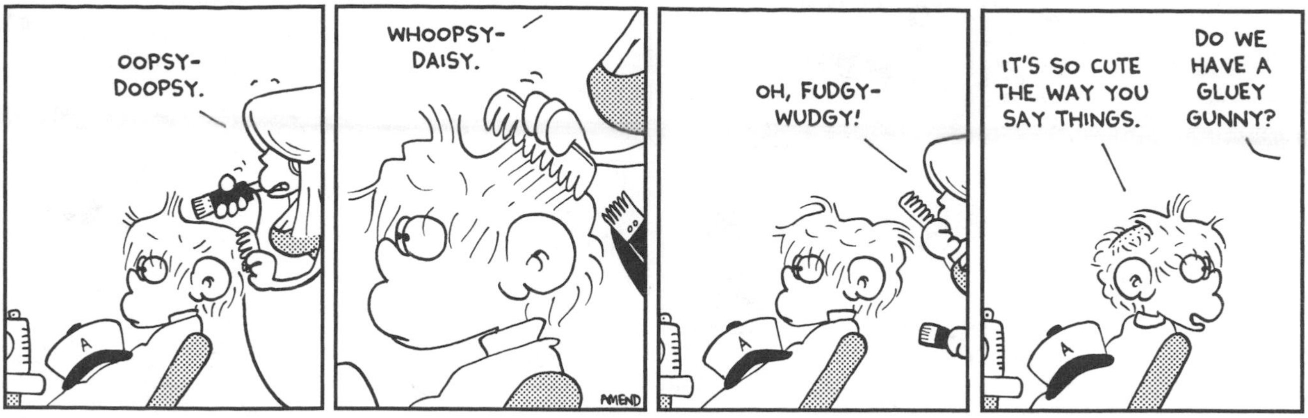
OOPSY-DOOPSY.
WHOOPSY-DAISY.
OH, FUDGY-WUDGY!
IT'S SO CUTE THE WAY YOU SAY THINGS.
DO WE HAVE A GLUEY GUNNY?
AMEND

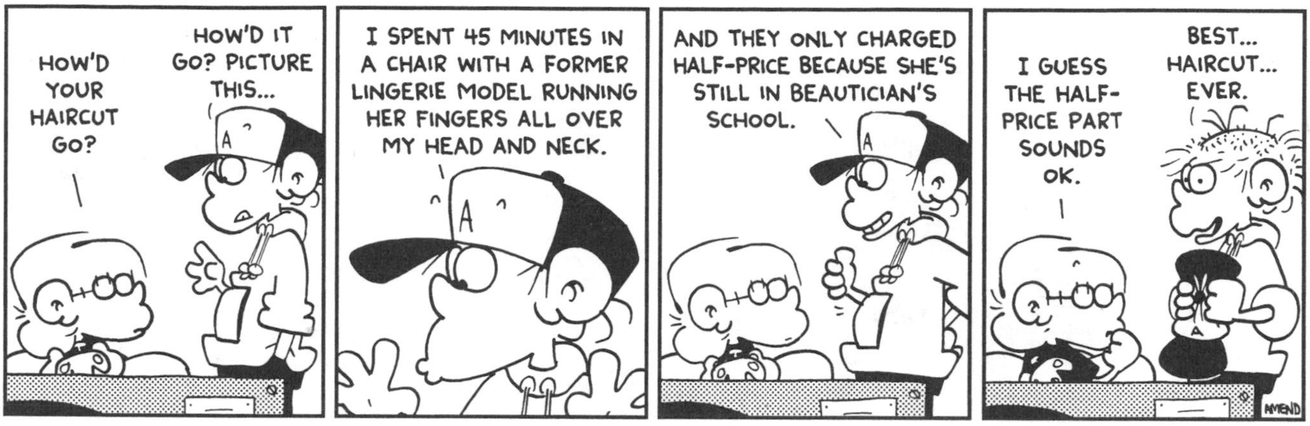
HOW'D YOUR HAIRCUT GO?
HOW'D IT GO? PICTURE THIS...
I SPENT 45 MINUTES IN A CHAIR WITH A FORMER LINGERIE MODEL RUNNING HER FINGERS ALL OVER MY HEAD AND NECK.
AND THEY ONLY CHARGED HALF-PRICE BECAUSE SHE'S STILL IN BEAUTICIAN'S SCHOOL.
I GUESS THE HALF-PRICE PART SOUNDS OK.
BEST... HAIRCUT... EVER.
AMEND

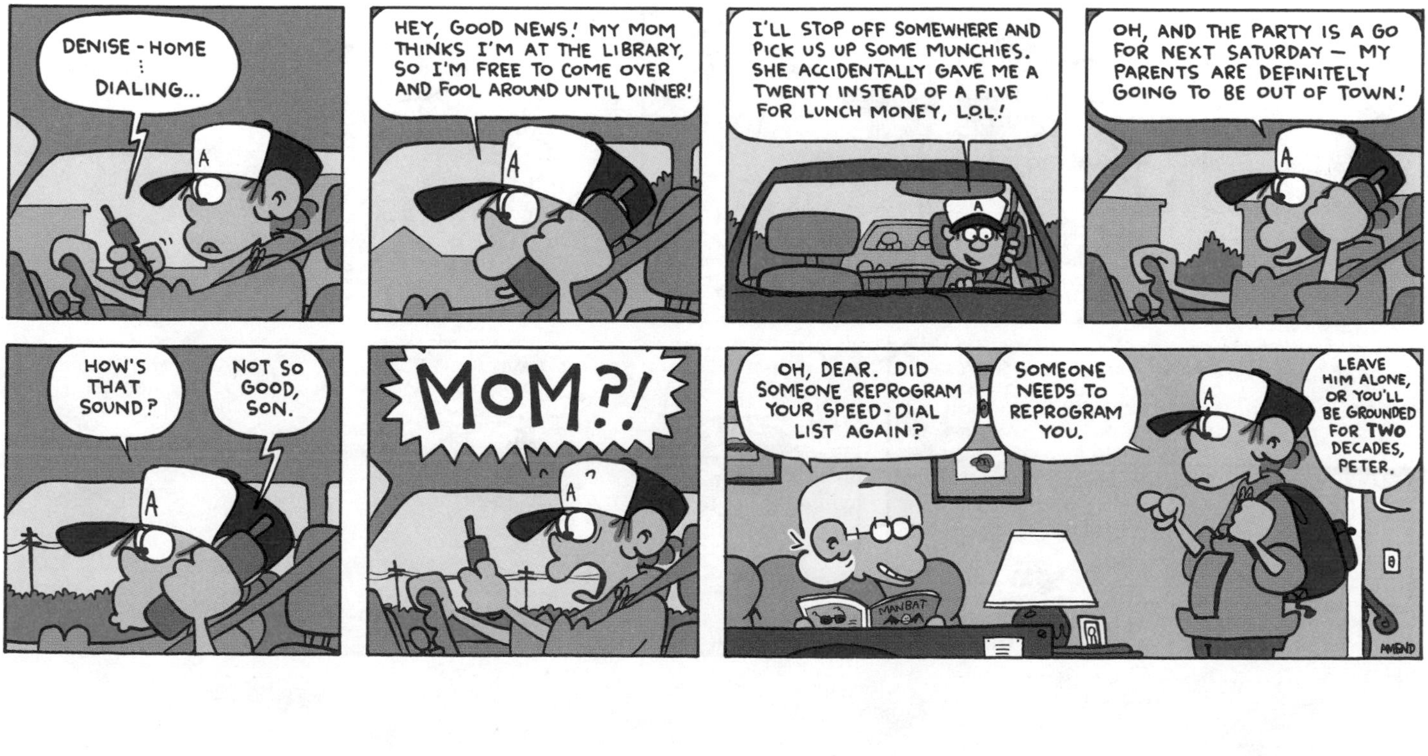
DENISE - HOME ⋮ DIALING...
HEY, GOOD NEWS! MY MOM THINKS I'M AT THE LIBRARY, SO I'M FREE TO COME OVER AND FOOL AROUND UNTIL DINNER!
I'LL STOP OFF SOMEWHERE AND PICK US UP SOME MUNCHIES. SHE ACCIDENTALLY GAVE ME A TWENTY INSTEAD OF A FIVE FOR LUNCH MONEY, L.O.L.!
OH, AND THE PARTY IS A GO FOR NEXT SATURDAY — MY PARENTS ARE DEFINITELY GOING TO BE OUT OF TOWN!
HOW'S THAT SOUND?
NOT SO GOOD, SON.
MOM?!
OH, DEAR. DID SOMEONE REPROGRAM YOUR SPEED-DIAL LIST AGAIN?
SOMEONE NEEDS TO REPROGRAM YOU.
LEAVE HIM ALONE, OR YOU'LL BE GROUNDED FOR TWO DECADES, PETER.
MANBAT
AMEND

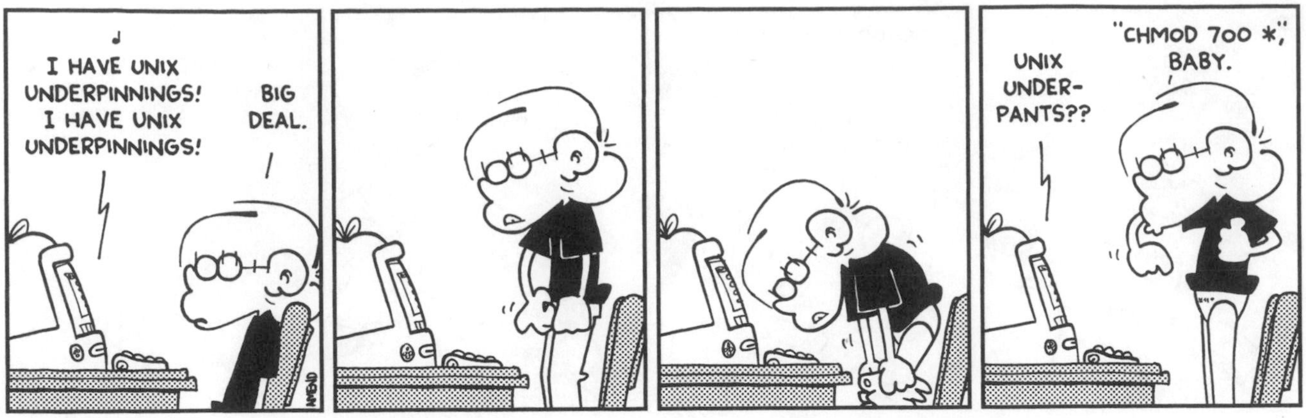
I HAVE UNIX UNDERPINNINGS! I HAVE UNIX UNDERPINNINGS!
BIG DEAL.
UNIX UNDER-PANTS??
"CHMOD 700 *," BABY.

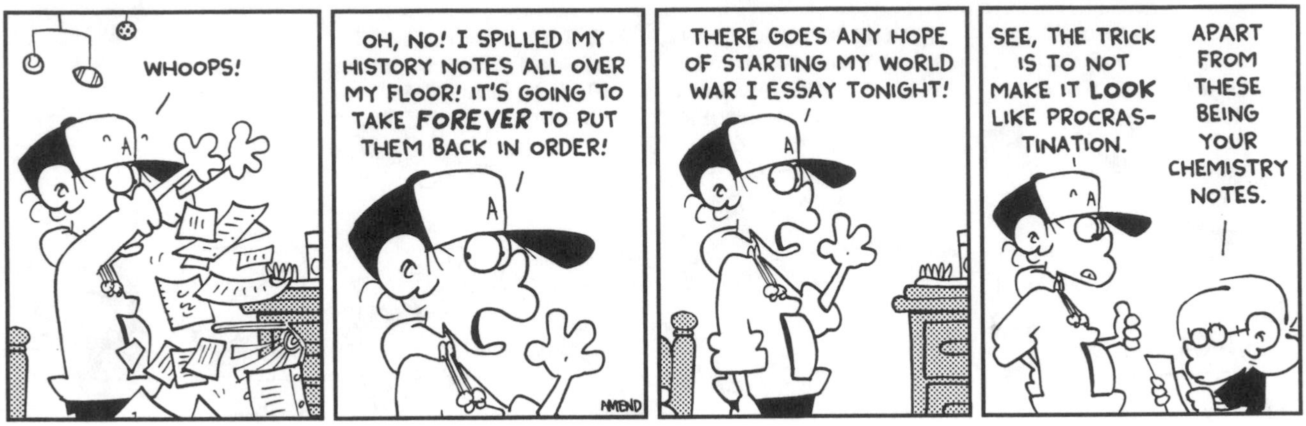
WHOOPS!
OH, NO! I SPILLED MY HISTORY NOTES ALL OVER MY FLOOR! IT'S GOING TO TAKE FOREVER TO PUT THEM BACK IN ORDER!
THERE GOES ANY HOPE OF STARTING MY WORLD WAR I ESSAY TONIGHT!
SEE, THE TRICK IS TO NOT MAKE IT LOOK LIKE PROCRAS-TINATION.
APART FROM THESE BEING YOUR CHEMISTRY NOTES.

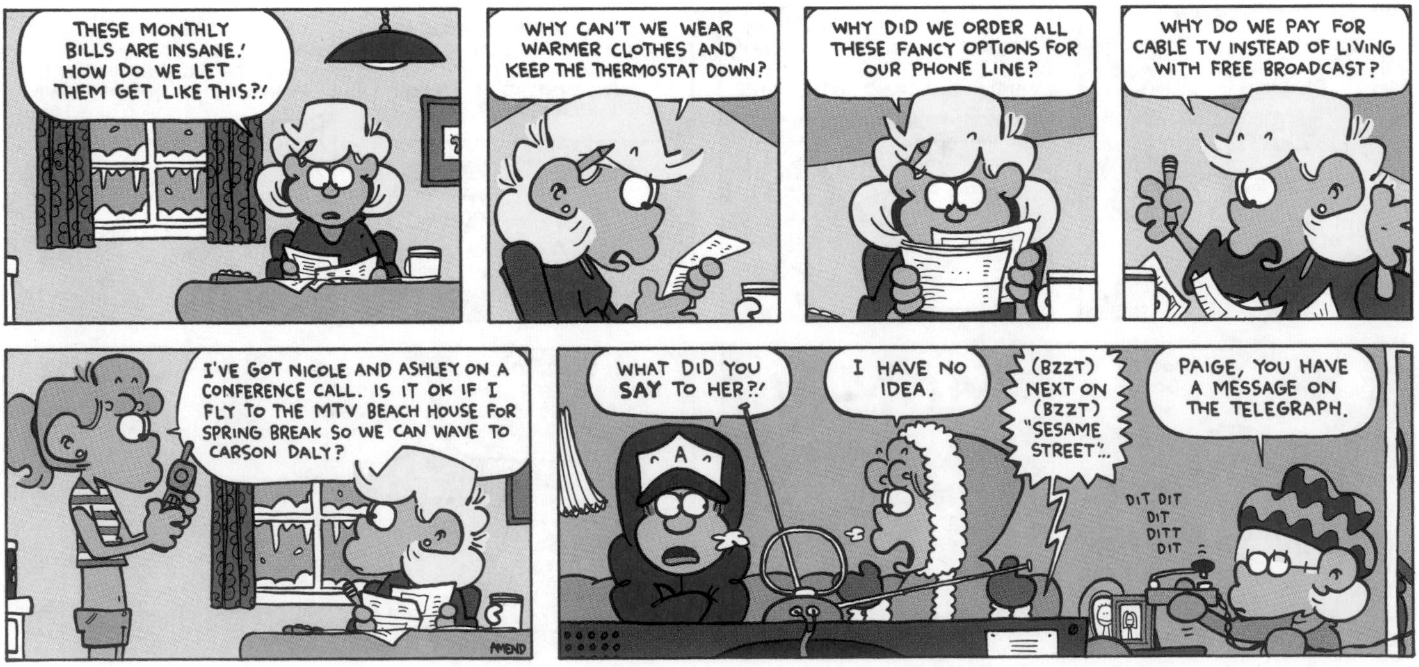
THESE MONTHLY BILLS ARE INSANE! HOW DO WE LET THEM GET LIKE THIS?!
WHY CAN'T WE WEAR WARMER CLOTHES AND KEEP THE THERMOSTAT DOWN?
WHY DID WE ORDER ALL THESE FANCY OPTIONS FOR OUR PHONE LINE?
WHY DO WE PAY FOR CABLE TV INSTEAD OF LIVING WITH FREE BROADCAST?
I'VE GOT NICOLE AND ASHLEY ON A CONFERENCE CALL. IS IT OK IF I FLY TO THE MTV BEACH HOUSE FOR SPRING BREAK SO WE CAN WAVE TO CARSON DALY?
WHAT DID YOU SAY TO HER?!
I HAVE NO IDEA.
(BZZT) NEXT ON (BZZT) "SESAME STREET"...
PAIGE, YOU HAVE A MESSAGE ON THE TELEGRAPH.
DIT DIT DIT DITT DIT

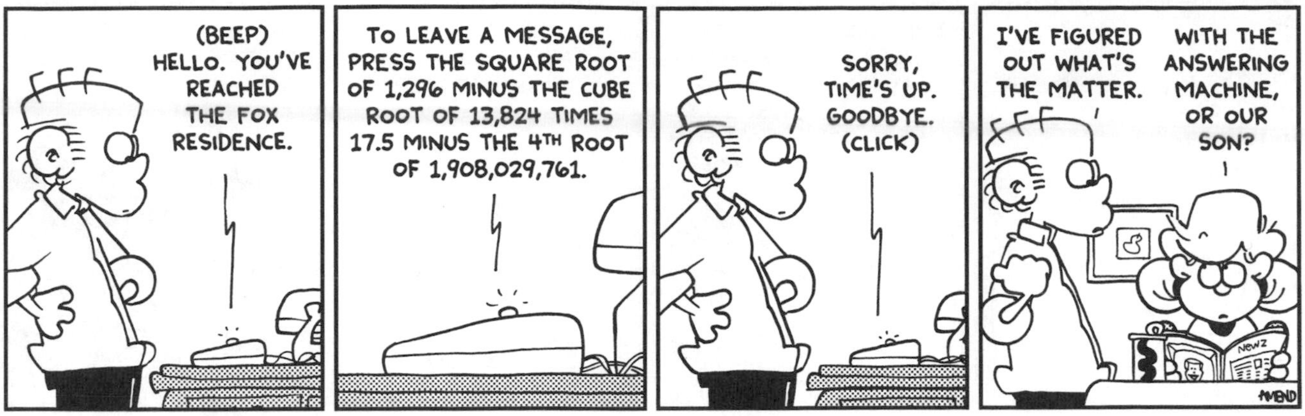
(BEEP) HELLO. YOU'VE REACHED THE FOX RESIDENCE.
TO LEAVE A MESSAGE, PRESS THE SQUARE ROOT OF 1,296 MINUS THE CUBE ROOT OF 13,824 TIMES 17.5 MINUS THE 4TH ROOT OF 1,908,029,761.
SORRY, TIME'S UP. GOODBYE. (CLICK)
I'VE FIGURED OUT WHAT'S THE MATTER.
WITH THE ANSWERING MACHINE, OR OUR SON?
NEWZ
AMEND

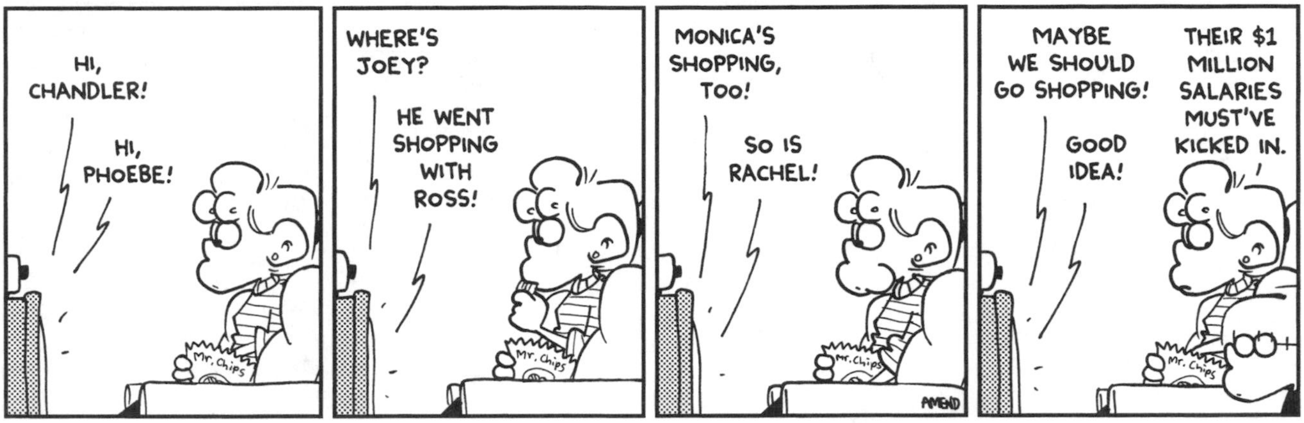
HI, CHANDLER!
HI, PHOEBE!
Mr. Chips
WHERE'S JOEY?
HE WENT SHOPPING WITH ROSS!
MONICA'S SHOPPING, TOO!
SO IS RACHEL!
AMEND
MAYBE WE SHOULD GO SHOPPING!
GOOD IDEA!
THEIR $1 MILLION SALARIES MUST'VE KICKED IN.

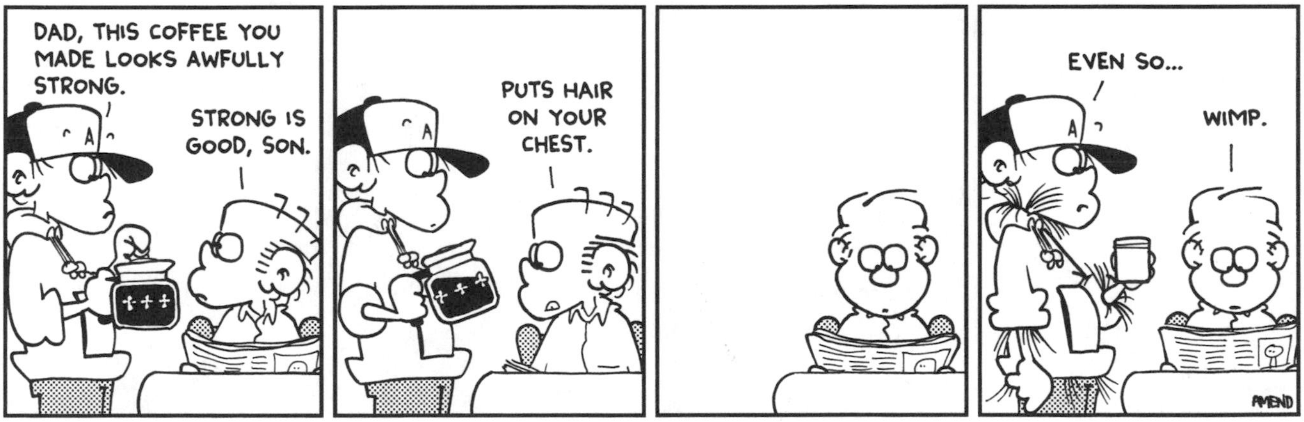
DAD, THIS COFFEE YOU MADE LOOKS AWFULLY STRONG.
STRONG IS GOOD, SON.
PUTS HAIR ON YOUR CHEST.
EVEN SO...
WIMP.
AMEND

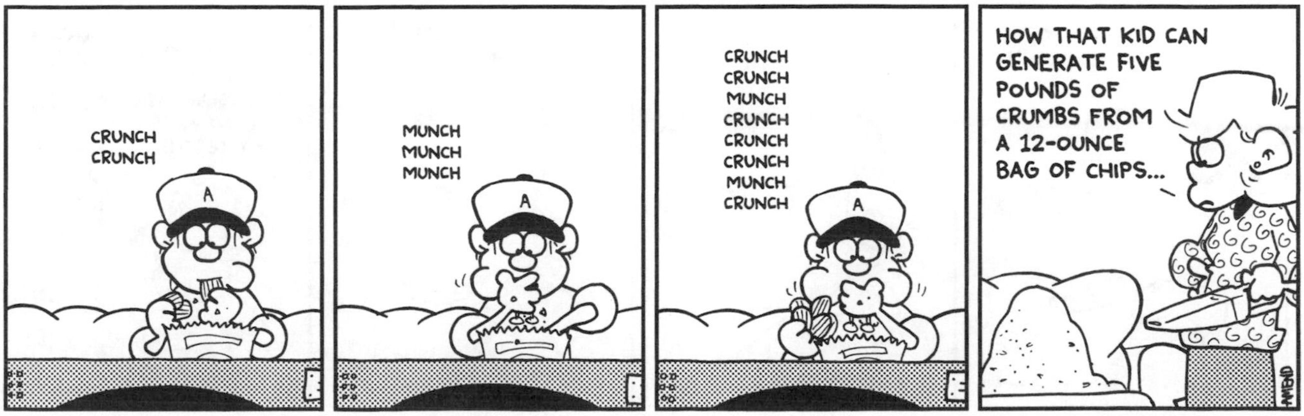
CRUNCH CRUNCH
MUNCH MUNCH MUNCH
CRUNCH CRUNCH MUNCH CRUNCH CRUNCH CRUNCH MUNCH CRUNCH
HOW THAT KID CAN GENERATE FIVE POUNDS OF CRUMBS FROM A 12-OUNCE BAG OF CHIPS...
AMEND

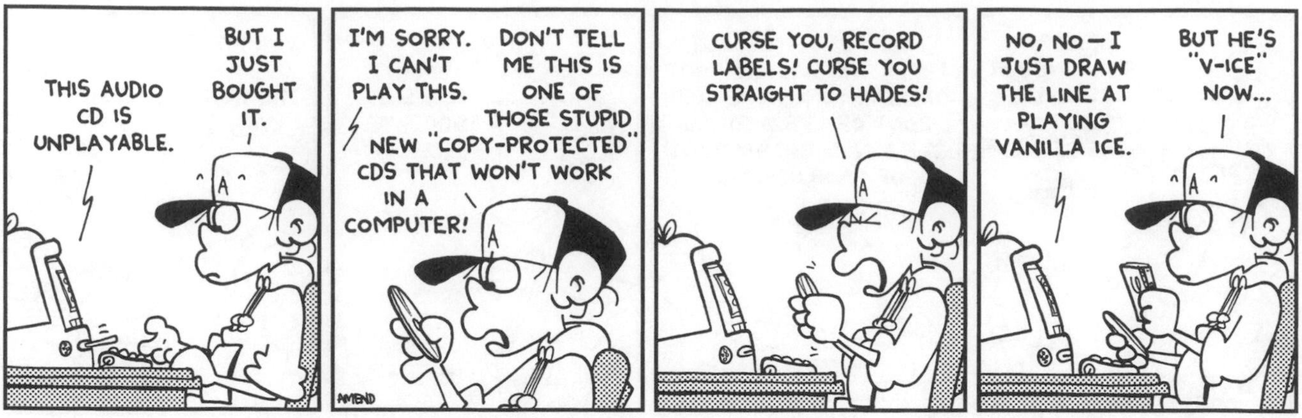
THIS AUDIO CD IS UNPLAYABLE.
BUT I JUST BOUGHT IT.
I'M SORRY. I CAN'T PLAY THIS.
DON'T TELL ME THIS IS ONE OF THOSE STUPID NEW "COPY-PROTECTED" CDS THAT WON'T WORK IN A COMPUTER!
CURSE YOU, RECORD LABELS! CURSE YOU STRAIGHT TO HADES!
NO, NO—I JUST DRAW THE LINE AT PLAYING VANILLA ICE.
BUT HE'S "V-ICE" NOW...

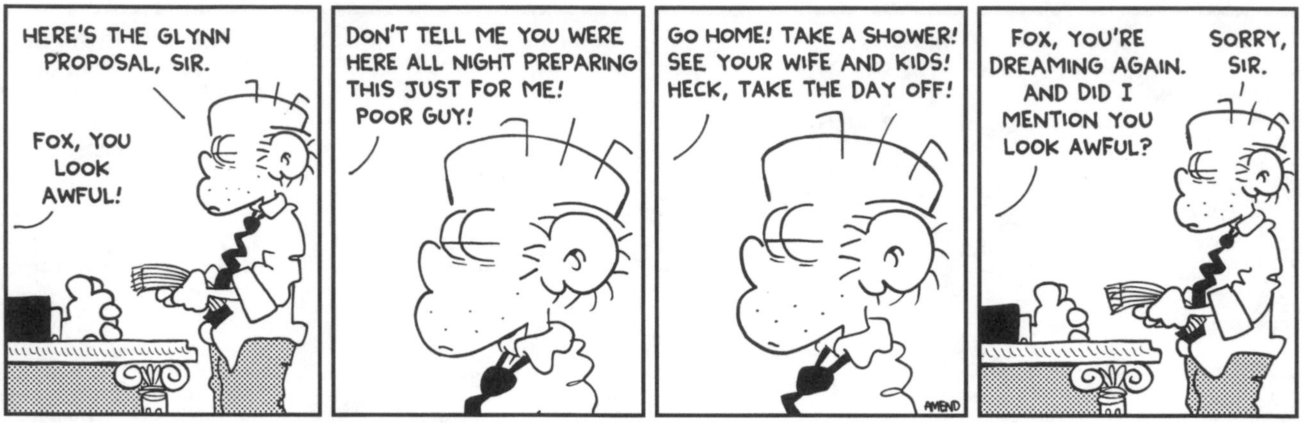
HERE'S THE GLYNN PROPOSAL, SIR.
FOX, YOU LOOK AWFUL!
DON'T TELL ME YOU WERE HERE ALL NIGHT PREPARING THIS JUST FOR ME! POOR GUY!
GO HOME! TAKE A SHOWER! SEE YOUR WIFE AND KIDS! HECK, TAKE THE DAY OFF!
FOX, YOU'RE DREAMING AGAIN. AND DID I MENTION YOU LOOK AWFUL?
SORRY, SIR.

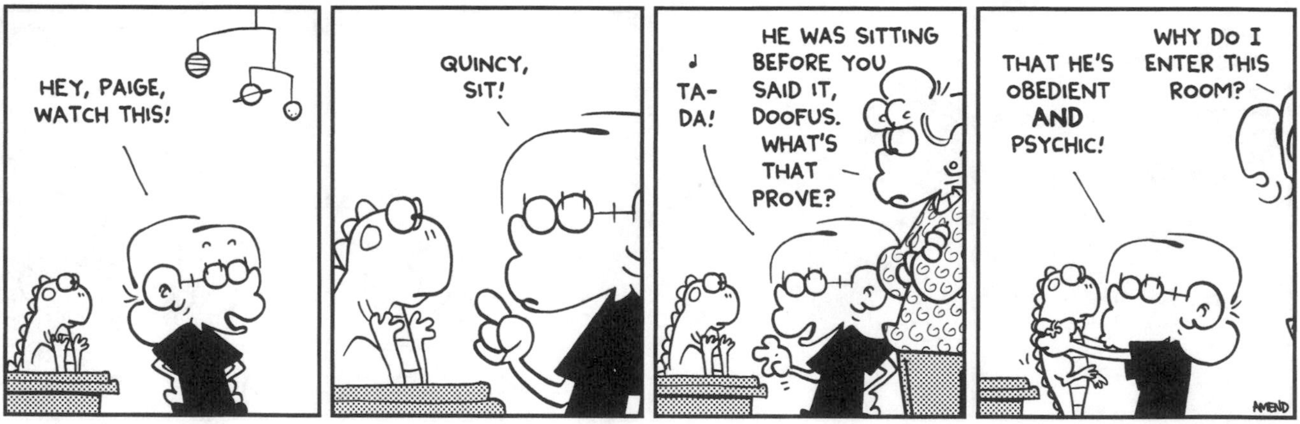
HEY, PAIGE, WATCH THIS!
QUINCY, SIT!
TA-DA!
HE WAS SITTING BEFORE YOU SAID IT, DOOFUS. WHAT'S THAT PROVE?
THAT HE'S OBEDIENT **AND** PSYCHIC!
WHY DO I ENTER THIS ROOM?

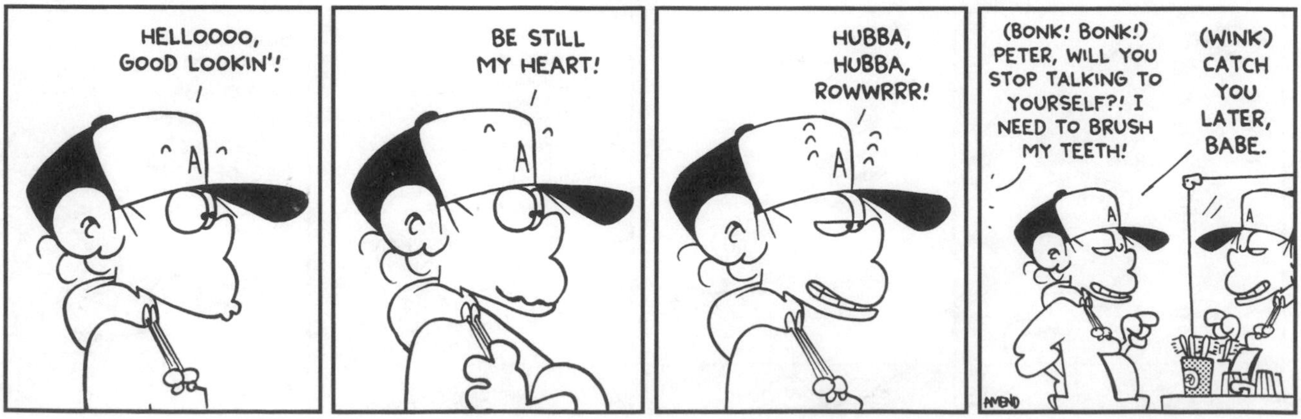
HELLOOOO, GOOD LOOKIN'!
BE STILL MY HEART!
HUBBA, HUBBA, ROWWRRR!
(BONK! BONK!) PETER, WILL YOU STOP TALKING TO YOURSELF?! I NEED TO BRUSH MY TEETH!
(WINK) CATCH YOU LATER, BABE.

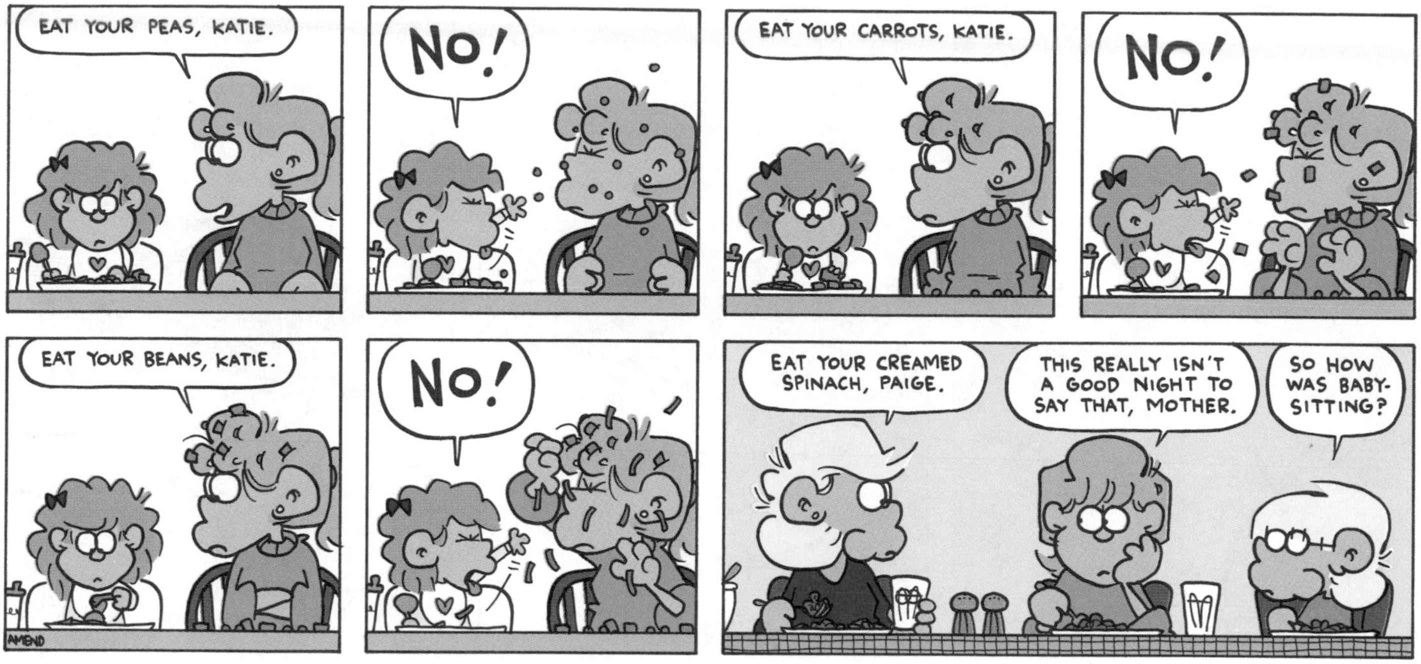
EAT YOUR PEAS, KATIE.
NO!
EAT YOUR CARROTS, KATIE.
NO!
EAT YOUR BEANS, KATIE.
NO!
EAT YOUR CREAMED SPINACH, PAIGE.
THIS REALLY ISN'T A GOOD NIGHT TO SAY THAT, MOTHER.
SO HOW WAS BABY-SITTING?

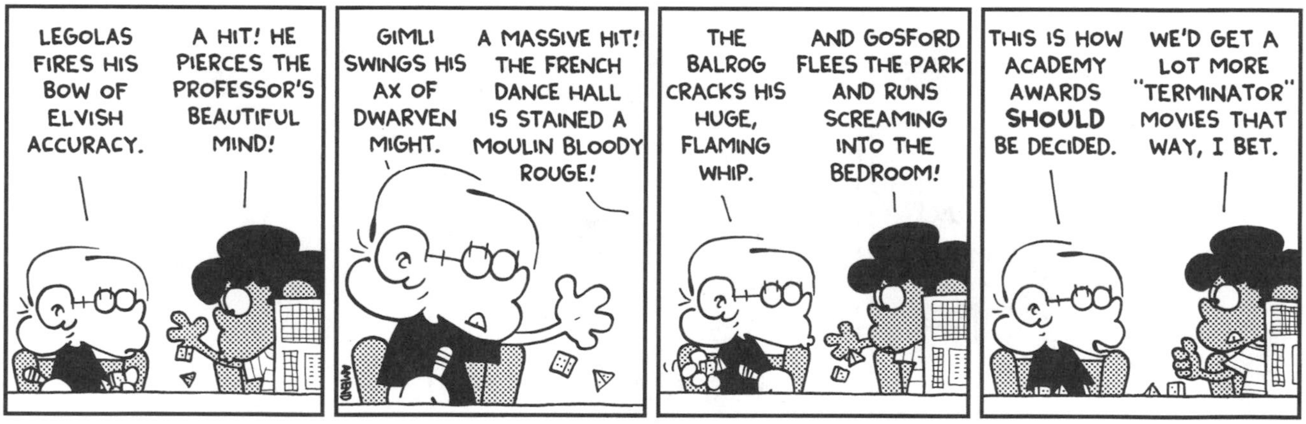
LEGOLAS FIRES HIS BOW OF ELVISH ACCURACY.
A HIT! HE PIERCES THE PROFESSOR'S BEAUTIFUL MIND!
GIMLI SWINGS HIS AX OF DWARVEN MIGHT.
A MASSIVE HIT! THE FRENCH DANCE HALL IS STAINED A MOULIN BLOODY ROUGE!
THE BALROG CRACKS HIS HUGE, FLAMING WHIP.
AND GOSFORD FLEES THE PARK AND RUNS SCREAMING INTO THE BEDROOM!
THIS IS HOW ACADEMY AWARDS **SHOULD** BE DECIDED.
WE'D GET A LOT MORE "TERMINATOR" MOVIES THAT WAY, I BET.

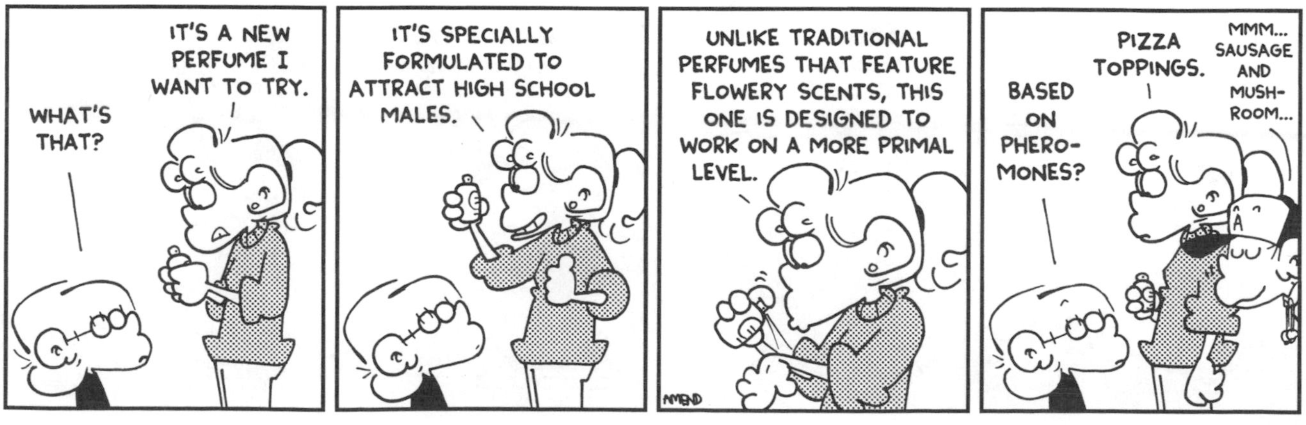
WHAT'S THAT?
IT'S A NEW PERFUME I WANT TO TRY.
IT'S SPECIALLY FORMULATED TO ATTRACT HIGH SCHOOL MALES.
UNLIKE TRADITIONAL PERFUMES THAT FEATURE FLOWERY SCENTS, THIS ONE IS DESIGNED TO WORK ON A MORE PRIMAL LEVEL.
BASED ON PHERO-MONES?
PIZZA TOPPINGS.
MMM... SAUSAGE AND MUSH-ROOM...

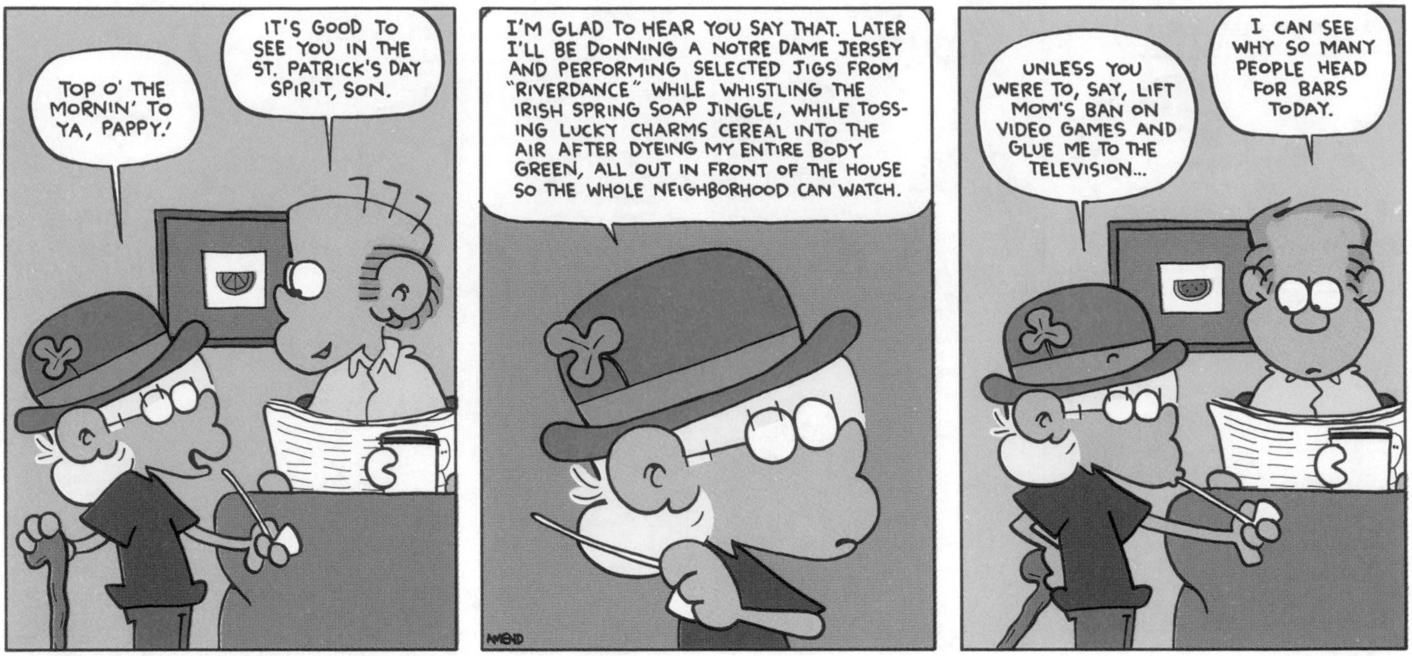
TOP O' THE MORNIN' TO YA, PAPPY!
IT'S GOOD TO SEE YOU IN THE ST. PATRICK'S DAY SPIRIT, SON.
I'M GLAD TO HEAR YOU SAY THAT. LATER I'LL BE DONNING A NOTRE DAME JERSEY AND PERFORMING SELECTED JIGS FROM "RIVERDANCE" WHILE WHISTLING THE IRISH SPRING SOAP JINGLE, WHILE TOSS-ING LUCKY CHARMS CEREAL INTO THE AIR AFTER DYEING MY ENTIRE BODY GREEN, ALL OUT IN FRONT OF THE HOUSE SO THE WHOLE NEIGHBORHOOD CAN WATCH.
UNLESS YOU WERE TO, SAY, LIFT MOM'S BAN ON VIDEO GAMES AND GLUE ME TO THE TELEVISION...
I CAN SEE WHY SO MANY PEOPLE HEAD FOR BARS TODAY.
AMEND

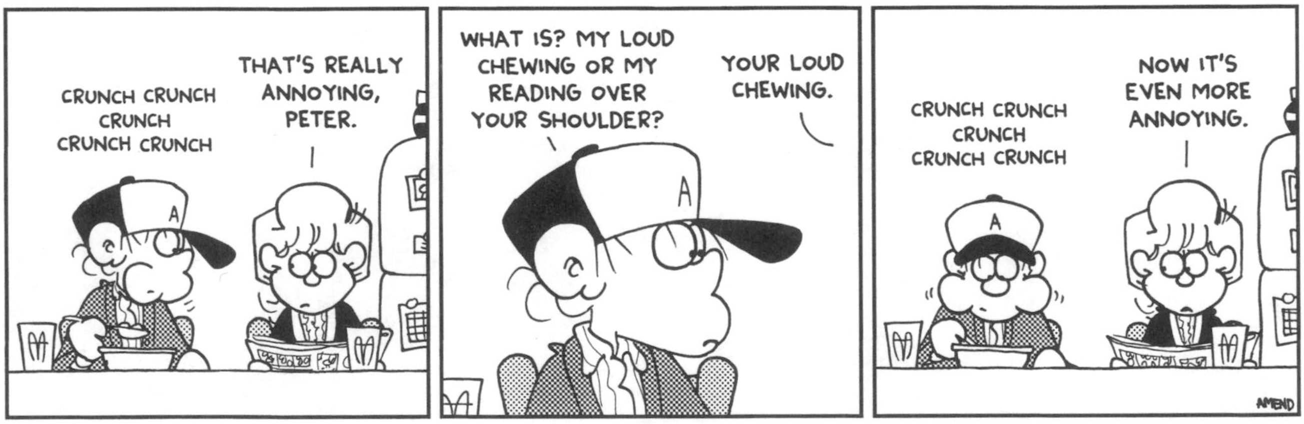
CRUNCH CRUNCH CRUNCH CRUNCH CRUNCH
THAT'S REALLY ANNOYING, PETER.
WHAT IS? MY LOUD CHEWING OR MY READING OVER YOUR SHOULDER?
YOUR LOUD CHEWING.
CRUNCH CRUNCH CRUNCH CRUNCH CRUNCH
NOW IT'S EVEN MORE ANNOYING.
AMEND

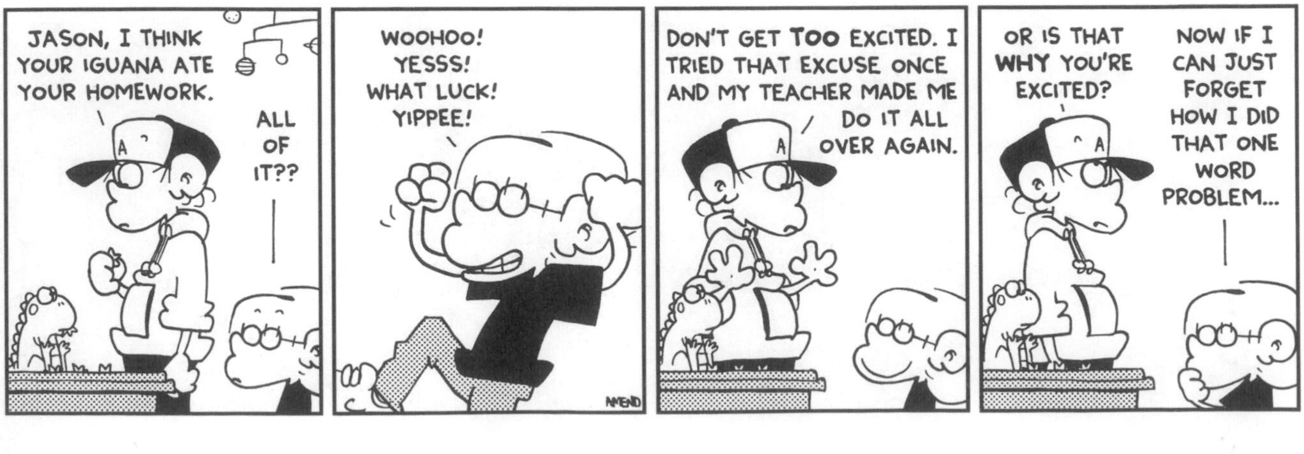
JASON, I THINK YOUR IGUANA ATE YOUR HOMEWORK.
ALL OF IT??
WOOHOO! YESSS! WHAT LUCK! YIPPEE!
DON'T GET TOO EXCITED. I TRIED THAT EXCUSE ONCE AND MY TEACHER MADE ME DO IT ALL OVER AGAIN.
OR IS THAT WHY YOU'RE EXCITED?
NOW IF I CAN JUST FORGET HOW I DID THAT ONE WORD PROBLEM...
AMEND

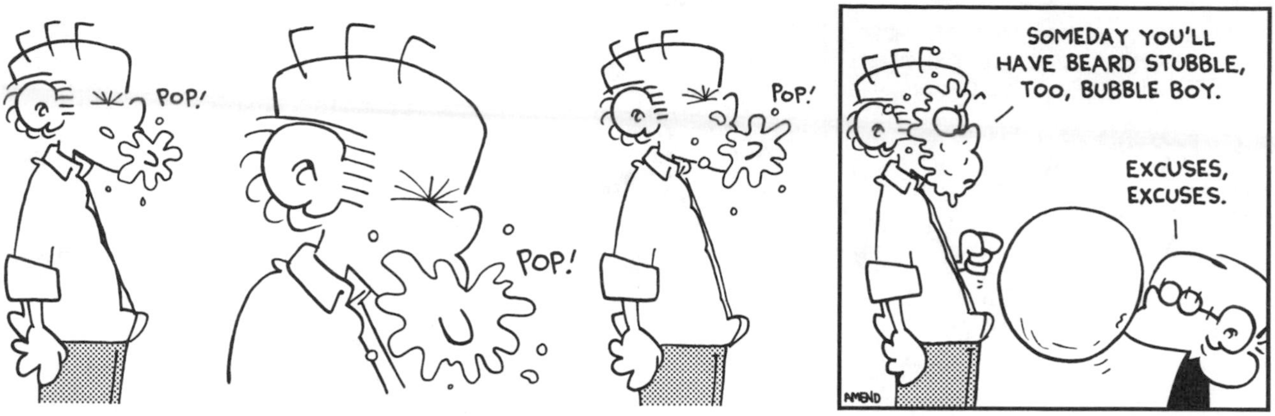
POP!
POP!
POP!
SOMEDAY YOU'LL HAVE BEARD STUBBLE, TOO, BUBBLE BOY.
EXCUSES, EXCUSES.
AMEND

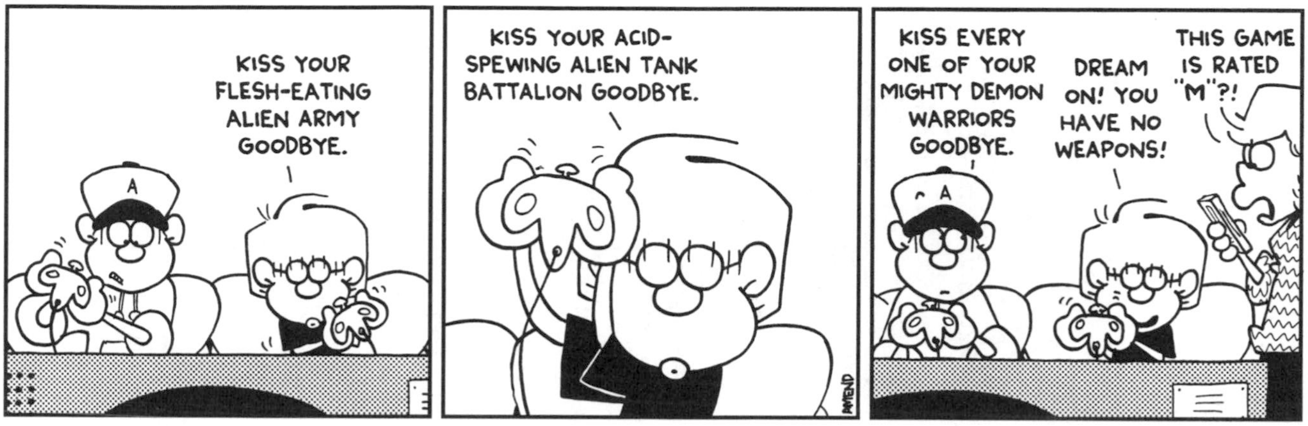
KISS YOUR FLESH-EATING ALIEN ARMY GOODBYE.
KISS YOUR ACID-SPEWING ALIEN TANK BATTALION GOODBYE.
AMEND
KISS EVERY ONE OF YOUR MIGHTY DEMON WARRIORS GOODBYE.
DREAM ON! YOU HAVE NO WEAPONS!
THIS GAME IS RATED "M"?!

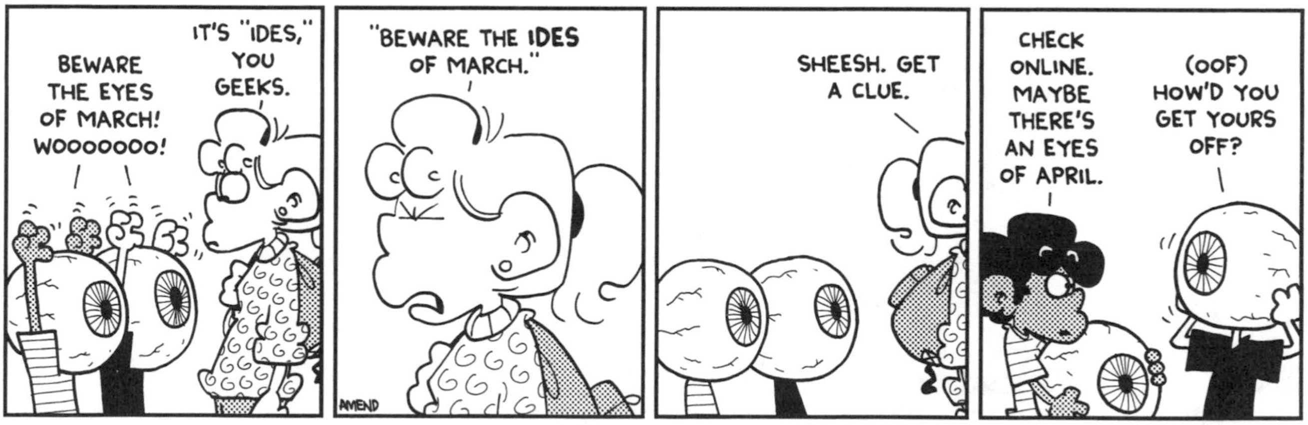
BEWARE THE EYES OF MARCH! WOOOOOOO!
IT'S "IDES," YOU GEEKS.
"BEWARE THE **IDES** OF MARCH."
AMEND
SHEESH. GET A CLUE.
CHECK ONLINE. MAYBE THERE'S AN EYES OF APRIL.
(OOF) HOW'D YOU GET YOURS OFF?

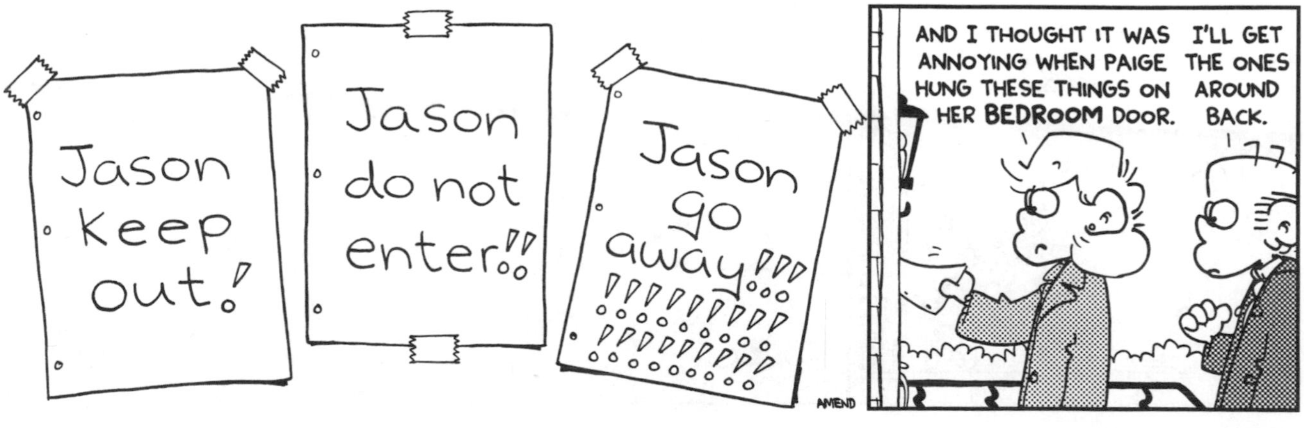
Jason keep out!
Jason do not enter!!
Jason go away!!!!!!!!!!!!!!!!!!!!!!!!!!!!!!!!!!
AMEND
AND I THOUGHT IT WAS ANNOYING WHEN PAIGE HUNG THESE THINGS ON HER **BEDROOM** DOOR.
I'LL GET THE ONES AROUND BACK.

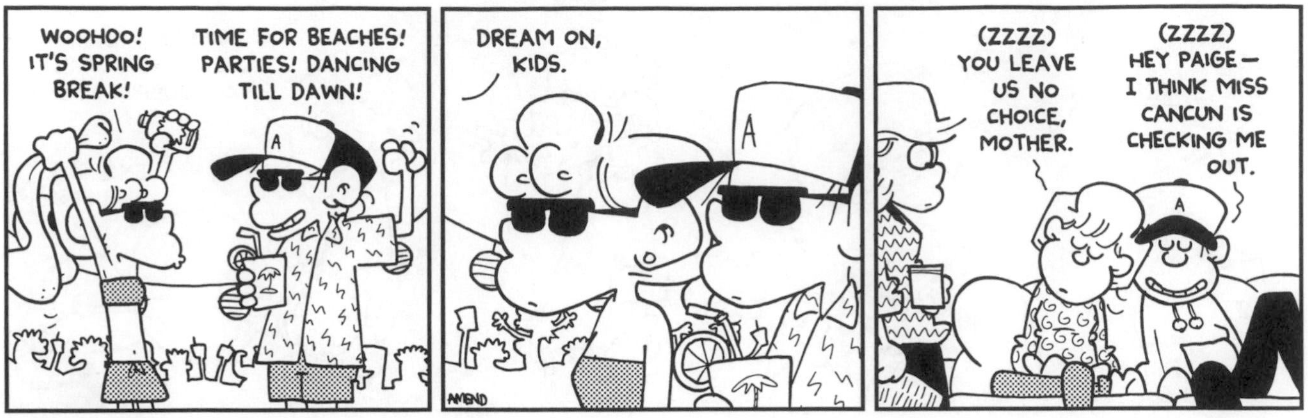
WOOHOO! IT'S SPRING BREAK!
TIME FOR BEACHES! PARTIES! DANCING TILL DAWN!
DREAM ON, KIDS.
AMEND
(ZZZZ) YOU LEAVE US NO CHOICE, MOTHER.
(ZZZZ) HEY PAIGE— I THINK MISS CANCUN IS CHECKING ME OUT.

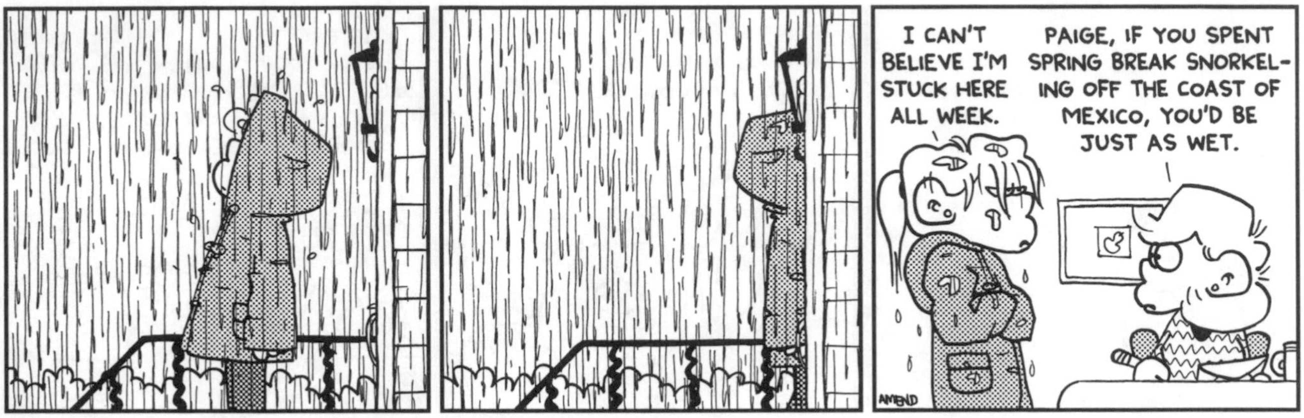
I CAN'T BELIEVE I'M STUCK HERE ALL WEEK.
PAIGE, IF YOU SPENT SPRING BREAK SNORKEL-ING OFF THE COAST OF MEXICO, YOU'D BE JUST AS WET.
AMEND

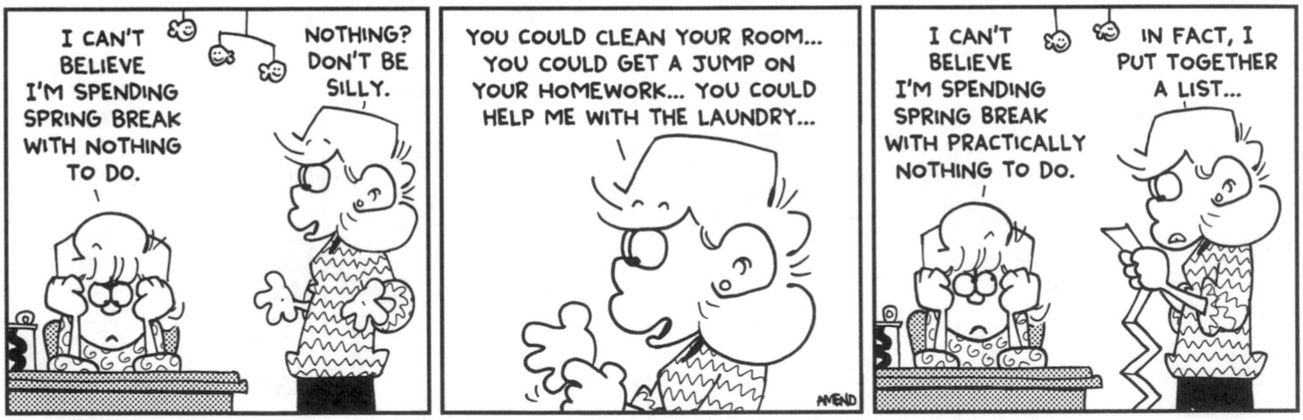
I CAN'T BELIEVE I'M SPENDING SPRING BREAK WITH NOTHING TO DO.
NOTHING? DON'T BE SILLY.
YOU COULD CLEAN YOUR ROOM... YOU COULD GET A JUMP ON YOUR HOMEWORK... YOU COULD HELP ME WITH THE LAUNDRY...
AMEND
I CAN'T BELIEVE I'M SPENDING SPRING BREAK WITH PRACTICALLY NOTHING TO DO.
IN FACT, I PUT TOGETHER A LIST...

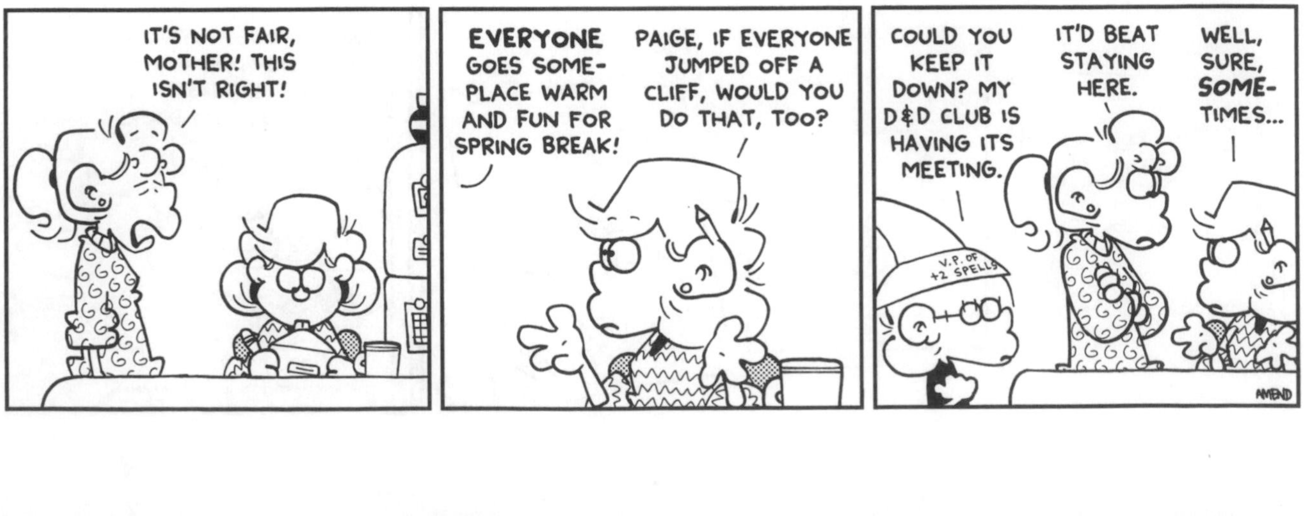
IT'S NOT FAIR, MOTHER! THIS ISN'T RIGHT!
EVERYONE GOES SOME-PLACE WARM AND FUN FOR SPRING BREAK!
PAIGE, IF EVERYONE JUMPED OFF A CLIFF, WOULD YOU DO THAT, TOO?
COULD YOU KEEP IT DOWN? MY D&D CLUB IS HAVING ITS MEETING.
V.P. OF +2 SPELLS
IT'D BEAT STAYING HERE.
WELL, SURE, SOME-TIMES...
AMEND

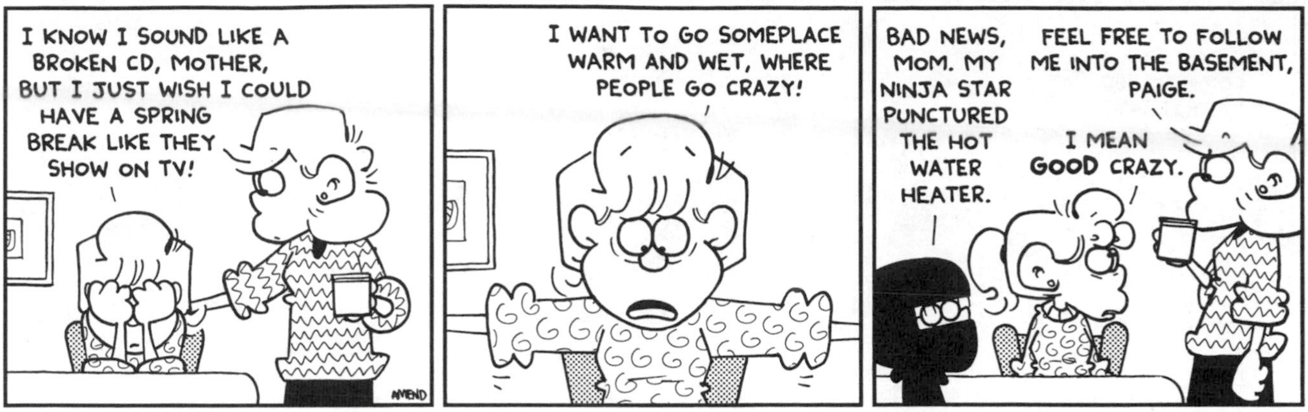
I KNOW I SOUND LIKE A BROKEN CD, MOTHER, BUT I JUST WISH I COULD HAVE A SPRING BREAK LIKE THEY SHOW ON TV!
I WANT TO GO SOMEPLACE WARM AND WET, WHERE PEOPLE GO CRAZY!
BAD NEWS, MOM. MY NINJA STAR PUNCTURED THE HOT WATER HEATER.
FEEL FREE TO FOLLOW ME INTO THE BASEMENT, PAIGE.
I MEAN GOOD CRAZY.
AMEND

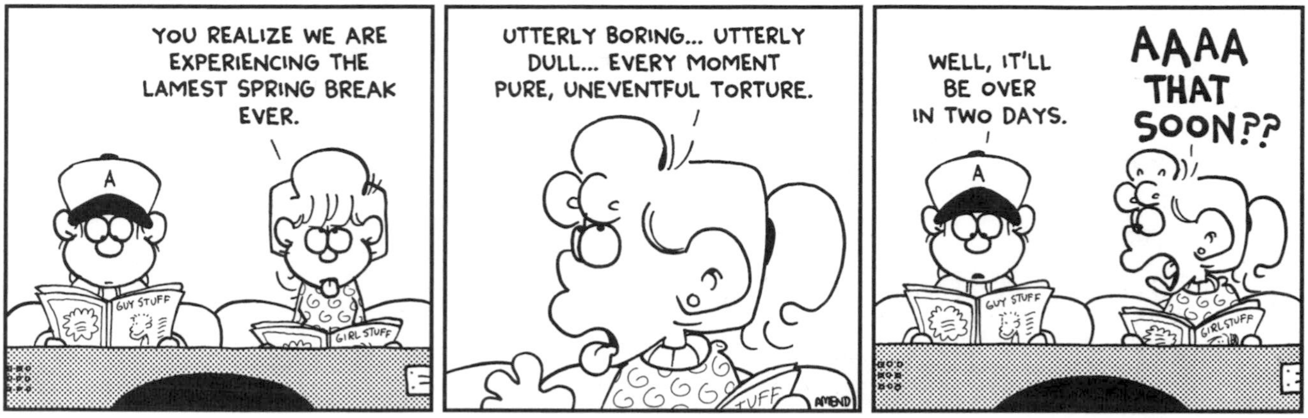
YOU REALIZE WE ARE EXPERIENCING THE LAMEST SPRING BREAK EVER.
GUY STUFF
GIRL STUFF
UTTERLY BORING... UTTERLY DULL... EVERY MOMENT PURE, UNEVENTFUL TORTURE.
AMEND
WELL, IT'LL BE OVER IN TWO DAYS.
AAAA THAT SOON??

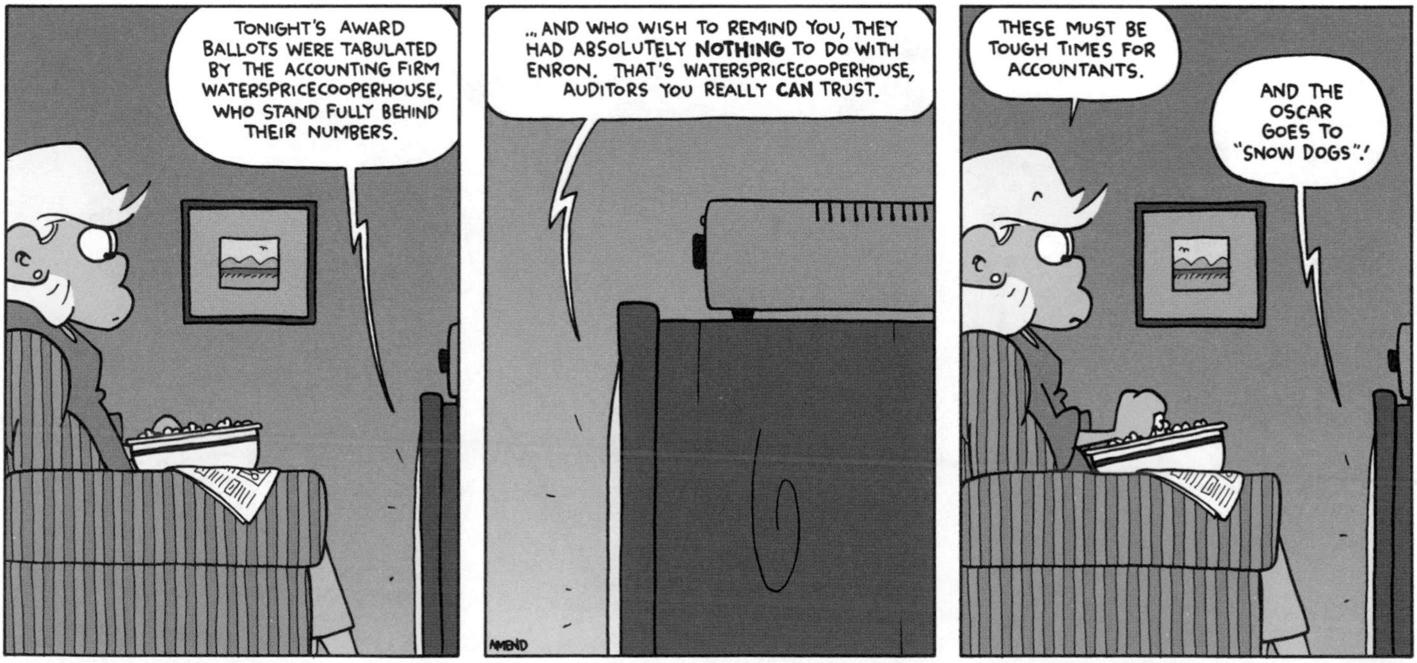
TONIGHT'S AWARD BALLOTS WERE TABULATED BY THE ACCOUNTING FIRM WATERSPRICECOOPERHOUSE, WHO STAND FULLY BEHIND THEIR NUMBERS.
...AND WHO WISH TO REMIND YOU, THEY HAD ABSOLUTELY NOTHING TO DO WITH ENRON. THAT'S WATERSPRICECOOPERHOUSE, AUDITORS YOU REALLY CAN TRUST.
AMEND
THESE MUST BE TOUGH TIMES FOR ACCOUNTANTS.
AND THE OSCAR GOES TO "SNOW DOGS"!

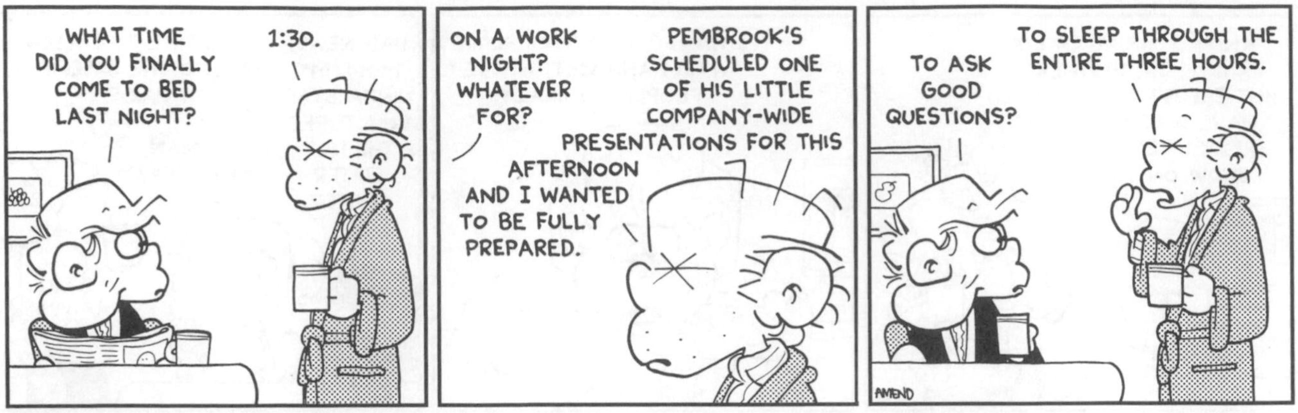
WHAT TIME DID YOU FINALLY COME TO BED LAST NIGHT?
1:30.
ON A WORK NIGHT? WHATEVER FOR?
PEMBROOK'S SCHEDULED ONE OF HIS LITTLE COMPANY-WIDE PRESENTATIONS FOR THIS AFTERNOON AND I WANTED TO BE FULLY PREPARED.
TO ASK GOOD QUESTIONS?
TO SLEEP THROUGH THE ENTIRE THREE HOURS.
AMEND

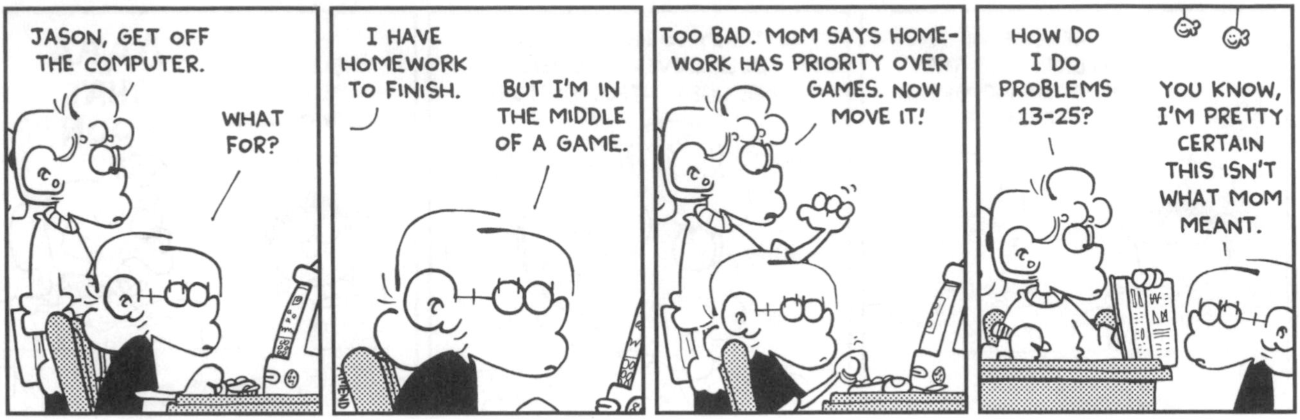
JASON, GET OFF THE COMPUTER.
WHAT FOR?
I HAVE HOMEWORK TO FINISH.
BUT I'M IN THE MIDDLE OF A GAME.
AMEND
TOO BAD. MOM SAYS HOMEWORK HAS PRIORITY OVER GAMES. NOW MOVE IT!
HOW DO I DO PROBLEMS 13-25?
YOU KNOW, I'M PRETTY CERTAIN THIS ISN'T WHAT MOM MEANT.

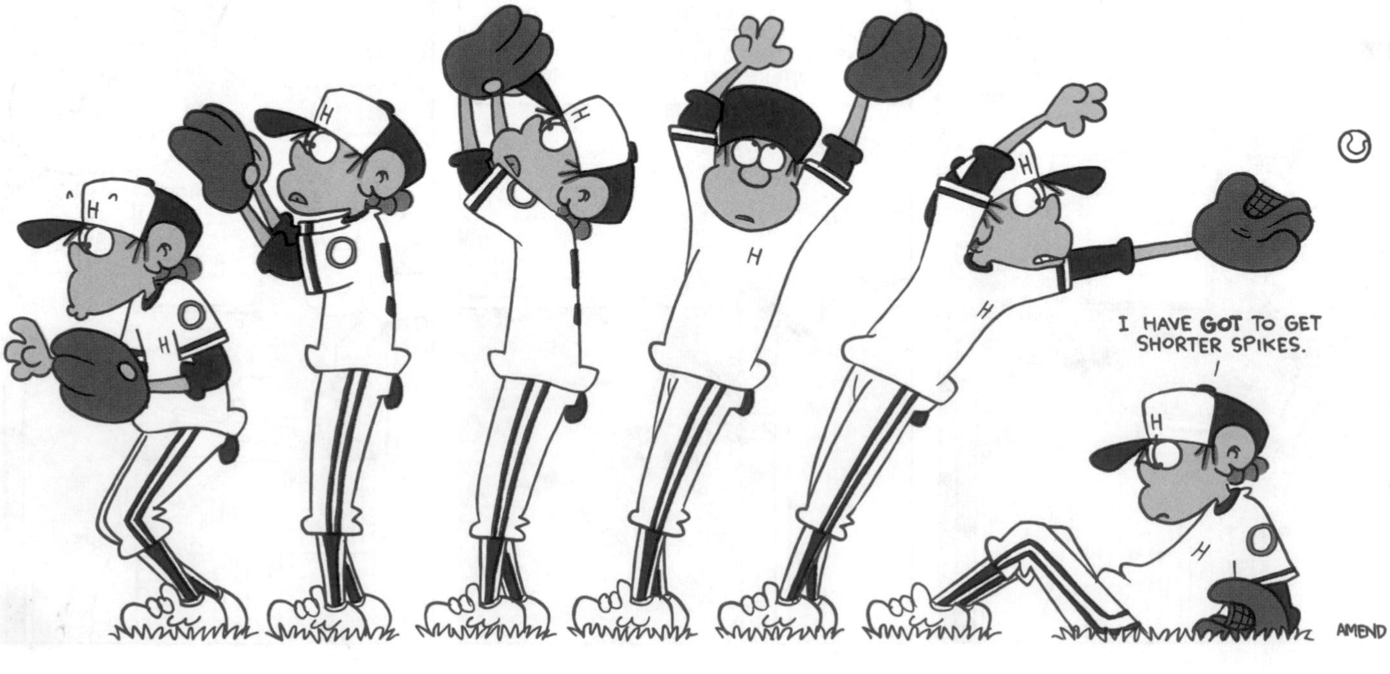
I HAVE GOT TO GET SHORTER SPIKES.
AMEND

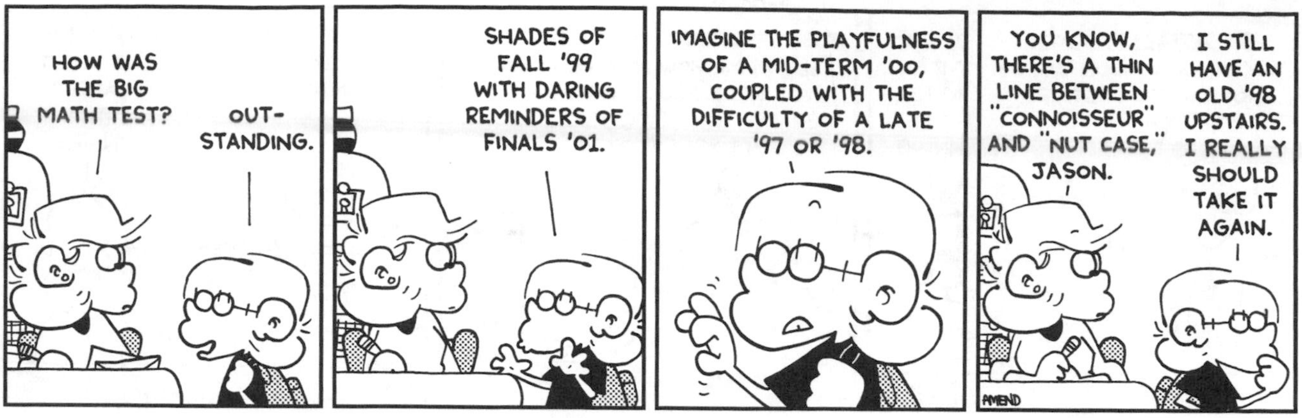
HOW WAS THE BIG MATH TEST?
OUT-STANDING.
SHADES OF FALL '99 WITH DARING REMINDERS OF FINALS '01.
IMAGINE THE PLAYFULNESS OF A MID-TERM '00, COUPLED WITH THE DIFFICULTY OF A LATE '97 OR '98.
YOU KNOW, THERE'S A THIN LINE BETWEEN "CONNOISSEUR" AND "NUT CASE," JASON.
I STILL HAVE AN OLD '98 UPSTAIRS. I REALLY SHOULD TAKE IT AGAIN.
AMEND

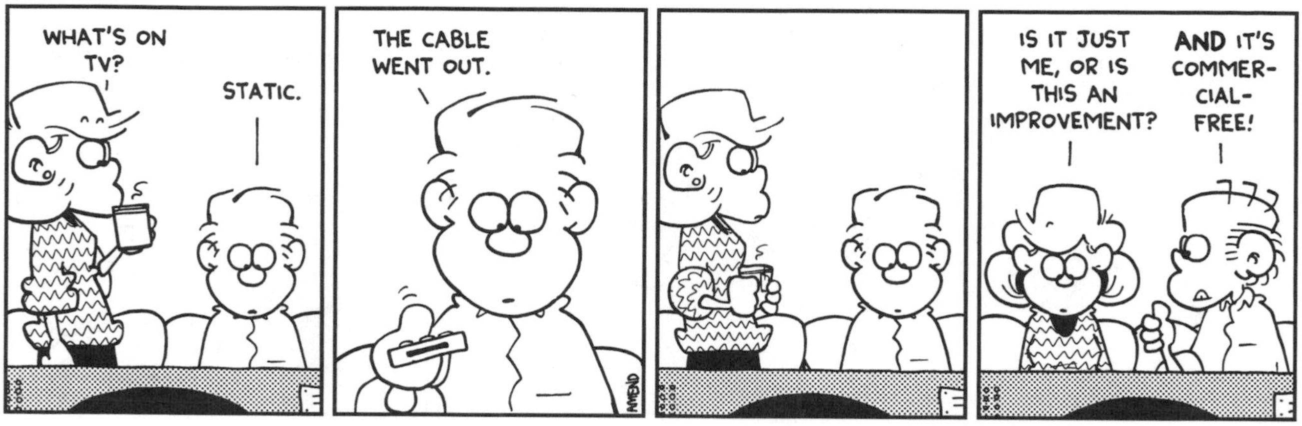
WHAT'S ON TV?
STATIC.
THE CABLE WENT OUT.
AMEND
IS IT JUST ME, OR IS THIS AN IMPROVEMENT?
AND IT'S COMMER-CIAL-FREE!

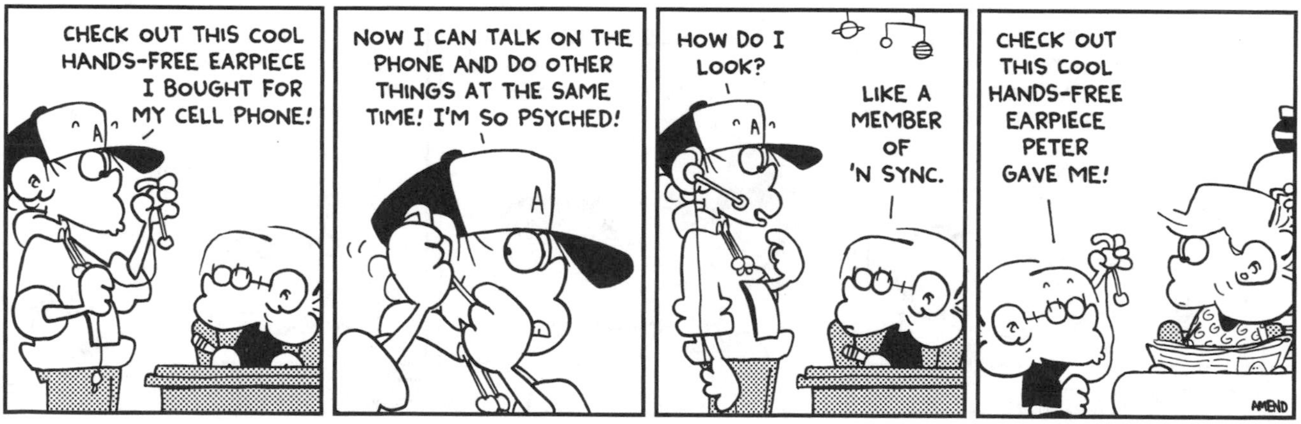
CHECK OUT THIS COOL HANDS-FREE EARPIECE I BOUGHT FOR MY CELL PHONE!
NOW I CAN TALK ON THE PHONE AND DO OTHER THINGS AT THE SAME TIME! I'M SO PSYCHED!
HOW DO I LOOK?
LIKE A MEMBER OF 'N SYNC.
CHECK OUT THIS COOL HANDS-FREE EARPIECE PETER GAVE ME!
AMEND

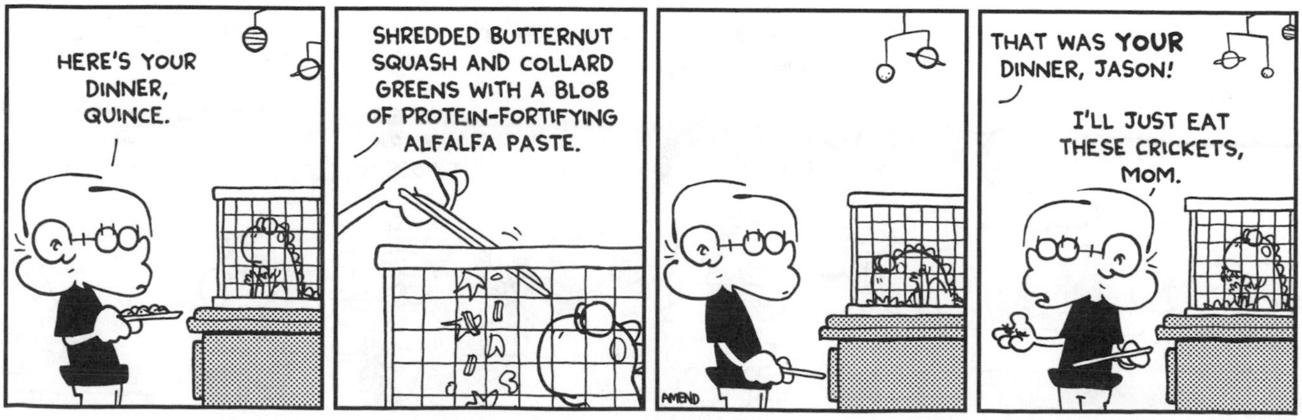
HERE'S YOUR DINNER, QUINCE.
SHREDDED BUTTERNUT SQUASH AND COLLARD GREENS WITH A BLOB OF PROTEIN-FORTIFYING ALFALFA PASTE.
AMEND
THAT WAS YOUR DINNER, JASON!
I'LL JUST EAT THESE CRICKETS, MOM.

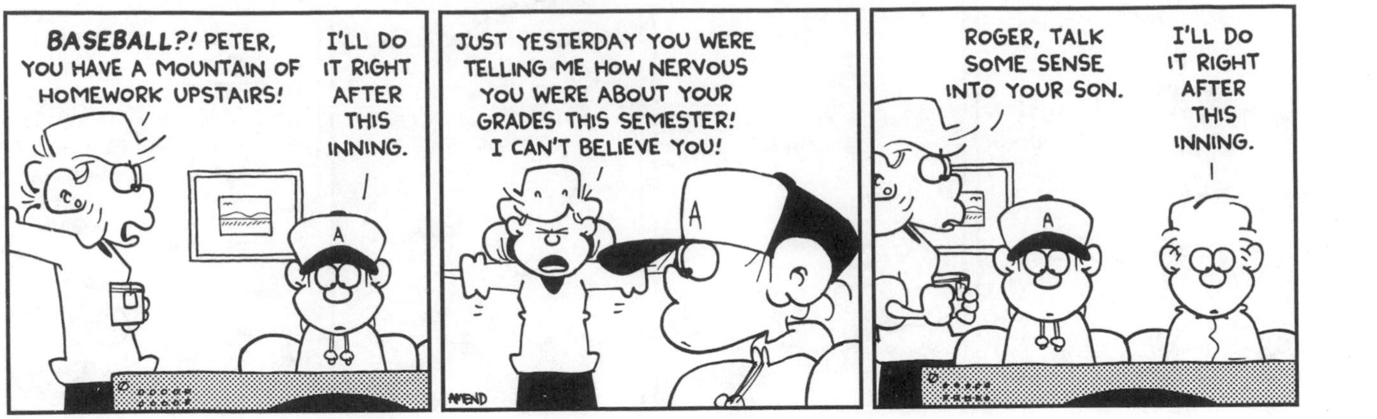
BASEBALL?! PETER, YOU HAVE A MOUNTAIN OF HOMEWORK UPSTAIRS!
I'LL DO IT RIGHT AFTER THIS INNING.
JUST YESTERDAY YOU WERE TELLING ME HOW NERVOUS YOU WERE ABOUT YOUR GRADES THIS SEMESTER! I CAN'T BELIEVE YOU!
AMEND
ROGER, TALK SOME SENSE INTO YOUR SON.
I'LL DO IT RIGHT AFTER THIS INNING.

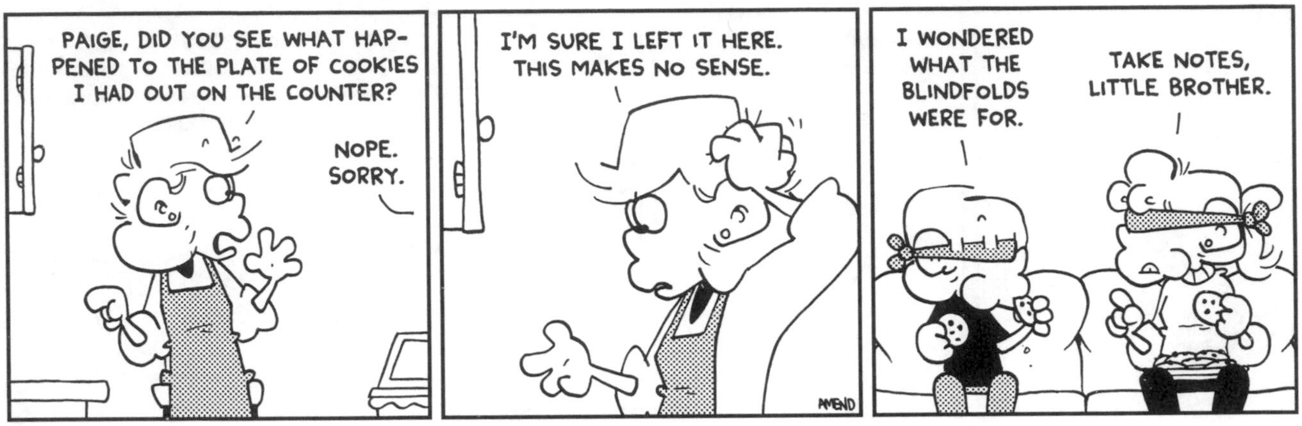
PAIGE, DID YOU SEE WHAT HAPPENED TO THE PLATE OF COOKIES I HAD OUT ON THE COUNTER?
NOPE. SORRY.
I'M SURE I LEFT IT HERE. THIS MAKES NO SENSE.
AMEND
I WONDERED WHAT THE BLINDFOLDS WERE FOR.
TAKE NOTES, LITTLE BROTHER.

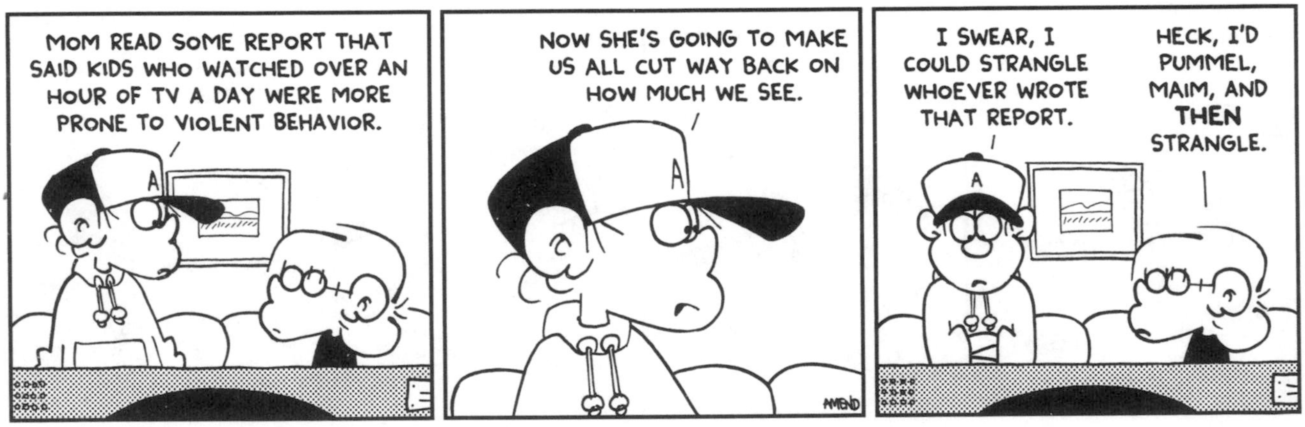
MOM READ SOME REPORT THAT SAID KIDS WHO WATCHED OVER AN HOUR OF TV A DAY WERE MORE PRONE TO VIOLENT BEHAVIOR.
NOW SHE'S GOING TO MAKE US ALL CUT WAY BACK ON HOW MUCH WE SEE.
AMEND
I SWEAR, I COULD STRANGLE WHOEVER WROTE THAT REPORT.
HECK, I'D PUMMEL, MAIM, AND **THEN** STRANGLE.

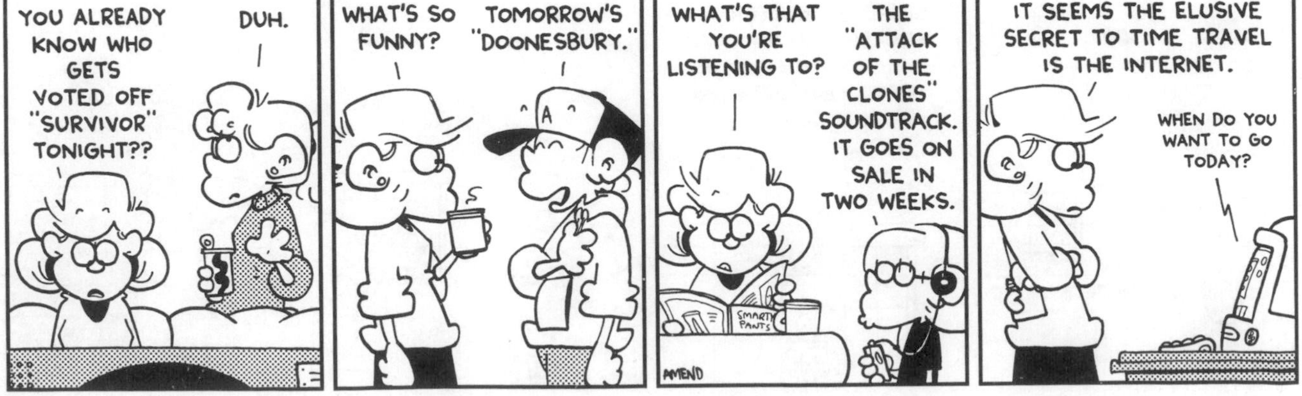
YOU ALREADY KNOW WHO GETS VOTED OFF "SURVIVOR" TONIGHT??
DUH.
WHAT'S SO FUNNY?
TOMORROW'S "DOONESBURY."
WHAT'S THAT YOU'RE LISTENING TO?
THE "ATTACK OF THE CLONES" SOUNDTRACK. IT GOES ON SALE IN TWO WEEKS.
SMARTY PANTS
AMEND
IT SEEMS THE ELUSIVE SECRET TO TIME TRAVEL IS THE INTERNET.
WHEN DO YOU WANT TO GO TODAY?

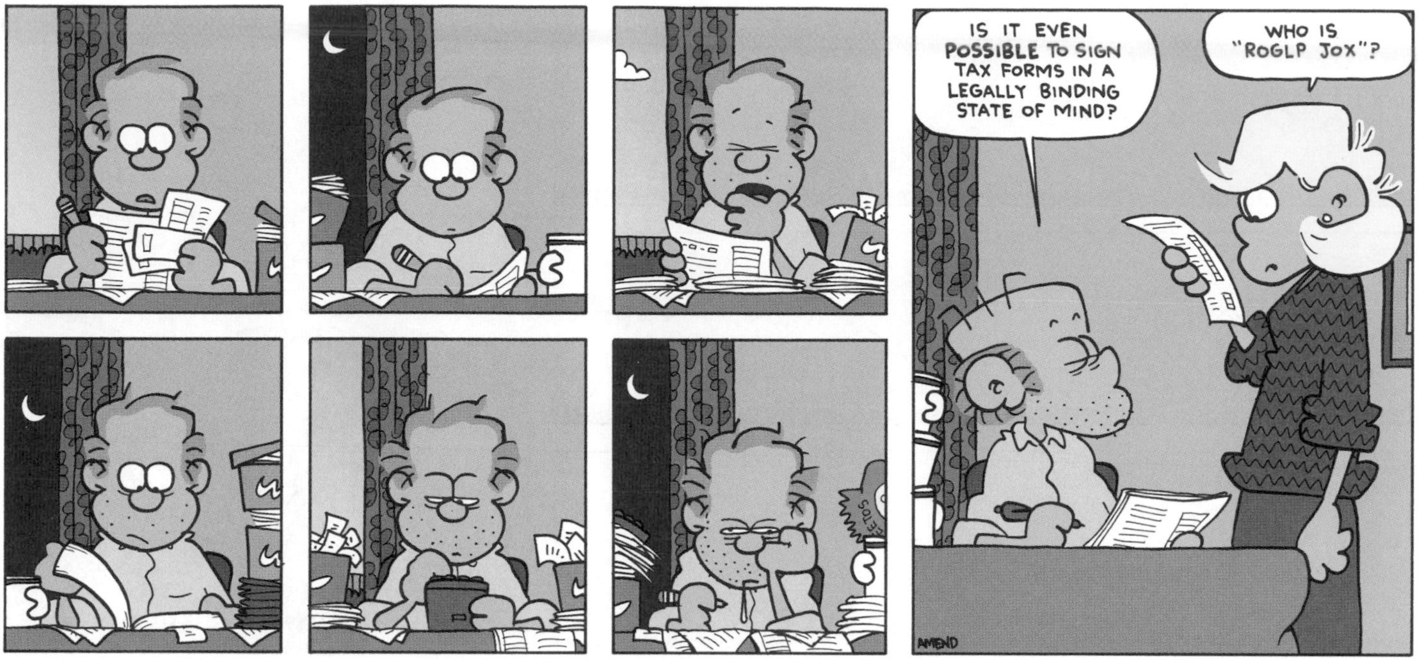
IS IT EVEN POSSIBLE TO SIGN TAX FORMS IN A LEGALLY BINDING STATE OF MIND?
WHO IS "ROGLP JOX"?
AMEND

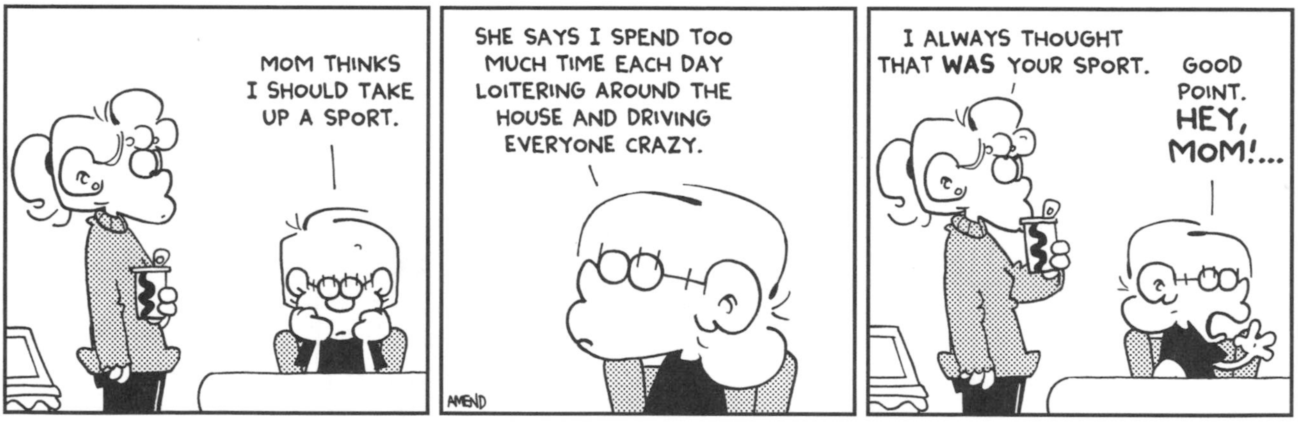
MOM THINKS I SHOULD TAKE UP A SPORT.
SHE SAYS I SPEND TOO MUCH TIME EACH DAY LOITERING AROUND THE HOUSE AND DRIVING EVERYONE CRAZY.
AMEND
I ALWAYS THOUGHT THAT WAS YOUR SPORT.
GOOD POINT. HEY, MOM!...

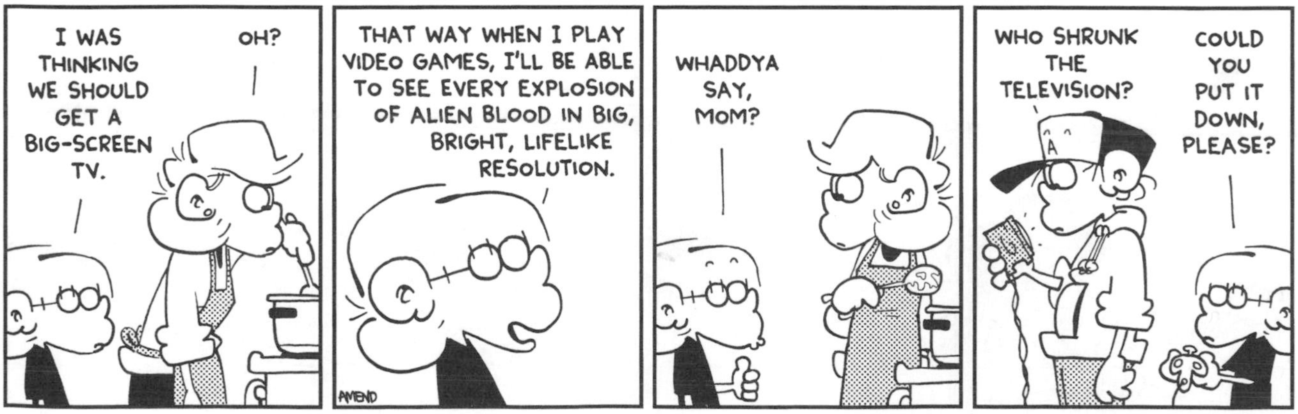
I WAS THINKING WE SHOULD GET A BIG-SCREEN TV.
OH?
THAT WAY WHEN I PLAY VIDEO GAMES, I'LL BE ABLE TO SEE EVERY EXPLOSION OF ALIEN BLOOD IN BIG, BRIGHT, LIFELIKE RESOLUTION.
AMEND
WHADDYA SAY, MOM?
WHO SHRUNK THE TELEVISION?
COULD YOU PUT IT DOWN, PLEASE?

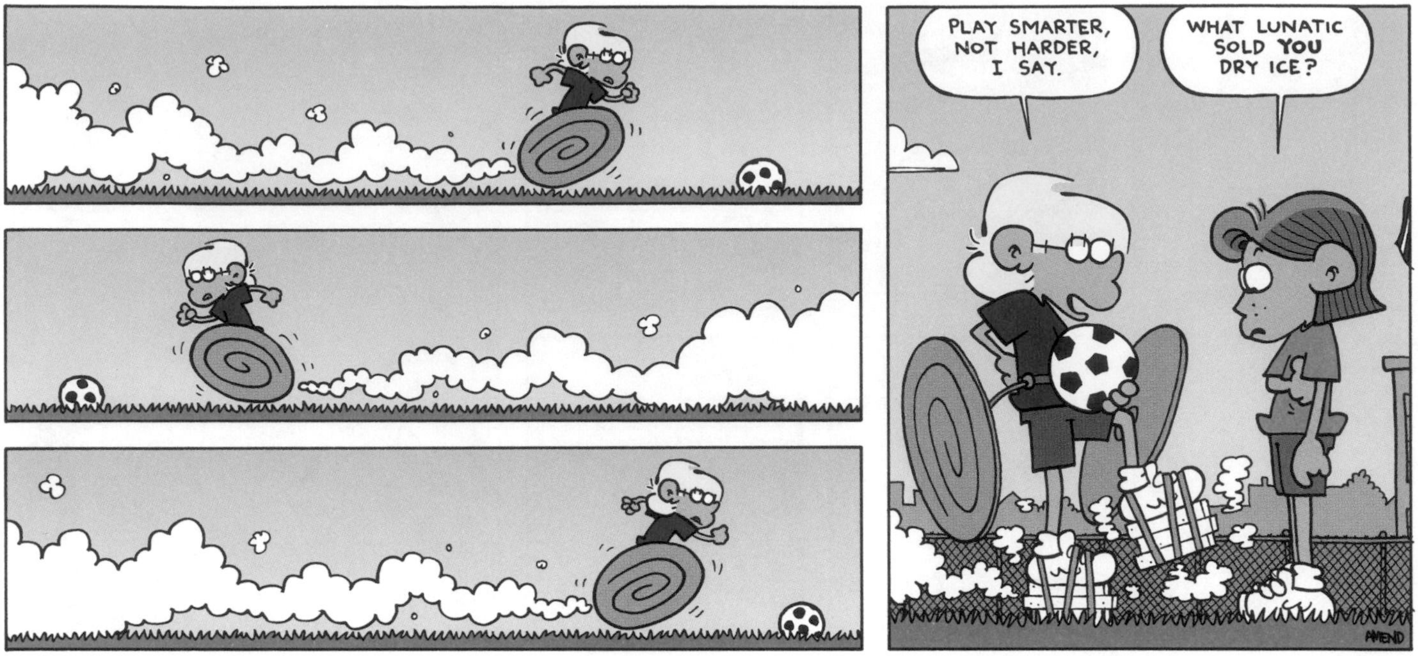
PLAY SMARTER, NOT HARDER, I SAY.
WHAT LUNATIC SOLD YOU DRY ICE?
AMEND

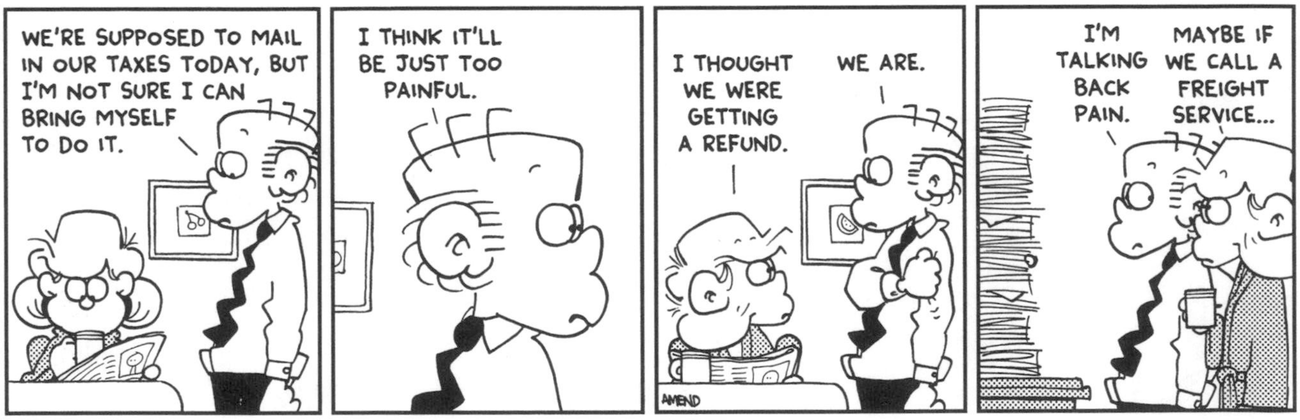
WE'RE SUPPOSED TO MAIL IN OUR TAXES TODAY, BUT I'M NOT SURE I CAN BRING MYSELF TO DO IT.
I THINK IT'LL BE JUST TOO PAINFUL.
I THOUGHT WE WERE GETTING A REFUND.
WE ARE.
AMEND
I'M TALKING BACK PAIN.
MAYBE IF WE CALL A FREIGHT SERVICE...

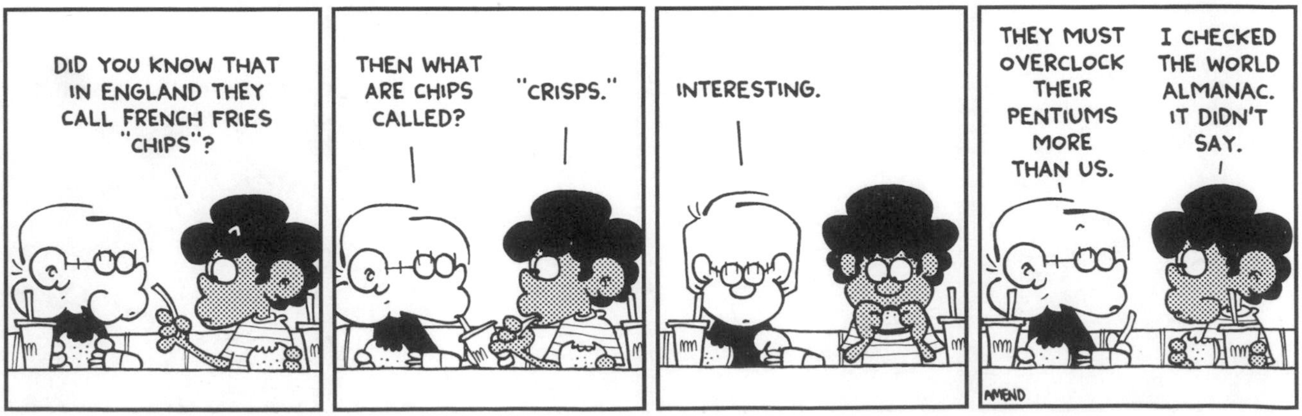
DID YOU KNOW THAT IN ENGLAND THEY CALL FRENCH FRIES "CHIPS"?
THEN WHAT ARE CHIPS CALLED?
"CRISPS."
INTERESTING.
THEY MUST OVERCLOCK THEIR PENTIUMS MORE THAN US.
I CHECKED THE WORLD ALMANAC. IT DIDN'T SAY.
AMEND

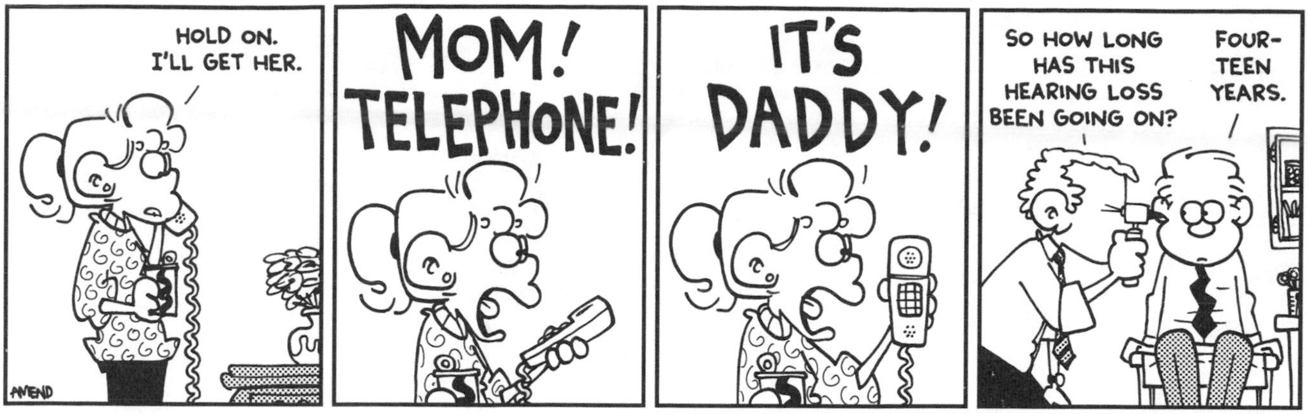
HOLD ON. I'LL GET HER.
MOM! TELEPHONE!
IT'S DADDY!
SO HOW LONG HAS THIS HEARING LOSS BEEN GOING ON?
FOURTEEN YEARS.
AMEND

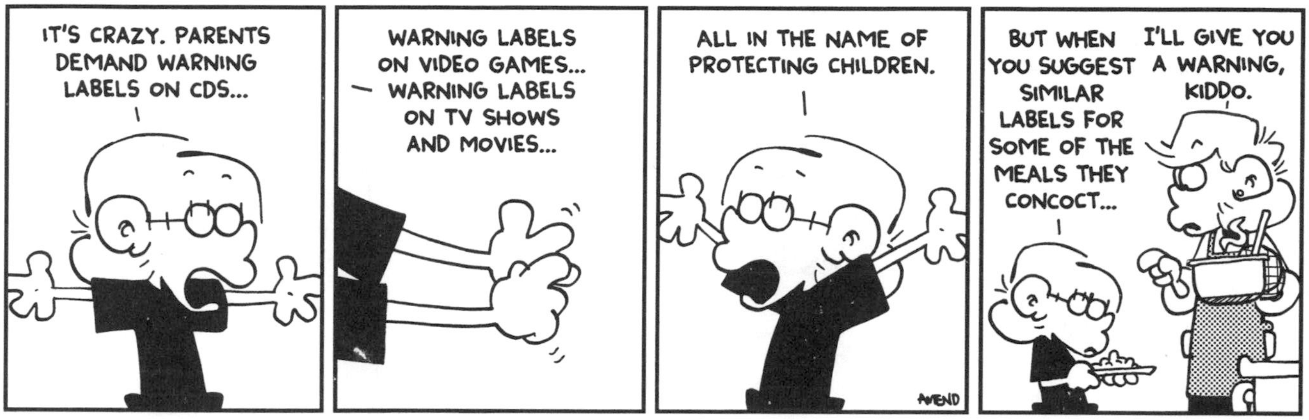
IT'S CRAZY. PARENTS DEMAND WARNING LABELS ON CDS...
WARNING LABELS ON VIDEO GAMES... WARNING LABELS ON TV SHOWS AND MOVIES...
ALL IN THE NAME OF PROTECTING CHILDREN.
BUT WHEN YOU SUGGEST SIMILAR LABELS FOR SOME OF THE MEALS THEY CONCOCT...
I'LL GIVE YOU A WARNING, KIDDO.
AMEND

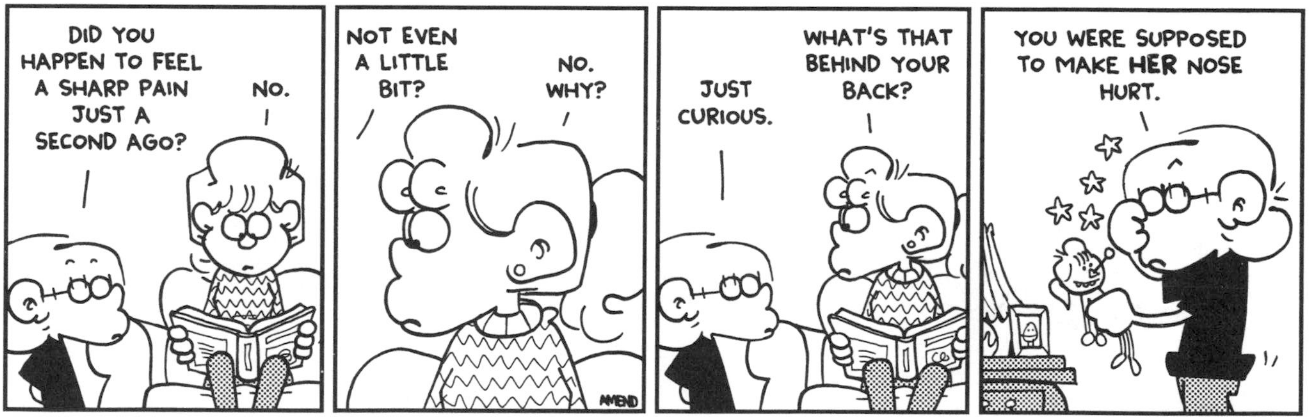
DID YOU HAPPEN TO FEEL A SHARP PAIN JUST A SECOND AGO?
NO.
NOT EVEN A LITTLE BIT?
NO. WHY?
JUST CURIOUS.
WHAT'S THAT BEHIND YOUR BACK?
YOU WERE SUPPOSED TO MAKE **HER** NOSE HURT.
AMEND

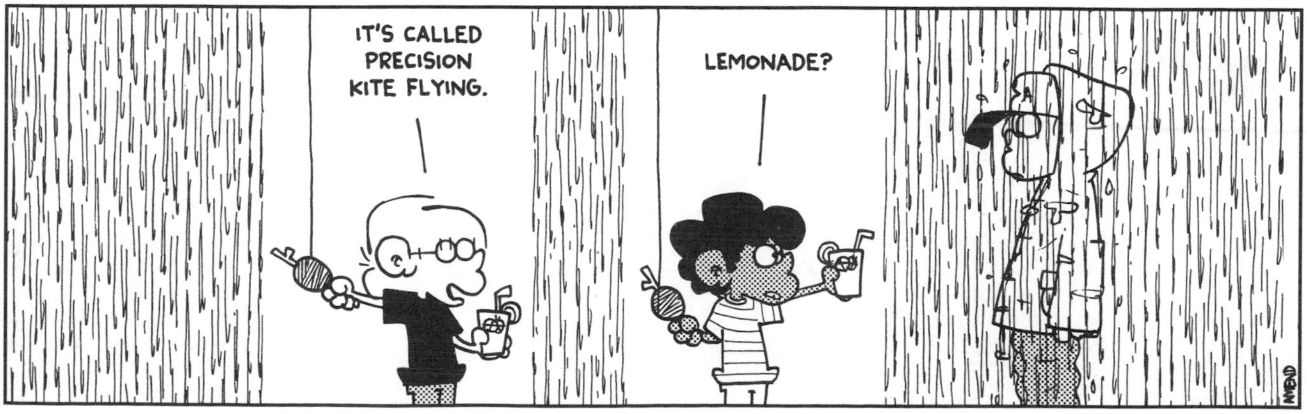
IT'S CALLED PRECISION KITE FLYING.
LEMONADE?
AMEND

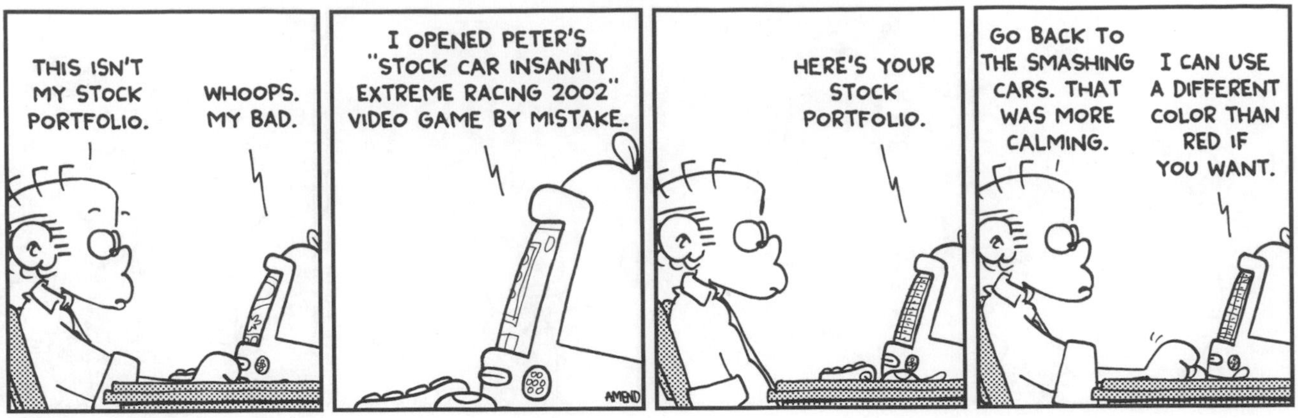

THIS ISN'T MY STOCK PORTFOLIO.
WHOOPS. MY BAD.
I OPENED PETER'S "STOCK CAR INSANITY EXTREME RACING 2002" VIDEO GAME BY MISTAKE.
AMEND
HERE'S YOUR STOCK PORTFOLIO.
GO BACK TO THE SMASHING CARS. THAT WAS MORE CALMING.
I CAN USE A DIFFERENT COLOR THAN RED IF YOU WANT.

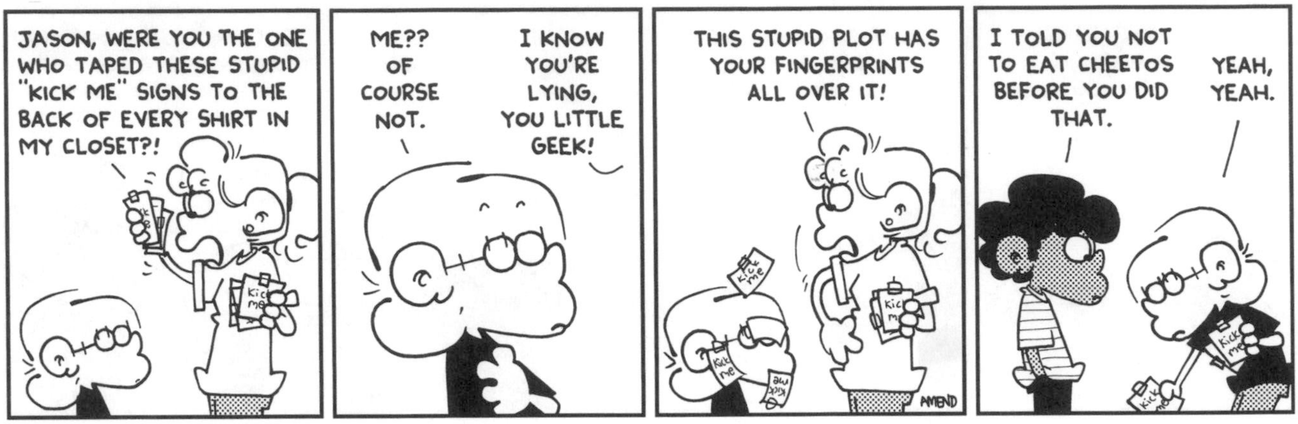

JASON, WERE YOU THE ONE WHO TAPED THESE STUPID "KICK ME" SIGNS TO THE BACK OF EVERY SHIRT IN MY CLOSET?!
ME?? OF COURSE NOT.
I KNOW YOU'RE LYING, YOU LITTLE GEEK!
THIS STUPID PLOT HAS YOUR FINGERPRINTS ALL OVER IT!
AMEND
I TOLD YOU NOT TO EAT CHEETOS BEFORE YOU DID THAT.
YEAH, YEAH.

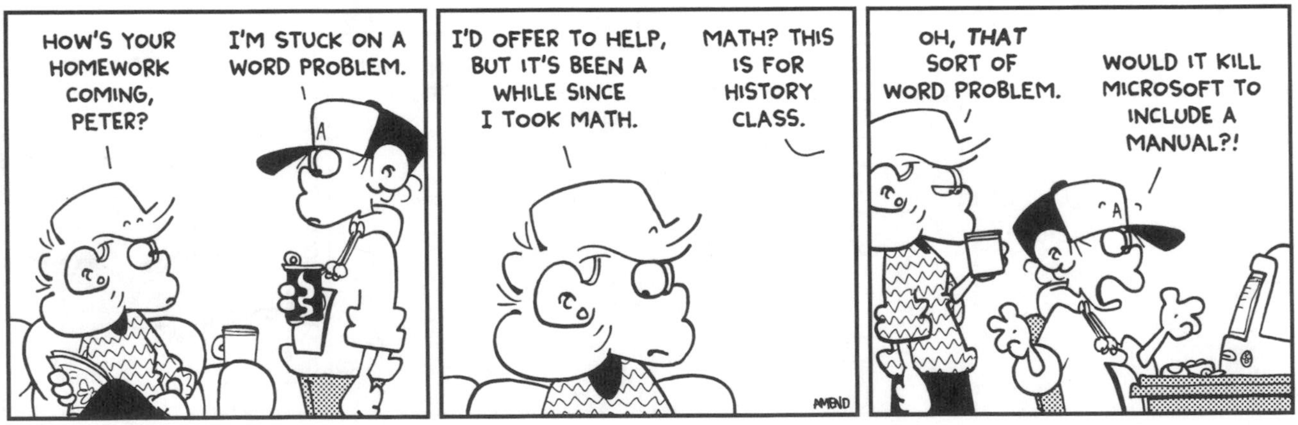

HOW'S YOUR HOMEWORK COMING, PETER?
I'M STUCK ON A WORD PROBLEM.
I'D OFFER TO HELP, BUT IT'S BEEN A WHILE SINCE I TOOK MATH.
MATH? THIS IS FOR HISTORY CLASS.
AMEND
OH, THAT SORT OF WORD PROBLEM.
WOULD IT KILL MICROSOFT TO INCLUDE A MANUAL?!

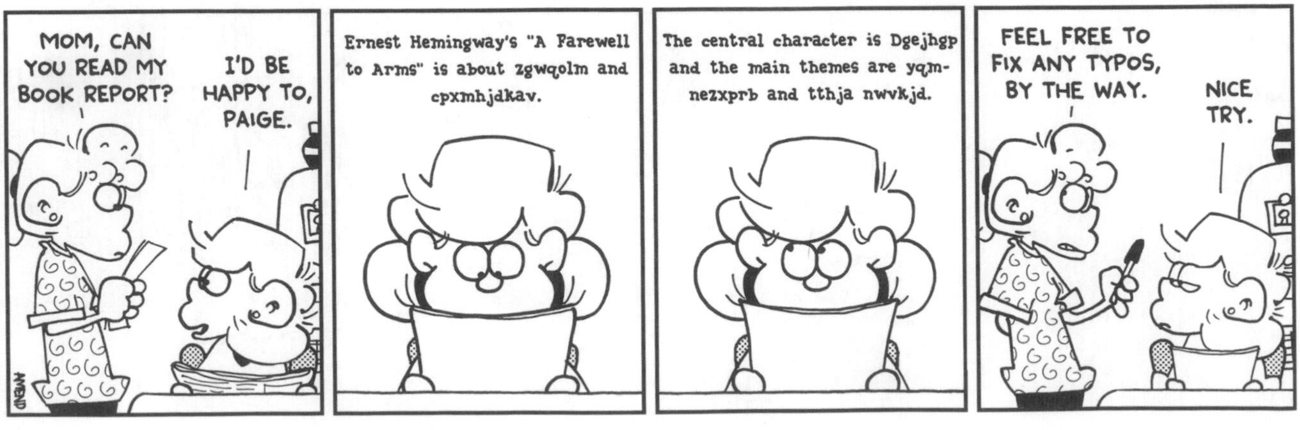

MOM, CAN YOU READ MY BOOK REPORT?
I'D BE HAPPY TO, PAIGE.
AMEND
Ernest Hemingway's "A Farewell to Arms" is about zgwqolm and cpxmhjdkav.
The central character is Dgejhgp and the main themes are yqm-nezxprb and tthja nwvkjd.
FEEL FREE TO FIX ANY TYPOS, BY THE WAY.
NICE TRY.

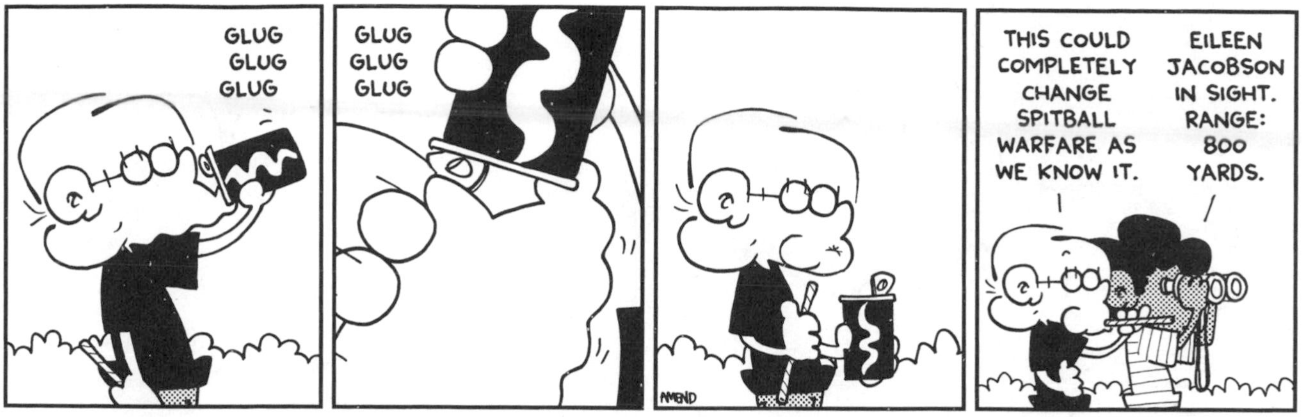
GLUG
GLUG
GLUG
GLUG
GLUG
GLUG
THIS COULD COMPLETELY CHANGE SPITBALL WARFARE AS WE KNOW IT.
EILEEN JACOBSON IN SIGHT. RANGE: 800 YARDS.

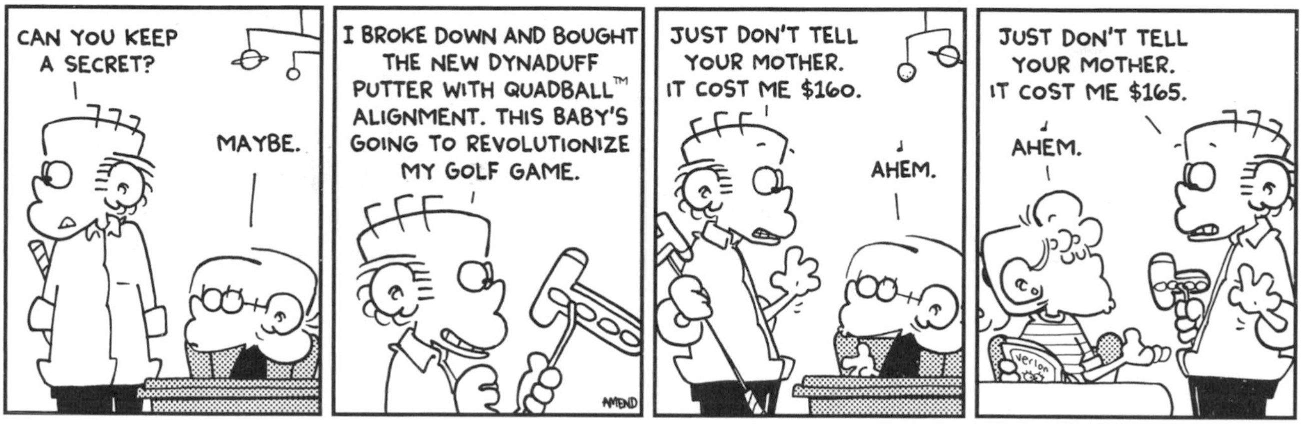
CAN YOU KEEP A SECRET?
MAYBE.
I BROKE DOWN AND BOUGHT THE NEW DYNADUFF PUTTER WITH QUADBALL™ ALIGNMENT. THIS BABY'S GOING TO REVOLUTIONIZE MY GOLF GAME.
JUST DON'T TELL YOUR MOTHER. IT COST ME $160.
AHEM.
JUST DON'T TELL YOUR MOTHER. IT COST ME $165.
AHEM.

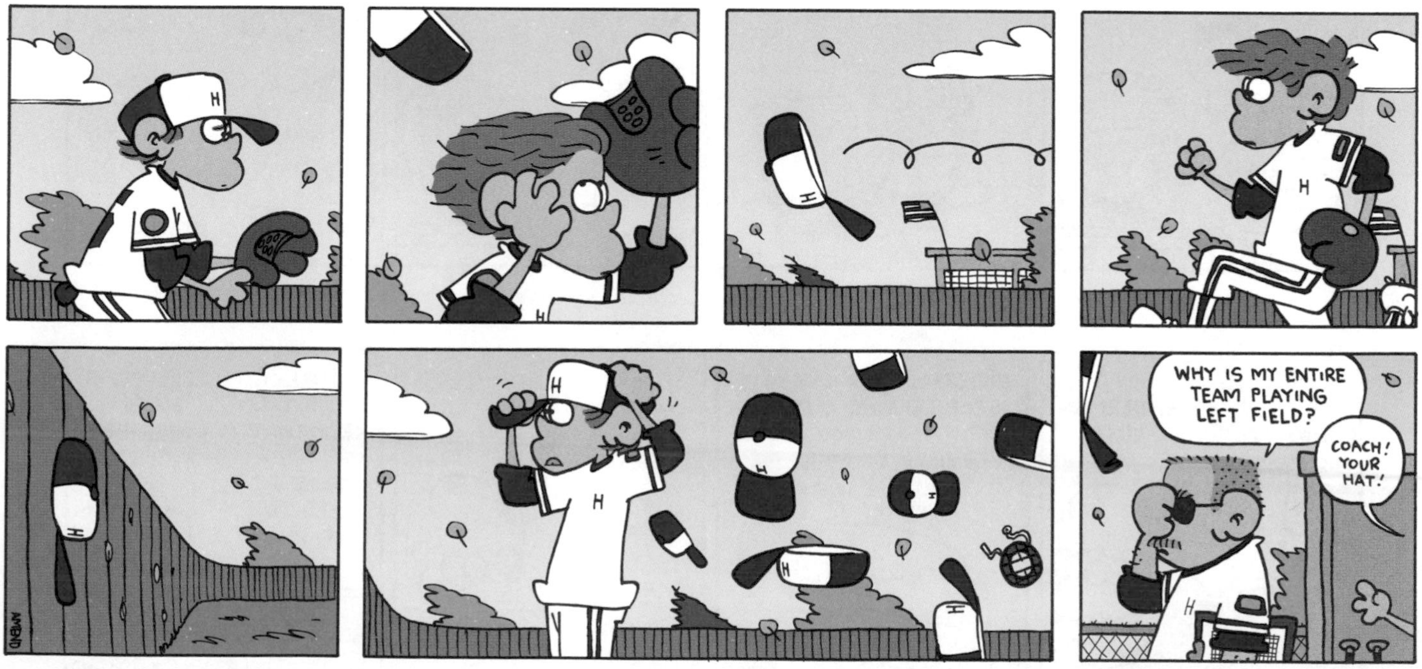
WHY IS MY ENTIRE TEAM PLAYING LEFT FIELD?
COACH! YOUR HAT!

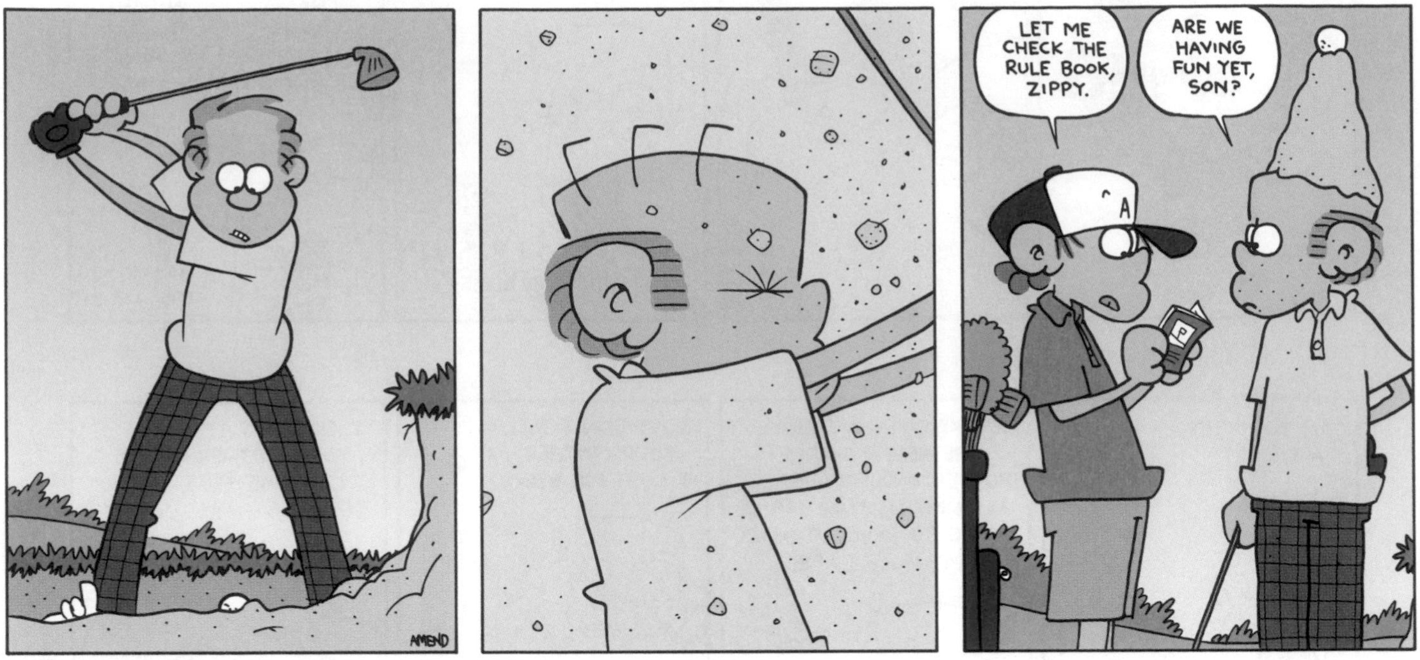
LET ME CHECK THE RULE BOOK, ZIPPY.
ARE WE HAVING FUN YET, SON?
AMEND

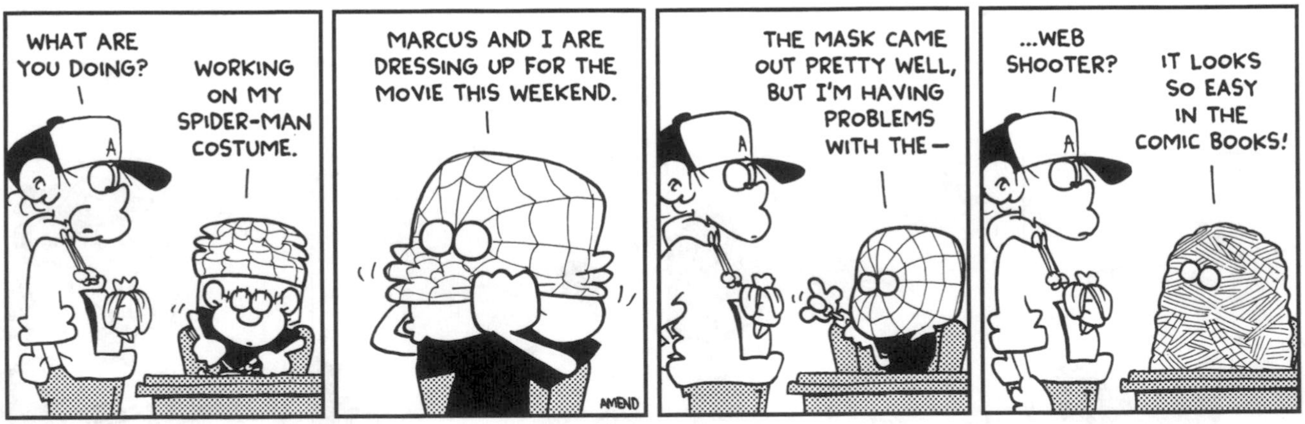
WHAT ARE YOU DOING?
WORKING ON MY SPIDER-MAN COSTUME.
MARCUS AND I ARE DRESSING UP FOR THE MOVIE THIS WEEKEND.
THE MASK CAME OUT PRETTY WELL, BUT I'M HAVING PROBLEMS WITH THE—
...WEB SHOOTER?
IT LOOKS SO EASY IN THE COMIC BOOKS!
AMEND

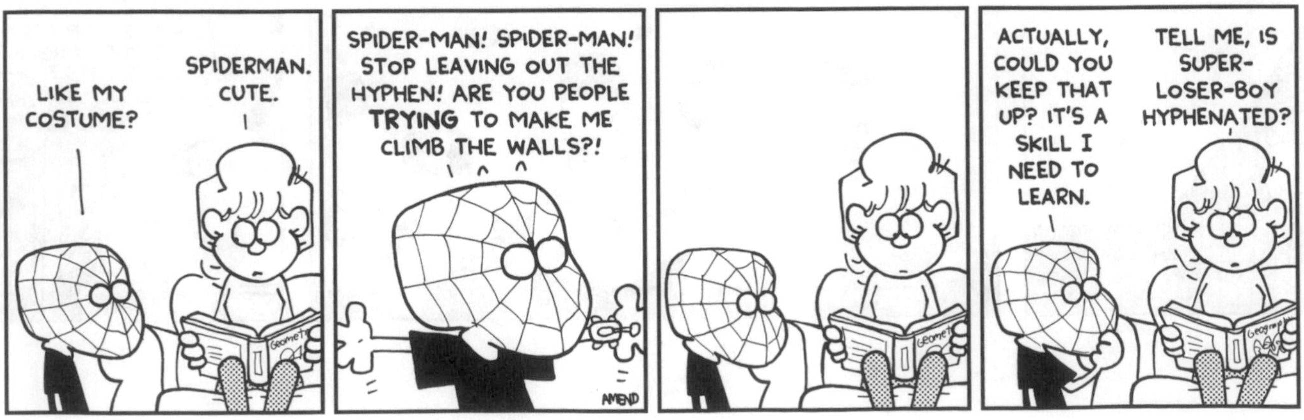
LIKE MY COSTUME?
SPIDERMAN. CUTE.
SPIDER-MAN! SPIDER-MAN! STOP LEAVING OUT THE HYPHEN! ARE YOU PEOPLE TRYING TO MAKE ME CLIMB THE WALLS?!
ACTUALLY, COULD YOU KEEP THAT UP? IT'S A SKILL I NEED TO LEARN.
TELL ME, IS SUPER-LOSER-BOY HYPHENATED?
AMEND

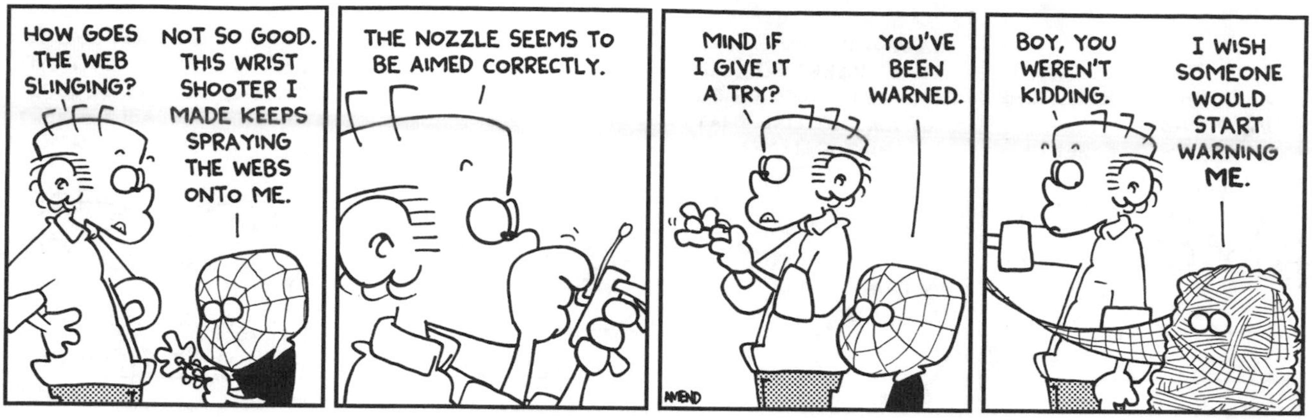
HOW GOES THE WEB SLINGING?
NOT SO GOOD. THIS WRIST SHOOTER I MADE KEEPS SPRAYING THE WEBS ONTO ME.
THE NOZZLE SEEMS TO BE AIMED CORRECTLY.
MIND IF I GIVE IT A TRY?
YOU'VE BEEN WARNED.
AMEND
BOY, YOU WEREN'T KIDDING.
I WISH SOMEONE WOULD START WARNING **ME.**

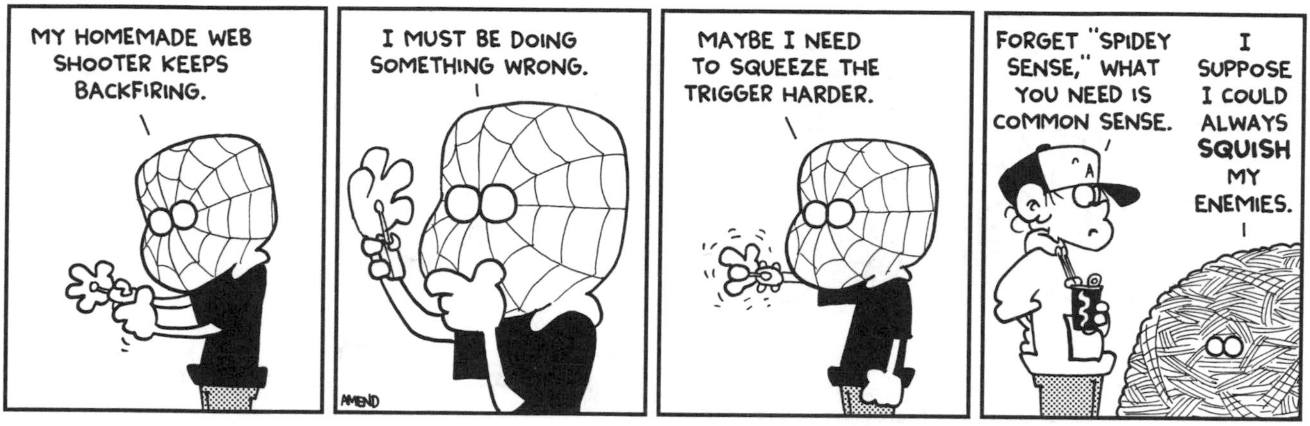
MY HOMEMADE WEB SHOOTER KEEPS BACKFIRING.
I MUST BE DOING SOMETHING WRONG.
AMEND
MAYBE I NEED TO SQUEEZE THE TRIGGER HARDER.
FORGET "SPIDEY SENSE," WHAT YOU NEED IS COMMON SENSE.
I SUPPOSE I COULD ALWAYS **SQUISH** MY ENEMIES.

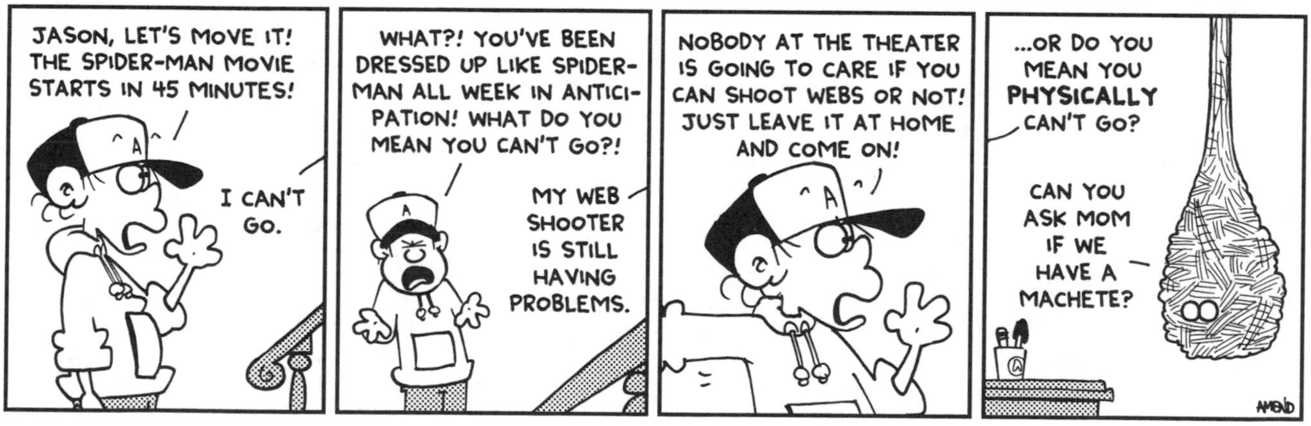
JASON, LET'S MOVE IT! THE SPIDER-MAN MOVIE STARTS IN 45 MINUTES!
I CAN'T GO.
WHAT?! YOU'VE BEEN DRESSED UP LIKE SPIDER-MAN ALL WEEK IN ANTICIPATION! WHAT DO YOU MEAN YOU CAN'T GO?!
MY WEB SHOOTER IS STILL HAVING PROBLEMS.
NOBODY AT THE THEATER IS GOING TO CARE IF YOU CAN SHOOT WEBS OR NOT! JUST LEAVE IT AT HOME AND COME ON!
...OR DO YOU MEAN YOU **PHYSICALLY** CAN'T GO?
CAN YOU ASK MOM IF WE HAVE A MACHETE?
AMEND

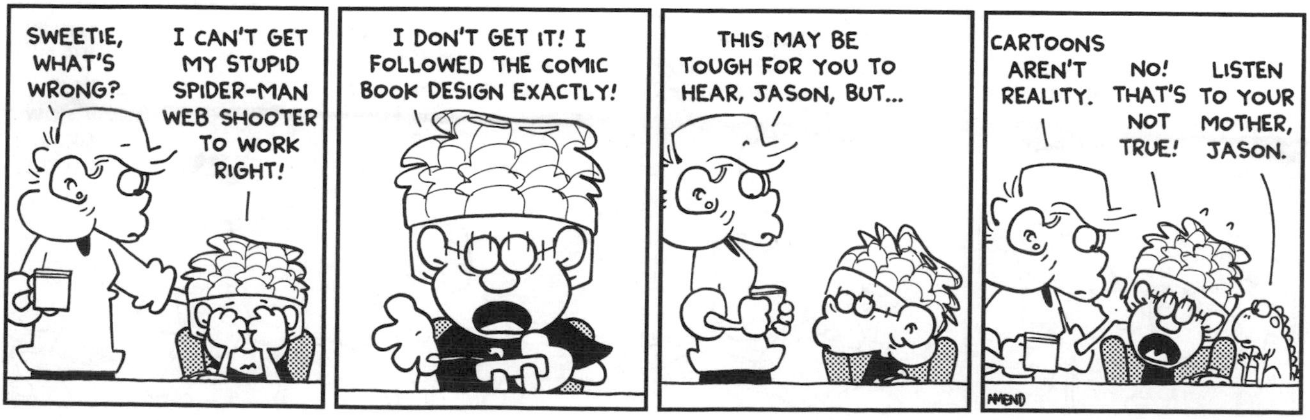
SWEETIE, WHAT'S WRONG?
I CAN'T GET MY STUPID SPIDER-MAN WEB SHOOTER TO WORK RIGHT!
I DON'T GET IT! I FOLLOWED THE COMIC BOOK DESIGN EXACTLY!
THIS MAY BE TOUGH FOR YOU TO HEAR, JASON, BUT...
AMEND
CARTOONS AREN'T REALITY.
NO! THAT'S NOT TRUE!
LISTEN TO YOUR MOTHER, JASON.

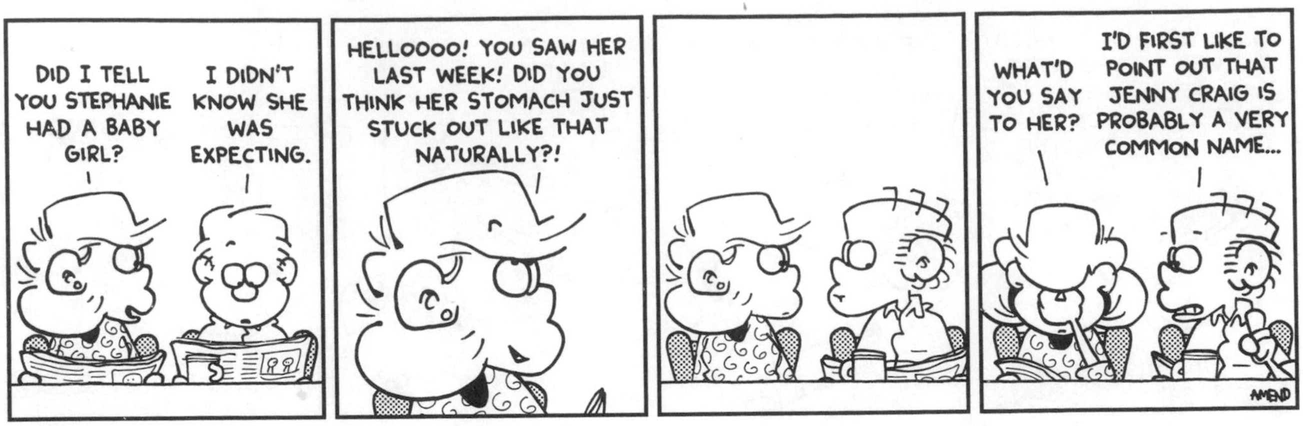
DID I TELL YOU STEPHANIE HAD A BABY GIRL?
I DIDN'T KNOW SHE WAS EXPECTING.
HELLOOOO! YOU SAW HER LAST WEEK! DID YOU THINK HER STOMACH JUST STUCK OUT LIKE THAT NATURALLY?!
WHAT'D YOU SAY TO HER?
I'D FIRST LIKE TO POINT OUT THAT JENNY CRAIG IS PROBABLY A VERY COMMON NAME...
AMEND

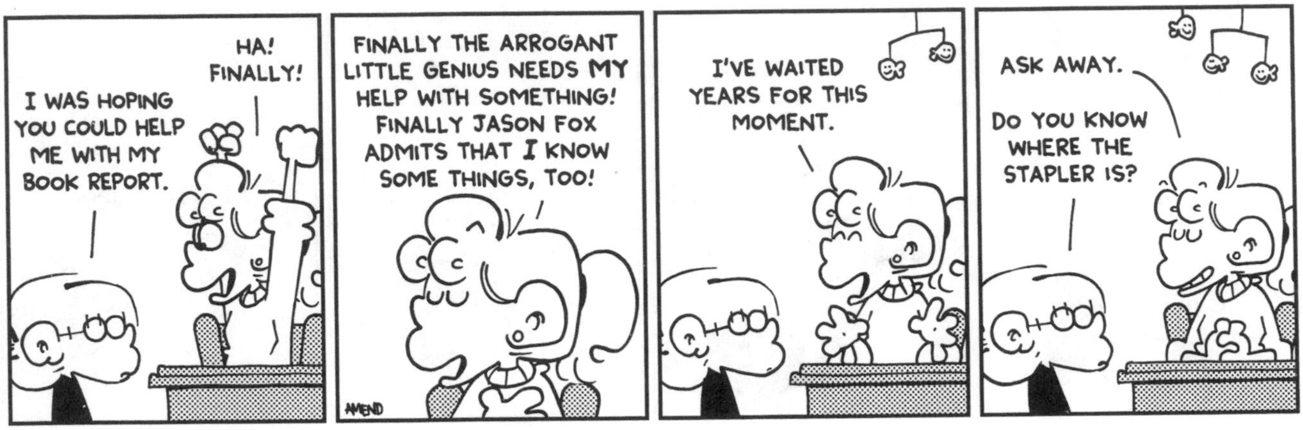
I WAS HOPING YOU COULD HELP ME WITH MY BOOK REPORT.
HA! FINALLY!
FINALLY THE ARROGANT LITTLE GENIUS NEEDS MY HELP WITH SOMETHING! FINALLY JASON FOX ADMITS THAT I KNOW SOME THINGS, TOO!
AMEND
I'VE WAITED YEARS FOR THIS MOMENT.
ASK AWAY.
DO YOU KNOW WHERE THE STAPLER IS?

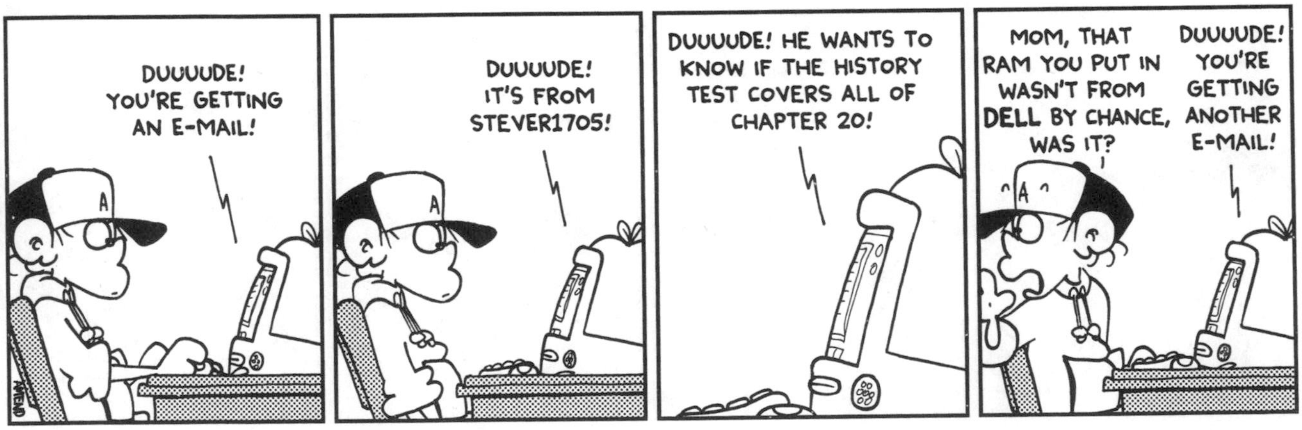
DUUUUDE! YOU'RE GETTING AN E-MAIL!
AMEND
DUUUUDE! IT'S FROM STEVER1705!
DUUUUDE! HE WANTS TO KNOW IF THE HISTORY TEST COVERS ALL OF CHAPTER 20!
MOM, THAT RAM YOU PUT IN WASN'T FROM DELL BY CHANCE, WAS IT?
DUUUUDE! YOU'RE GETTING ANOTHER E-MAIL!

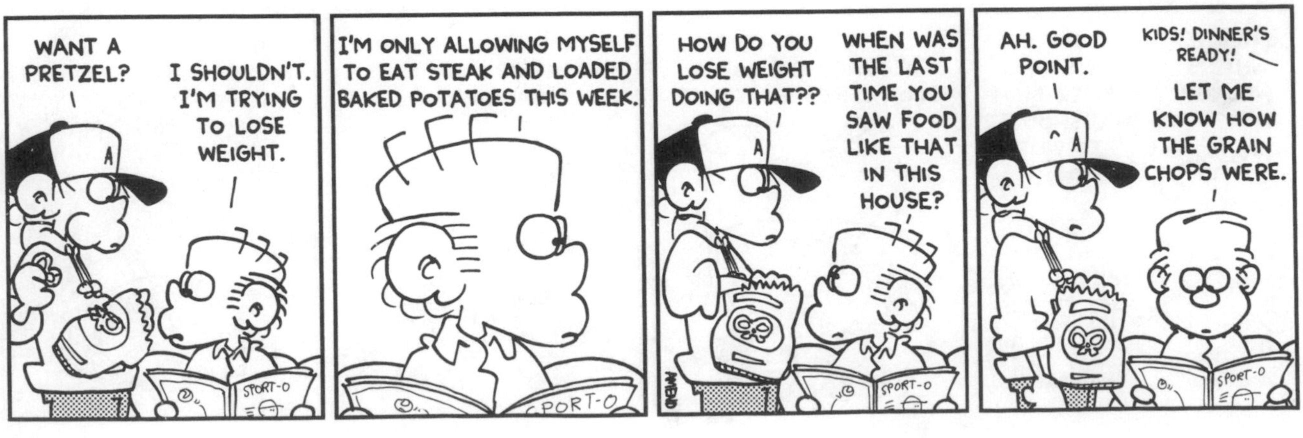
WANT A PRETZEL?
I SHOULDN'T. I'M TRYING TO LOSE WEIGHT.
SPORT-O
I'M ONLY ALLOWING MYSELF TO EAT STEAK AND LOADED BAKED POTATOES THIS WEEK.
SPORT-O
HOW DO YOU LOSE WEIGHT DOING THAT??
WHEN WAS THE LAST TIME YOU SAW FOOD LIKE THAT IN THIS HOUSE?
AMEND
SPORT-O
AH. GOOD POINT.
KIDS! DINNER'S READY!
LET ME KNOW HOW THE GRAIN CHOPS WERE.
SPORT-O

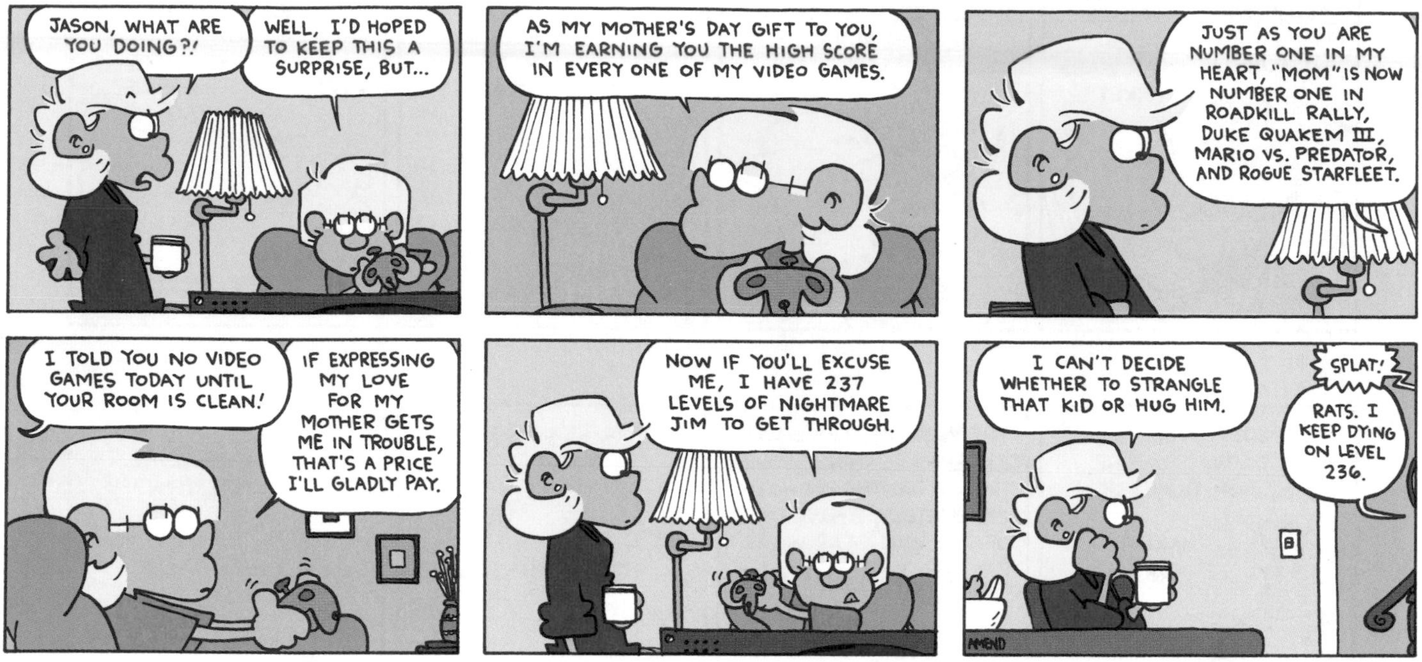
JASON, WHAT ARE YOU DOING?!
WELL, I'D HOPED TO KEEP THIS A SURPRISE, BUT...
AS MY MOTHER'S DAY GIFT TO YOU, I'M EARNING YOU THE HIGH SCORE IN EVERY ONE OF MY VIDEO GAMES.
JUST AS YOU ARE NUMBER ONE IN MY HEART, "MOM" IS NOW NUMBER ONE IN ROADKILL RALLY, DUKE QUAKEM III, MARIO VS. PREDATOR, AND ROGUE STARFLEET.
I TOLD YOU NO VIDEO GAMES TODAY UNTIL YOUR ROOM IS CLEAN!
IF EXPRESSING MY LOVE FOR MY MOTHER GETS ME IN TROUBLE, THAT'S A PRICE I'LL GLADLY PAY.
NOW IF YOU'LL EXCUSE ME, I HAVE 237 LEVELS OF NIGHTMARE JIM TO GET THROUGH.
I CAN'T DECIDE WHETHER TO STRANGLE THAT KID OR HUG HIM.
SPLAT!
RATS. I KEEP DYING ON LEVEL 236.
AMEND

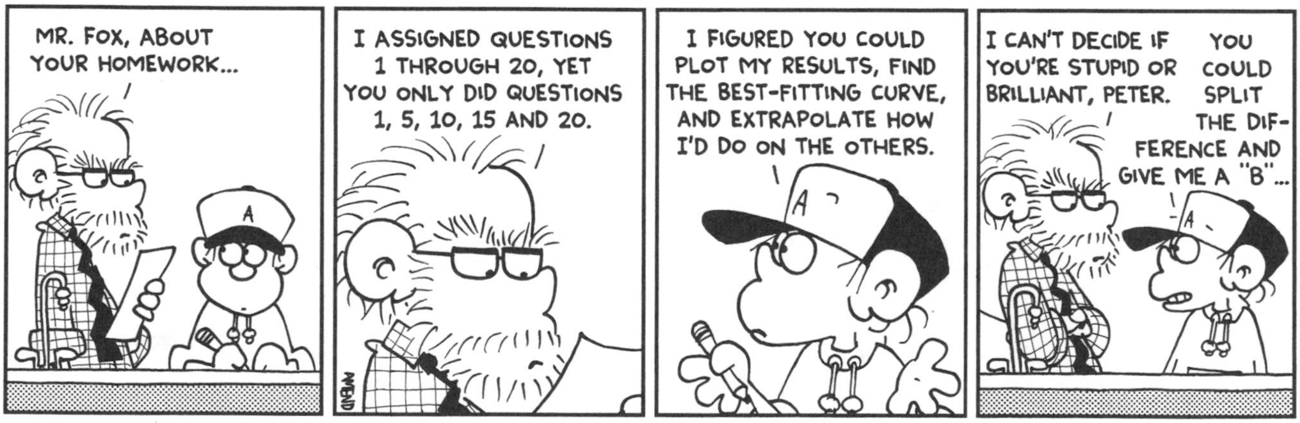
MR. FOX, ABOUT YOUR HOMEWORK...
I ASSIGNED QUESTIONS 1 THROUGH 20, YET YOU ONLY DID QUESTIONS 1, 5, 10, 15 AND 20.
AMEND
I FIGURED YOU COULD PLOT MY RESULTS, FIND THE BEST-FITTING CURVE, AND EXTRAPOLATE HOW I'D DO ON THE OTHERS.
I CAN'T DECIDE IF YOU'RE STUPID OR BRILLIANT, PETER.
YOU COULD SPLIT THE DIFFERENCE AND GIVE ME A "B"...

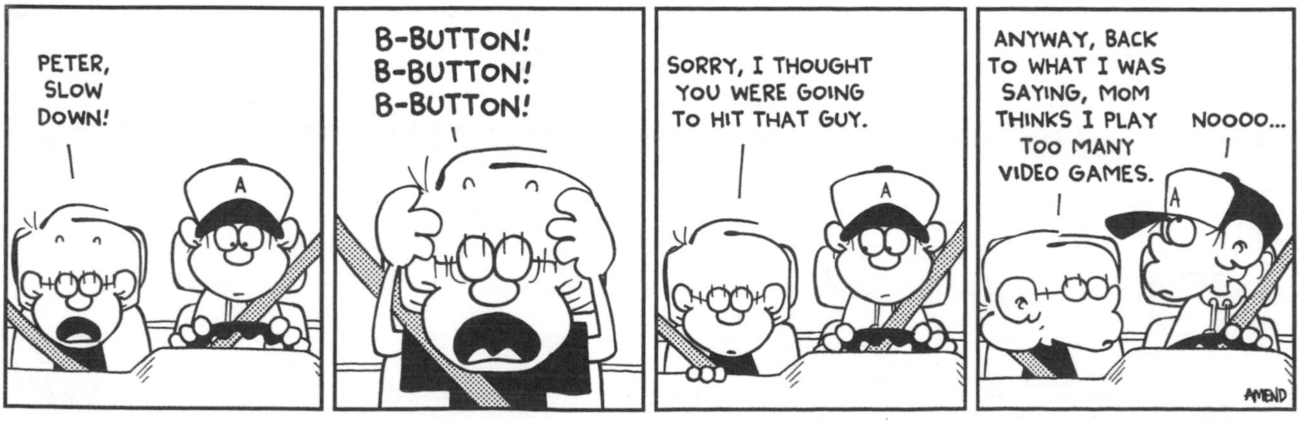
PETER, SLOW DOWN!
B-BUTTON! B-BUTTON! B-BUTTON!
SORRY, I THOUGHT YOU WERE GOING TO HIT THAT GUY.
ANYWAY, BACK TO WHAT I WAS SAYING, MOM THINKS I PLAY TOO MANY VIDEO GAMES.
NOOOO...
AMEND

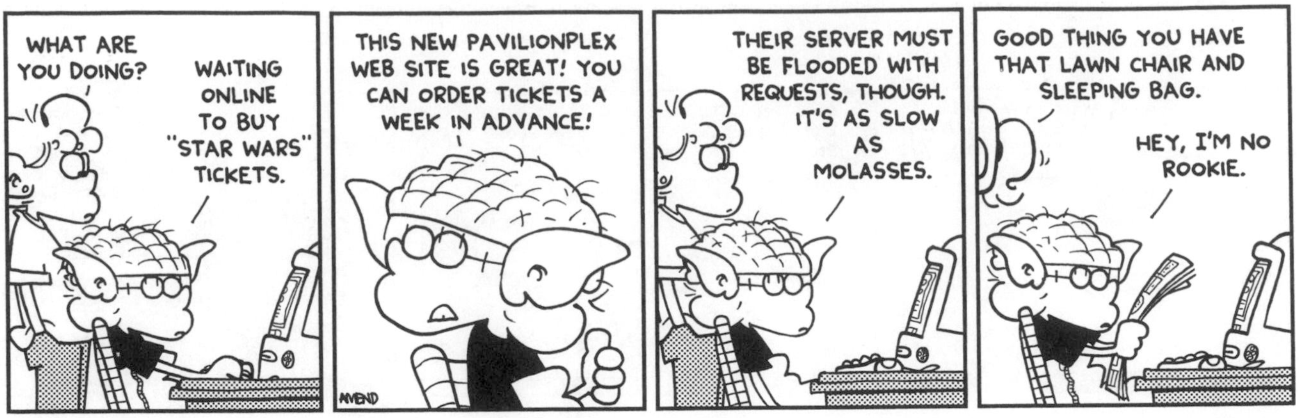
WHAT ARE YOU DOING?
WAITING ONLINE TO BUY "STAR WARS" TICKETS.
THIS NEW PAVILIONPLEX WEB SITE IS GREAT! YOU CAN ORDER TICKETS A WEEK IN ADVANCE!
AMEND
THEIR SERVER MUST BE FLOODED WITH REQUESTS, THOUGH. IT'S AS SLOW AS MOLASSES.
GOOD THING YOU HAVE THAT LAWN CHAIR AND SLEEPING BAG.
HEY, I'M NO ROOKIE.

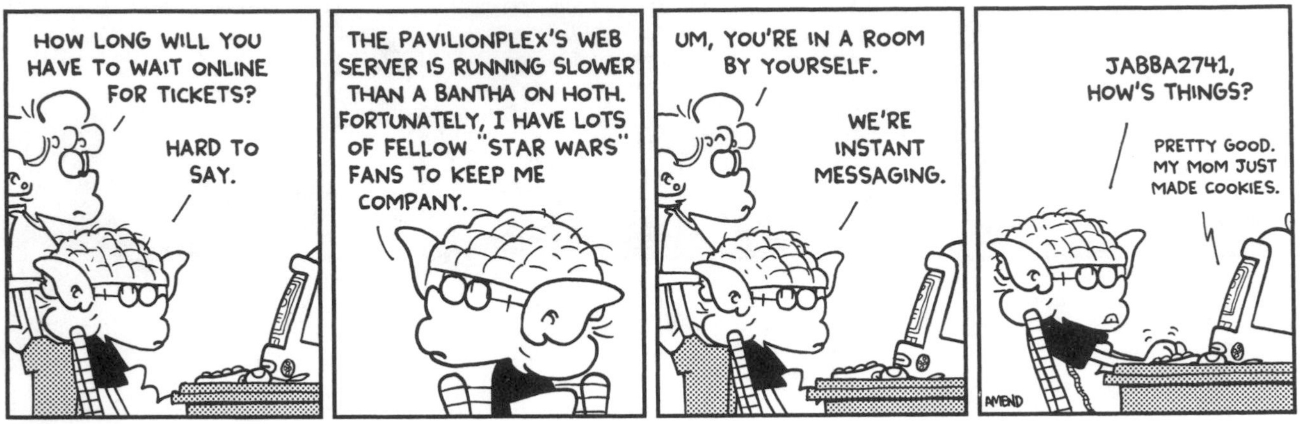
HOW LONG WILL YOU HAVE TO WAIT ONLINE FOR TICKETS?
HARD TO SAY.
THE PAVILIONPLEX'S WEB SERVER IS RUNNING SLOWER THAN A BANTHA ON HOTH. FORTUNATELY, I HAVE LOTS OF FELLOW "STAR WARS" FANS TO KEEP ME COMPANY.
UM, YOU'RE IN A ROOM BY YOURSELF.
WE'RE INSTANT MESSAGING.
JABBA2741, HOW'S THINGS?
PRETTY GOOD. MY MOM JUST MADE COOKIES.
AMEND

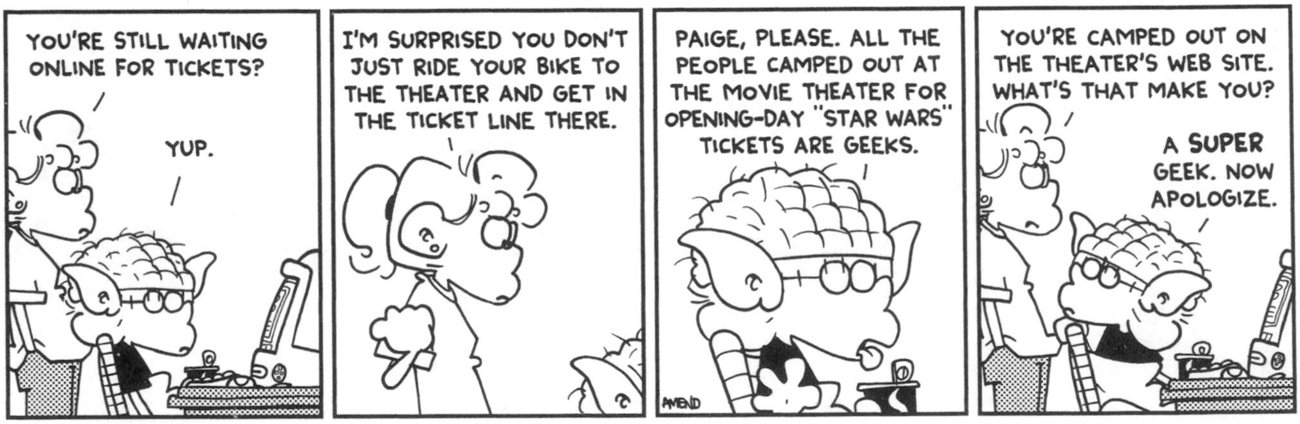
YOU'RE STILL WAITING ONLINE FOR TICKETS?
YUP.
I'M SURPRISED YOU DON'T JUST RIDE YOUR BIKE TO THE THEATER AND GET IN THE TICKET LINE THERE.
PAIGE, PLEASE. ALL THE PEOPLE CAMPED OUT AT THE MOVIE THEATER FOR OPENING-DAY "STAR WARS" TICKETS ARE GEEKS.
AMEND
YOU'RE CAMPED OUT ON THE THEATER'S WEB SITE. WHAT'S THAT MAKE YOU?
A SUPER GEEK. NOW APOLOGIZE.

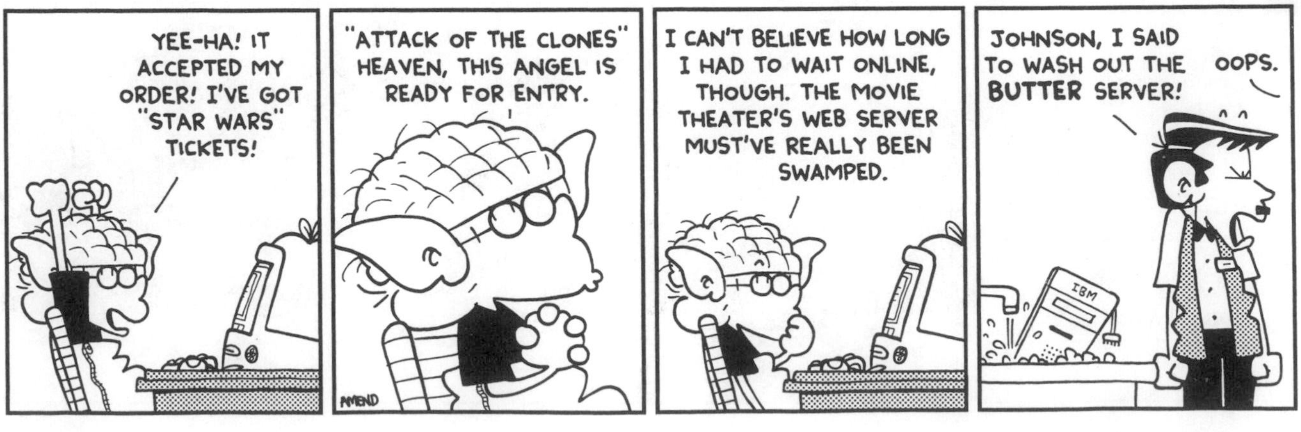
YEE-HA! IT ACCEPTED MY ORDER! I'VE GOT "STAR WARS" TICKETS!
"ATTACK OF THE CLONES" HEAVEN, THIS ANGEL IS READY FOR ENTRY.
AMEND
I CAN'T BELIEVE HOW LONG I HAD TO WAIT ONLINE, THOUGH. THE MOVIE THEATER'S WEB SERVER MUST'VE REALLY BEEN SWAMPED.
JOHNSON, I SAID TO WASH OUT THE BUTTER SERVER!
OOPS.
IBM

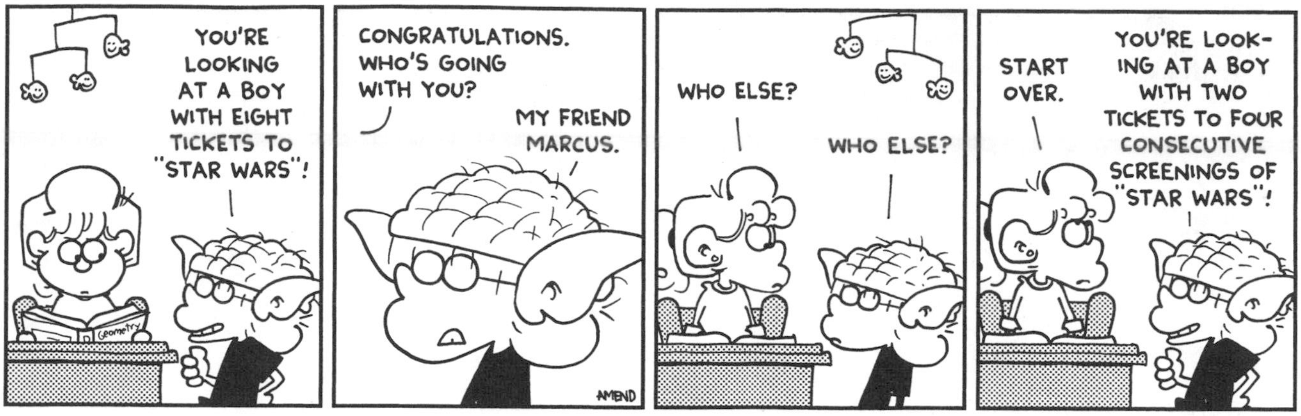

YOU'RE LOOKING AT A BOY WITH EIGHT TICKETS TO "STAR WARS"!
Geometry
CONGRATULATIONS. WHO'S GOING WITH YOU?
MY FRIEND MARCUS.
WHO ELSE?
WHO ELSE?
START OVER.
YOU'RE LOOK-ING AT A BOY WITH TWO TICKETS TO FOUR CONSECUTIVE SCREENINGS OF "STAR WARS"!
AMEND

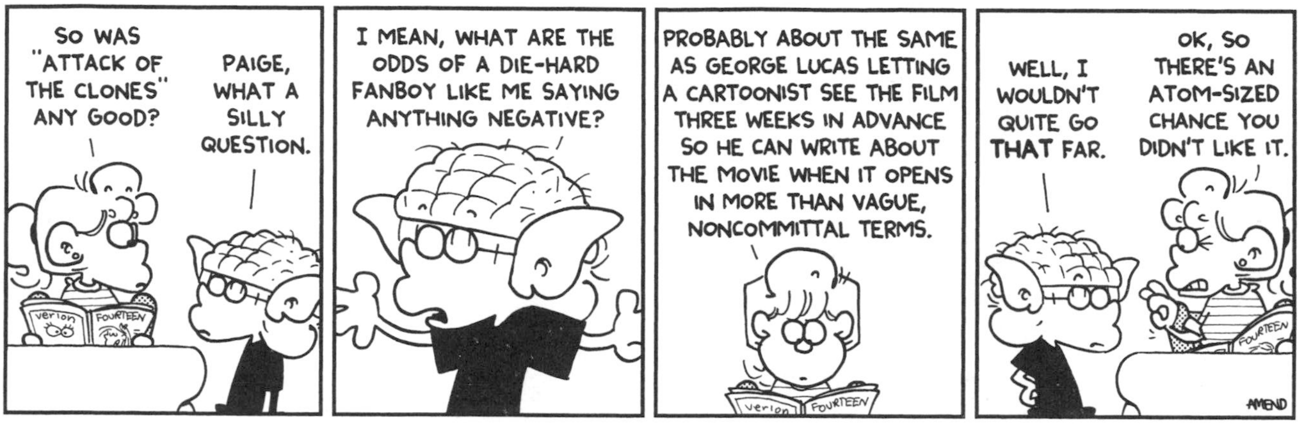

SO WAS "ATTACK OF THE CLONES" ANY GOOD?
PAIGE, WHAT A SILLY QUESTION.
verion
FOURTEEN
I MEAN, WHAT ARE THE ODDS OF A DIE-HARD FANBOY LIKE ME SAYING ANYTHING NEGATIVE?
PROBABLY ABOUT THE SAME AS GEORGE LUCAS LETTING A CARTOONIST SEE THE FILM THREE WEEKS IN ADVANCE SO HE CAN WRITE ABOUT THE MOVIE WHEN IT OPENS IN MORE THAN VAGUE, NONCOMMITTAL TERMS.
WELL, I WOULDN'T QUITE GO THAT FAR.
OK, SO THERE'S AN ATOM-SIZED CHANCE YOU DIDN'T LIKE IT.
AMEND

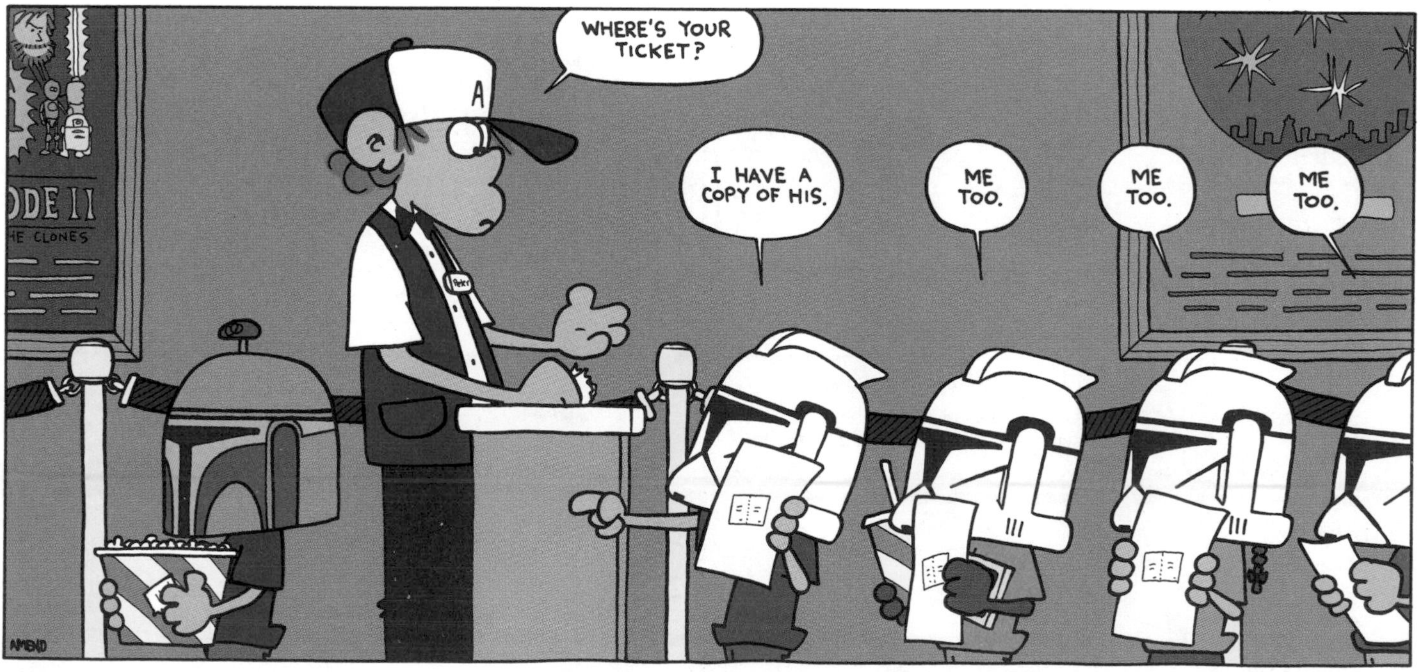

WHERE'S YOUR TICKET?
I HAVE A COPY OF HIS.
ME TOO.
ME TOO.
ME TOO.
AMEND

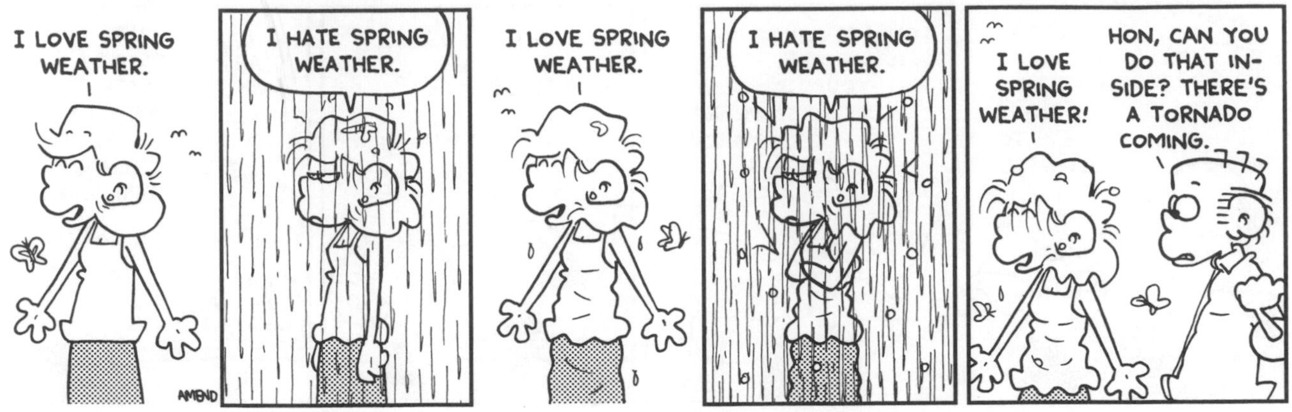
I LOVE SPRING WEATHER.
I HATE SPRING WEATHER.
I LOVE SPRING WEATHER.
I HATE SPRING WEATHER.
I LOVE SPRING WEATHER!
HON, CAN YOU DO THAT IN-SIDE? THERE'S A TORNADO COMING.
AMEND

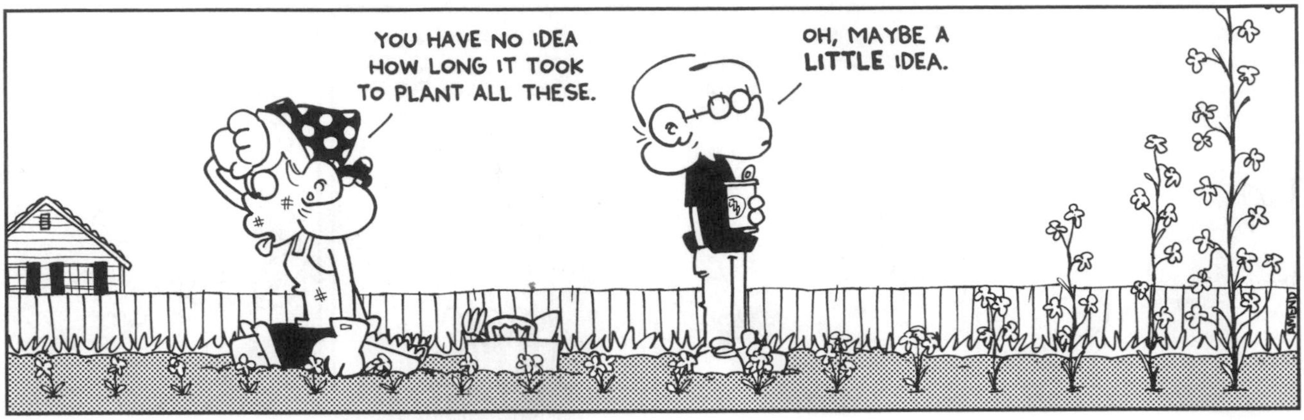
YOU HAVE NO IDEA HOW LONG IT TOOK TO PLANT ALL THESE.
OH, MAYBE A LITTLE IDEA.
AMEND

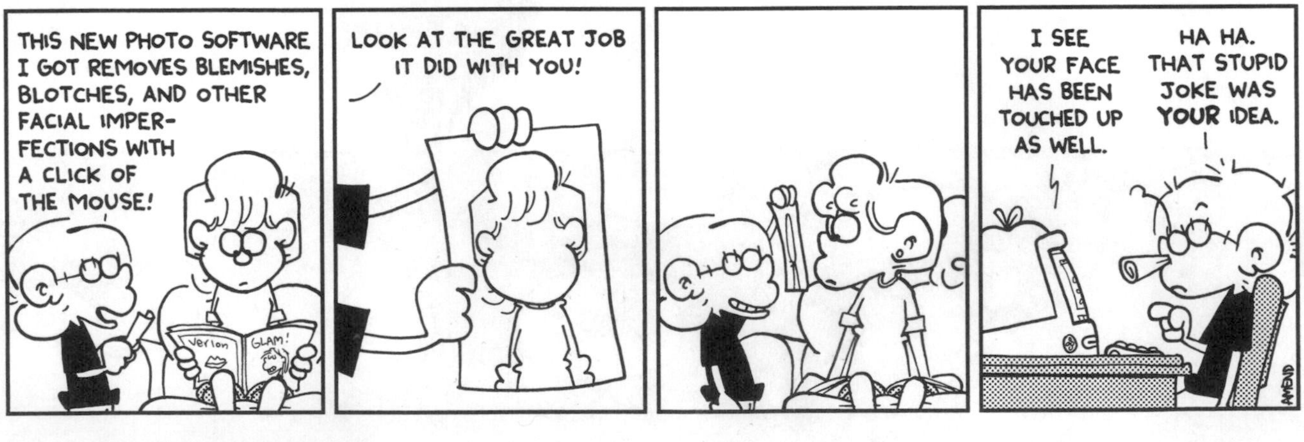
THIS NEW PHOTO SOFTWARE I GOT REMOVES BLEMISHES, BLOTCHES, AND OTHER FACIAL IMPER-FECTIONS WITH A CLICK OF THE MOUSE!
Verlon
GLAM!
LOOK AT THE GREAT JOB IT DID WITH YOU!
I SEE YOUR FACE HAS BEEN TOUCHED UP AS WELL.
HA HA. THAT STUPID JOKE WAS YOUR IDEA.
AMEND

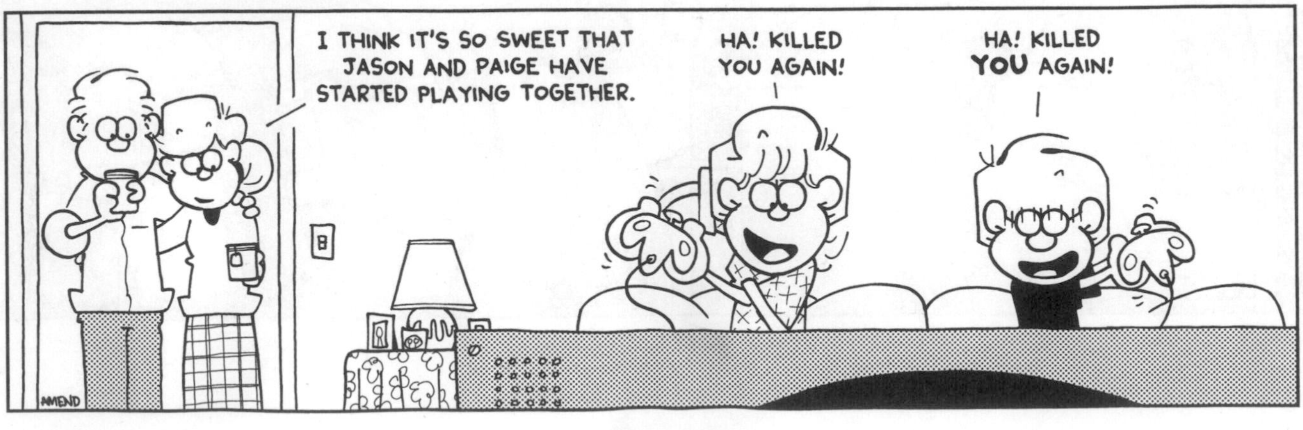
I THINK IT'S SO SWEET THAT JASON AND PAIGE HAVE STARTED PLAYING TOGETHER.
HA! KILLED YOU AGAIN!
HA! KILLED YOU AGAIN!
AMEND

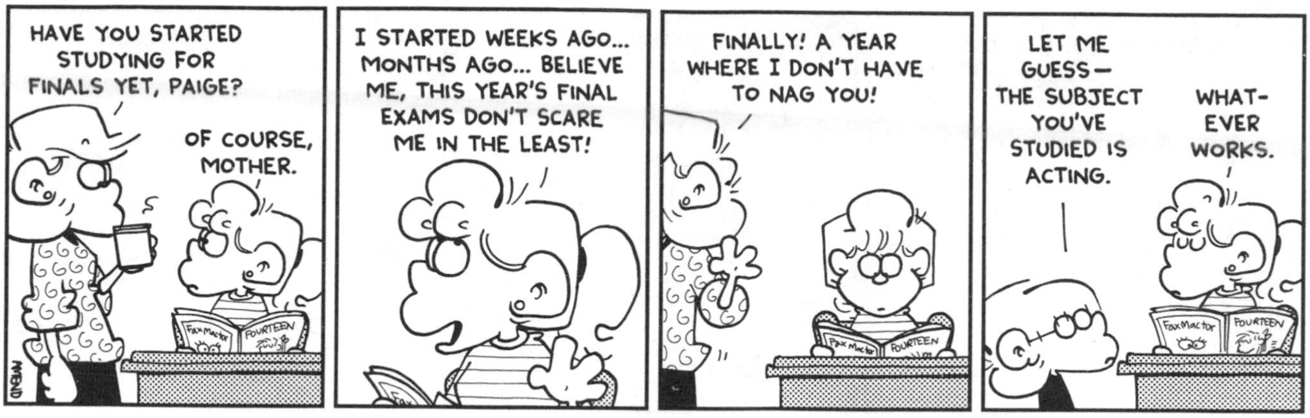
HAVE YOU STARTED STUDYING FOR FINALS YET, PAIGE?
OF COURSE, MOTHER.
I STARTED WEEKS AGO... MONTHS AGO... BELIEVE ME, THIS YEAR'S FINAL EXAMS DON'T SCARE ME IN THE LEAST!
FINALLY! A YEAR WHERE I DON'T HAVE TO NAG YOU!
LET ME GUESS— THE SUBJECT YOU'VE STUDIED IS ACTING.
WHAT-EVER WORKS.
AMEND

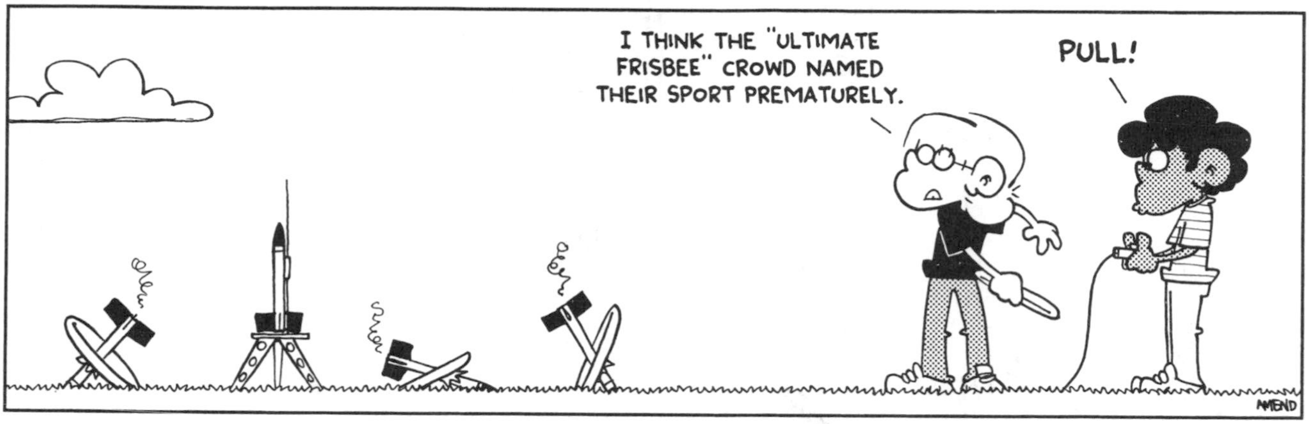
I THINK THE "ULTIMATE FRISBEE" CROWD NAMED THEIR SPORT PREMATURELY.
PULL!
AMEND

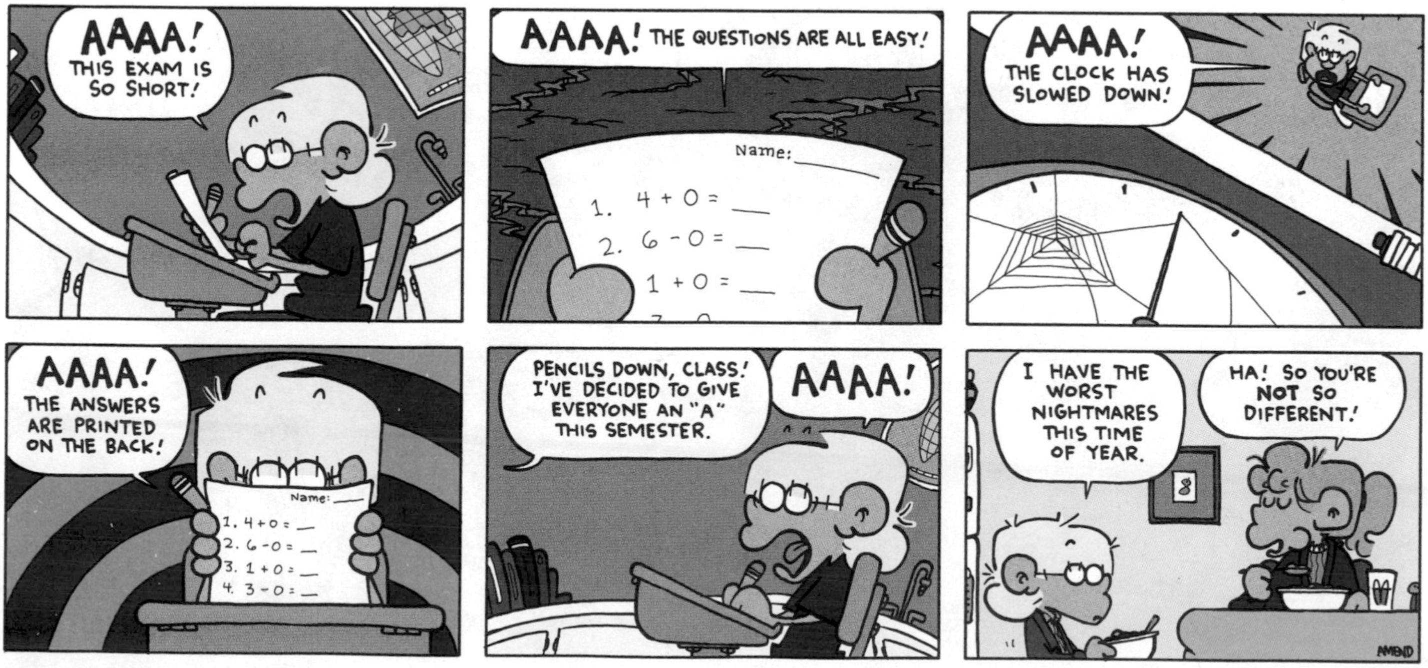
AAAA! THIS EXAM IS SO SHORT!
AAAA! THE QUESTIONS ARE ALL EASY!
Name:
1. 4 + 0 =
2. 6 - 0 =
1 + 0 =
AAAA! THE CLOCK HAS SLOWED DOWN!
AAAA! THE ANSWERS ARE PRINTED ON THE BACK!
Name:
1. 4 + 0 =
2. 6 - 0 =
3. 1 + 0 =
4. 3 - 0 =
PENCILS DOWN, CLASS! I'VE DECIDED TO GIVE EVERYONE AN "A" THIS SEMESTER.
AAAA!
I HAVE THE WORST NIGHTMARES THIS TIME OF YEAR.
HA! SO YOU'RE NOT SO DIFFERENT!
AMEND

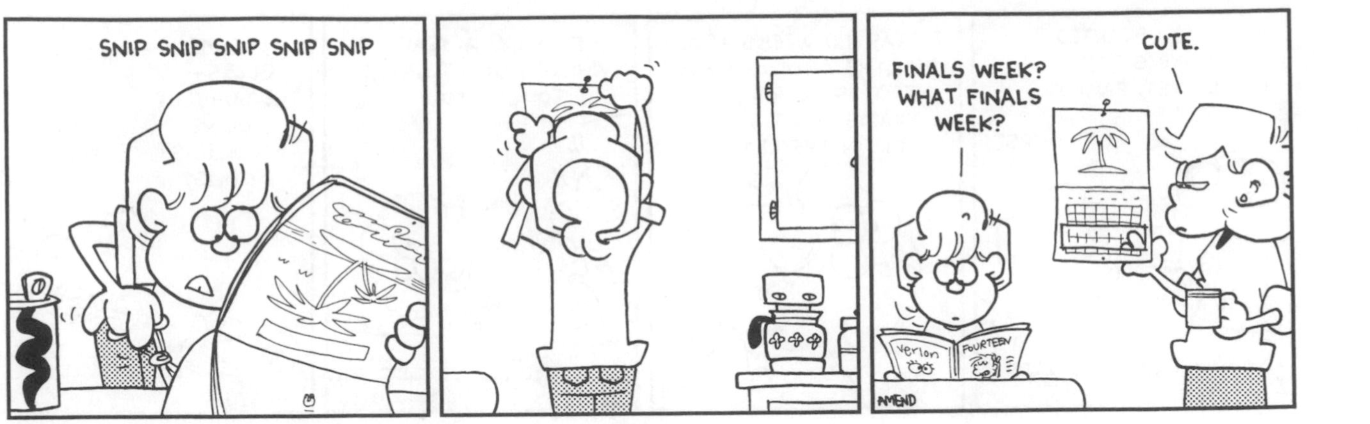
SNIP SNIP SNIP SNIP SNIP
FINALS WEEK? WHAT FINALS WEEK?
CUTE.

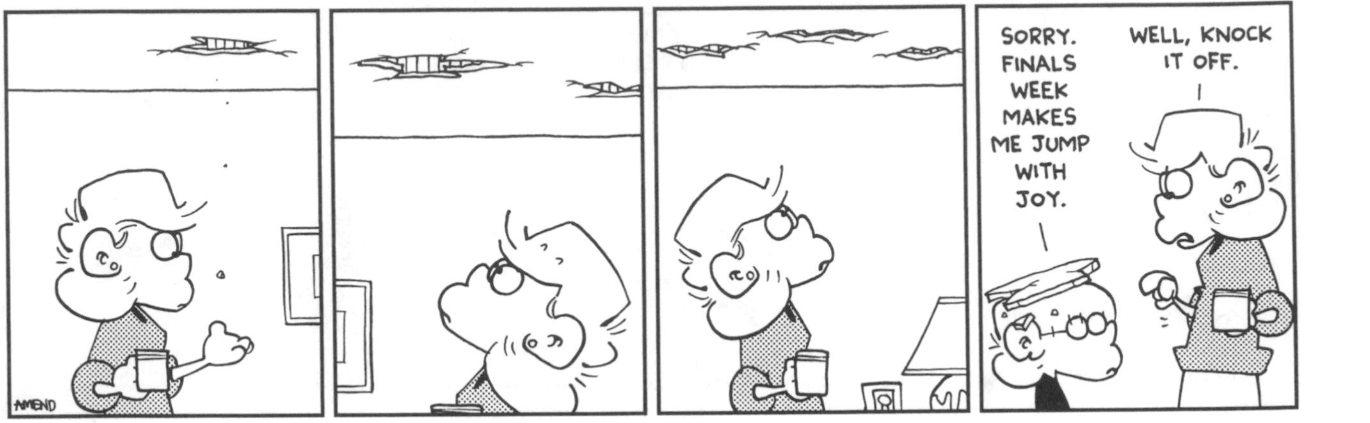
SORRY. FINALS WEEK MAKES ME JUMP WITH JOY.
WELL, KNOCK IT OFF.

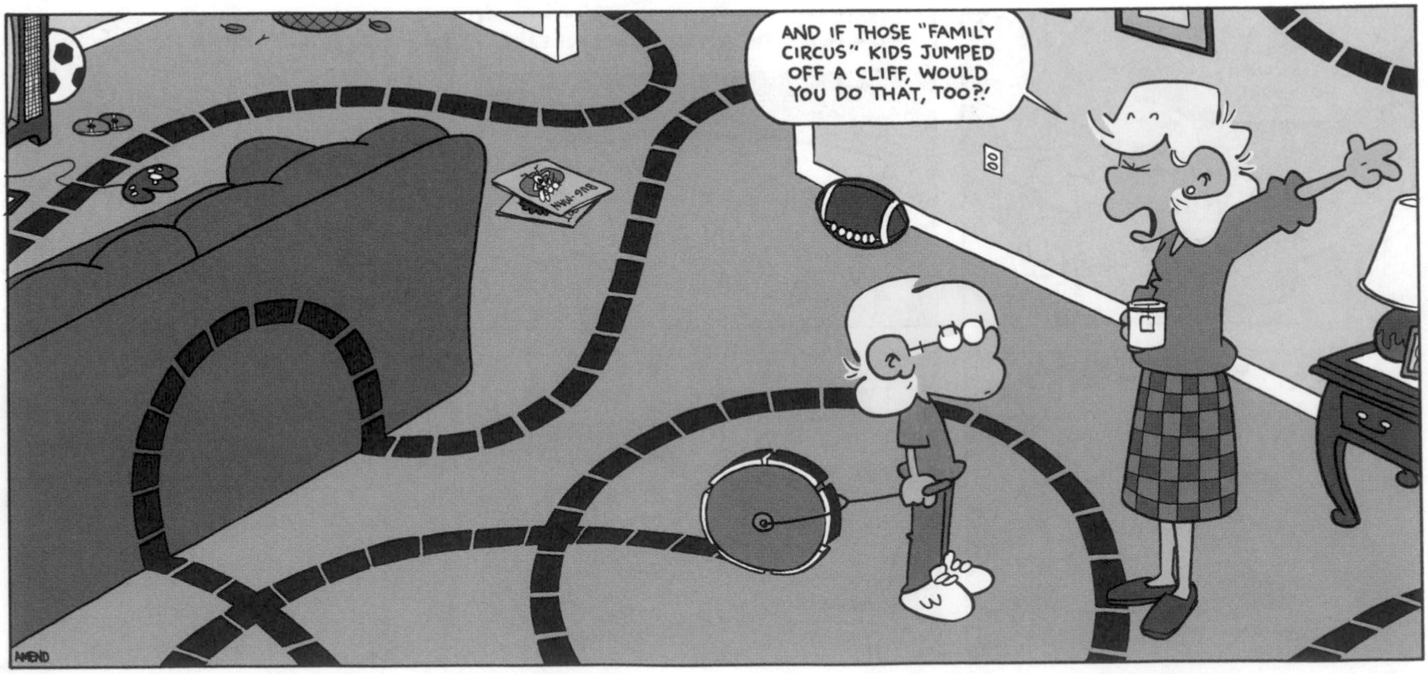
AND IF THOSE "FAMILY CIRCUS" KIDS JUMPED OFF A CLIFF, WOULD YOU DO THAT, TOO?!

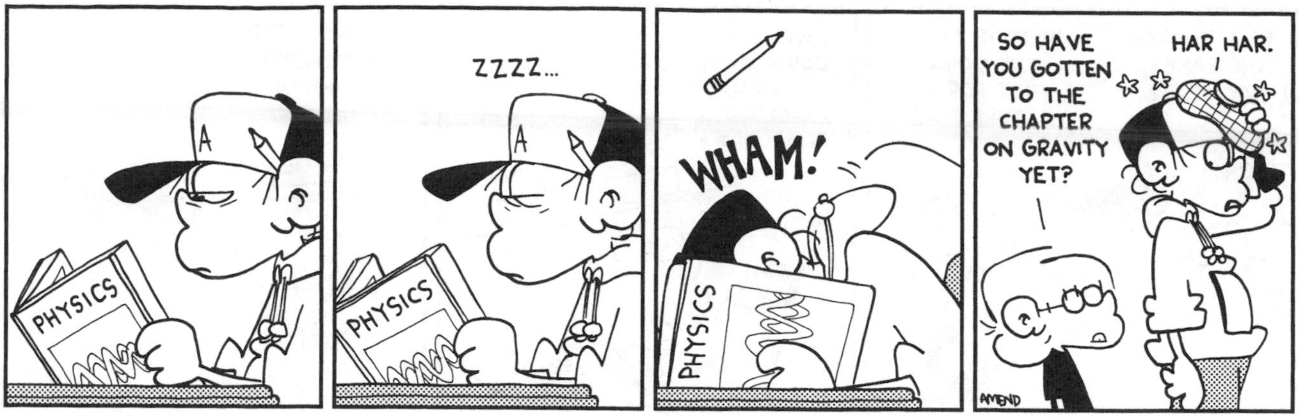
ZZZZ...
WHAM!
SO HAVE YOU GOTTEN TO THE CHAPTER ON GRAVITY YET?
HAR HAR.
PHYSICS
AMEND

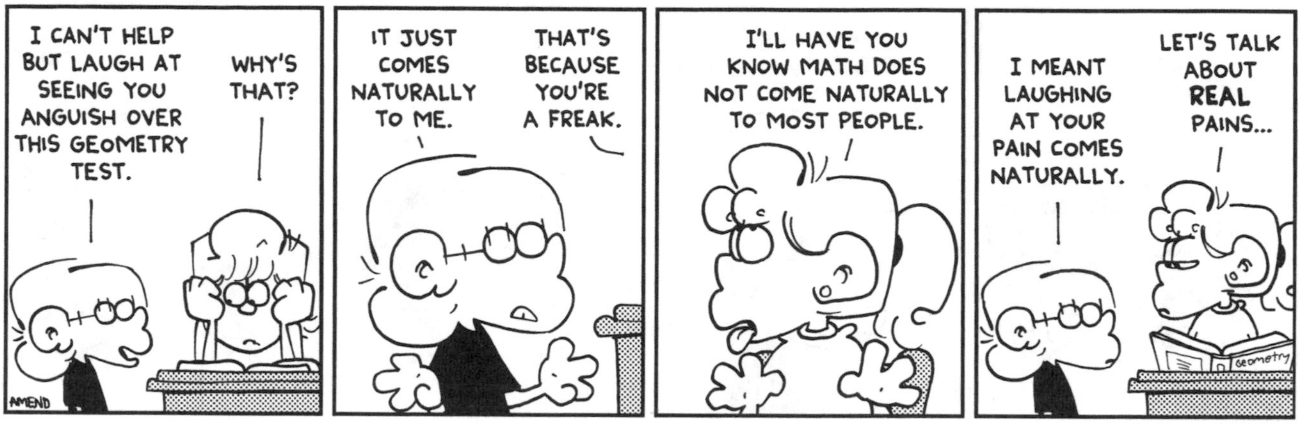
I CAN'T HELP BUT LAUGH AT SEEING YOU ANGUISH OVER THIS GEOMETRY TEST.
WHY'S THAT?
IT JUST COMES NATURALLY TO ME.
THAT'S BECAUSE YOU'RE A FREAK.
I'LL HAVE YOU KNOW MATH DOES NOT COME NATURALLY TO MOST PEOPLE.
I MEANT LAUGHING AT YOUR PAIN COMES NATURALLY.
LET'S TALK ABOUT **REAL** PAINS...
Geometry
AMEND

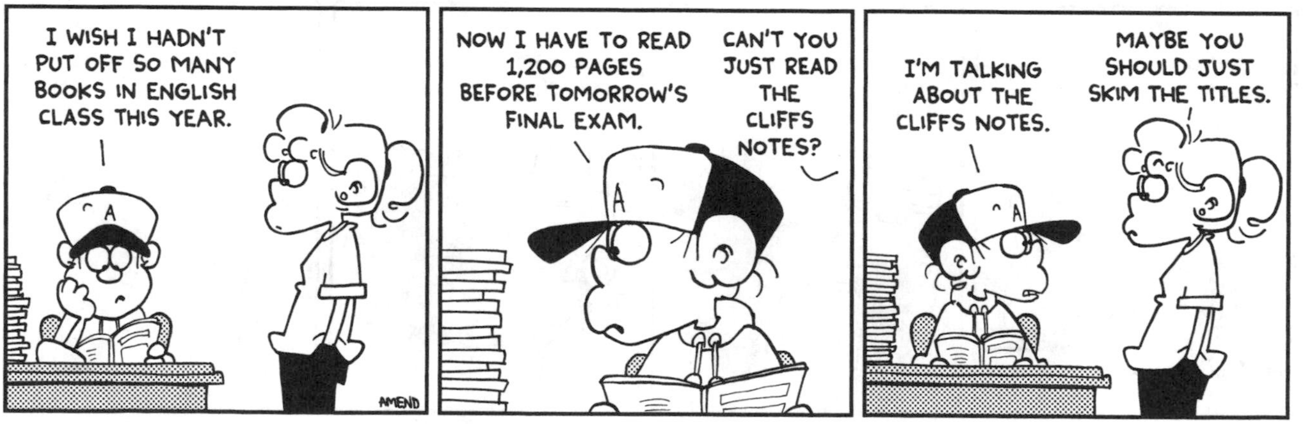
I WISH I HADN'T PUT OFF SO MANY BOOKS IN ENGLISH CLASS THIS YEAR.
NOW I HAVE TO READ 1,200 PAGES BEFORE TOMORROW'S FINAL EXAM.
CAN'T YOU JUST READ THE CLIFFS NOTES?
I'M TALKING ABOUT THE CLIFFS NOTES.
MAYBE YOU SHOULD JUST SKIM THE TITLES.
AMEND

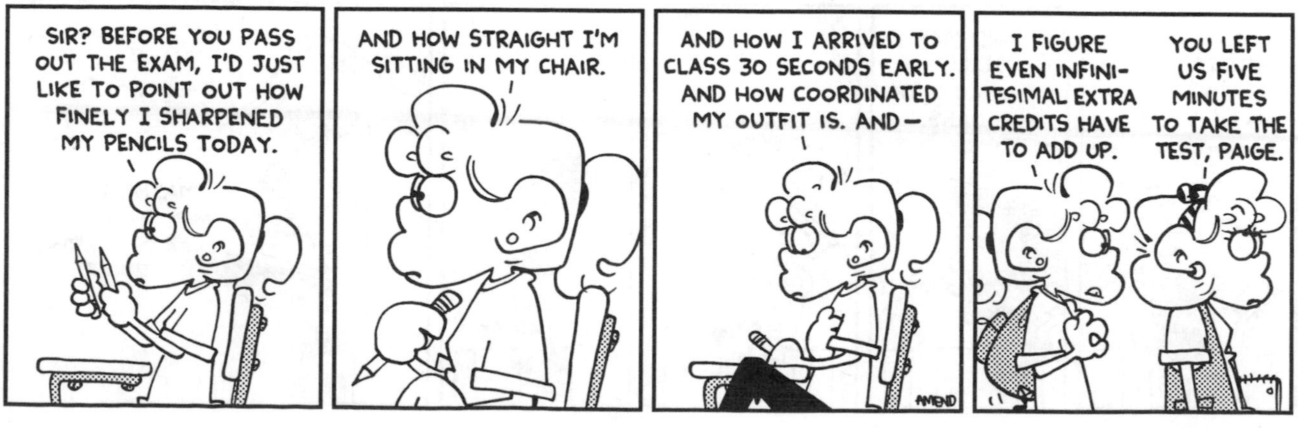
SIR? BEFORE YOU PASS OUT THE EXAM, I'D JUST LIKE TO POINT OUT HOW FINELY I SHARPENED MY PENCILS TODAY.
AND HOW STRAIGHT I'M SITTING IN MY CHAIR.
AND HOW I ARRIVED TO CLASS 30 SECONDS EARLY. AND HOW COORDINATED MY OUTFIT IS. AND—
I FIGURE EVEN INFINI-TESIMAL EXTRA CREDITS HAVE TO ADD UP.
YOU LEFT US FIVE MINUTES TO TAKE THE TEST, PAIGE.
AMEND

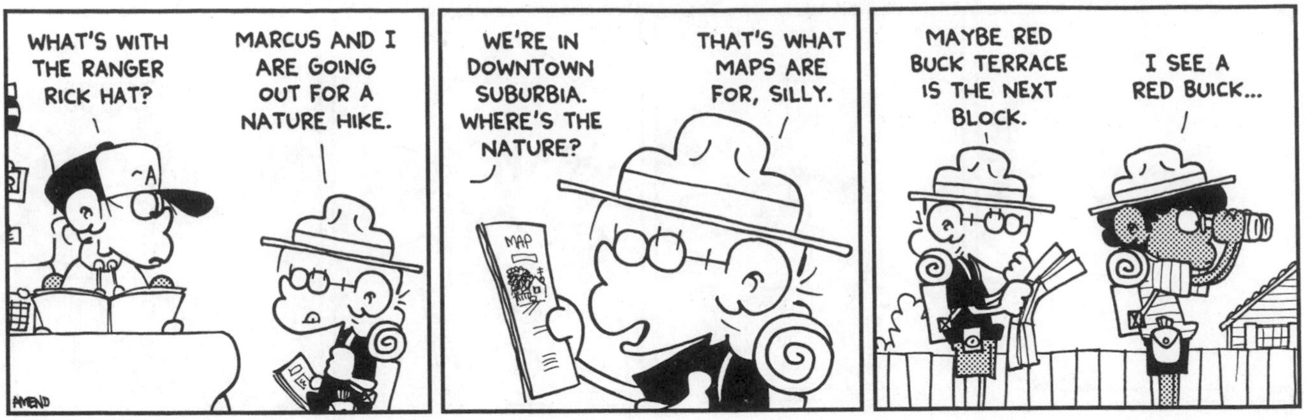
WHAT'S WITH THE RANGER RICK HAT?
MARCUS AND I ARE GOING OUT FOR A NATURE HIKE.
WE'RE IN DOWNTOWN SUBURBIA. WHERE'S THE NATURE?
THAT'S WHAT MAPS ARE FOR, SILLY.
MAP
MAYBE RED BUCK TERRACE IS THE NEXT BLOCK.
I SEE A RED BUICK...
AMEND

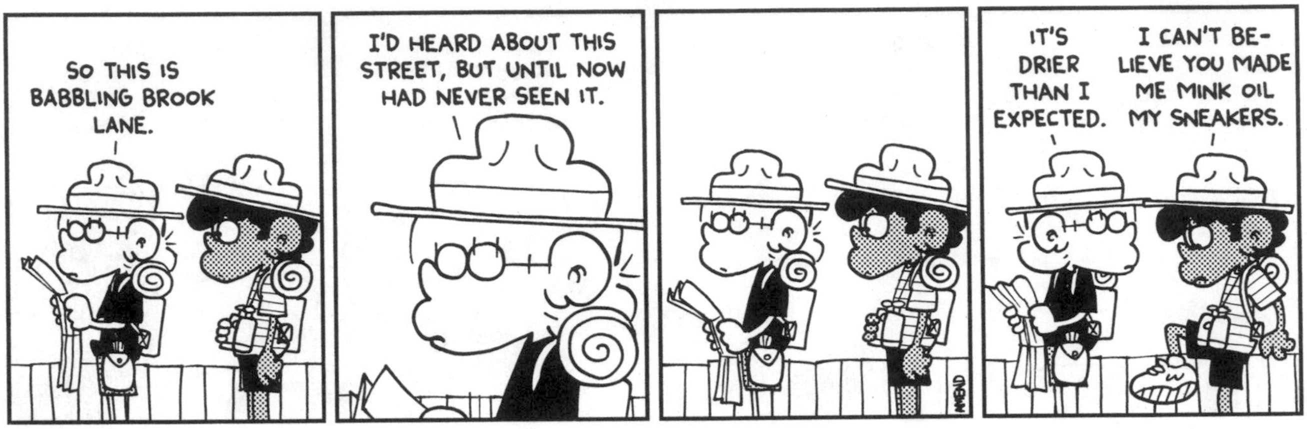
SO THIS IS BABBLING BROOK LANE.
I'D HEARD ABOUT THIS STREET, BUT UNTIL NOW HAD NEVER SEEN IT.
IT'S DRIER THAN I EXPECTED.
I CAN'T BE-LIEVE YOU MADE ME MINK OIL MY SNEAKERS.
AMEND

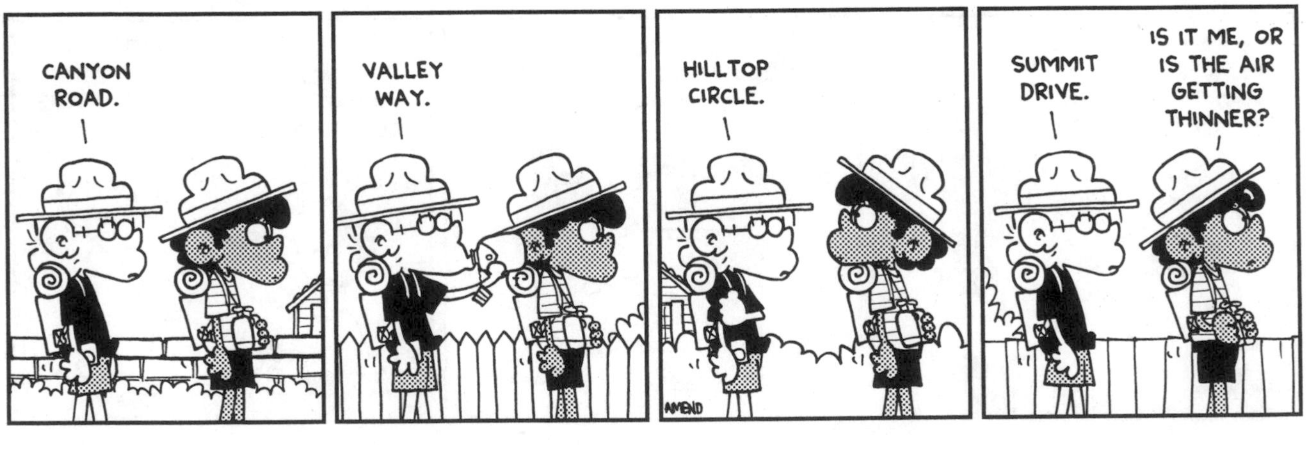
CANYON ROAD.
VALLEY WAY.
HILLTOP CIRCLE.
SUMMIT DRIVE.
IS IT ME, OR IS THE AIR GETTING THINNER?
AMEND

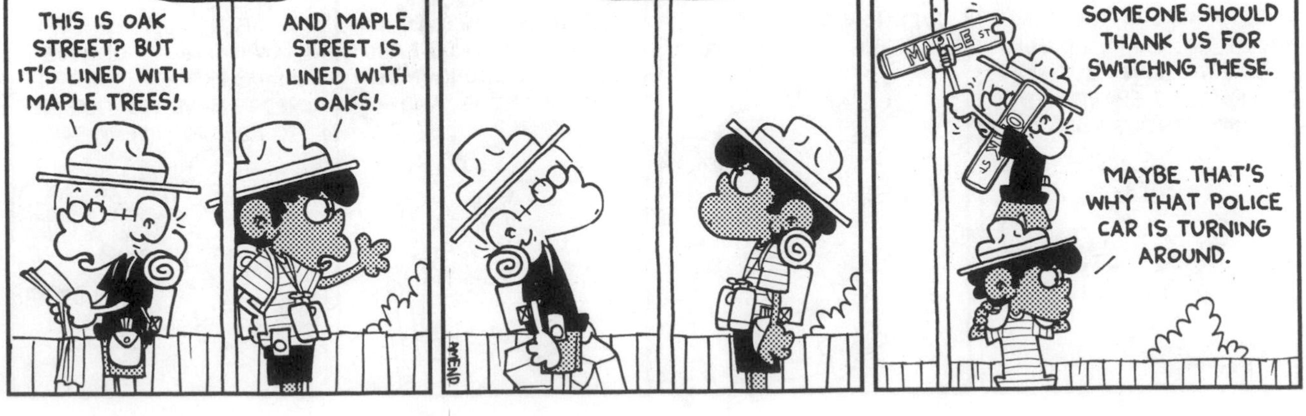
THIS IS OAK STREET? BUT IT'S LINED WITH MAPLE TREES!
AND MAPLE STREET IS LINED WITH OAKS!
AMEND
MAPLE ST
SOMEONE SHOULD THANK US FOR SWITCHING THESE.
MAYBE THAT'S WHY THAT POLICE CAR IS TURNING AROUND.

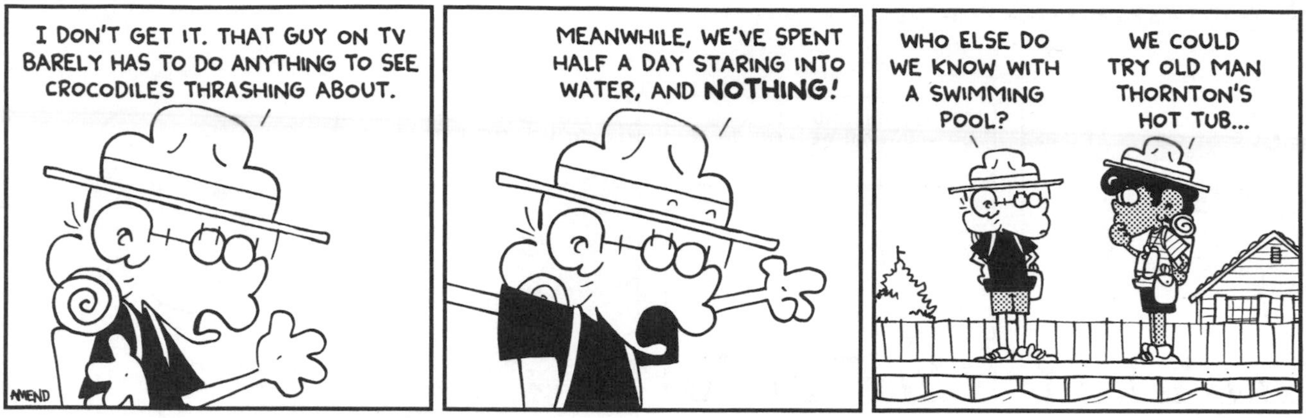
I DON'T GET IT. THAT GUY ON TV BARELY HAS TO DO ANYTHING TO SEE CROCODILES THRASHING ABOUT.
MEANWHILE, WE'VE SPENT HALF A DAY STARING INTO WATER, AND **NOTHING!**
WHO ELSE DO WE KNOW WITH A SWIMMING POOL?
WE COULD TRY OLD MAN THORNTON'S HOT TUB...
AMEND

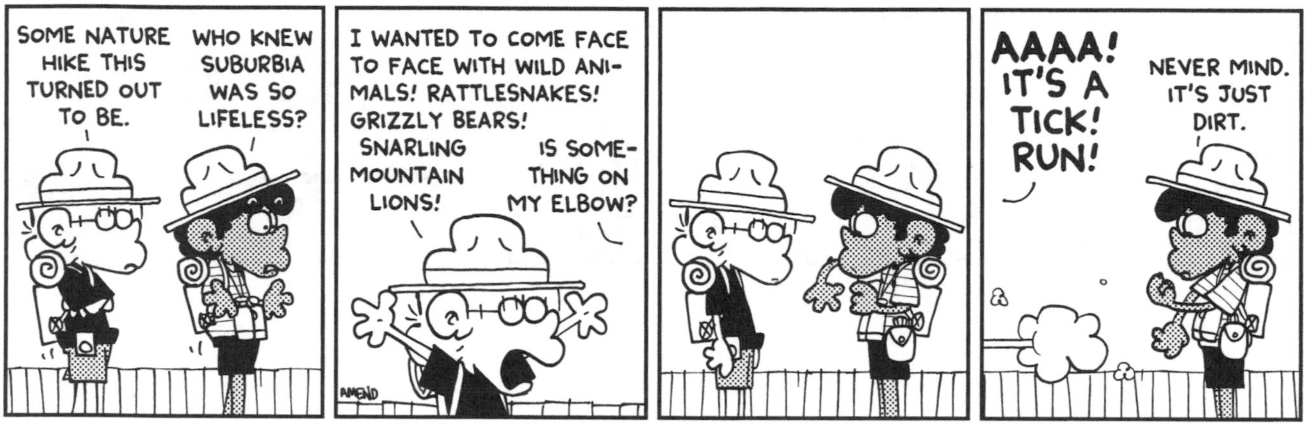
SOME NATURE HIKE THIS TURNED OUT TO BE.
WHO KNEW SUBURBIA WAS SO LIFELESS?
I WANTED TO COME FACE TO FACE WITH WILD ANIMALS! RATTLESNAKES! GRIZZLY BEARS!
SNARLING MOUNTAIN LIONS!
IS SOMETHING ON MY ELBOW?
AAAA! IT'S A TICK! RUN!
NEVER MIND. IT'S JUST DIRT.
AMEND

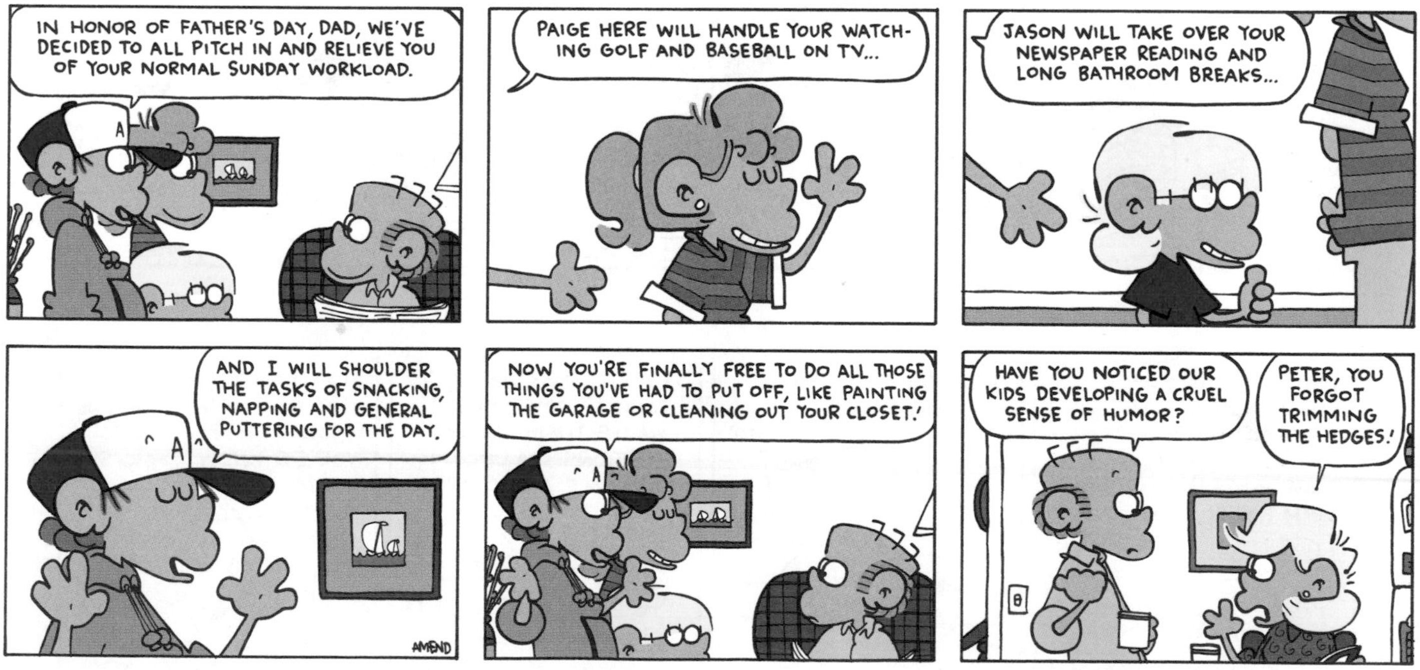
IN HONOR OF FATHER'S DAY, DAD, WE'VE DECIDED TO ALL PITCH IN AND RELIEVE YOU OF YOUR NORMAL SUNDAY WORKLOAD.
PAIGE HERE WILL HANDLE YOUR WATCHING GOLF AND BASEBALL ON TV...
JASON WILL TAKE OVER YOUR NEWSPAPER READING AND LONG BATHROOM BREAKS...
AND I WILL SHOULDER THE TASKS OF SNACKING, NAPPING AND GENERAL PUTTERING FOR THE DAY.
NOW YOU'RE FINALLY FREE TO DO ALL THOSE THINGS YOU'VE HAD TO PUT OFF, LIKE PAINTING THE GARAGE OR CLEANING OUT YOUR CLOSET!
HAVE YOU NOTICED OUR KIDS DEVELOPING A CRUEL SENSE OF HUMOR?
PETER, YOU FORGOT TRIMMING THE HEDGES!
AMEND

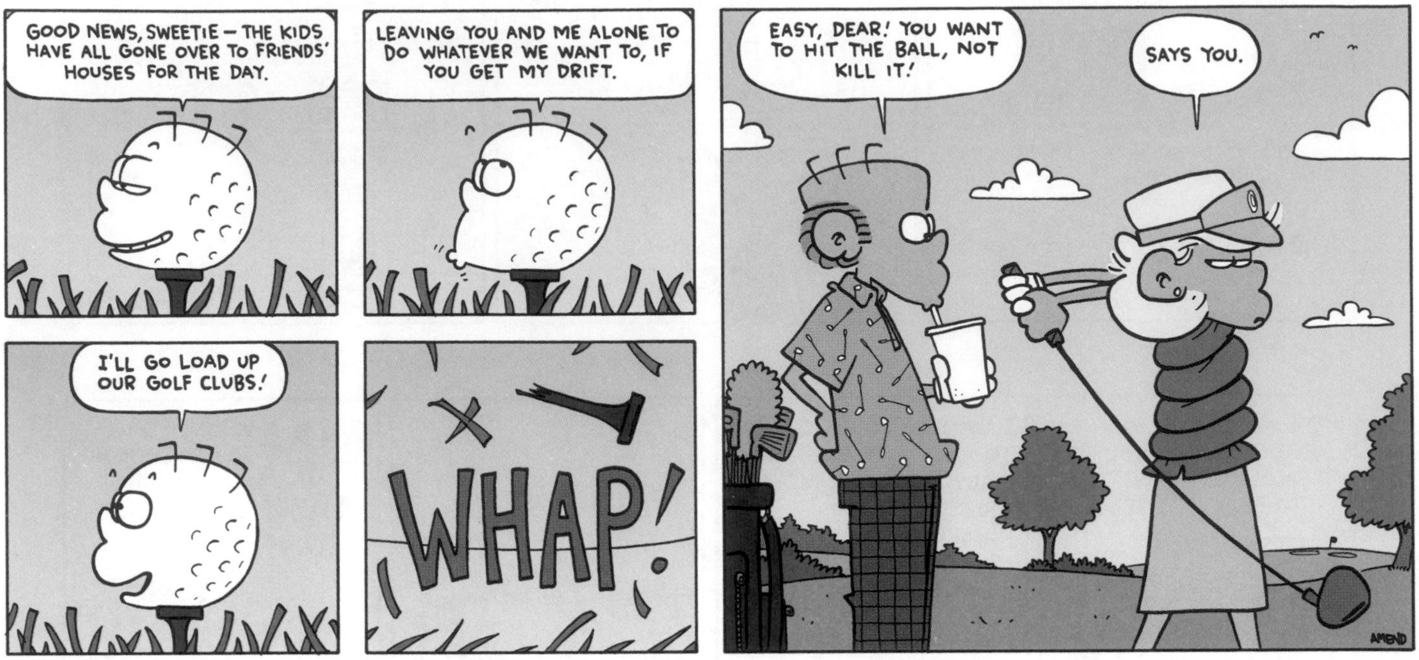
GOOD NEWS, SWEETIE — THE KIDS HAVE ALL GONE OVER TO FRIENDS' HOUSES FOR THE DAY.
LEAVING YOU AND ME ALONE TO DO WHATEVER WE WANT TO, IF YOU GET MY DRIFT.
I'LL GO LOAD UP OUR GOLF CLUBS!
WHAP!
EASY, DEAR! YOU WANT TO HIT THE BALL, NOT KILL IT!
SAYS YOU.
AMEND

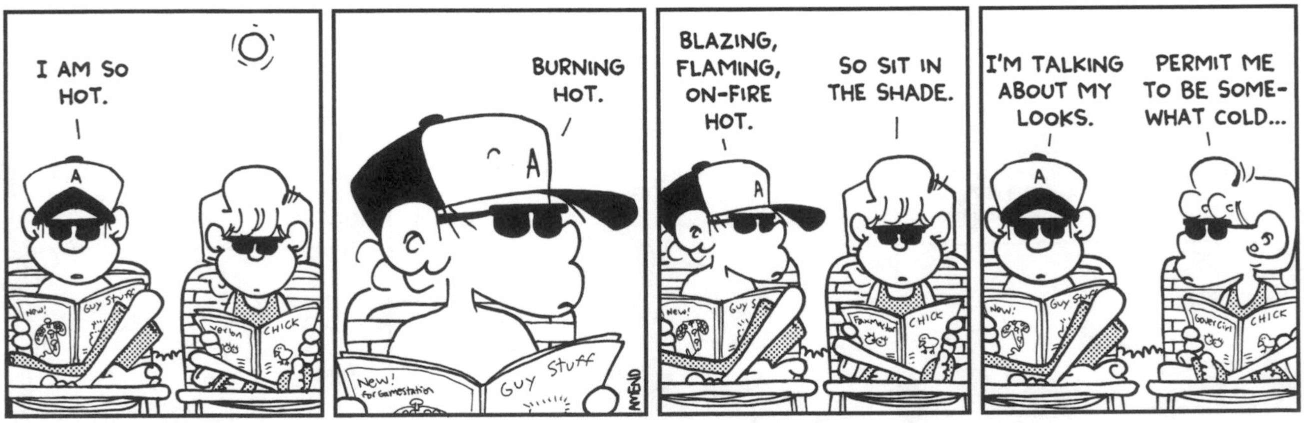
I AM SO HOT.
BURNING HOT.
BLAZING, FLAMING, ON-FIRE HOT.
SO SIT IN THE SHADE.
I'M TALKING ABOUT MY LOOKS.
PERMIT ME TO BE SOME-WHAT COLD...
AMEND

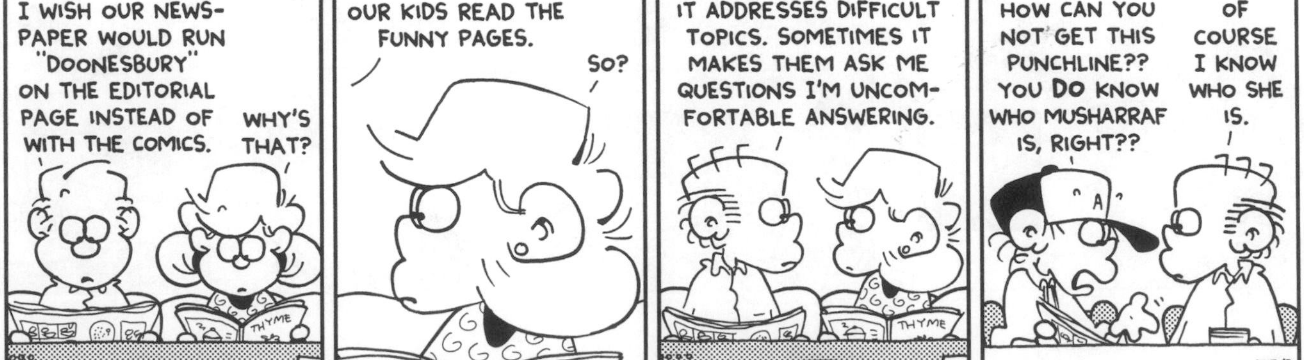
I WISH OUR NEWS-PAPER WOULD RUN "DOONESBURY" ON THE EDITORIAL PAGE INSTEAD OF WITH THE COMICS.
WHY'S THAT?
OUR KIDS READ THE FUNNY PAGES.
SO?
IT ADDRESSES DIFFICULT TOPICS. SOMETIMES IT MAKES THEM ASK ME QUESTIONS I'M UNCOM-FORTABLE ANSWERING.
HOW CAN YOU NOT GET THIS PUNCHLINE?? YOU DO KNOW WHO MUSHARRAF IS, RIGHT??
OF COURSE I KNOW WHO SHE IS.
AMEND

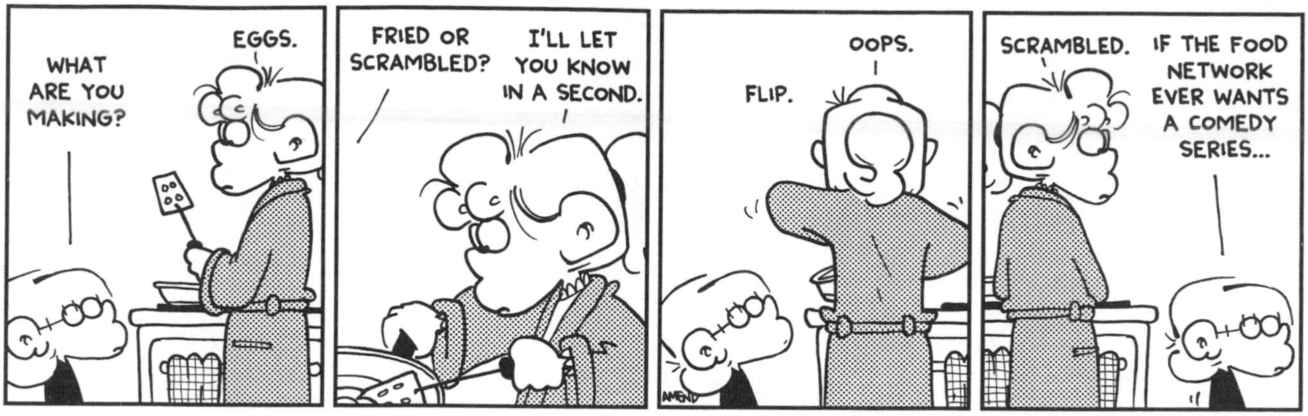
WHAT ARE YOU MAKING?
EGGS.
FRIED OR SCRAMBLED?
I'LL LET YOU KNOW IN A SECOND.
FLIP.
OOPS.
SCRAMBLED.
IF THE FOOD NETWORK EVER WANTS A COMEDY SERIES...
AMEND

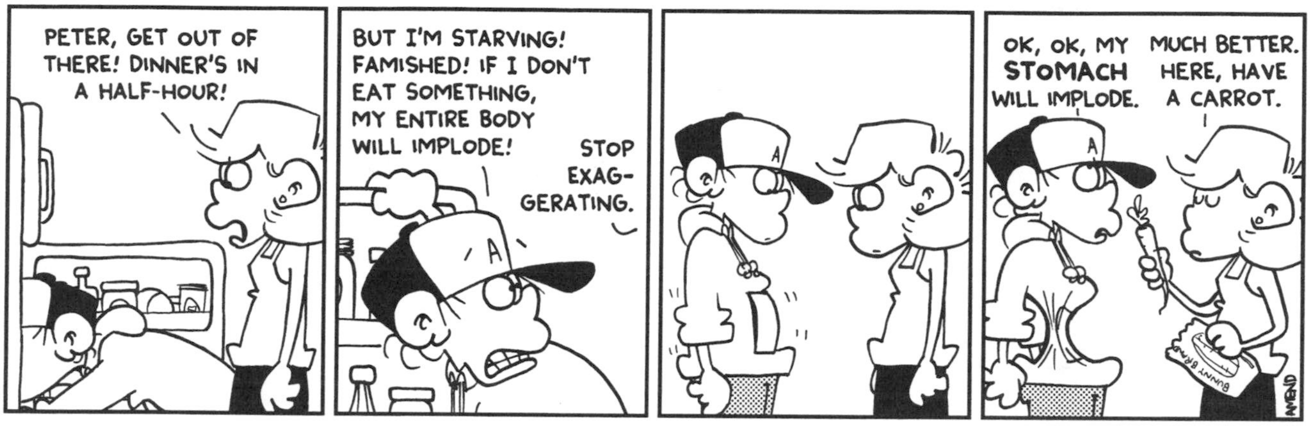
PETER, GET OUT OF THERE! DINNER'S IN A HALF-HOUR!
BUT I'M STARVING! FAMISHED! IF I DON'T EAT SOMETHING, MY ENTIRE BODY WILL IMPLODE!
STOP EXAG-GERATING.
OK, OK, MY STOMACH WILL IMPLODE.
MUCH BETTER. HERE, HAVE A CARROT.
BUNNY BRAND
AMEND

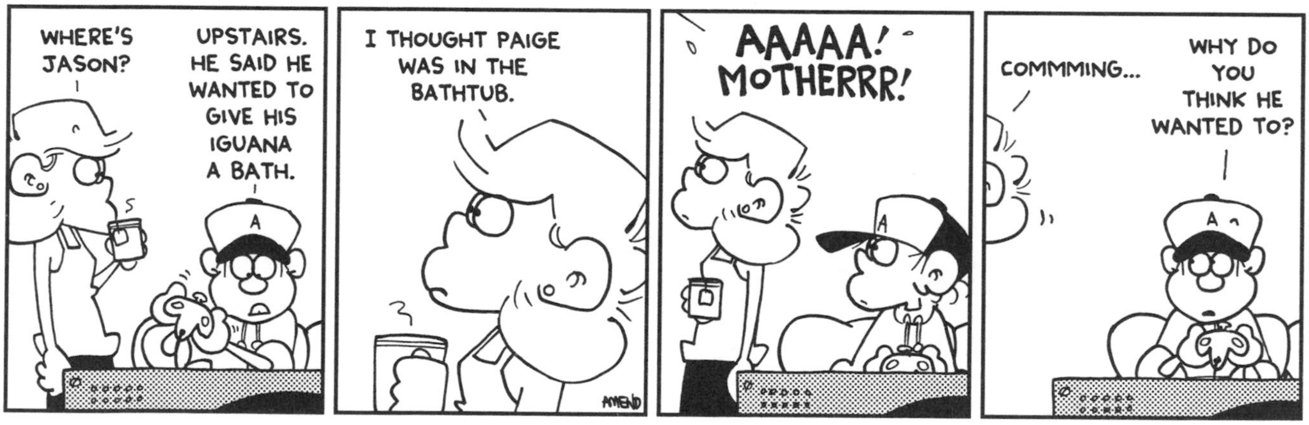
WHERE'S JASON?
UPSTAIRS. HE SAID HE WANTED TO GIVE HIS IGUANA A BATH.
I THOUGHT PAIGE WAS IN THE BATHTUB.
AMEND
AAAAA! MOTHERRR!
COMMMING...
WHY DO YOU THINK HE WANTED TO?

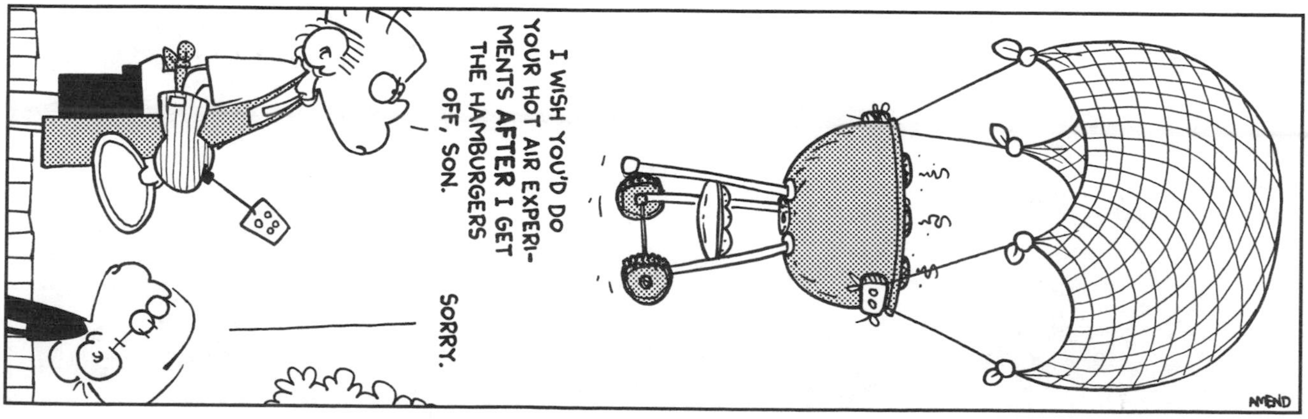
I WISH YOU'D DO YOUR HOT AIR EXPERI-MENTS AFTER I GET THE HAMBURGERS OFF, SON.
SORRY.
AMEND

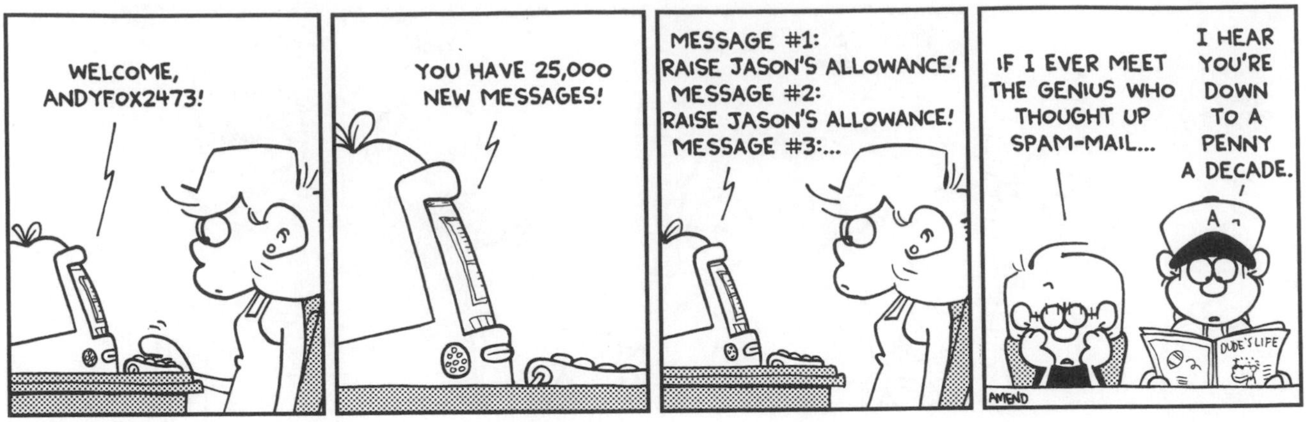
WELCOME, ANDYFOX2473!
YOU HAVE 25,000 NEW MESSAGES!
MESSAGE #1: RAISE JASON'S ALLOWANCE! MESSAGE #2: RAISE JASON'S ALLOWANCE! MESSAGE #3:...
IF I EVER MEET THE GENIUS WHO THOUGHT UP SPAM-MAIL...
I HEAR YOU'RE DOWN TO A PENNY A DECADE.
DUDE'S LIFE
AMEND

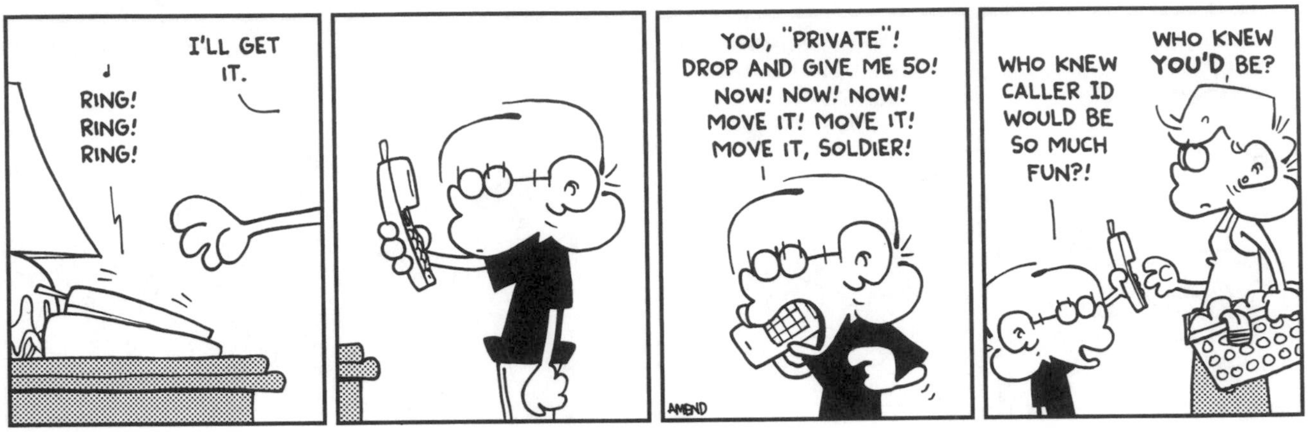
RING! RING! RING!
I'LL GET IT.
YOU, "PRIVATE"! DROP AND GIVE ME 50! NOW! NOW! NOW! MOVE IT! MOVE IT! MOVE IT, SOLDIER!
AMEND
WHO KNEW CALLER ID WOULD BE SO MUCH FUN?!
WHO KNEW YOU'D BE?

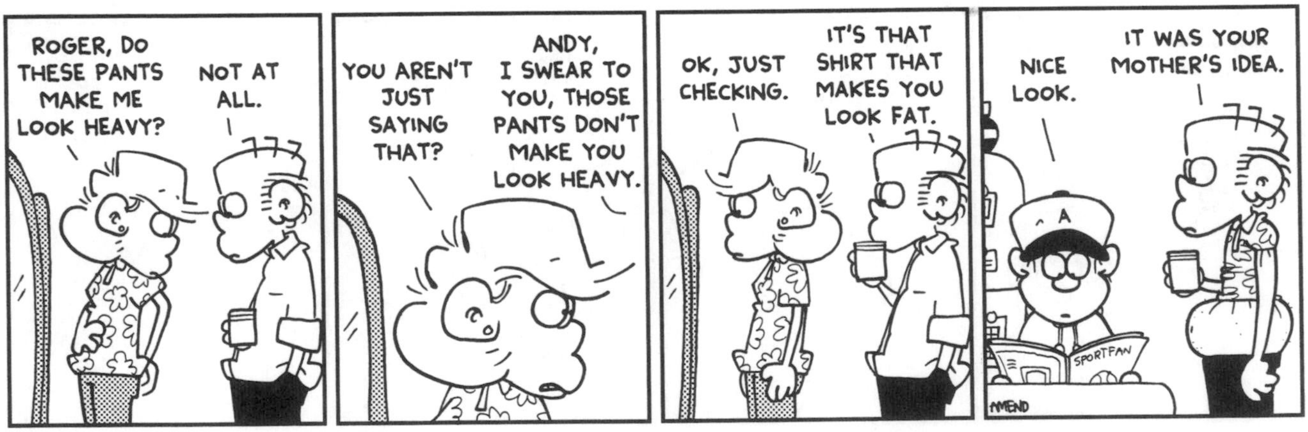
ROGER, DO THESE PANTS MAKE ME LOOK HEAVY?
NOT AT ALL.
YOU AREN'T JUST SAYING THAT?
ANDY, I SWEAR TO YOU, THOSE PANTS DON'T MAKE YOU LOOK HEAVY.
OK, JUST CHECKING.
IT'S THAT SHIRT THAT MAKES YOU LOOK FAT.
NICE LOOK.
IT WAS YOUR MOTHER'S IDEA.
SPORTFAN
AMEND

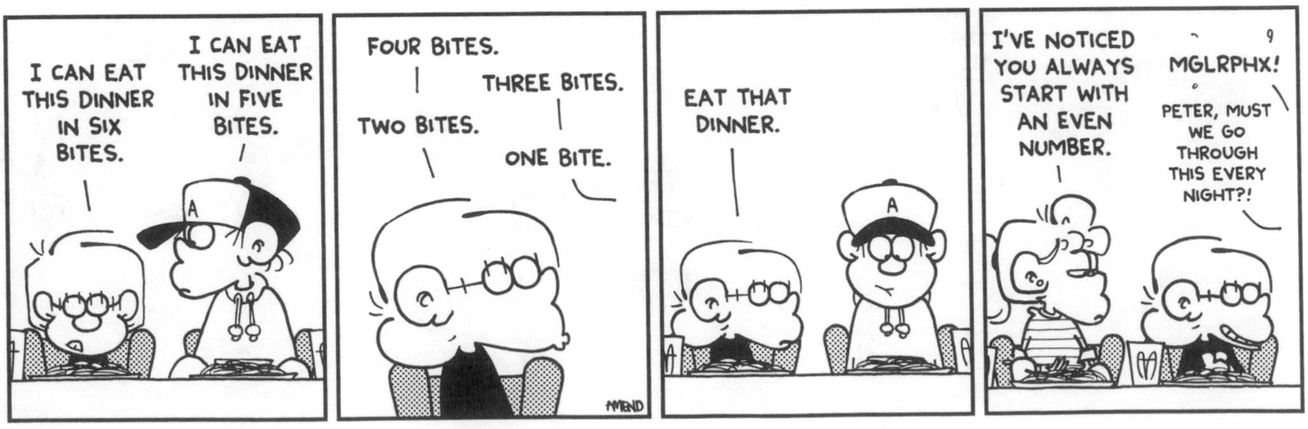
I CAN EAT THIS DINNER IN SIX BITES.
I CAN EAT THIS DINNER IN FIVE BITES.
FOUR BITES.
THREE BITES.
TWO BITES.
ONE BITE.
AMEND
EAT THAT DINNER.
I'VE NOTICED YOU ALWAYS START WITH AN EVEN NUMBER.
MGLRPHX!
PETER, MUST WE GO THROUGH THIS EVERY NIGHT?!

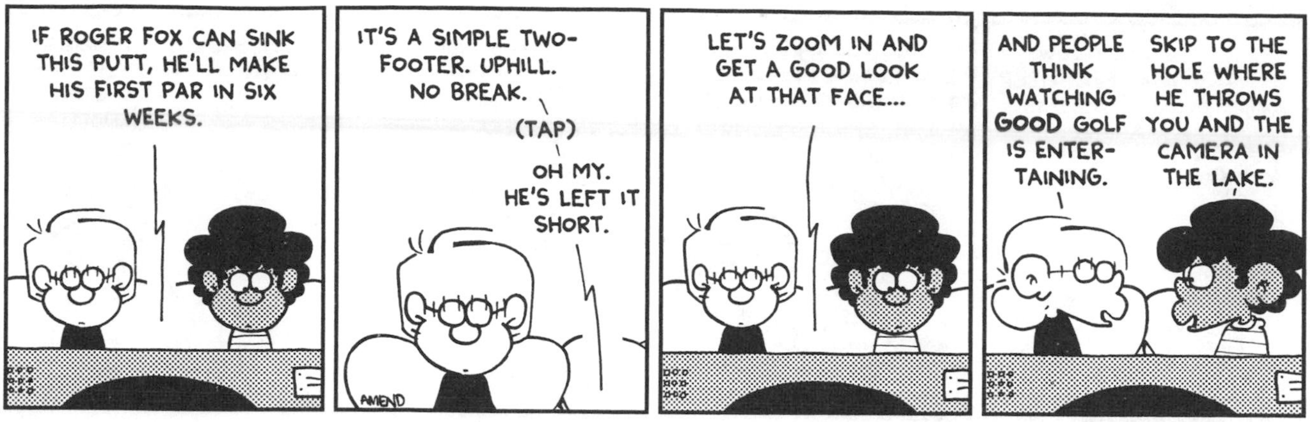
IF ROGER FOX CAN SINK THIS PUTT, HE'LL MAKE HIS FIRST PAR IN SIX WEEKS.
IT'S A SIMPLE TWO-FOOTER. UPHILL. NO BREAK.
(TAP)
OH MY. HE'S LEFT IT SHORT.
LET'S ZOOM IN AND GET A GOOD LOOK AT THAT FACE...
AND PEOPLE THINK WATCHING GOOD GOLF IS ENTERTAINING.
SKIP TO THE HOLE WHERE HE THROWS YOU AND THE CAMERA IN THE LAKE.
AMEND

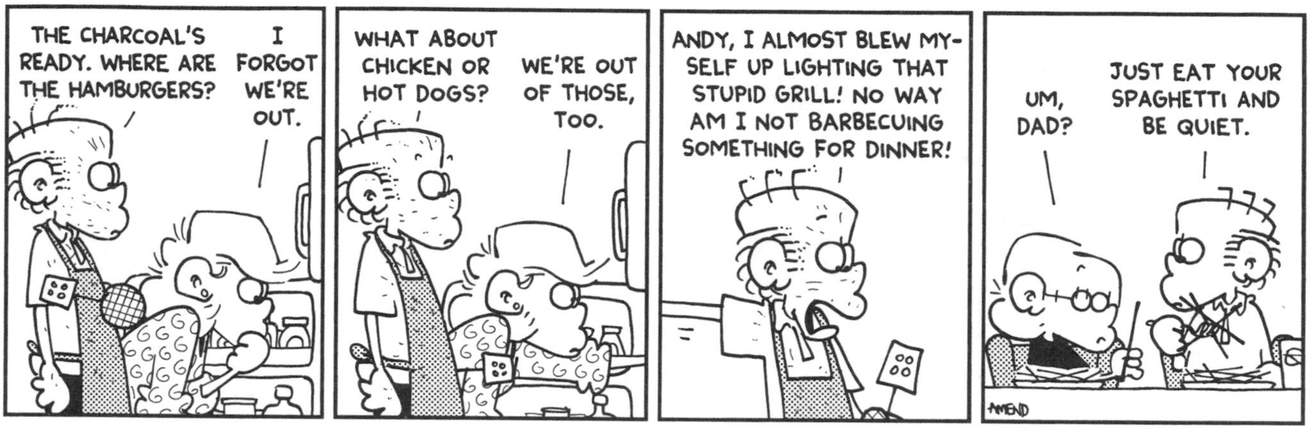
THE CHARCOAL'S READY. WHERE ARE THE HAMBURGERS?
I FORGOT WE'RE OUT.
WHAT ABOUT CHICKEN OR HOT DOGS?
WE'RE OUT OF THOSE, TOO.
ANDY, I ALMOST BLEW MYSELF UP LIGHTING THAT STUPID GRILL! NO WAY AM I NOT BARBECUING SOMETHING FOR DINNER!
UM, DAD?
JUST EAT YOUR SPAGHETTI AND BE QUIET.
AMEND

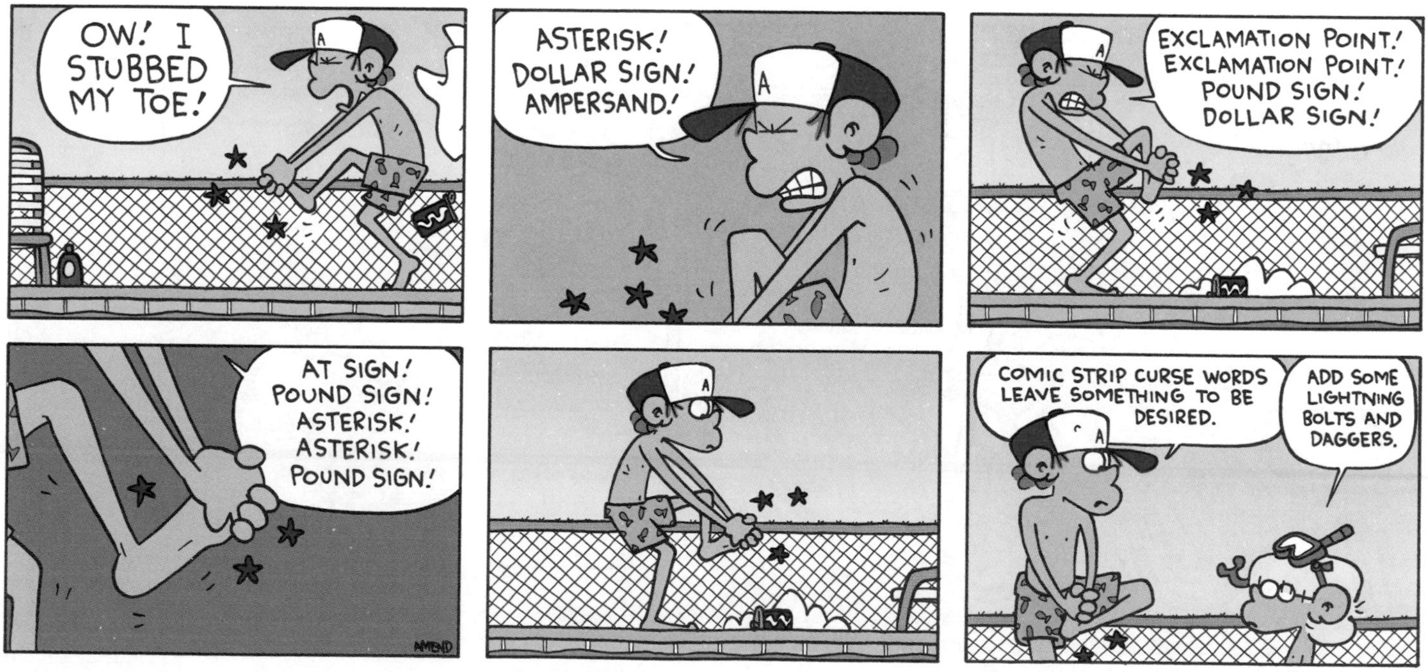
OW! I STUBBED MY TOE!
ASTERISK! DOLLAR SIGN! AMPERSAND!
EXCLAMATION POINT! EXCLAMATION POINT! POUND SIGN! DOLLAR SIGN!
AT SIGN! POUND SIGN! ASTERISK! ASTERISK! POUND SIGN!
AMEND
COMIC STRIP CURSE WORDS LEAVE SOMETHING TO BE DESIRED.
ADD SOME LIGHTNING BOLTS AND DAGGERS.

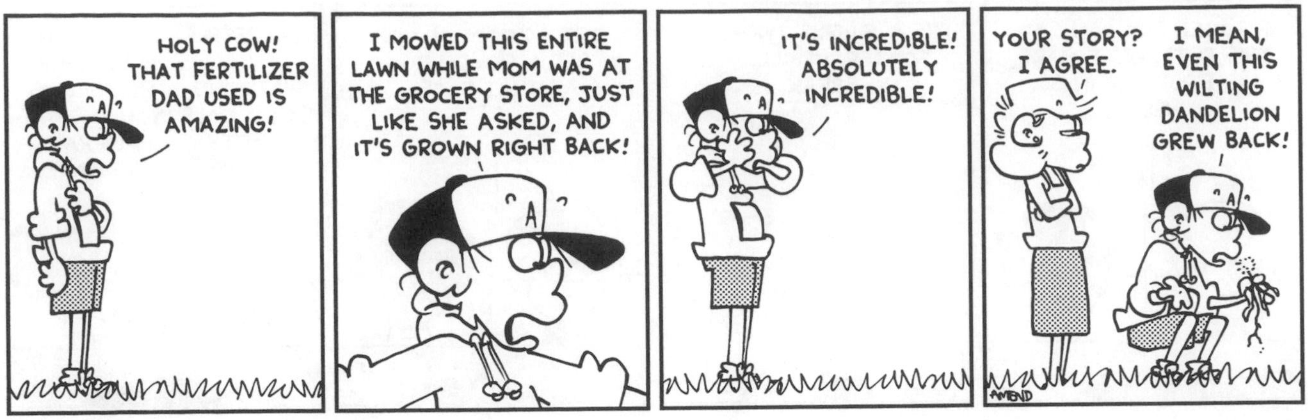
HOLY COW! THAT FERTILIZER DAD USED IS AMAZING!
I MOWED THIS ENTIRE LAWN WHILE MOM WAS AT THE GROCERY STORE, JUST LIKE SHE ASKED, AND IT'S GROWN RIGHT BACK!
IT'S INCREDIBLE! ABSOLUTELY INCREDIBLE!
YOUR STORY? I AGREE.
I MEAN, EVEN THIS WILTING DANDELION GREW BACK!
AMEND

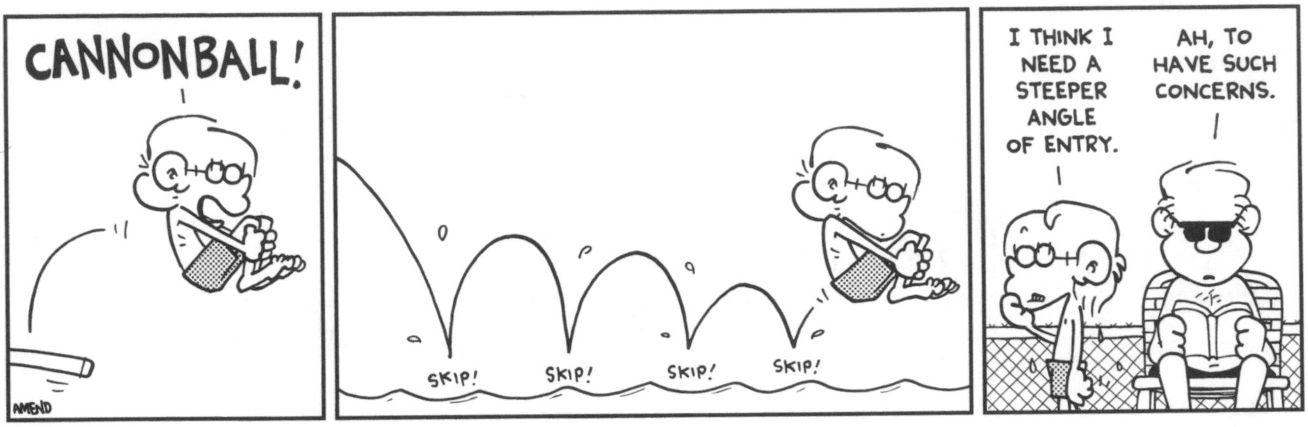
CANNONBALL!
AMEND
SKIP!
SKIP!
SKIP!
SKIP!
I THINK I NEED A STEEPER ANGLE OF ENTRY.
AH, TO HAVE SUCH CONCERNS.

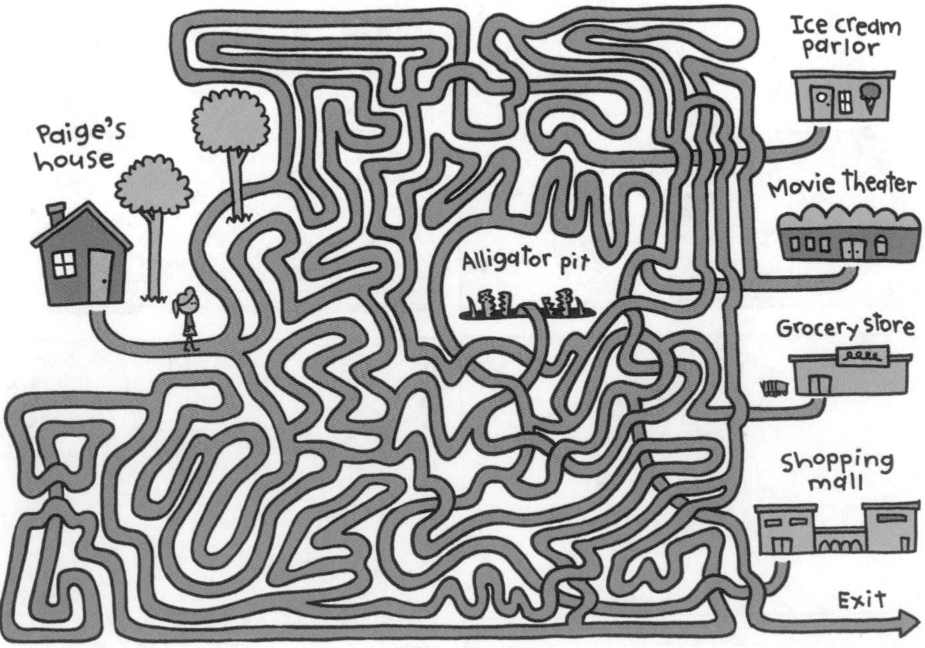
Paige's house
Ice cream parlor
Movie theater
Alligator pit
Grocery store
Shopping mall
Exit

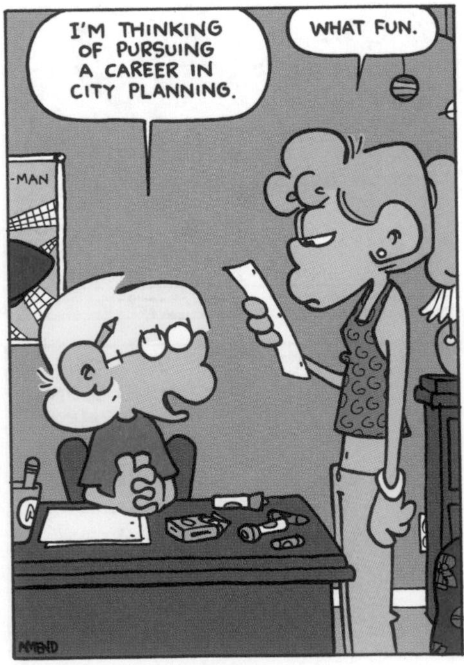
I'M THINKING OF PURSUING A CAREER IN CITY PLANNING.
WHAT FUN.
-MAN
AMEND

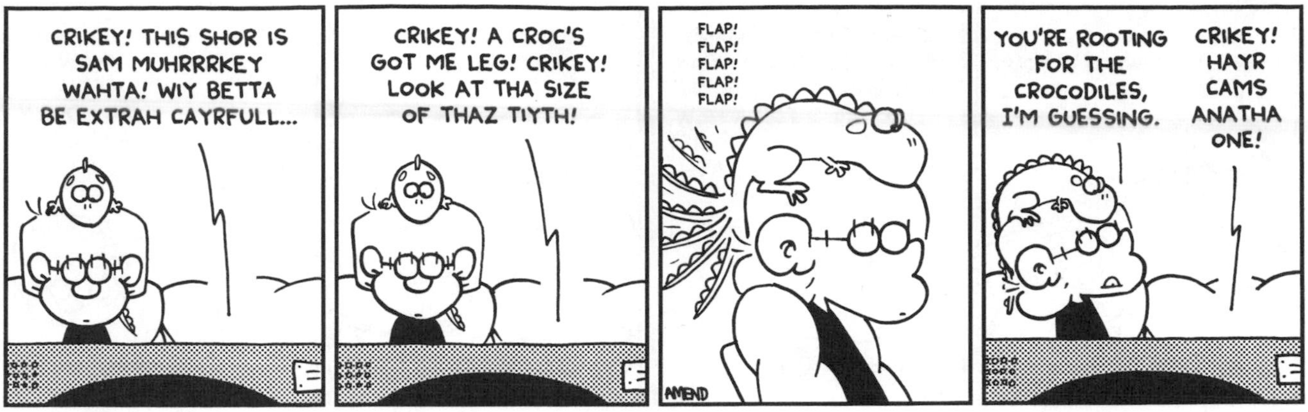
CRIKEY! THIS SHOR IS SAM MUHRRRKEY WAHTA! WIY BETTA BE EXTRAH CAYRFULL...
CRIKEY! A CROC'S GOT ME LEG! CRIKEY! LOOK AT THA SIZE OF THAZ TIYTH!
FLAP! FLAP! FLAP! FLAP! FLAP!
YOU'RE ROOTING FOR THE CROCODILES, I'M GUESSING.
CRIKEY! HAYR CAMS ANATHA ONE!
AMEND

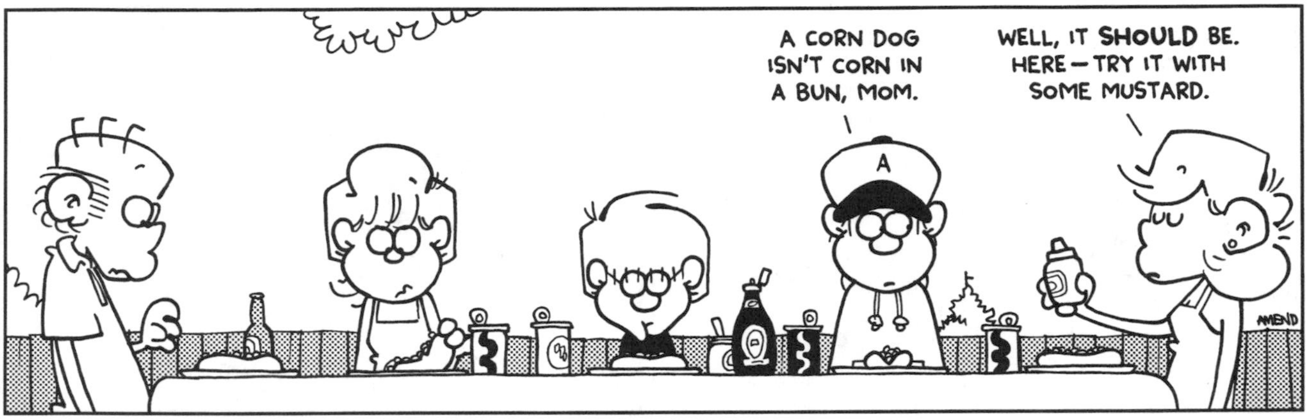
A CORN DOG ISN'T CORN IN A BUN, MOM.
WELL, IT **SHOULD** BE. HERE—TRY IT WITH SOME MUSTARD.
AMEND

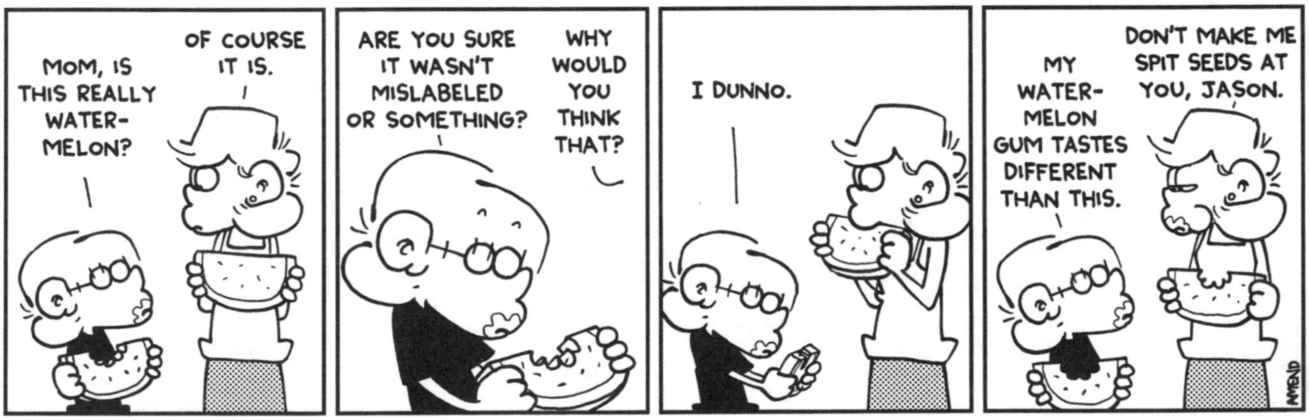
MOM, IS THIS REALLY WATER-MELON?
OF COURSE IT IS.
ARE YOU SURE IT WASN'T MISLABELED OR SOMETHING?
WHY WOULD YOU THINK THAT?
I DUNNO.
MY WATER-MELON GUM TASTES DIFFERENT THAN THIS.
DON'T MAKE ME SPIT SEEDS AT YOU, JASON.
AMEND

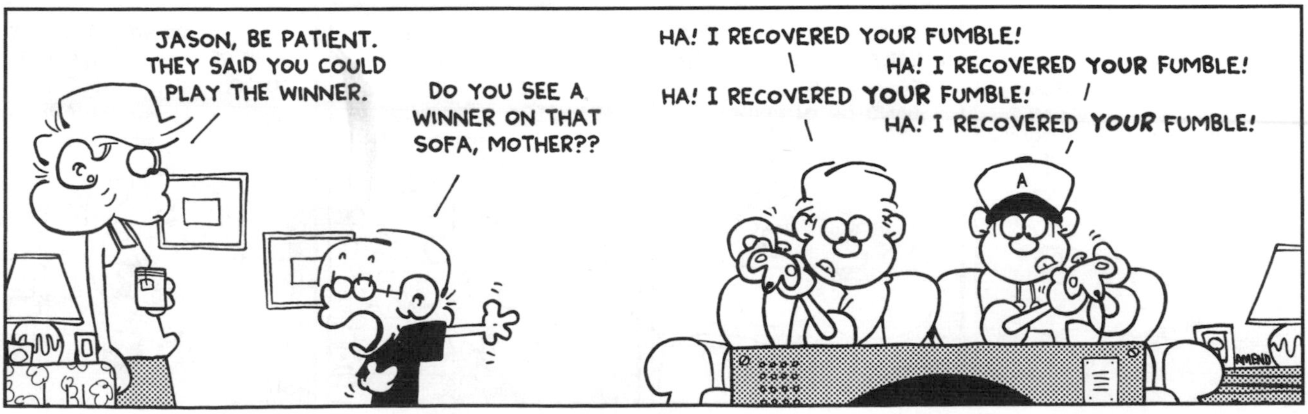
JASON, BE PATIENT. THEY SAID YOU COULD PLAY THE WINNER.
DO YOU SEE A WINNER ON THAT SOFA, MOTHER??
HA! I RECOVERED YOUR FUMBLE!
HA! I RECOVERED **YOUR** FUMBLE!
HA! I RECOVERED **YOUR** FUMBLE!
HA! I RECOVERED **YOUR** FUMBLE!
AMEND

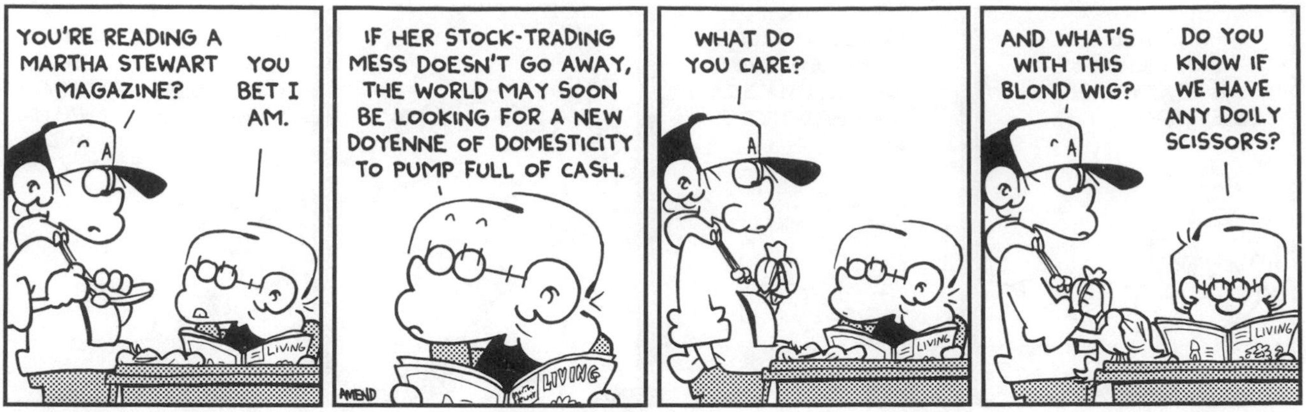
YOU'RE READING A MARTHA STEWART MAGAZINE?
YOU BET I AM.
LIVING
IF HER STOCK-TRADING MESS DOESN'T GO AWAY, THE WORLD MAY SOON BE LOOKING FOR A NEW DOYENNE OF DOMESTICITY TO PUMP FULL OF CASH.
AMEND
LIVING
WHAT DO YOU CARE?
LIVING
AND WHAT'S WITH THIS BLOND WIG?
DO YOU KNOW IF WE HAVE ANY DOILY SCISSORS?
LIVING

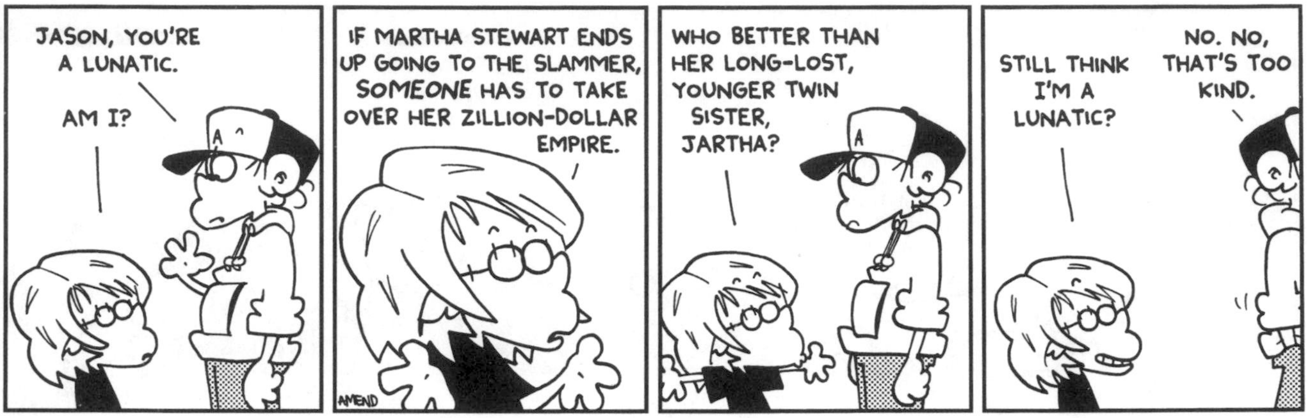
JASON, YOU'RE A LUNATIC.
AM I?
IF MARTHA STEWART ENDS UP GOING TO THE SLAMMER, SOMEONE HAS TO TAKE OVER HER ZILLION-DOLLAR EMPIRE.
AMEND
WHO BETTER THAN HER LONG-LOST, YOUNGER TWIN SISTER, JARTHA?
STILL THINK I'M A LUNATIC?
NO. NO, THAT'S TOO KIND.

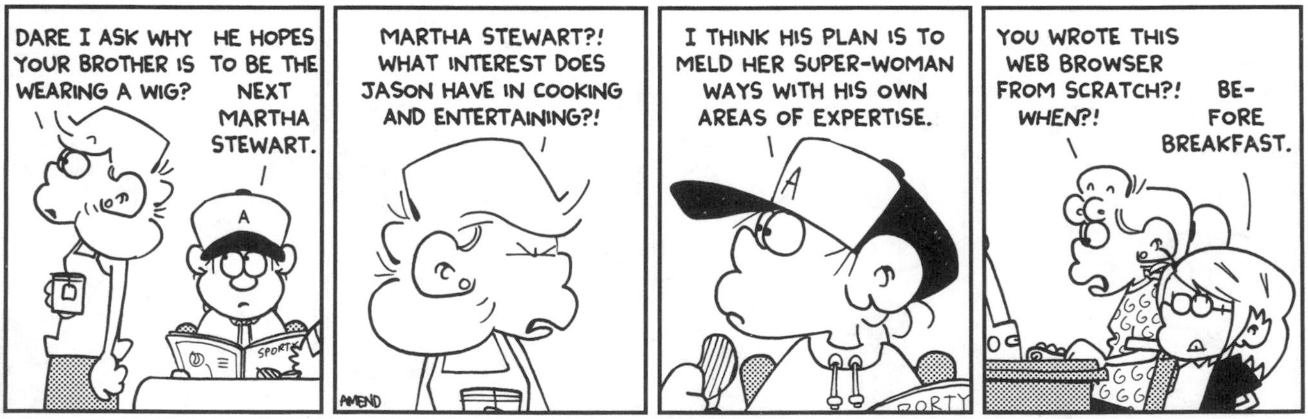
DARE I ASK WHY YOUR BROTHER IS WEARING A WIG?
HE HOPES TO BE THE NEXT MARTHA STEWART.
MARTHA STEWART?! WHAT INTEREST DOES JASON HAVE IN COOKING AND ENTERTAINING?!
AMEND
I THINK HIS PLAN IS TO MELD HER SUPER-WOMAN WAYS WITH HIS OWN AREAS OF EXPERTISE.
YOU WROTE THIS WEB BROWSER FROM SCRATCH?! WHEN?!
BE-FORE BREAKFAST.

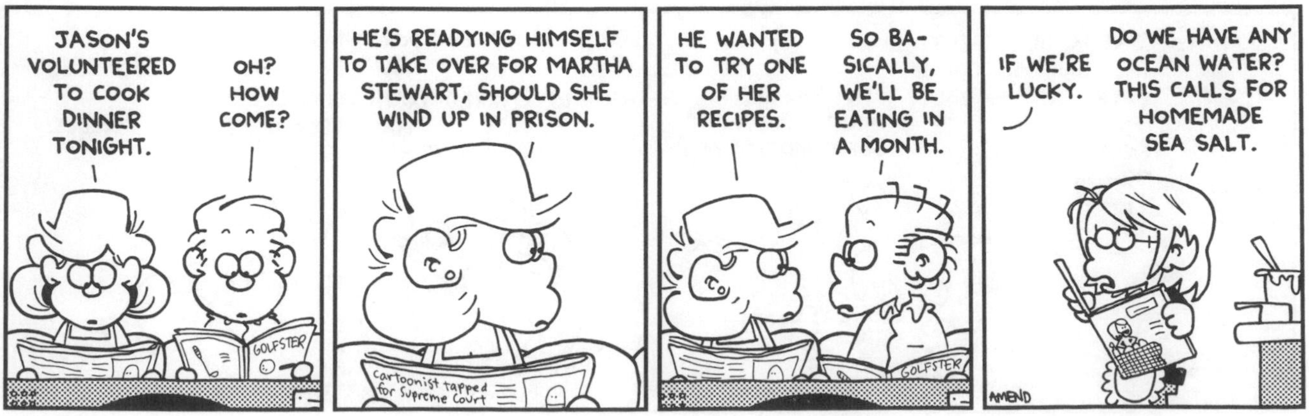
JASON'S VOLUNTEERED TO COOK DINNER TONIGHT.
OH? HOW COME?
GOLFSTER
HE'S READYING HIMSELF TO TAKE OVER FOR MARTHA STEWART, SHOULD SHE WIND UP IN PRISON.
Cartoonist tapped for Supreme Court
HE WANTED TO TRY ONE OF HER RECIPES.
SO BA-SICALLY, WE'LL BE EATING IN A MONTH.
GOLFSTER
IF WE'RE LUCKY.
DO WE HAVE ANY OCEAN WATER? THIS CALLS FOR HOMEMADE SEA SALT.
AMEND

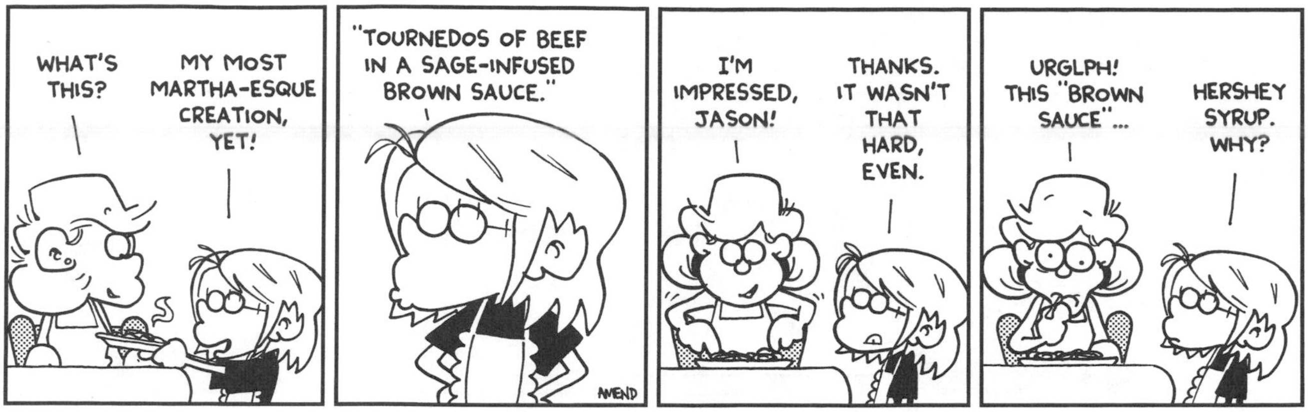
WHAT'S THIS?
MY MOST MARTHA-ESQUE CREATION, YET!
"TOURNEDOS OF BEEF IN A SAGE-INFUSED BROWN SAUCE."
I'M IMPRESSED, JASON!
THANKS. IT WASN'T THAT HARD, EVEN.
URGLPH! THIS "BROWN SAUCE"...
HERSHEY SYRUP. WHY?
AMEND

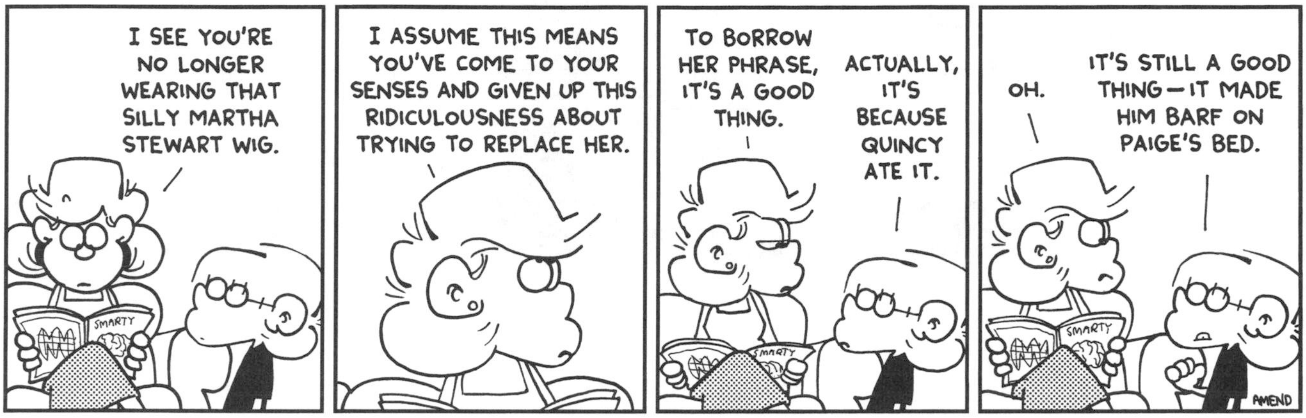
I SEE YOU'RE NO LONGER WEARING THAT SILLY MARTHA STEWART WIG.
I ASSUME THIS MEANS YOU'VE COME TO YOUR SENSES AND GIVEN UP THIS RIDICULOUSNESS ABOUT TRYING TO REPLACE HER.
TO BORROW HER PHRASE, IT'S A GOOD THING.
ACTUALLY, IT'S BECAUSE QUINCY ATE IT.
OH.
IT'S STILL A GOOD THING—IT MADE HIM BARF ON PAIGE'S BED.
SMARTY
AMEND

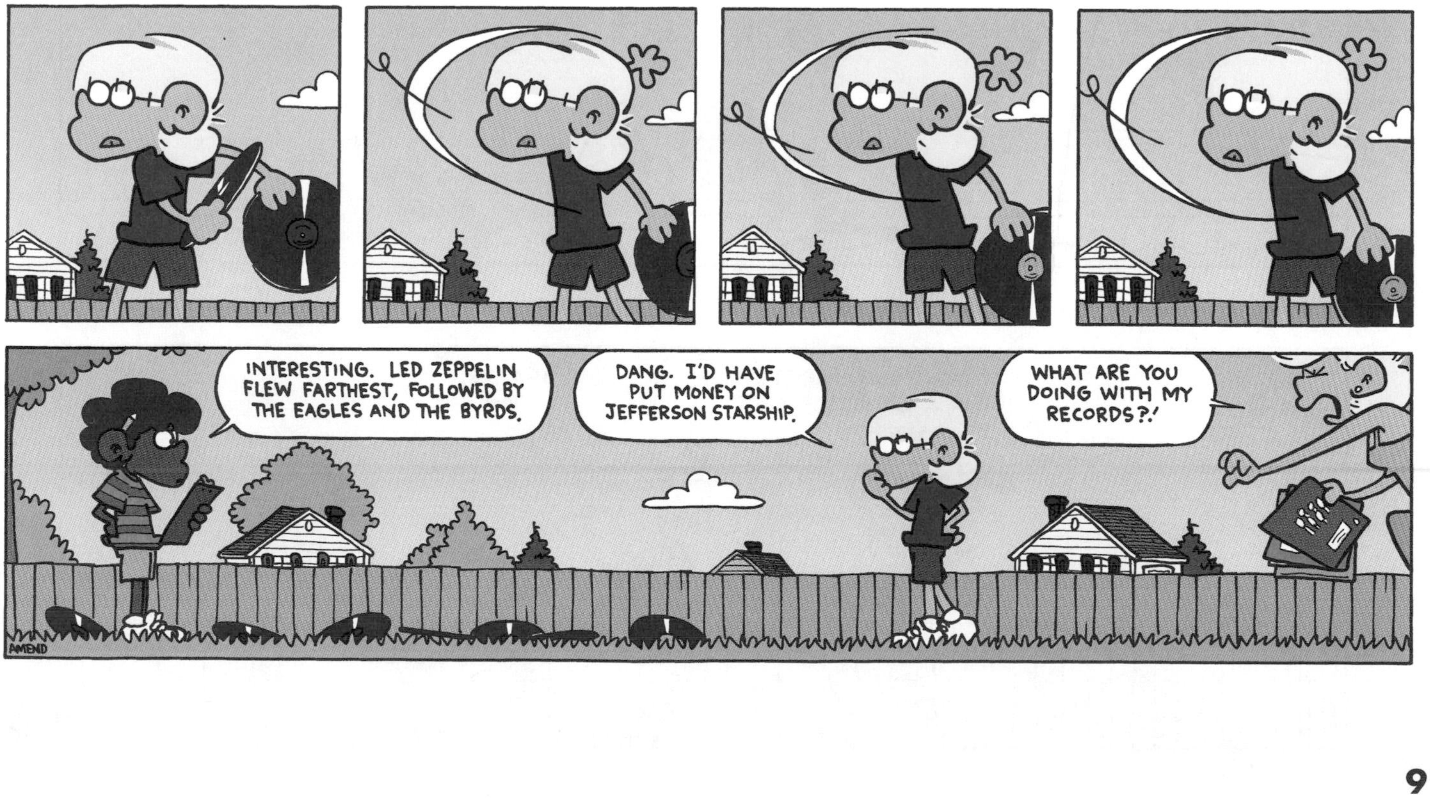
INTERESTING. LED ZEPPELIN FLEW FARTHEST, FOLLOWED BY THE EAGLES AND THE BYRDS.
DANG. I'D HAVE PUT MONEY ON JEFFERSON STARSHIP.
WHAT ARE YOU DOING WITH MY RECORDS?!
AMEND

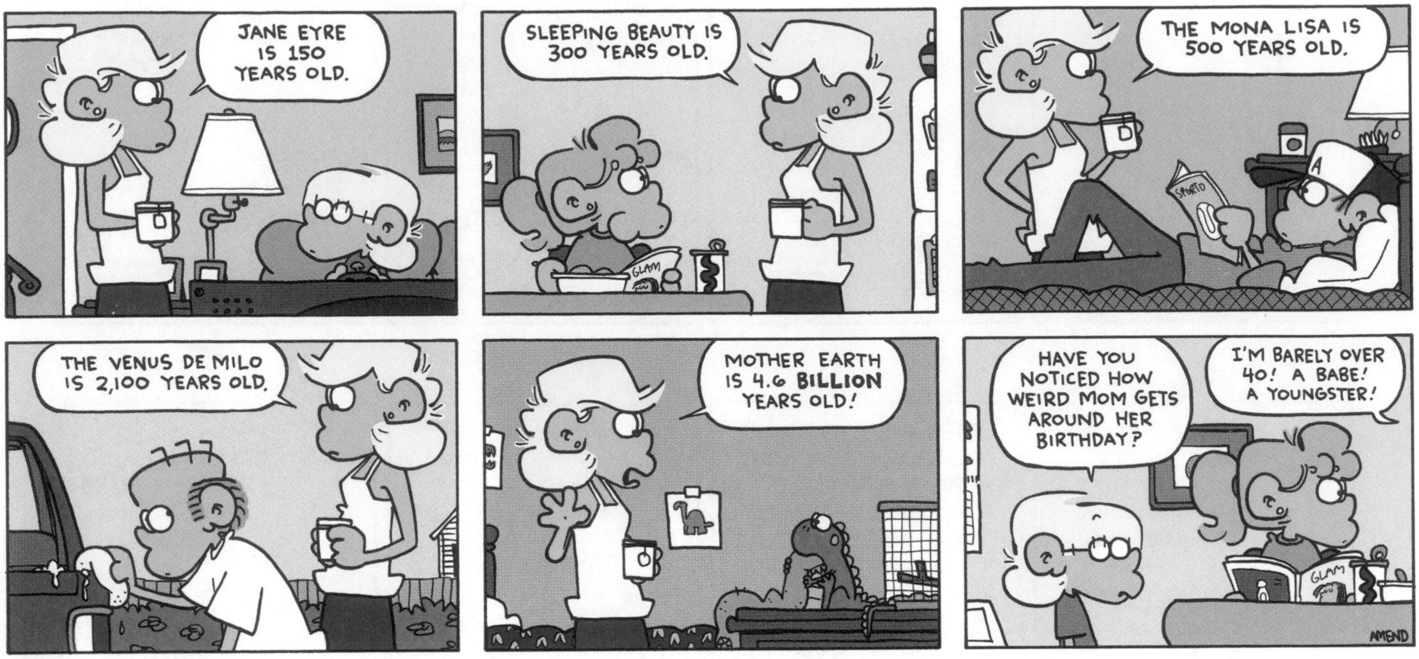
JANE EYRE IS 150 YEARS OLD.
SLEEPING BEAUTY IS 300 YEARS OLD.
THE MONA LISA IS 500 YEARS OLD.
THE VENUS DE MILO IS 2,100 YEARS OLD.
MOTHER EARTH IS 4.6 **BILLION** YEARS OLD!
HAVE YOU NOTICED HOW WEIRD MOM GETS AROUND HER BIRTHDAY?
I'M BARELY OVER 40! A BABE! A YOUNGSTER!
AMEND

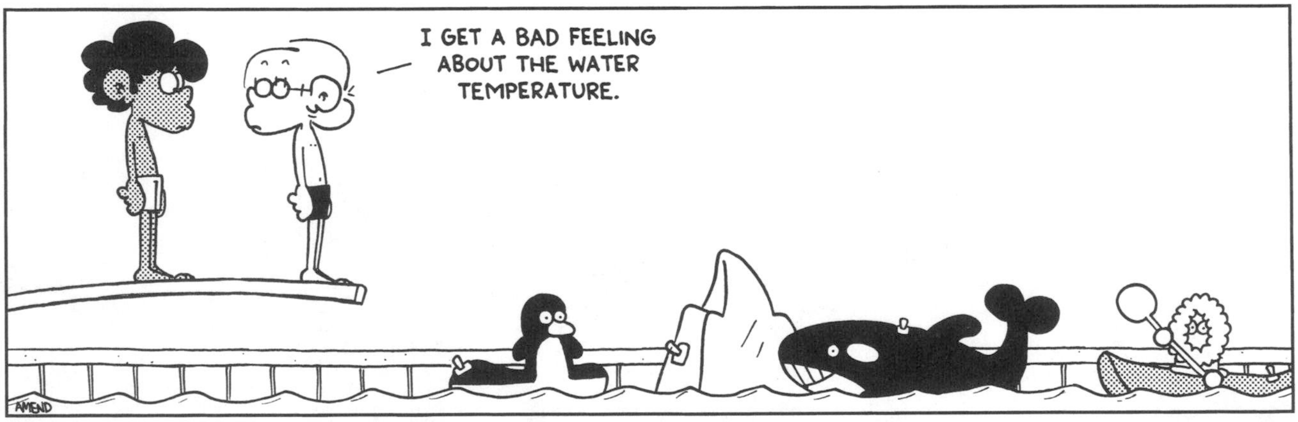
I GET A BAD FEELING ABOUT THE WATER TEMPERATURE.
AMEND

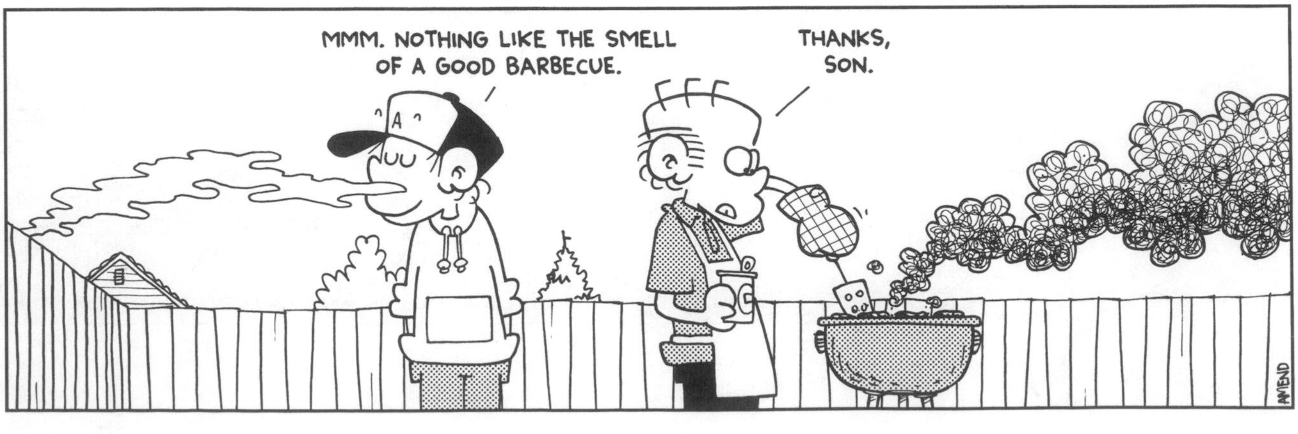
MMM. NOTHING LIKE THE SMELL OF A GOOD BARBECUE.
THANKS, SON.
AMEND

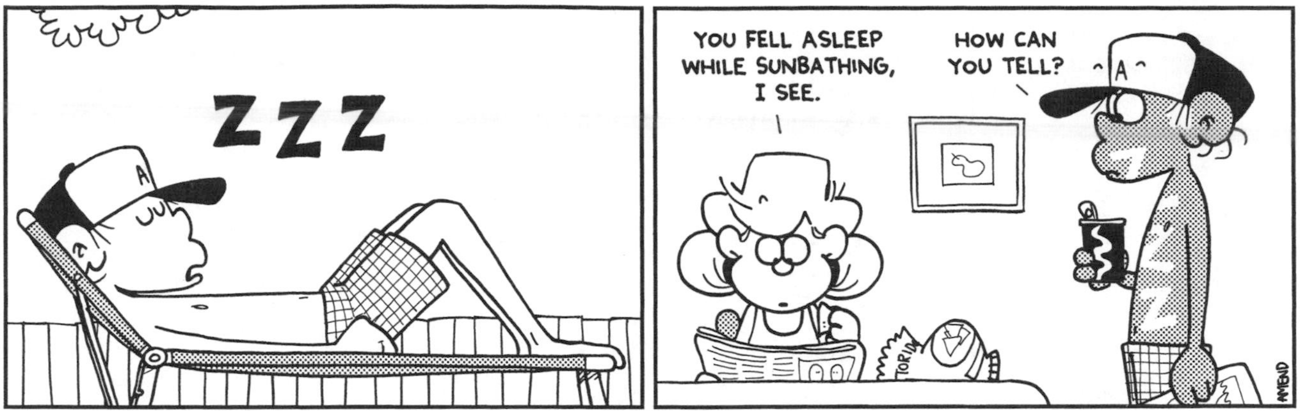
ZZZ
YOU FELL ASLEEP WHILE SUNBATHING, I SEE.
HOW CAN YOU TELL?
AMEND

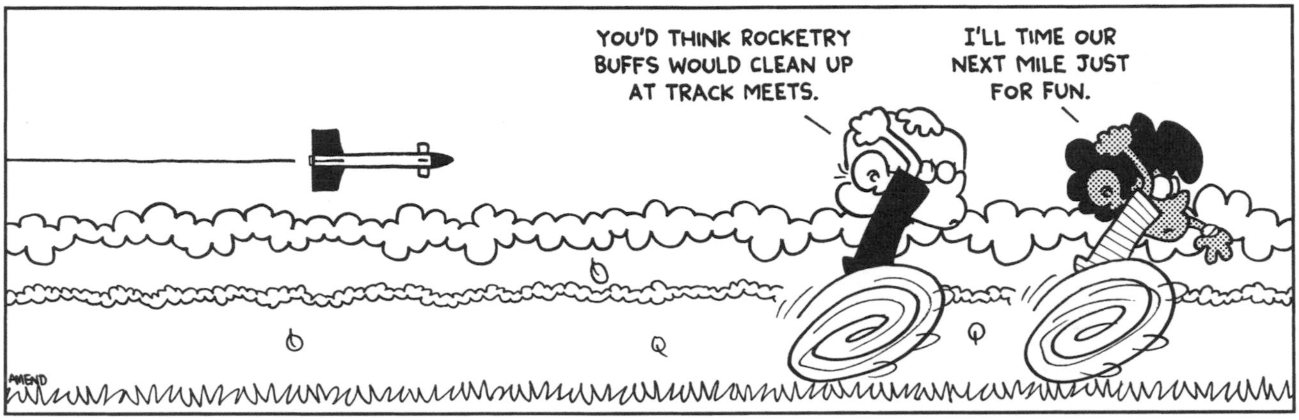
YOU'D THINK ROCKETRY BUFFS WOULD CLEAN UP AT TRACK MEETS.
I'LL TIME OUR NEXT MILE JUST FOR FUN.
AMEND

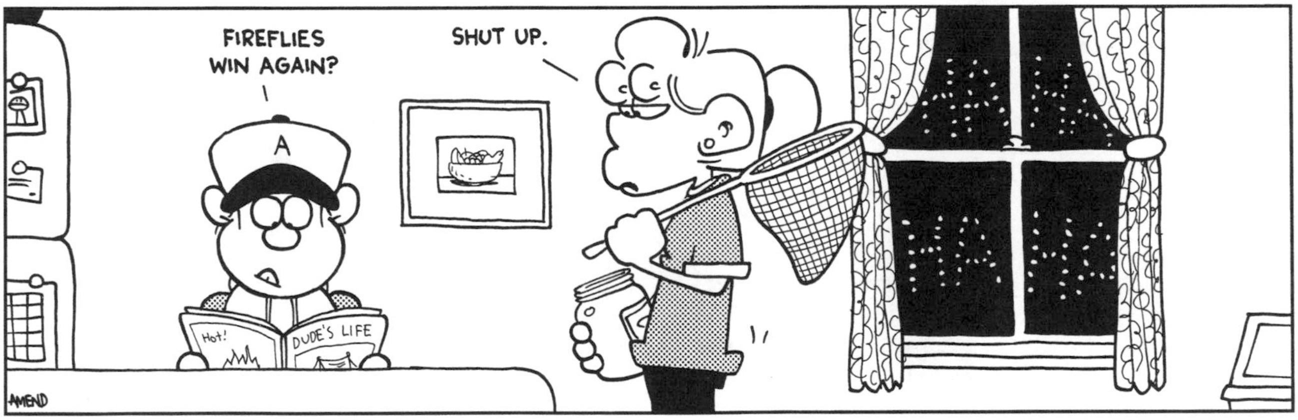
FIREFLIES WIN AGAIN?
SHUT UP.
Hot!
DUDE'S LIFE
AMEND

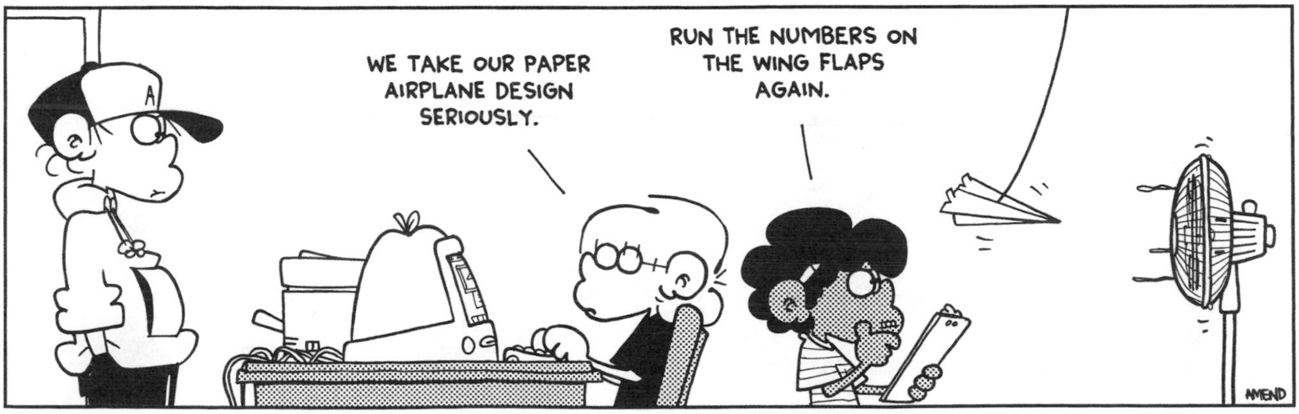
WE TAKE OUR PAPER AIRPLANE DESIGN SERIOUSLY.
RUN THE NUMBERS ON THE WING FLAPS AGAIN.
AMEND

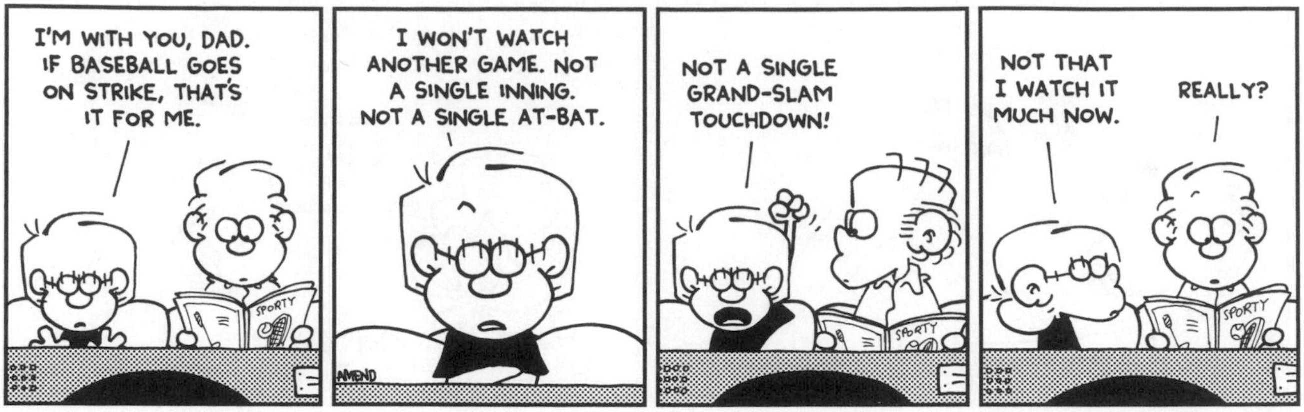
I'M WITH YOU, DAD. IF BASEBALL GOES ON STRIKE, THAT'S IT FOR ME.
I WON'T WATCH ANOTHER GAME. NOT A SINGLE INNING. NOT A SINGLE AT-BAT.
NOT A SINGLE GRAND-SLAM TOUCHDOWN!
NOT THAT I WATCH IT MUCH NOW.
REALLY?
SPORTY
AMEND

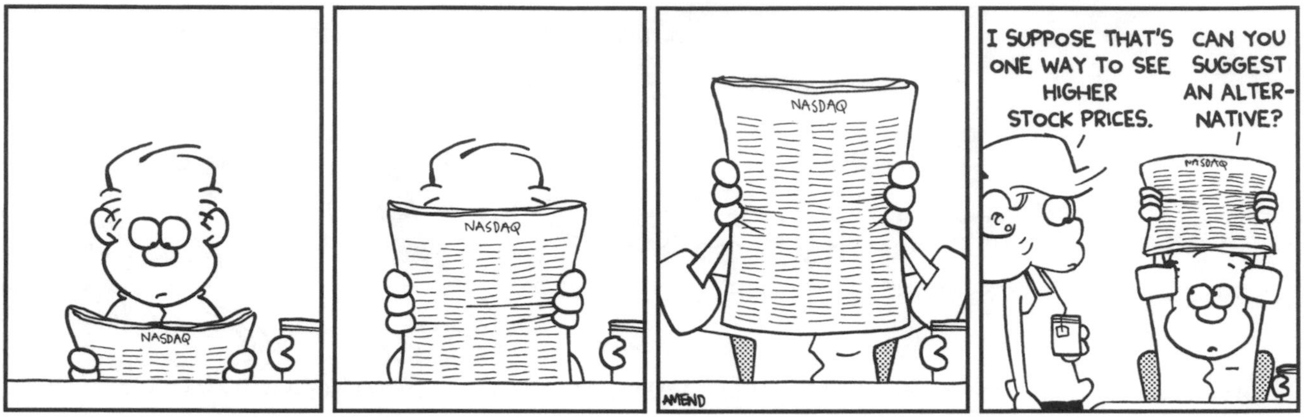
NASDAQ
I SUPPOSE THAT'S ONE WAY TO SEE HIGHER STOCK PRICES.
CAN YOU SUGGEST AN ALTER-NATIVE?
AMEND

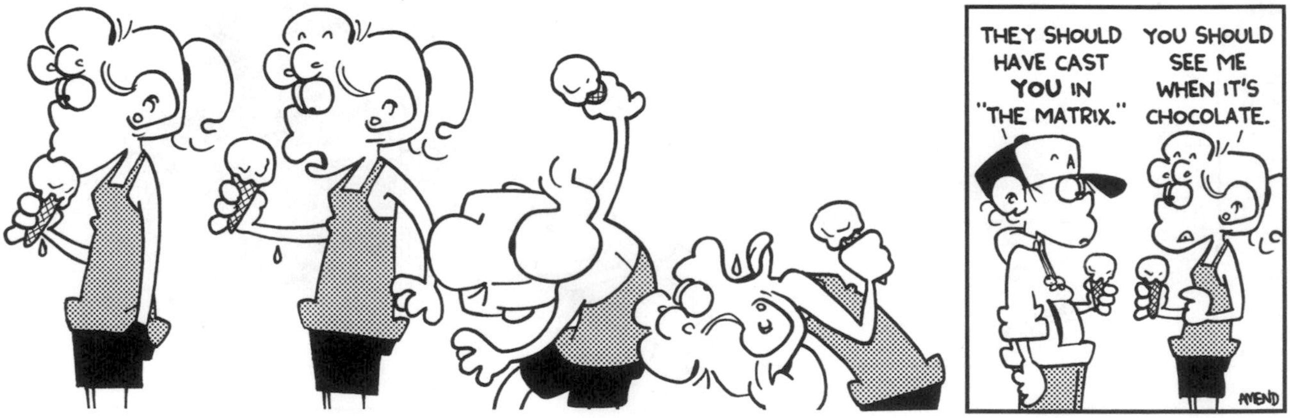
THEY SHOULD HAVE CAST YOU IN "THE MATRIX."
YOU SHOULD SEE ME WHEN IT'S CHOCOLATE.
AMEND

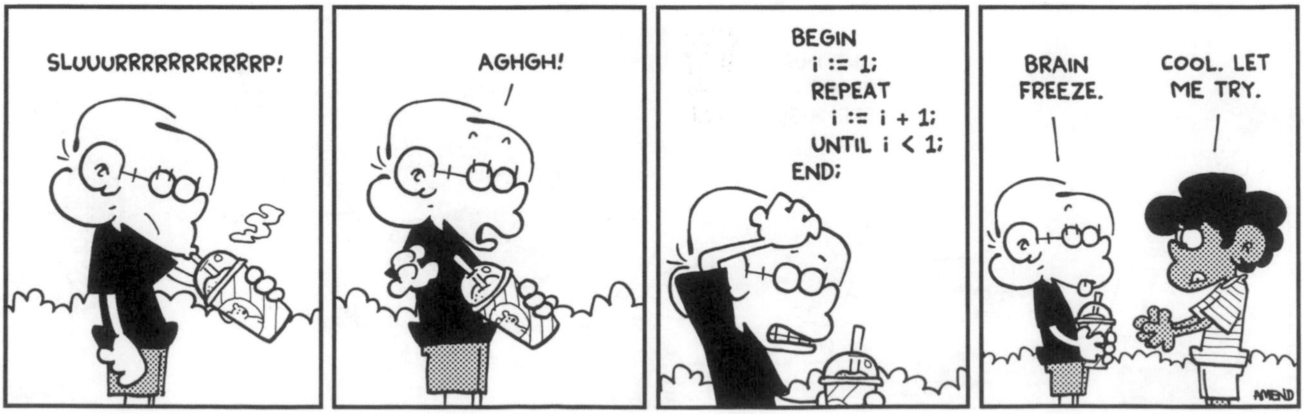
SLUUURRRRRRRRRRRP!
AGHGH!
BEGIN
i := 1;
REPEAT
i := i + 1;
UNTIL i < 1;
END;
BRAIN FREEZE.
COOL. LET ME TRY.
AMEND

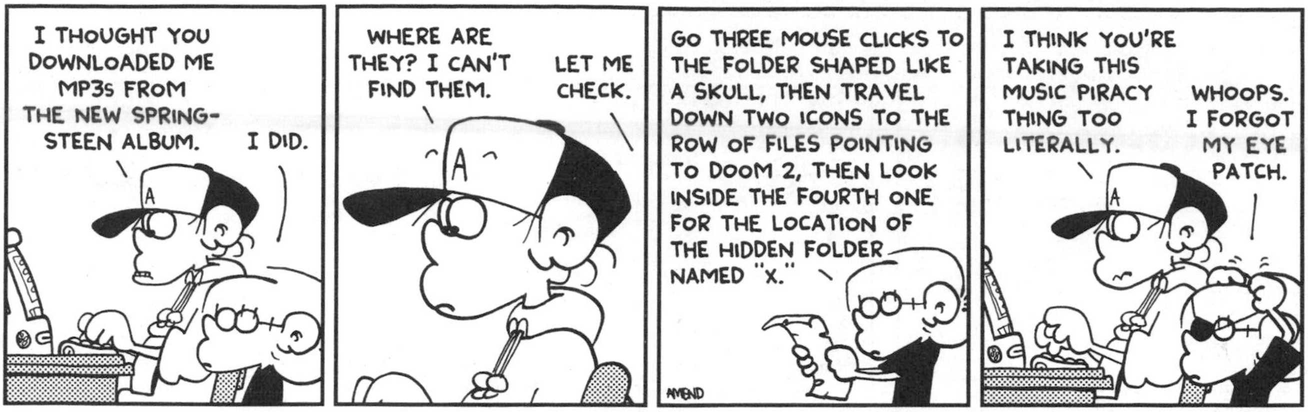
I THOUGHT YOU DOWNLOADED ME MP3s FROM THE NEW SPRING-STEEN ALBUM.
I DID.
WHERE ARE THEY? I CAN'T FIND THEM.
LET ME CHECK.
GO THREE MOUSE CLICKS TO THE FOLDER SHAPED LIKE A SKULL, THEN TRAVEL DOWN TWO ICONS TO THE ROW OF FILES POINTING TO DOOM 2, THEN LOOK INSIDE THE FOURTH ONE FOR THE LOCATION OF THE HIDDEN FOLDER NAMED "X."
AMEND
I THINK YOU'RE TAKING THIS MUSIC PIRACY THING TOO LITERALLY.
WHOOPS. I FORGOT MY EYE PATCH.

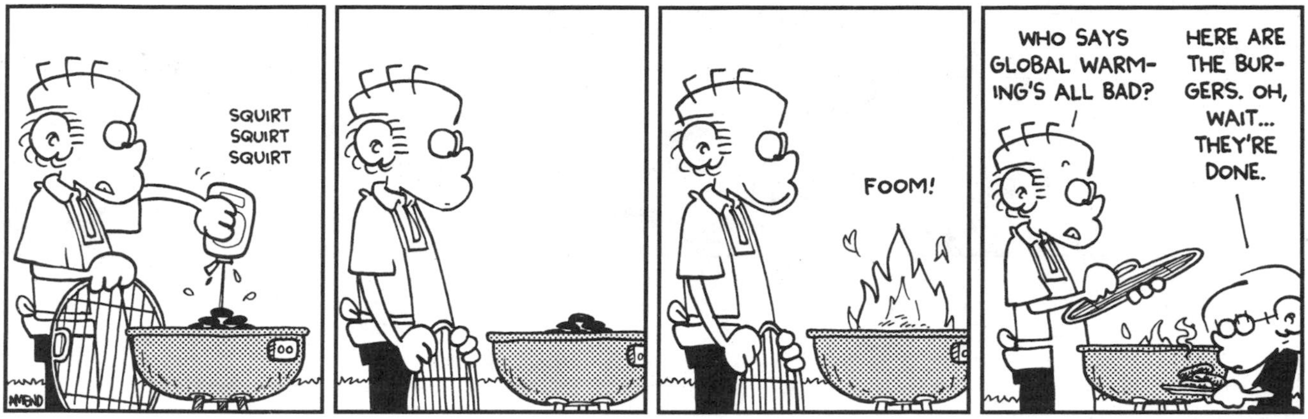
SQUIRT SQUIRT SQUIRT
AMEND
FOOM!
WHO SAYS GLOBAL WARM-ING'S ALL BAD?
HERE ARE THE BUR-GERS. OH, WAIT... THEY'RE DONE.

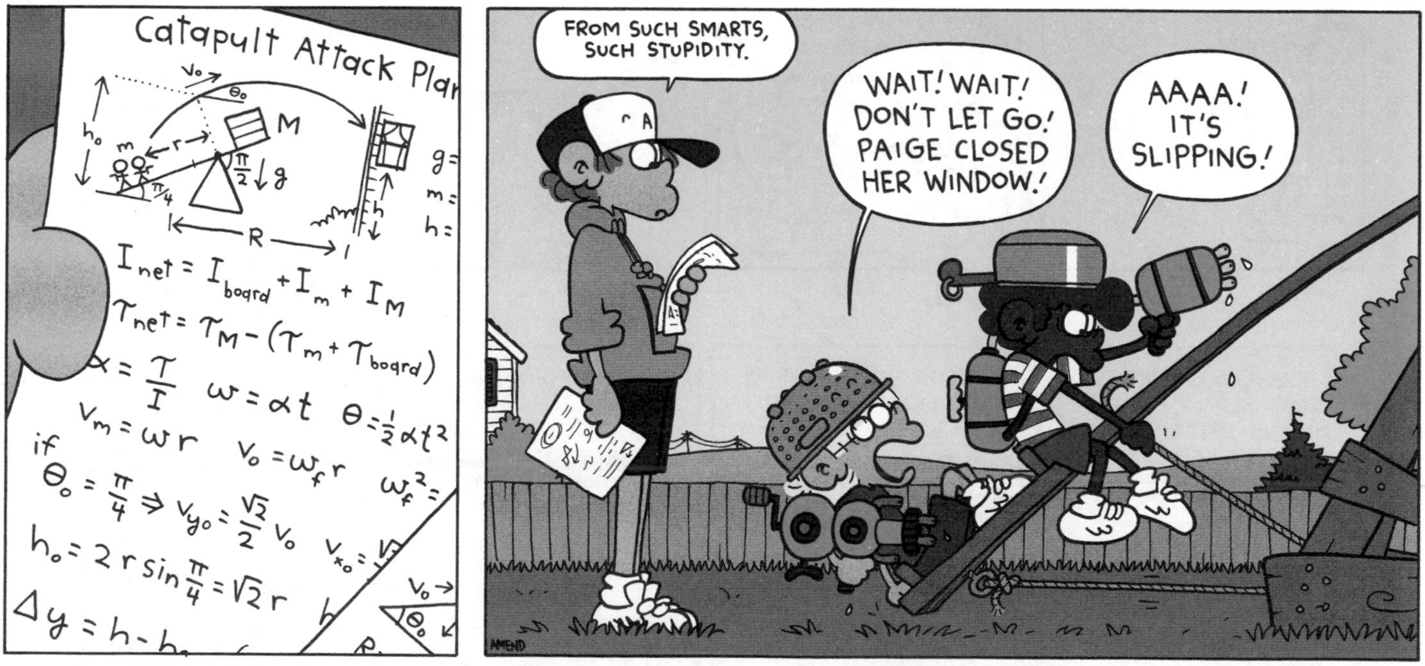
Catapult Attack Pla
FROM SUCH SMARTS, SUCH STUPIDITY.
WAIT! WAIT! DON'T LET GO! PAIGE CLOSED HER WINDOW!
AAAA! IT'S SLIPPING!
AMEND

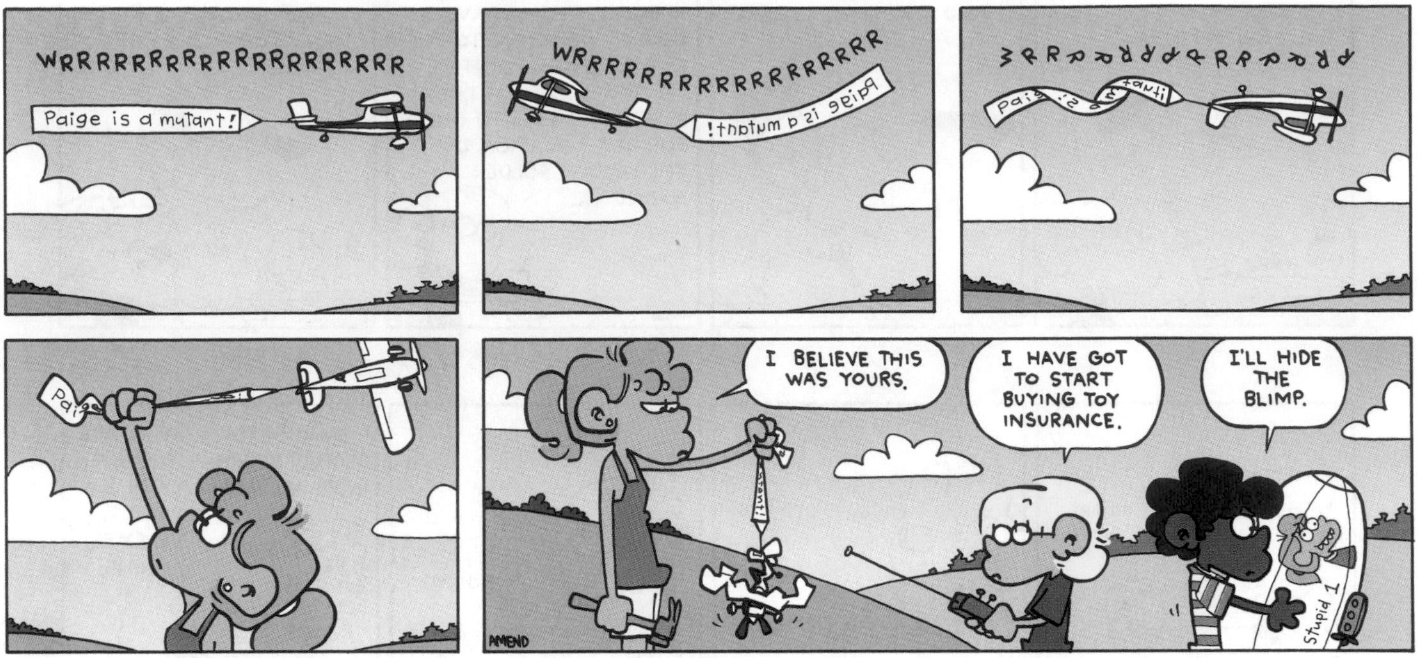
WRRRRRRRRRRRRRRRRRRRR
Paige is a mutant!
WRRRRRRRRRRRRRRRRRR
Paige is a mutant!
I BELIEVE THIS WAS YOURS.
I HAVE GOT TO START BUYING TOY INSURANCE.
I'LL HIDE THE BLIMP.
Stupid 1
AMEND

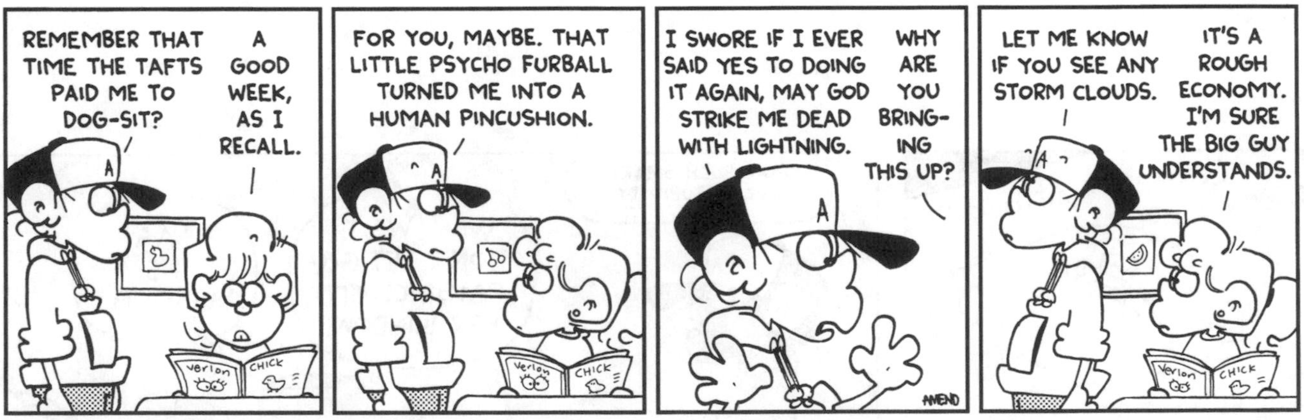
REMEMBER THAT TIME THE TAFTS PAID ME TO DOG-SIT?
A GOOD WEEK, AS I RECALL.
FOR YOU, MAYBE. THAT LITTLE PSYCHO FURBALL TURNED ME INTO A HUMAN PINCUSHION.
I SWORE IF I EVER SAID YES TO DOING IT AGAIN, MAY GOD STRIKE ME DEAD WITH LIGHTNING.
WHY ARE YOU BRINGING THIS UP?
LET ME KNOW IF YOU SEE ANY STORM CLOUDS.
IT'S A ROUGH ECONOMY. I'M SURE THE BIG GUY UNDERSTANDS.
Verlon
CHICK
AMEND

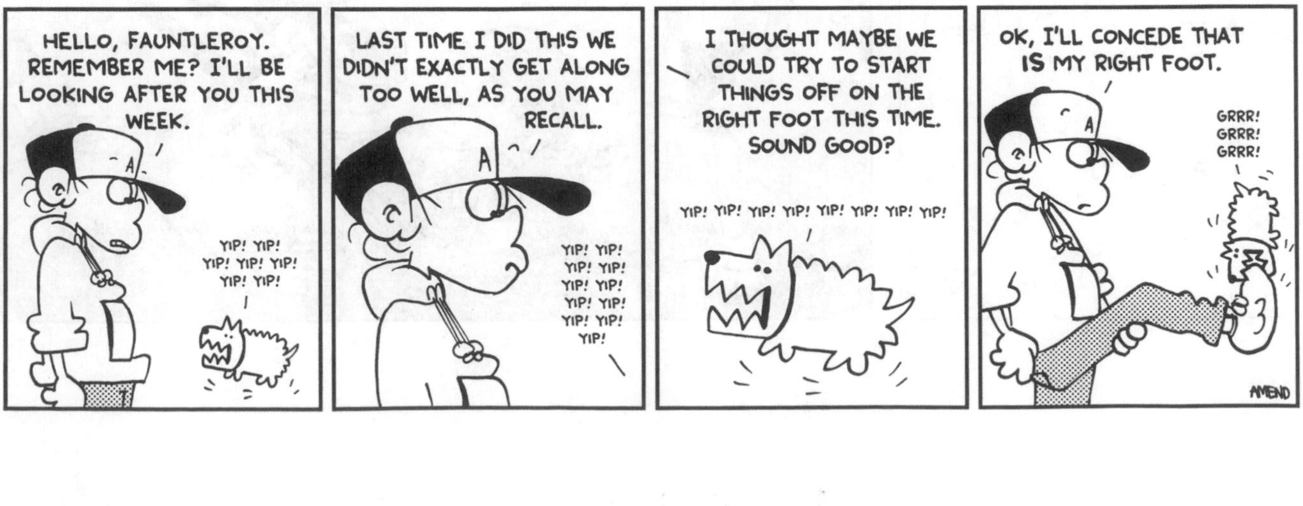
HELLO, FAUNTLEROY. REMEMBER ME? I'LL BE LOOKING AFTER YOU THIS WEEK.
YIP! YIP! YIP! YIP! YIP! YIP! YIP!
LAST TIME I DID THIS WE DIDN'T EXACTLY GET ALONG TOO WELL, AS YOU MAY RECALL.
YIP! YIP! YIP! YIP! YIP! YIP! YIP! YIP! YIP! YIP! YIP!
I THOUGHT MAYBE WE COULD TRY TO START THINGS OFF ON THE RIGHT FOOT THIS TIME. SOUND GOOD?
YIP! YIP! YIP! YIP! YIP! YIP! YIP! YIP!
OK, I'LL CONCEDE THAT IS MY RIGHT FOOT.
GRRR! GRRR! GRRR!
AMEND

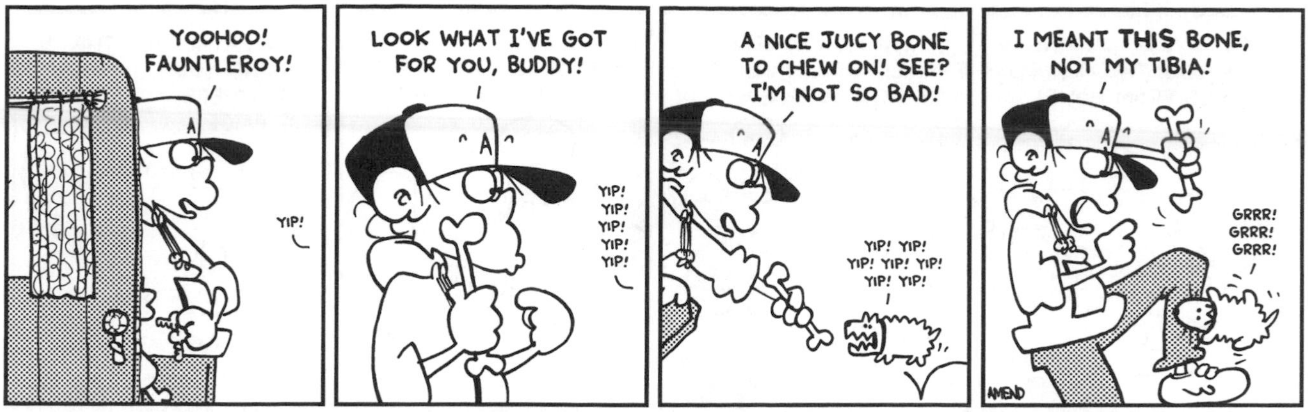
YOOHOO! FAUNTLEROY!
YIP!
LOOK WHAT I'VE GOT FOR YOU, BUDDY!
YIP! YIP! YIP! YIP! YIP!
A NICE JUICY BONE TO CHEW ON! SEE? I'M NOT SO BAD!
YIP! YIP! YIP! YIP! YIP! YIP! YIP!
I MEANT **THIS** BONE, NOT MY TIBIA!
GRRR! GRRR! GRRR!
AMEND

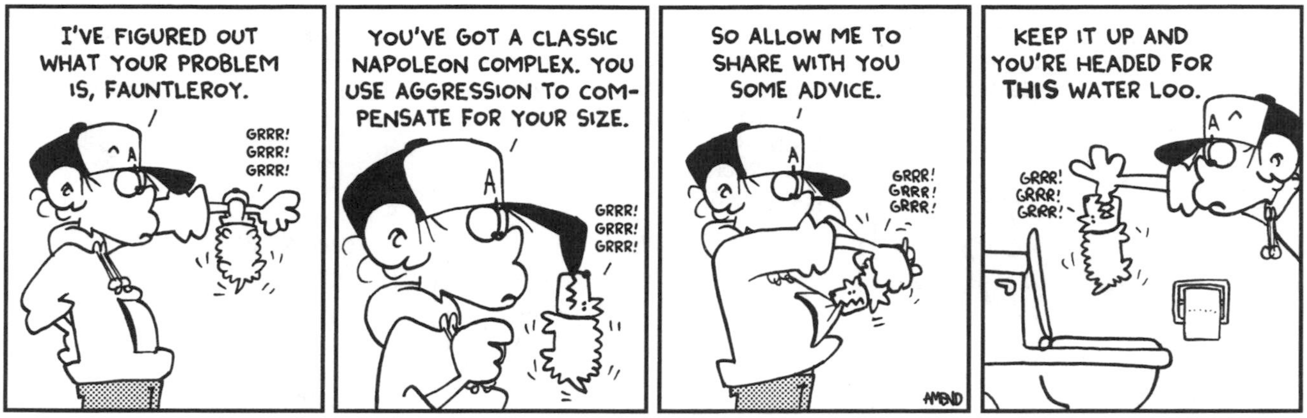
I'VE FIGURED OUT WHAT YOUR PROBLEM IS, FAUNTLEROY.
GRRR! GRRR! GRRR!
YOU'VE GOT A CLASSIC NAPOLEON COMPLEX. YOU USE AGGRESSION TO COMPENSATE FOR YOUR SIZE.
GRRR! GRRR! GRRR!
SO ALLOW ME TO SHARE WITH YOU SOME ADVICE.
GRRR! GRRR! GRRR!
AMEND
KEEP IT UP AND YOU'RE HEADED FOR **THIS** WATER LOO.
GRRR! GRRR! GRRR!

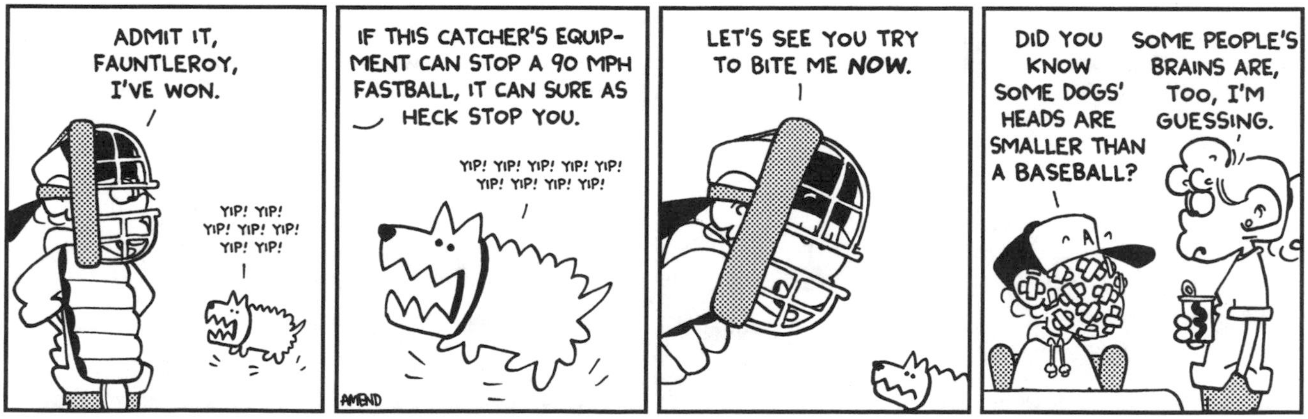
ADMIT IT, FAUNTLEROY, I'VE WON.
YIP! YIP! YIP! YIP! YIP! YIP! YIP!
IF THIS CATCHER'S EQUIPMENT CAN STOP A 90 MPH FASTBALL, IT CAN SURE AS HECK STOP YOU.
YIP! YIP! YIP! YIP! YIP! YIP! YIP! YIP! YIP!
AMEND
LET'S SEE YOU TRY TO BITE ME ***NOW***.
DID YOU KNOW SOME DOGS' HEADS ARE SMALLER THAN A BASEBALL?
SOME PEOPLE'S BRAINS ARE, TOO, I'M GUESSING.

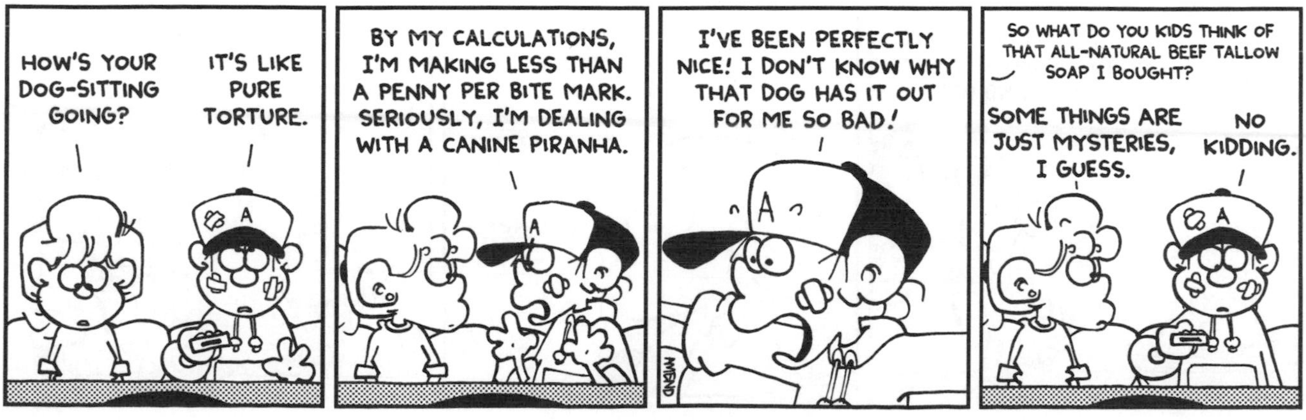
HOW'S YOUR DOG-SITTING GOING?
IT'S LIKE PURE TORTURE.
BY MY CALCULATIONS, I'M MAKING LESS THAN A PENNY PER BITE MARK. SERIOUSLY, I'M DEALING WITH A CANINE PIRANHA.
I'VE BEEN PERFECTLY NICE! I DON'T KNOW WHY THAT DOG HAS IT OUT FOR ME SO BAD!
AMEND
SO WHAT DO YOU KIDS THINK OF THAT ALL-NATURAL BEEF TALLOW SOAP I BOUGHT?
SOME THINGS ARE JUST MYSTERIES, I GUESS.
NO KIDDING.

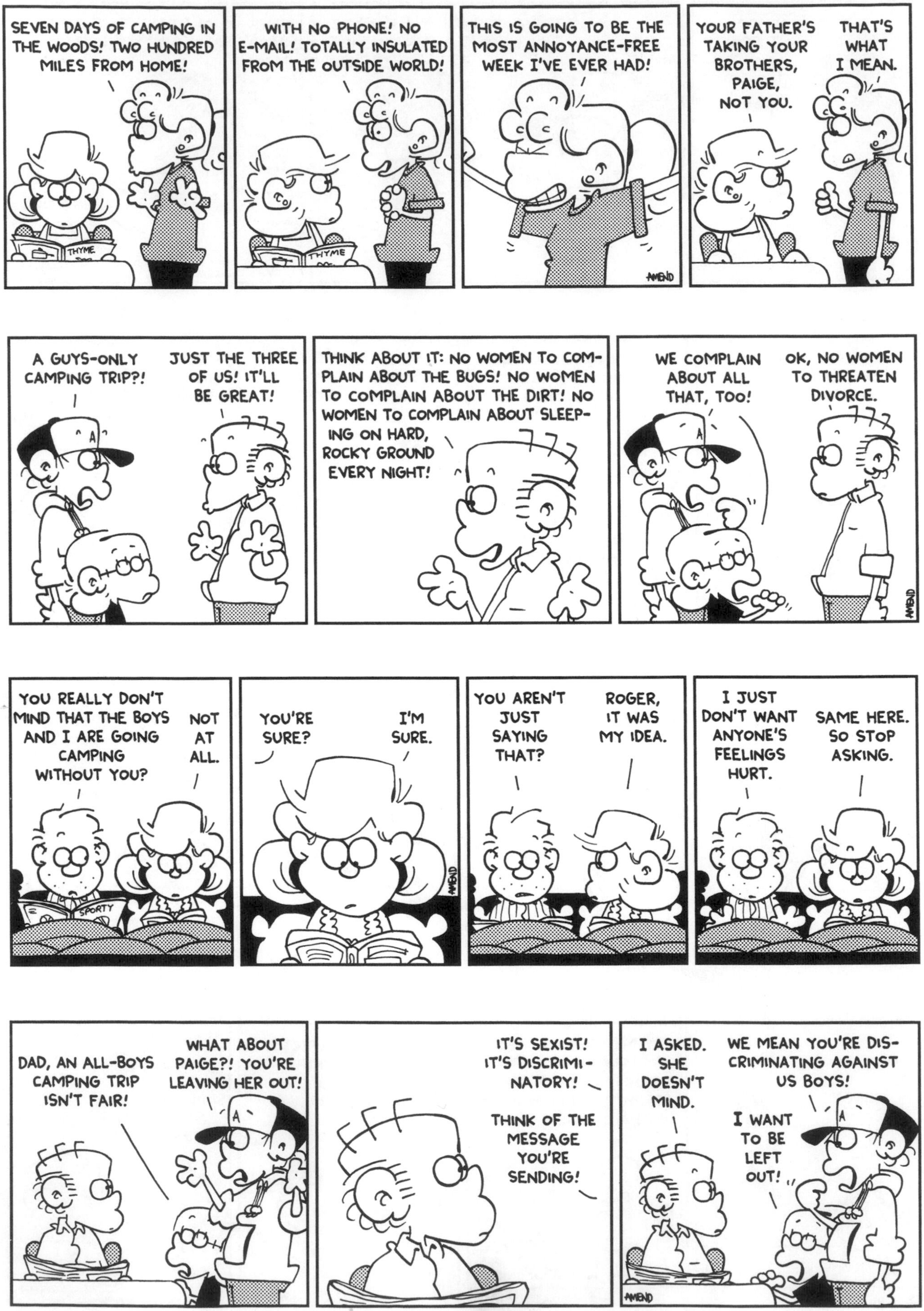
SEVEN DAYS OF CAMPING IN THE WOODS! TWO HUNDRED MILES FROM HOME!
WITH NO PHONE! NO E-MAIL! TOTALLY INSULATED FROM THE OUTSIDE WORLD!
THIS IS GOING TO BE THE MOST ANNOYANCE-FREE WEEK I'VE EVER HAD!
YOUR FATHER'S TAKING YOUR BROTHERS, PAIGE, NOT YOU.
THAT'S WHAT I MEAN.
THYME
AMEND
A GUYS-ONLY CAMPING TRIP?!
JUST THE THREE OF US! IT'LL BE GREAT!
THINK ABOUT IT: NO WOMEN TO COMPLAIN ABOUT THE BUGS! NO WOMEN TO COMPLAIN ABOUT THE DIRT! NO WOMEN TO COMPLAIN ABOUT SLEEPING ON HARD, ROCKY GROUND EVERY NIGHT!
WE COMPLAIN ABOUT ALL THAT, TOO!
OK, NO WOMEN TO THREATEN DIVORCE.
AMEND
YOU REALLY DON'T MIND THAT THE BOYS AND I ARE GOING CAMPING WITHOUT YOU?
NOT AT ALL.
SPORTY
YOU'RE SURE?
I'M SURE.
AMEND
YOU AREN'T JUST SAYING THAT?
ROGER, IT WAS MY IDEA.
I JUST DON'T WANT ANYONE'S FEELINGS HURT.
SAME HERE. SO STOP ASKING.
DAD, AN ALL-BOYS CAMPING TRIP ISN'T FAIR!
WHAT ABOUT PAIGE?! YOU'RE LEAVING HER OUT!
IT'S SEXIST! IT'S DISCRIMINATORY!
THINK OF THE MESSAGE YOU'RE SENDING!
I ASKED. SHE DOESN'T MIND.
WE MEAN YOU'RE DISCRIMINATING AGAINST US BOYS!
I WANT TO BE LEFT OUT!
AMEND

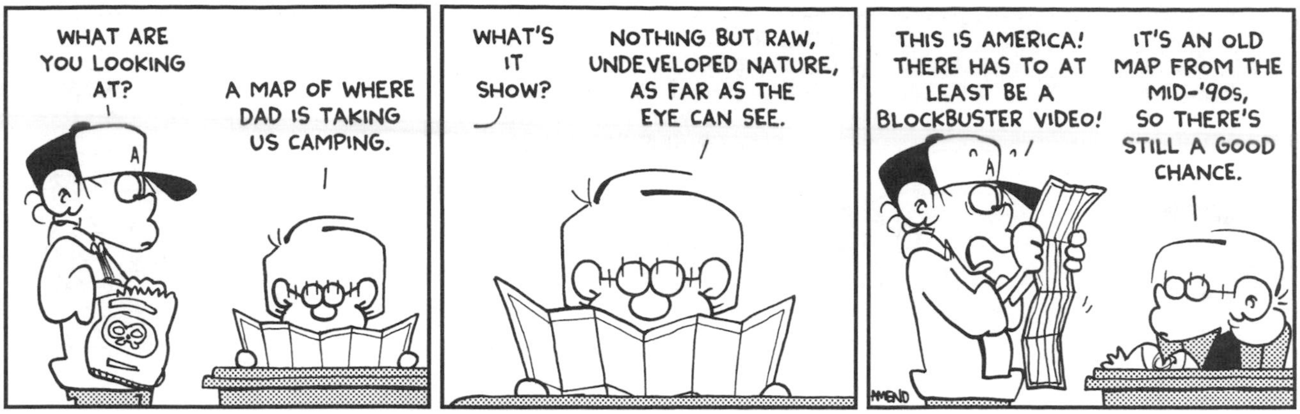
WHAT ARE YOU LOOKING AT?
A MAP OF WHERE DAD IS TAKING US CAMPING.
WHAT'S IT SHOW?
NOTHING BUT RAW, UNDEVELOPED NATURE, AS FAR AS THE EYE CAN SEE.
THIS IS AMERICA! THERE HAS TO AT LEAST BE A BLOCKBUSTER VIDEO!
IT'S AN OLD MAP FROM THE MID-'90s, SO THERE'S STILL A GOOD CHANCE.

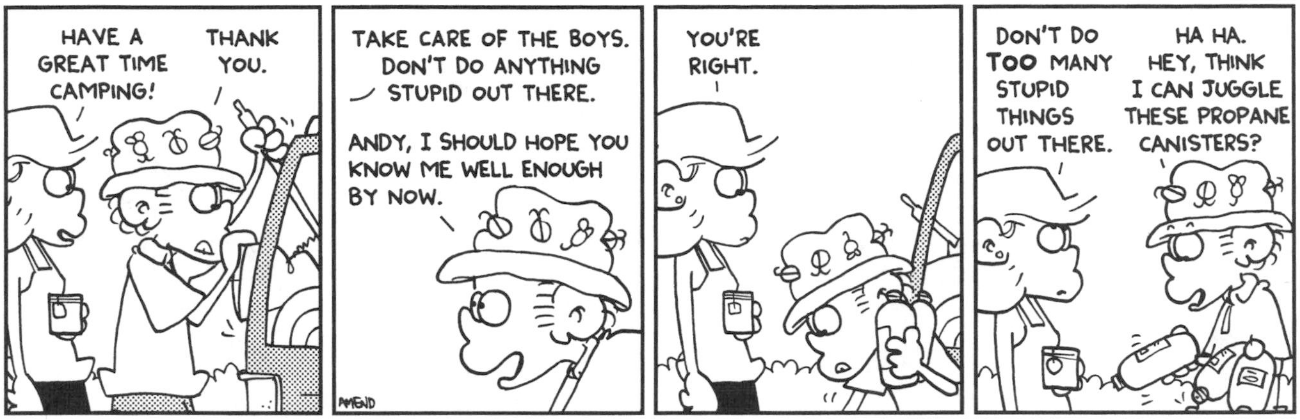
HAVE A GREAT TIME CAMPING!
THANK YOU.
TAKE CARE OF THE BOYS. DON'T DO ANYTHING STUPID OUT THERE.
ANDY, I SHOULD HOPE YOU KNOW ME WELL ENOUGH BY NOW.
YOU'RE RIGHT.
DON'T DO **TOO** MANY STUPID THINGS OUT THERE.
HA HA. HEY, THINK I CAN JUGGLE THESE PROPANE CANISTERS?

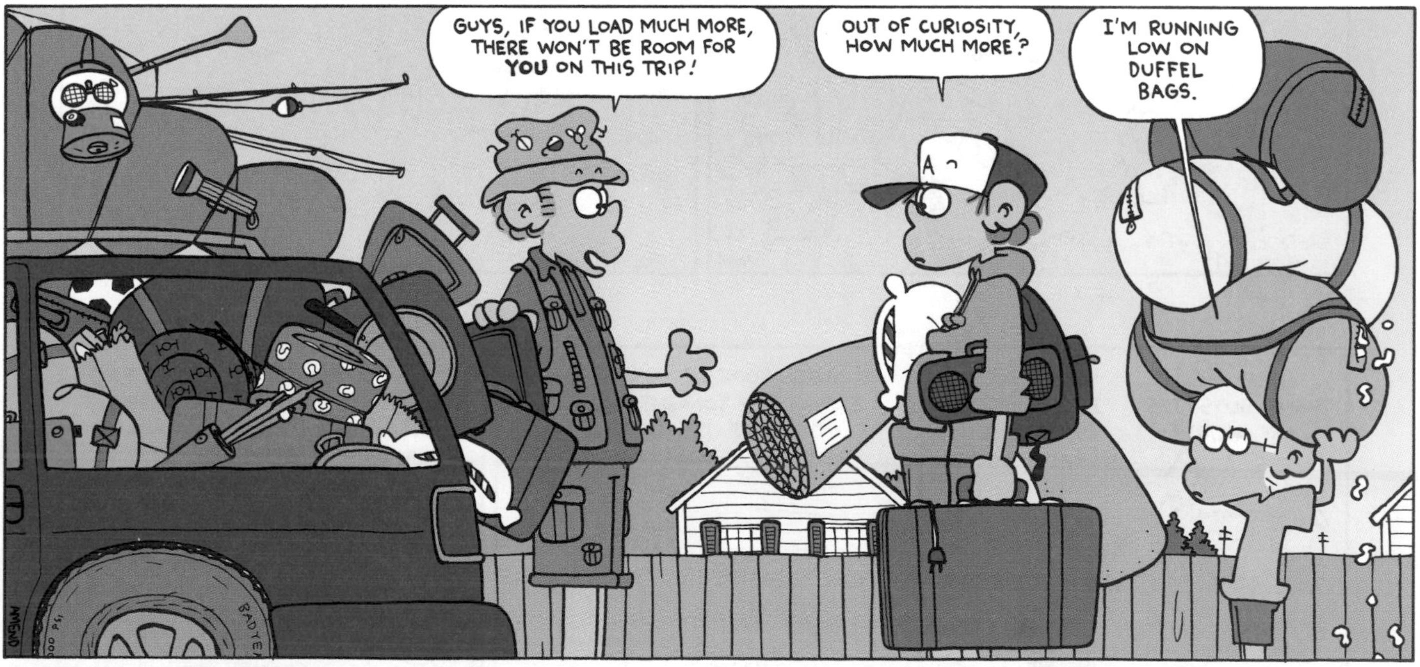
GUYS, IF YOU LOAD MUCH MORE, THERE WON'T BE ROOM FOR **YOU** ON THIS TRIP!
OUT OF CURIOSITY, HOW MUCH MORE?
I'M RUNNING LOW ON DUFFEL BAGS.

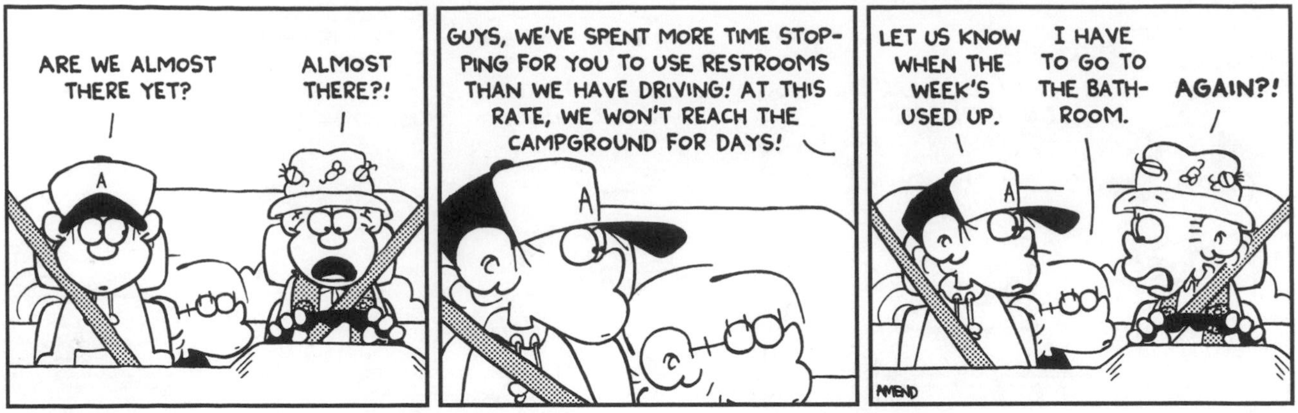
ARE WE ALMOST THERE YET?
ALMOST THERE?!
GUYS, WE'VE SPENT MORE TIME STOPPING FOR YOU TO USE RESTROOMS THAN WE HAVE DRIVING! AT THIS RATE, WE WON'T REACH THE CAMPGROUND FOR DAYS!
LET US KNOW WHEN THE WEEK'S USED UP.
I HAVE TO GO TO THE BATHROOM.
AGAIN?!

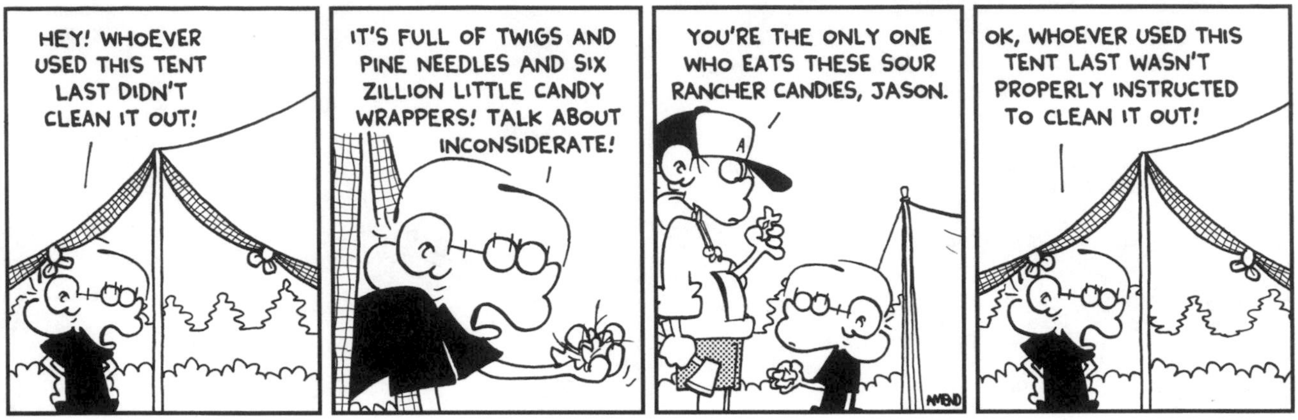
HEY! WHOEVER USED THIS TENT LAST DIDN'T CLEAN IT OUT!
IT'S FULL OF TWIGS AND PINE NEEDLES AND SIX ZILLION LITTLE CANDY WRAPPERS! TALK ABOUT INCONSIDERATE!
YOU'RE THE ONLY ONE WHO EATS THESE SOUR RANCHER CANDIES, JASON.
OK, WHOEVER USED THIS TENT LAST WASN'T PROPERLY INSTRUCTED TO CLEAN IT OUT!

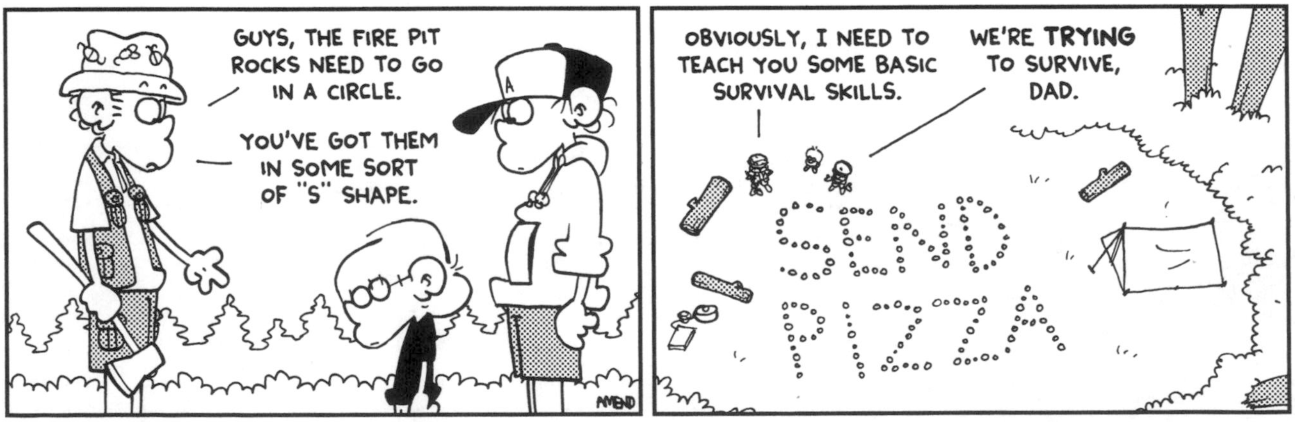
GUYS, THE FIRE PIT ROCKS NEED TO GO IN A CIRCLE.
YOU'VE GOT THEM IN SOME SORT OF "S" SHAPE.
OBVIOUSLY, I NEED TO TEACH YOU SOME BASIC SURVIVAL SKILLS.
WE'RE TRYING TO SURVIVE, DAD.
SEND PIZZA

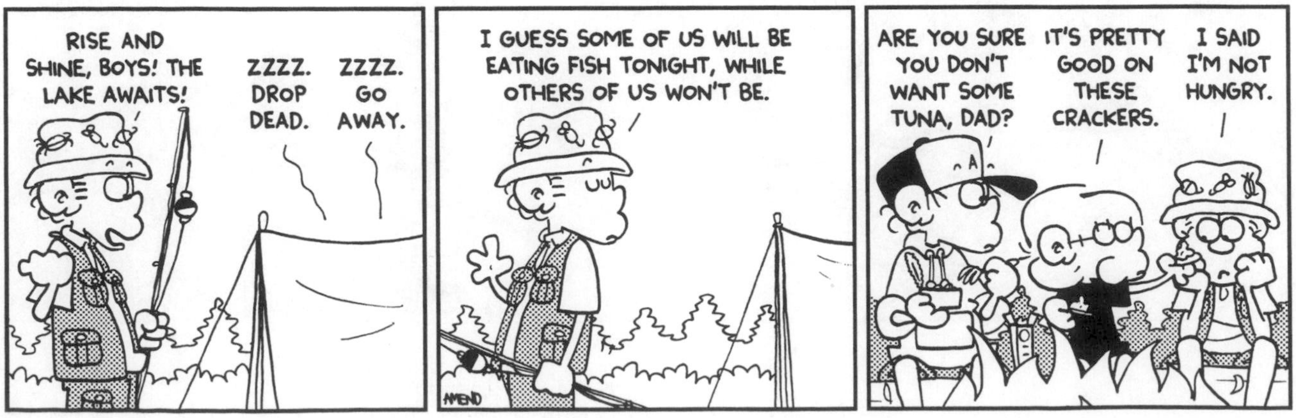
RISE AND SHINE, BOYS! THE LAKE AWAITS!
ZZZZ. DROP DEAD.
ZZZZ. GO AWAY.
I GUESS SOME OF US WILL BE EATING FISH TONIGHT, WHILE OTHERS OF US WON'T BE.
ARE YOU SURE YOU DON'T WANT SOME TUNA, DAD?
IT'S PRETTY GOOD ON THESE CRACKERS.
I SAID I'M NOT HUNGRY.

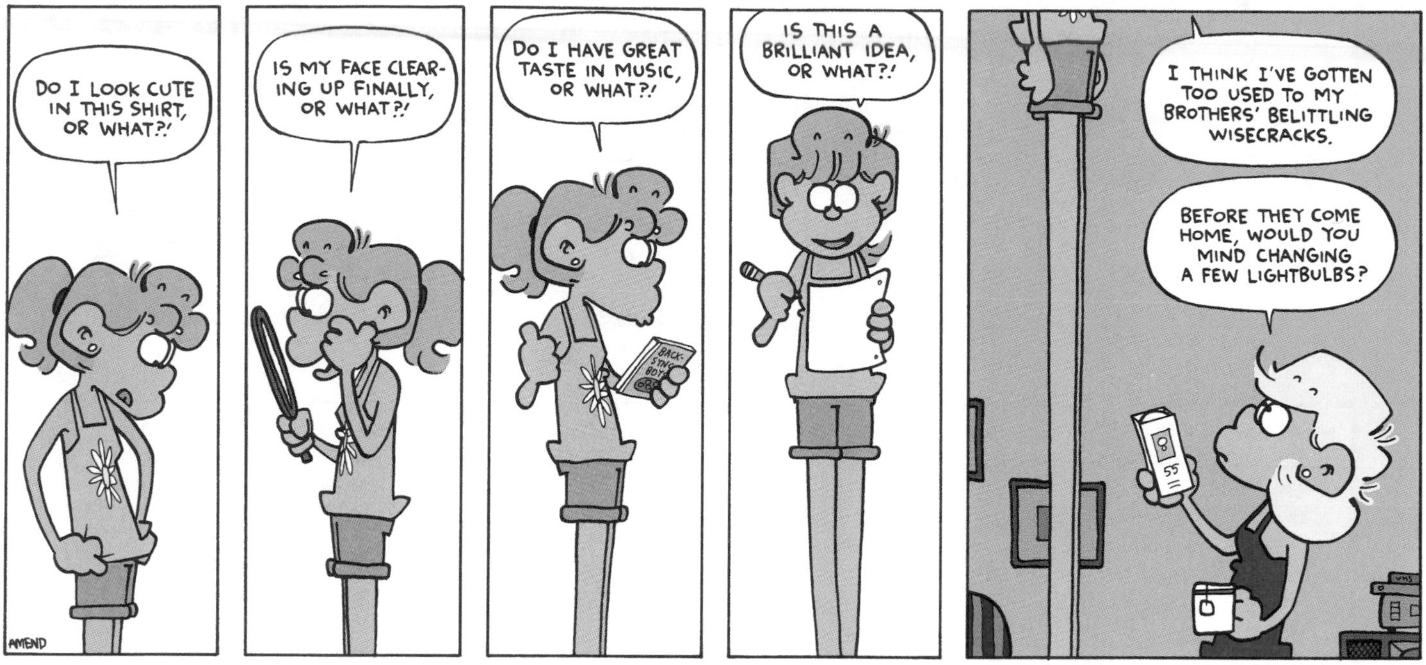
DO I LOOK CUTE IN THIS SHIRT, OR WHAT?!
AMEND
IS MY FACE CLEARING UP FINALLY, OR WHAT?!
DO I HAVE GREAT TASTE IN MUSIC, OR WHAT?!
IS THIS A BRILLIANT IDEA, OR WHAT?!
I THINK I'VE GOTTEN TOO USED TO MY BROTHERS' BELITTLING WISECRACKS.
BEFORE THEY COME HOME, WOULD YOU MIND CHANGING A FEW LIGHTBULBS?

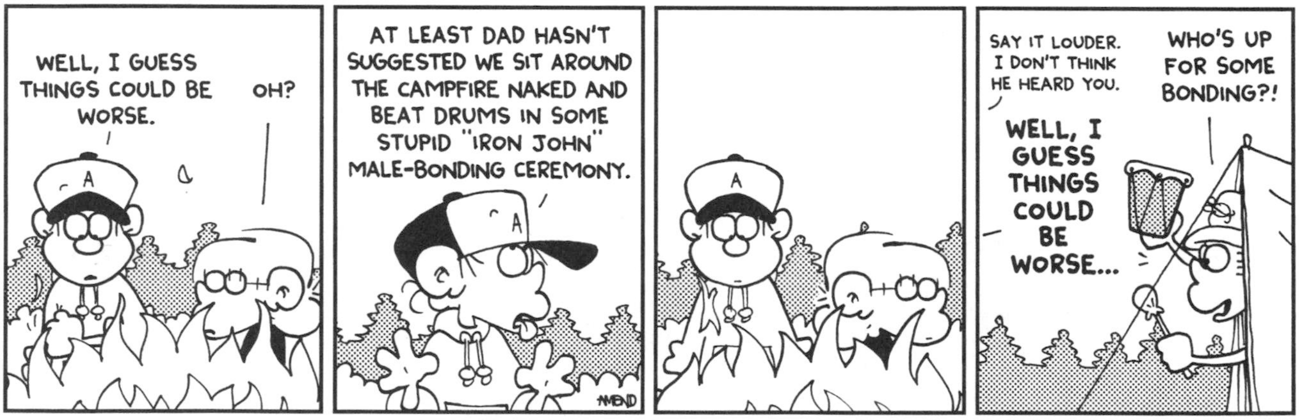
WELL, I GUESS THINGS COULD BE WORSE.
OH?
AT LEAST DAD HASN'T SUGGESTED WE SIT AROUND THE CAMPFIRE NAKED AND BEAT DRUMS IN SOME STUPID "IRON JOHN" MALE-BONDING CEREMONY.
AMEND
SAY IT LOUDER. I DON'T THINK HE HEARD YOU.
WELL, I GUESS THINGS COULD BE WORSE...
WHO'S UP FOR SOME BONDING?!

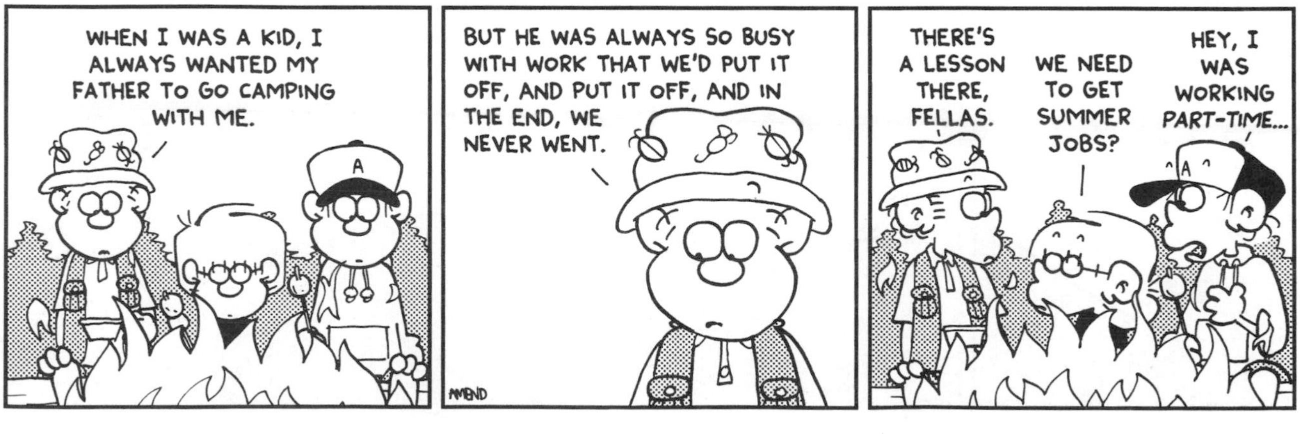
WHEN I WAS A KID, I ALWAYS WANTED MY FATHER TO GO CAMPING WITH ME.
BUT HE WAS ALWAYS SO BUSY WITH WORK THAT WE'D PUT IT OFF, AND PUT IT OFF, AND IN THE END, WE NEVER WENT.
AMEND
THERE'S A LESSON THERE, FELLAS.
WE NEED TO GET SUMMER JOBS?
HEY, I WAS WORKING PART-TIME...

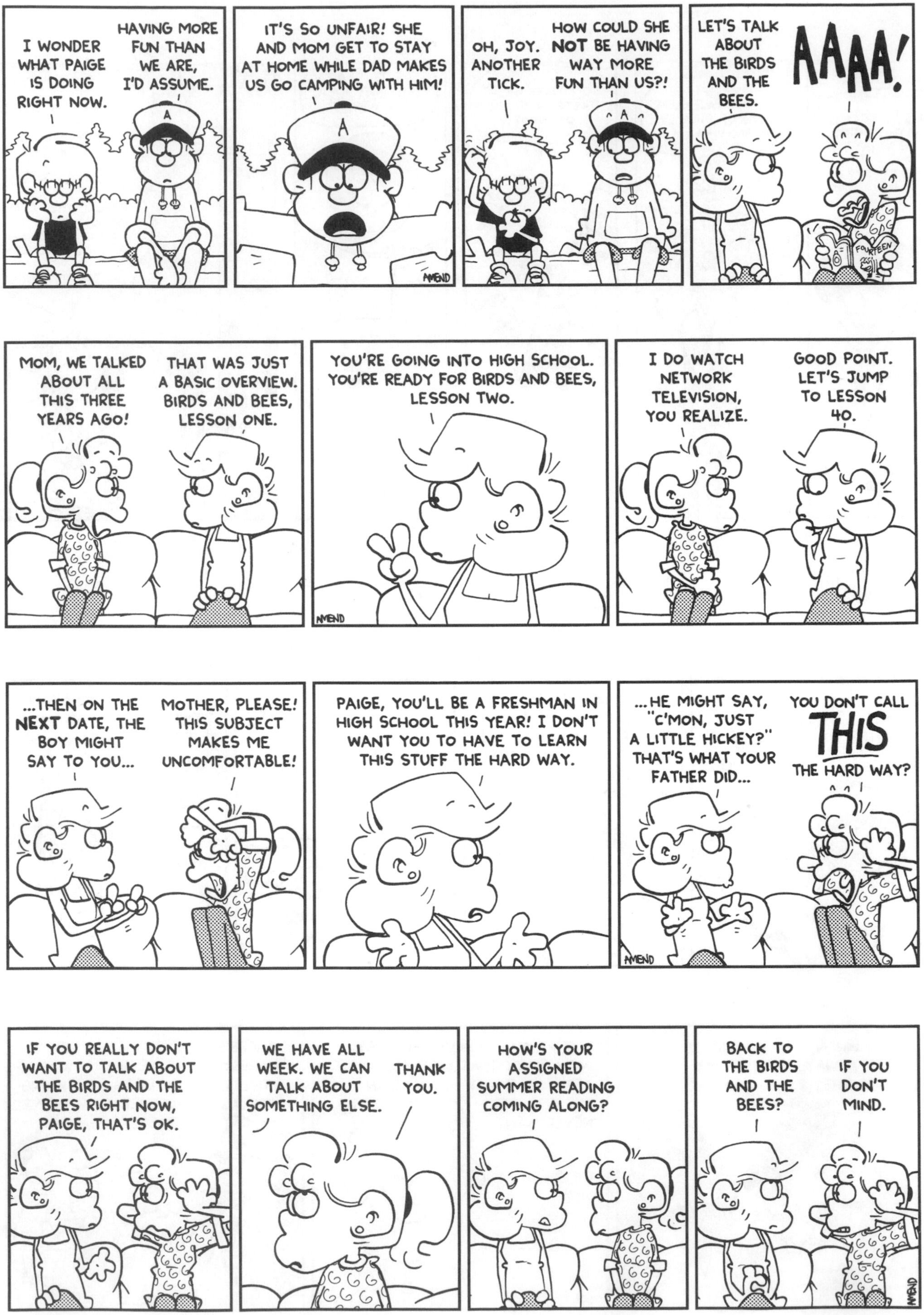

I WONDER WHAT PAIGE IS DOING RIGHT NOW.
HAVING MORE FUN THAN WE ARE, I'D ASSUME.
IT'S SO UNFAIR! SHE AND MOM GET TO STAY AT HOME WHILE DAD MAKES US GO CAMPING WITH HIM!
OH, JOY. ANOTHER TICK.
HOW COULD SHE NOT BE HAVING WAY MORE FUN THAN US?!
LET'S TALK ABOUT THE BIRDS AND THE BEES.
AAAA!
FOURTEEN
AMEND
MOM, WE TALKED ABOUT ALL THIS THREE YEARS AGO!
THAT WAS JUST A BASIC OVERVIEW. BIRDS AND BEES, LESSON ONE.
YOU'RE GOING INTO HIGH SCHOOL. YOU'RE READY FOR BIRDS AND BEES, LESSON TWO.
I DO WATCH NETWORK TELEVISION, YOU REALIZE.
GOOD POINT. LET'S JUMP TO LESSON 40.
AMEND
...THEN ON THE NEXT DATE, THE BOY MIGHT SAY TO YOU...
MOTHER, PLEASE! THIS SUBJECT MAKES ME UNCOMFORTABLE!
PAIGE, YOU'LL BE A FRESHMAN IN HIGH SCHOOL THIS YEAR! I DON'T WANT YOU TO HAVE TO LEARN THIS STUFF THE HARD WAY.
...HE MIGHT SAY, "C'MON, JUST A LITTLE HICKEY?" THAT'S WHAT YOUR FATHER DID...
YOU DON'T CALL THIS THE HARD WAY?
AMEND
IF YOU REALLY DON'T WANT TO TALK ABOUT THE BIRDS AND THE BEES RIGHT NOW, PAIGE, THAT'S OK.
WE HAVE ALL WEEK. WE CAN TALK ABOUT SOMETHING ELSE.
THANK YOU.
HOW'S YOUR ASSIGNED SUMMER READING COMING ALONG?
BACK TO THE BIRDS AND THE BEES?
IF YOU DON'T MIND.
AMEND

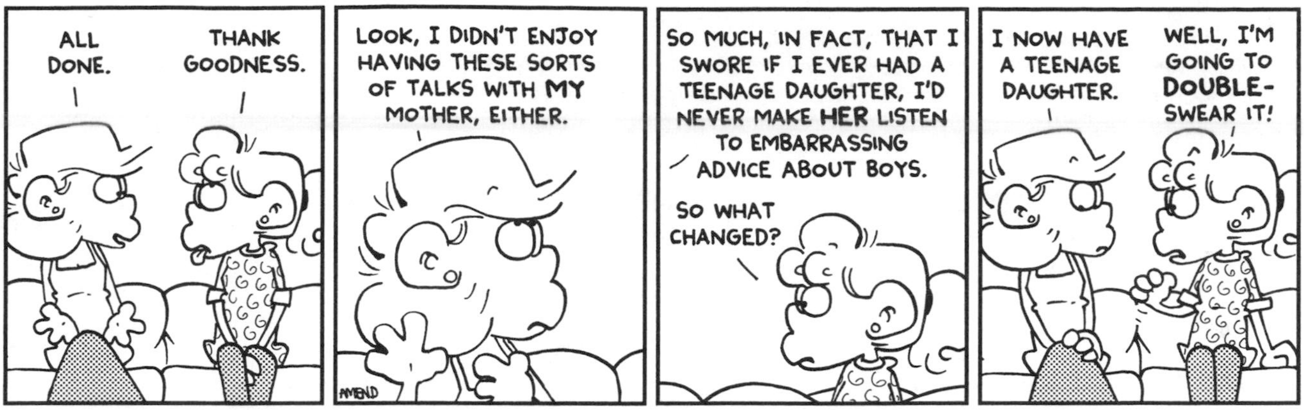
ALL DONE.
THANK GOODNESS.
LOOK, I DIDN'T ENJOY HAVING THESE SORTS OF TALKS WITH MY MOTHER, EITHER.
SO MUCH, IN FACT, THAT I SWORE IF I EVER HAD A TEENAGE DAUGHTER, I'D NEVER MAKE HER LISTEN TO EMBARRASSING ADVICE ABOUT BOYS.
SO WHAT CHANGED?
I NOW HAVE A TEENAGE DAUGHTER.
WELL, I'M GOING TO DOUBLE-SWEAR IT!
AMEND

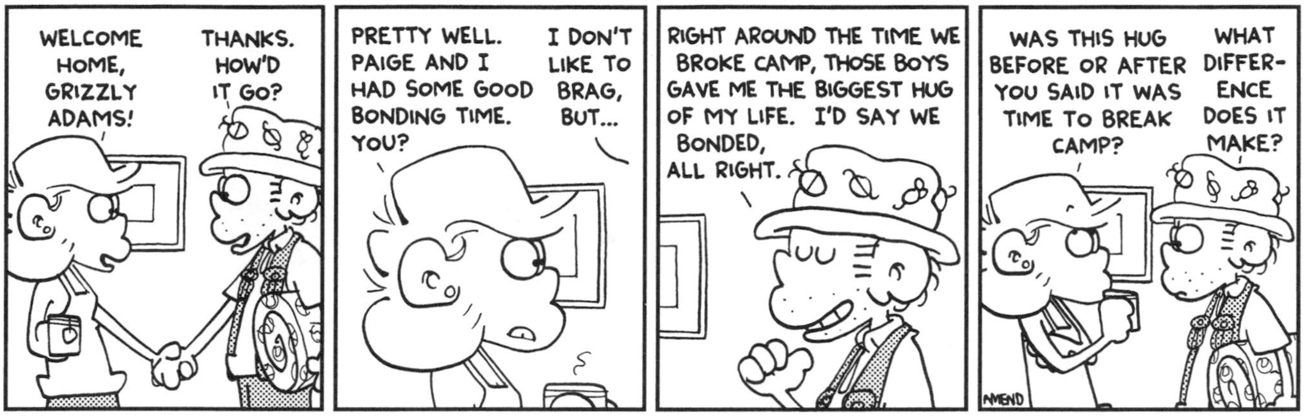
WELCOME HOME, GRIZZLY ADAMS!
THANKS. HOW'D IT GO?
PRETTY WELL. PAIGE AND I HAD SOME GOOD BONDING TIME. YOU?
I DON'T LIKE TO BRAG, BUT...
RIGHT AROUND THE TIME WE BROKE CAMP, THOSE BOYS GAVE ME THE BIGGEST HUG OF MY LIFE. I'D SAY WE BONDED, ALL RIGHT.
WAS THIS HUG BEFORE OR AFTER YOU SAID IT WAS TIME TO BREAK CAMP?
WHAT DIFFERENCE DOES IT MAKE?
AMEND

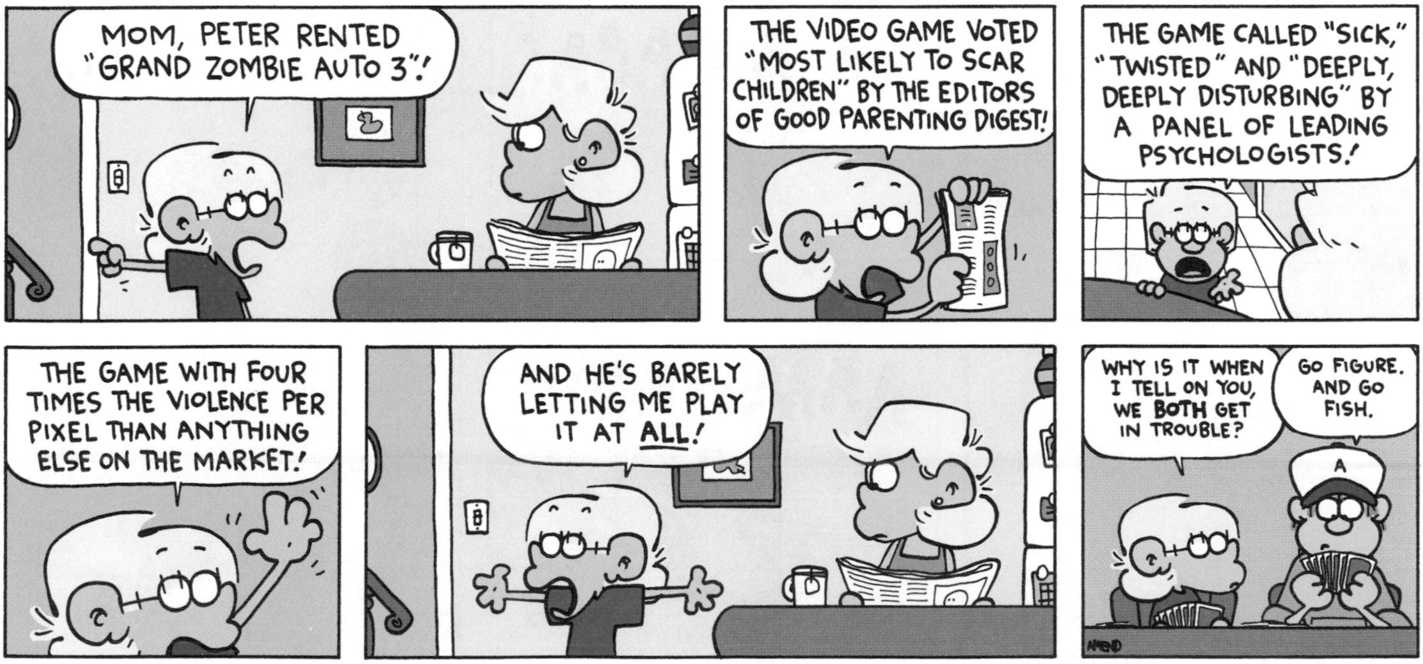
MOM, PETER RENTED "GRAND ZOMBIE AUTO 3"!
THE VIDEO GAME VOTED "MOST LIKELY TO SCAR CHILDREN" BY THE EDITORS OF GOOD PARENTING DIGEST!
THE GAME CALLED "SICK," "TWISTED" AND "DEEPLY, DEEPLY DISTURBING" BY A PANEL OF LEADING PSYCHOLOGISTS!
THE GAME WITH FOUR TIMES THE VIOLENCE PER PIXEL THAN ANYTHING ELSE ON THE MARKET!
AND HE'S BARELY LETTING ME PLAY IT AT ALL!
WHY IS IT WHEN I TELL ON YOU, WE BOTH GET IN TROUBLE?
GO FIGURE. AND GO FISH.
AMEND

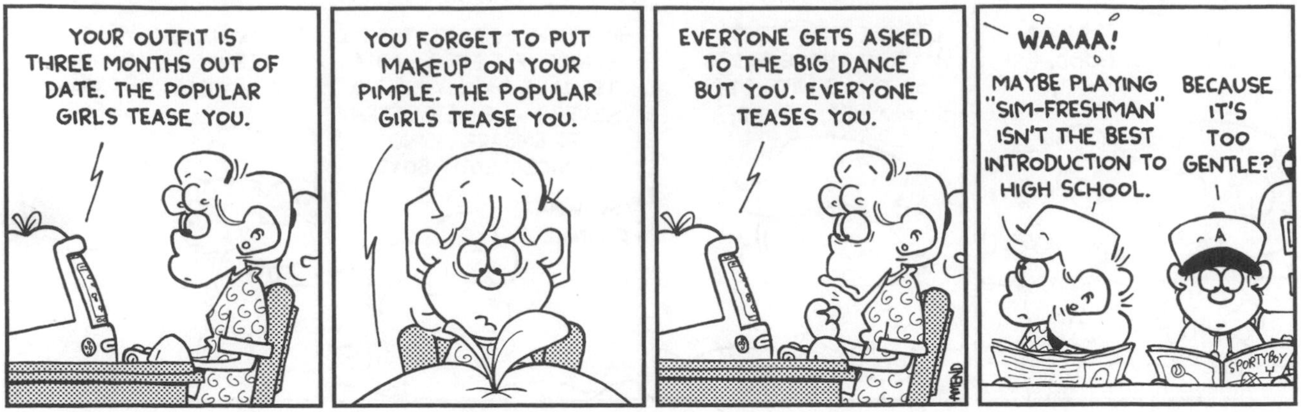
YOUR OUTFIT IS THREE MONTHS OUT OF DATE. THE POPULAR GIRLS TEASE YOU.
YOU FORGET TO PUT MAKEUP ON YOUR PIMPLE. THE POPULAR GIRLS TEASE YOU.
EVERYONE GETS ASKED TO THE BIG DANCE BUT YOU. EVERYONE TEASES YOU.
AMEND
WAAAA!
MAYBE PLAYING "SIM-FRESHMAN" ISN'T THE BEST INTRODUCTION TO HIGH SCHOOL.
BECAUSE IT'S TOO GENTLE?
SPORTYBOY

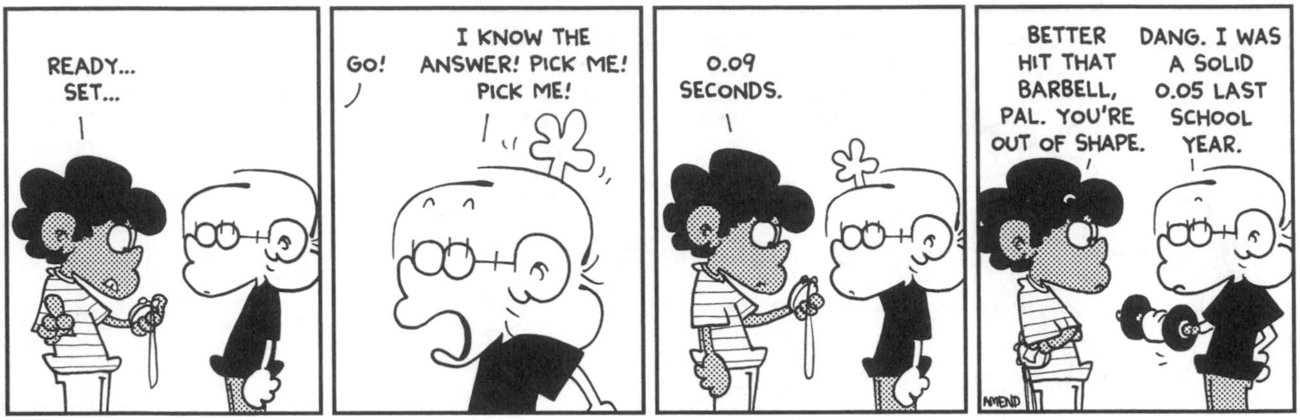
READY... SET...
GO!
I KNOW THE ANSWER! PICK ME! PICK ME!
0.09 SECONDS.
BETTER HIT THAT BARBELL, PAL. YOU'RE OUT OF SHAPE.
DANG. I WAS A SOLID 0.05 LAST SCHOOL YEAR.
AMEND

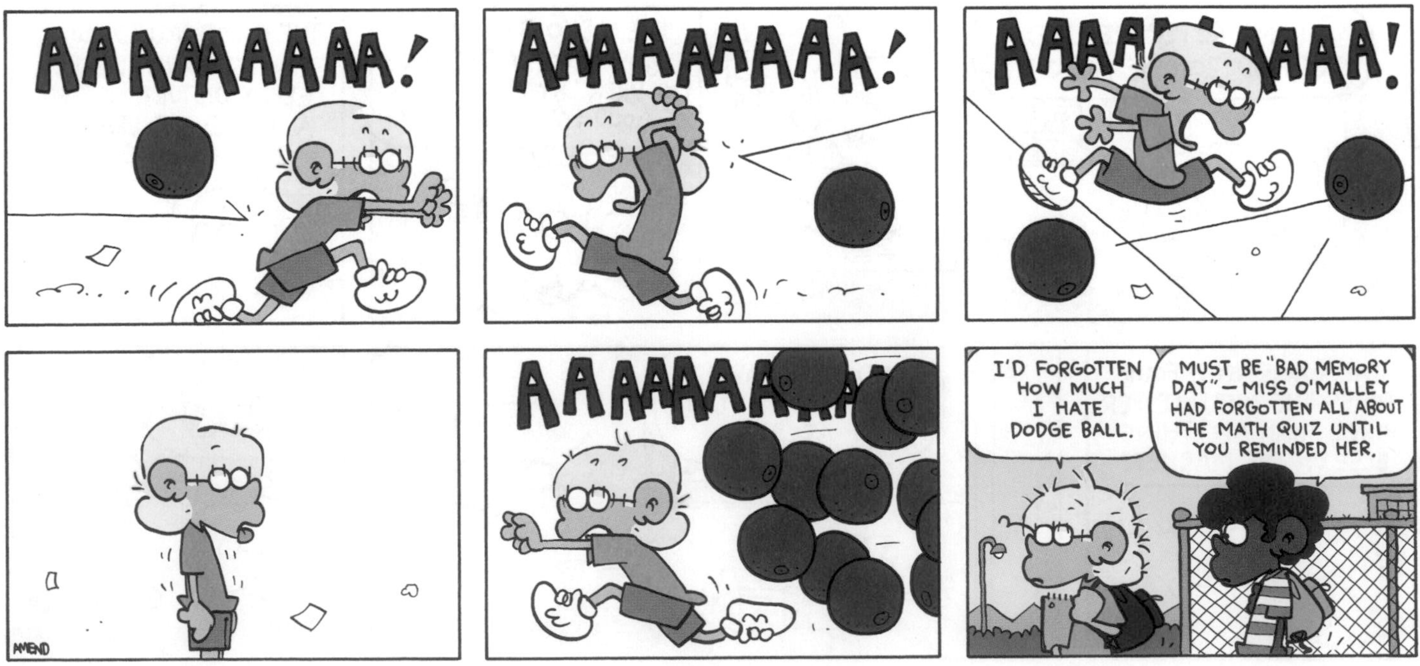
AAAAAAAAA!
AAAAAAAAA!
AAAAAAA!
AMEND
AAAAAAA
I'D FORGOTTEN HOW MUCH I HATE DODGE BALL.
MUST BE "BAD MEMORY DAY" — MISS O'MALLEY HAD FORGOTTEN ALL ABOUT THE MATH QUIZ UNTIL YOU REMINDED HER.

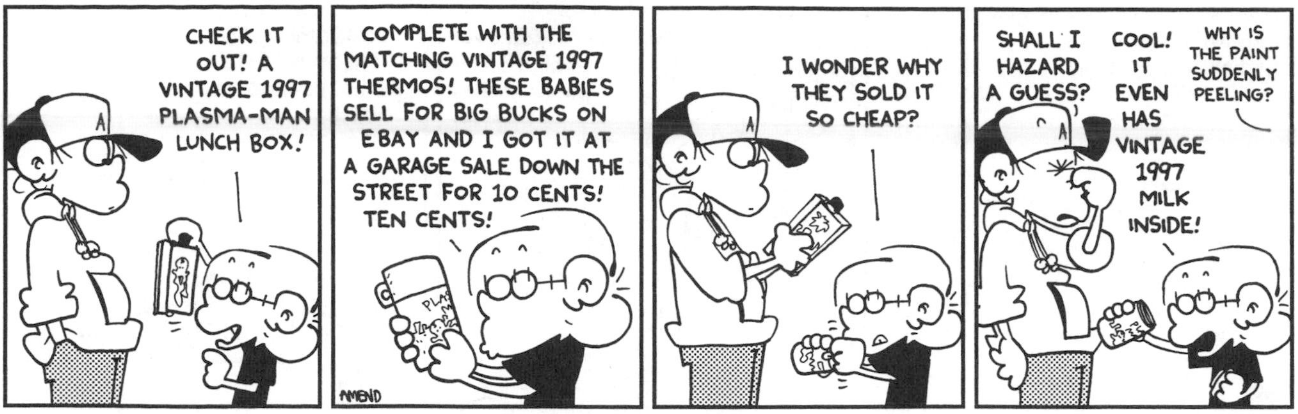
CHECK IT OUT! A VINTAGE 1997 PLASMA-MAN LUNCH BOX!
COMPLETE WITH THE MATCHING VINTAGE 1997 THERMOS! THESE BABIES SELL FOR BIG BUCKS ON EBAY AND I GOT IT AT A GARAGE SALE DOWN THE STREET FOR 10 CENTS! TEN CENTS!
AMEND
I WONDER WHY THEY SOLD IT SO CHEAP?
SHALL I HAZARD A GUESS?
COOL! IT EVEN HAS VINTAGE 1997 MILK INSIDE!
WHY IS THE PAINT SUDDENLY PEELING?

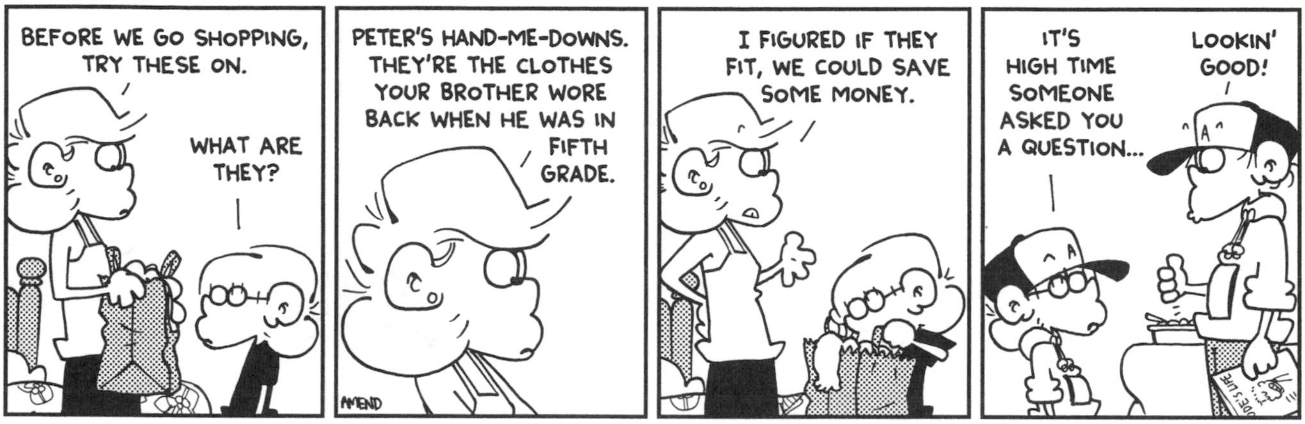
BEFORE WE GO SHOPPING, TRY THESE ON.
WHAT ARE THEY?
PETER'S HAND-ME-DOWNS. THEY'RE THE CLOTHES YOUR BROTHER WORE BACK WHEN HE WAS IN FIFTH GRADE.
AMEND
I FIGURED IF THEY FIT, WE COULD SAVE SOME MONEY.
IT'S HIGH TIME SOMEONE ASKED YOU A QUESTION...
LOOKIN' GOOD!

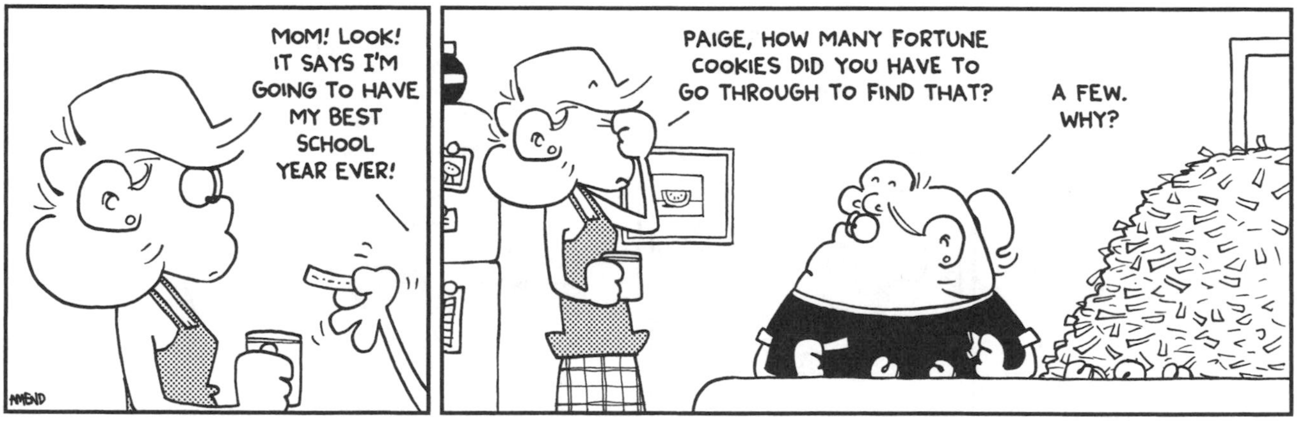
MOM! LOOK! IT SAYS I'M GOING TO HAVE MY BEST SCHOOL YEAR EVER!
AMEND
PAIGE, HOW MANY FORTUNE COOKIES DID YOU HAVE TO GO THROUGH TO FIND THAT?
A FEW. WHY?

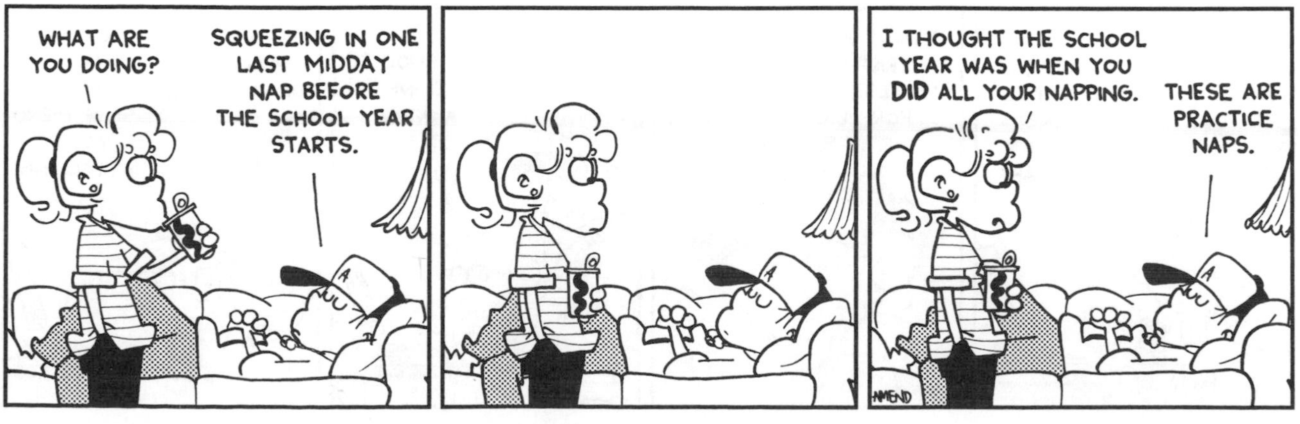
WHAT ARE YOU DOING?
SQUEEZING IN ONE LAST MIDDAY NAP BEFORE THE SCHOOL YEAR STARTS.
I THOUGHT THE SCHOOL YEAR WAS WHEN YOU DID ALL YOUR NAPPING.
THESE ARE PRACTICE NAPS.
AMEND

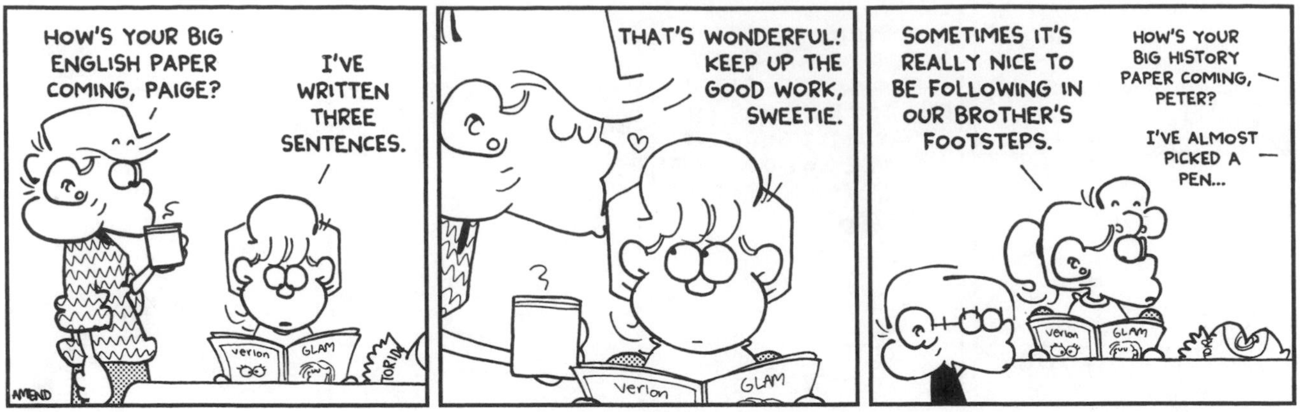
HOW'S YOUR BIG ENGLISH PAPER COMING, PAIGE?
I'VE WRITTEN THREE SENTENCES.
THAT'S WONDERFUL! KEEP UP THE GOOD WORK, SWEETIE.
SOMETIMES IT'S REALLY NICE TO BE FOLLOWING IN OUR BROTHER'S FOOTSTEPS.
HOW'S YOUR BIG HISTORY PAPER COMING, PETER?
I'VE ALMOST PICKED A PEN...

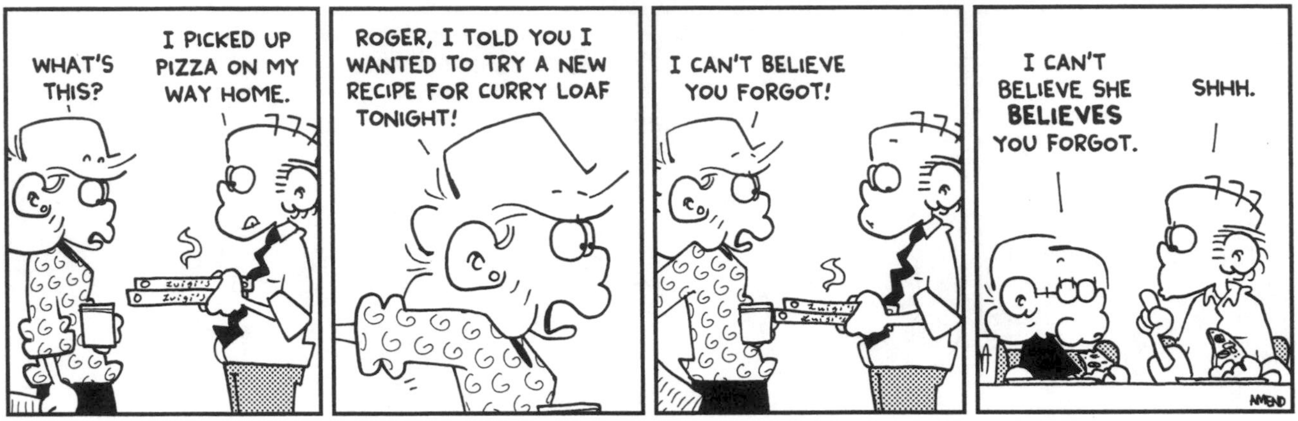
WHAT'S THIS?
I PICKED UP PIZZA ON MY WAY HOME.
ROGER, I TOLD YOU I WANTED TO TRY A NEW RECIPE FOR CURRY LOAF TONIGHT!
I CAN'T BELIEVE YOU FORGOT!
I CAN'T BELIEVE SHE **BELIEVES** YOU FORGOT.
SHHH.

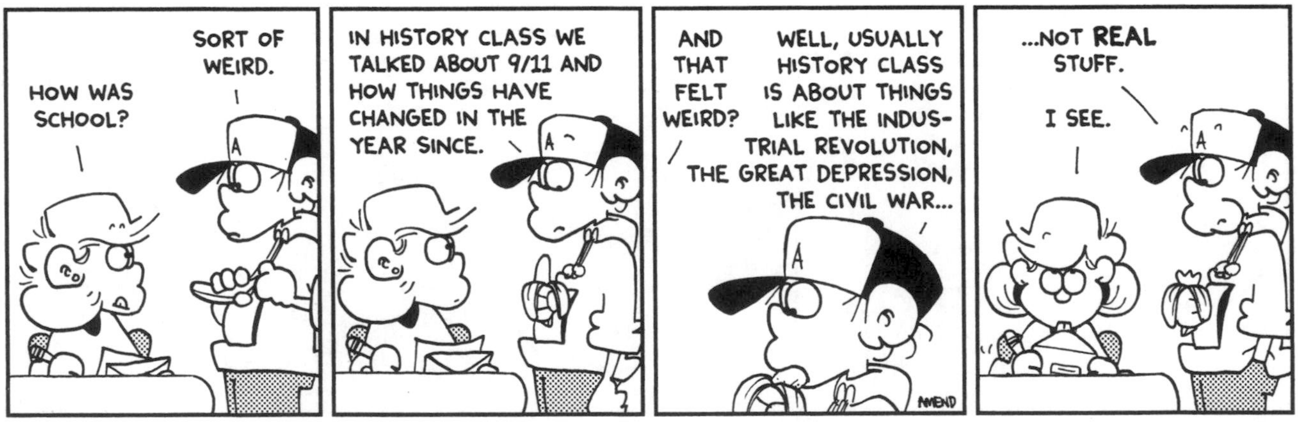
HOW WAS SCHOOL?
SORT OF WEIRD.
IN HISTORY CLASS WE TALKED ABOUT 9/11 AND HOW THINGS HAVE CHANGED IN THE YEAR SINCE.
AND THAT FELT WEIRD?
WELL, USUALLY HISTORY CLASS IS ABOUT THINGS LIKE THE INDUSTRIAL REVOLUTION, THE GREAT DEPRESSION, THE CIVIL WAR...
...NOT **REAL** STUFF.
I SEE.

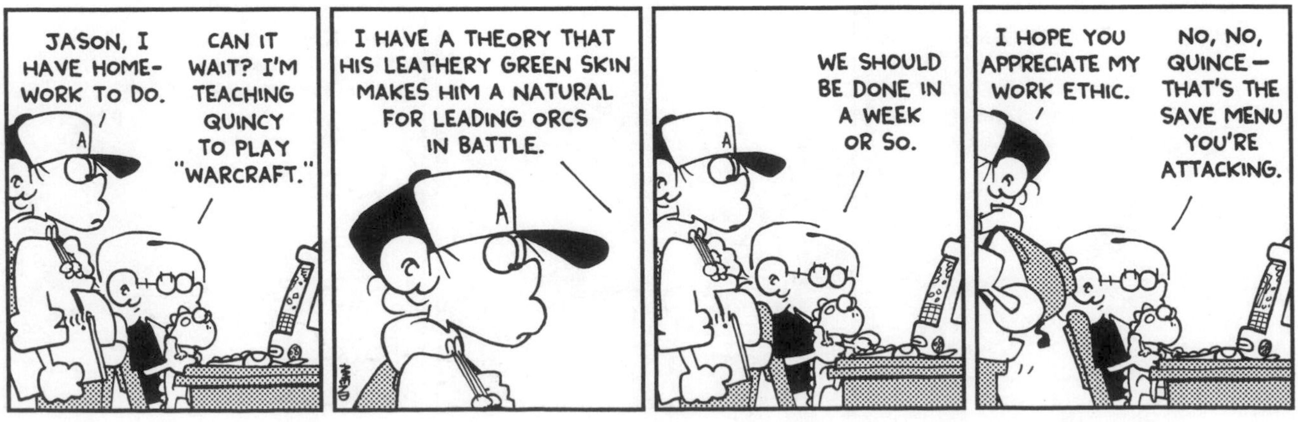
JASON, I HAVE HOMEWORK TO DO.
CAN IT WAIT? I'M TEACHING QUINCY TO PLAY "WARCRAFT."
I HAVE A THEORY THAT HIS LEATHERY GREEN SKIN MAKES HIM A NATURAL FOR LEADING ORCS IN BATTLE.
WE SHOULD BE DONE IN A WEEK OR SO.
I HOPE YOU APPRECIATE MY WORK ETHIC.
NO, NO, QUINCE—THAT'S THE SAVE MENU YOU'RE ATTACKING.

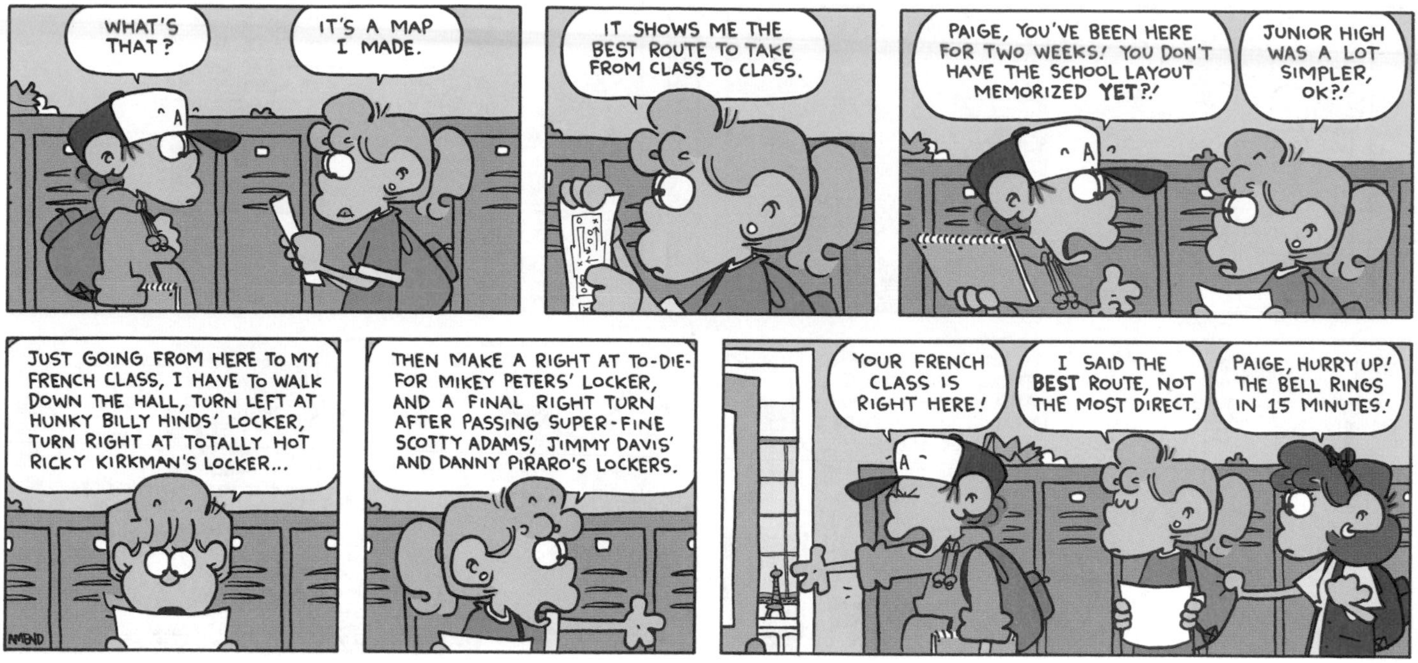
WHAT'S THAT?
IT'S A MAP I MADE.
IT SHOWS ME THE BEST ROUTE TO TAKE FROM CLASS TO CLASS.
PAIGE, YOU'VE BEEN HERE FOR TWO WEEKS! YOU DON'T HAVE THE SCHOOL LAYOUT MEMORIZED YET?!
JUNIOR HIGH WAS A LOT SIMPLER, OK?!
JUST GOING FROM HERE TO MY FRENCH CLASS, I HAVE TO WALK DOWN THE HALL, TURN LEFT AT HUNKY BILLY HINDS' LOCKER, TURN RIGHT AT TOTALLY HOT RICKY KIRKMAN'S LOCKER...
THEN MAKE A RIGHT AT TO-DIE-FOR MIKEY PETERS' LOCKER, AND A FINAL RIGHT TURN AFTER PASSING SUPER-FINE SCOTTY ADAMS', JIMMY DAVIS' AND DANNY PIRARO'S LOCKERS.
YOUR FRENCH CLASS IS RIGHT HERE!
I SAID THE BEST ROUTE, NOT THE MOST DIRECT.
PAIGE, HURRY UP! THE BELL RINGS IN 15 MINUTES!
AMEND

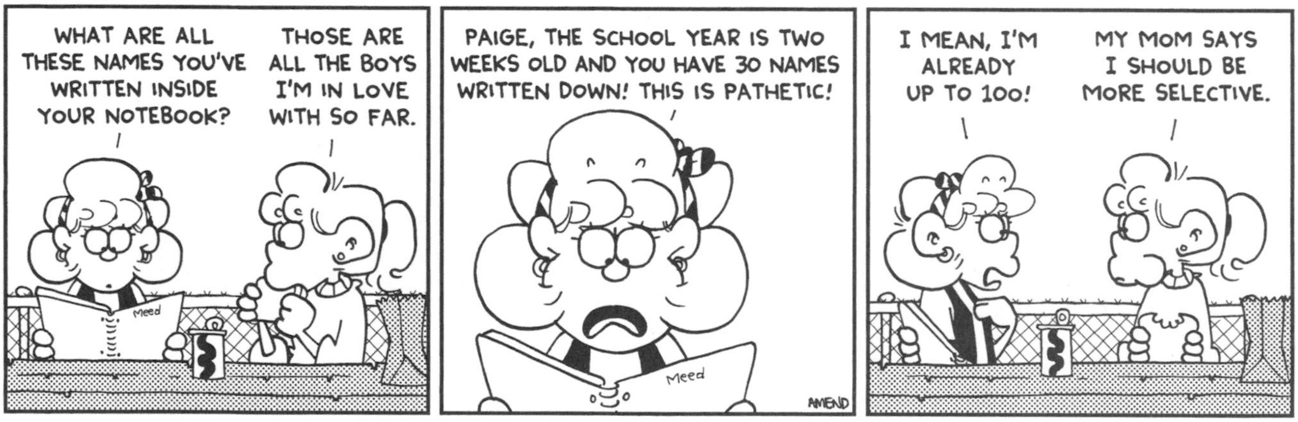
WHAT ARE ALL THESE NAMES YOU'VE WRITTEN INSIDE YOUR NOTEBOOK?
THOSE ARE ALL THE BOYS I'M IN LOVE WITH SO FAR.
Meed
PAIGE, THE SCHOOL YEAR IS TWO WEEKS OLD AND YOU HAVE 30 NAMES WRITTEN DOWN! THIS IS PATHETIC!
Meed
AMEND
I MEAN, I'M ALREADY UP TO 100!
MY MOM SAYS I SHOULD BE MORE SELECTIVE.

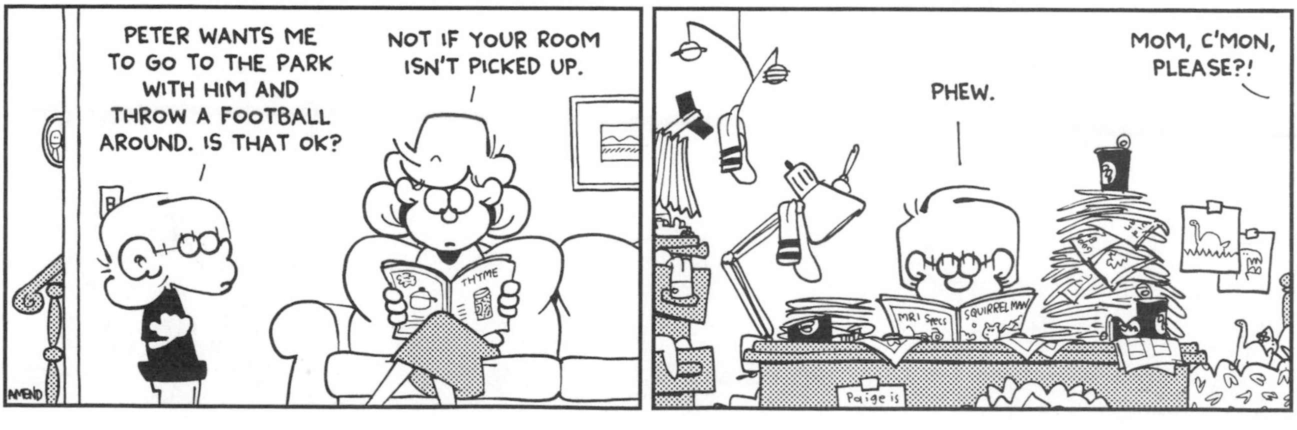
PETER WANTS ME TO GO TO THE PARK WITH HIM AND THROW A FOOTBALL AROUND. IS THAT OK?
NOT IF YOUR ROOM ISN'T PICKED UP.
THYME
AMEND
MOM, C'MON, PLEASE?!
PHEW.
SQUIRREL MAN
Paige is

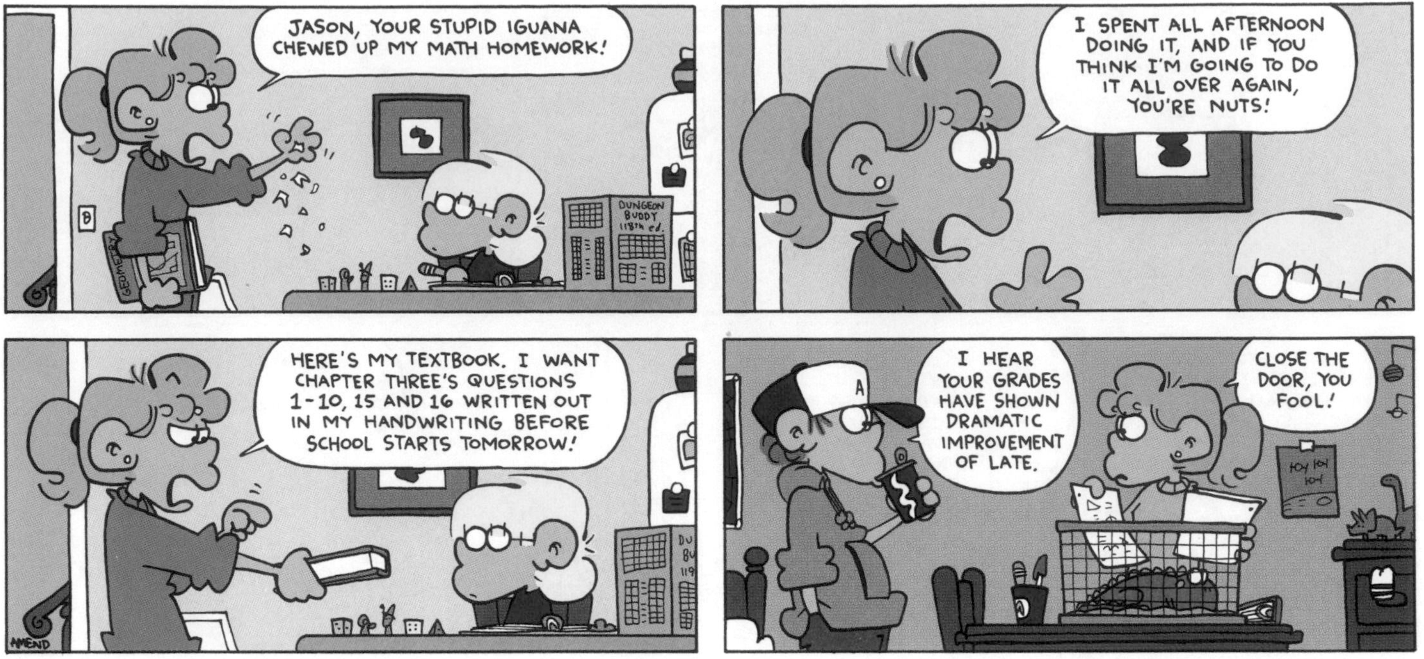
JASON, YOUR STUPID IGUANA CHEWED UP MY MATH HOMEWORK!
GEOMETRY
DUNGEON BUDDY 118th ed.
I SPENT ALL AFTERNOON DOING IT, AND IF YOU THINK I'M GOING TO DO IT ALL OVER AGAIN, YOU'RE NUTS!
HERE'S MY TEXTBOOK. I WANT CHAPTER THREE'S QUESTIONS 1-10, 15 AND 16 WRITTEN OUT IN MY HANDWRITING BEFORE SCHOOL STARTS TOMORROW!
AMEND
I HEAR YOUR GRADES HAVE SHOWN DRAMATIC IMPROVEMENT OF LATE.
CLOSE THE DOOR, YOU FOOL!

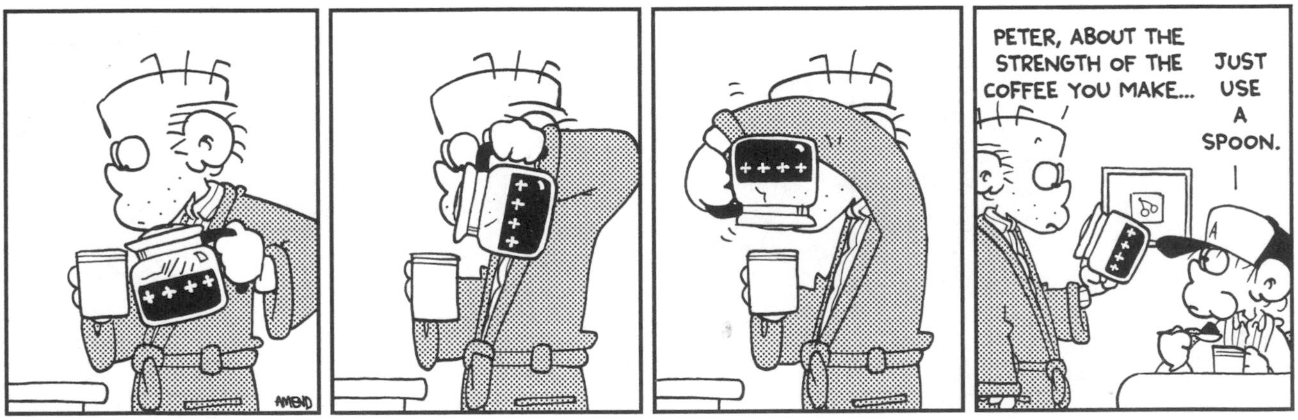
AMEND
PETER, ABOUT THE STRENGTH OF THE COFFEE YOU MAKE...
JUST USE A SPOON.

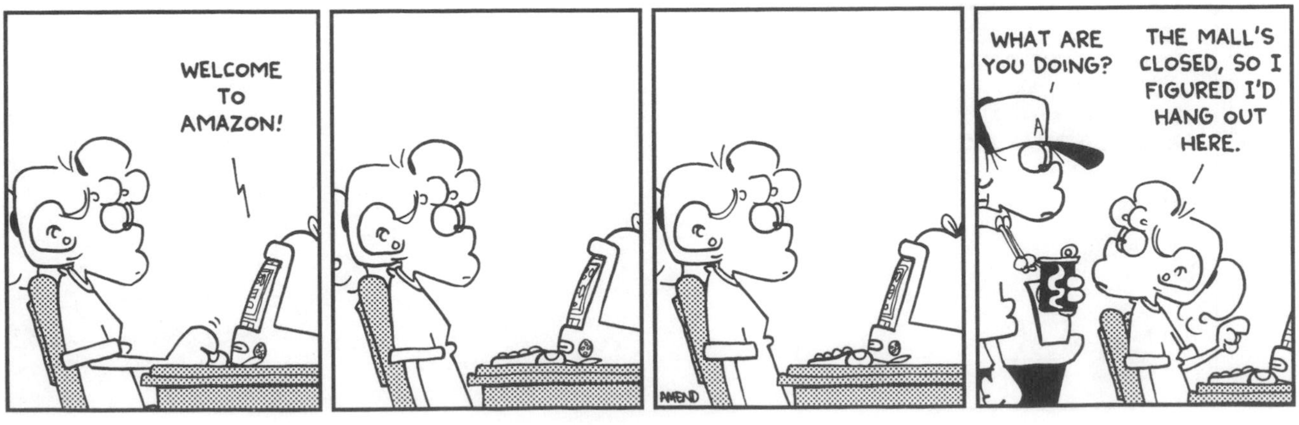
WELCOME TO AMAZON!
AMEND
WHAT ARE YOU DOING?
THE MALL'S CLOSED, SO I FIGURED I'D HANG OUT HERE.

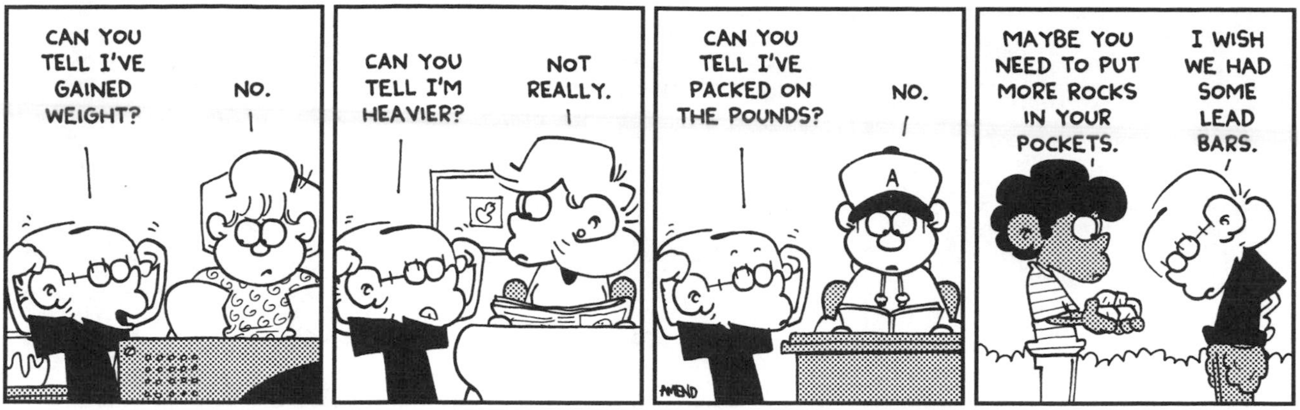
CAN YOU TELL I'VE GAINED WEIGHT?
NO.
CAN YOU TELL I'M HEAVIER?
NOT REALLY.
CAN YOU TELL I'VE PACKED ON THE POUNDS?
NO.
AMEND
MAYBE YOU NEED TO PUT MORE ROCKS IN YOUR POCKETS.
I WISH WE HAD SOME LEAD BARS.

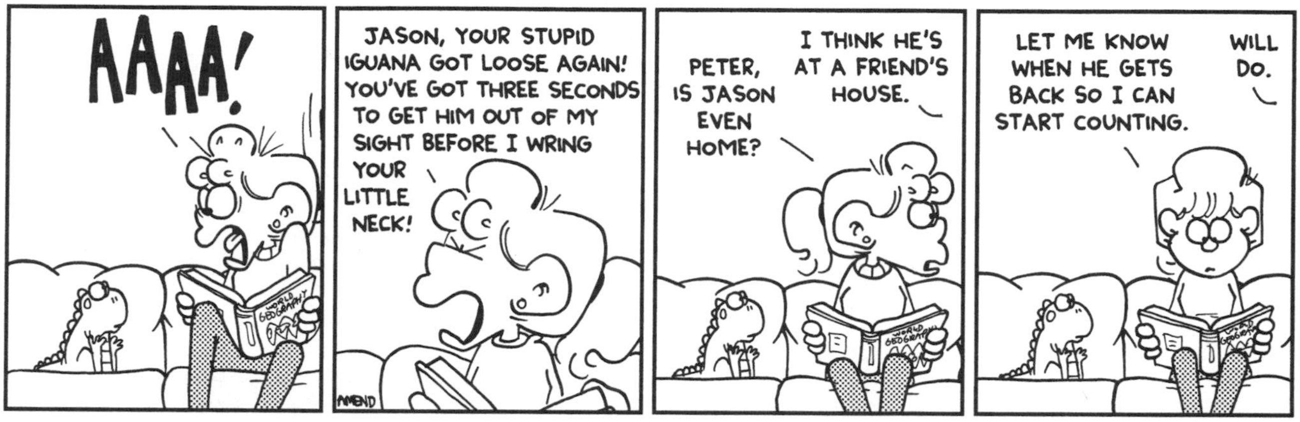
AAAA!
AMEND
JASON, YOUR STUPID IGUANA GOT LOOSE AGAIN! YOU'VE GOT THREE SECONDS TO GET HIM OUT OF MY SIGHT BEFORE I WRING YOUR LITTLE NECK!
PETER, IS JASON EVEN HOME?
I THINK HE'S AT A FRIEND'S HOUSE.
LET ME KNOW WHEN HE GETS BACK SO I CAN START COUNTING.
WILL DO.

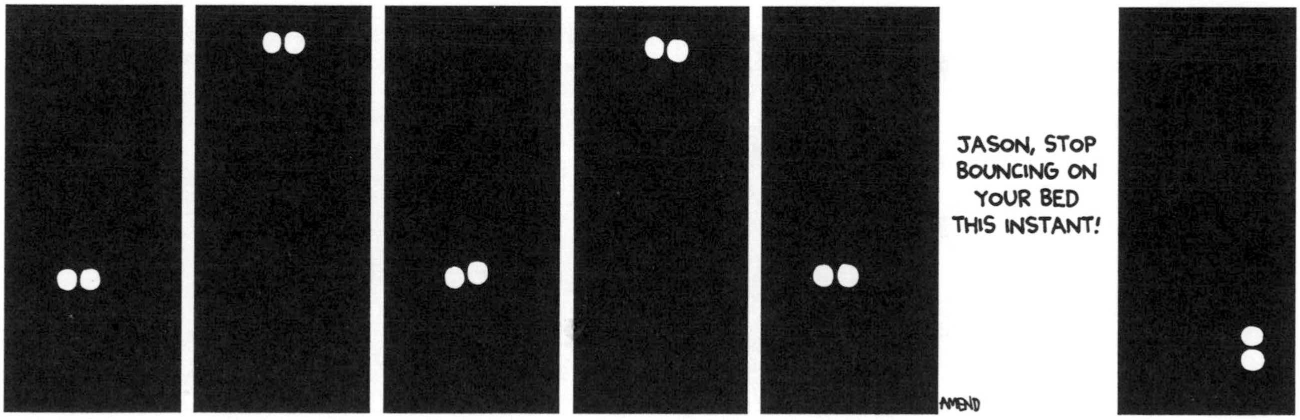
AMEND
JASON, STOP BOUNCING ON YOUR BED THIS INSTANT!

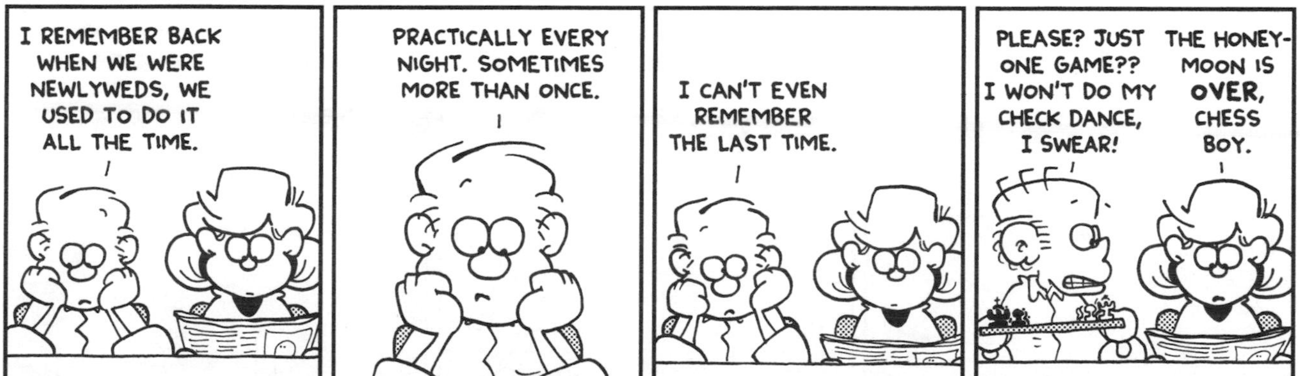
I REMEMBER BACK WHEN WE WERE NEWLYWEDS, WE USED TO DO IT ALL THE TIME.
PRACTICALLY EVERY NIGHT. SOMETIMES MORE THAN ONCE.
I CAN'T EVEN REMEMBER THE LAST TIME.
PLEASE? JUST ONE GAME?? I WON'T DO MY CHECK DANCE, I SWEAR!
THE HONEY-MOON IS OVER, CHESS BOY.
AMEND

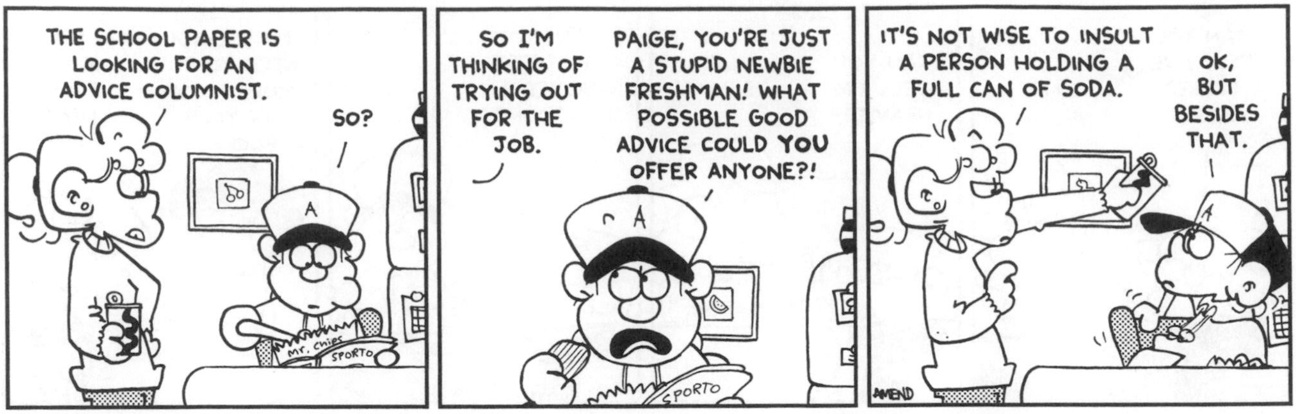
THE SCHOOL PAPER IS LOOKING FOR AN ADVICE COLUMNIST.
SO?
SO I'M THINKING OF TRYING OUT FOR THE JOB.
PAIGE, YOU'RE JUST A STUPID NEWBIE FRESHMAN! WHAT POSSIBLE GOOD ADVICE COULD YOU OFFER ANYONE?!
IT'S NOT WISE TO INSULT A PERSON HOLDING A FULL CAN OF SODA.
OK, BUT BESIDES THAT.

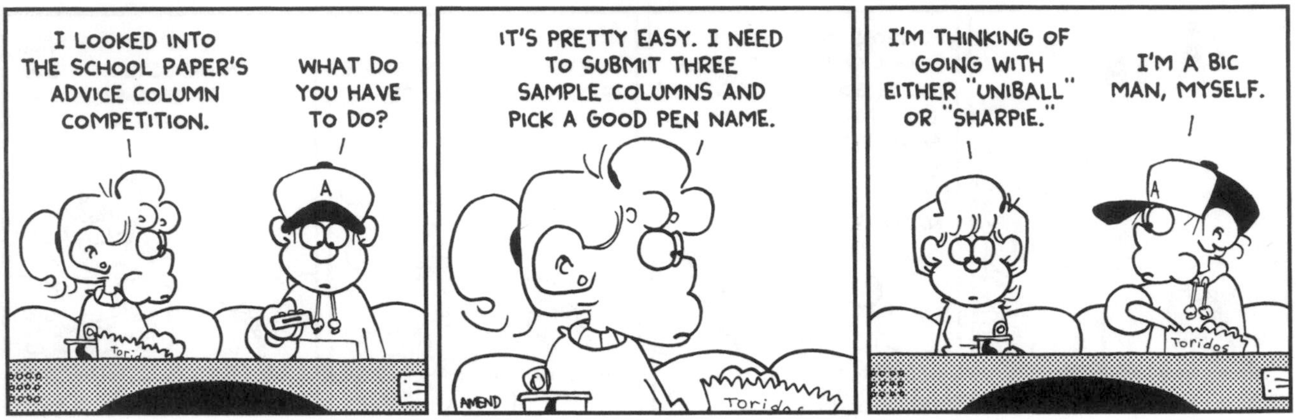
I LOOKED INTO THE SCHOOL PAPER'S ADVICE COLUMN COMPETITION.
WHAT DO YOU HAVE TO DO?
IT'S PRETTY EASY. I NEED TO SUBMIT THREE SAMPLE COLUMNS AND PICK A GOOD PEN NAME.
I'M THINKING OF GOING WITH EITHER "UNIBALL" OR "SHARPIE."
I'M A BIC MAN, MYSELF.

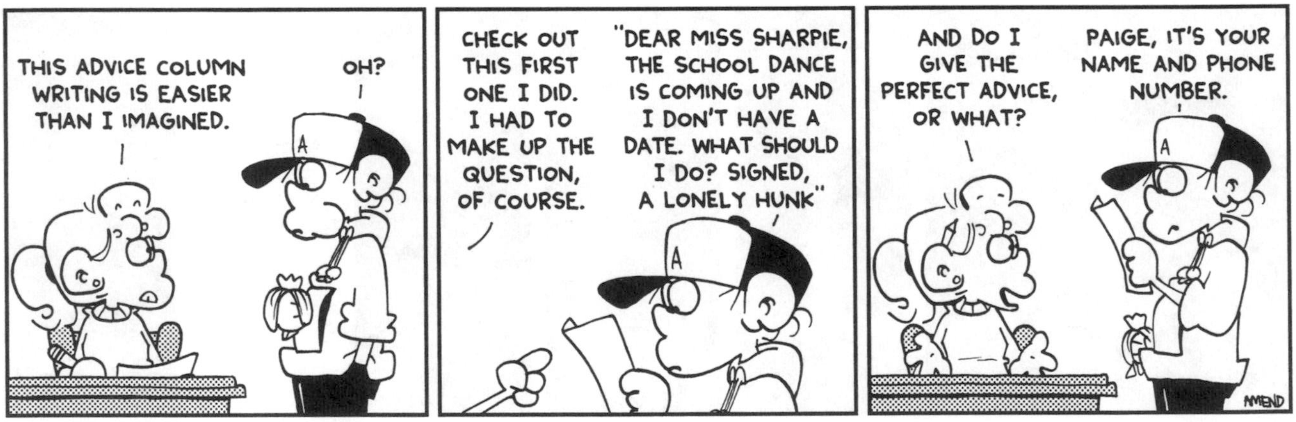
THIS ADVICE COLUMN WRITING IS EASIER THAN I IMAGINED.
OH?
CHECK OUT THIS FIRST ONE I DID. I HAD TO MAKE UP THE QUESTION, OF COURSE.
"DEAR MISS SHARPIE, THE SCHOOL DANCE IS COMING UP AND I DON'T HAVE A DATE. WHAT SHOULD I DO? SIGNED, A LONELY HUNK"
AND DO I GIVE THE PERFECT ADVICE, OR WHAT?
PAIGE, IT'S YOUR NAME AND PHONE NUMBER.

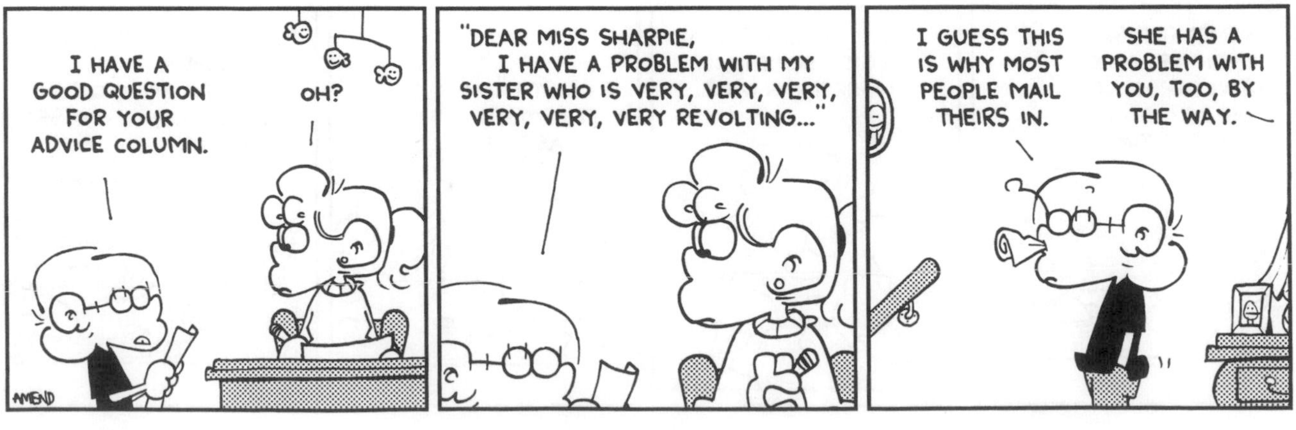
I HAVE A GOOD QUESTION FOR YOUR ADVICE COLUMN.
OH?
"DEAR MISS SHARPIE, I HAVE A PROBLEM WITH MY SISTER WHO IS VERY, VERY, VERY, VERY, VERY, VERY REVOLTING..."
I GUESS THIS IS WHY MOST PEOPLE MAIL THEIRS IN.
SHE HAS A PROBLEM WITH YOU, TOO, BY THE WAY.

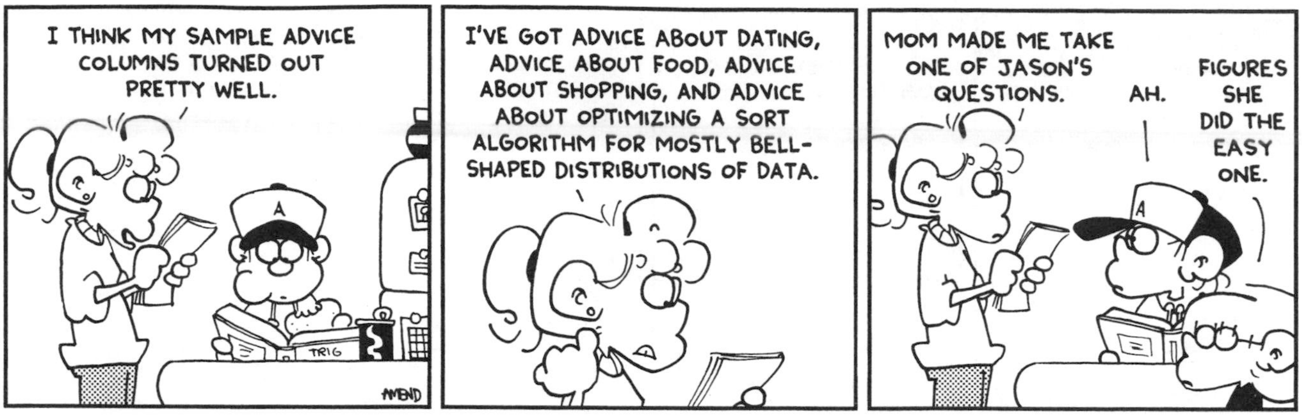
I THINK MY SAMPLE ADVICE COLUMNS TURNED OUT PRETTY WELL.
TRIG
AMEND
I'VE GOT ADVICE ABOUT DATING, ADVICE ABOUT FOOD, ADVICE ABOUT SHOPPING, AND ADVICE ABOUT OPTIMIZING A SORT ALGORITHM FOR MOSTLY BELL-SHAPED DISTRIBUTIONS OF DATA.
MOM MADE ME TAKE ONE OF JASON'S QUESTIONS.
AH.
FIGURES SHE DID THE EASY ONE.

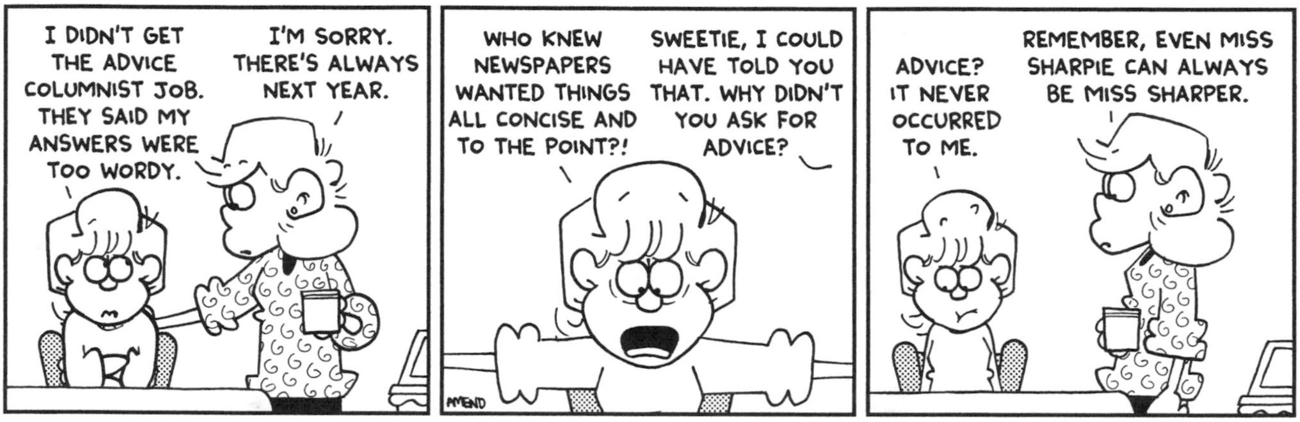
I DIDN'T GET THE ADVICE COLUMNIST JOB. THEY SAID MY ANSWERS WERE TOO WORDY.
I'M SORRY. THERE'S ALWAYS NEXT YEAR.
WHO KNEW NEWSPAPERS WANTED THINGS ALL CONCISE AND TO THE POINT?!
SWEETIE, I COULD HAVE TOLD YOU THAT. WHY DIDN'T YOU ASK FOR ADVICE?
AMEND
ADVICE? IT NEVER OCCURRED TO ME.
REMEMBER, EVEN MISS SHARPIE CAN ALWAYS BE MISS SHARPER.

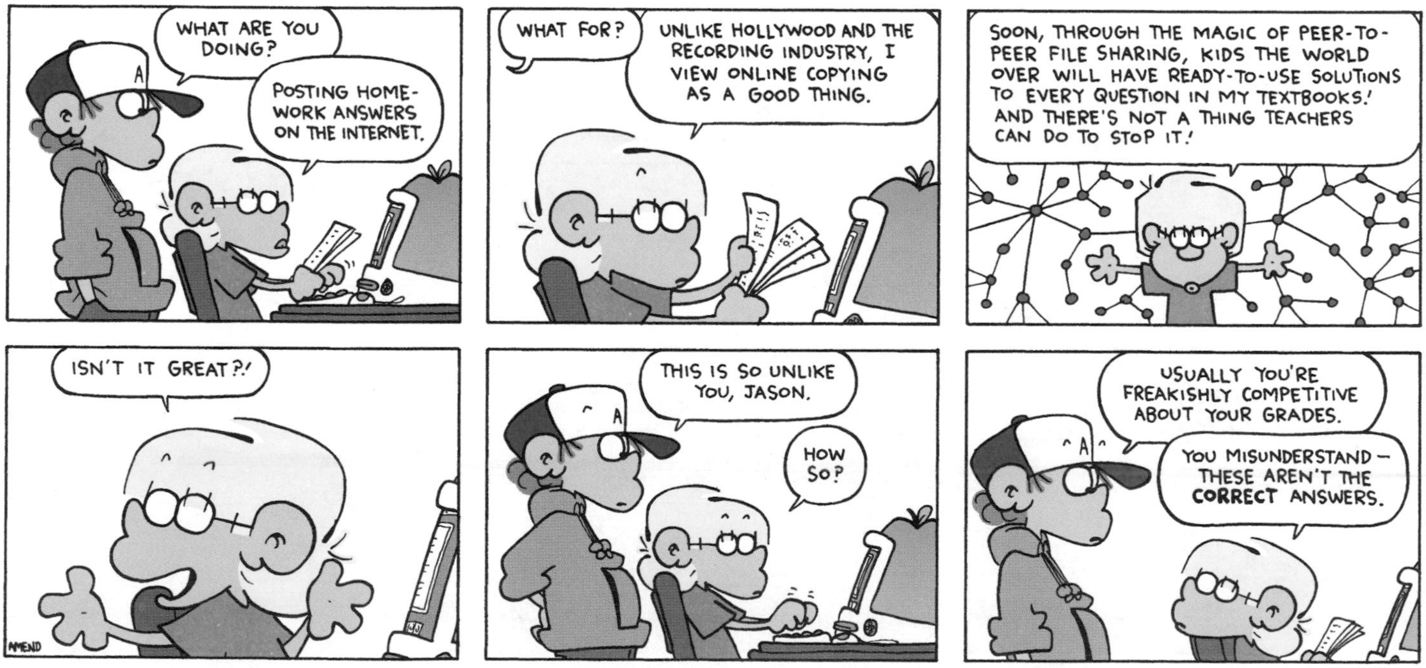
WHAT ARE YOU DOING?
POSTING HOME-WORK ANSWERS ON THE INTERNET.
WHAT FOR?
UNLIKE HOLLYWOOD AND THE RECORDING INDUSTRY, I VIEW ONLINE COPYING AS A GOOD THING.
SOON, THROUGH THE MAGIC OF PEER-TO-PEER FILE SHARING, KIDS THE WORLD OVER WILL HAVE READY-TO-USE SOLUTIONS TO EVERY QUESTION IN MY TEXTBOOKS! AND THERE'S NOT A THING TEACHERS CAN DO TO STOP IT!
ISN'T IT GREAT?!
AMEND
THIS IS SO UNLIKE YOU, JASON.
HOW SO?
USUALLY YOU'RE FREAKISHLY COMPETITIVE ABOUT YOUR GRADES.
YOU MISUNDERSTAND — THESE AREN'T THE CORRECT ANSWERS.

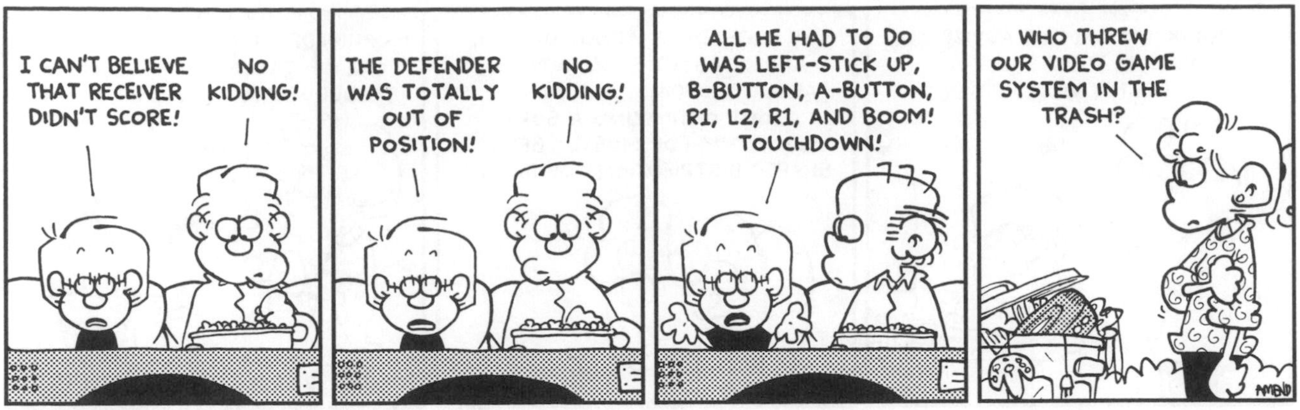
I CAN'T BELIEVE THAT RECEIVER DIDN'T SCORE!
NO KIDDING!
THE DEFENDER WAS TOTALLY OUT OF POSITION!
NO KIDDING!
ALL HE HAD TO DO WAS LEFT-STICK UP, B-BUTTON, A-BUTTON, R1, L2, R1, AND BOOM! TOUCHDOWN!
WHO THREW OUR VIDEO GAME SYSTEM IN THE TRASH?
AMEND

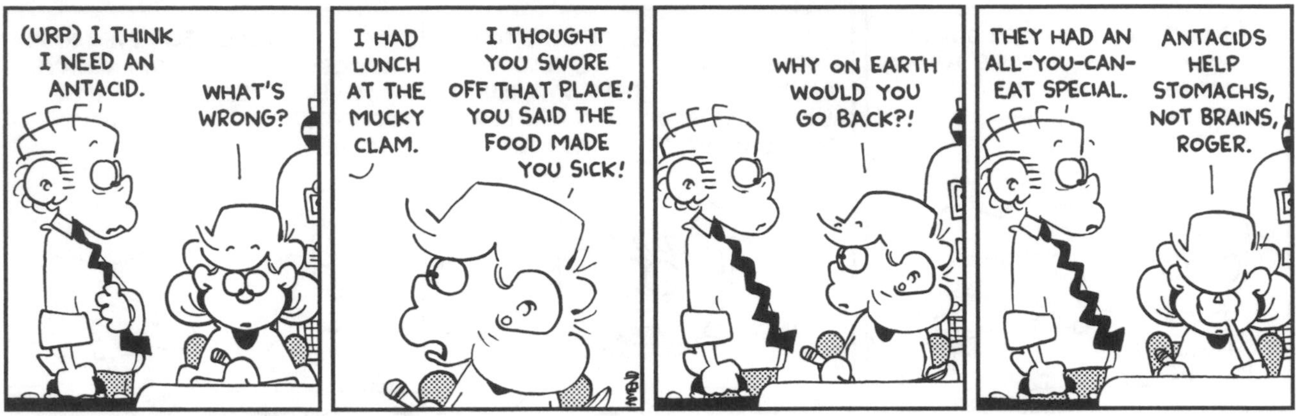
(URP) I THINK I NEED AN ANTACID.
WHAT'S WRONG?
I HAD LUNCH AT THE MUCKY CLAM.
I THOUGHT YOU SWORE OFF THAT PLACE! YOU SAID THE FOOD MADE YOU SICK!
AMEND
WHY ON EARTH WOULD YOU GO BACK?!
THEY HAD AN ALL-YOU-CAN-EAT SPECIAL.
ANTACIDS HELP STOMACHS, NOT BRAINS, ROGER.

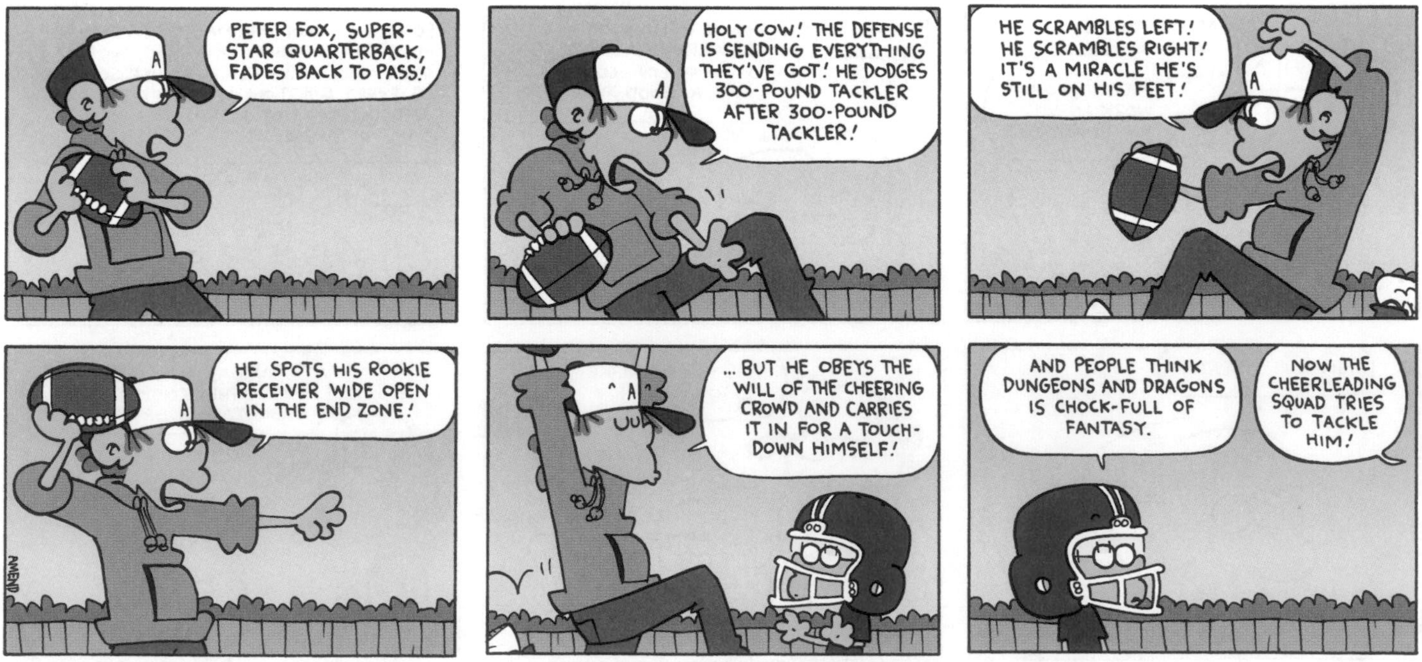
PETER FOX, SUPER-STAR QUARTERBACK, FADES BACK TO PASS!
HOLY COW! THE DEFENSE IS SENDING EVERYTHING THEY'VE GOT! HE DODGES 300-POUND TACKLER AFTER 300-POUND TACKLER!
HE SCRAMBLES LEFT! HE SCRAMBLES RIGHT! IT'S A MIRACLE HE'S STILL ON HIS FEET!
HE SPOTS HIS ROOKIE RECEIVER WIDE OPEN IN THE END ZONE!
AMEND
... BUT HE OBEYS THE WILL OF THE CHEERING CROWD AND CARRIES IT IN FOR A TOUCH-DOWN HIMSELF!
AND PEOPLE THINK DUNGEONS AND DRAGONS IS CHOCK-FULL OF FANTASY.
NOW THE CHEERLEADING SQUAD TRIES TO TACKLE HIM!

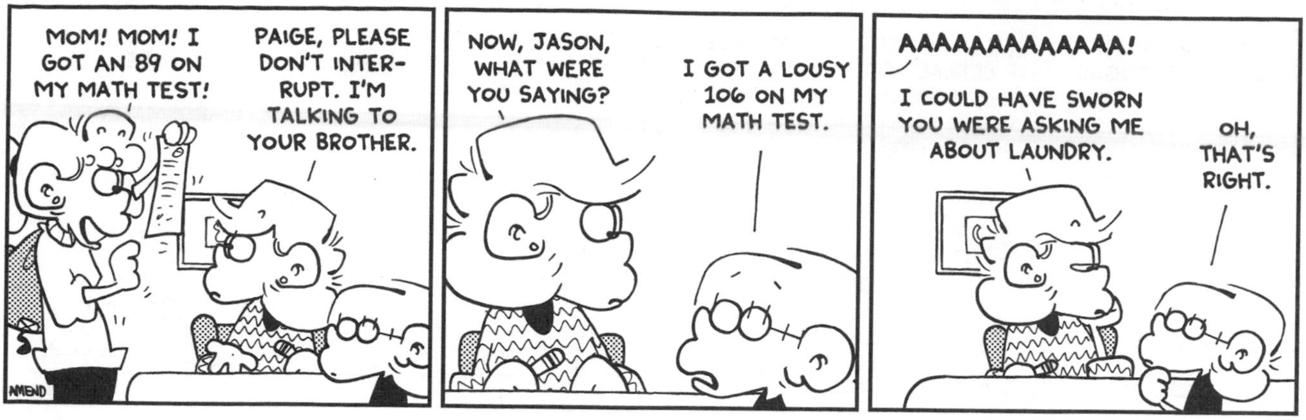
MOM! MOM! I GOT AN 89 ON MY MATH TEST!
PAIGE, PLEASE DON'T INTER-RUPT. I'M TALKING TO YOUR BROTHER.
NOW, JASON, WHAT WERE YOU SAYING?
I GOT A LOUSY 106 ON MY MATH TEST.
AAAAAAAAAAAA!
I COULD HAVE SWORN YOU WERE ASKING ME ABOUT LAUNDRY.
OH, THAT'S RIGHT.
AMEND

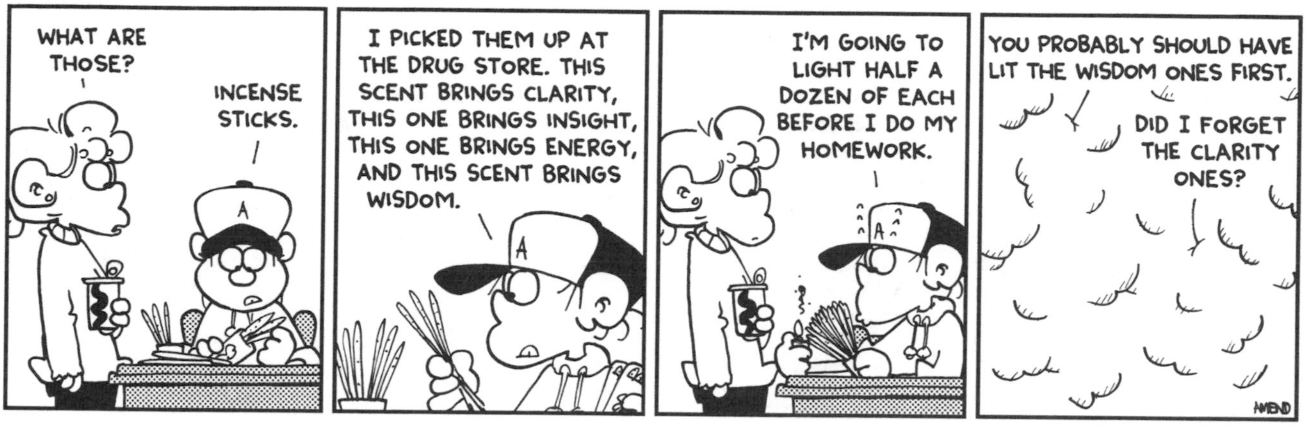
WHAT ARE THOSE?
INCENSE STICKS.
I PICKED THEM UP AT THE DRUG STORE. THIS SCENT BRINGS CLARITY, THIS ONE BRINGS INSIGHT, THIS ONE BRINGS ENERGY, AND THIS SCENT BRINGS WISDOM.
I'M GOING TO LIGHT HALF A DOZEN OF EACH BEFORE I DO MY HOMEWORK.
YOU PROBABLY SHOULD HAVE LIT THE WISDOM ONES FIRST.
DID I FORGET THE CLARITY ONES?
AMEND

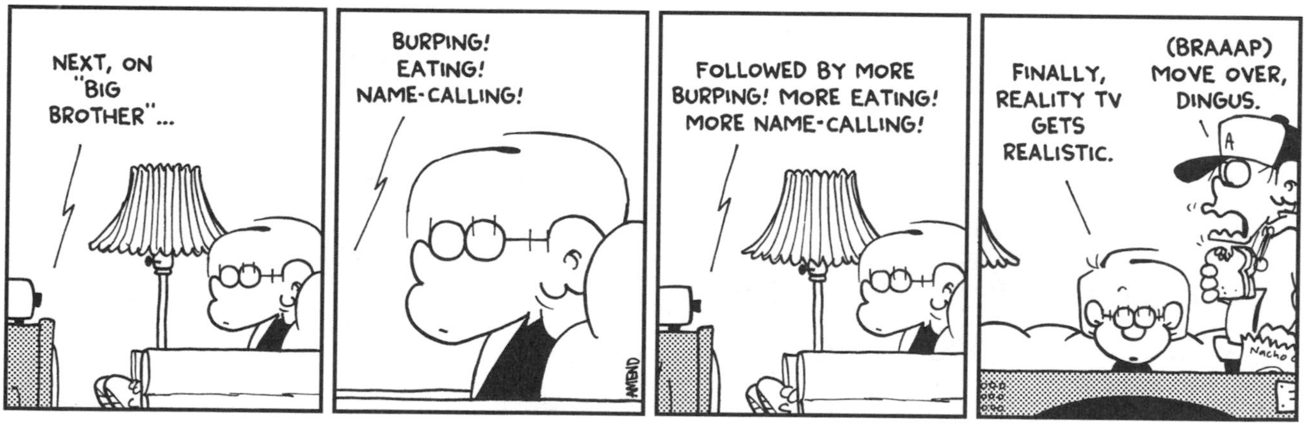
NEXT, ON "BIG BROTHER"...
BURPING! EATING! NAME-CALLING!
AMEND
FOLLOWED BY MORE BURPING! MORE EATING! MORE NAME-CALLING!
FINALLY, REALITY TV GETS REALISTIC.
(BRAAAP) MOVE OVER, DINGUS.

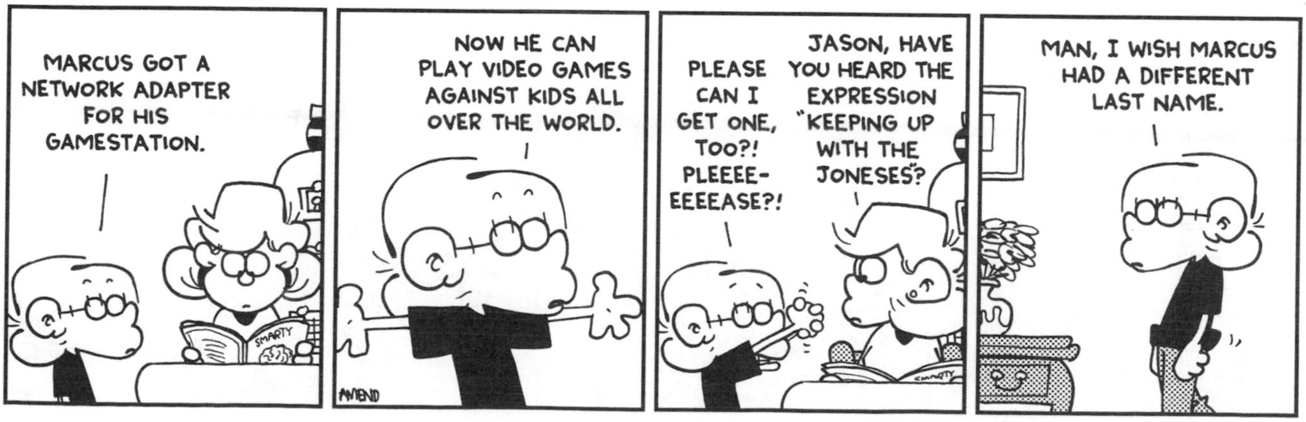
MARCUS GOT A NETWORK ADAPTER FOR HIS GAMESTATION.
SMARTY
NOW HE CAN PLAY VIDEO GAMES AGAINST KIDS ALL OVER THE WORLD.
AMEND
PLEASE CAN I GET ONE, TOO?! PLEEEE-EEEEASE?!
JASON, HAVE YOU HEARD THE EXPRESSION "KEEPING UP WITH THE JONESES"?
MAN, I WISH MARCUS HAD A DIFFERENT LAST NAME.

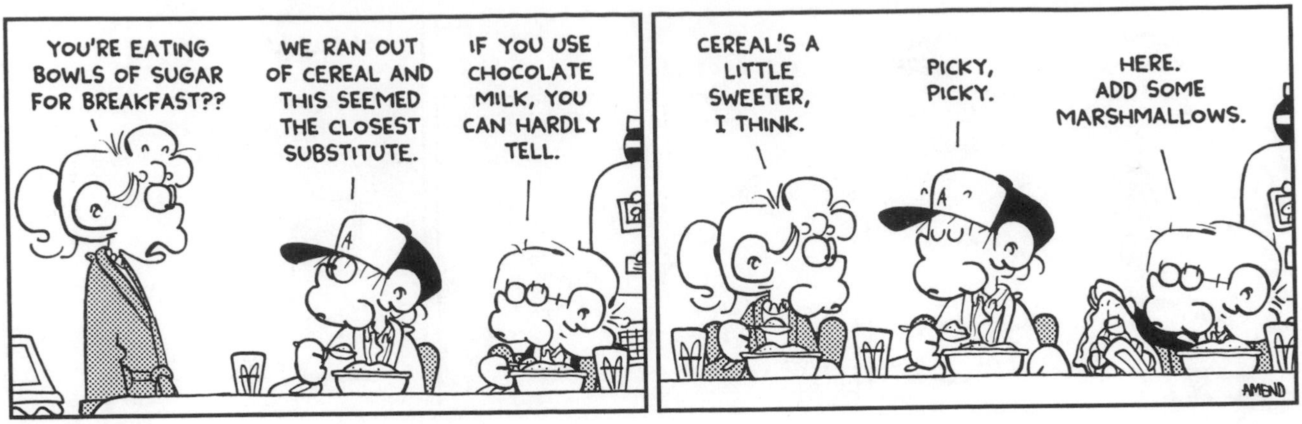
YOU'RE EATING BOWLS OF SUGAR FOR BREAKFAST??
WE RAN OUT OF CEREAL AND THIS SEEMED THE CLOSEST SUBSTITUTE.
IF YOU USE CHOCOLATE MILK, YOU CAN HARDLY TELL.
CEREAL'S A LITTLE SWEETER, I THINK.
PICKY, PICKY.
HERE. ADD SOME MARSHMALLOWS.
AMEND

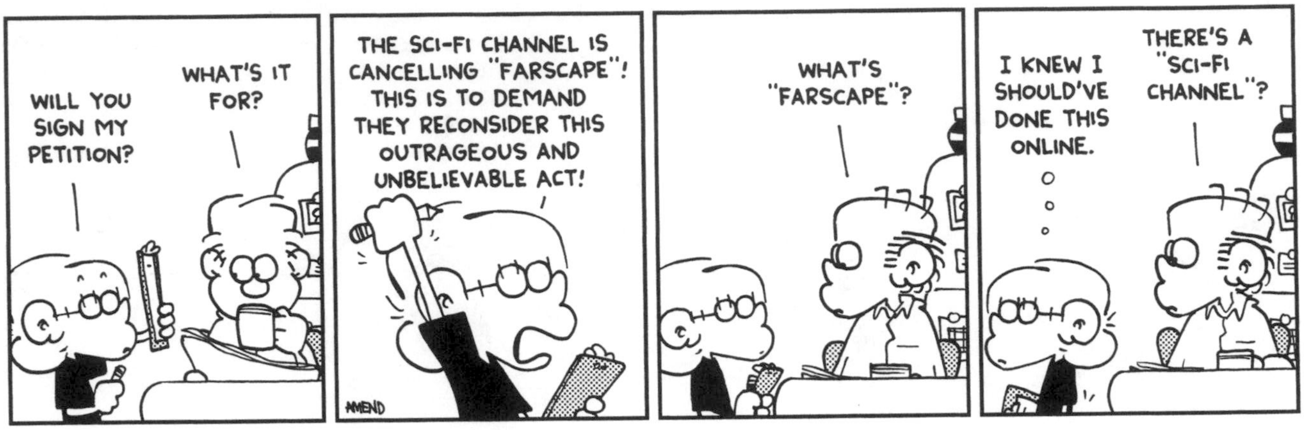
WILL YOU SIGN MY PETITION?
WHAT'S IT FOR?
THE SCI-FI CHANNEL IS CANCELLING "FARSCAPE"! THIS IS TO DEMAND THEY RECONSIDER THIS OUTRAGEOUS AND UNBELIEVABLE ACT!
AMEND
WHAT'S "FARSCAPE"?
I KNEW I SHOULD'VE DONE THIS ONLINE.
THERE'S A "SCI-FI CHANNEL"?

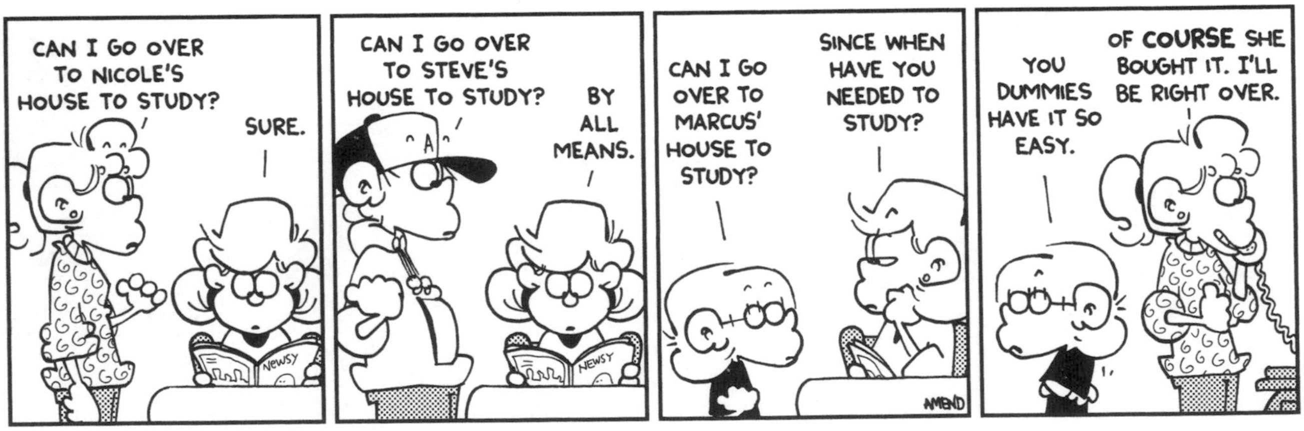
CAN I GO OVER TO NICOLE'S HOUSE TO STUDY?
SURE.
NEWSY
CAN I GO OVER TO STEVE'S HOUSE TO STUDY?
BY ALL MEANS.
NEWSY
CAN I GO OVER TO MARCUS' HOUSE TO STUDY?
SINCE WHEN HAVE YOU NEEDED TO STUDY?
AMEND
YOU DUMMIES HAVE IT SO EASY.
OF COURSE SHE BOUGHT IT. I'LL BE RIGHT OVER.

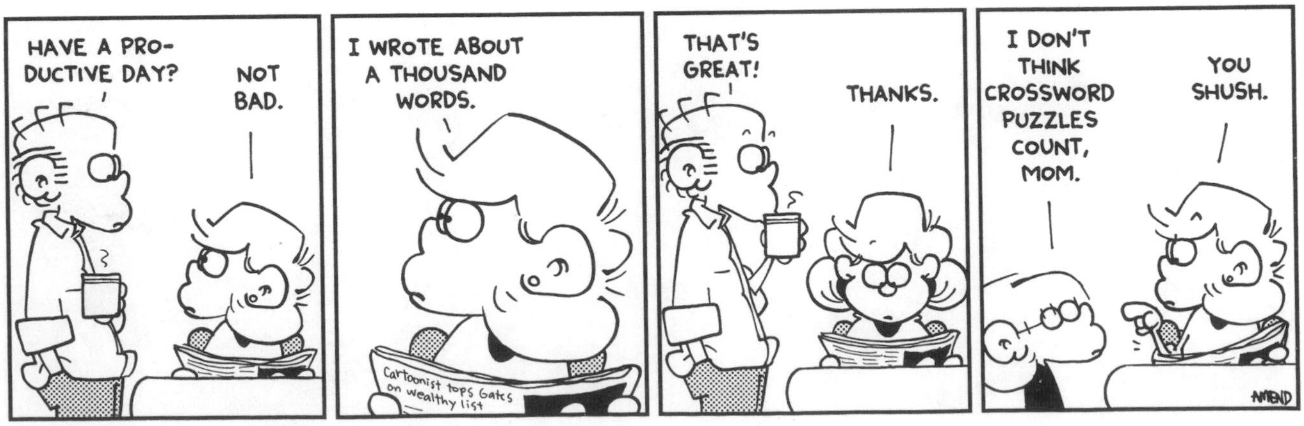
HAVE A PRO-DUCTIVE DAY?
NOT BAD.
I WROTE ABOUT A THOUSAND WORDS.
Cartoonist tops Gates on wealthy list
THAT'S GREAT!
THANKS.
I DON'T THINK CROSSWORD PUZZLES COUNT, MOM.
YOU SHUSH.
AMEND

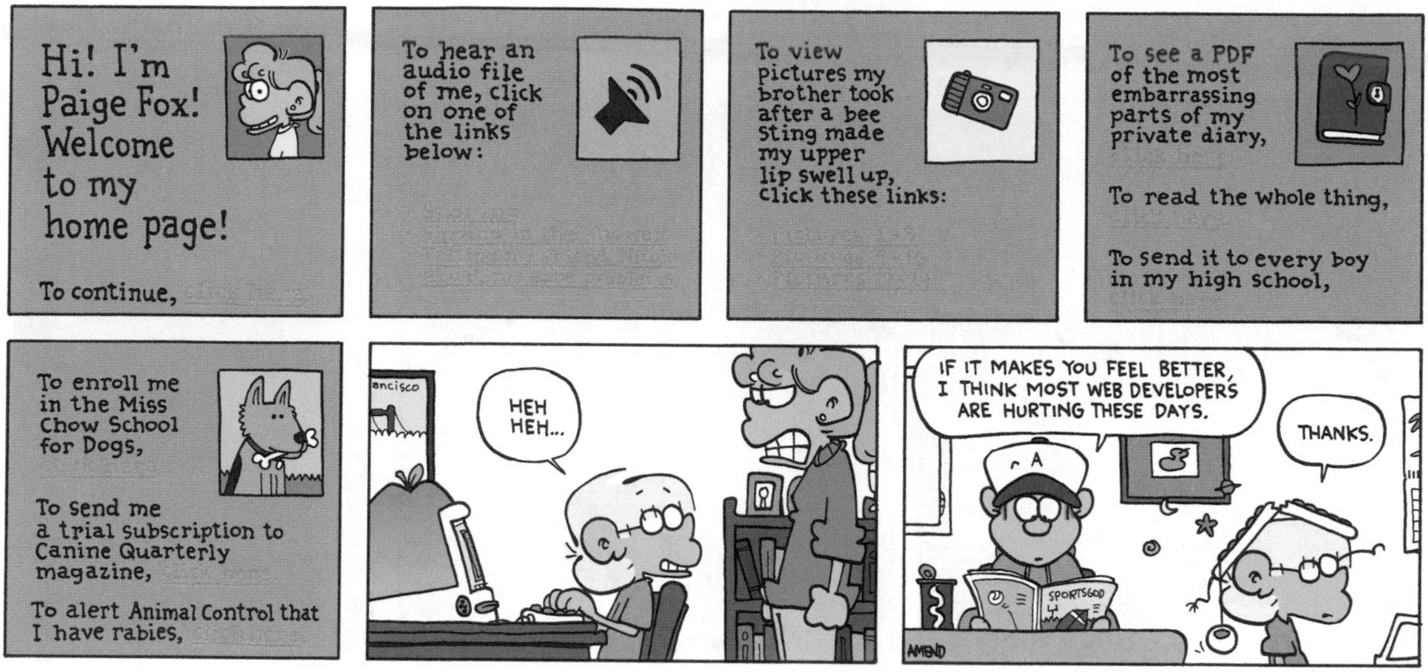
Hi! I'm Paige Fox! Welcome to my home page!
To continue,
To hear an audio file of me, click on one of the links below:
To view pictures my brother took after a bee sting made my upper lip swell up, click these links:
To see a PDF of the most embarrassing parts of my private diary,
To read the whole thing,
To send it to every boy in my high school,
To enroll me in the Miss Chow School for Dogs,
To send me a trial subscription to Canine Quarterly magazine,
To alert Animal Control that I have rabies,
HEH HEH...
IF IT MAKES YOU FEEL BETTER, I THINK MOST WEB DEVELOPERS ARE HURTING THESE DAYS.
THANKS.
SPORTSGOD
AMEND

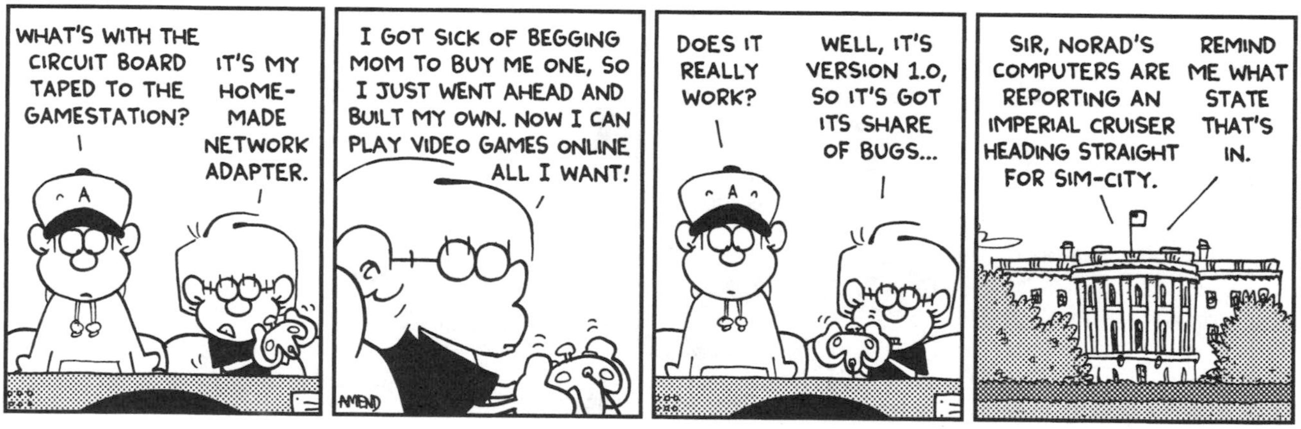
WHAT'S WITH THE CIRCUIT BOARD TAPED TO THE GAMESTATION?
IT'S MY HOME-MADE NETWORK ADAPTER.
I GOT SICK OF BEGGING MOM TO BUY ME ONE, SO I JUST WENT AHEAD AND BUILT MY OWN. NOW I CAN PLAY VIDEO GAMES ONLINE ALL I WANT!
DOES IT REALLY WORK?
WELL, IT'S VERSION 1.0, SO IT'S GOT ITS SHARE OF BUGS...
SIR, NORAD'S COMPUTERS ARE REPORTING AN IMPERIAL CRUISER HEADING STRAIGHT FOR SIM-CITY.
REMIND ME WHAT STATE THAT'S IN.
AMEND

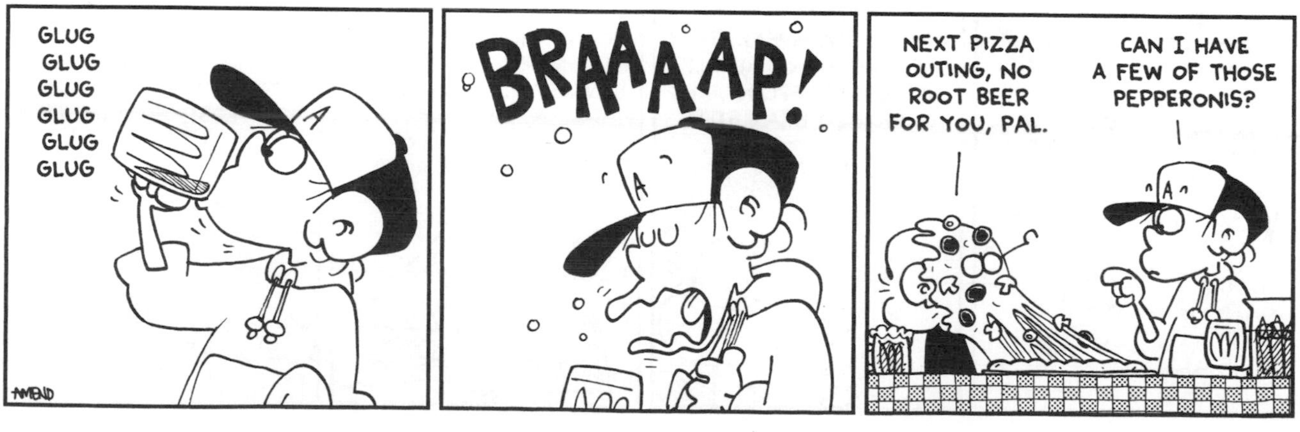
GLUG GLUG GLUG GLUG GLUG GLUG
BRAAAAP!
NEXT PIZZA OUTING, NO ROOT BEER FOR YOU, PAL.
CAN I HAVE A FEW OF THOSE PEPPERONIS?
AMEND

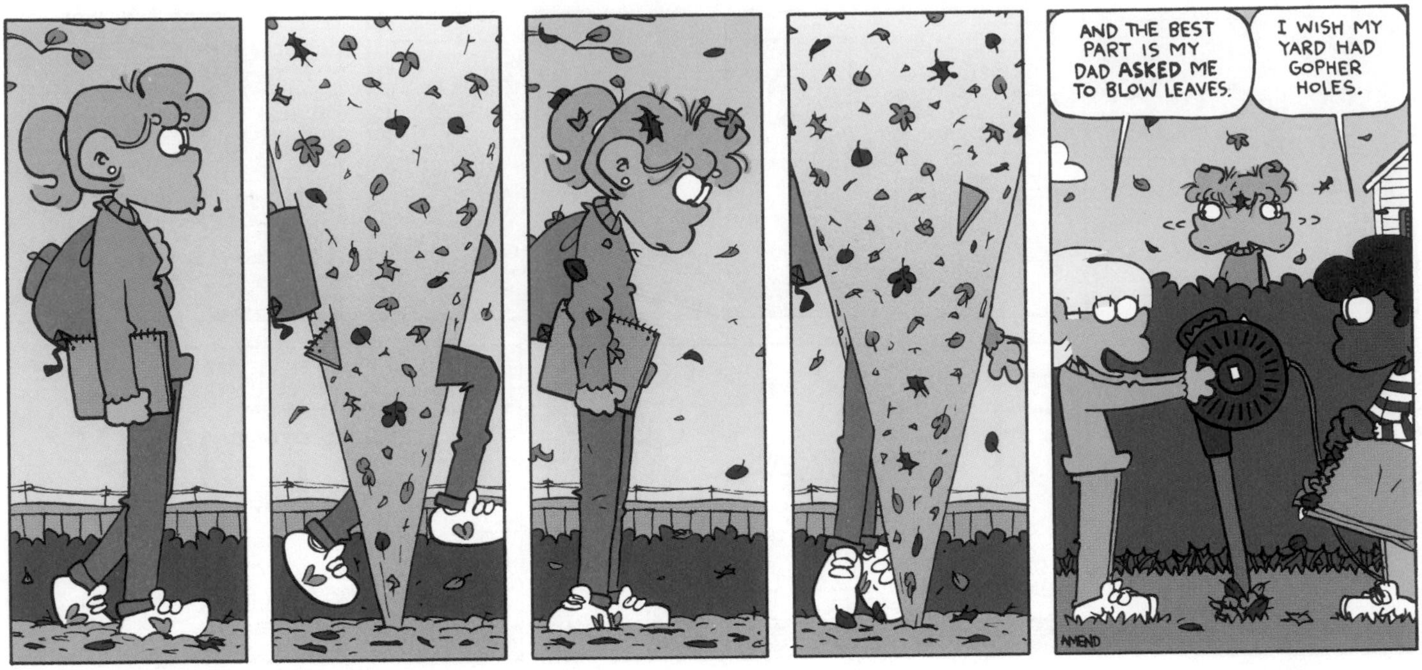
AND THE BEST PART IS MY DAD ASKED ME TO BLOW LEAVES.
I WISH MY YARD HAD GOPHER HOLES.
AMEND

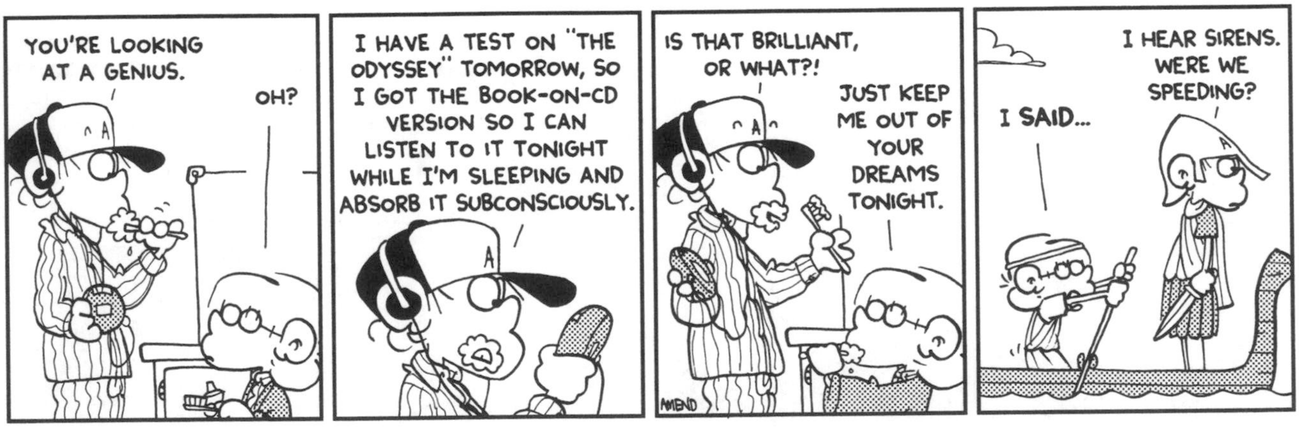
YOU'RE LOOKING AT A GENIUS.
OH?
I HAVE A TEST ON "THE ODYSSEY" TOMORROW, SO I GOT THE BOOK-ON-CD VERSION SO I CAN LISTEN TO IT TONIGHT WHILE I'M SLEEPING AND ABSORB IT SUBCONSCIOUSLY.
IS THAT BRILLIANT, OR WHAT?!
JUST KEEP ME OUT OF YOUR DREAMS TONIGHT.
AMEND
I SAID...
I HEAR SIRENS. WERE WE SPEEDING?

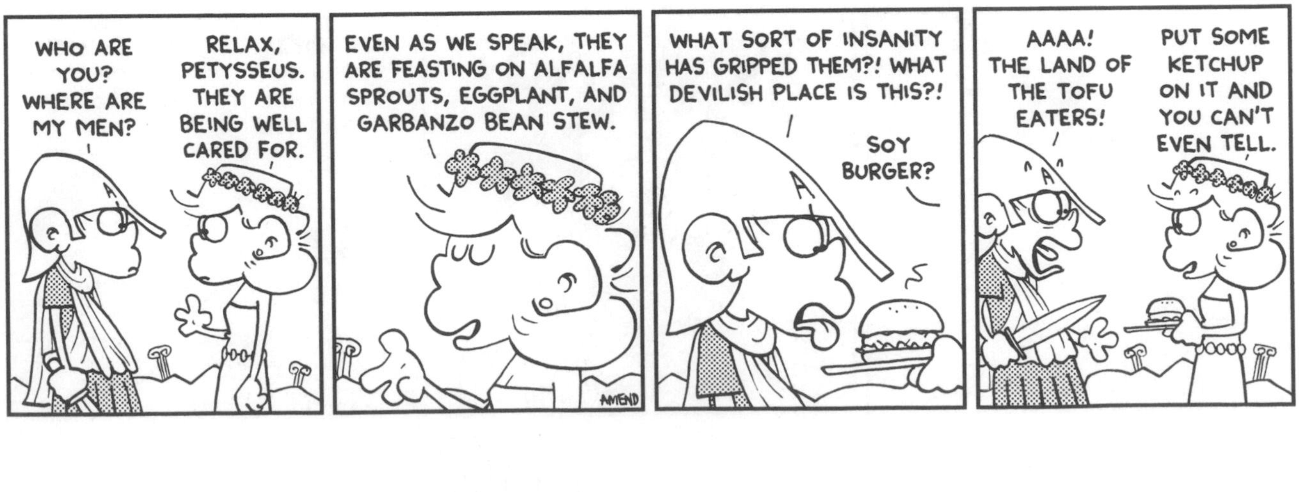
WHO ARE YOU? WHERE ARE MY MEN?
RELAX, PETYSSEUS. THEY ARE BEING WELL CARED FOR.
EVEN AS WE SPEAK, THEY ARE FEASTING ON ALFALFA SPROUTS, EGGPLANT, AND GARBANZO BEAN STEW.
AMEND
WHAT SORT OF INSANITY HAS GRIPPED THEM?! WHAT DEVILISH PLACE IS THIS?!
SOY BURGER?
AAAA! THE LAND OF THE TOFU EATERS!
PUT SOME KETCHUP ON IT AND YOU CAN'T EVEN TELL.

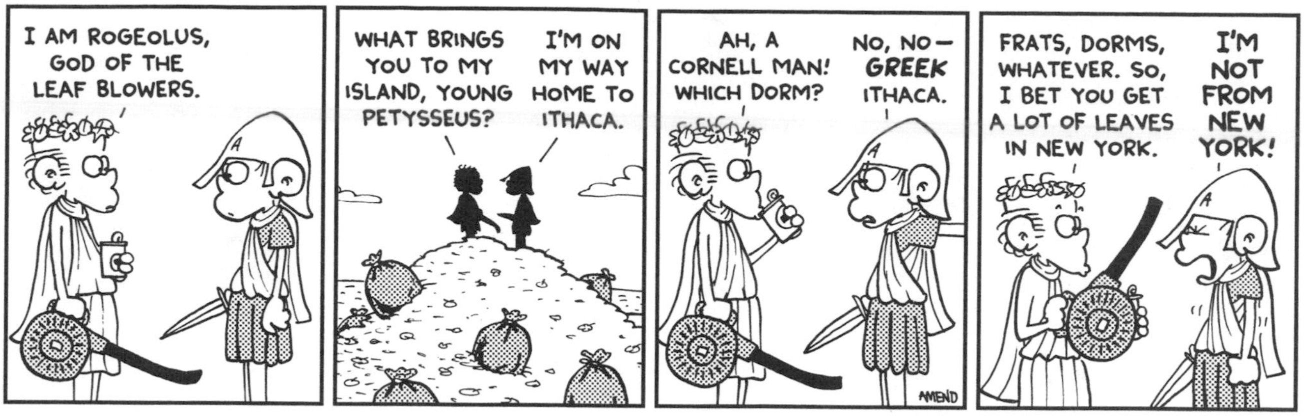
I AM ROGEOLUS, GOD OF THE LEAF BLOWERS.
WHAT BRINGS YOU TO MY ISLAND, YOUNG PETYSSEUS?
I'M ON MY WAY HOME TO ITHACA.
AH, A CORNELL MAN! WHICH DORM?
NO, NO— GREEK ITHACA.
FRATS, DORMS, WHATEVER. SO, I BET YOU GET A LOT OF LEAVES IN NEW YORK.
I'M NOT FROM NEW YORK!
AMEND

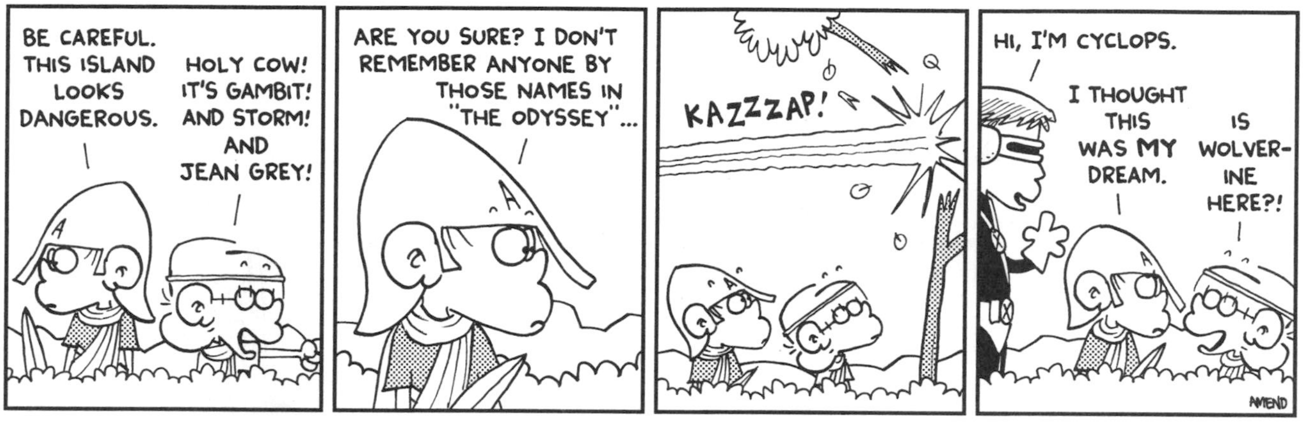
BE CAREFUL. THIS ISLAND LOOKS DANGEROUS.
HOLY COW! IT'S GAMBIT! AND STORM! AND JEAN GREY!
ARE YOU SURE? I DON'T REMEMBER ANYONE BY THOSE NAMES IN "THE ODYSSEY"...
KAZZZAP!
HI, I'M CYCLOPS.
I THOUGHT THIS WAS MY DREAM.
IS WOLVERINE HERE?!
AMEND

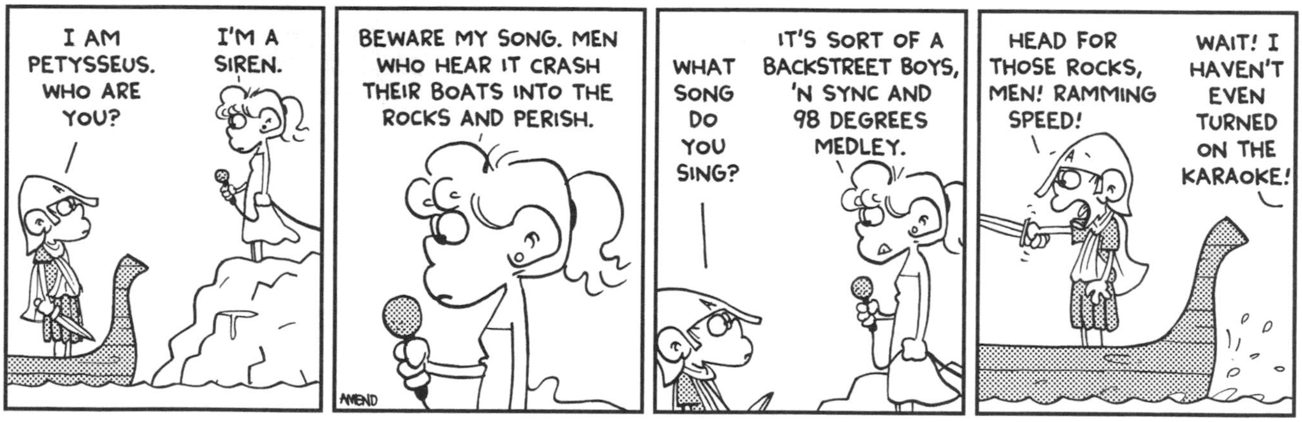
I AM PETYSSEUS. WHO ARE YOU?
I'M A SIREN.
BEWARE MY SONG. MEN WHO HEAR IT CRASH THEIR BOATS INTO THE ROCKS AND PERISH.
AMEND
WHAT SONG DO YOU SING?
IT'S SORT OF A BACKSTREET BOYS, 'N SYNC AND 98 DEGREES MEDLEY.
HEAD FOR THOSE ROCKS, MEN! RAMMING SPEED!
WAIT! I HAVEN'T EVEN TURNED ON THE KARAOKE!

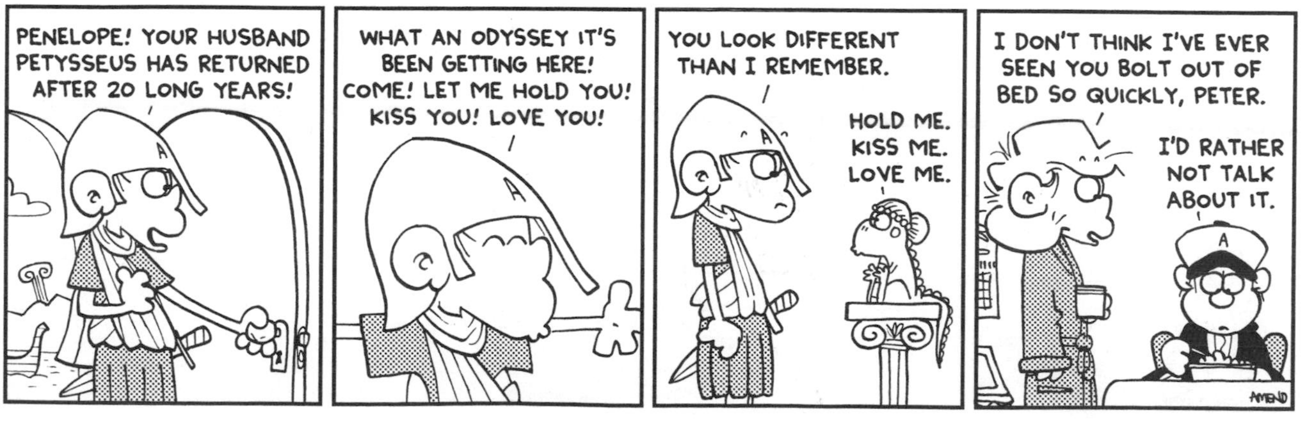
PENELOPE! YOUR HUSBAND PETYSSEUS HAS RETURNED AFTER 20 LONG YEARS!
WHAT AN ODYSSEY IT'S BEEN GETTING HERE! COME! LET ME HOLD YOU! KISS YOU! LOVE YOU!
YOU LOOK DIFFERENT THAN I REMEMBER.
HOLD ME. KISS ME. LOVE ME.
I DON'T THINK I'VE EVER SEEN YOU BOLT OUT OF BED SO QUICKLY, PETER.
I'D RATHER NOT TALK ABOUT IT.
AMEND

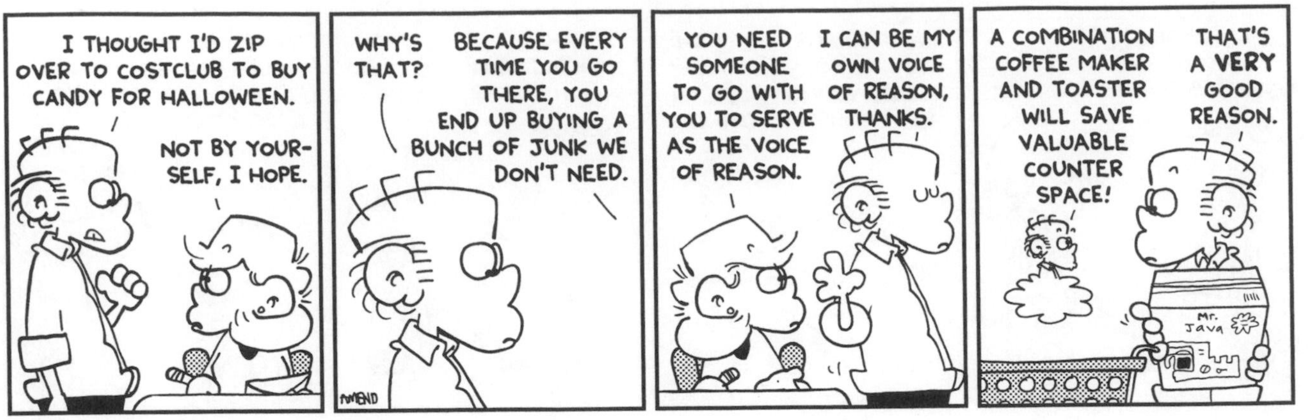
I THOUGHT I'D ZIP OVER TO COSTCLUB TO BUY CANDY FOR HALLOWEEN.
NOT BY YOURSELF, I HOPE.
WHY'S THAT?
BECAUSE EVERY TIME YOU GO THERE, YOU END UP BUYING A BUNCH OF JUNK WE DON'T NEED.
YOU NEED SOMEONE TO GO WITH YOU TO SERVE AS THE VOICE OF REASON.
I CAN BE MY OWN VOICE OF REASON, THANKS.
A COMBINATION COFFEE MAKER AND TOASTER WILL SAVE VALUABLE COUNTER SPACE!
THAT'S A **VERY** GOOD REASON.
Mr. Java

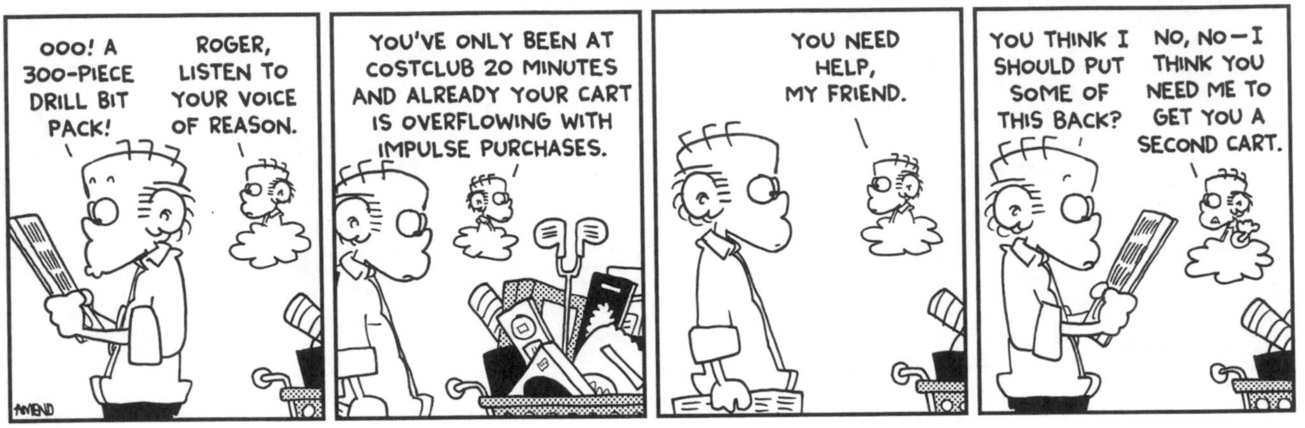
OOO! A 300-PIECE DRILL BIT PACK!
ROGER, LISTEN TO YOUR VOICE OF REASON.
YOU'VE ONLY BEEN AT COSTCLUB 20 MINUTES AND ALREADY YOUR CART IS OVERFLOWING WITH IMPULSE PURCHASES.
YOU NEED HELP, MY FRIEND.
YOU THINK I SHOULD PUT SOME OF THIS BACK?
NO, NO—I THINK YOU NEED ME TO GET YOU A SECOND CART.

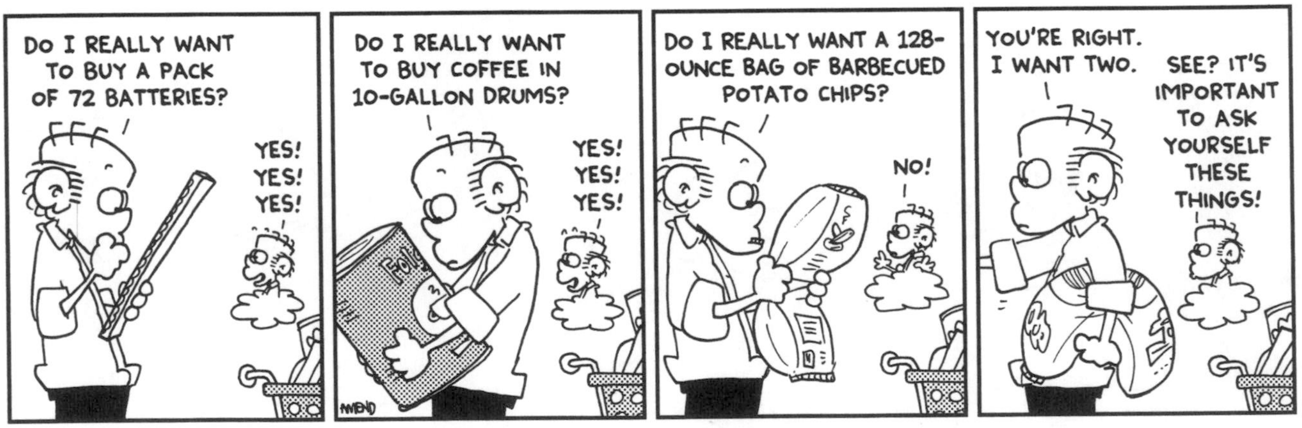
DO I REALLY WANT TO BUY A PACK OF 72 BATTERIES?
YES! YES! YES!
DO I REALLY WANT TO BUY COFFEE IN 10-GALLON DRUMS?
YES! YES! YES!
DO I REALLY WANT A 128-OUNCE BAG OF BARBECUED POTATO CHIPS?
NO!
YOU'RE RIGHT. I WANT TWO.
SEE? IT'S IMPORTANT TO ASK YOURSELF THESE THINGS!

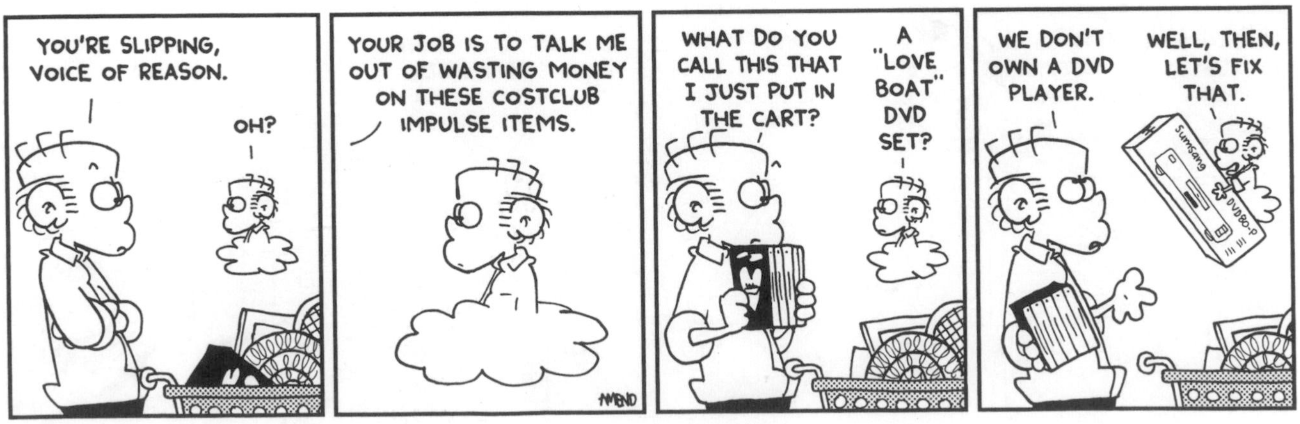
YOU'RE SLIPPING, VOICE OF REASON.
OH?
YOUR JOB IS TO TALK ME OUT OF WASTING MONEY ON THESE COSTCLUB IMPULSE ITEMS.
WHAT DO YOU CALL THIS THAT I JUST PUT IN THE CART?
A "LOVE BOAT" DVD SET?
WE DON'T OWN A DVD PLAYER.
WELL, THEN, LET'S FIX THAT.

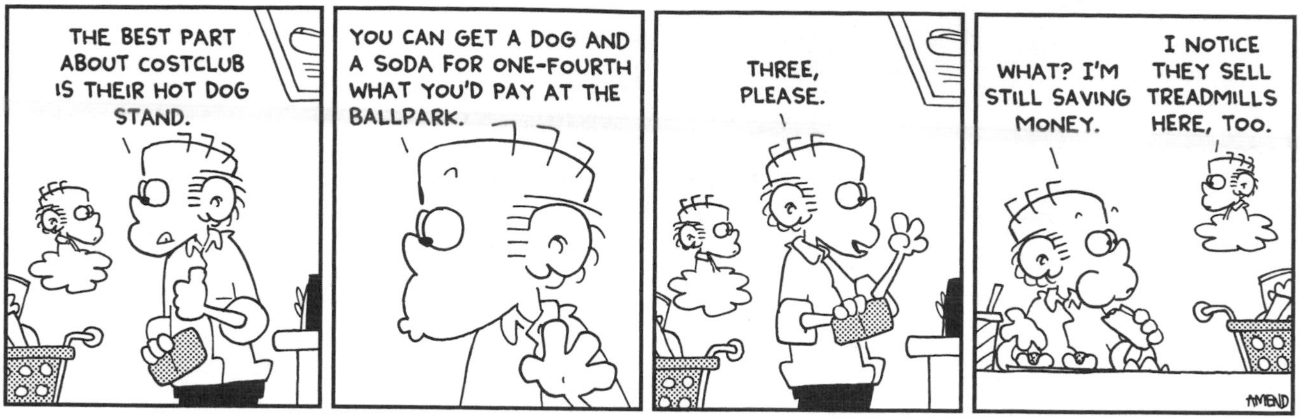
THE BEST PART ABOUT COSTCLUB IS THEIR HOT DOG STAND.
YOU CAN GET A DOG AND A SODA FOR ONE-FOURTH WHAT YOU'D PAY AT THE BALLPARK.
THREE, PLEASE.
WHAT? I'M STILL SAVING MONEY.
I NOTICE THEY SELL TREADMILLS HERE, TOO.
AMEND

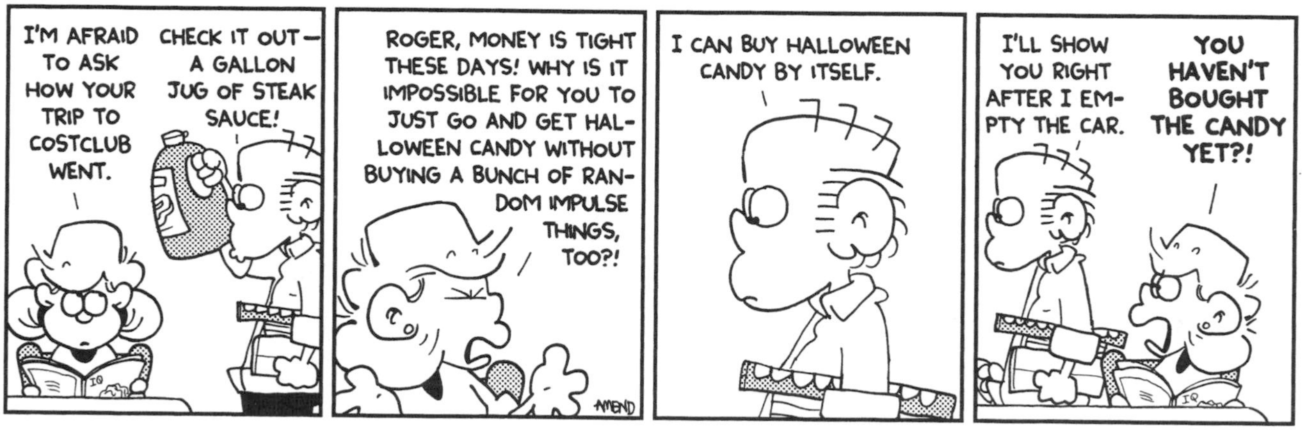
I'M AFRAID TO ASK HOW YOUR TRIP TO COSTCLUB WENT.
CHECK IT OUT— A GALLON JUG OF STEAK SAUCE!
ROGER, MONEY IS TIGHT THESE DAYS! WHY IS IT IMPOSSIBLE FOR YOU TO JUST GO AND GET HALLOWEEN CANDY WITHOUT BUYING A BUNCH OF RANDOM IMPULSE THINGS, TOO?!
I CAN BUY HALLOWEEN CANDY BY ITSELF.
I'LL SHOW YOU RIGHT AFTER I EMPTY THE CAR.
YOU HAVEN'T BOUGHT THE CANDY YET?!
AMEND

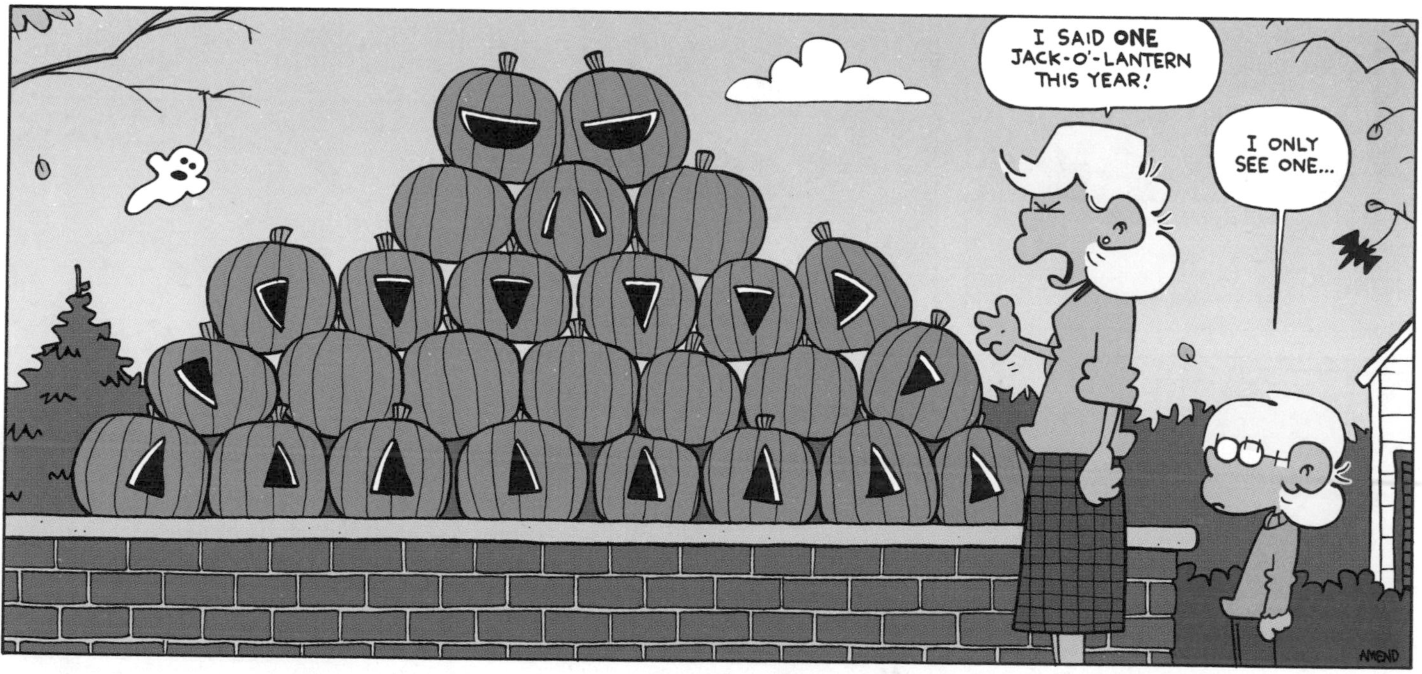
I SAID ONE JACK-O'-LANTERN THIS YEAR!
I ONLY SEE ONE...
AMEND

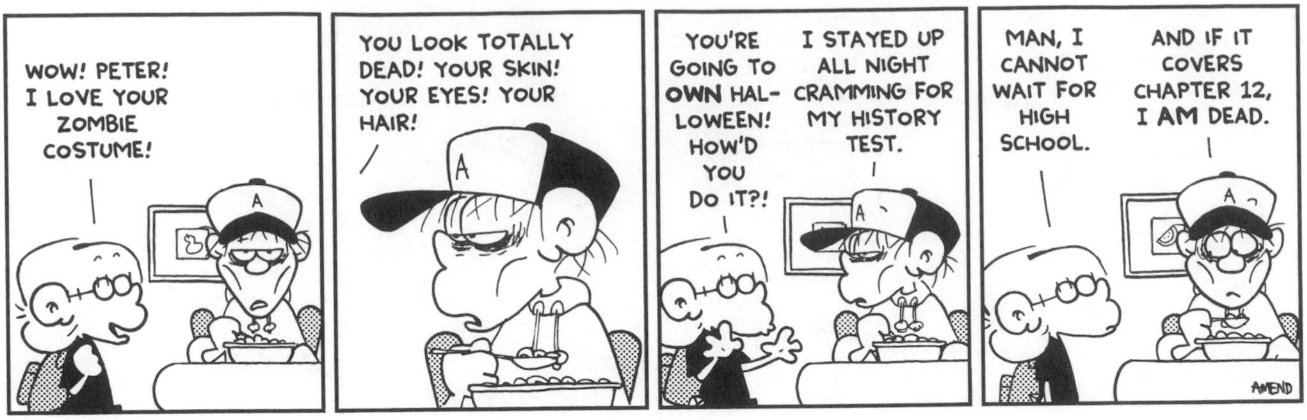
WOW! PETER! I LOVE YOUR ZOMBIE COSTUME!
YOU LOOK TOTALLY DEAD! YOUR SKIN! YOUR EYES! YOUR HAIR!
YOU'RE GOING TO OWN HALLOWEEN! HOW'D YOU DO IT?!
I STAYED UP ALL NIGHT CRAMMING FOR MY HISTORY TEST.
MAN, I CANNOT WAIT FOR HIGH SCHOOL.
AND IF IT COVERS CHAPTER 12, I AM DEAD.
AMEND

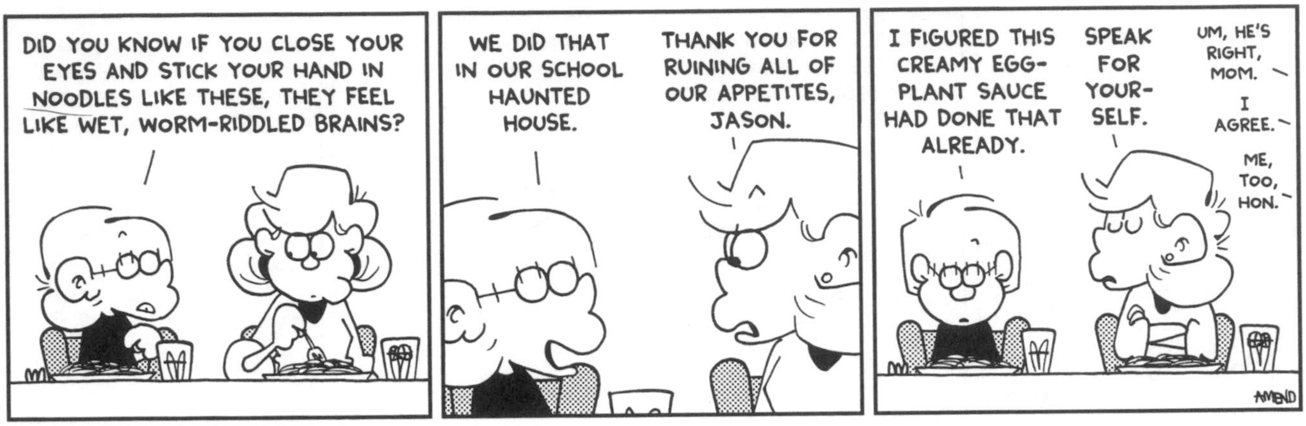
DID YOU KNOW IF YOU CLOSE YOUR EYES AND STICK YOUR HAND IN NOODLES LIKE THESE, THEY FEEL LIKE WET, WORM-RIDDLED BRAINS?
WE DID THAT IN OUR SCHOOL HAUNTED HOUSE.
THANK YOU FOR RUINING ALL OF OUR APPETITES, JASON.
I FIGURED THIS CREAMY EGGPLANT SAUCE HAD DONE THAT ALREADY.
SPEAK FOR YOURSELF.
UM, HE'S RIGHT, MOM.
I AGREE.
ME, TOO, HON.
AMEND

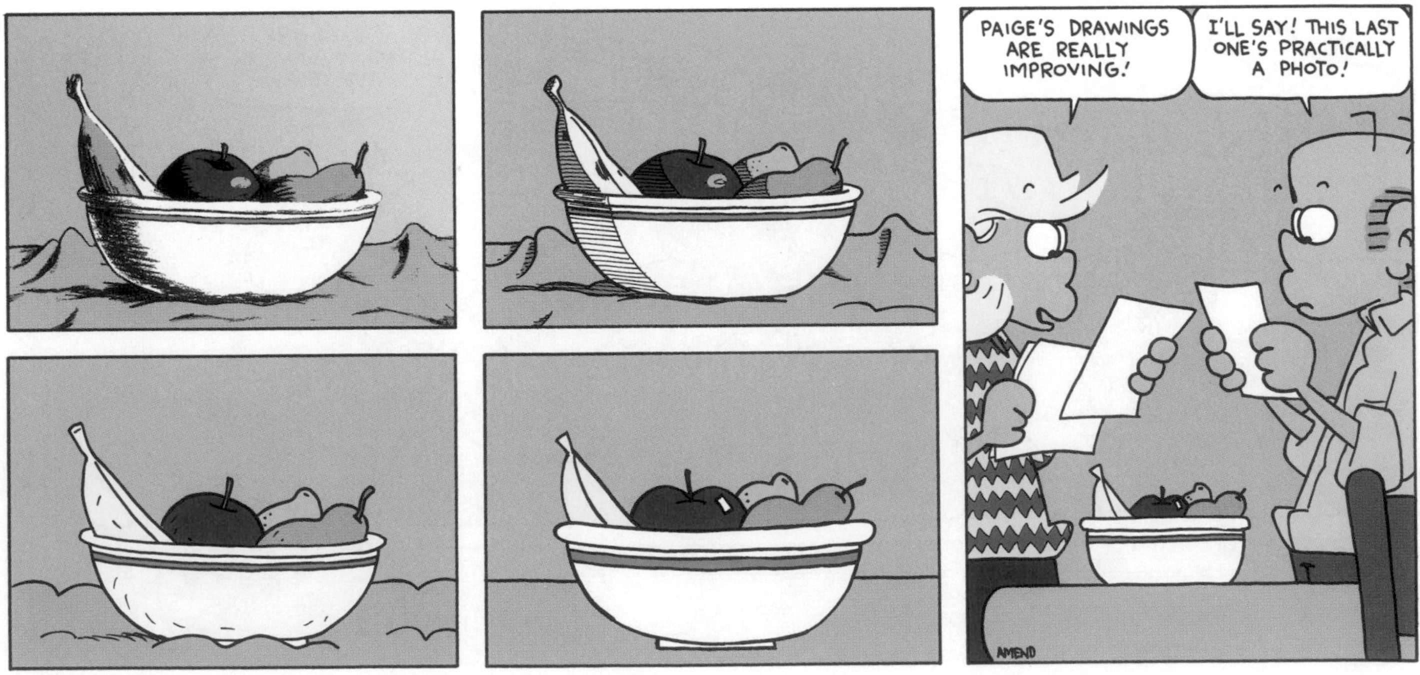
PAIGE'S DRAWINGS ARE REALLY IMPROVING!
I'LL SAY! THIS LAST ONE'S PRACTICALLY A PHOTO!
AMEND

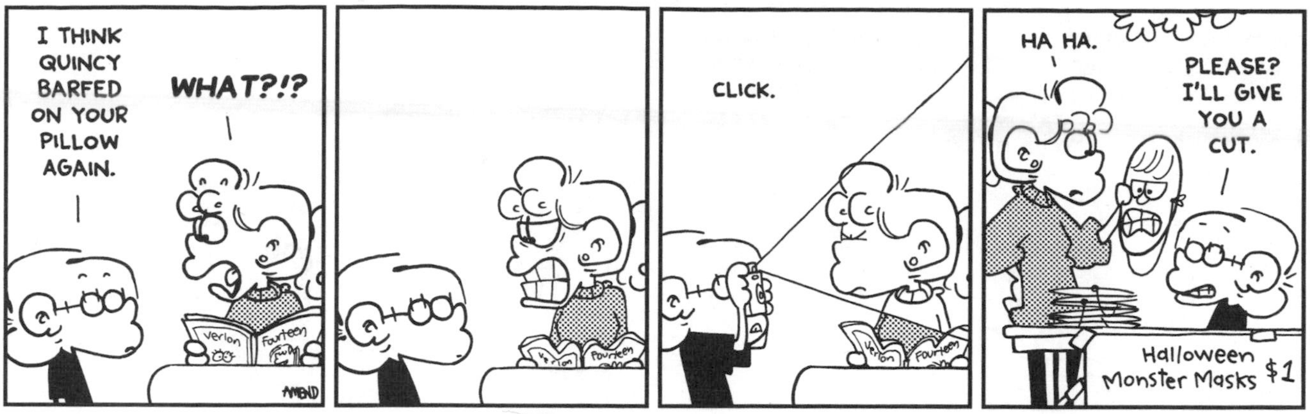

I THINK QUINCY BARFED ON YOUR PILLOW AGAIN.
WHAT?!?
CLICK.
HA HA.
PLEASE? I'LL GIVE YOU A CUT.
Halloween Monster Masks $1

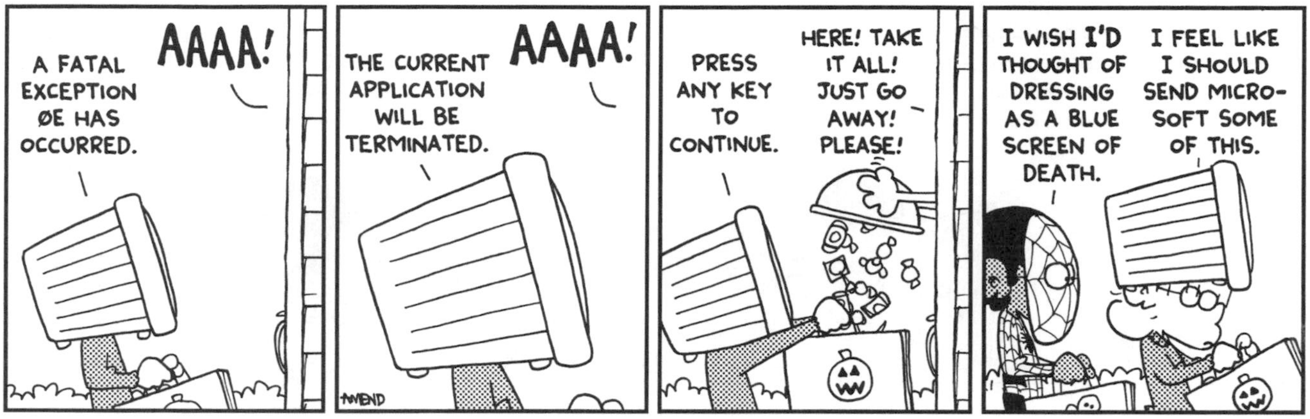

A FATAL EXCEPTION ØE HAS OCCURRED.
AAAA!
THE CURRENT APPLICATION WILL BE TERMINATED.
AAAA!
PRESS ANY KEY TO CONTINUE.
HERE! TAKE IT ALL! JUST GO AWAY! PLEASE!
I WISH I'D THOUGHT OF DRESSING AS A BLUE SCREEN OF DEATH.
I FEEL LIKE I SHOULD SEND MICRO-SOFT SOME OF THIS.

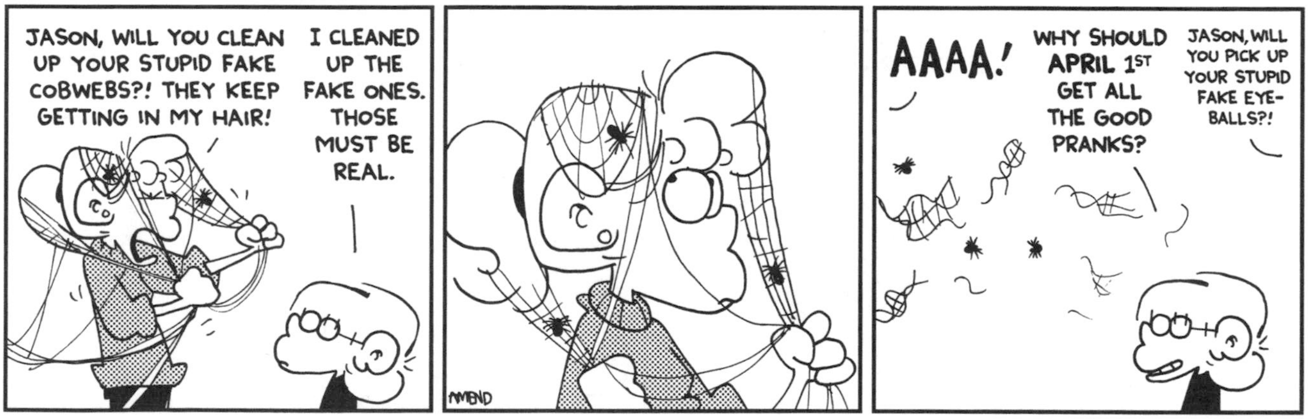

JASON, WILL YOU CLEAN UP YOUR STUPID FAKE COBWEBS?! THEY KEEP GETTING IN MY HAIR!
I CLEANED UP THE FAKE ONES. THOSE MUST BE REAL.
AAAA!
WHY SHOULD APRIL 1ST GET ALL THE GOOD PRANKS?
JASON, WILL YOU PICK UP YOUR STUPID FAKE EYE-BALLS?!

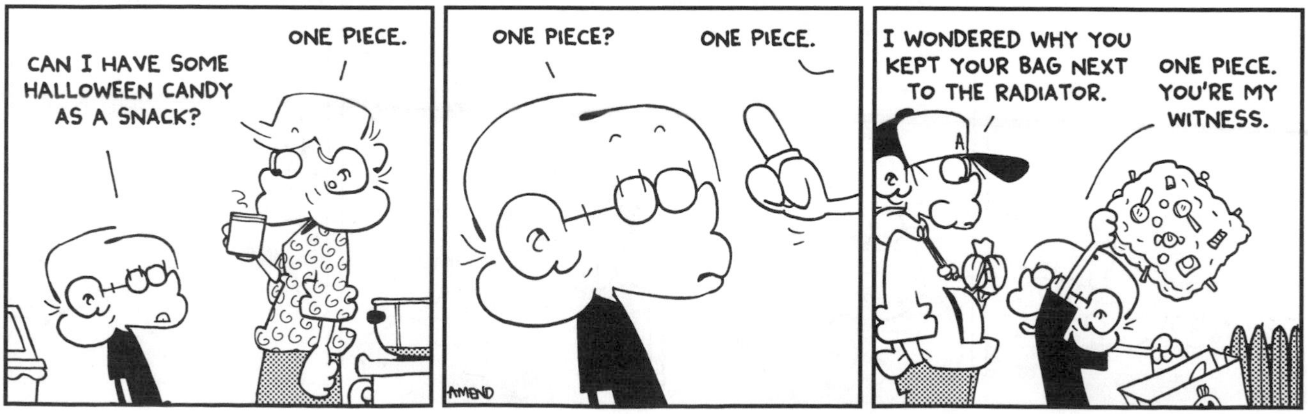

CAN I HAVE SOME HALLOWEEN CANDY AS A SNACK?
ONE PIECE.
ONE PIECE?
ONE PIECE.
I WONDERED WHY YOU KEPT YOUR BAG NEXT TO THE RADIATOR.
ONE PIECE. YOU'RE MY WITNESS.

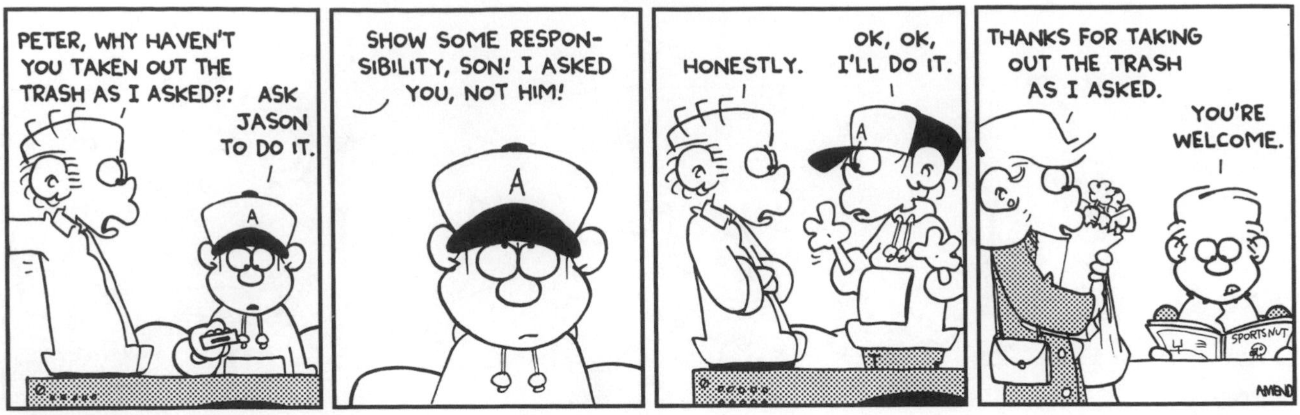
PETER, WHY HAVEN'T YOU TAKEN OUT THE TRASH AS I ASKED?!
ASK JASON TO DO IT.
SHOW SOME RESPONSIBILITY, SON! I ASKED YOU, NOT HIM!
HONESTLY.
OK, OK, I'LL DO IT.
THANKS FOR TAKING OUT THE TRASH AS I ASKED.
YOU'RE WELCOME.
SPORTS NUT
AMEND

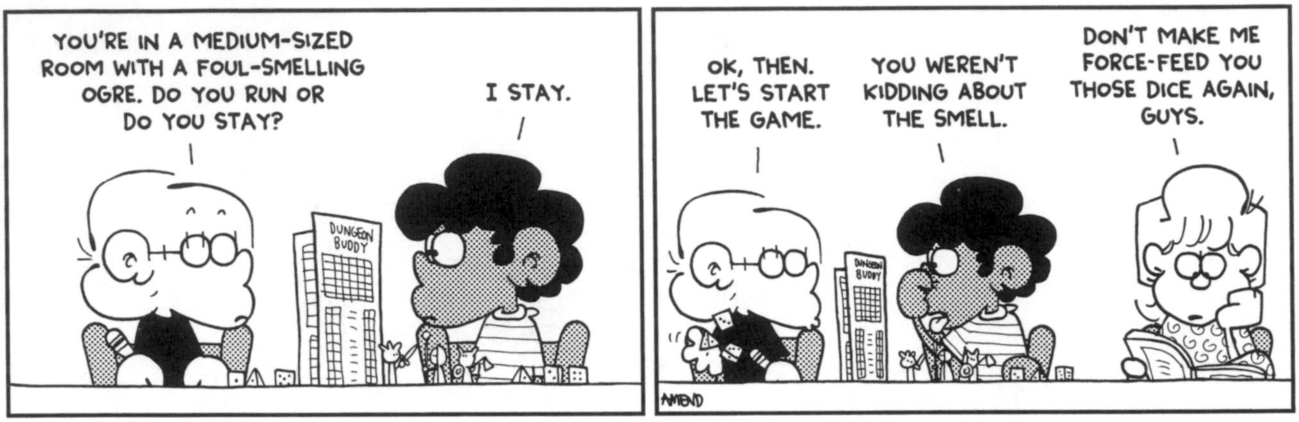
YOU'RE IN A MEDIUM-SIZED ROOM WITH A FOUL-SMELLING OGRE. DO YOU RUN OR DO YOU STAY?
I STAY.
DUNGEON BUDDY
OK, THEN. LET'S START THE GAME.
YOU WEREN'T KIDDING ABOUT THE SMELL.
DON'T MAKE ME FORCE-FEED YOU THOSE DICE AGAIN, GUYS.
AMEND

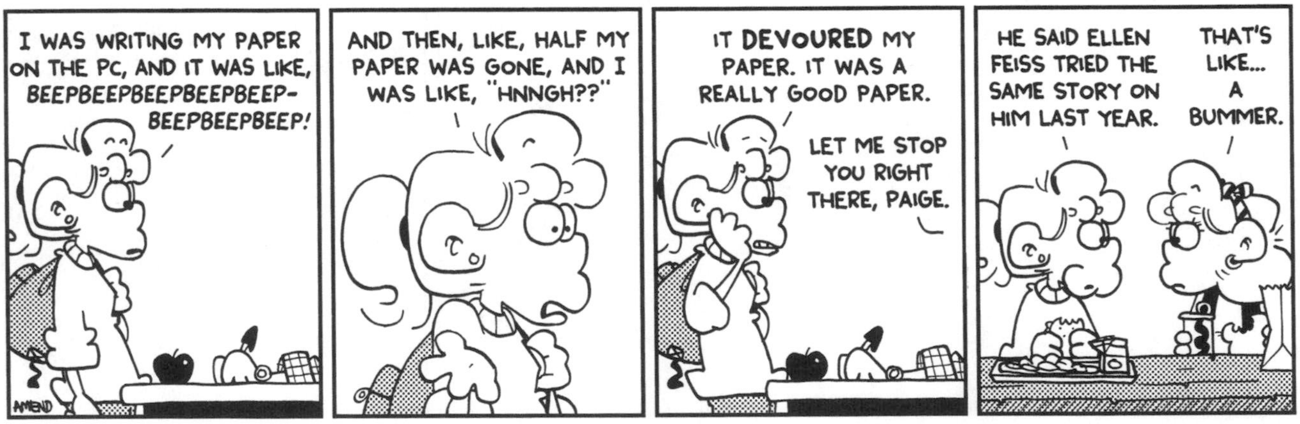
I WAS WRITING MY PAPER ON THE PC, AND IT WAS LIKE, *BEEPBEEPBEEPBEEPBEEP-BEEPBEEPBEEP!*
AND THEN, LIKE, HALF MY PAPER WAS GONE, AND I WAS LIKE, "HNNGH??"
IT **DEVOURED** MY PAPER. IT WAS A REALLY GOOD PAPER.
LET ME STOP YOU RIGHT THERE, PAIGE.
HE SAID ELLEN FEISS TRIED THE SAME STORY ON HIM LAST YEAR.
THAT'S LIKE... A BUMMER.
AMEND

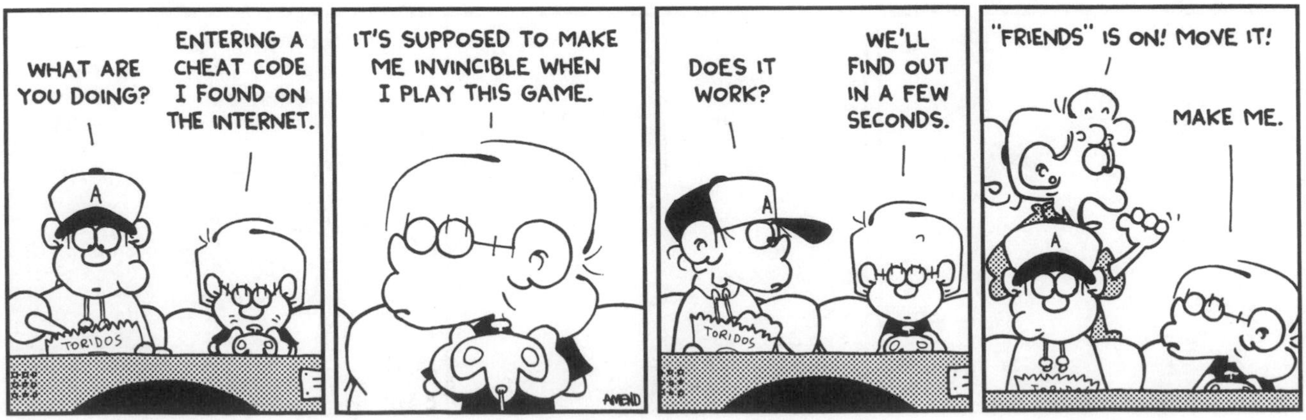
WHAT ARE YOU DOING?
ENTERING A CHEAT CODE I FOUND ON THE INTERNET.
TORIDOS
IT'S SUPPOSED TO MAKE ME INVINCIBLE WHEN I PLAY THIS GAME.
DOES IT WORK?
WE'LL FIND OUT IN A FEW SECONDS.
"FRIENDS" IS ON! MOVE IT!
MAKE ME.
AMEND

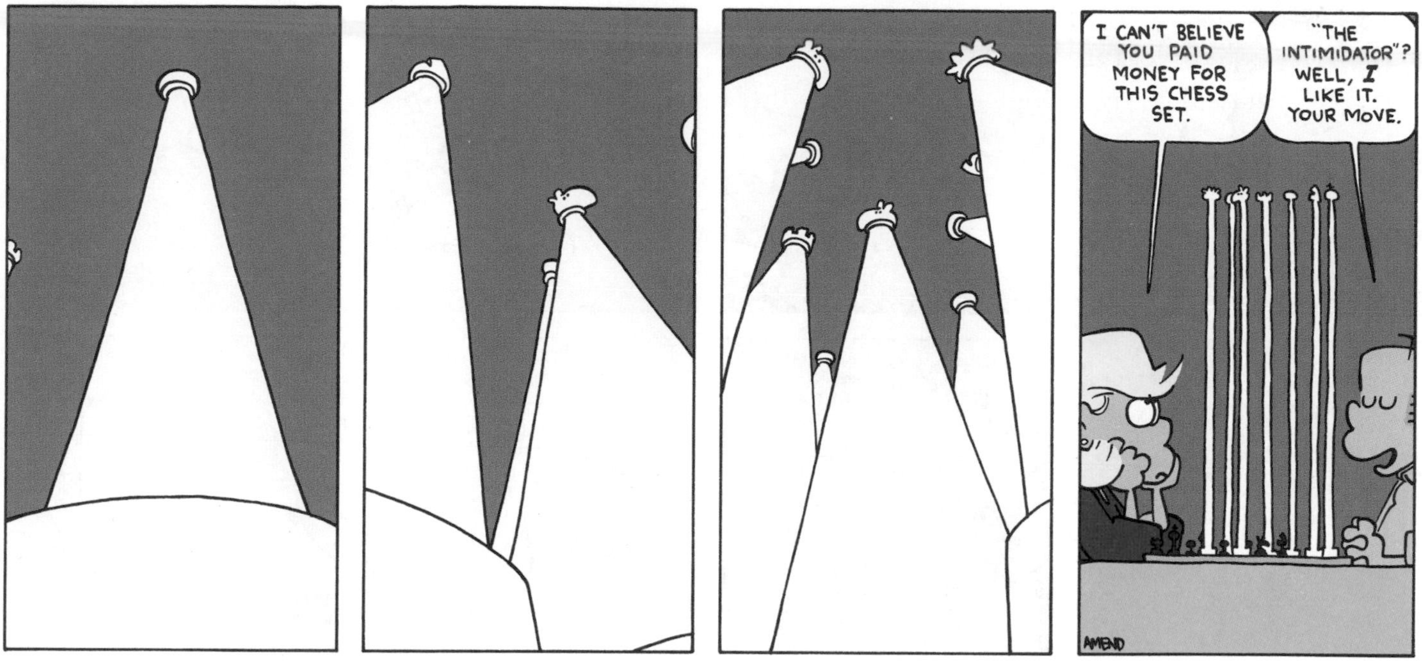
I CAN'T BELIEVE YOU PAID MONEY FOR THIS CHESS SET.
"THE INTIMIDATOR"? WELL, I LIKE IT. YOUR MOVE.
AMEND

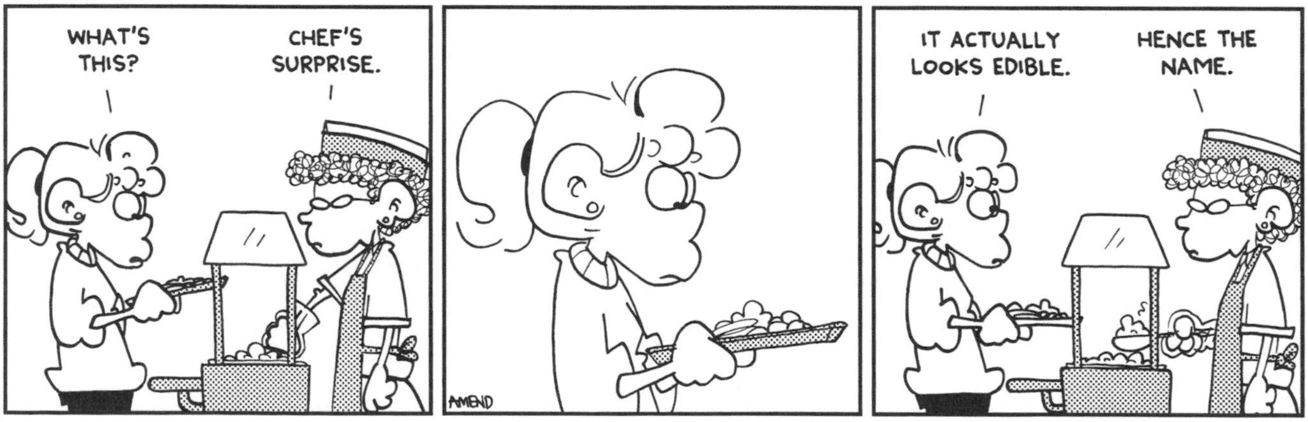
WHAT'S THIS?
CHEF'S SURPRISE.
AMEND
IT ACTUALLY LOOKS EDIBLE.
HENCE THE NAME.

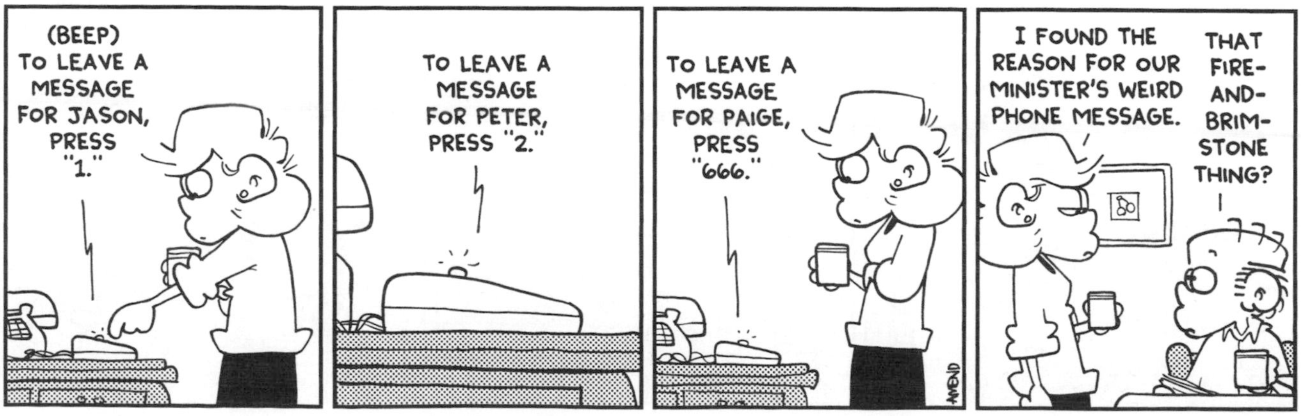
(BEEP) TO LEAVE A MESSAGE FOR JASON, PRESS "1."
TO LEAVE A MESSAGE FOR PETER, PRESS "2."
TO LEAVE A MESSAGE FOR PAIGE, PRESS "666."
AMEND
I FOUND THE REASON FOR OUR MINISTER'S WEIRD PHONE MESSAGE.
THAT FIRE-AND-BRIMSTONE THING?

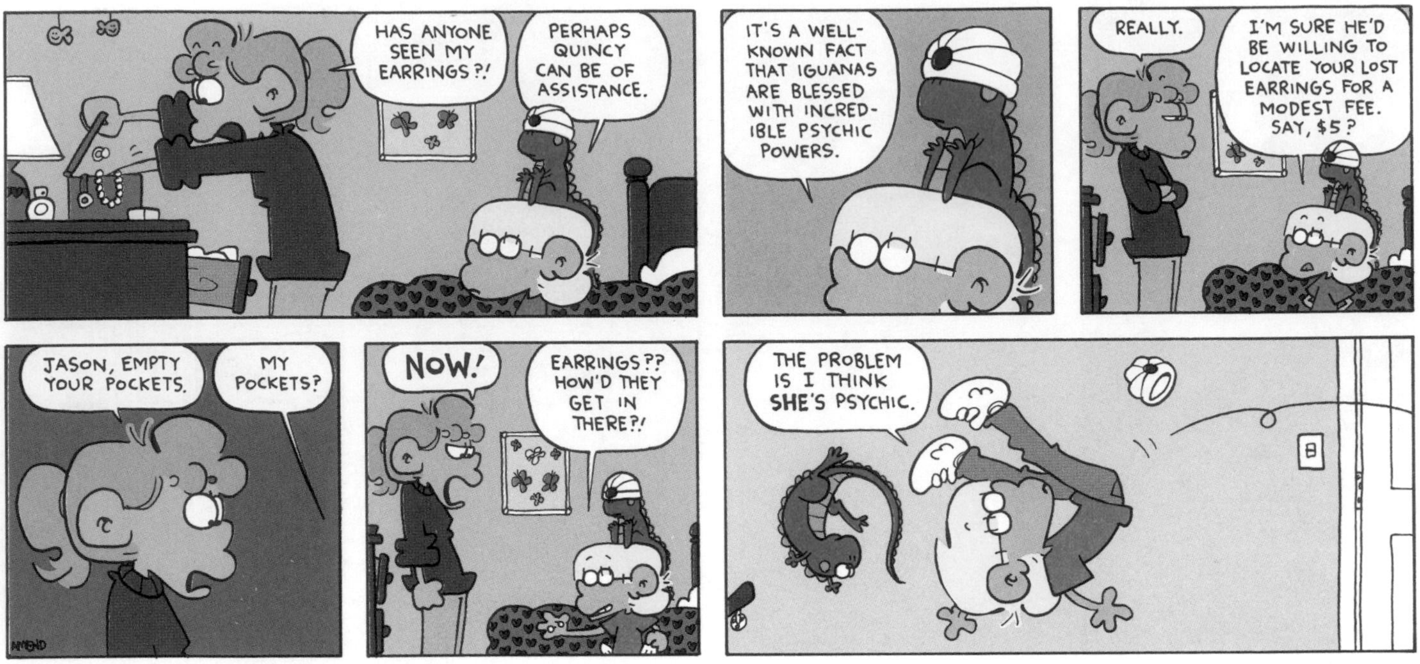
HAS ANYONE SEEN MY EARRINGS?!
PERHAPS QUINCY CAN BE OF ASSISTANCE.
IT'S A WELL-KNOWN FACT THAT IGUANAS ARE BLESSED WITH INCREDIBLE PSYCHIC POWERS.
REALLY.
I'M SURE HE'D BE WILLING TO LOCATE YOUR LOST EARRINGS FOR A MODEST FEE. SAY, $5?
JASON, EMPTY YOUR POCKETS.
MY POCKETS?
NOW!
EARRINGS?? HOW'D THEY GET IN THERE?!
THE PROBLEM IS I THINK SHE'S PSYCHIC.
AMEND

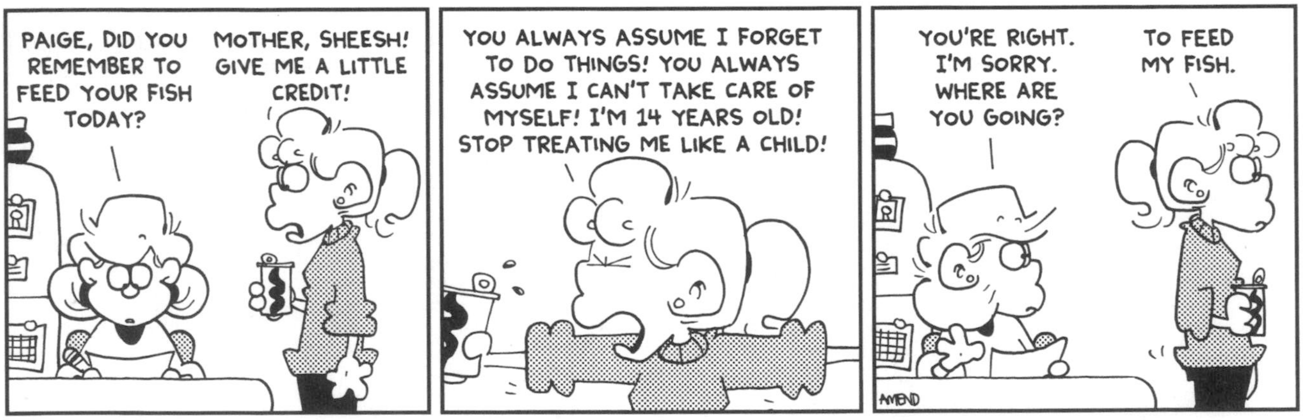
PAIGE, DID YOU REMEMBER TO FEED YOUR FISH TODAY?
MOTHER, SHEESH! GIVE ME A LITTLE CREDIT!
YOU ALWAYS ASSUME I FORGET TO DO THINGS! YOU ALWAYS ASSUME I CAN'T TAKE CARE OF MYSELF! I'M 14 YEARS OLD! STOP TREATING ME LIKE A CHILD!
YOU'RE RIGHT. I'M SORRY. WHERE ARE YOU GOING?
TO FEED MY FISH.
AMEND

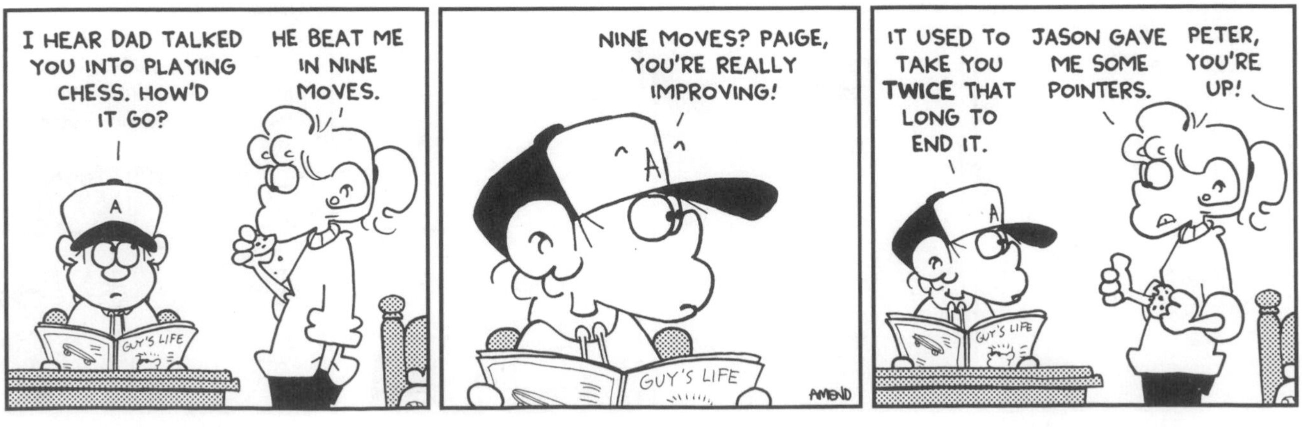
I HEAR DAD TALKED YOU INTO PLAYING CHESS. HOW'D IT GO?
HE BEAT ME IN NINE MOVES.
GUY'S LIFE
NINE MOVES? PAIGE, YOU'RE REALLY IMPROVING!
GUY'S LIFE
AMEND
IT USED TO TAKE YOU TWICE THAT LONG TO END IT.
JASON GAVE ME SOME POINTERS.
PETER, YOU'RE UP!
GUY'S LIFE

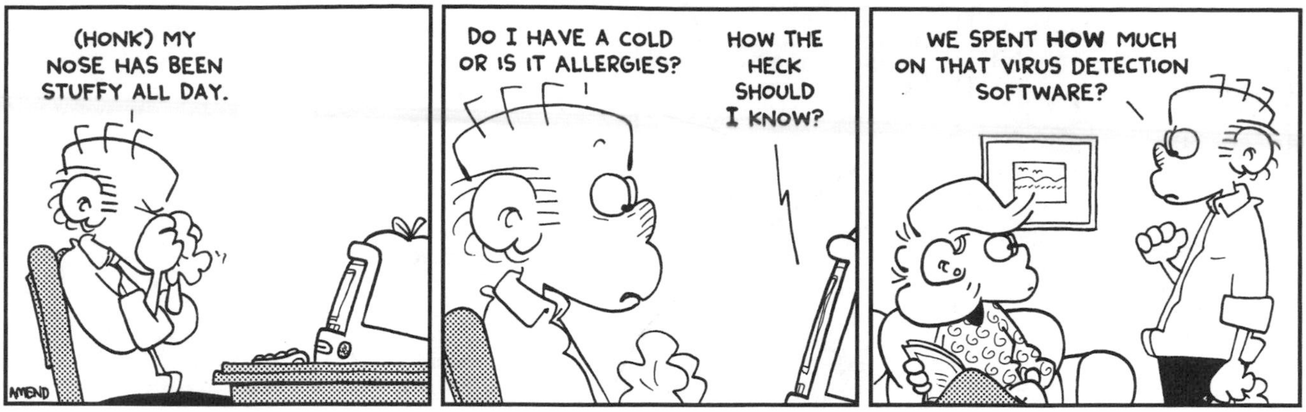
(HONK) MY NOSE HAS BEEN STUFFY ALL DAY.
DO I HAVE A COLD OR IS IT ALLERGIES?
HOW THE HECK SHOULD I KNOW?
WE SPENT HOW MUCH ON THAT VIRUS DETECTION SOFTWARE?

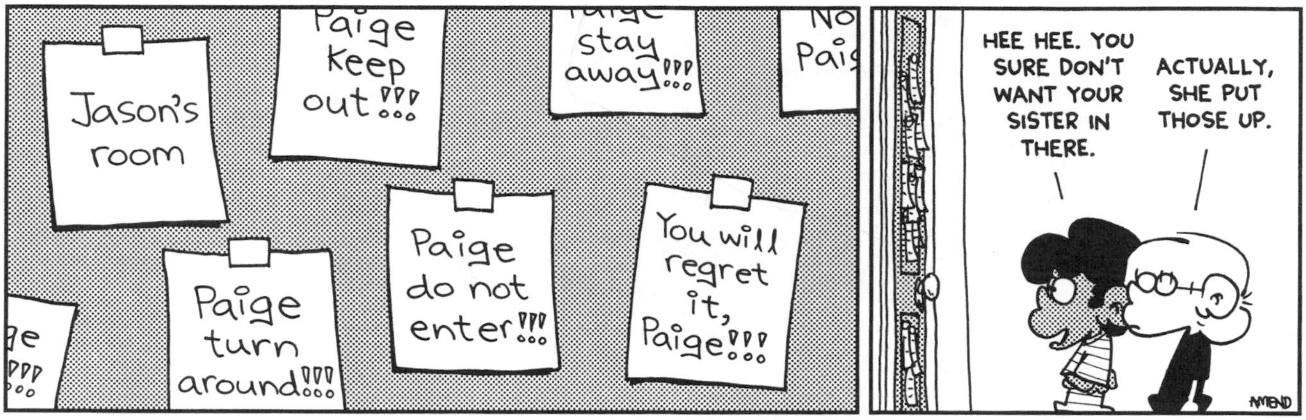
Jason's room
Paige keep out!!!
stay away!!!
Paige do not enter!!!
You will regret it, Paige!!!
Paige turn around!!!
HEE HEE. YOU SURE DON'T WANT YOUR SISTER IN THERE.
ACTUALLY, SHE PUT THOSE UP.

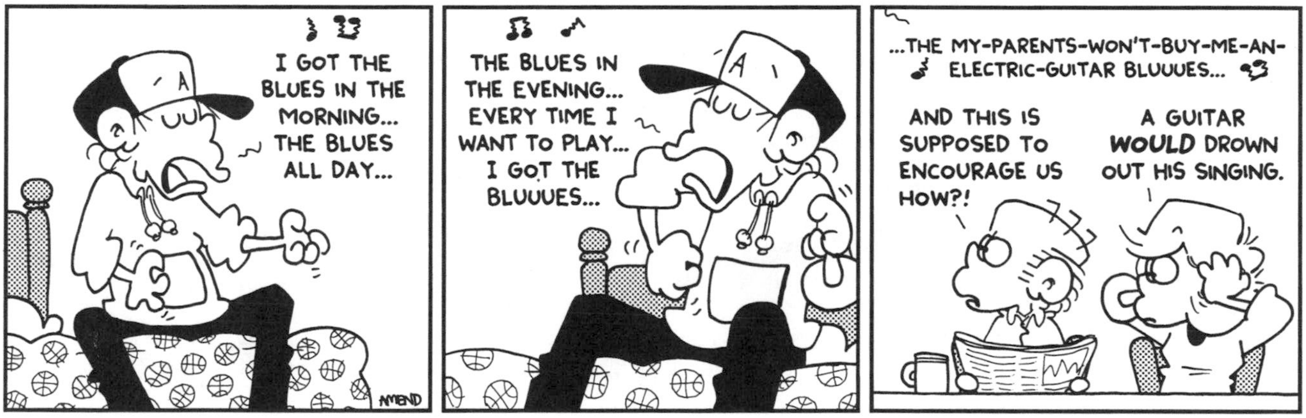
I GOT THE BLUES IN THE MORNING... THE BLUES ALL DAY...
THE BLUES IN THE EVENING... EVERY TIME I WANT TO PLAY... I GOT THE BLUUUES...
...THE MY-PARENTS-WON'T-BUY-ME-AN-ELECTRIC-GUITAR BLUUUES...
AND THIS IS SUPPOSED TO ENCOURAGE US HOW?!
A GUITAR WOULD DROWN OUT HIS SINGING.

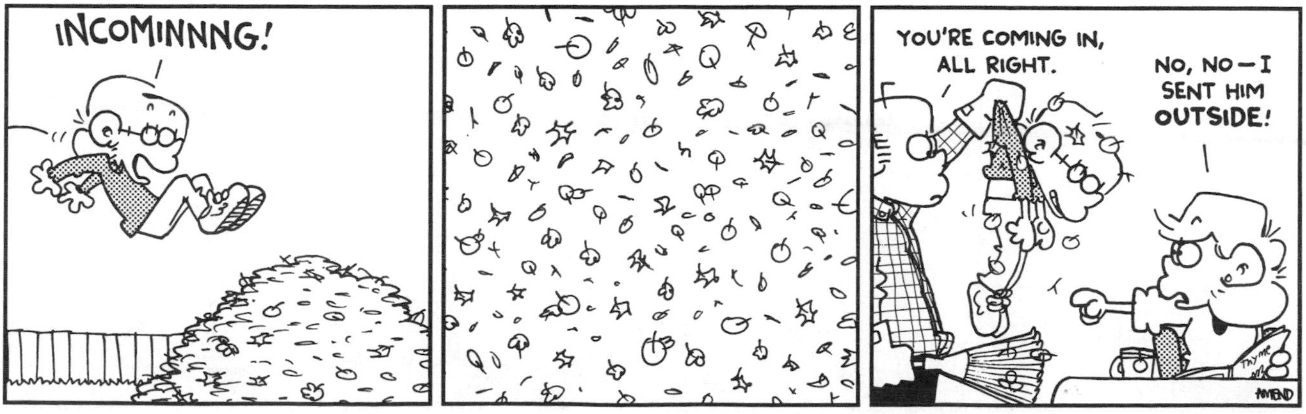
INCOMINNNG!
YOU'RE COMING IN, ALL RIGHT.
NO, NO—I SENT HIM OUTSIDE!

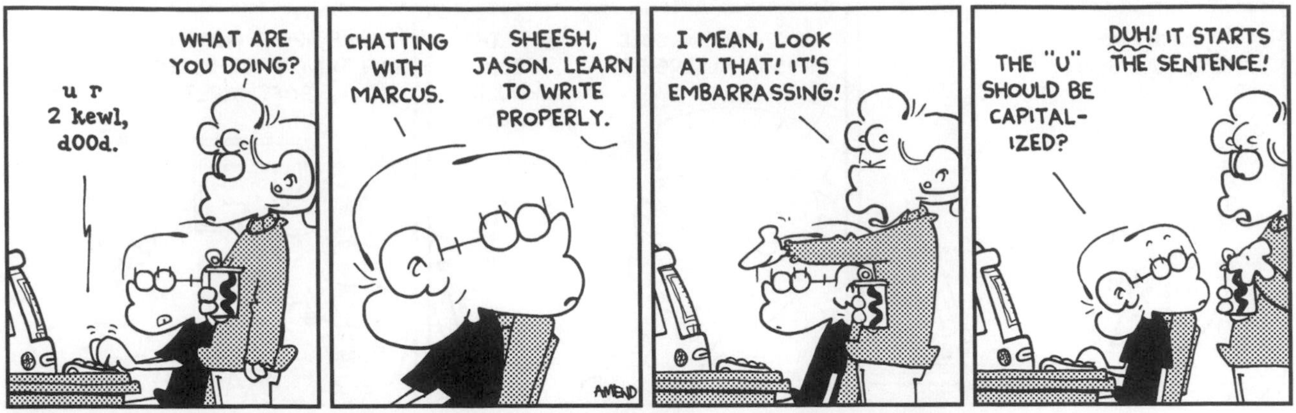
u r 2 kewl, d00d.
WHAT ARE YOU DOING?
CHATTING WITH MARCUS.
SHEESH, JASON. LEARN TO WRITE PROPERLY.
I MEAN, LOOK AT THAT! IT'S EMBARRASSING!
THE "U" SHOULD BE CAPITAL-IZED?
DUH! IT STARTS THE SENTENCE!
AMEND

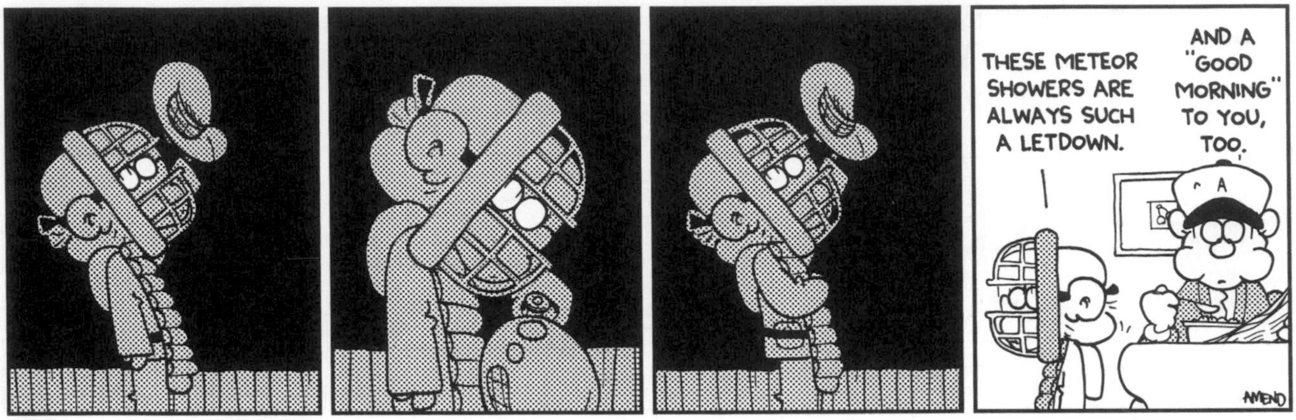
THESE METEOR SHOWERS ARE ALWAYS SUCH A LETDOWN.
AND A "GOOD MORNING" TO YOU, TOO.
AMEND

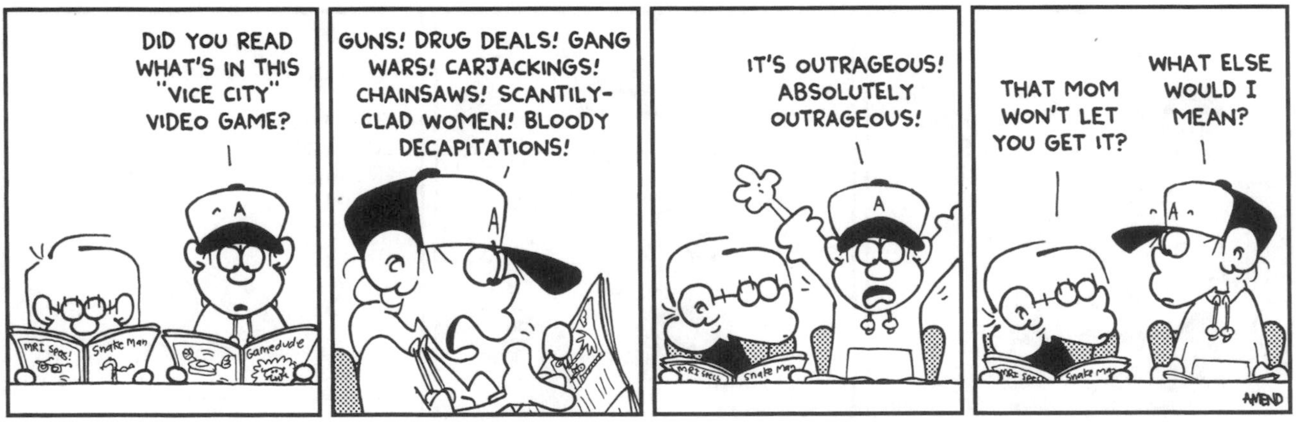
DID YOU READ WHAT'S IN THIS "VICE CITY" VIDEO GAME?
MRI Specs!
Snake Man
Gamedude
GUNS! DRUG DEALS! GANG WARS! CARJACKINGS! CHAINSAWS! SCANTILY-CLAD WOMEN! BLOODY DECAPITATIONS!
IT'S OUTRAGEOUS! ABSOLUTELY OUTRAGEOUS!
THAT MOM WON'T LET YOU GET IT?
WHAT ELSE WOULD I MEAN?
AMEND

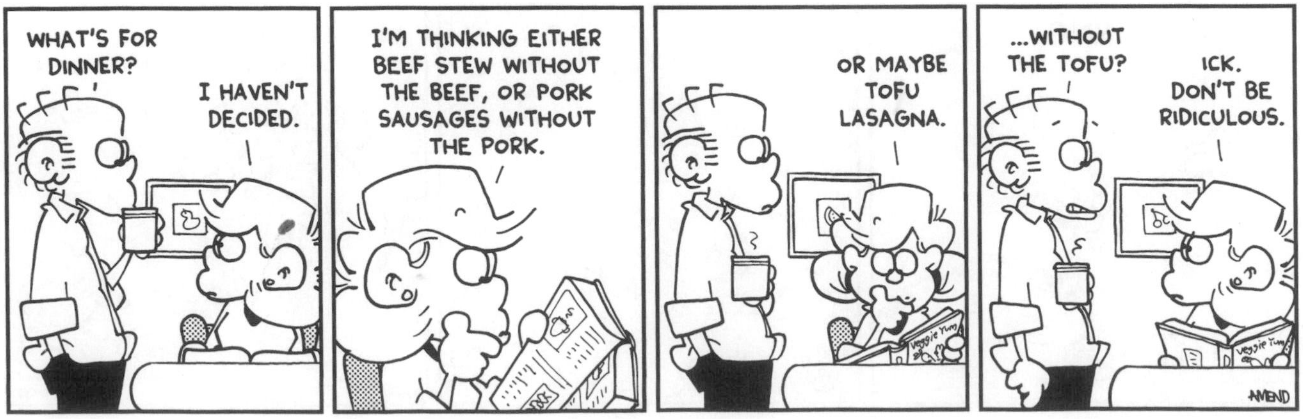
WHAT'S FOR DINNER?
I HAVEN'T DECIDED.
I'M THINKING EITHER BEEF STEW WITHOUT THE BEEF, OR PORK SAUSAGES WITHOUT THE PORK.
OR MAYBE TOFU LASAGNA.
...WITHOUT THE TOFU?
ICK. DON'T BE RIDICULOUS.
AMEND

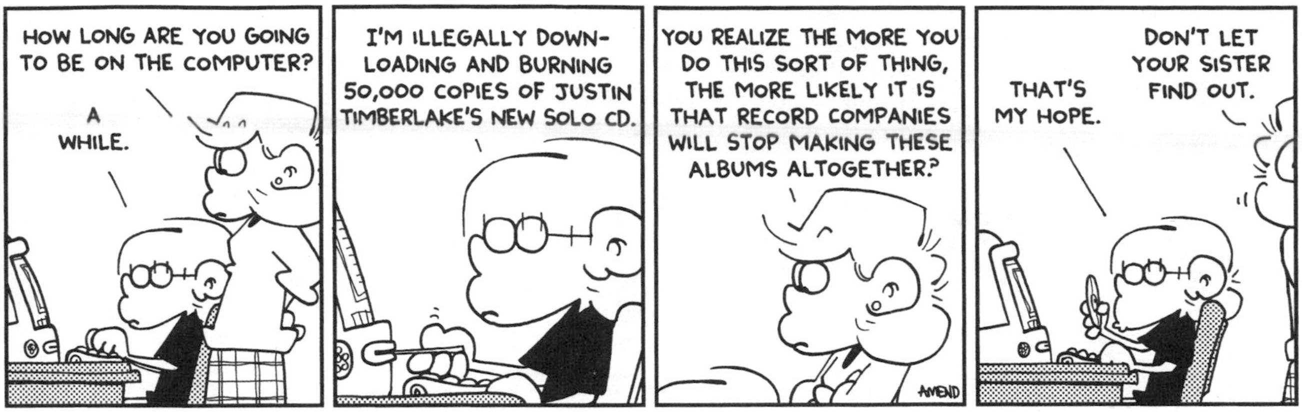
HOW LONG ARE YOU GOING TO BE ON THE COMPUTER?
A WHILE.
I'M ILLEGALLY DOWN-LOADING AND BURNING 50,000 COPIES OF JUSTIN TIMBERLAKE'S NEW SOLO CD.
YOU REALIZE THE MORE YOU DO THIS SORT OF THING, THE MORE LIKELY IT IS THAT RECORD COMPANIES WILL STOP MAKING THESE ALBUMS ALTOGETHER?
THAT'S MY HOPE.
DON'T LET YOUR SISTER FIND OUT.
AMEND

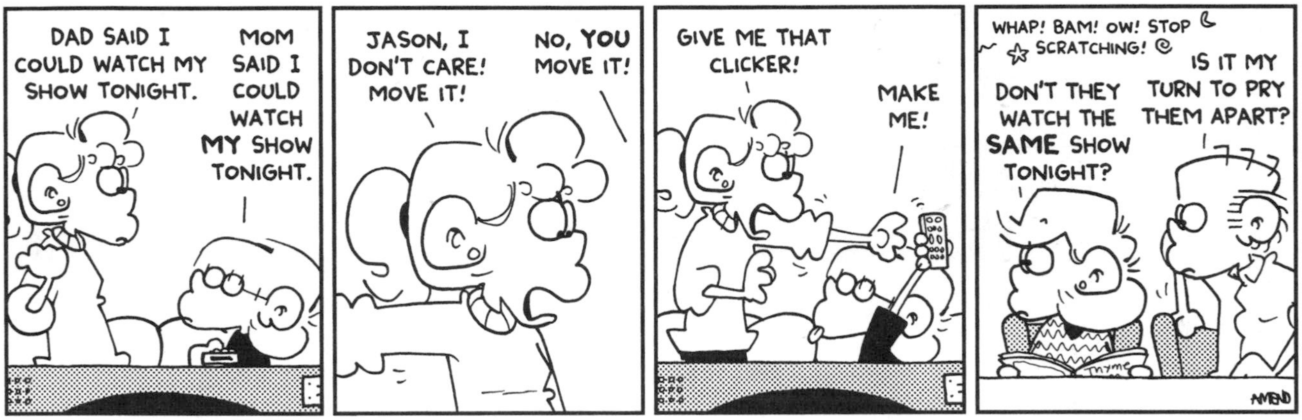
DAD SAID I COULD WATCH MY SHOW TONIGHT.
MOM SAID I COULD WATCH MY SHOW TONIGHT.
JASON, I DON'T CARE! MOVE IT!
NO, YOU MOVE IT!
GIVE ME THAT CLICKER!
MAKE ME!
WHAP! BAM! OW! STOP SCRATCHING!
DON'T THEY WATCH THE SAME SHOW TONIGHT?
IS IT MY TURN TO PRY THEM APART?
AMEND

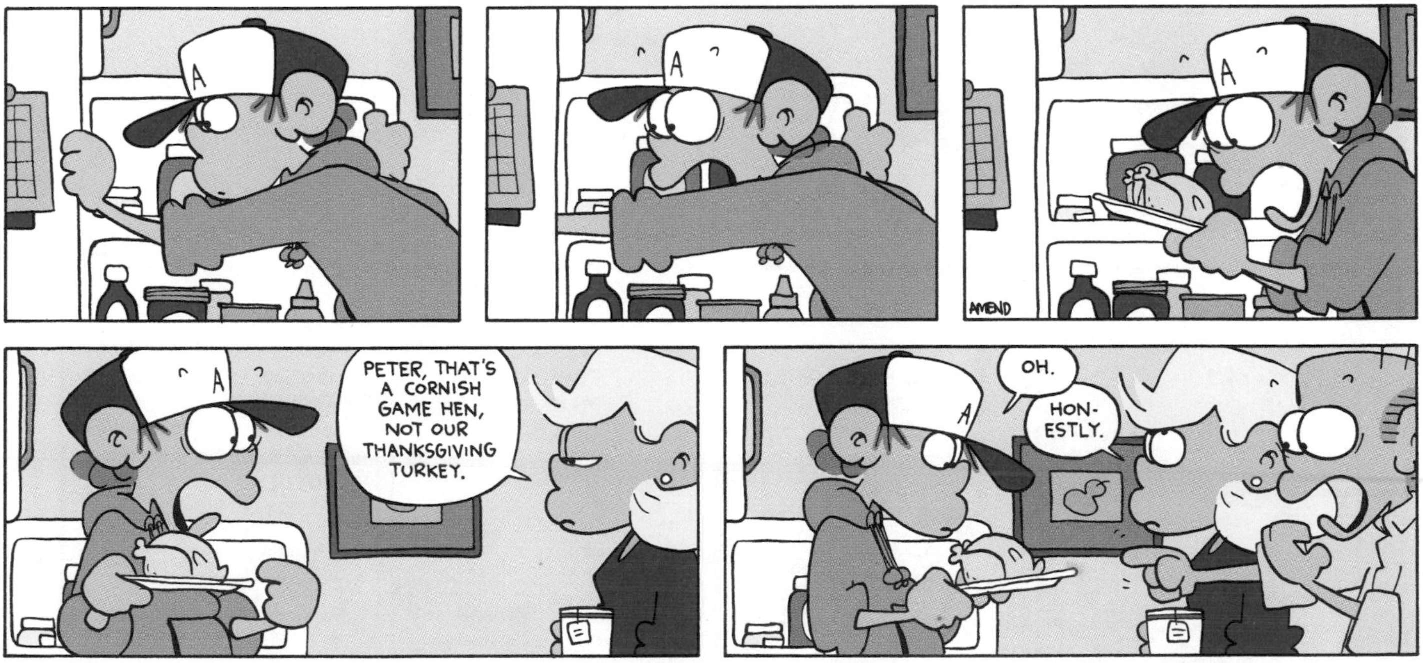
AMEND
PETER, THAT'S A CORNISH GAME HEN, NOT OUR THANKSGIVING TURKEY.
OH.
HON-ESTLY.

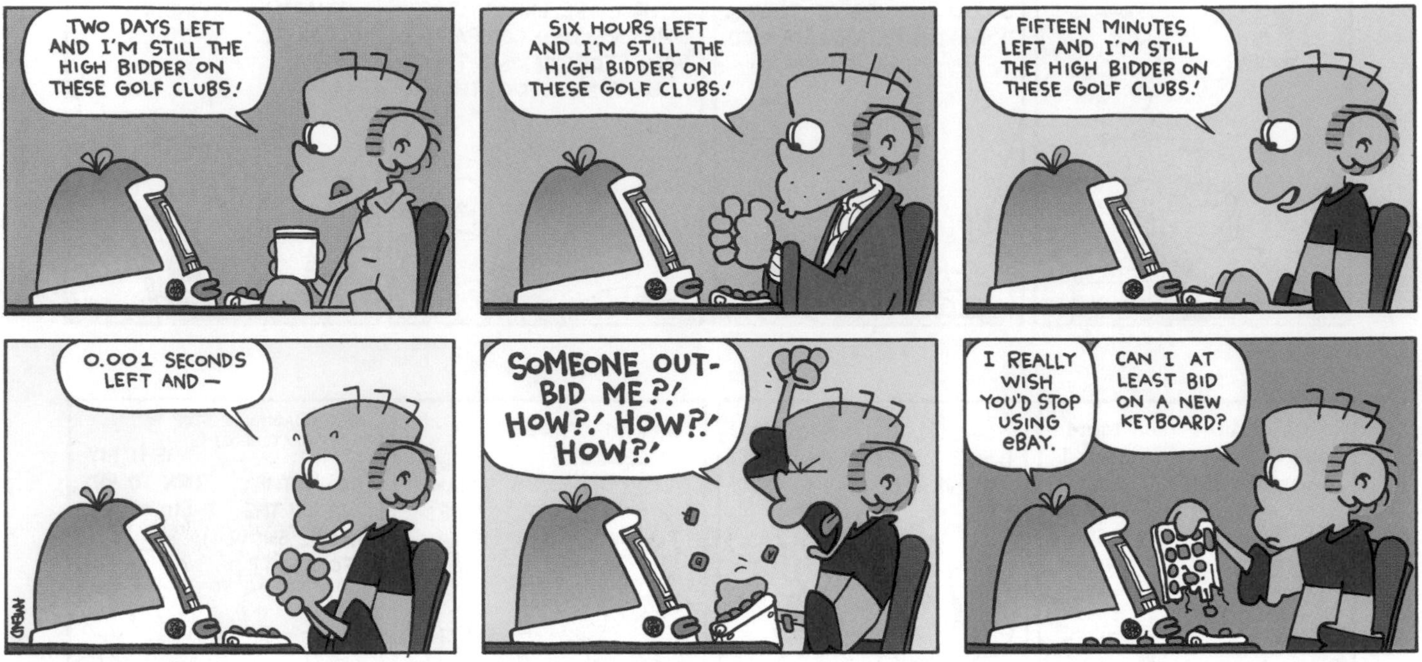
TWO DAYS LEFT AND I'M STILL THE HIGH BIDDER ON THESE GOLF CLUBS!
SIX HOURS LEFT AND I'M STILL THE HIGH BIDDER ON THESE GOLF CLUBS!
FIFTEEN MINUTES LEFT AND I'M STILL THE HIGH BIDDER ON THESE GOLF CLUBS!
0.001 SECONDS LEFT AND—
SOMEONE OUT-BID ME?! HOW?! HOW?! HOW?!
I REALLY WISH YOU'D STOP USING eBAY.
CAN I AT LEAST BID ON A NEW KEYBOARD?

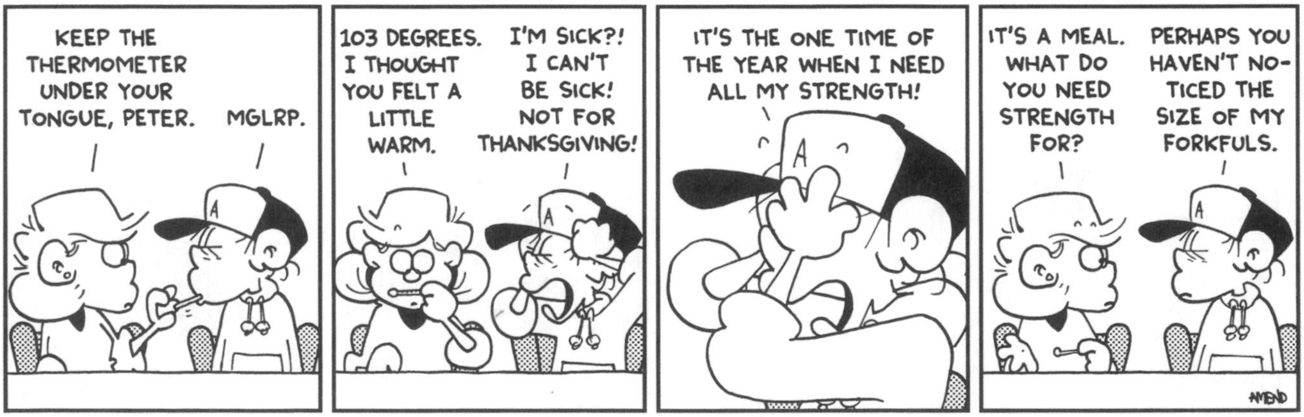
KEEP THE THERMOMETER UNDER YOUR TONGUE, PETER.
MGLRP.
103 DEGREES. I THOUGHT YOU FELT A LITTLE WARM.
I'M SICK?! I CAN'T BE SICK! NOT FOR THANKSGIVING!
IT'S THE ONE TIME OF THE YEAR WHEN I NEED ALL MY STRENGTH!
IT'S A MEAL. WHAT DO YOU NEED STRENGTH FOR?
PERHAPS YOU HAVEN'T NOTICED THE SIZE OF MY FORKFULS.

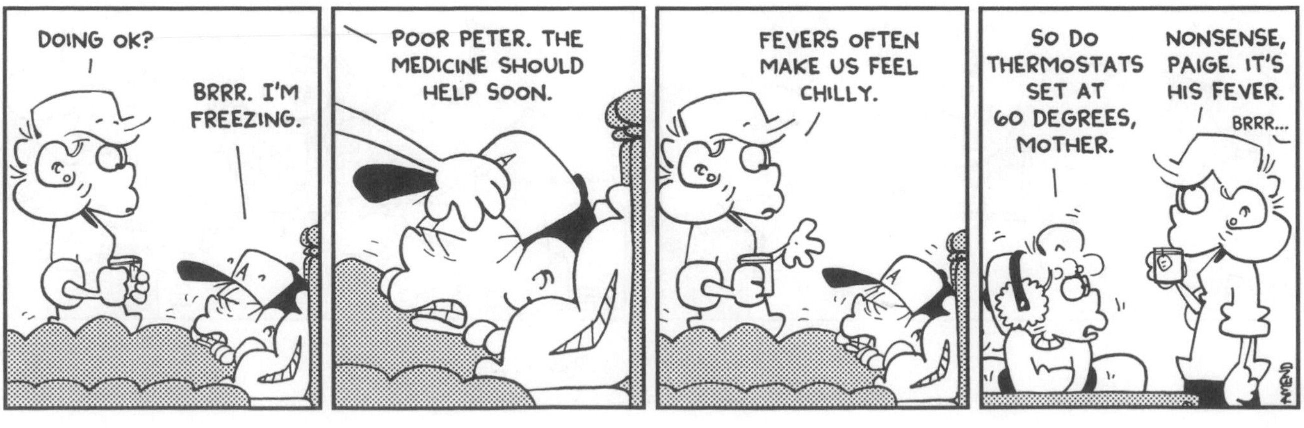
DOING OK?
BRRR. I'M FREEZING.
POOR PETER. THE MEDICINE SHOULD HELP SOON.
FEVERS OFTEN MAKE US FEEL CHILLY.
SO DO THERMOSTATS SET AT 60 DEGREES, MOTHER.
NONSENSE, PAIGE. IT'S HIS FEVER.
BRRR...

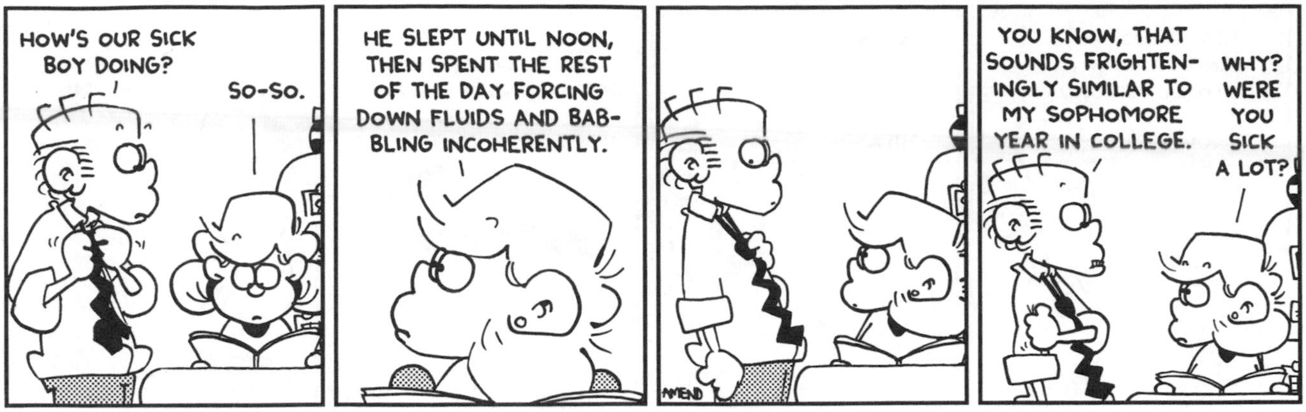
HOW'S OUR SICK BOY DOING?
SO-SO.
HE SLEPT UNTIL NOON, THEN SPENT THE REST OF THE DAY FORCING DOWN FLUIDS AND BAB-BLING INCOHERENTLY.
AMEND
YOU KNOW, THAT SOUNDS FRIGHTEN-INGLY SIMILAR TO MY SOPHOMORE YEAR IN COLLEGE.
WHY? WERE YOU SICK A LOT?

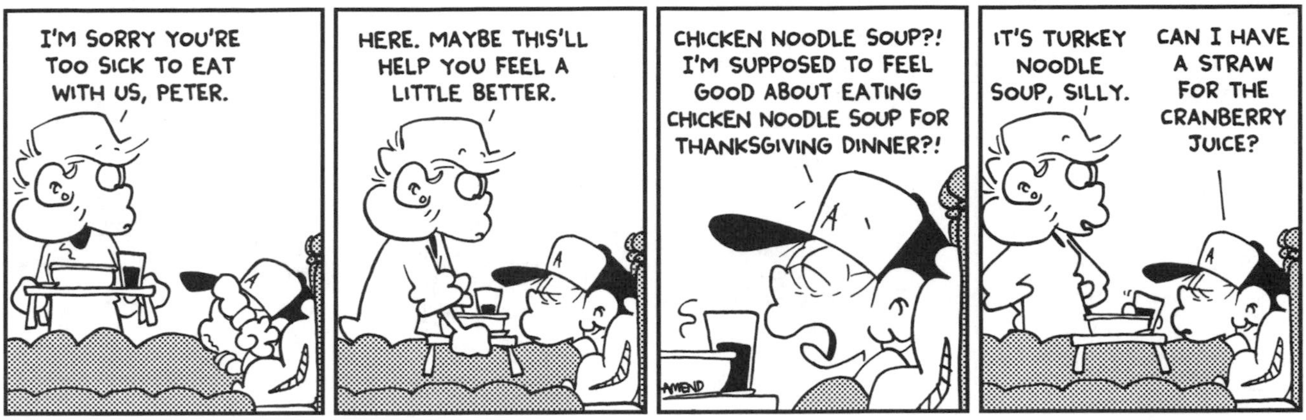
I'M SORRY YOU'RE TOO SICK TO EAT WITH US, PETER.
HERE. MAYBE THIS'LL HELP YOU FEEL A LITTLE BETTER.
CHICKEN NOODLE SOUP?! I'M SUPPOSED TO FEEL GOOD ABOUT EATING CHICKEN NOODLE SOUP FOR THANKSGIVING DINNER?!
AMEND
IT'S TURKEY NOODLE SOUP, SILLY.
CAN I HAVE A STRAW FOR THE CRANBERRY JUICE?

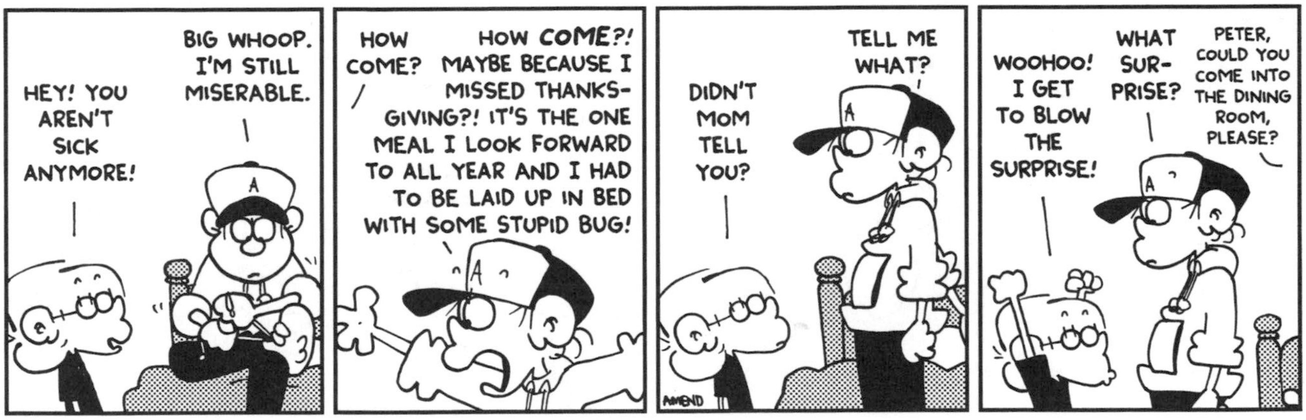
HEY! YOU AREN'T SICK ANYMORE!
BIG WHOOP. I'M STILL MISERABLE.
HOW COME?
HOW COME?! MAYBE BECAUSE I MISSED THANKS-GIVING?! IT'S THE ONE MEAL I LOOK FORWARD TO ALL YEAR AND I HAD TO BE LAID UP IN BED WITH SOME STUPID BUG!
DIDN'T MOM TELL YOU?
TELL ME WHAT?
AMEND
WOOHOO! I GET TO BLOW THE SURPRISE!
WHAT SUR-PRISE?
PETER, COULD YOU COME INTO THE DINING ROOM, PLEASE?

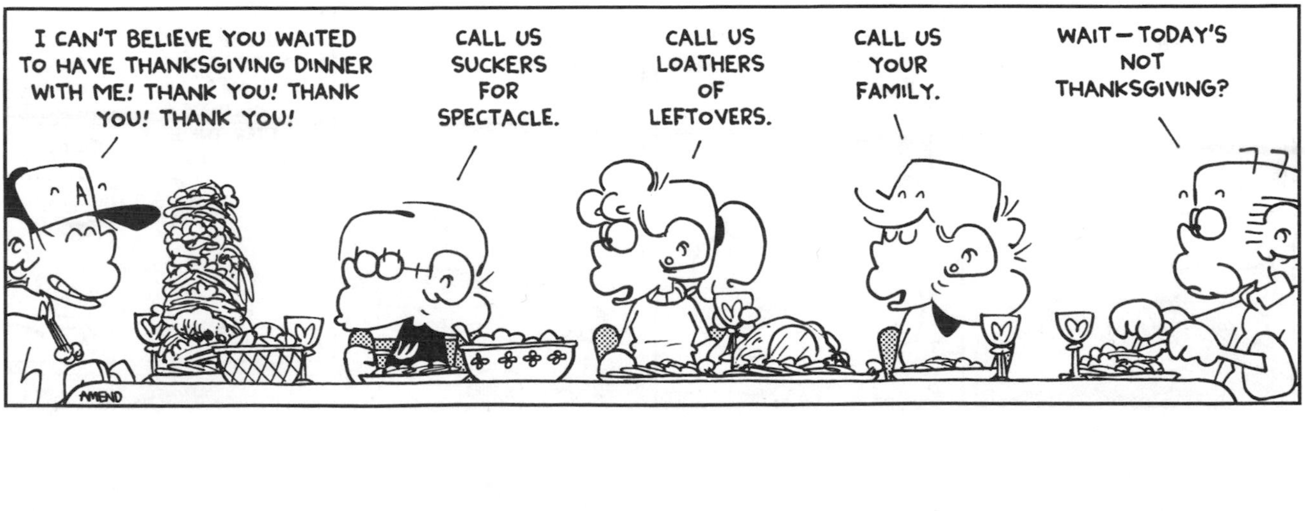
I CAN'T BELIEVE YOU WAITED TO HAVE THANKSGIVING DINNER WITH ME! THANK YOU! THANK YOU! THANK YOU!
CALL US SUCKERS FOR SPECTACLE.
CALL US LOATHERS OF LEFTOVERS.
CALL US YOUR FAMILY.
WAIT—TODAY'S NOT THANKSGIVING?
AMEND

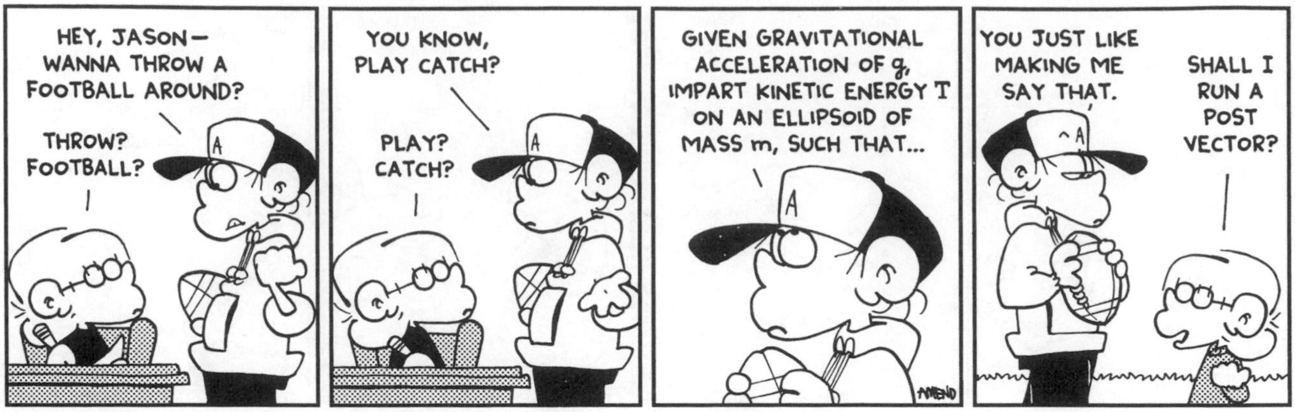
HEY, JASON— WANNA THROW A FOOTBALL AROUND?
THROW? FOOTBALL?
YOU KNOW, PLAY CATCH?
PLAY? CATCH?
GIVEN GRAVITATIONAL ACCELERATION OF g, IMPART KINETIC ENERGY T ON AN ELLIPSOID OF MASS m, SUCH THAT...
YOU JUST LIKE MAKING ME SAY THAT.
SHALL I RUN A POST VECTOR?

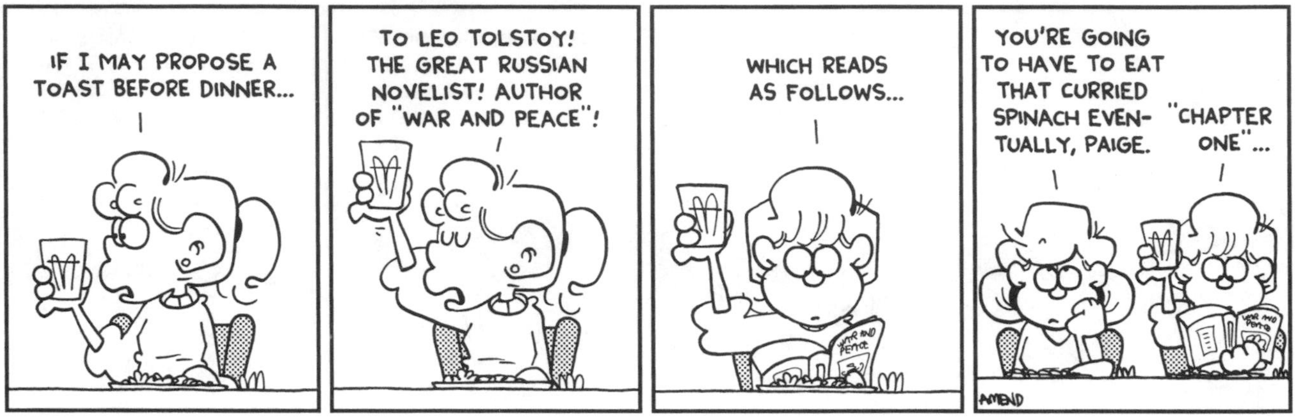
IF I MAY PROPOSE A TOAST BEFORE DINNER...
TO LEO TOLSTOY! THE GREAT RUSSIAN NOVELIST! AUTHOR OF "WAR AND PEACE"!
WHICH READS AS FOLLOWS...
YOU'RE GOING TO HAVE TO EAT THAT CURRIED SPINACH EVENTUALLY, PAIGE.
"CHAPTER ONE"...

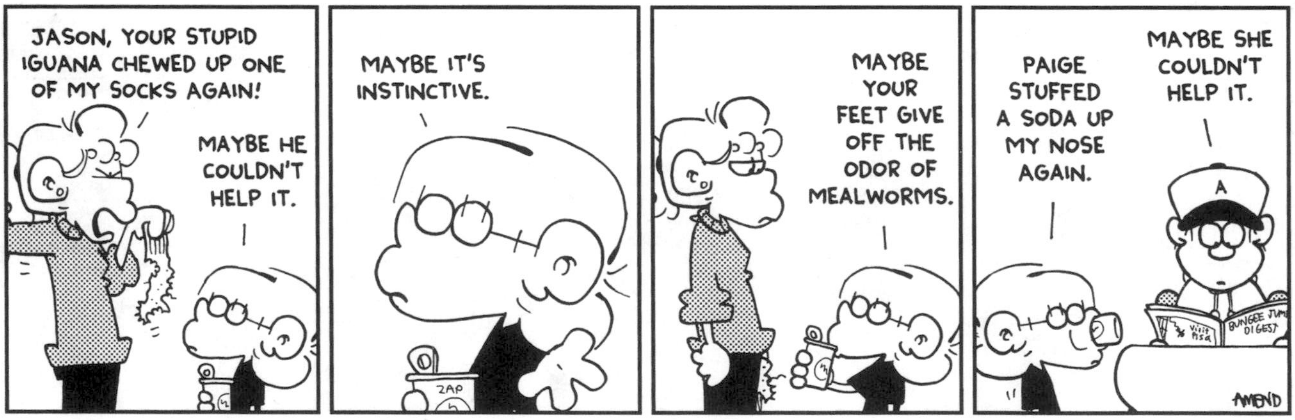
JASON, YOUR STUPID IGUANA CHEWED UP ONE OF MY SOCKS AGAIN!
MAYBE HE COULDN'T HELP IT.
MAYBE IT'S INSTINCTIVE.
MAYBE YOUR FEET GIVE OFF THE ODOR OF MEALWORMS.
PAIGE STUFFED A SODA UP MY NOSE AGAIN.
MAYBE SHE COULDN'T HELP IT.

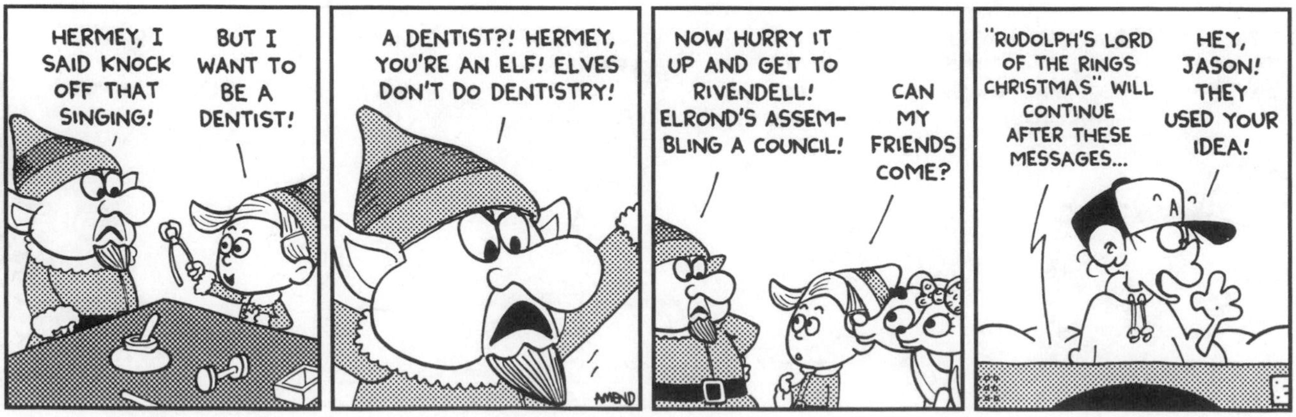
HERMEY, I SAID KNOCK OFF THAT SINGING!
BUT I WANT TO BE A DENTIST!
A DENTIST?! HERMEY, YOU'RE AN ELF! ELVES DON'T DO DENTISTRY!
NOW HURRY IT UP AND GET TO RIVENDELL! ELROND'S ASSEMBLING A COUNCIL!
CAN MY FRIENDS COME?
"RUDOLPH'S LORD OF THE RINGS CHRISTMAS" WILL CONTINUE AFTER THESE MESSAGES...
HEY, JASON! THEY USED YOUR IDEA!

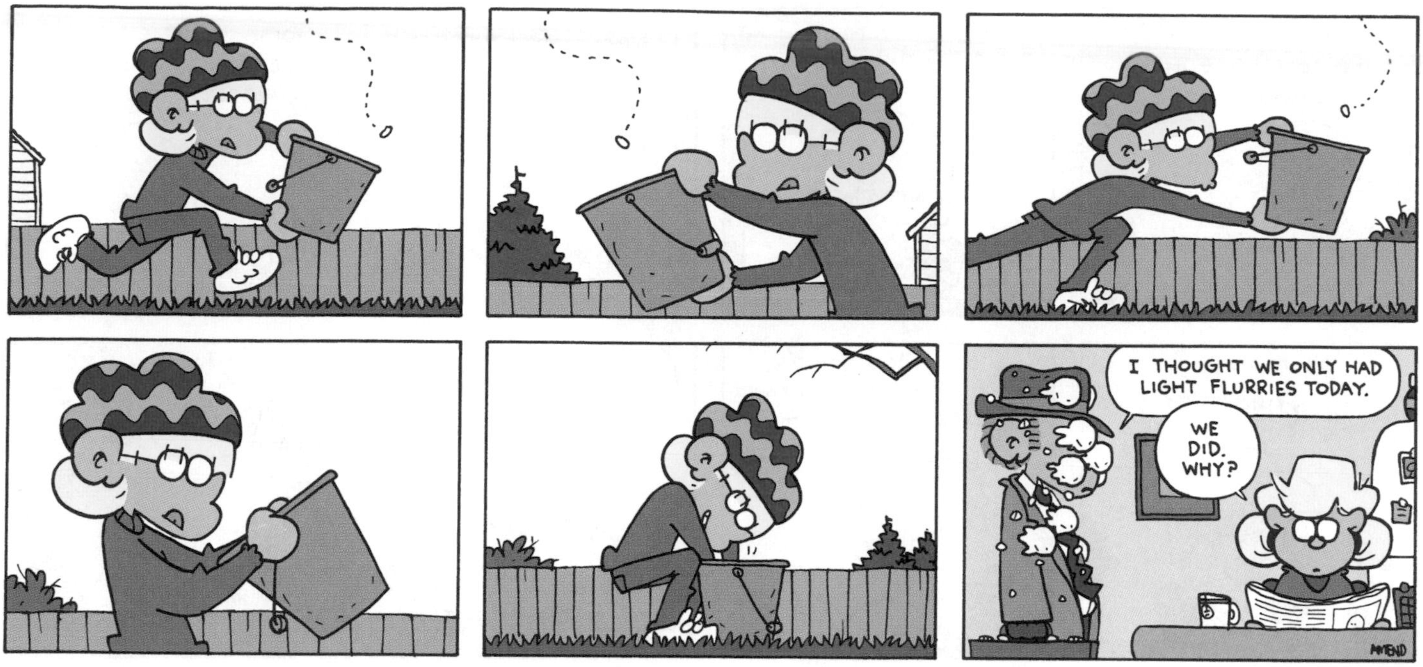
I THOUGHT WE ONLY HAD LIGHT FLURRIES TODAY.
WE DID. WHY?
AMEND

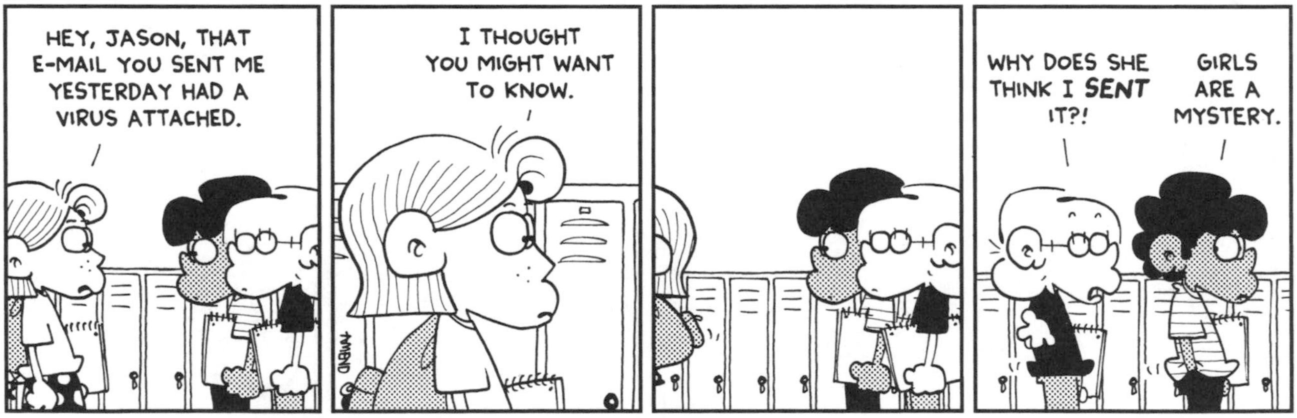
HEY, JASON, THAT E-MAIL YOU SENT ME YESTERDAY HAD A VIRUS ATTACHED.
I THOUGHT YOU MIGHT WANT TO KNOW.
AMEND
WHY DOES SHE THINK I **SENT** IT?!
GIRLS ARE A MYSTERY.

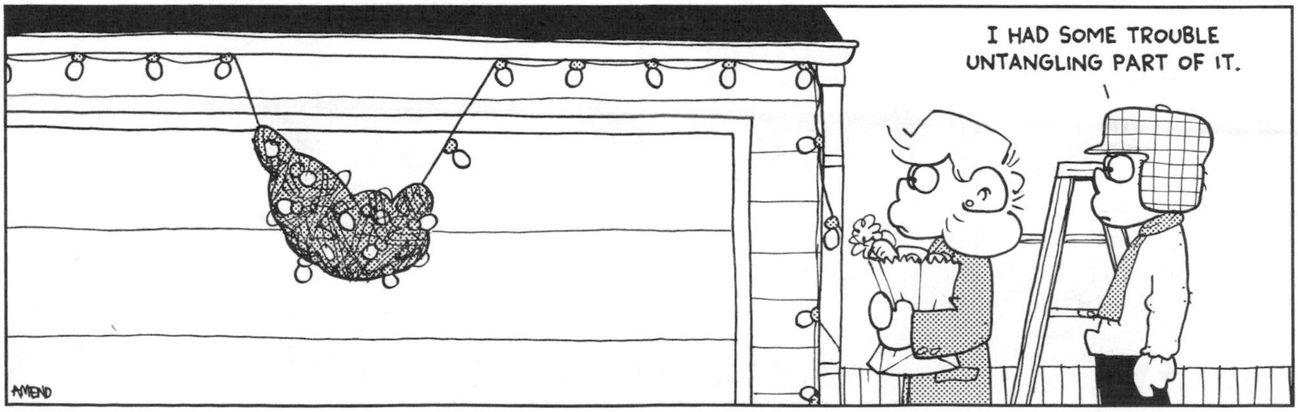
I HAD SOME TROUBLE UNTANGLING PART OF IT.
AMEND

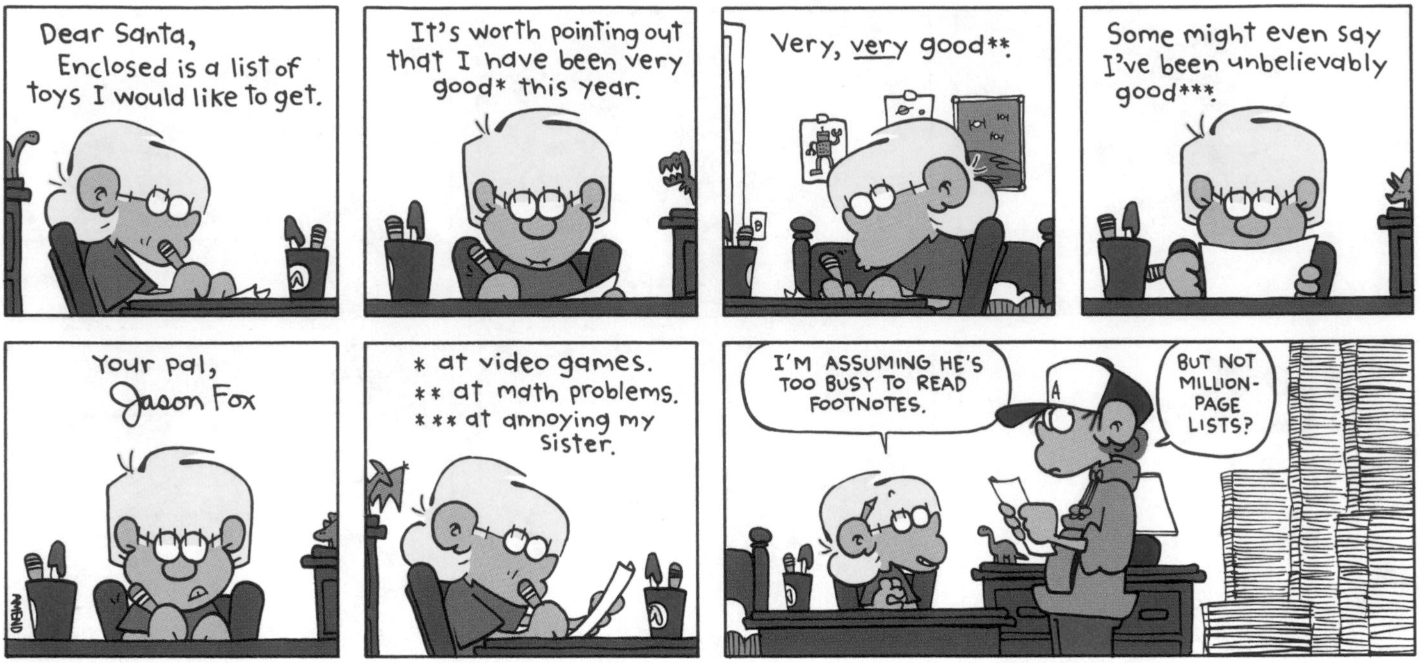
Dear Santa,
Enclosed is a list of toys I would like to get.
It's worth pointing out that I have been very good* this year.
Very, very good**.
Some might even say I've been unbelievably good***.
Your pal,
Jason Fox
* at video games.
** at math problems.
*** at annoying my sister.
I'M ASSUMING HE'S TOO BUSY TO READ FOOTNOTES.
BUT NOT MILLION-PAGE LISTS?
AMEND

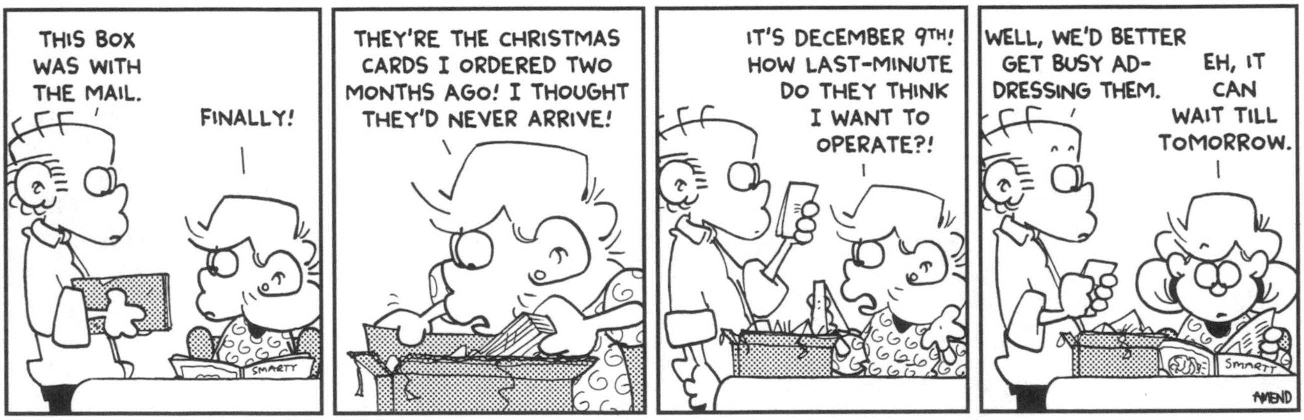
THIS BOX WAS WITH THE MAIL.
FINALLY!
SMARTT
THEY'RE THE CHRISTMAS CARDS I ORDERED TWO MONTHS AGO! I THOUGHT THEY'D NEVER ARRIVE!
IT'S DECEMBER 9TH! HOW LAST-MINUTE DO THEY THINK I WANT TO OPERATE?!
WELL, WE'D BETTER GET BUSY ADDRESSING THEM.
EH, IT CAN WAIT TILL TOMORROW.
SMARTT
AMEND

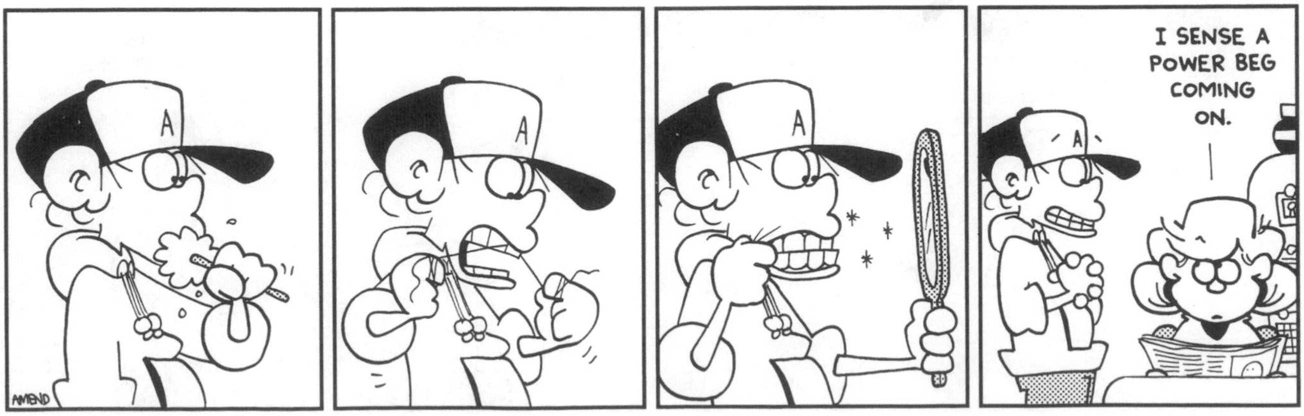
A
AMEND
A
A
A
I SENSE A POWER BEG COMING ON.

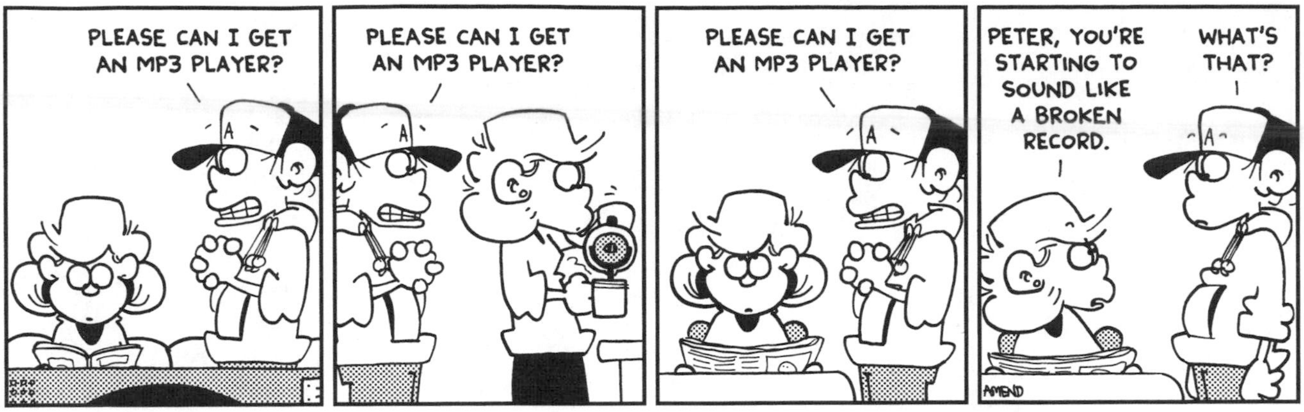
PLEASE CAN I GET AN MP3 PLAYER?
PLEASE CAN I GET AN MP3 PLAYER?
PLEASE CAN I GET AN MP3 PLAYER?
PETER, YOU'RE STARTING TO SOUND LIKE A BROKEN RECORD.
WHAT'S THAT?
AMEND

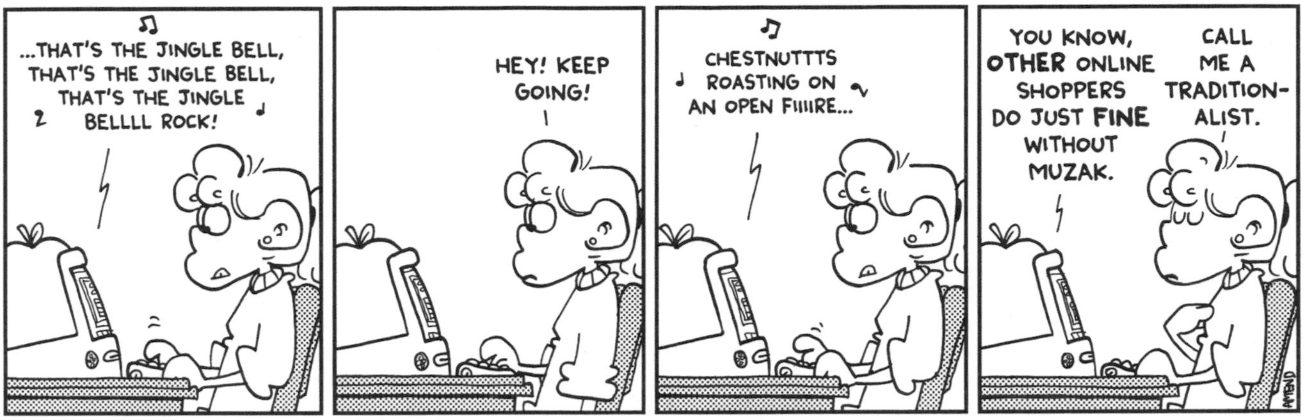
...THAT'S THE JINGLE BELL, THAT'S THE JINGLE BELL, THAT'S THE JINGLE BELLLL ROCK!
HEY! KEEP GOING!
CHESTNUTTTS ROASTING ON AN OPEN FIIIIRE...
YOU KNOW, OTHER ONLINE SHOPPERS DO JUST FINE WITHOUT MUZAK.
CALL ME A TRADITION-ALIST.
AMEND

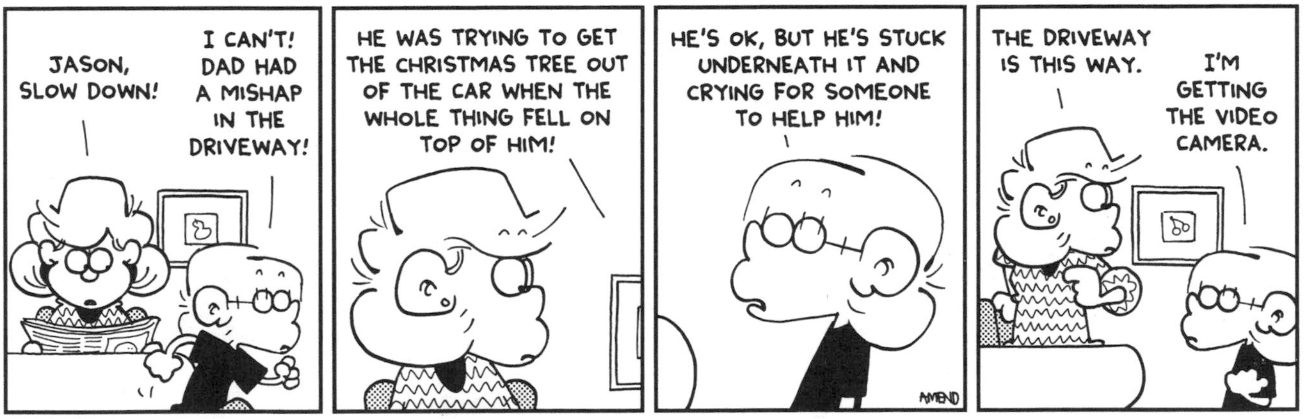
JASON, SLOW DOWN!
I CAN'T! DAD HAD A MISHAP IN THE DRIVEWAY!
HE WAS TRYING TO GET THE CHRISTMAS TREE OUT OF THE CAR WHEN THE WHOLE THING FELL ON TOP OF HIM!
HE'S OK, BUT HE'S STUCK UNDERNEATH IT AND CRYING FOR SOMEONE TO HELP HIM!
AMEND
THE DRIVEWAY IS THIS WAY.
I'M GETTING THE VIDEO CAMERA.

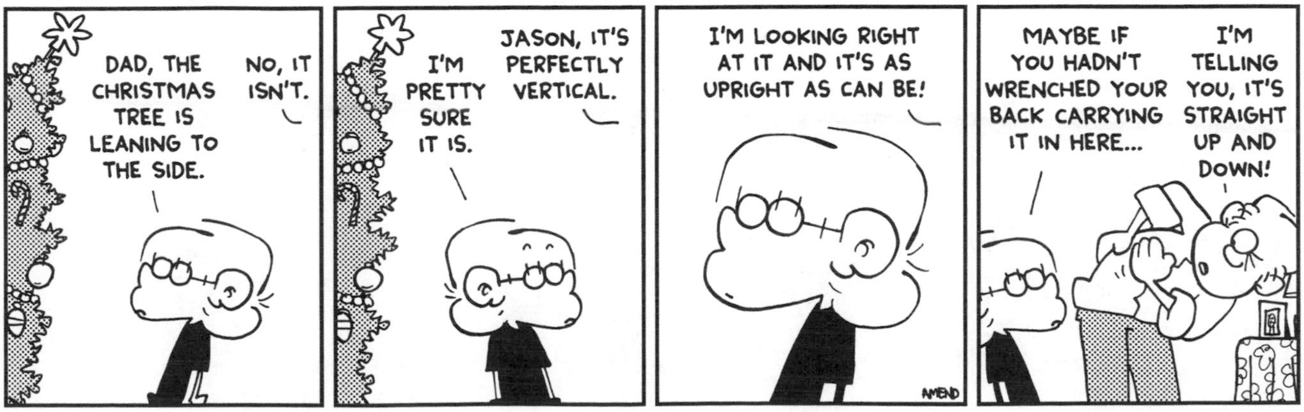
DAD, THE CHRISTMAS TREE IS LEANING TO THE SIDE.
NO, IT ISN'T.
I'M PRETTY SURE IT IS.
JASON, IT'S PERFECTLY VERTICAL.
I'M LOOKING RIGHT AT IT AND IT'S AS UPRIGHT AS CAN BE!
AMEND
MAYBE IF YOU HADN'T WRENCHED YOUR BACK CARRYING IT IN HERE...
I'M TELLING YOU, IT'S STRAIGHT UP AND DOWN!

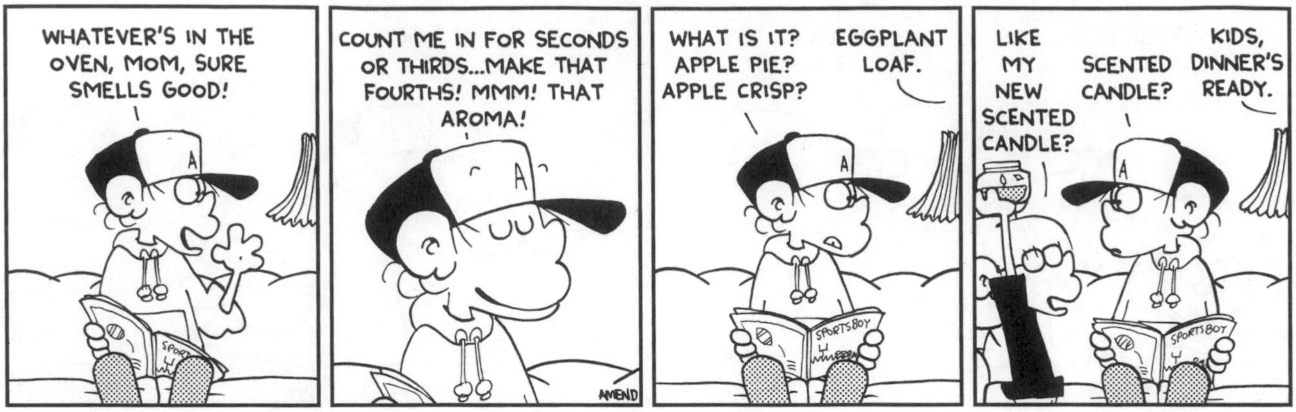
WHATEVER'S IN THE OVEN, MOM, SURE SMELLS GOOD!
COUNT ME IN FOR SECONDS OR THIRDS...MAKE THAT FOURTHS! MMM! THAT AROMA!
WHAT IS IT? APPLE PIE? APPLE CRISP?
EGGPLANT LOAF.
LIKE MY NEW SCENTED CANDLE?
SCENTED CANDLE?
KIDS, DINNER'S READY.

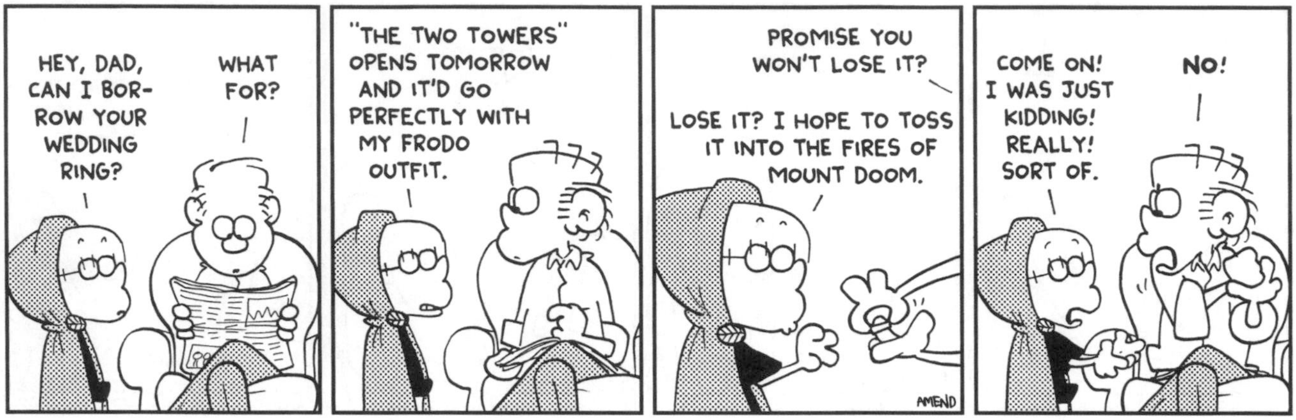
HEY, DAD, CAN I BOR-ROW YOUR WEDDING RING?
WHAT FOR?
"THE TWO TOWERS" OPENS TOMORROW AND IT'D GO PERFECTLY WITH MY FRODO OUTFIT.
PROMISE YOU WON'T LOSE IT?
LOSE IT? I HOPE TO TOSS IT INTO THE FIRES OF MOUNT DOOM.
COME ON! I WAS JUST KIDDING! REALLY! SORT OF.
NO!

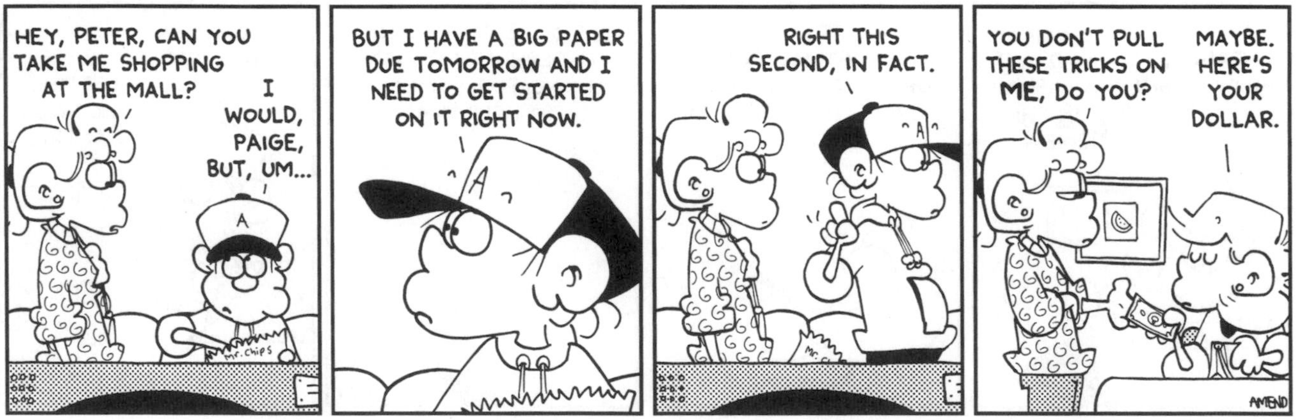
HEY, PETER, CAN YOU TAKE ME SHOPPING AT THE MALL?
I WOULD, PAIGE, BUT, UM...
BUT I HAVE A BIG PAPER DUE TOMORROW AND I NEED TO GET STARTED ON IT RIGHT NOW.
RIGHT THIS SECOND, IN FACT.
YOU DON'T PULL THESE TRICKS ON ME, DO YOU?
MAYBE. HERE'S YOUR DOLLAR.

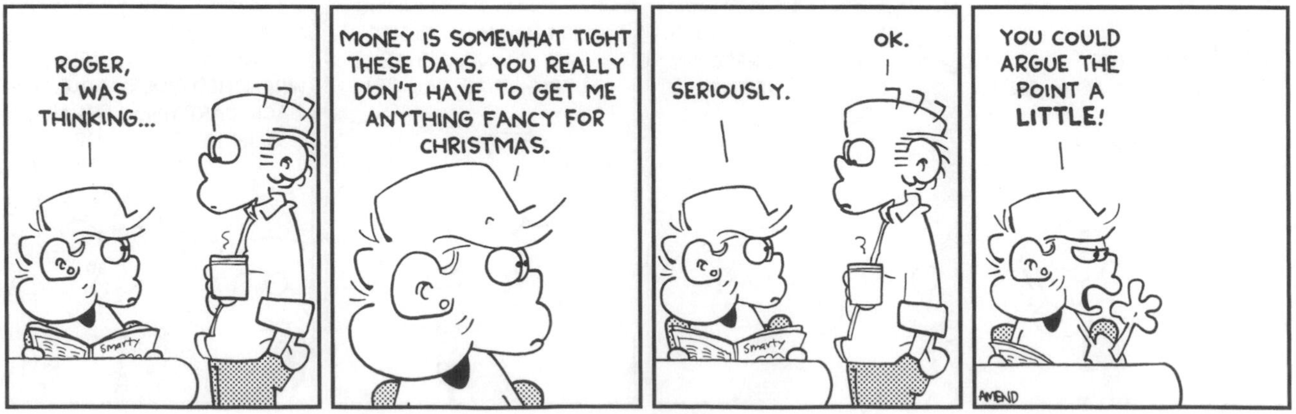
ROGER, I WAS THINKING...
MONEY IS SOMEWHAT TIGHT THESE DAYS. YOU REALLY DON'T HAVE TO GET ME ANYTHING FANCY FOR CHRISTMAS.
SERIOUSLY.
OK.
YOU COULD ARGUE THE POINT A LITTLE!

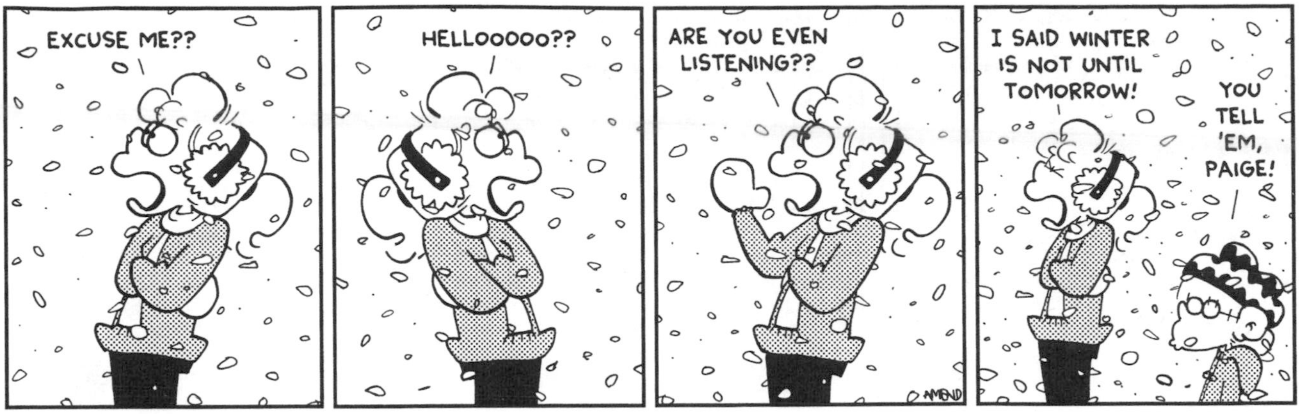
EXCUSE ME??
HELLOOOOO??
ARE YOU EVEN LISTENING??
I SAID WINTER IS NOT UNTIL TOMORROW!
YOU TELL 'EM, PAIGE!
AMEND

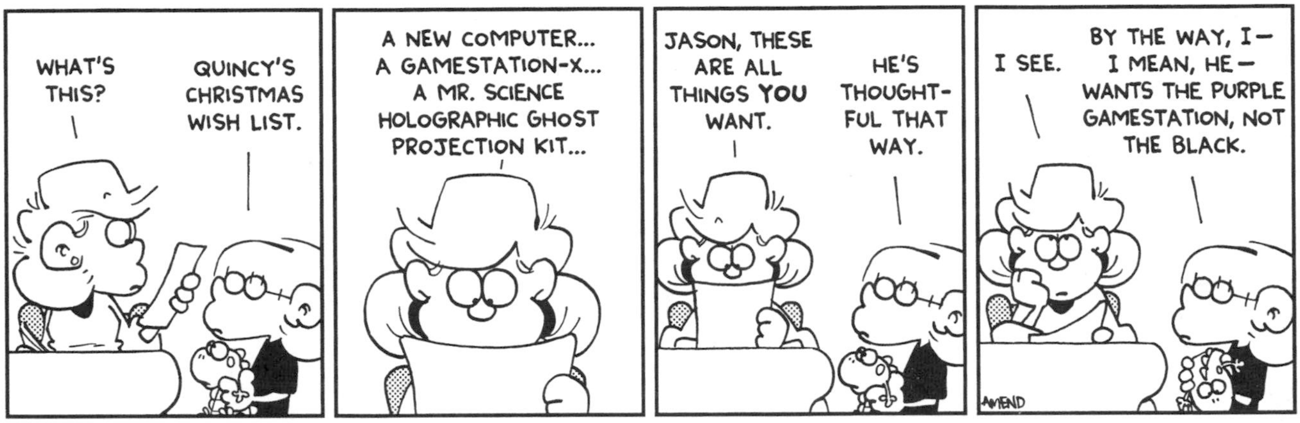
WHAT'S THIS?
QUINCY'S CHRISTMAS WISH LIST.
A NEW COMPUTER... A GAMESTATION-X... A MR. SCIENCE HOLOGRAPHIC GHOST PROJECTION KIT...
JASON, THESE ARE ALL THINGS YOU WANT.
HE'S THOUGHT-FUL THAT WAY.
I SEE.
BY THE WAY, I— I MEAN, HE— WANTS THE PURPLE GAMESTATION, NOT THE BLACK.
AMEND

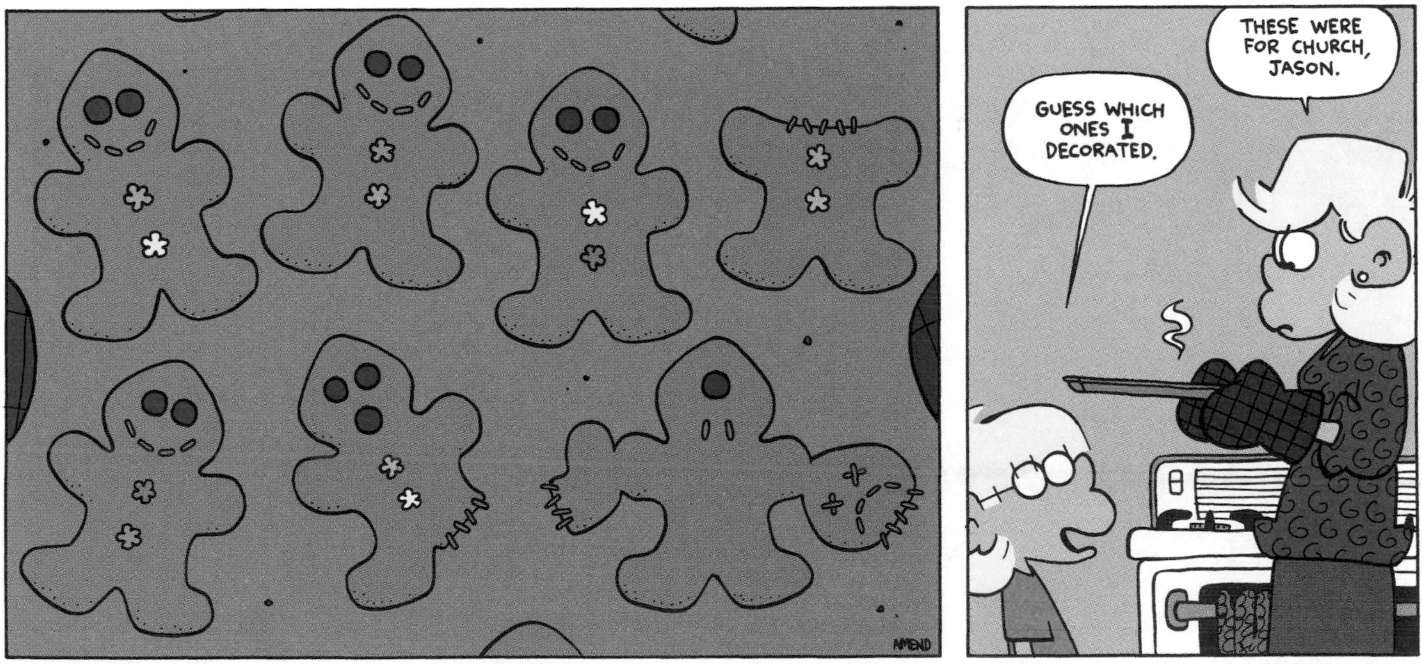
AMEND
THESE WERE FOR CHURCH, JASON.
GUESS WHICH ONES I DECORATED.

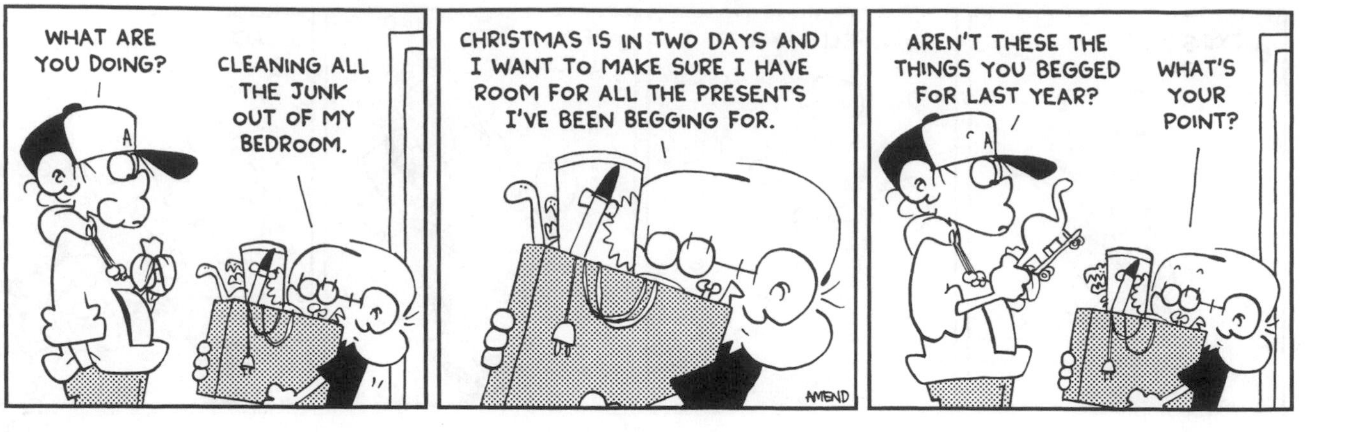
WHAT ARE YOU DOING?
CLEANING ALL THE JUNK OUT OF MY BEDROOM.
CHRISTMAS IS IN TWO DAYS AND I WANT TO MAKE SURE I HAVE ROOM FOR ALL THE PRESENTS I'VE BEEN BEGGING FOR.
AREN'T THESE THE THINGS YOU BEGGED FOR LAST YEAR?
WHAT'S YOUR POINT?
AMEND

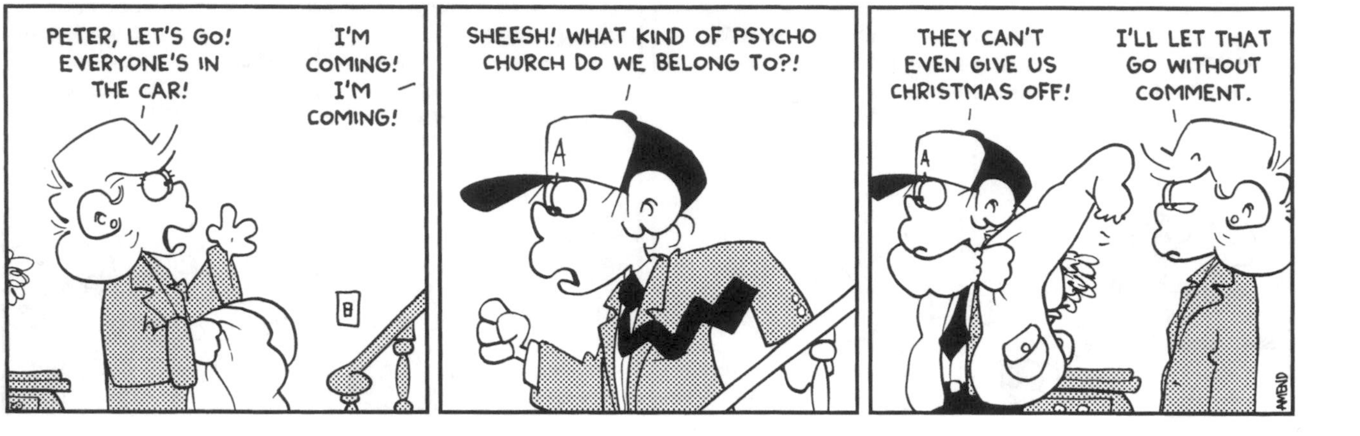
PETER, LET'S GO! EVERYONE'S IN THE CAR!
I'M COMING! I'M COMING!
SHEESH! WHAT KIND OF PSYCHO CHURCH DO WE BELONG TO?!
THEY CAN'T EVEN GIVE US CHRISTMAS OFF!
I'LL LET THAT GO WITHOUT COMMENT.
AMEND

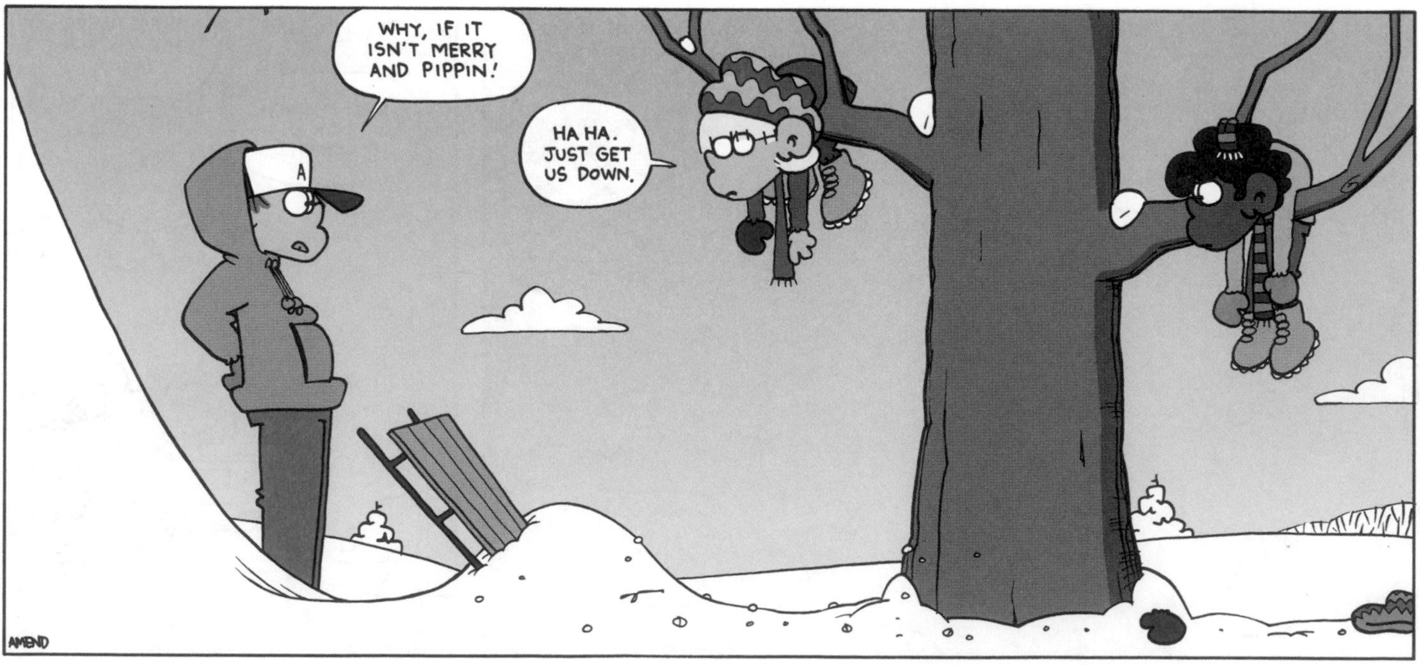
WHY, IF IT ISN'T MERRY AND PIPPIN!
HA HA. JUST GET US DOWN.
AMEND

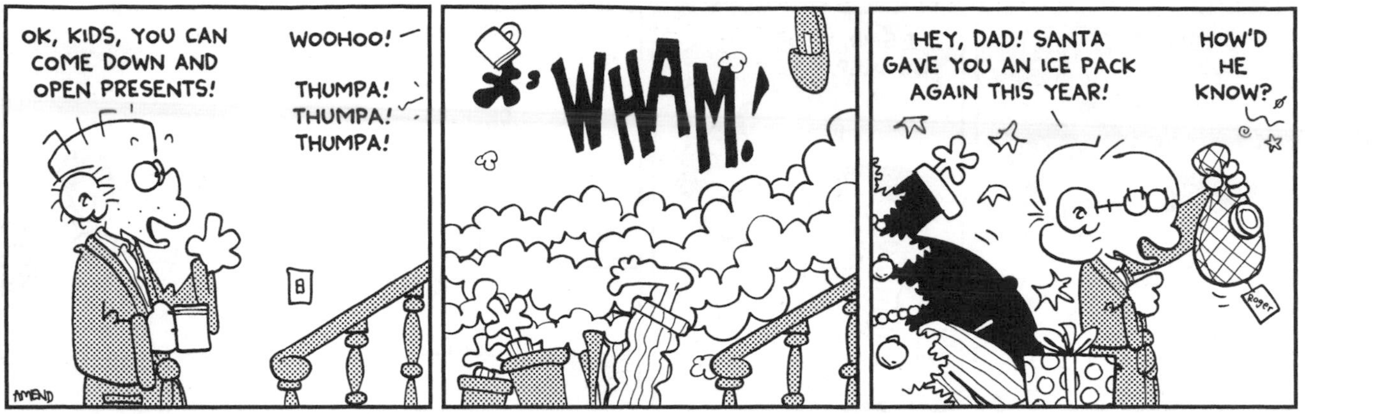
OK, KIDS, YOU CAN COME DOWN AND OPEN PRESENTS!
WOOHOO!
THUMPA! THUMPA! THUMPA!
AMEND
WHAM!
HEY, DAD! SANTA GAVE YOU AN ICE PACK AGAIN THIS YEAR!
HOW'D HE KNOW?

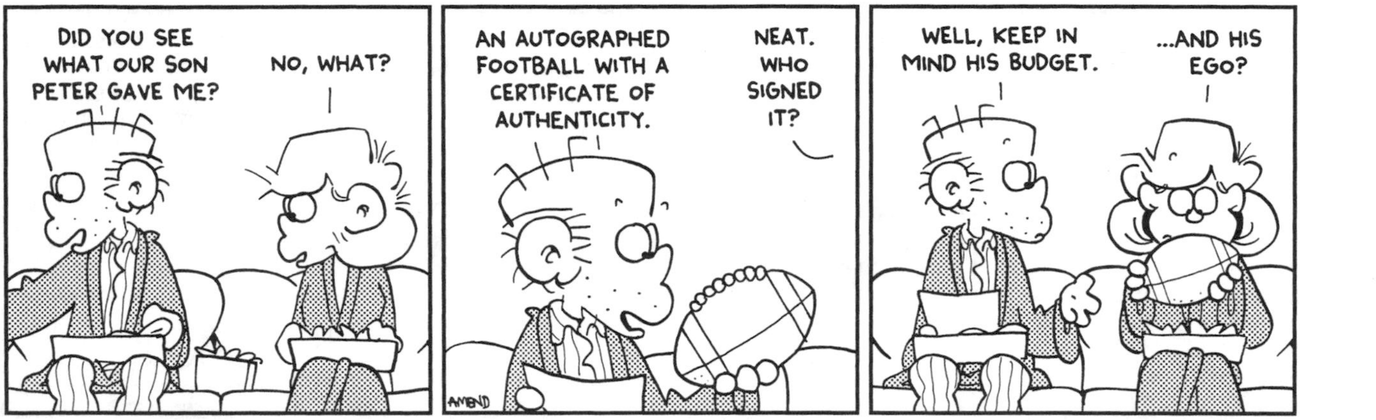
DID YOU SEE WHAT OUR SON PETER GAVE ME?
NO, WHAT?
AN AUTOGRAPHED FOOTBALL WITH A CERTIFICATE OF AUTHENTICITY.
NEAT. WHO SIGNED IT?
AMEND
WELL, KEEP IN MIND HIS BUDGET.
...AND HIS EGO?

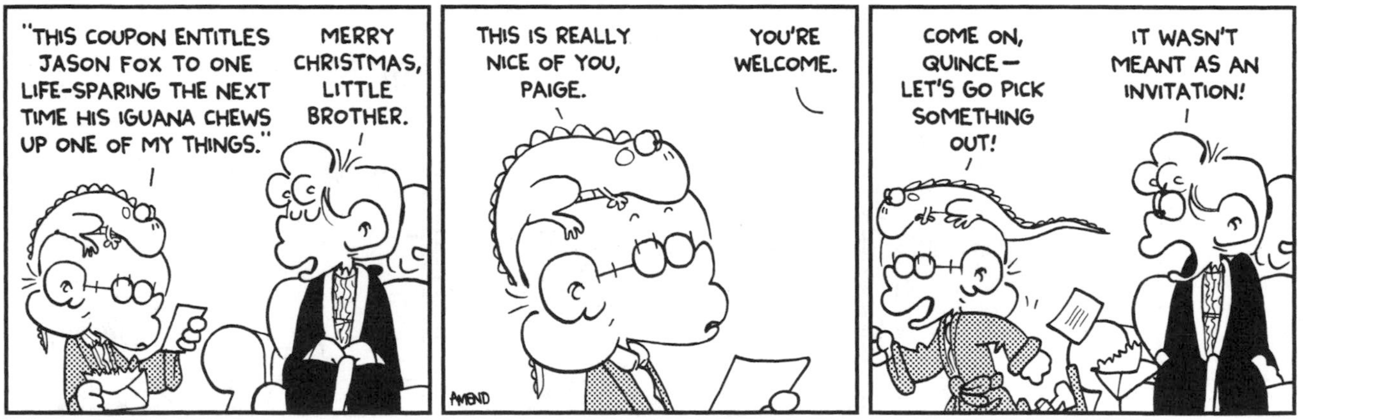
"THIS COUPON ENTITLES JASON FOX TO ONE LIFE-SPARING THE NEXT TIME HIS IGUANA CHEWS UP ONE OF MY THINGS."
MERRY CHRISTMAS, LITTLE BROTHER.
THIS IS REALLY NICE OF YOU, PAIGE.
YOU'RE WELCOME.
AMEND
COME ON, QUINCE— LET'S GO PICK SOMETHING OUT!
IT WASN'T MEANT AS AN INVITATION!

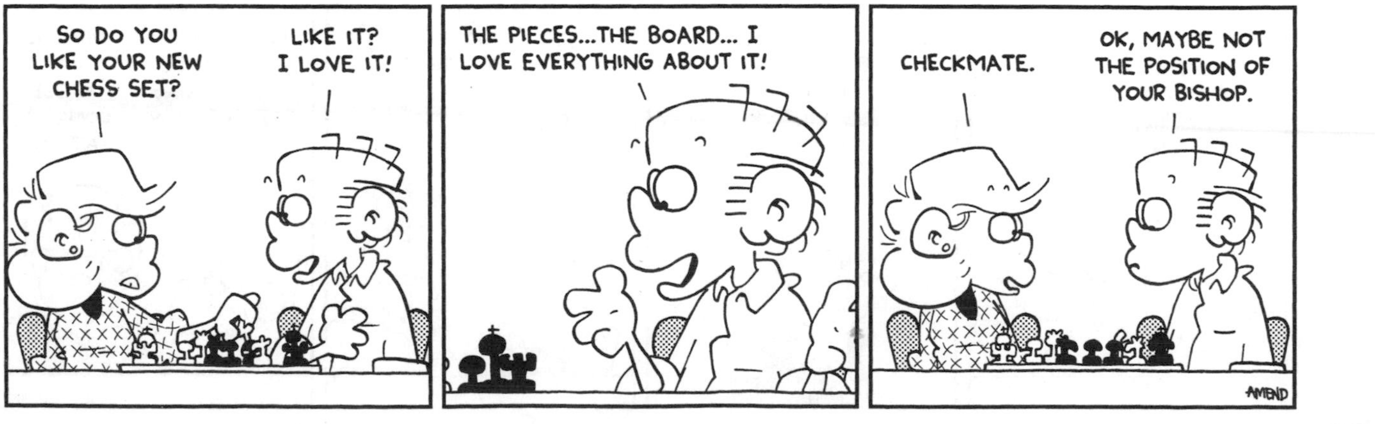
SO DO YOU LIKE YOUR NEW CHESS SET?
LIKE IT? I LOVE IT!
THE PIECES...THE BOARD... I LOVE EVERYTHING ABOUT IT!
CHECKMATE.
OK, MAYBE NOT THE POSITION OF YOUR BISHOP.
AMEND

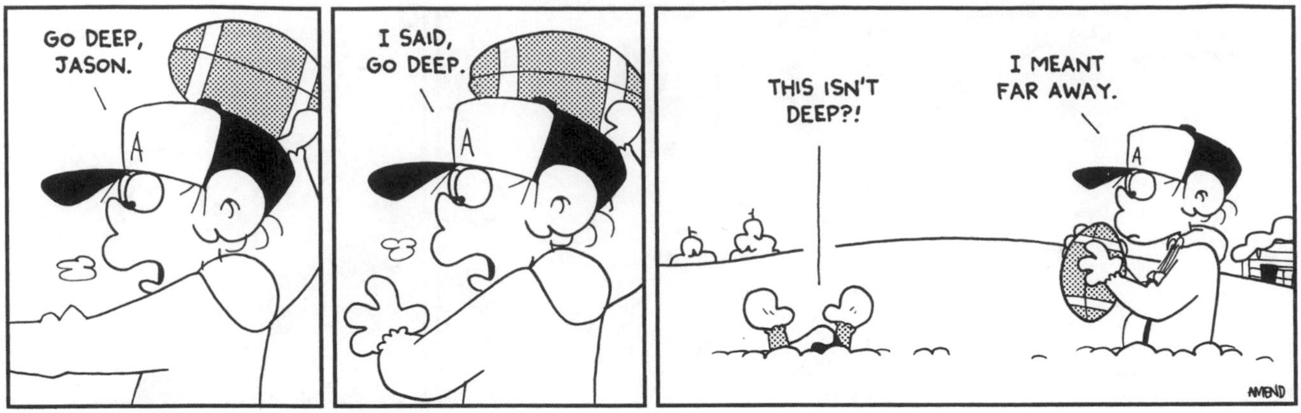
GO DEEP, JASON.
I SAID, GO DEEP.
THIS ISN'T DEEP?!
I MEANT FAR AWAY.
AMEND

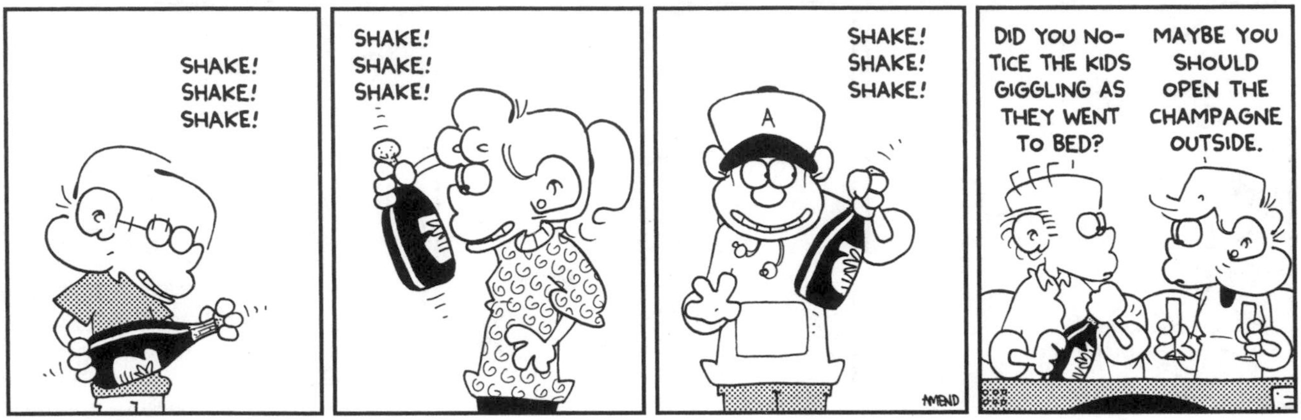
SHAKE! SHAKE! SHAKE!
SHAKE! SHAKE! SHAKE!
SHAKE! SHAKE! SHAKE!
AMEND
DID YOU NOTICE THE KIDS GIGGLING AS THEY WENT TO BED?
MAYBE YOU SHOULD OPEN THE CHAMPAGNE OUTSIDE.

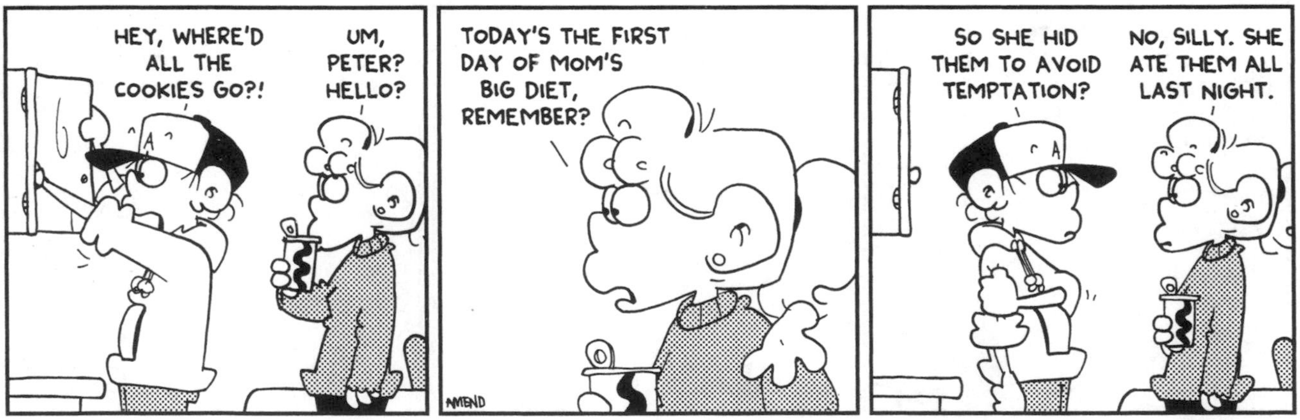
HEY, WHERE'D ALL THE COOKIES GO?!
UM, PETER? HELLO?
TODAY'S THE FIRST DAY OF MOM'S BIG DIET, REMEMBER?
AMEND
SO SHE HID THEM TO AVOID TEMPTATION?
NO, SILLY. SHE ATE THEM ALL LAST NIGHT.

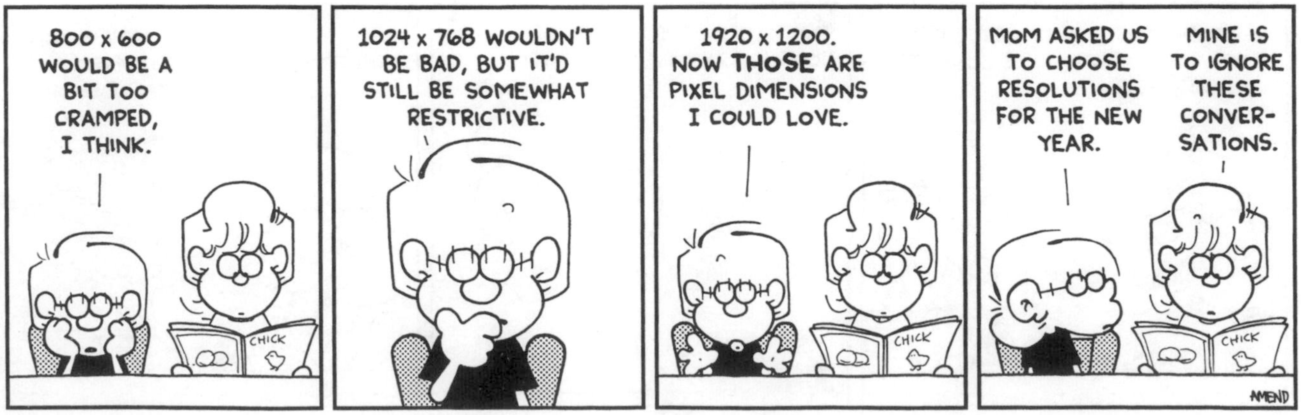
800 x 600 WOULD BE A BIT TOO CRAMPED, I THINK.
CHICK
1024 x 768 WOULDN'T BE BAD, BUT IT'D STILL BE SOMEWHAT RESTRICTIVE.
1920 x 1200. NOW THOSE ARE PIXEL DIMENSIONS I COULD LOVE.
CHICK
MOM ASKED US TO CHOOSE RESOLUTIONS FOR THE NEW YEAR.
MINE IS TO IGNORE THESE CONVERSATIONS.
CHICK
AMEND

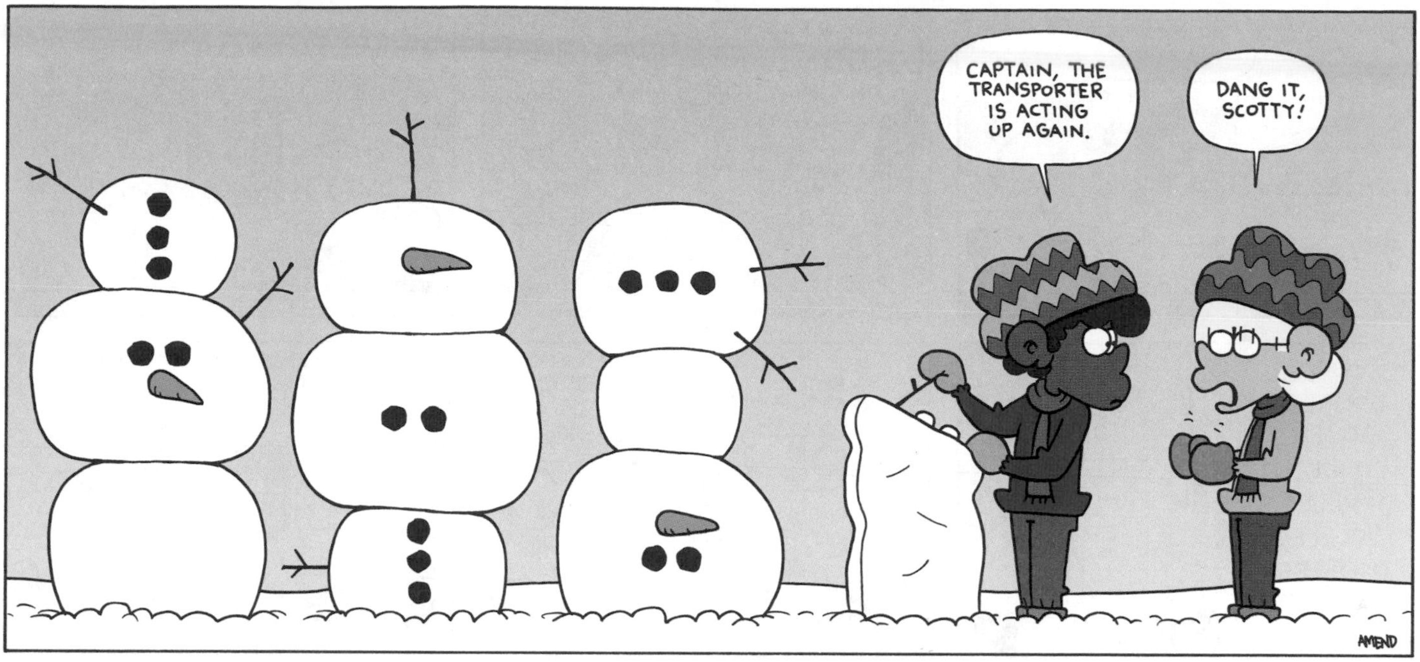
CAPTAIN, THE TRANSPORTER IS ACTING UP AGAIN.
DANG IT, SCOTTY!
AMEND

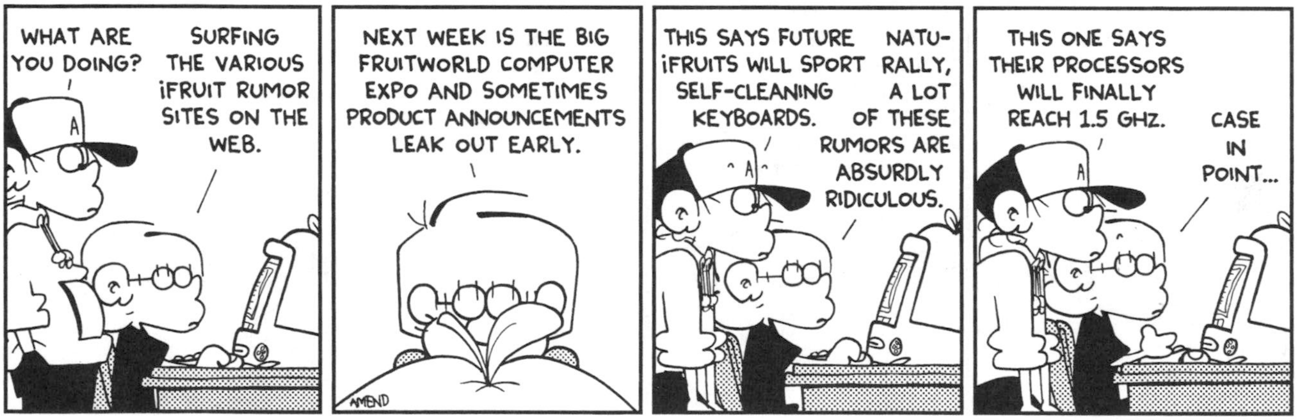
WHAT ARE YOU DOING?
SURFING THE VARIOUS iFRUIT RUMOR SITES ON THE WEB.
NEXT WEEK IS THE BIG FRUITWORLD COMPUTER EXPO AND SOMETIMES PRODUCT ANNOUNCEMENTS LEAK OUT EARLY.
THIS SAYS FUTURE iFRUITS WILL SPORT SELF-CLEANING KEYBOARDS.
NATURALLY, A LOT OF THESE RUMORS ARE ABSURDLY RIDICULOUS.
THIS ONE SAYS THEIR PROCESSORS WILL FINALLY REACH 1.5 GHZ.
CASE IN POINT...
AMEND

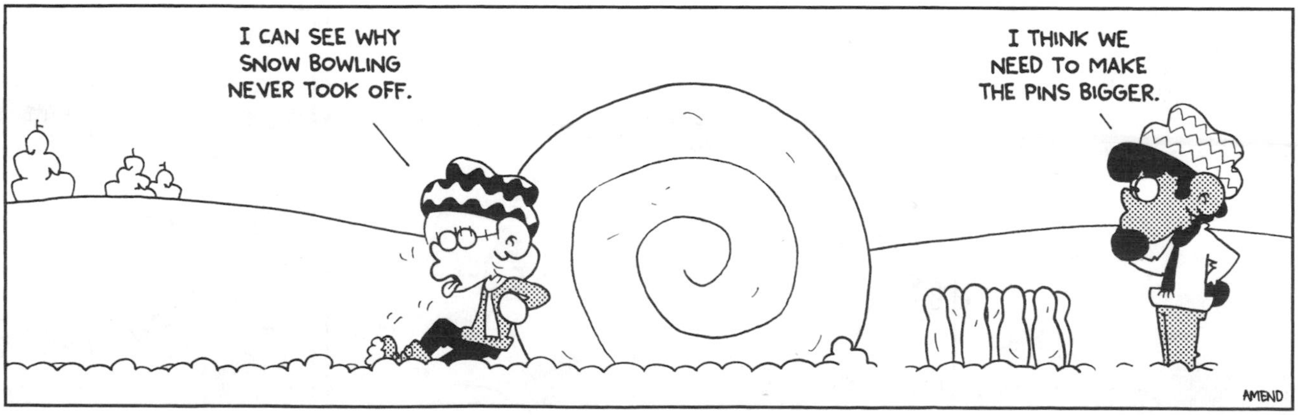
I CAN SEE WHY SNOW BOWLING NEVER TOOK OFF.
I THINK WE NEED TO MAKE THE PINS BIGGER.
AMEND

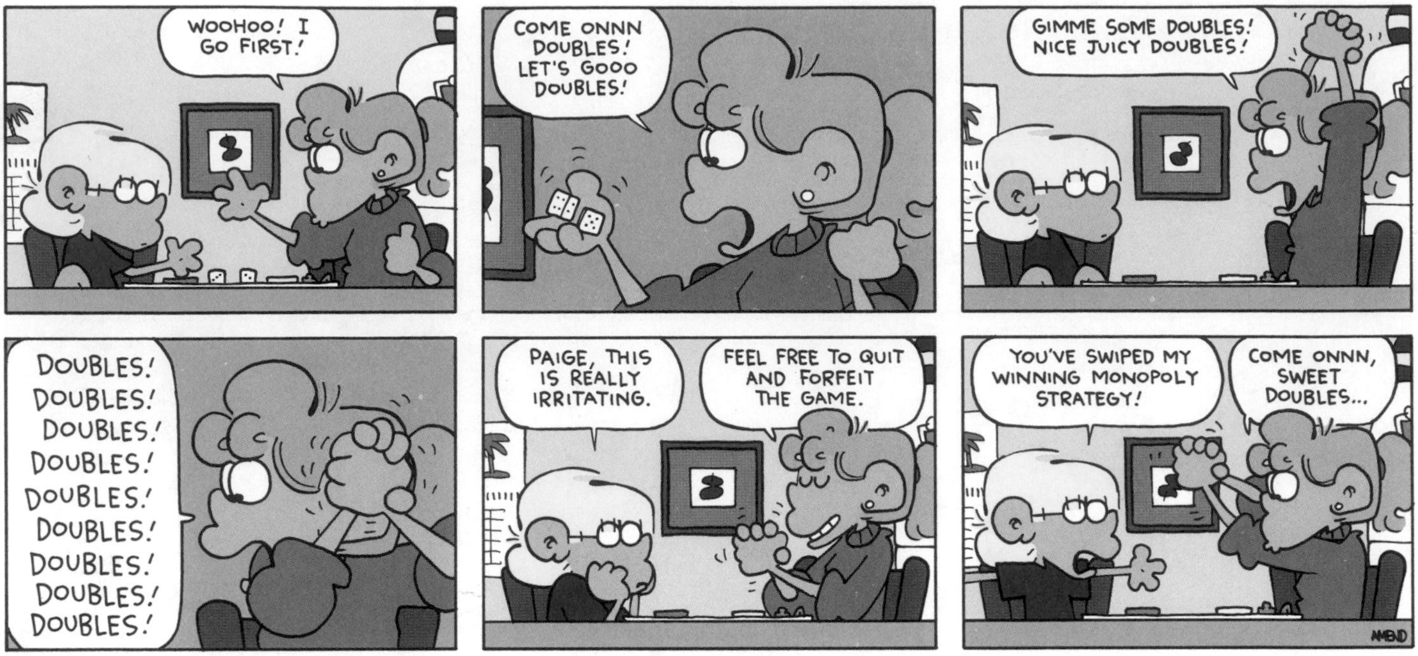
WOOHOO! I GO FIRST!
COME ONNN DOUBLES! LET'S GOOO DOUBLES!
GIMME SOME DOUBLES! NICE JUICY DOUBLES!
DOUBLES! DOUBLES! DOUBLES! DOUBLES! DOUBLES! DOUBLES! DOUBLES! DOUBLES! DOUBLES!
PAIGE, THIS IS REALLY IRRITATING.
FEEL FREE TO QUIT AND FORFEIT THE GAME.
YOU'VE SWIPED MY WINNING MONOPOLY STRATEGY!
COME ONNN, SWEET DOUBLES...
AMEND

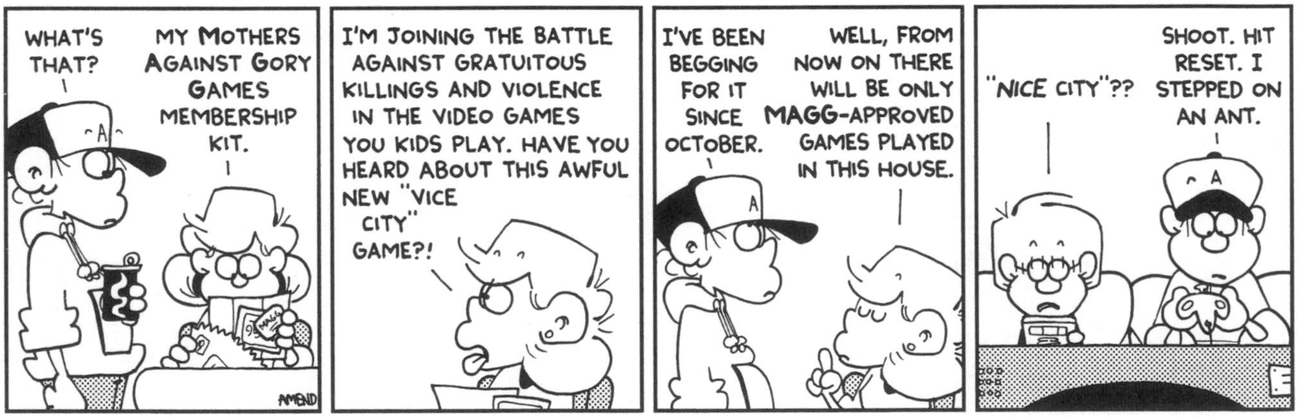
WHAT'S THAT?
MY MOTHERS AGAINST GORY GAMES MEMBERSHIP KIT.
I'M JOINING THE BATTLE AGAINST GRATUITOUS KILLINGS AND VIOLENCE IN THE VIDEO GAMES YOU KIDS PLAY. HAVE YOU HEARD ABOUT THIS AWFUL NEW "VICE CITY" GAME?!
I'VE BEEN BEGGING FOR IT SINCE OCTOBER.
WELL, FROM NOW ON THERE WILL BE ONLY MAGG-APPROVED GAMES PLAYED IN THIS HOUSE.
"NICE CITY"??
SHOOT. HIT RESET. I STEPPED ON AN ANT.
AMEND

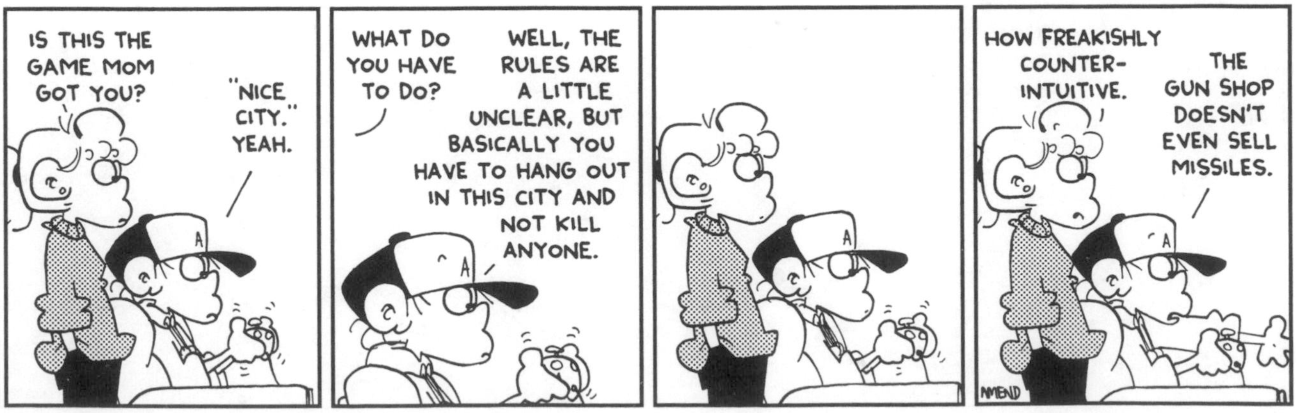
IS THIS THE GAME MOM GOT YOU?
"NICE CITY." YEAH.
WHAT DO YOU HAVE TO DO?
WELL, THE RULES ARE A LITTLE UNCLEAR, BUT BASICALLY YOU HAVE TO HANG OUT IN THIS CITY AND NOT KILL ANYONE.
HOW FREAKISHLY COUNTER-INTUITIVE.
THE GUN SHOP DOESN'T EVEN SELL MISSILES.
AMEND

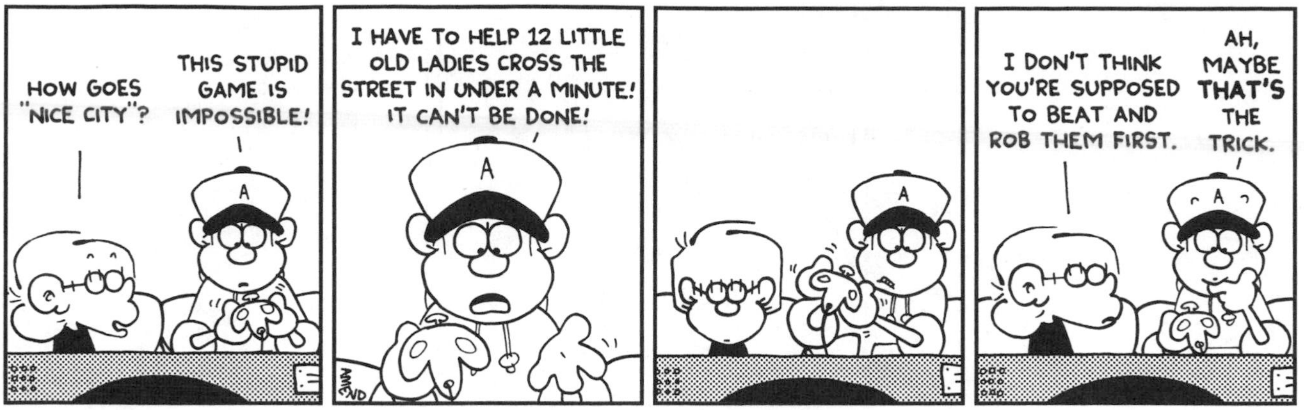
HOW GOES "NICE CITY"?
THIS STUPID GAME IS IMPOSSIBLE!
I HAVE TO HELP 12 LITTLE OLD LADIES CROSS THE STREET IN UNDER A MINUTE! IT CAN'T BE DONE!
I DON'T THINK YOU'RE SUPPOSED TO BEAT AND ROB THEM FIRST.
AH, MAYBE **THAT'S** THE TRICK.
AMEND

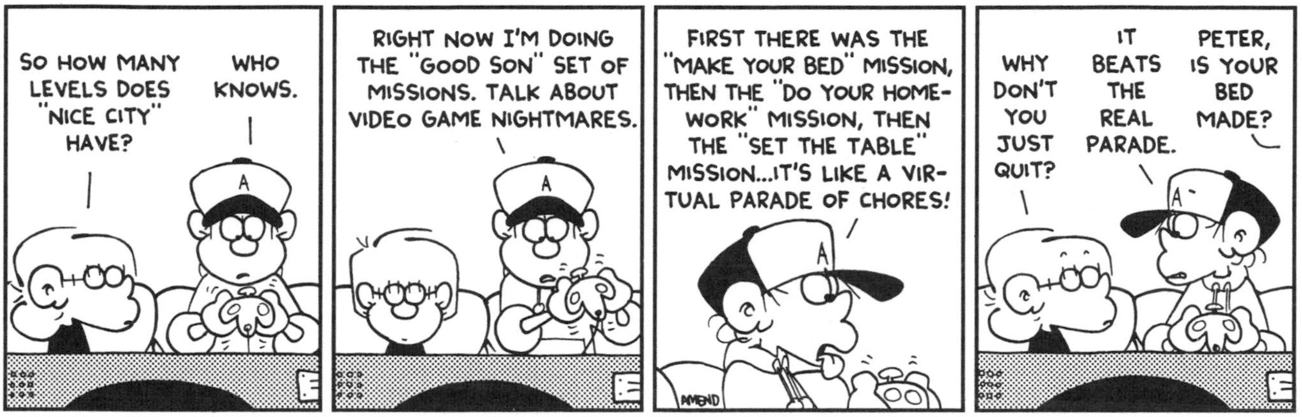
SO HOW MANY LEVELS DOES "NICE CITY" HAVE?
WHO KNOWS.
RIGHT NOW I'M DOING THE "GOOD SON" SET OF MISSIONS. TALK ABOUT VIDEO GAME NIGHTMARES.
FIRST THERE WAS THE "MAKE YOUR BED" MISSION, THEN THE "DO YOUR HOME-WORK" MISSION, THEN THE "SET THE TABLE" MISSION...IT'S LIKE A VIR-TUAL PARADE OF CHORES!
WHY DON'T YOU JUST QUIT?
IT BEATS THE REAL PARADE.
PETER, IS YOUR BED MADE?
AMEND

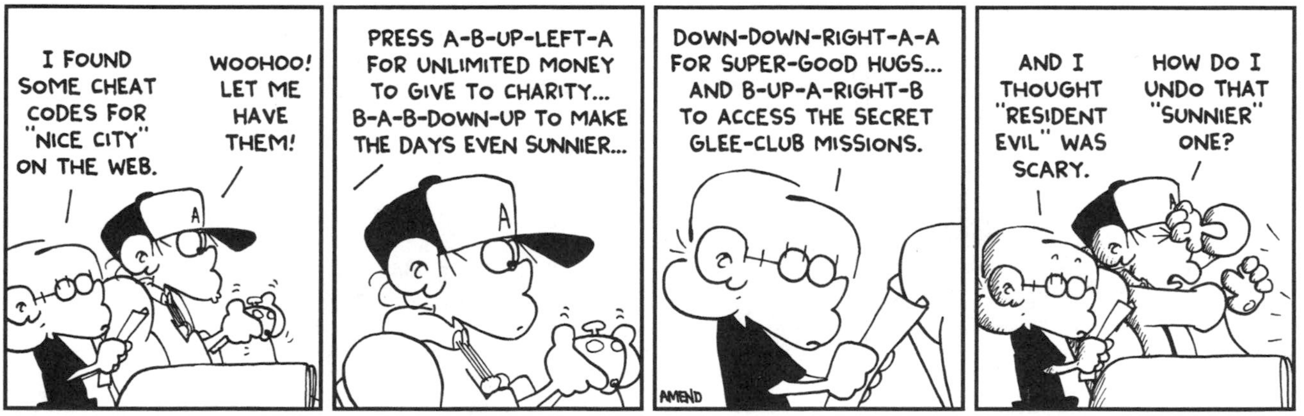
I FOUND SOME CHEAT CODES FOR "NICE CITY" ON THE WEB.
WOOHOO! LET ME HAVE THEM!
PRESS A-B-UP-LEFT-A FOR UNLIMITED MONEY TO GIVE TO CHARITY... B-A-B-DOWN-UP TO MAKE THE DAYS EVEN SUNNIER...
DOWN-DOWN-RIGHT-A-A FOR SUPER-GOOD HUGS... AND B-UP-A-RIGHT-B TO ACCESS THE SECRET GLEE-CLUB MISSIONS.
AND I THOUGHT "RESIDENT EVIL" WAS SCARY.
HOW DO I UNDO THAT "SUNNIER" ONE?
AMEND

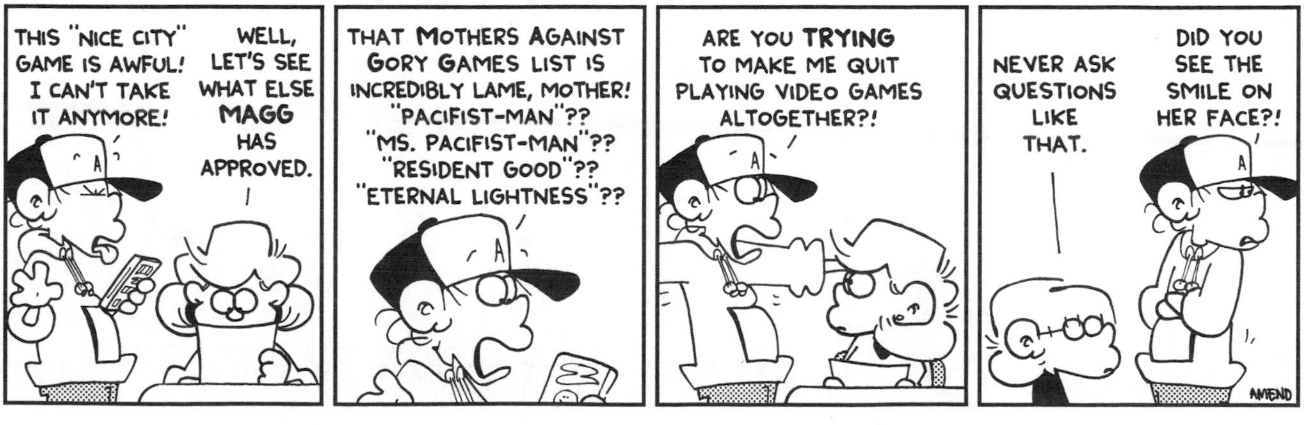
THIS "NICE CITY" GAME IS AWFUL! I CAN'T TAKE IT ANYMORE!
WELL, LET'S SEE WHAT ELSE **MAGG** HAS APPROVED.
THAT **MOTHERS AGAINST GORY GAMES** LIST IS INCREDIBLY LAME, MOTHER! "PACIFIST-MAN"?? "MS. PACIFIST-MAN"?? "RESIDENT GOOD"?? "ETERNAL LIGHTNESS"??
ARE YOU **TRYING** TO MAKE ME QUIT PLAYING VIDEO GAMES ALTOGETHER?!
NEVER ASK QUESTIONS LIKE THAT.
DID YOU SEE THE SMILE ON HER FACE?!
AMEND

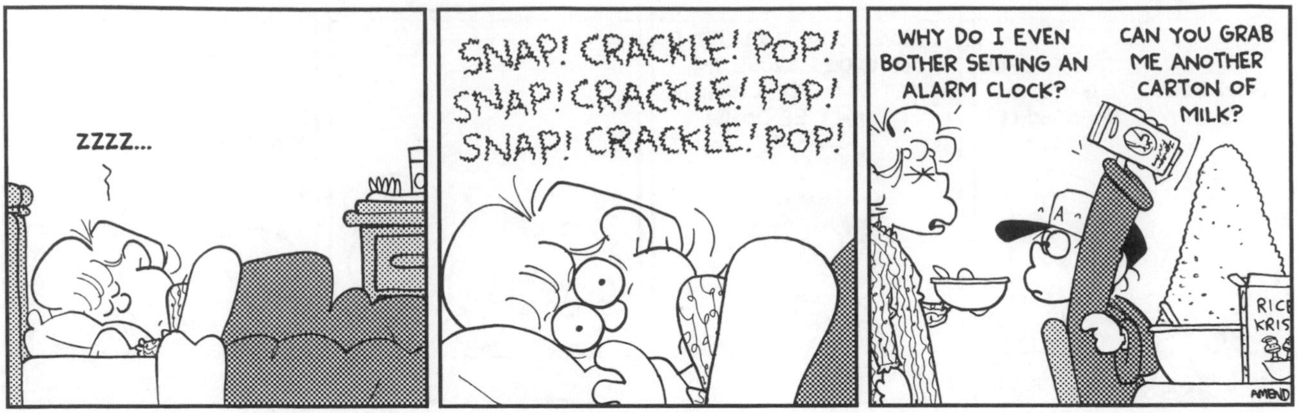
ZZZZ...
SNAP! CRACKLE! POP!
SNAP! CRACKLE! POP!
SNAP! CRACKLE! POP!
WHY DO I EVEN BOTHER SETTING AN ALARM CLOCK?
CAN YOU GRAB ME ANOTHER CARTON OF MILK?
AMEND

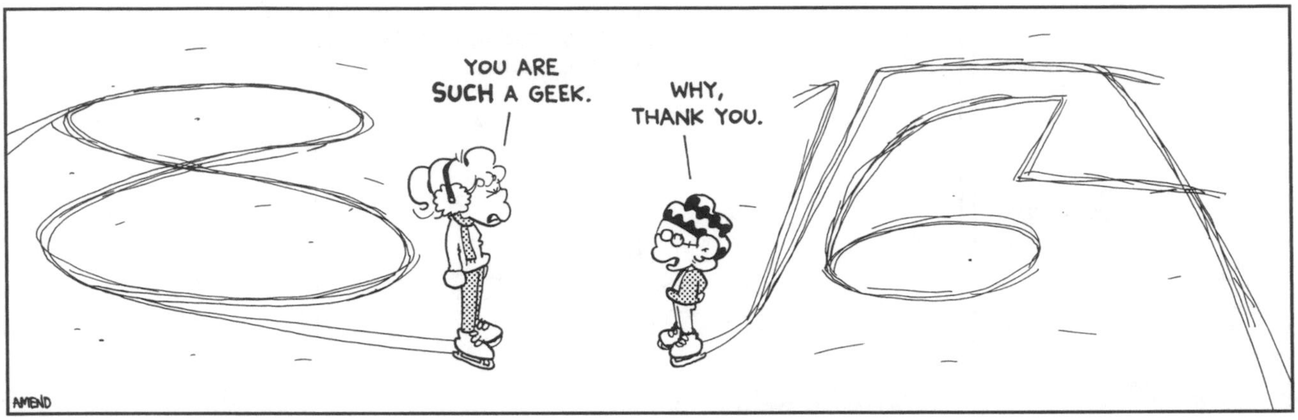
YOU ARE SUCH A GEEK.
WHY, THANK YOU.
AMEND

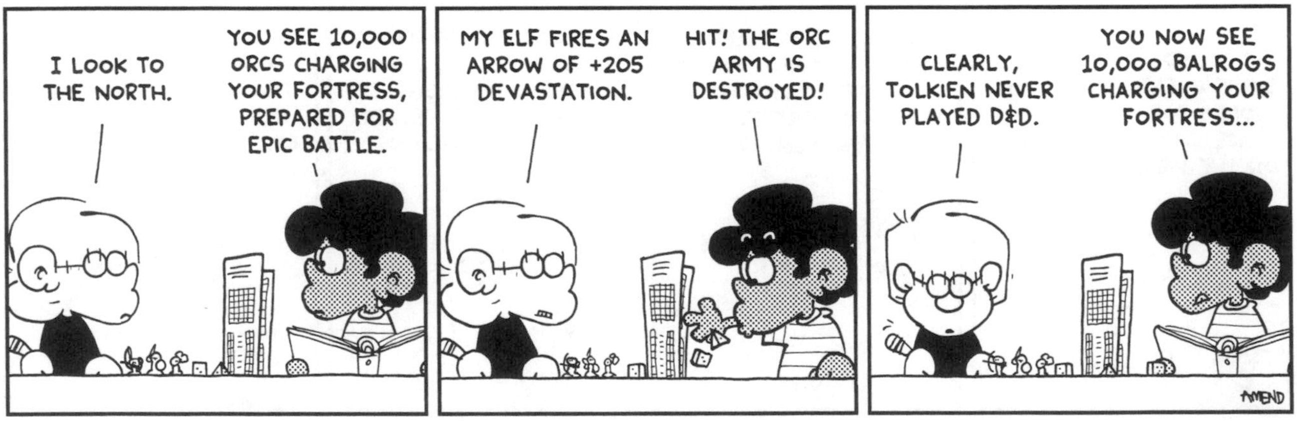
I LOOK TO THE NORTH.
YOU SEE 10,000 ORCS CHARGING YOUR FORTRESS, PREPARED FOR EPIC BATTLE.
MY ELF FIRES AN ARROW OF +205 DEVASTATION.
HIT! THE ORC ARMY IS DESTROYED!
CLEARLY, TOLKIEN NEVER PLAYED D&D.
YOU NOW SEE 10,000 BALROGS CHARGING YOUR FORTRESS...
AMEND

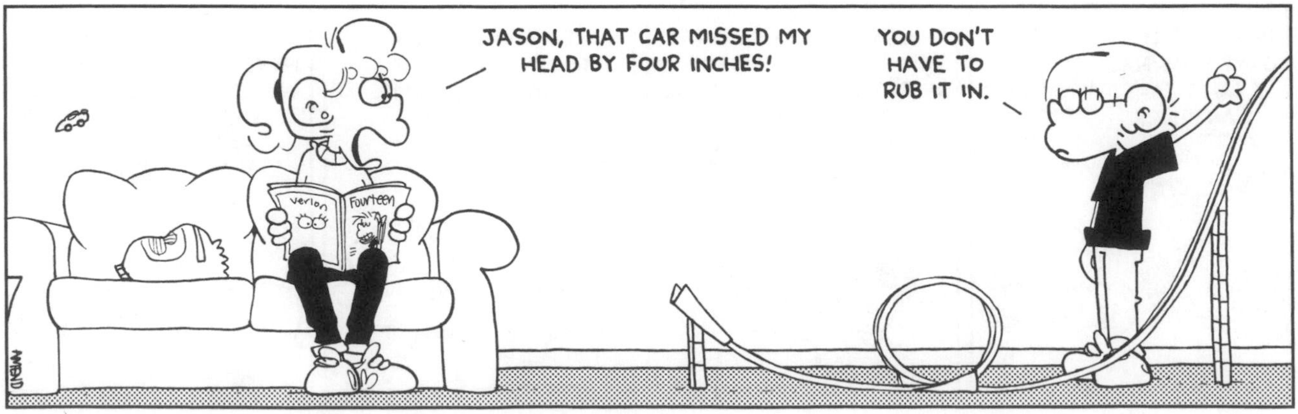
JASON, THAT CAR MISSED MY HEAD BY FOUR INCHES!
YOU DON'T HAVE TO RUB IT IN.
AMEND

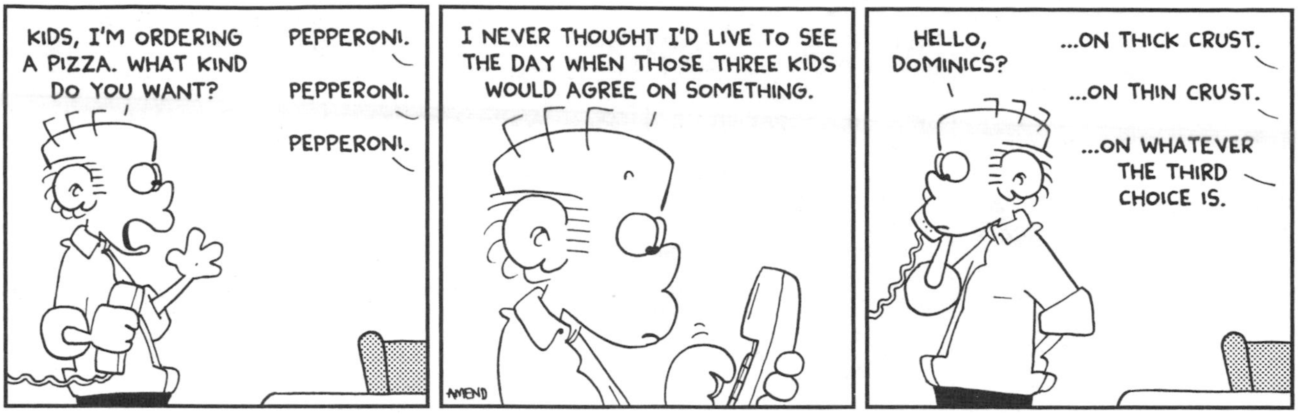
KIDS, I'M ORDERING A PIZZA. WHAT KIND DO YOU WANT?
PEPPERONI.
PEPPERONI.
PEPPERONI.
I NEVER THOUGHT I'D LIVE TO SEE THE DAY WHEN THOSE THREE KIDS WOULD AGREE ON SOMETHING.
HELLO, DOMINICS?
...ON THICK CRUST.
...ON THIN CRUST.
...ON WHATEVER THE THIRD CHOICE IS.
AMEND

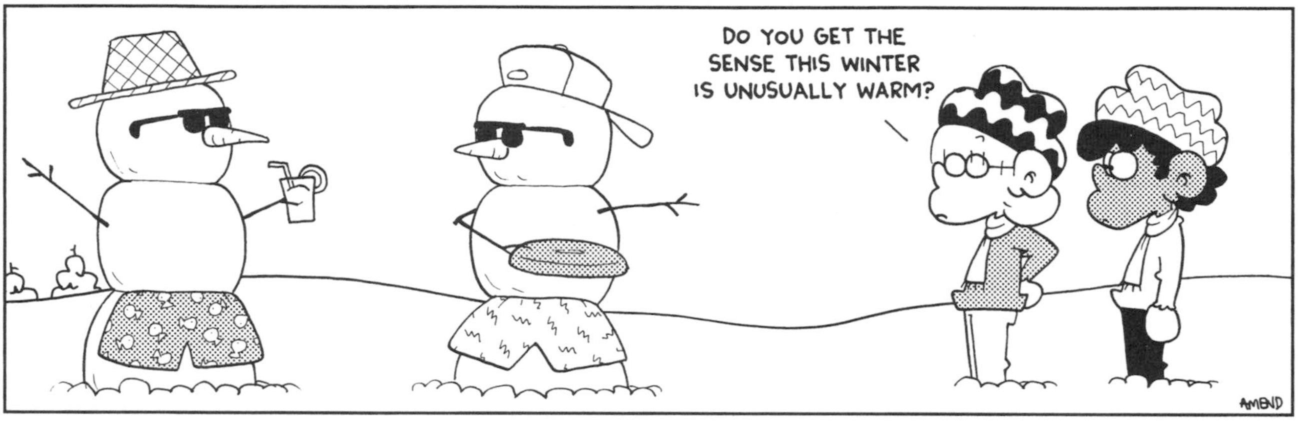
DO YOU GET THE SENSE THIS WINTER IS UNUSUALLY WARM?
AMEND

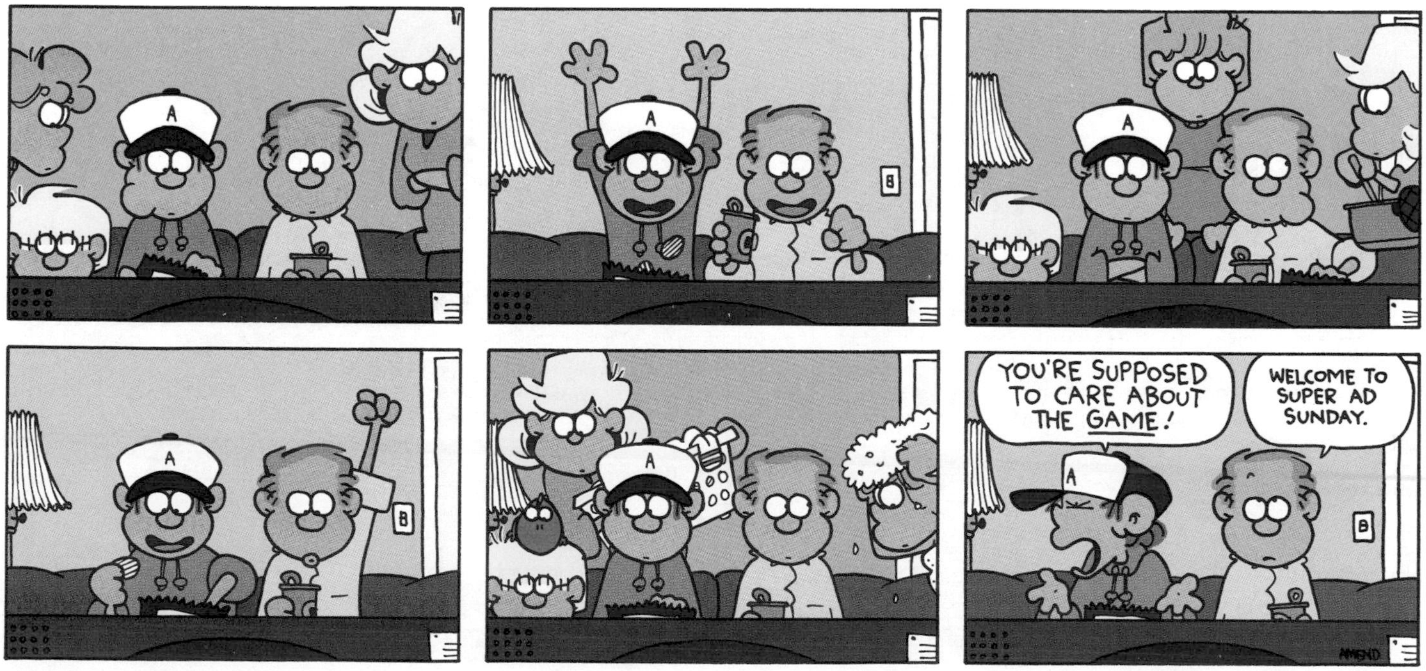
YOU'RE SUPPOSED TO CARE ABOUT THE GAME!
WELCOME TO SUPER AD SUNDAY.
AMEND

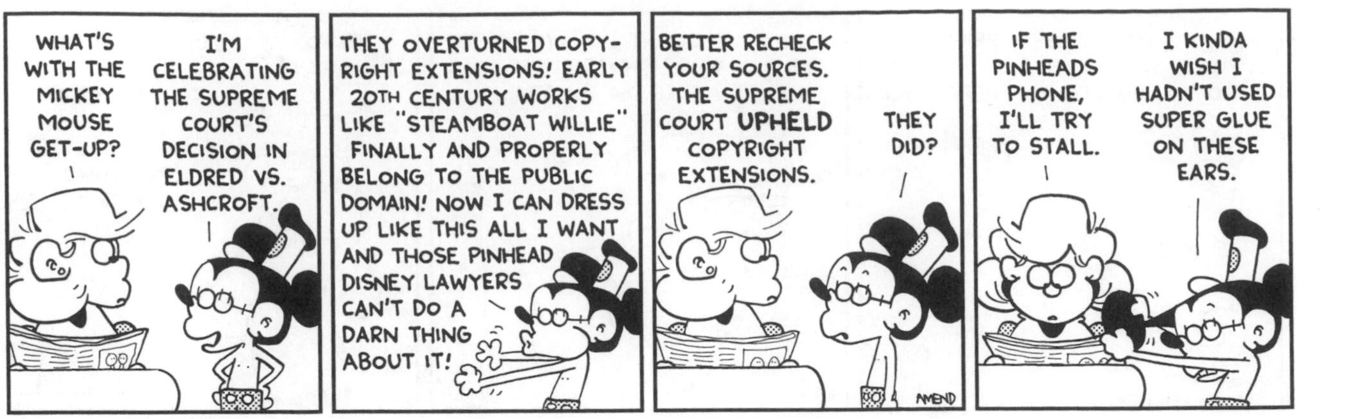
WHAT'S WITH THE MICKEY MOUSE GET-UP?
I'M CELEBRATING THE SUPREME COURT'S DECISION IN ELDRED VS. ASHCROFT.
THEY OVERTURNED COPYRIGHT EXTENSIONS! EARLY 20TH CENTURY WORKS LIKE "STEAMBOAT WILLIE" FINALLY AND PROPERLY BELONG TO THE PUBLIC DOMAIN! NOW I CAN DRESS UP LIKE THIS ALL I WANT AND THOSE PINHEAD DISNEY LAWYERS CAN'T DO A DARN THING ABOUT IT!
BETTER RECHECK YOUR SOURCES. THE SUPREME COURT **UPHELD** COPYRIGHT EXTENSIONS.
THEY DID?
IF THE PINHEADS PHONE, I'LL TRY TO STALL.
I KINDA WISH I HADN'T USED SUPER GLUE ON THESE EARS.
AMEND

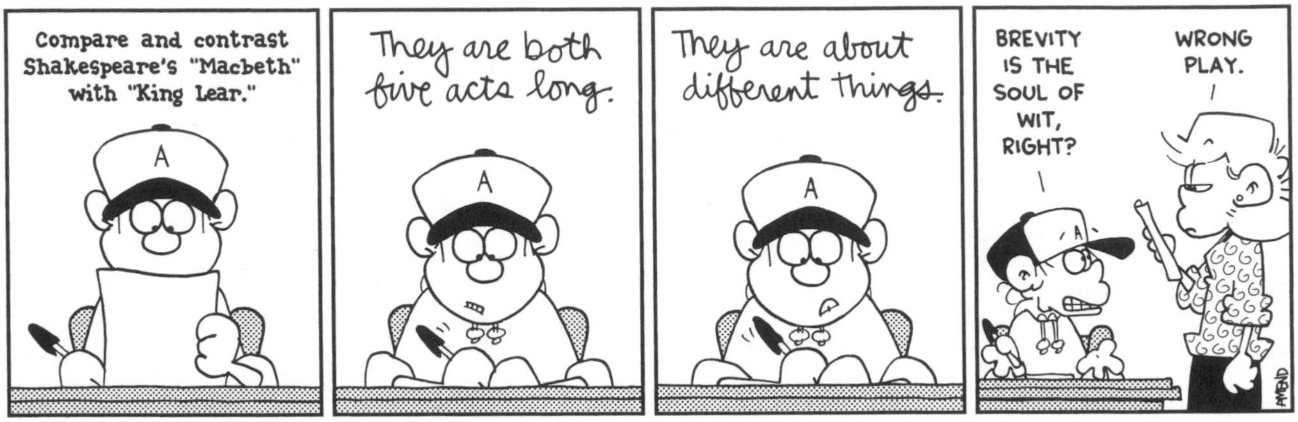
Compare and contrast Shakespeare's "Macbeth" with "King Lear."
They are both five acts long.
They are about different things.
BREVITY IS THE SOUL OF WIT, RIGHT?
WRONG PLAY.
AMEND

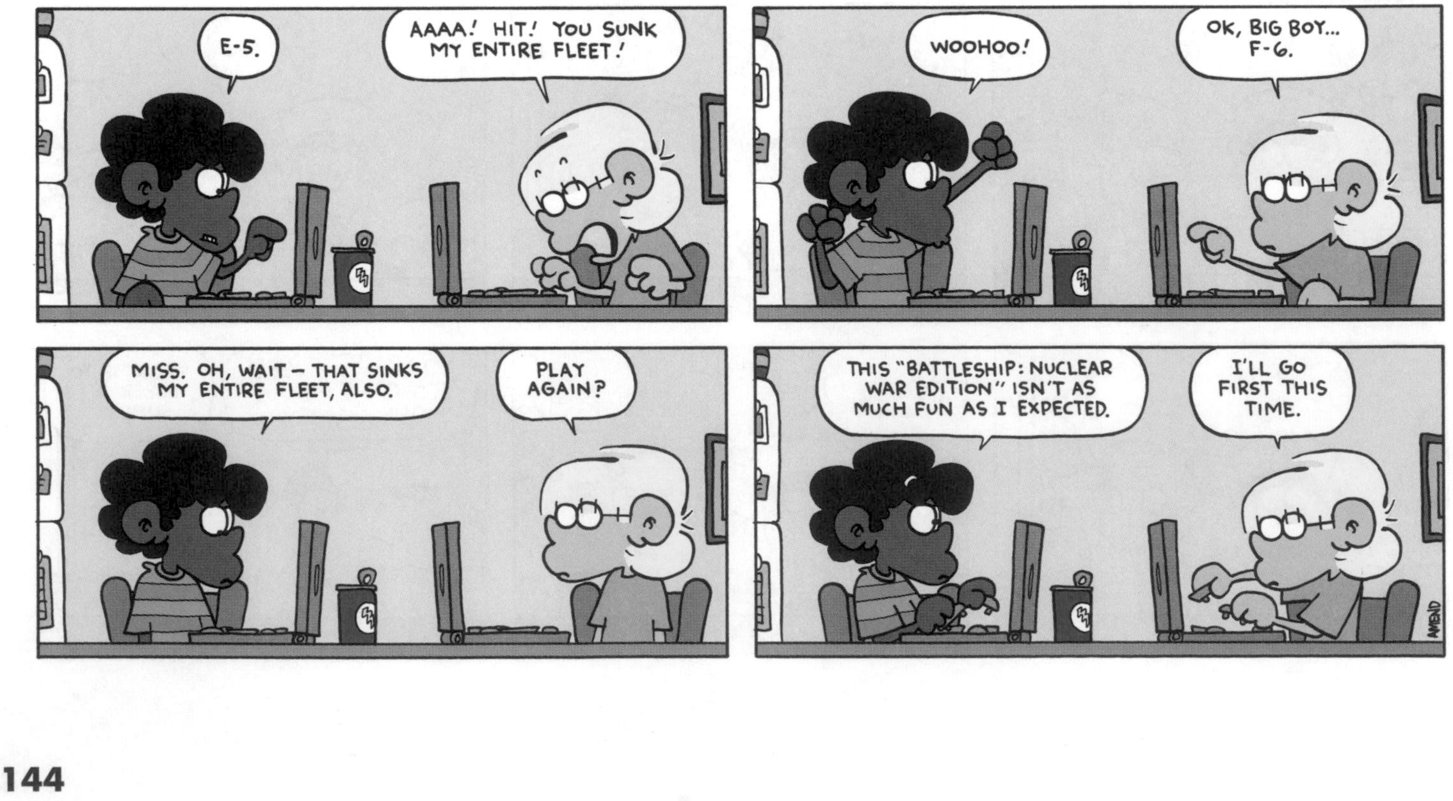
E-5.
AAAA! HIT! YOU SUNK MY ENTIRE FLEET!
WOOHOO!
OK, BIG BOY... F-6.
MISS. OH, WAIT – THAT SINKS MY ENTIRE FLEET, ALSO.
PLAY AGAIN?
THIS "BATTLESHIP: NUCLEAR WAR EDITION" ISN'T AS MUCH FUN AS I EXPECTED.
I'LL GO FIRST THIS TIME.
AMEND

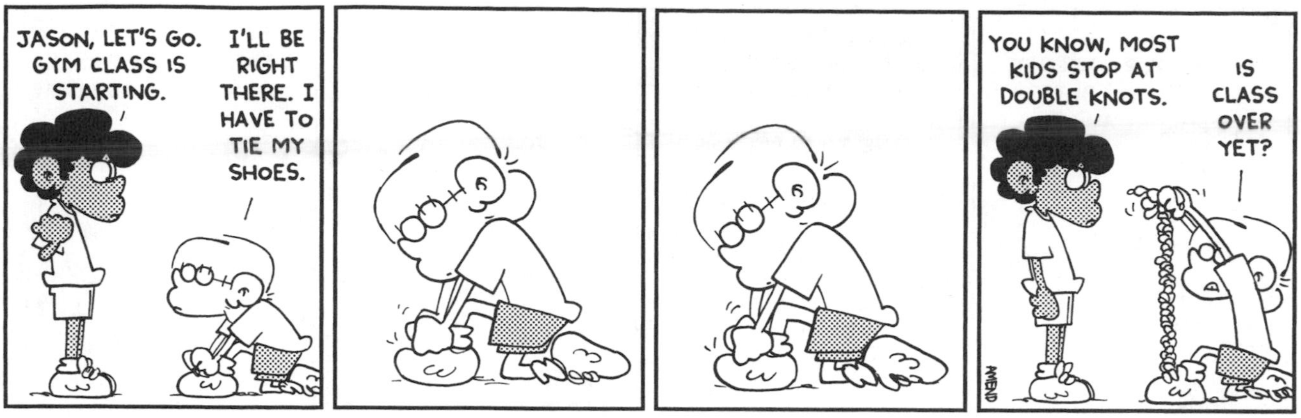
JASON, LET'S GO. GYM CLASS IS STARTING.
I'LL BE RIGHT THERE. I HAVE TO TIE MY SHOES.
YOU KNOW, MOST KIDS STOP AT DOUBLE KNOTS.
IS CLASS OVER YET?
AMEND

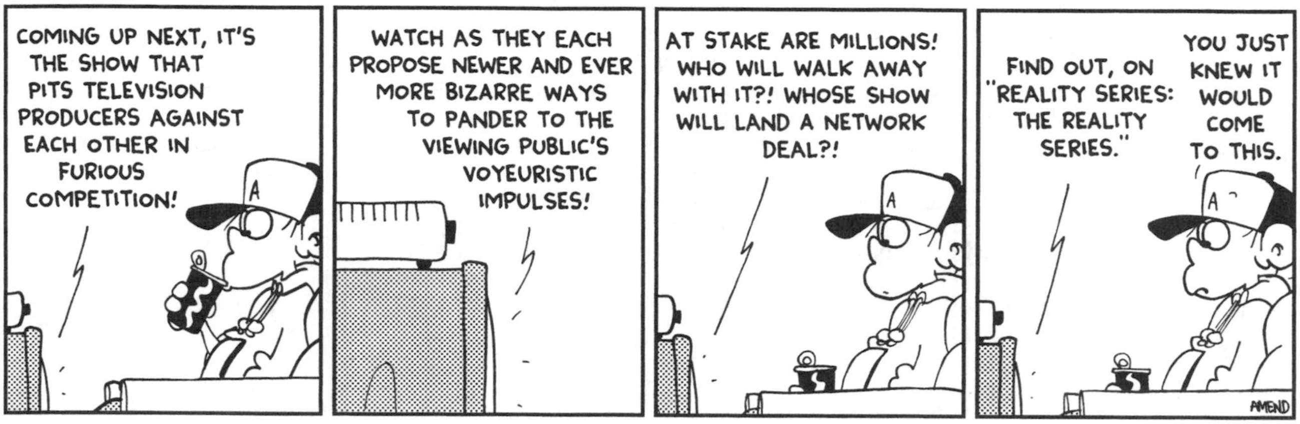
COMING UP NEXT, IT'S THE SHOW THAT PITS TELEVISION PRODUCERS AGAINST EACH OTHER IN FURIOUS COMPETITION!
WATCH AS THEY EACH PROPOSE NEWER AND EVER MORE BIZARRE WAYS TO PANDER TO THE VIEWING PUBLIC'S VOYEURISTIC IMPULSES!
AT STAKE ARE MILLIONS! WHO WILL WALK AWAY WITH IT?! WHOSE SHOW WILL LAND A NETWORK DEAL?!
FIND OUT, ON "REALITY SERIES: THE REALITY SERIES."
YOU JUST KNEW IT WOULD COME TO THIS.
AMEND

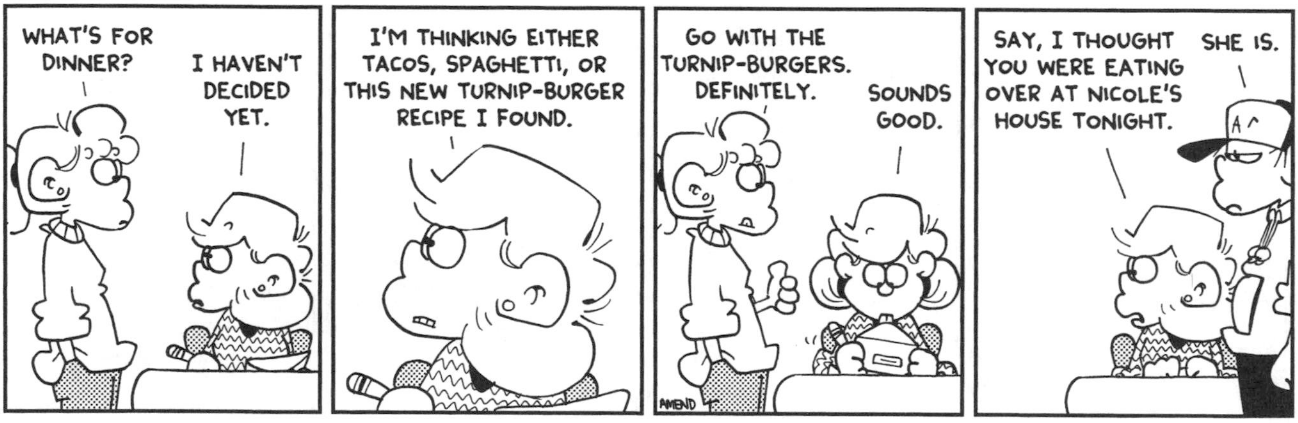
WHAT'S FOR DINNER?
I HAVEN'T DECIDED YET.
I'M THINKING EITHER TACOS, SPAGHETTI, OR THIS NEW TURNIP-BURGER RECIPE I FOUND.
GO WITH THE TURNIP-BURGERS. DEFINITELY.
SOUNDS GOOD.
AMEND
SAY, I THOUGHT YOU WERE EATING OVER AT NICOLE'S HOUSE TONIGHT.
SHE IS.

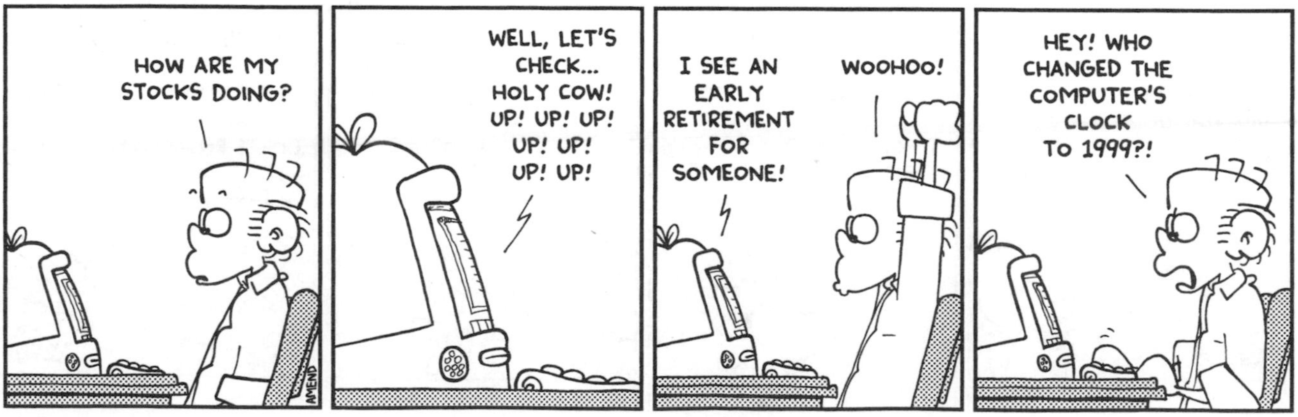
HOW ARE MY STOCKS DOING?
AMEND
WELL, LET'S CHECK... HOLY COW! UP! UP! UP! UP! UP! UP! UP!
I SEE AN EARLY RETIREMENT FOR SOMEONE!
WOOHOO!
HEY! WHO CHANGED THE COMPUTER'S CLOCK TO 1999?!

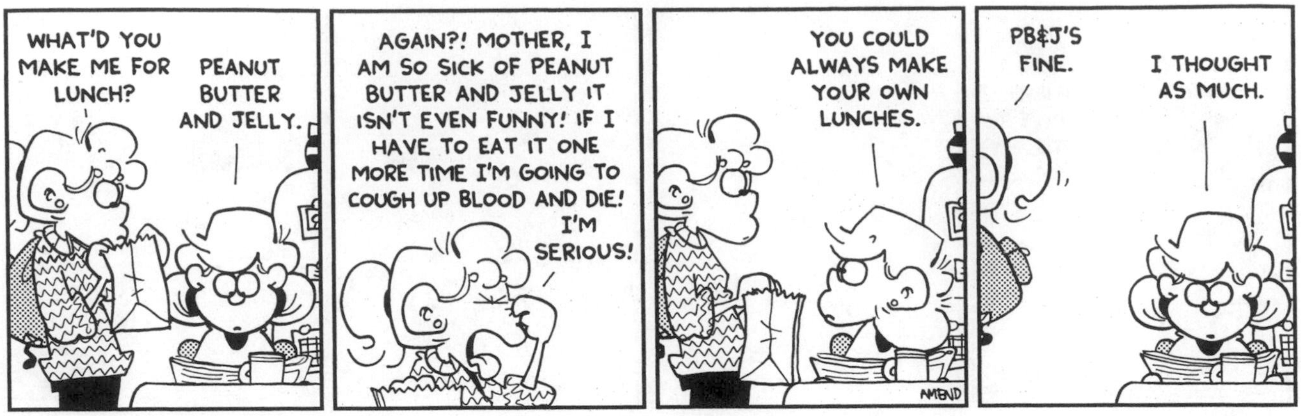
WHAT'D YOU MAKE ME FOR LUNCH?
PEANUT BUTTER AND JELLY.
AGAIN?! MOTHER, I AM SO SICK OF PEANUT BUTTER AND JELLY IT ISN'T EVEN FUNNY! IF I HAVE TO EAT IT ONE MORE TIME I'M GOING TO COUGH UP BLOOD AND DIE!
I'M SERIOUS!
YOU COULD ALWAYS MAKE YOUR OWN LUNCHES.
PB&J'S FINE.
I THOUGHT AS MUCH.
AMEND

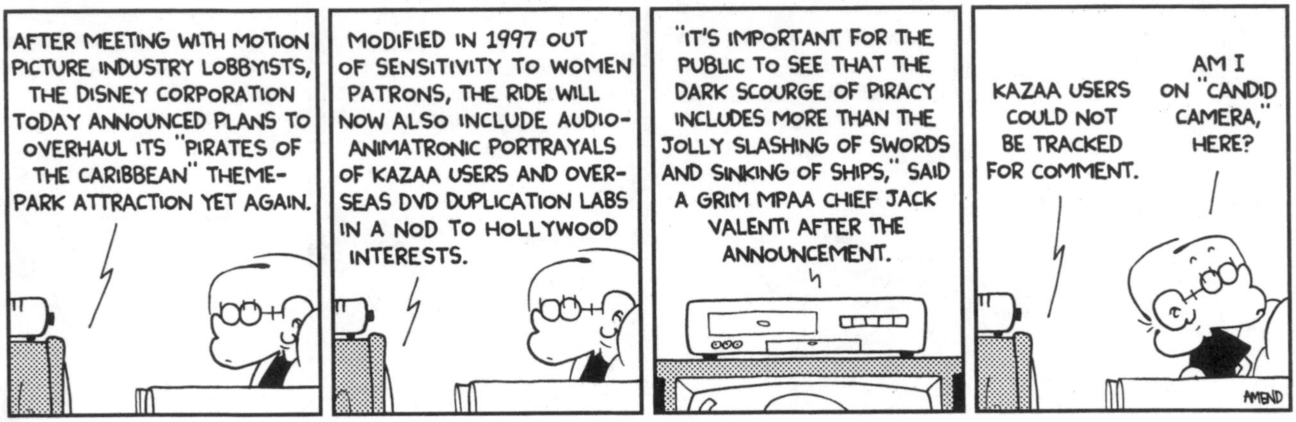
AFTER MEETING WITH MOTION PICTURE INDUSTRY LOBBYISTS, THE DISNEY CORPORATION TODAY ANNOUNCED PLANS TO OVERHAUL ITS "PIRATES OF THE CARIBBEAN" THEME-PARK ATTRACTION YET AGAIN.
MODIFIED IN 1997 OUT OF SENSITIVITY TO WOMEN PATRONS, THE RIDE WILL NOW ALSO INCLUDE AUDIO-ANIMATRONIC PORTRAYALS OF KAZAA USERS AND OVERSEAS DVD DUPLICATION LABS IN A NOD TO HOLLYWOOD INTERESTS.
"IT'S IMPORTANT FOR THE PUBLIC TO SEE THAT THE DARK SCOURGE OF PIRACY INCLUDES MORE THAN THE JOLLY SLASHING OF SWORDS AND SINKING OF SHIPS," SAID A GRIM MPAA CHIEF JACK VALENTI AFTER THE ANNOUNCEMENT.
KAZAA USERS COULD NOT BE TRACKED FOR COMMENT.
AM I ON "CANDID CAMERA," HERE?
AMEND

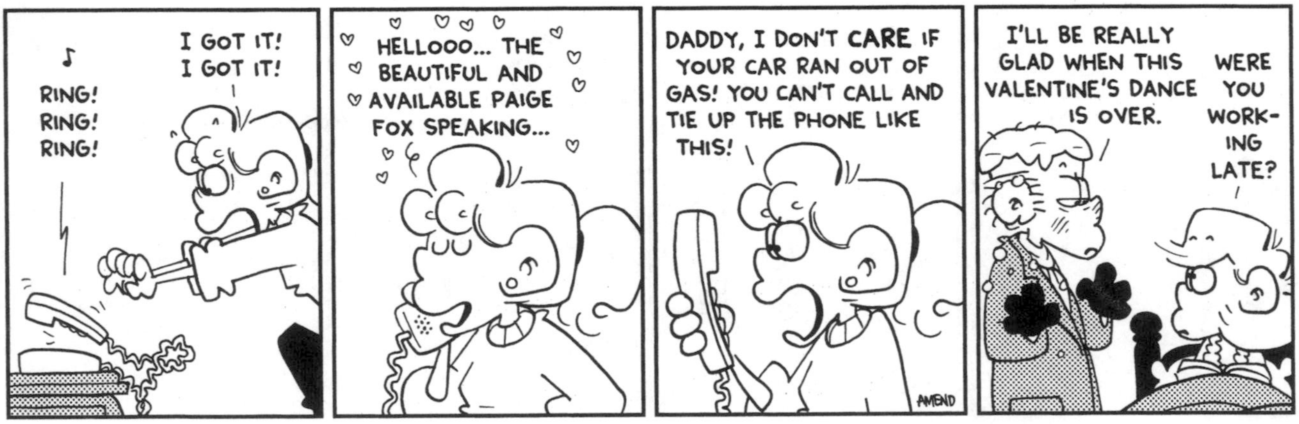
RING! RING! RING!
I GOT IT! I GOT IT!
HELLOOO... THE BEAUTIFUL AND AVAILABLE PAIGE FOX SPEAKING...
DADDY, I DON'T **CARE** IF YOUR CAR RAN OUT OF GAS! YOU CAN'T CALL AND TIE UP THE PHONE LIKE THIS!
AMEND
I'LL BE REALLY GLAD WHEN THIS VALENTINE'S DANCE IS OVER.
WERE YOU WORKING LATE?

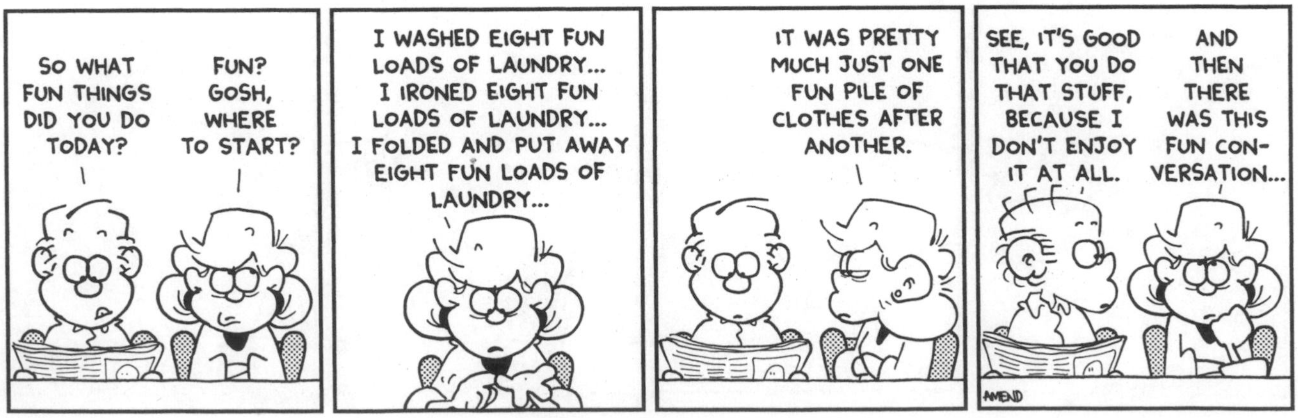
SO WHAT FUN THINGS DID YOU DO TODAY?
FUN? GOSH, WHERE TO START?
I WASHED EIGHT FUN LOADS OF LAUNDRY... I IRONED EIGHT FUN LOADS OF LAUNDRY... I FOLDED AND PUT AWAY EIGHT FUN LOADS OF LAUNDRY...
IT WAS PRETTY MUCH JUST ONE FUN PILE OF CLOTHES AFTER ANOTHER.
SEE, IT'S GOOD THAT YOU DO THAT STUFF, BECAUSE I DON'T ENJOY IT AT ALL.
AND THEN THERE WAS THIS FUN CONVERSATION...
AMEND

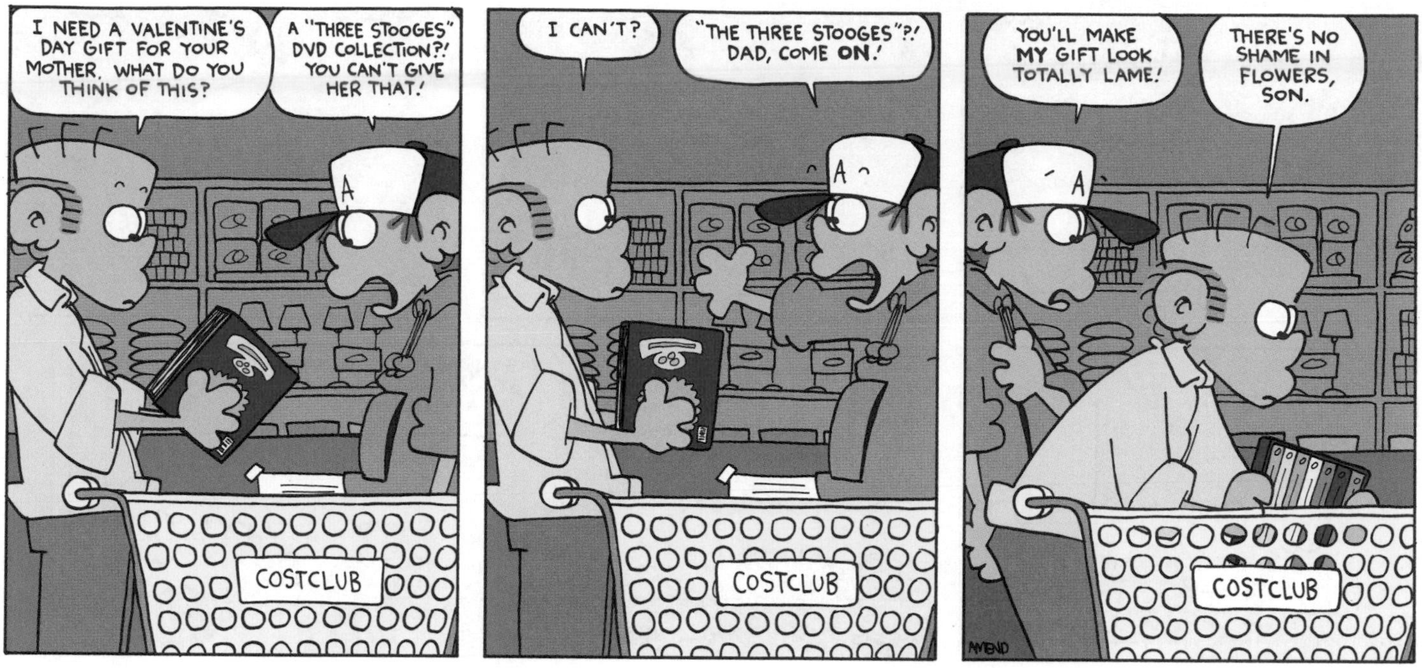
I NEED A VALENTINE'S DAY GIFT FOR YOUR MOTHER. WHAT DO YOU THINK OF THIS?
A "THREE STOOGES" DVD COLLECTION?! YOU CAN'T GIVE HER THAT!
COSTCLUB
I CAN'T?
"THE THREE STOOGES"?! DAD, COME **ON**!
COSTCLUB
YOU'LL MAKE **MY** GIFT LOOK TOTALLY LAME!
THERE'S NO SHAME IN FLOWERS, SON.
COSTCLUB
AMEND

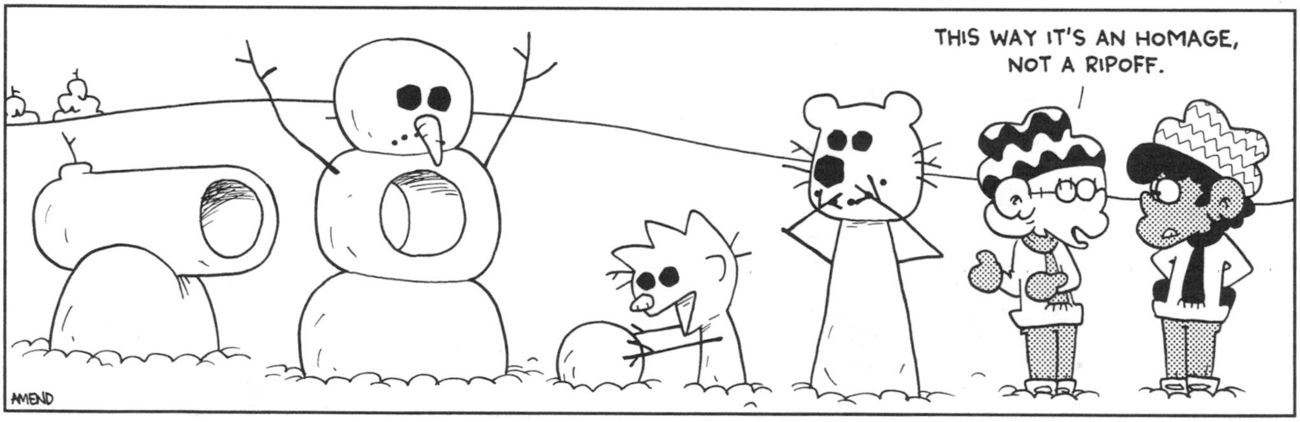
THIS WAY IT'S AN HOMAGE, NOT A RIPOFF.
AMEND

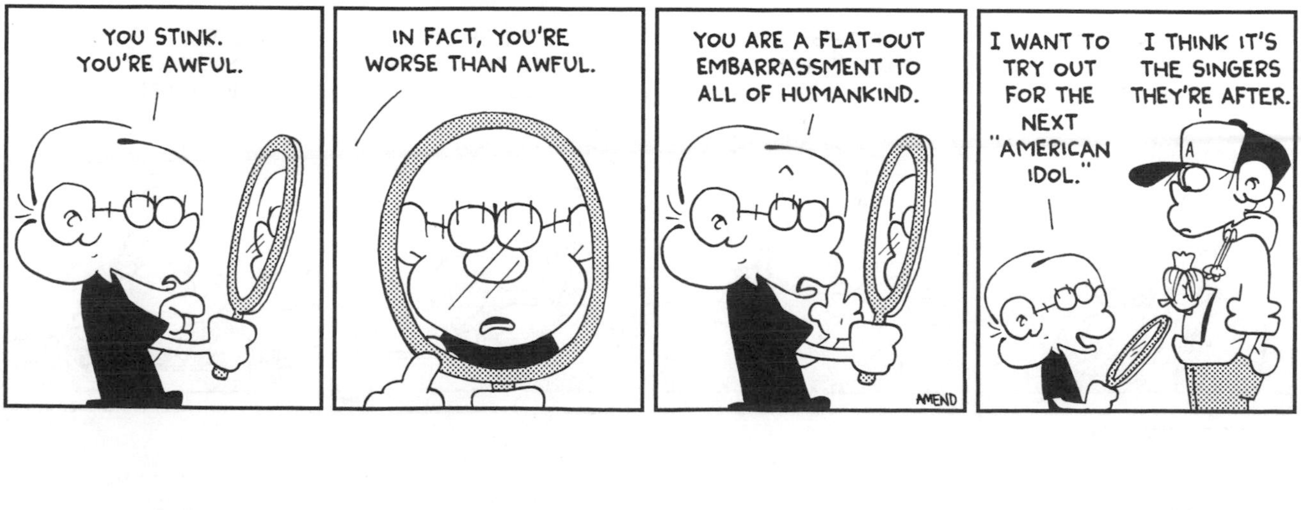
YOU STINK. YOU'RE AWFUL.
IN FACT, YOU'RE WORSE THAN AWFUL.
YOU ARE A FLAT-OUT EMBARRASSMENT TO ALL OF HUMANKIND.
AMEND
I WANT TO TRY OUT FOR THE NEXT "AMERICAN IDOL."
I THINK IT'S THE SINGERS THEY'RE AFTER.

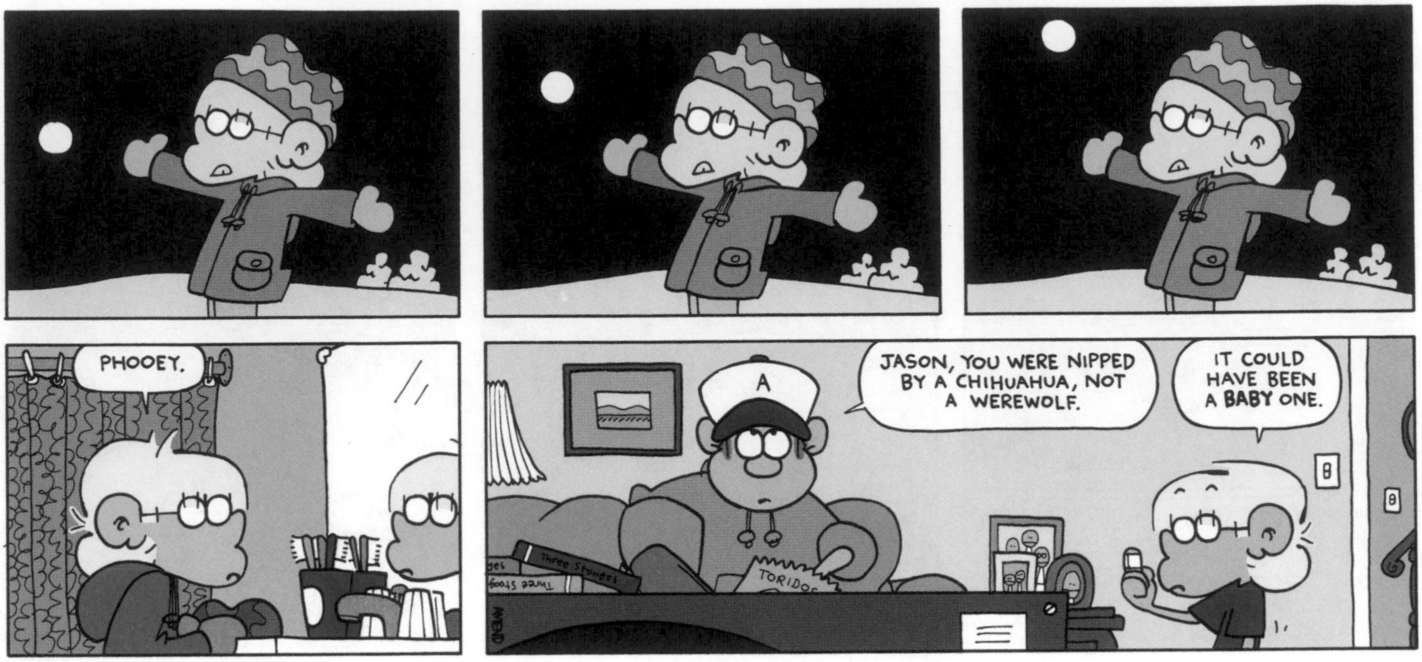
PHOOEY.
JASON, YOU WERE NIPPED BY A CHIHUAHUA, NOT A WEREWOLF.
IT COULD HAVE BEEN A BABY ONE.

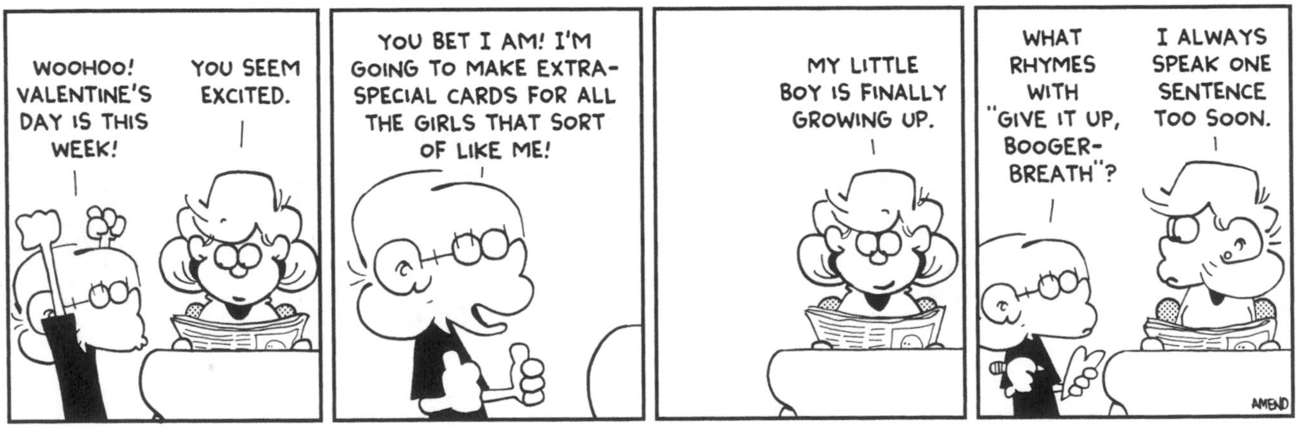
WOOHOO! VALENTINE'S DAY IS THIS WEEK!
YOU SEEM EXCITED.
YOU BET I AM! I'M GOING TO MAKE EXTRA-SPECIAL CARDS FOR ALL THE GIRLS THAT SORT OF LIKE ME!
MY LITTLE BOY IS FINALLY GROWING UP.
WHAT RHYMES WITH "GIVE IT UP, BOOGER-BREATH"?
I ALWAYS SPEAK ONE SENTENCE TOO SOON.
AMEND

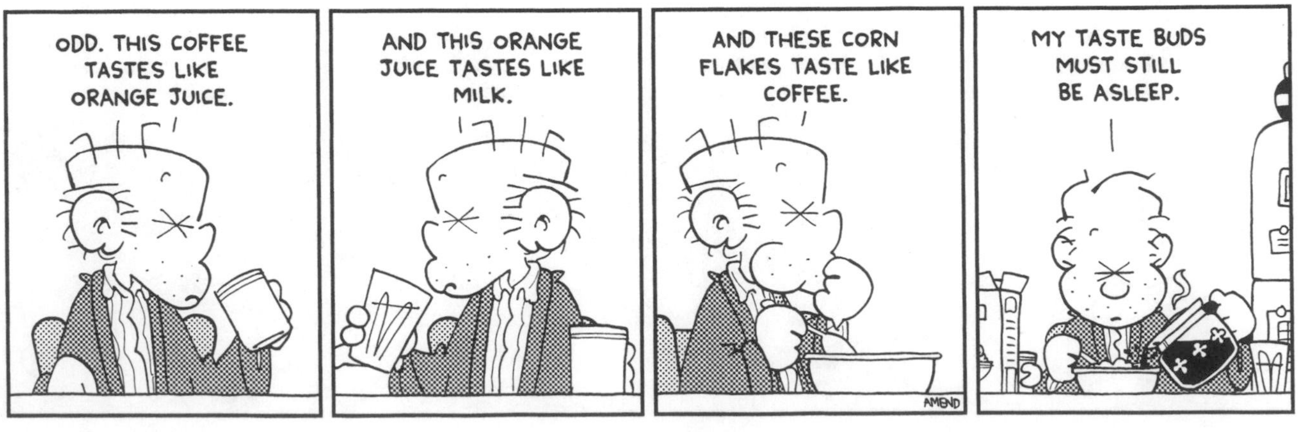
ODD. THIS COFFEE TASTES LIKE ORANGE JUICE.
AND THIS ORANGE JUICE TASTES LIKE MILK.
AND THESE CORN FLAKES TASTE LIKE COFFEE.
MY TASTE BUDS MUST STILL BE ASLEEP.
AMEND

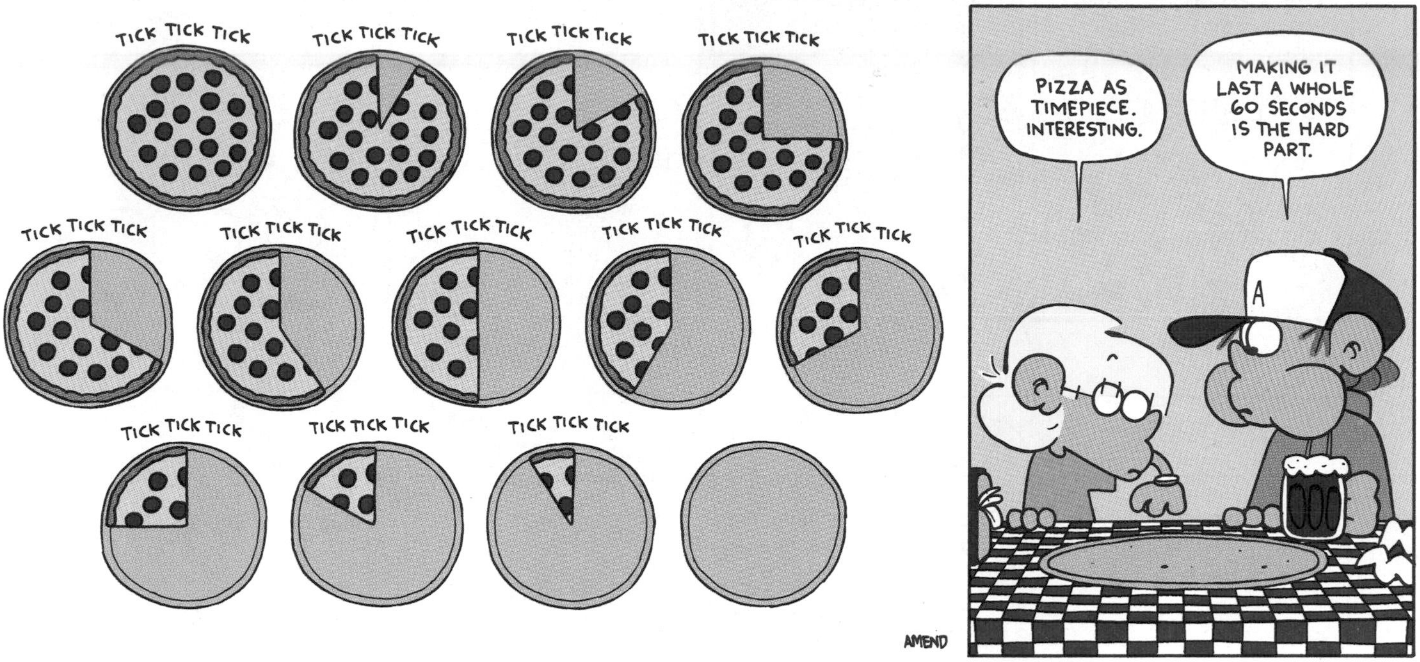
TICK TICK TICK
TICK TICK TICK
TICK TICK TICK
TICK TICK TICK
TICK TICK TICK
TICK TICK TICK
TICK TICK TICK
TICK TICK TICK
TICK TICK TICK
TICK TICK TICK
TICK TICK TICK
TICK TICK TICK
PIZZA AS TIMEPIECE. INTERESTING.
MAKING IT LAST A WHOLE 60 SECONDS IS THE HARD PART.
AMEND

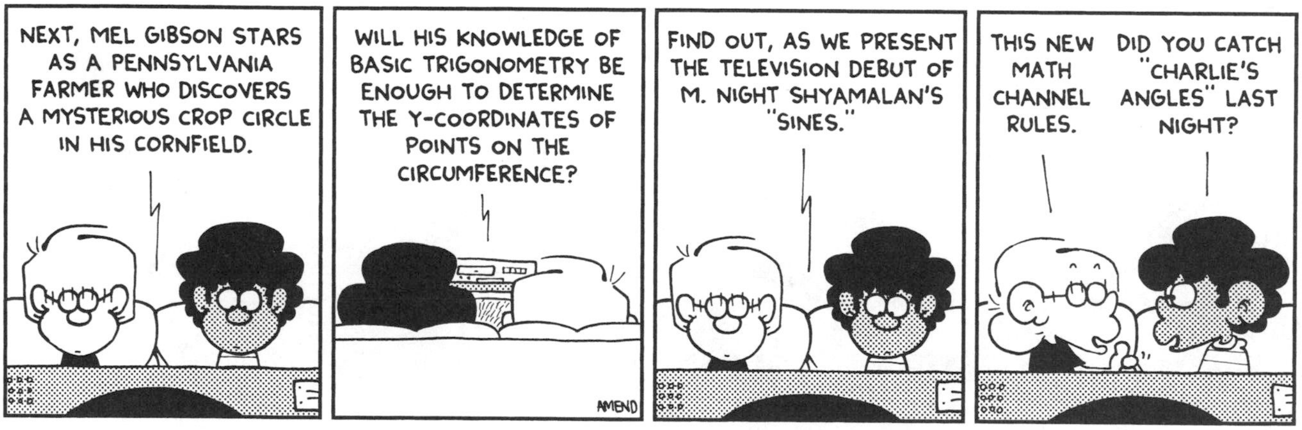
NEXT, MEL GIBSON STARS AS A PENNSYLVANIA FARMER WHO DISCOVERS A MYSTERIOUS CROP CIRCLE IN HIS CORNFIELD.
WILL HIS KNOWLEDGE OF BASIC TRIGONOMETRY BE ENOUGH TO DETERMINE THE Y-COORDINATES OF POINTS ON THE CIRCUMFERENCE?
AMEND
FIND OUT, AS WE PRESENT THE TELEVISION DEBUT OF M. NIGHT SHYAMALAN'S "SINES."
THIS NEW MATH CHANNEL RULES.
DID YOU CATCH "CHARLIE'S ANGLES" LAST NIGHT?

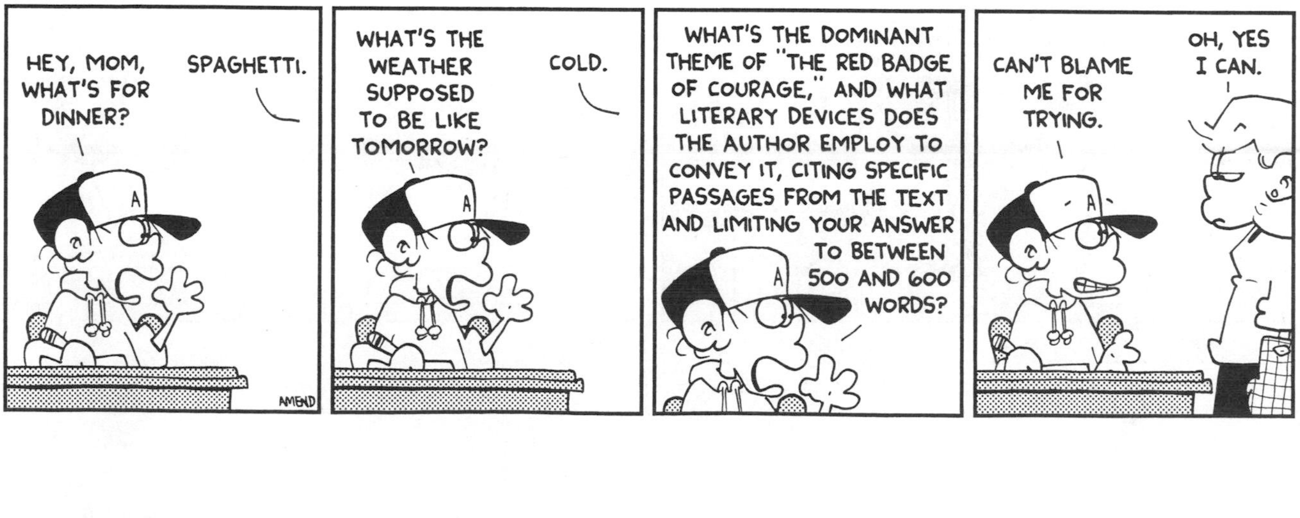
HEY, MOM, WHAT'S FOR DINNER?
SPAGHETTI.
AMEND
WHAT'S THE WEATHER SUPPOSED TO BE LIKE TOMORROW?
COLD.
WHAT'S THE DOMINANT THEME OF "THE RED BADGE OF COURAGE," AND WHAT LITERARY DEVICES DOES THE AUTHOR EMPLOY TO CONVEY IT, CITING SPECIFIC PASSAGES FROM THE TEXT AND LIMITING YOUR ANSWER TO BETWEEN 500 AND 600 WORDS?
CAN'T BLAME ME FOR TRYING.
OH, YES I CAN.

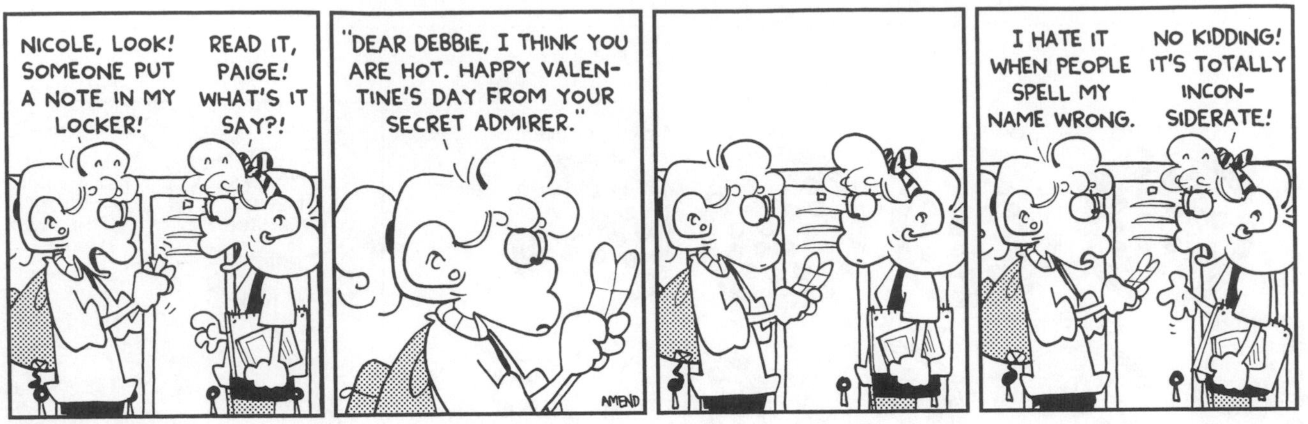
NICOLE, LOOK! SOMEONE PUT A NOTE IN MY LOCKER!
READ IT, PAIGE! WHAT'S IT SAY?!
"DEAR DEBBIE, I THINK YOU ARE HOT. HAPPY VALENTINE'S DAY FROM YOUR SECRET ADMIRER."
AMEND
I HATE IT WHEN PEOPLE SPELL MY NAME WRONG.
NO KIDDING! IT'S TOTALLY INCONSIDERATE!

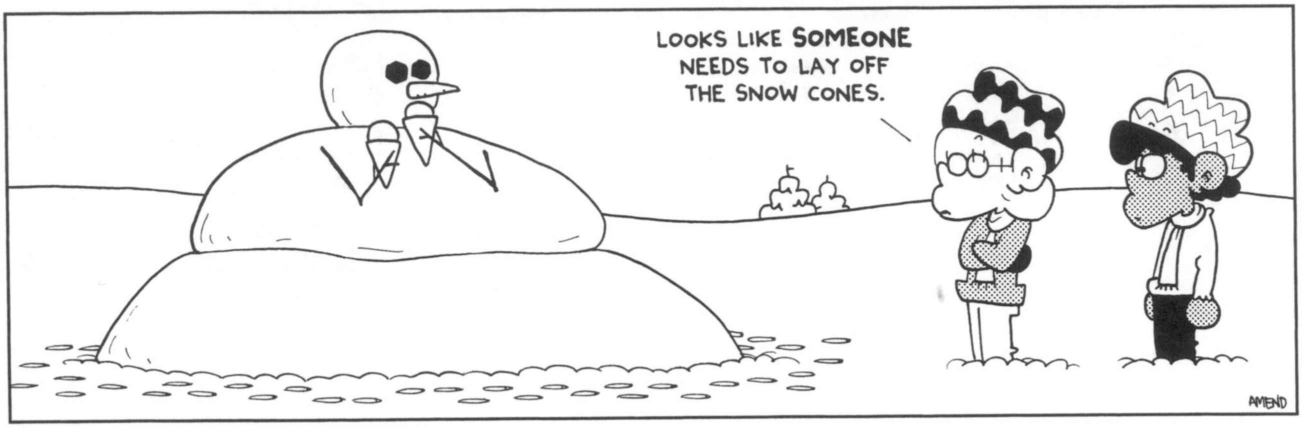
LOOKS LIKE SOMEONE NEEDS TO LAY OFF THE SNOW CONES.
AMEND

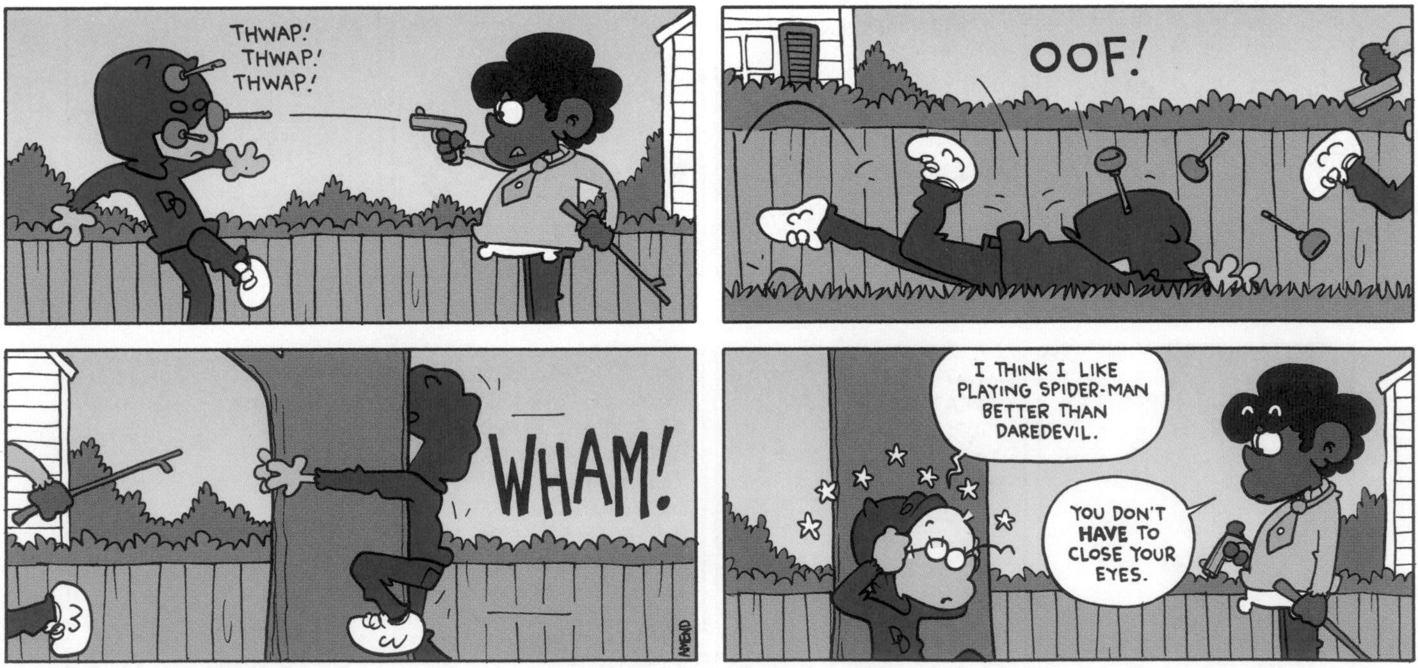
THWAP! THWAP! THWAP!
OOF!
WHAM!
AMEND
I THINK I LIKE PLAYING SPIDER-MAN BETTER THAN DAREDEVIL.
YOU DON'T HAVE TO CLOSE YOUR EYES.

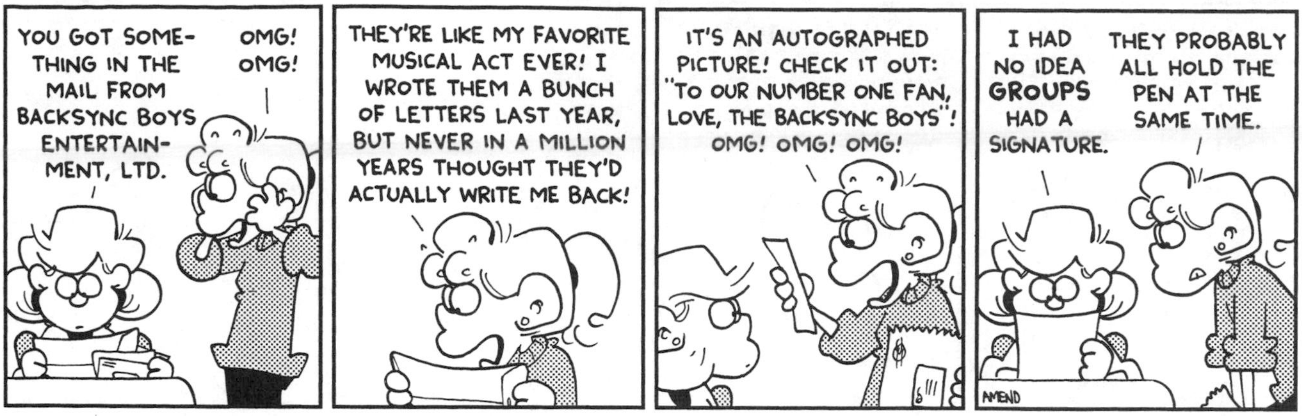
YOU GOT SOMETHING IN THE MAIL FROM BACKSYNC BOYS ENTERTAINMENT, LTD.
OMG! OMG!
THEY'RE LIKE MY FAVORITE MUSICAL ACT EVER! I WROTE THEM A BUNCH OF LETTERS LAST YEAR, BUT NEVER IN A MILLION YEARS THOUGHT THEY'D ACTUALLY WRITE ME BACK!
IT'S AN AUTOGRAPHED PICTURE! CHECK IT OUT: "TO OUR NUMBER ONE FAN, LOVE, THE BACKSYNC BOYS"! OMG! OMG! OMG!
I HAD NO IDEA **GROUPS** HAD A SIGNATURE.
THEY PROBABLY ALL HOLD THE PEN AT THE SAME TIME.
AMEND

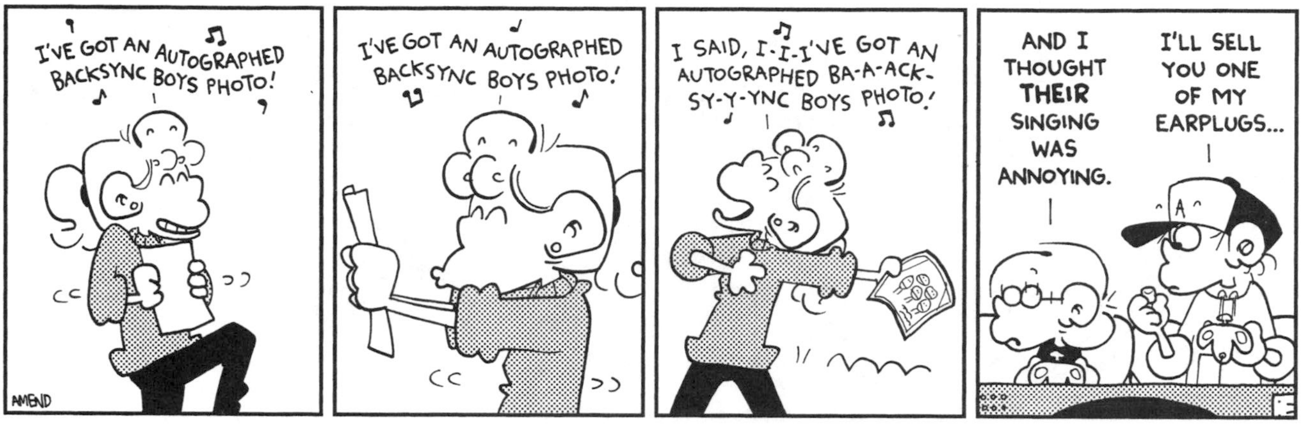
I'VE GOT AN AUTOGRAPHED BACKSYNC BOYS PHOTO!
AMEND
I'VE GOT AN AUTOGRAPHED BACKSYNC BOYS PHOTO!
I SAID, I-I-I'VE GOT AN AUTOGRAPHED BA-A-ACK-SY-Y-YNC BOYS PHOTO!
AND I THOUGHT **THEIR** SINGING WAS ANNOYING.
I'LL SELL YOU ONE OF MY EARPLUGS...

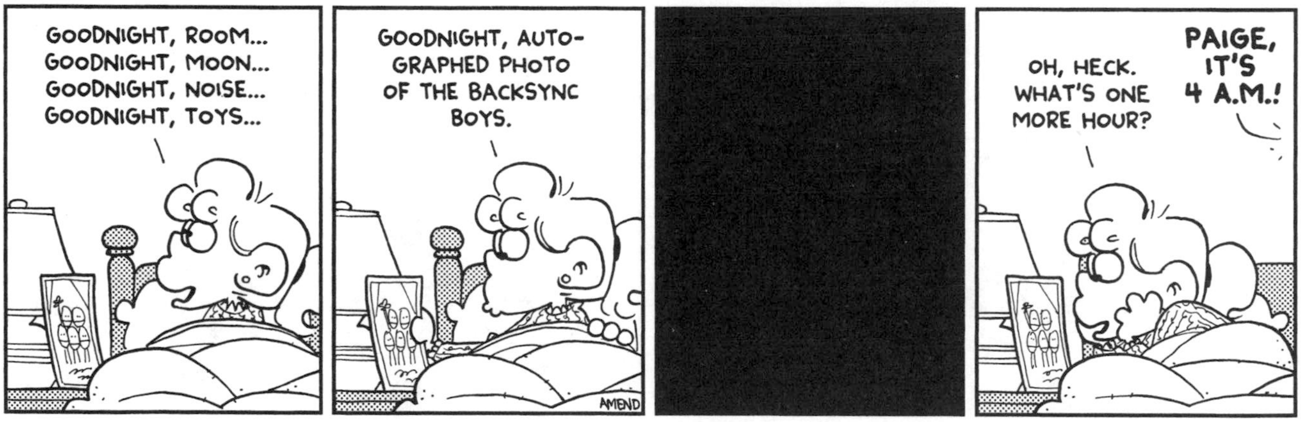
GOODNIGHT, ROOM... GOODNIGHT, MOON... GOODNIGHT, NOISE... GOODNIGHT, TOYS...
GOODNIGHT, AUTOGRAPHED PHOTO OF THE BACKSYNC BOYS.
AMEND
OH, HECK. WHAT'S ONE MORE HOUR?
PAIGE, IT'S 4 A.M.!

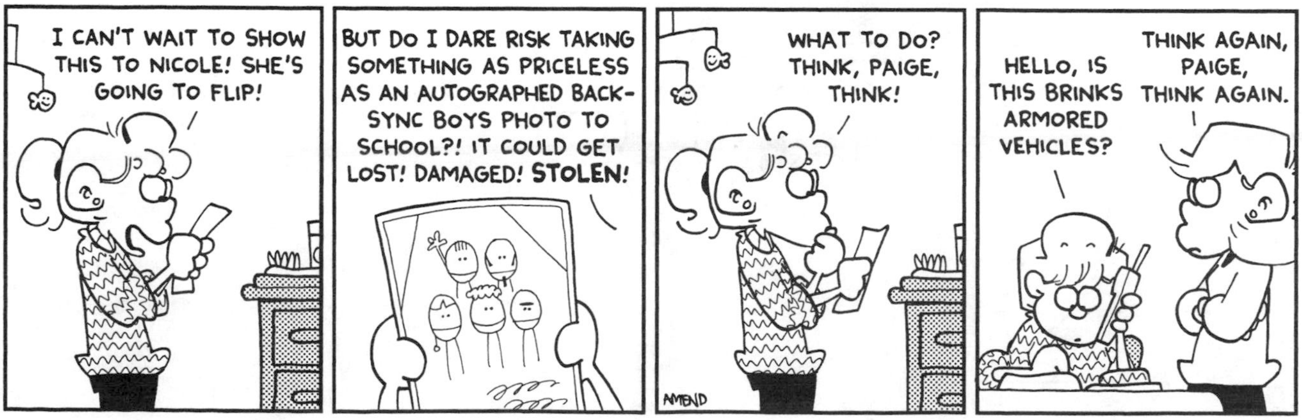
I CAN'T WAIT TO SHOW THIS TO NICOLE! SHE'S GOING TO FLIP!
BUT DO I DARE RISK TAKING SOMETHING AS PRICELESS AS AN AUTOGRAPHED BACKSYNC BOYS PHOTO TO SCHOOL?! IT COULD GET LOST! DAMAGED! **STOLEN**!
WHAT TO DO? THINK, PAIGE, THINK!
AMEND
HELLO, IS THIS BRINKS ARMORED VEHICLES?
THINK AGAIN, PAIGE, THINK AGAIN.

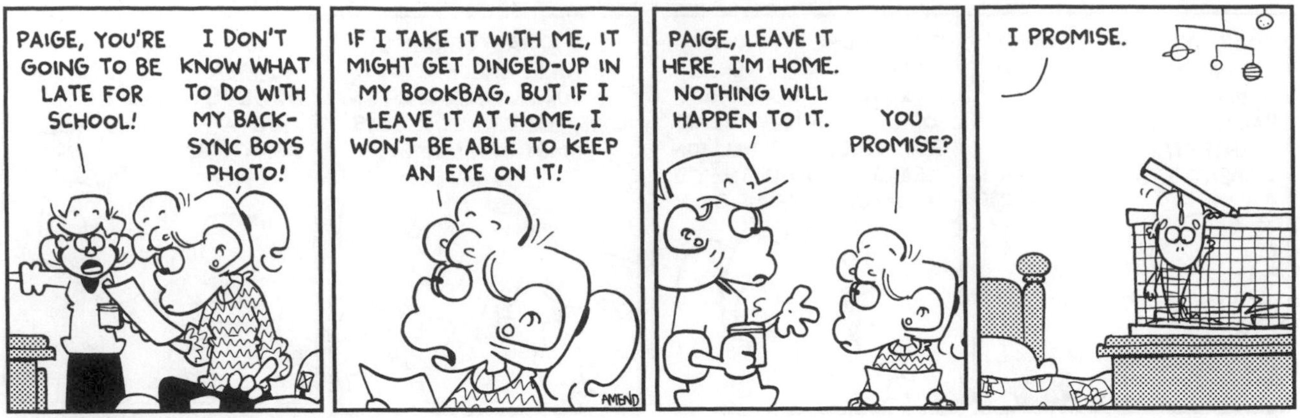
PAIGE, YOU'RE GOING TO BE LATE FOR SCHOOL!
I DON'T KNOW WHAT TO DO WITH MY BACK-SYNC BOYS PHOTO!
IF I TAKE IT WITH ME, IT MIGHT GET DINGED-UP IN MY BOOKBAG, BUT IF I LEAVE IT AT HOME, I WON'T BE ABLE TO KEEP AN EYE ON IT!
PAIGE, LEAVE IT HERE. I'M HOME. NOTHING WILL HAPPEN TO IT.
YOU PROMISE?
I PROMISE.
AMEND

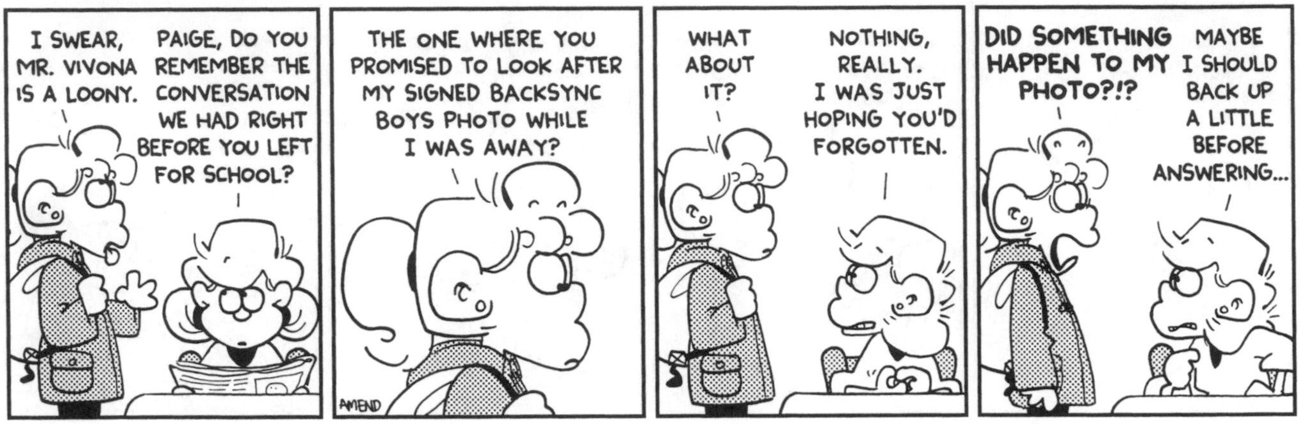
I SWEAR, MR. VIVONA IS A LOONY.
PAIGE, DO YOU REMEMBER THE CONVERSATION WE HAD RIGHT BEFORE YOU LEFT FOR SCHOOL?
THE ONE WHERE YOU PROMISED TO LOOK AFTER MY SIGNED BACKSYNC BOYS PHOTO WHILE I WAS AWAY?
WHAT ABOUT IT?
NOTHING, REALLY. I WAS JUST HOPING YOU'D FORGOTTEN.
DID SOMETHING HAPPEN TO MY PHOTO?!?
MAYBE I SHOULD BACK UP A LITTLE BEFORE ANSWERING...
AMEND

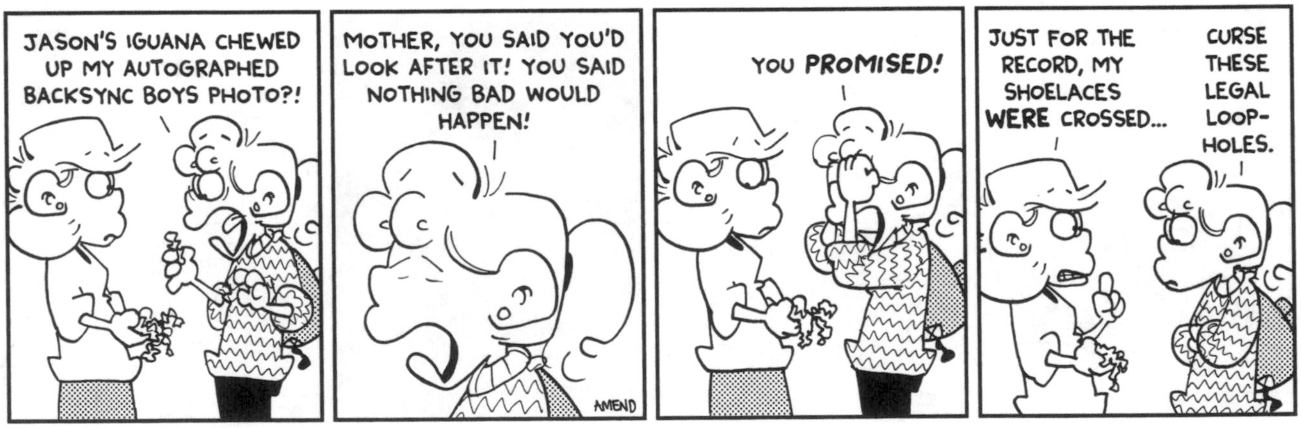
JASON'S IGUANA CHEWED UP MY AUTOGRAPHED BACKSYNC BOYS PHOTO?!
MOTHER, YOU SAID YOU'D LOOK AFTER IT! YOU SAID NOTHING BAD WOULD HAPPEN!
YOU PROMISED!
JUST FOR THE RECORD, MY SHOELACES WERE CROSSED...
CURSE THESE LEGAL LOOP-HOLES.
AMEND

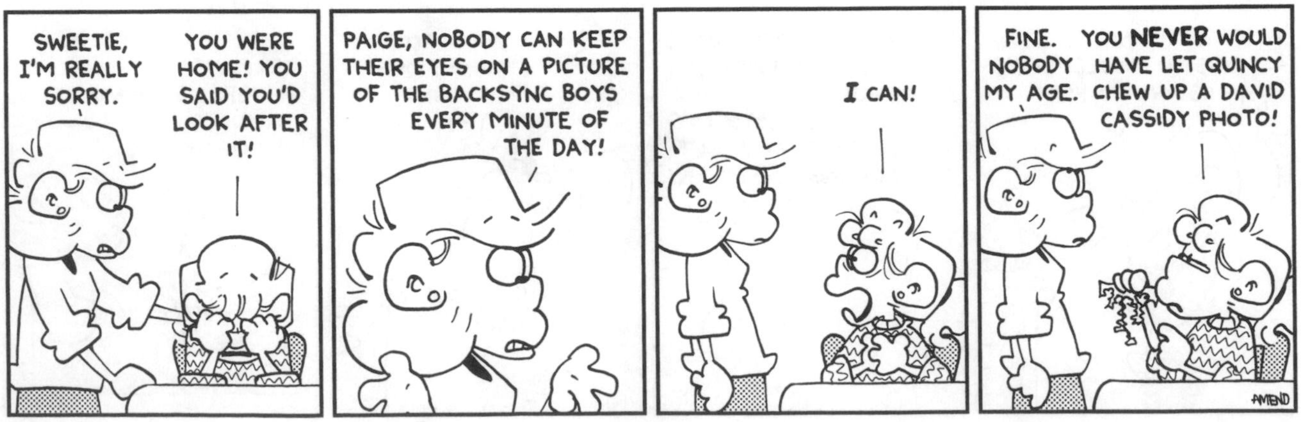
SWEETIE, I'M REALLY SORRY.
YOU WERE HOME! YOU SAID YOU'D LOOK AFTER IT!
PAIGE, NOBODY CAN KEEP THEIR EYES ON A PICTURE OF THE BACKSYNC BOYS EVERY MINUTE OF THE DAY!
I CAN!
FINE. NOBODY MY AGE.
YOU NEVER WOULD HAVE LET QUINCY CHEW UP A DAVID CASSIDY PHOTO!
AMEND

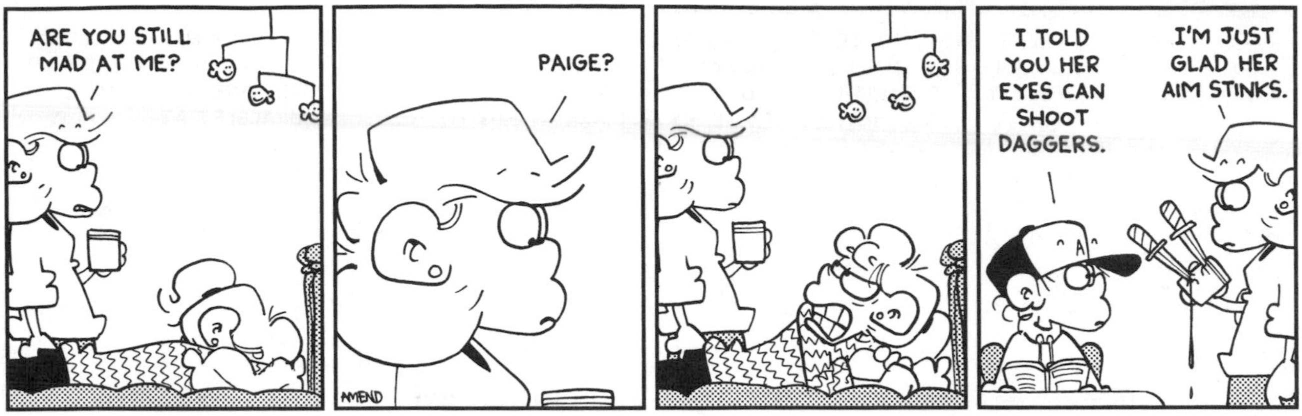
ARE YOU STILL MAD AT ME?
PAIGE?
AMEND
I TOLD YOU HER EYES CAN SHOOT DAGGERS.
I'M JUST GLAD HER AIM STINKS.

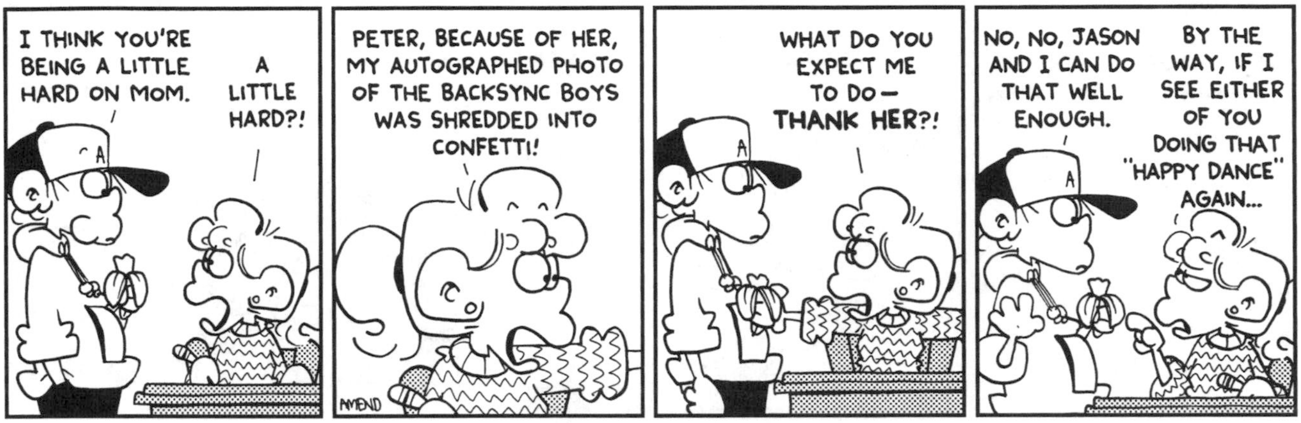
I THINK YOU'RE BEING A LITTLE HARD ON MOM.
A LITTLE HARD?!
PETER, BECAUSE OF HER, MY AUTOGRAPHED PHOTO OF THE BACKSYNC BOYS WAS SHREDDED INTO CONFETTI!
AMEND
WHAT DO YOU EXPECT ME TO DO— **THANK HER**?!
NO, NO, JASON AND I CAN DO THAT WELL ENOUGH.
BY THE WAY, IF I SEE EITHER OF YOU DOING THAT "HAPPY DANCE" AGAIN...

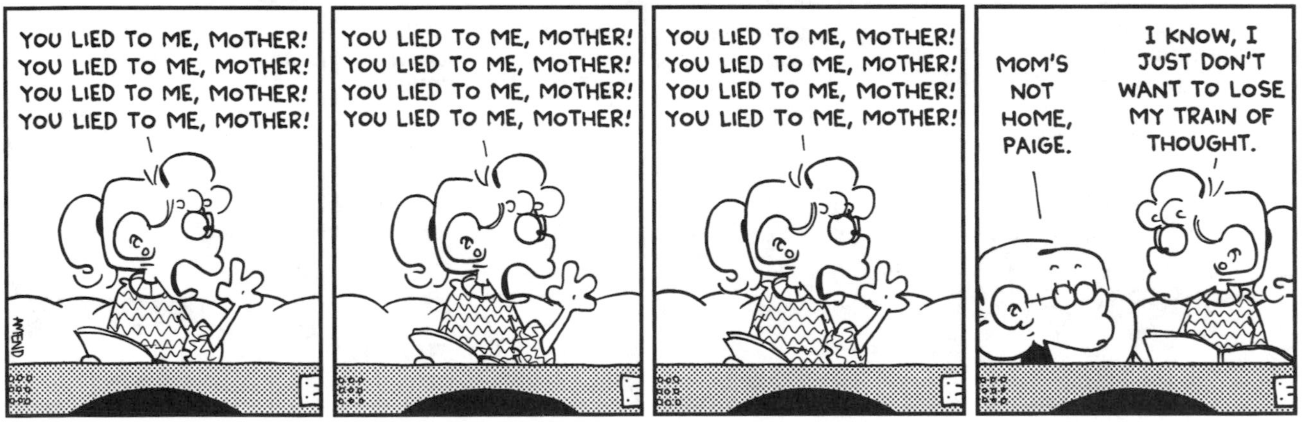
YOU LIED TO ME, MOTHER! YOU LIED TO ME, MOTHER! YOU LIED TO ME, MOTHER! YOU LIED TO ME, MOTHER!
AMEND
YOU LIED TO ME, MOTHER! YOU LIED TO ME, MOTHER! YOU LIED TO ME, MOTHER! YOU LIED TO ME, MOTHER!
YOU LIED TO ME, MOTHER! YOU LIED TO ME, MOTHER! YOU LIED TO ME, MOTHER! YOU LIED TO ME, MOTHER!
MOM'S NOT HOME, PAIGE.
I KNOW, I JUST DON'T WANT TO LOSE MY TRAIN OF THOUGHT.

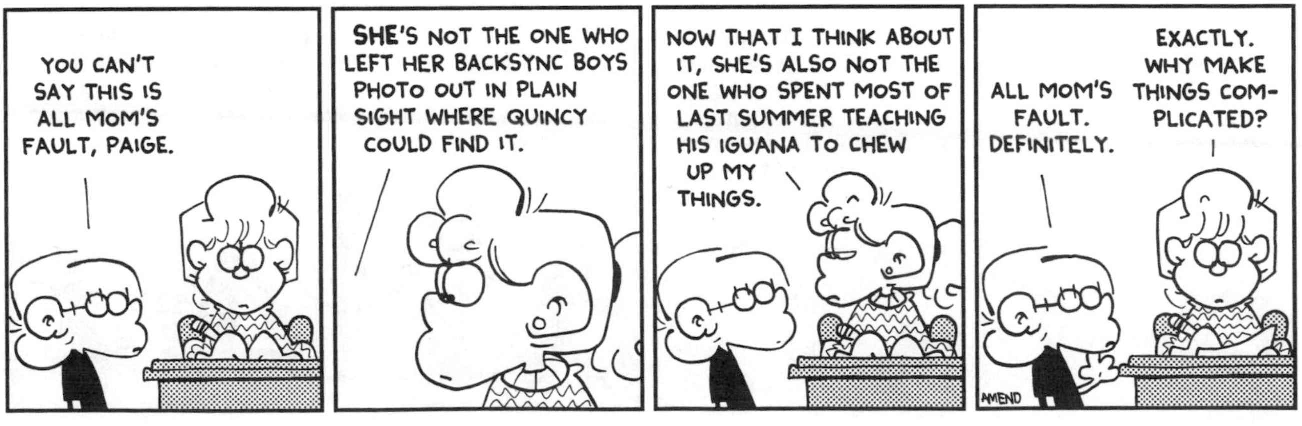
YOU CAN'T SAY THIS IS ALL MOM'S FAULT, PAIGE.
SHE'S NOT THE ONE WHO LEFT HER BACKSYNC BOYS PHOTO OUT IN PLAIN SIGHT WHERE QUINCY COULD FIND IT.
NOW THAT I THINK ABOUT IT, SHE'S ALSO NOT THE ONE WHO SPENT MOST OF LAST SUMMER TEACHING HIS IGUANA TO CHEW UP MY THINGS.
ALL MOM'S FAULT. DEFINITELY.
EXACTLY. WHY MAKE THINGS COMPLICATED?
AMEND

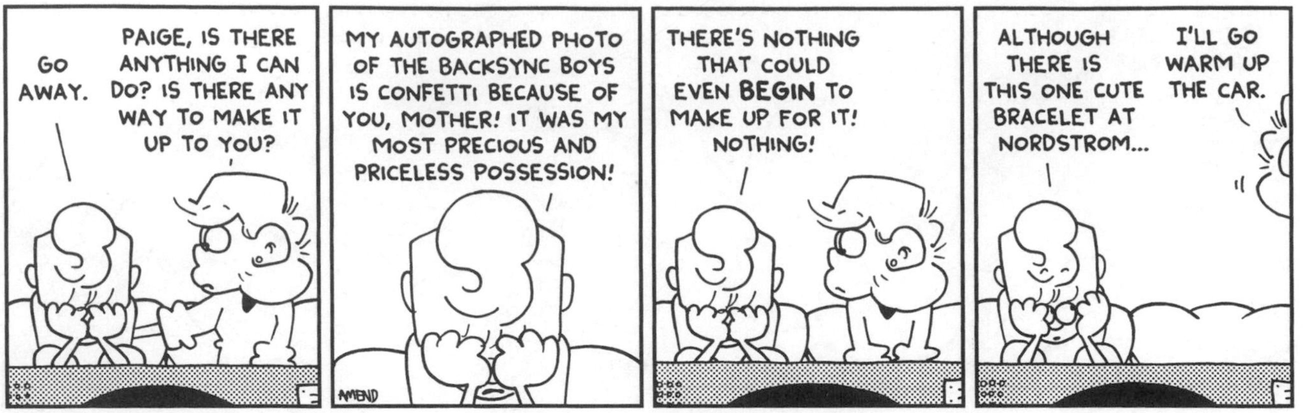
GO AWAY.
PAIGE, IS THERE ANYTHING I CAN DO? IS THERE ANY WAY TO MAKE IT UP TO YOU?
MY AUTOGRAPHED PHOTO OF THE BACKSYNC BOYS IS CONFETTI BECAUSE OF YOU, MOTHER! IT WAS MY MOST PRECIOUS AND PRICELESS POSSESSION!
THERE'S NOTHING THAT COULD EVEN **BEGIN** TO MAKE UP FOR IT! NOTHING!
ALTHOUGH THERE IS THIS ONE CUTE BRACELET AT NORDSTROM...
I'LL GO WARM UP THE CAR.

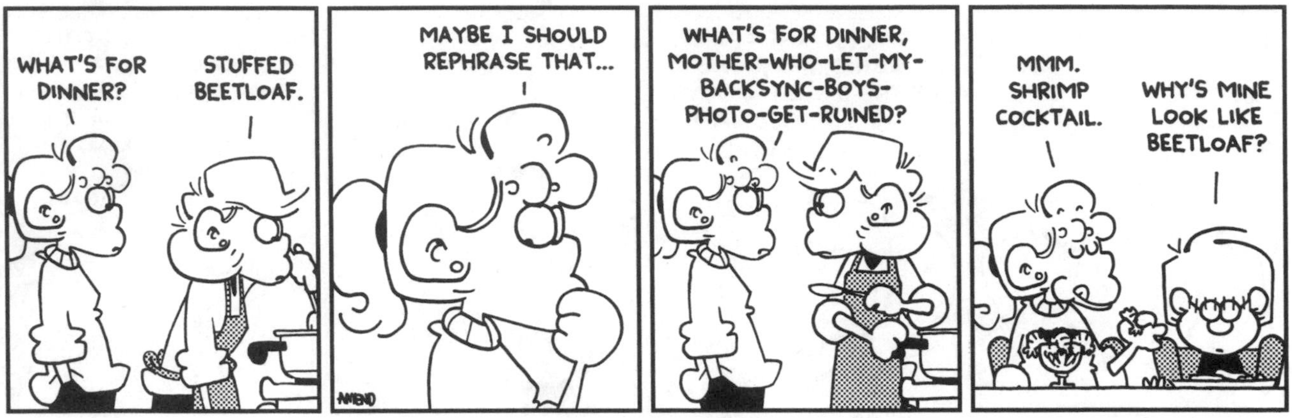
WHAT'S FOR DINNER?
STUFFED BEETLOAF.
MAYBE I SHOULD REPHRASE THAT...
WHAT'S FOR DINNER, MOTHER-WHO-LET-MY-BACKSYNC-BOYS-PHOTO-GET-RUINED?
MMM. SHRIMP COCKTAIL.
WHY'S MINE LOOK LIKE BEETLOAF?

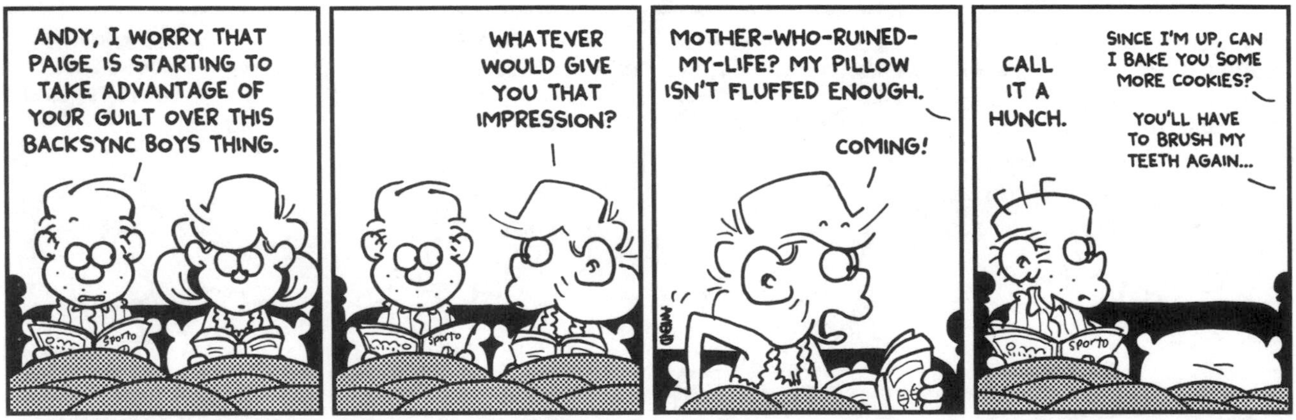
ANDY, I WORRY THAT PAIGE IS STARTING TO TAKE ADVANTAGE OF YOUR GUILT OVER THIS BACKSYNC BOYS THING.
WHATEVER WOULD GIVE YOU THAT IMPRESSION?
MOTHER-WHO-RUINED-MY-LIFE? MY PILLOW ISN'T FLUFFED ENOUGH.
COMING!
CALL IT A HUNCH.
SINCE I'M UP, CAN I BAKE YOU SOME MORE COOKIES?
YOU'LL HAVE TO BRUSH MY TEETH AGAIN...

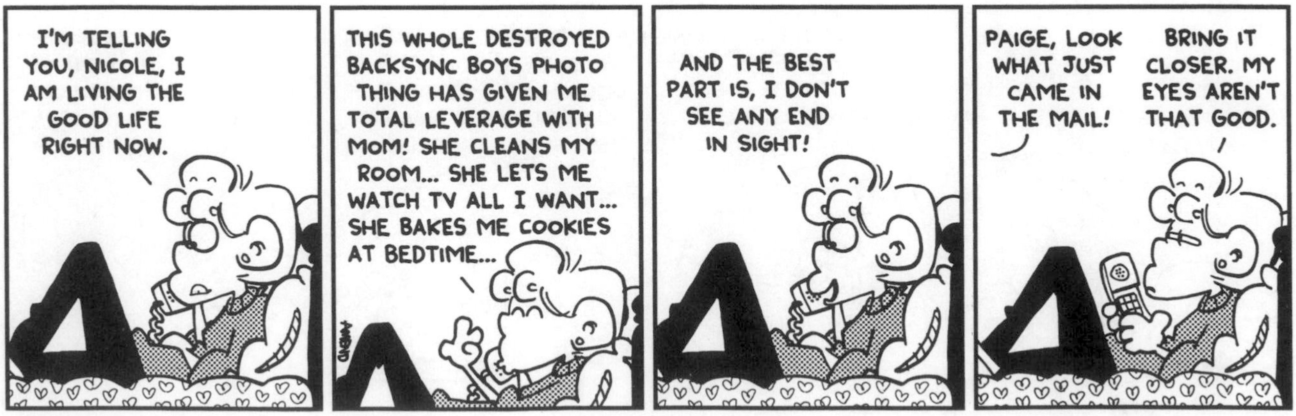
I'M TELLING YOU, NICOLE, I AM LIVING THE GOOD LIFE RIGHT NOW.
THIS WHOLE DESTROYED BACKSYNC BOYS PHOTO THING HAS GIVEN ME TOTAL LEVERAGE WITH MOM! SHE CLEANS MY ROOM... SHE LETS ME WATCH TV ALL I WANT... SHE BAKES ME COOKIES AT BEDTIME...
AND THE BEST PART IS, I DON'T SEE ANY END IN SIGHT!
PAIGE, LOOK WHAT JUST CAME IN THE MAIL!
BRING IT CLOSER. MY EYES AREN'T THAT GOOD.

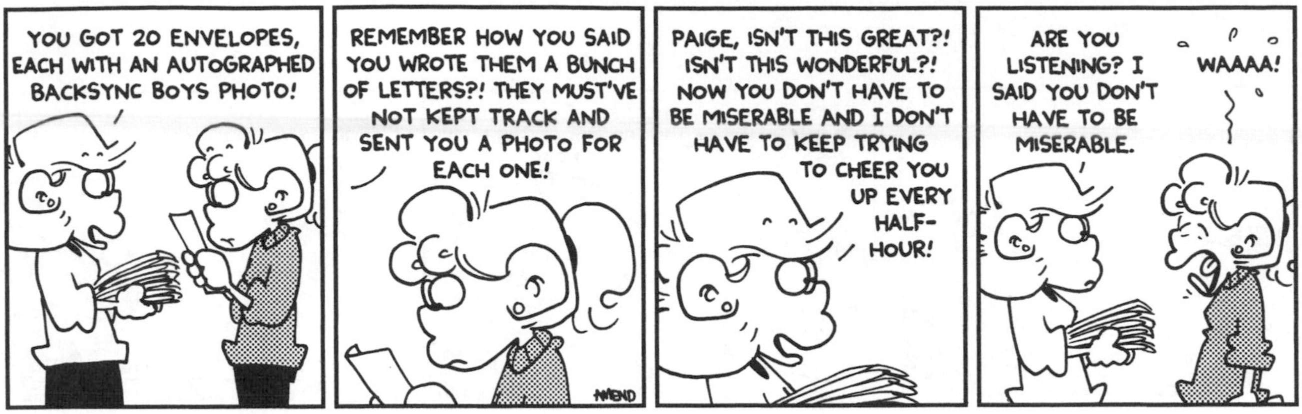
YOU GOT 20 ENVELOPES, EACH WITH AN AUTOGRAPHED BACKSYNC BOYS PHOTO!
REMEMBER HOW YOU SAID YOU WROTE THEM A BUNCH OF LETTERS?! THEY MUST'VE NOT KEPT TRACK AND SENT YOU A PHOTO FOR EACH ONE!
PAIGE, ISN'T THIS GREAT?! ISN'T THIS WONDERFUL?! NOW YOU DON'T HAVE TO BE MISERABLE AND I DON'T HAVE TO KEEP TRYING TO CHEER YOU UP EVERY HALF-HOUR!
ARE YOU LISTENING? I SAID YOU DON'T HAVE TO BE MISERABLE.
WAAAA!
AMEND

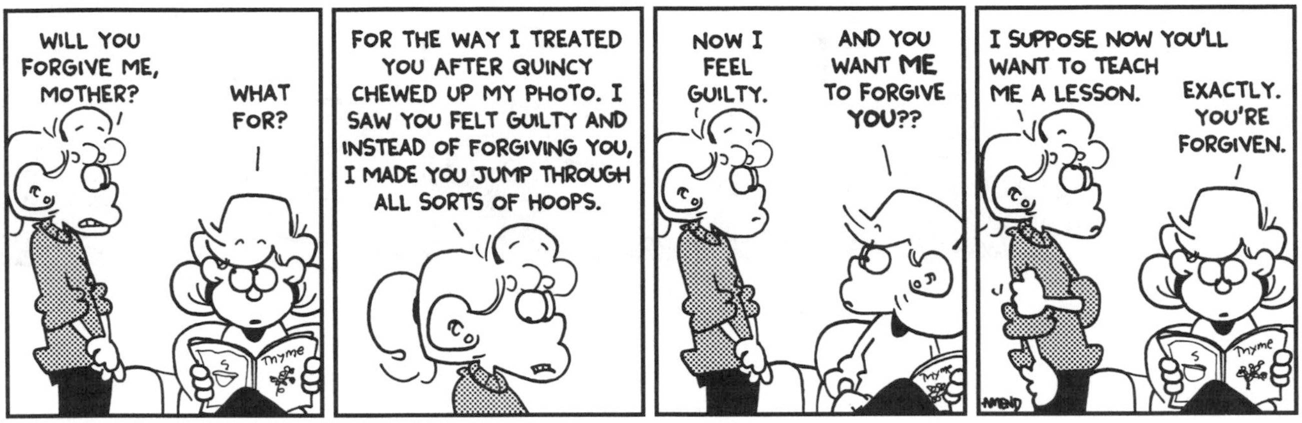
WILL YOU FORGIVE ME, MOTHER?
WHAT FOR?
Thyme
FOR THE WAY I TREATED YOU AFTER QUINCY CHEWED UP MY PHOTO. I SAW YOU FELT GUILTY AND INSTEAD OF FORGIVING YOU, I MADE YOU JUMP THROUGH ALL SORTS OF HOOPS.
NOW I FEEL GUILTY.
AND YOU WANT ME TO FORGIVE YOU??
I SUPPOSE NOW YOU'LL WANT TO TEACH ME A LESSON.
EXACTLY. YOU'RE FORGIVEN.
Thyme
AMEND

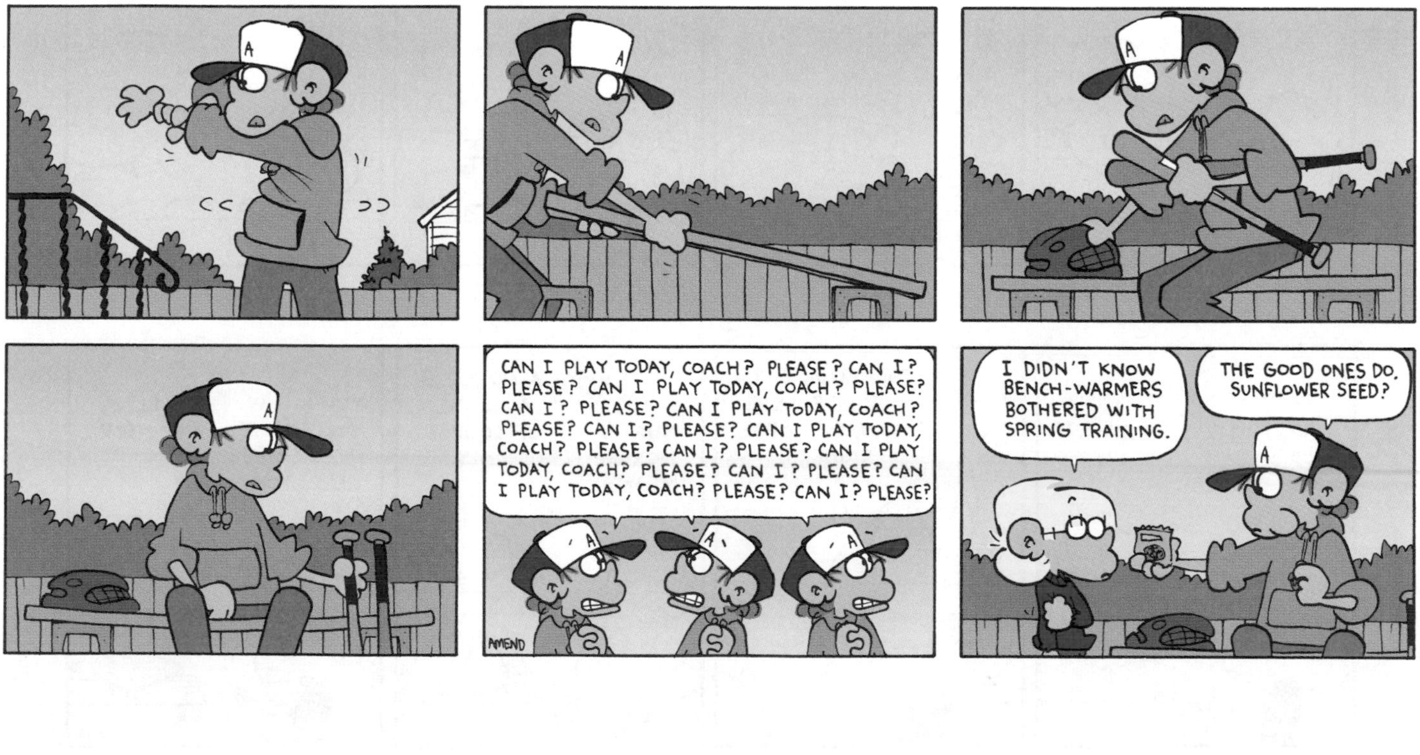
CAN I PLAY TODAY, COACH? PLEASE? CAN I? PLEASE? CAN I PLAY TODAY, COACH? PLEASE? CAN I? PLEASE? CAN I PLAY TODAY, COACH? PLEASE? CAN I? PLEASE? CAN I PLAY TODAY, COACH? PLEASE? CAN I? PLEASE? CAN I PLAY TODAY, COACH? PLEASE? CAN I? PLEASE? CAN I PLAY TODAY, COACH? PLEASE? CAN I? PLEASE?
AMEND
I DIDN'T KNOW BENCH-WARMERS BOTHERED WITH SPRING TRAINING.
THE GOOD ONES DO, SUNFLOWER SEED?

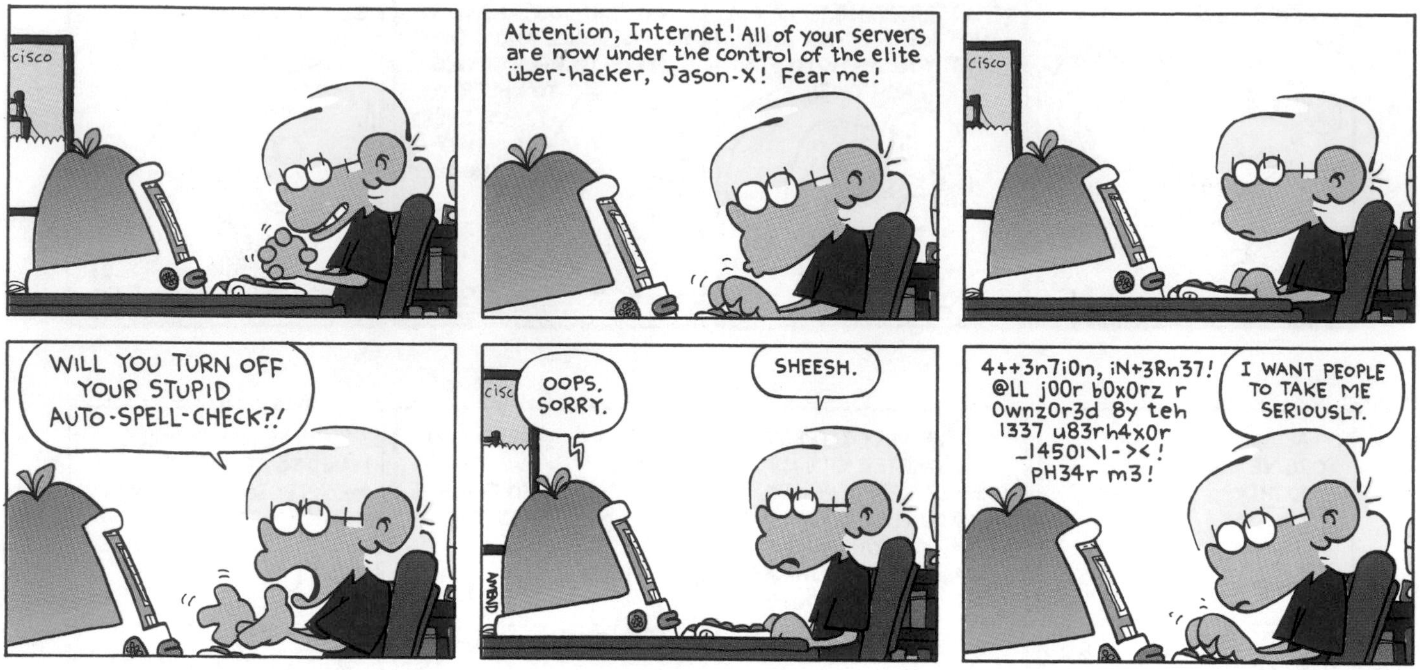
cisco
Attention, Internet! All of your servers are now under the control of the elite über-hacker, Jason-X! Fear me!
cisco
WILL YOU TURN OFF YOUR STUPID AUTO-SPELL-CHECK?!
OOPS. SORRY.
SHEESH.
4++3n7i0n, iN+3Rn37! @LL j00r b0x0rz r 0wnz0r3d 8y teh 1337 u83rh4x0r _|450|\|->< ! pH34r m3!
I WANT PEOPLE TO TAKE ME SERIOUSLY.
AMEND

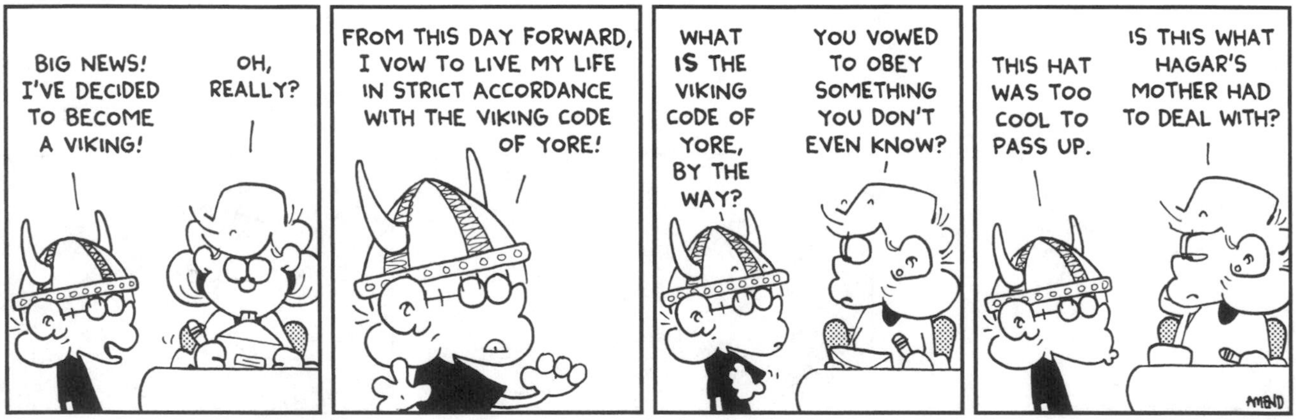
BIG NEWS! I'VE DECIDED TO BECOME A VIKING!
OH, REALLY?
FROM THIS DAY FORWARD, I VOW TO LIVE MY LIFE IN STRICT ACCORDANCE WITH THE VIKING CODE OF YORE!
WHAT IS THE VIKING CODE OF YORE, BY THE WAY?
YOU VOWED TO OBEY SOMETHING YOU DON'T EVEN KNOW?
THIS HAT WAS TOO COOL TO PASS UP.
IS THIS WHAT HAGAR'S MOTHER HAD TO DEAL WITH?
AMEND

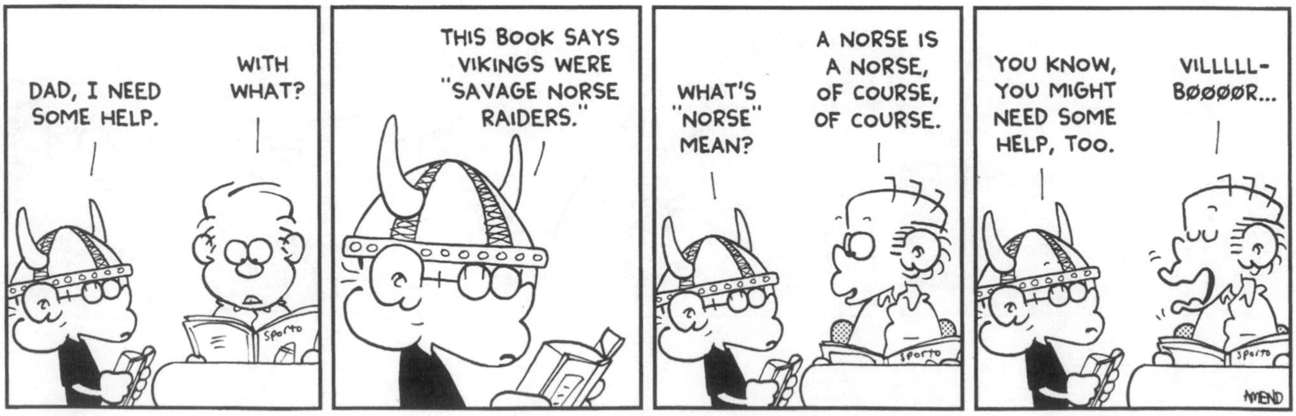
DAD, I NEED SOME HELP.
WITH WHAT?
THIS BOOK SAYS VIKINGS WERE "SAVAGE NORSE RAIDERS."
WHAT'S "NORSE" MEAN?
A NORSE IS A NORSE, OF COURSE, OF COURSE.
YOU KNOW, YOU MIGHT NEED SOME HELP, TOO.
VILLLLL-BØØØØR...
AMEND

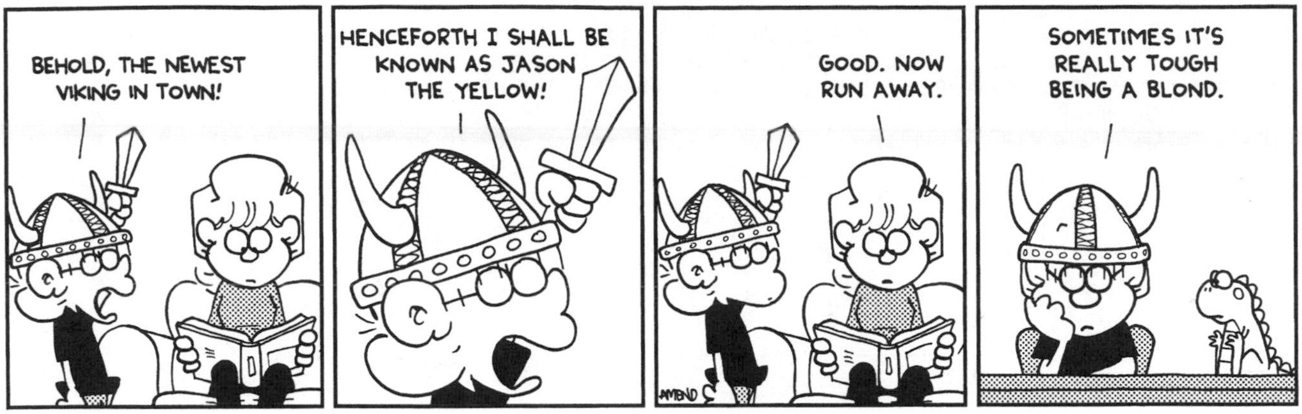
BEHOLD, THE NEWEST VIKING IN TOWN!
HENCEFORTH I SHALL BE KNOWN AS JASON THE YELLOW!
GOOD. NOW RUN AWAY.
AMEND
SOMETIMES IT'S REALLY TOUGH BEING A BLOND.

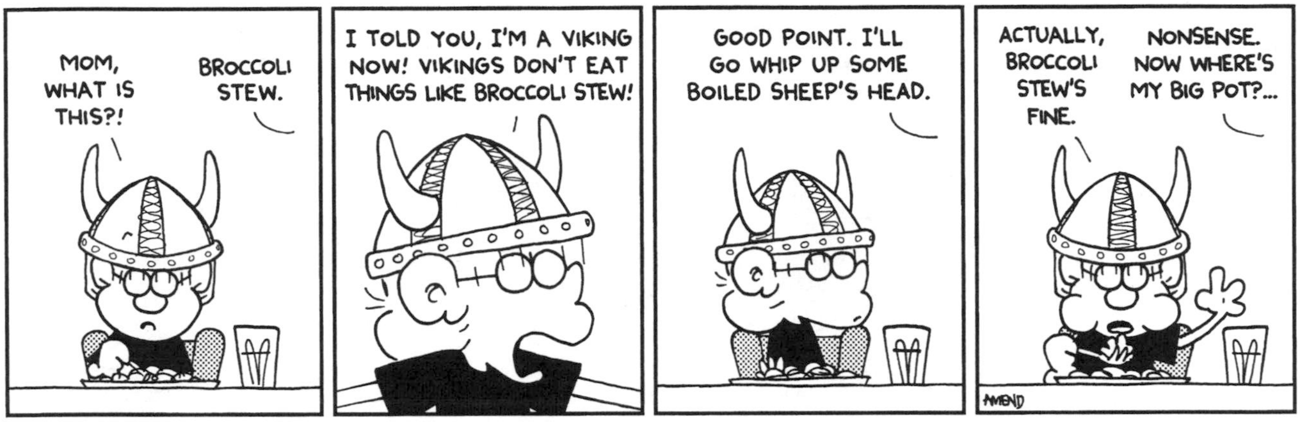
MOM, WHAT IS THIS?!
BROCCOLI STEW.
I TOLD YOU, I'M A VIKING NOW! VIKINGS DON'T EAT THINGS LIKE BROCCOLI STEW!
GOOD POINT. I'LL GO WHIP UP SOME BOILED SHEEP'S HEAD.
ACTUALLY, BROCCOLI STEW'S FINE.
NONSENSE. NOW WHERE'S MY BIG POT?...
AMEND

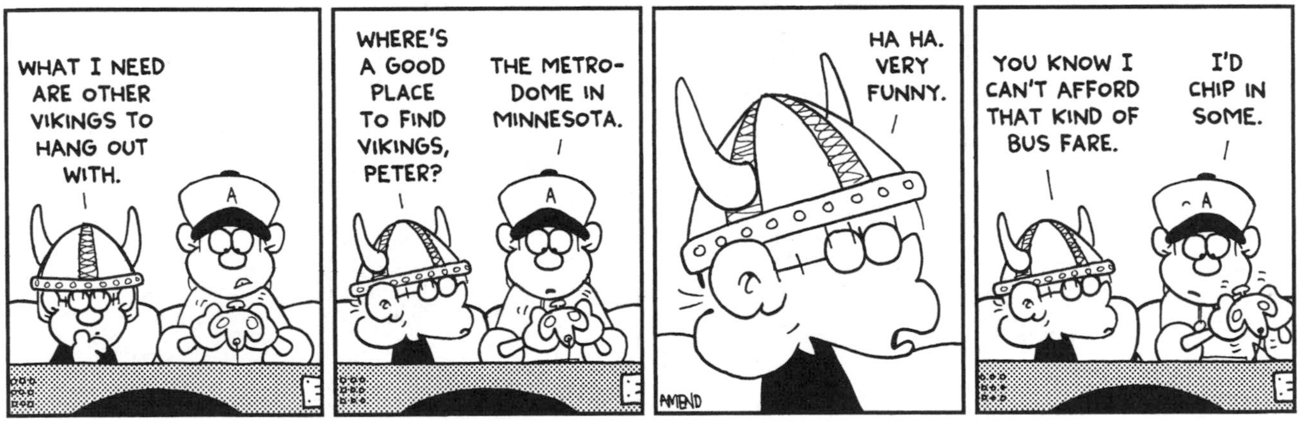
WHAT I NEED ARE OTHER VIKINGS TO HANG OUT WITH.
WHERE'S A GOOD PLACE TO FIND VIKINGS, PETER?
THE METRO-DOME IN MINNESOTA.
HA HA. VERY FUNNY.
AMEND
YOU KNOW I CAN'T AFFORD THAT KIND OF BUS FARE.
I'D CHIP IN SOME.

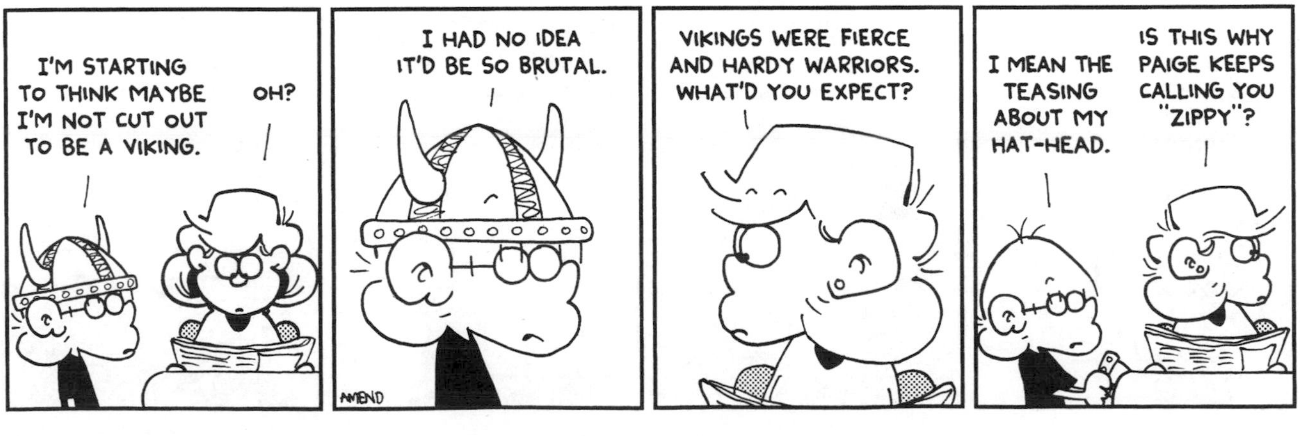
I'M STARTING TO THINK MAYBE I'M NOT CUT OUT TO BE A VIKING.
OH?
I HAD NO IDEA IT'D BE SO BRUTAL.
AMEND
VIKINGS WERE FIERCE AND HARDY WARRIORS. WHAT'D YOU EXPECT?
I MEAN THE TEASING ABOUT MY HAT-HEAD.
IS THIS WHY PAIGE KEEPS CALLING YOU "ZIPPY"?

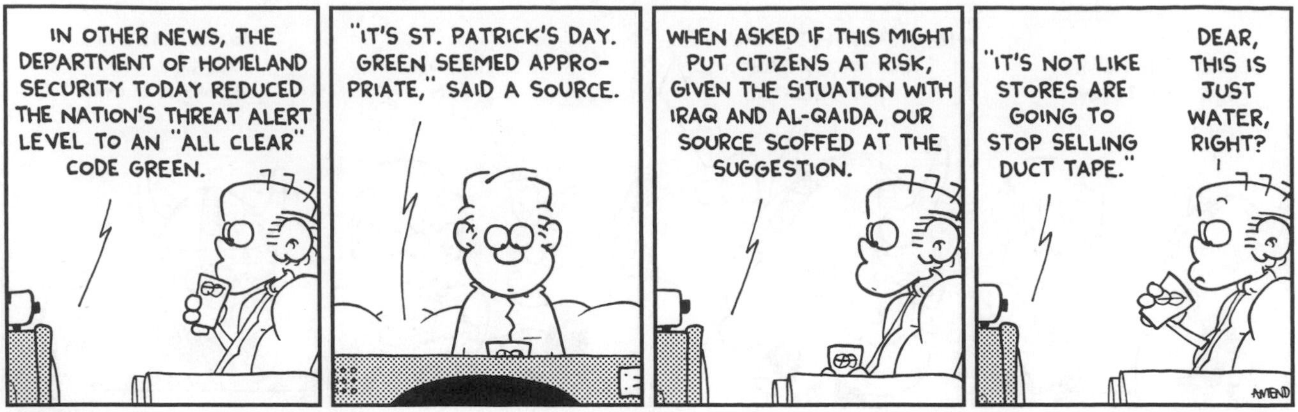
IN OTHER NEWS, THE DEPARTMENT OF HOMELAND SECURITY TODAY REDUCED THE NATION'S THREAT ALERT LEVEL TO AN "ALL CLEAR" CODE GREEN.
"IT'S ST. PATRICK'S DAY. GREEN SEEMED APPROPRIATE," SAID A SOURCE.
WHEN ASKED IF THIS MIGHT PUT CITIZENS AT RISK, GIVEN THE SITUATION WITH IRAQ AND AL-QAIDA, OUR SOURCE SCOFFED AT THE SUGGESTION.
"IT'S NOT LIKE STORES ARE GOING TO STOP SELLING DUCT TAPE."
DEAR, THIS IS JUST WATER, RIGHT?
AMEND

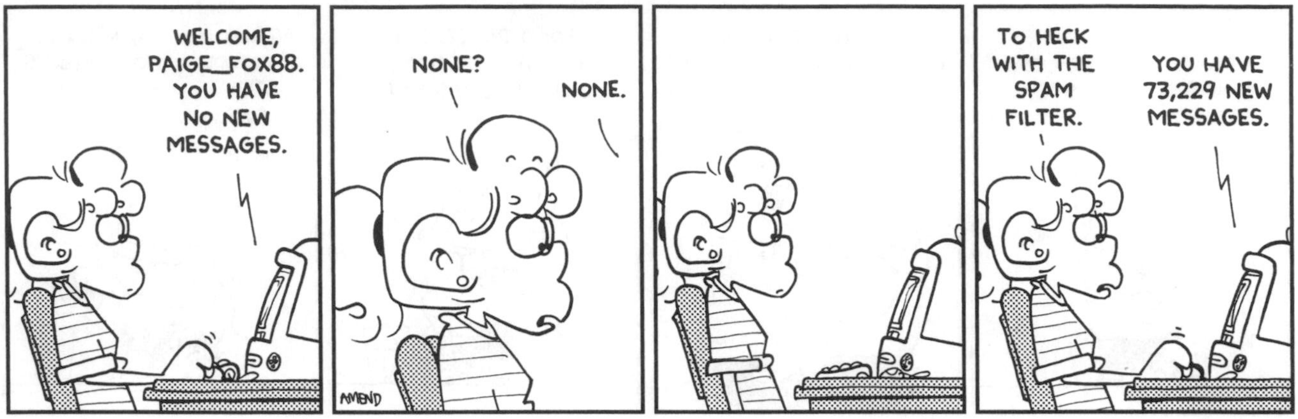
WELCOME, PAIGE_FOX88. YOU HAVE NO NEW MESSAGES.
NONE?
NONE.
AMEND
TO HECK WITH THE SPAM FILTER.
YOU HAVE 73,229 NEW MESSAGES.

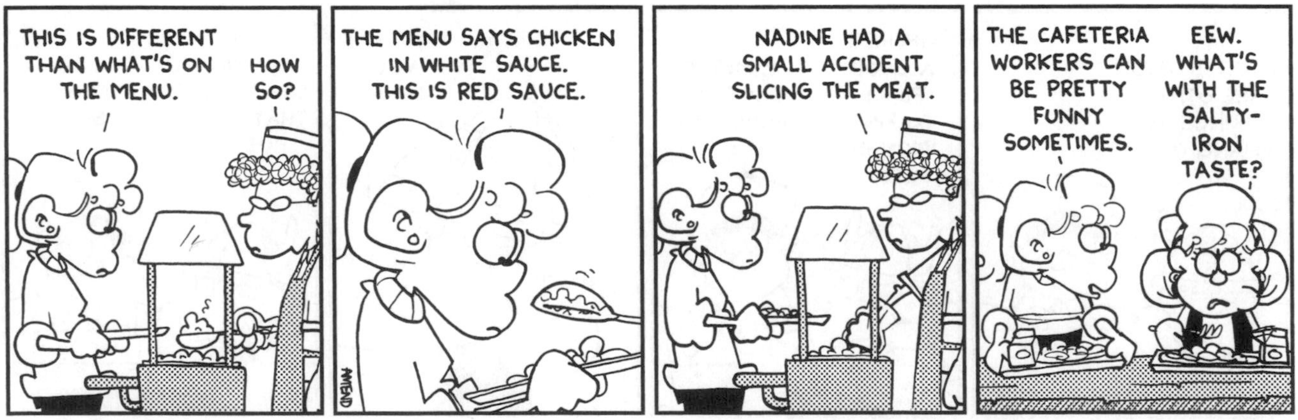
THIS IS DIFFERENT THAN WHAT'S ON THE MENU.
HOW SO?
THE MENU SAYS CHICKEN IN WHITE SAUCE. THIS IS RED SAUCE.
AMEND
NADINE HAD A SMALL ACCIDENT SLICING THE MEAT.
THE CAFETERIA WORKERS CAN BE PRETTY FUNNY SOMETIMES.
EEW. WHAT'S WITH THE SALTY-IRON TASTE?

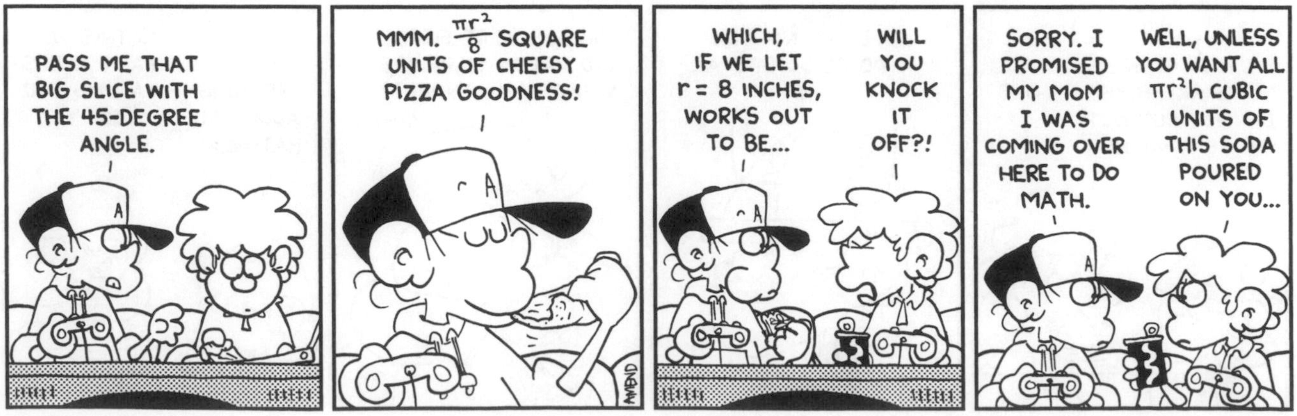
PASS ME THAT BIG SLICE WITH THE 45-DEGREE ANGLE.
MMM. $\frac{\pi r^2}{8}$ SQUARE UNITS OF CHEESY PIZZA GOODNESS!
AMEND
WHICH, IF WE LET $r = 8$ INCHES, WORKS OUT TO BE...
WILL YOU KNOCK IT OFF?!
SORRY. I PROMISED MY MOM I WAS COMING OVER HERE TO DO MATH.
WELL, UNLESS YOU WANT ALL $\pi r^2 h$ CUBIC UNITS OF THIS SODA POURED ON YOU...

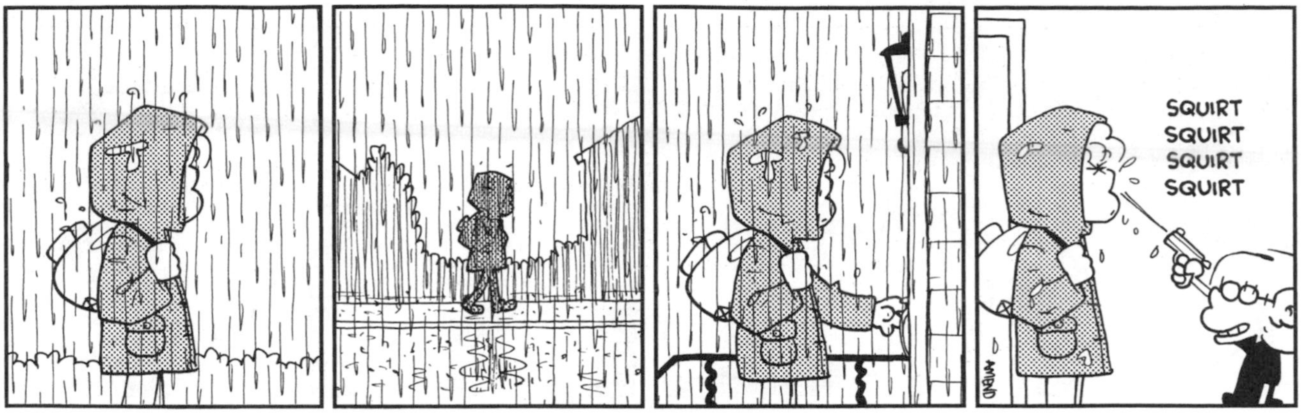
SQUIRT
SQUIRT
SQUIRT
SQUIRT
AMEND

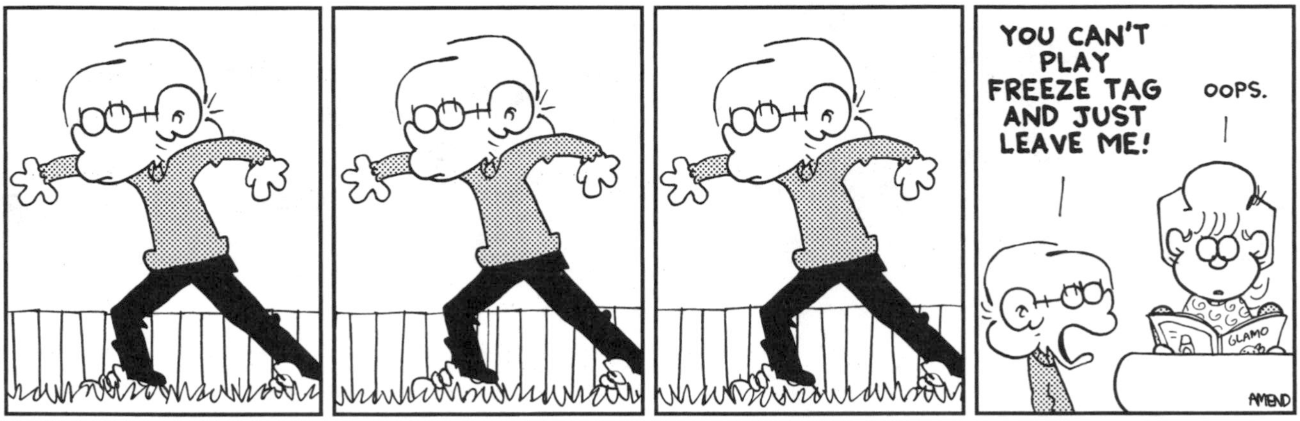
YOU CAN'T PLAY FREEZE TAG AND JUST LEAVE ME!
OOPS.
GLAMO
AMEND

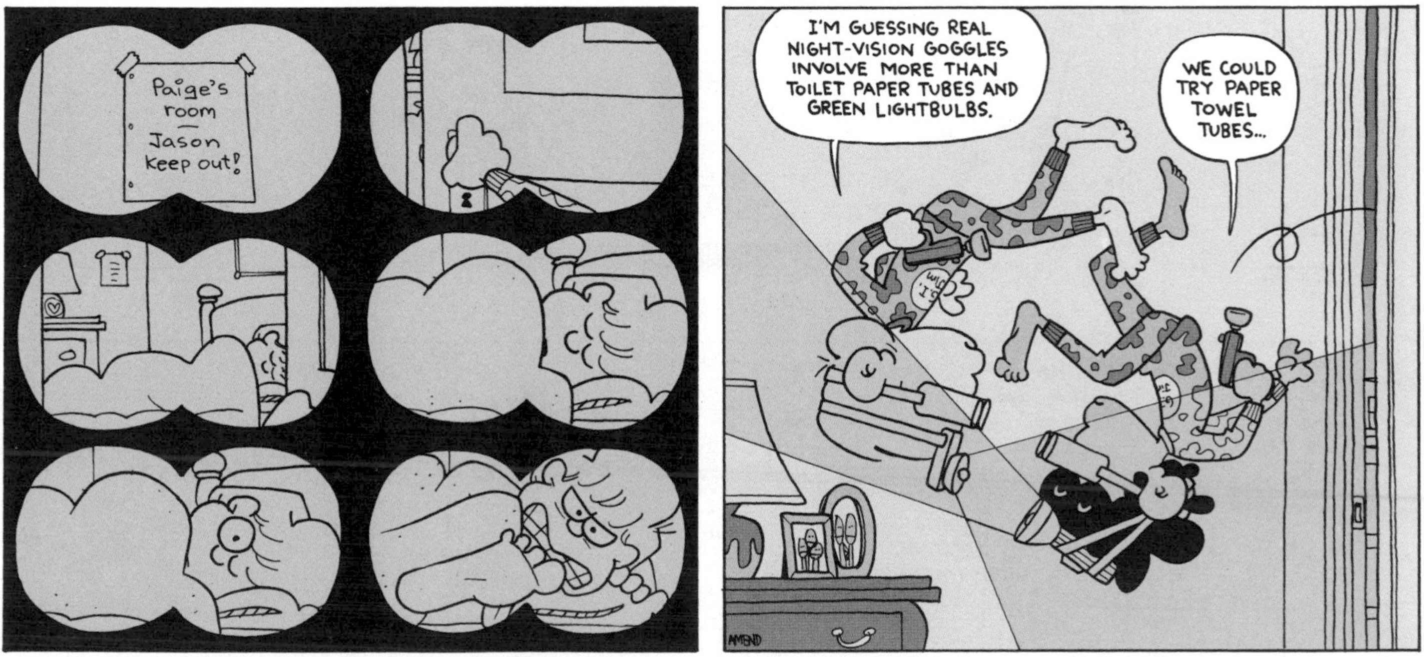
Paige's room — Jason keep out!
I'M GUESSING REAL NIGHT-VISION GOGGLES INVOLVE MORE THAN TOILET PAPER TUBES AND GREEN LIGHTBULBS.
WE COULD TRY PAPER TOWEL TUBES...
AMEND

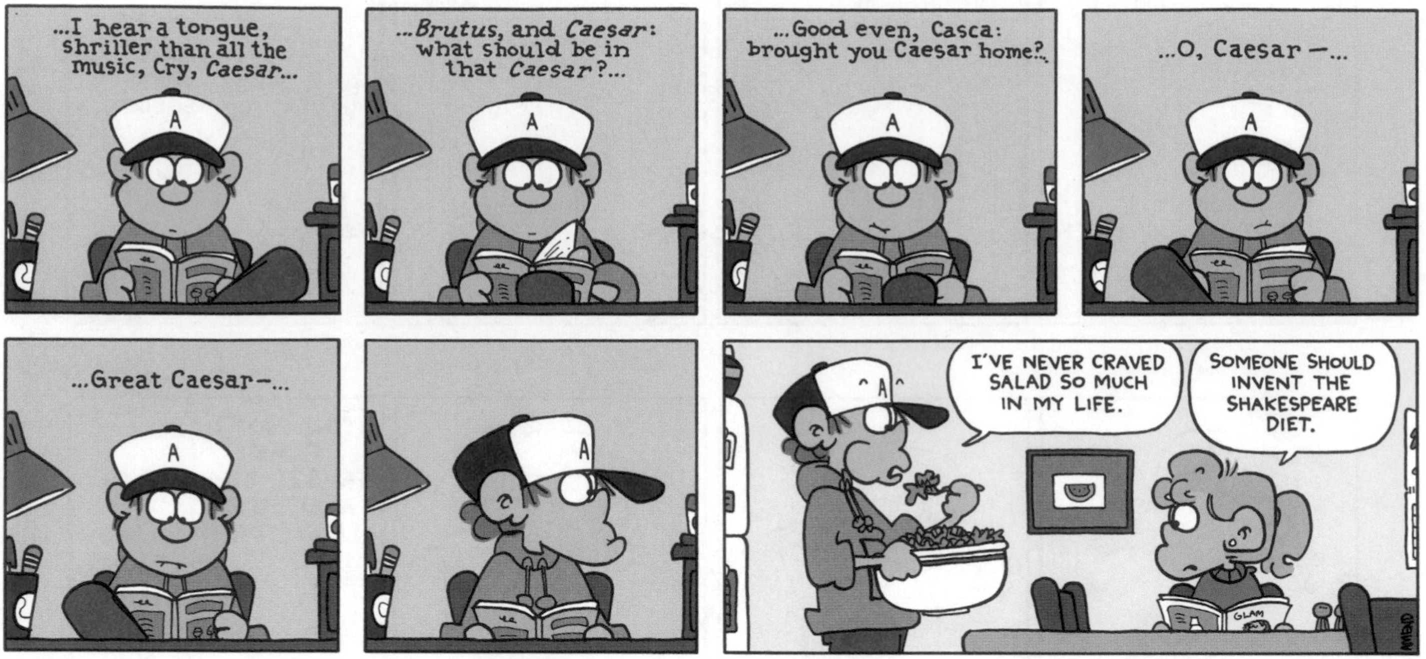
...I hear a tongue, shriller than all the music, Cry, *Caesar*...
...*Brutus*, and *Caesar*: what should be in that *Caesar*?...
...Good even, Casca: brought you Caesar home?...
...O, Caesar —...
...Great Caesar—...
I'VE NEVER CRAVED SALAD SO MUCH IN MY LIFE.
SOMEONE SHOULD INVENT THE SHAKESPEARE DIET.
AMEND

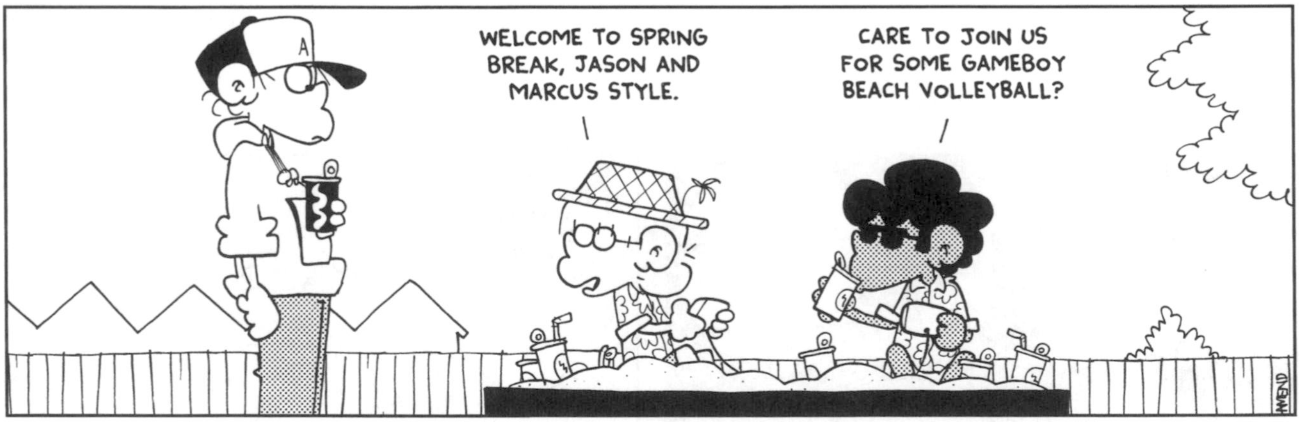
WELCOME TO SPRING BREAK, JASON AND MARCUS STYLE.
CARE TO JOIN US FOR SOME GAMEBOY BEACH VOLLEYBALL?
AMEND

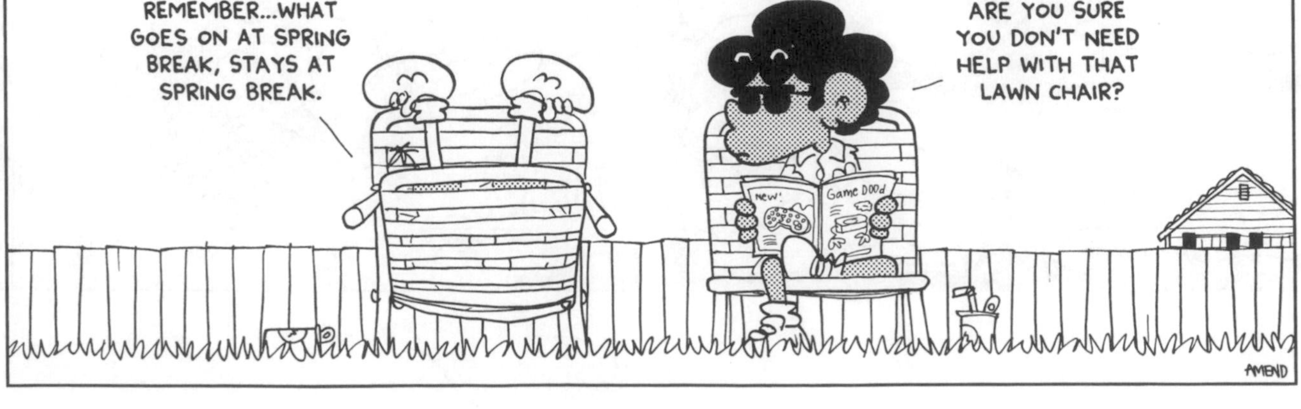
REMEMBER...WHAT GOES ON AT SPRING BREAK, STAYS AT SPRING BREAK.
ARE YOU SURE YOU DON'T NEED HELP WITH THAT LAWN CHAIR?
New!
Game DOOd
AMEND

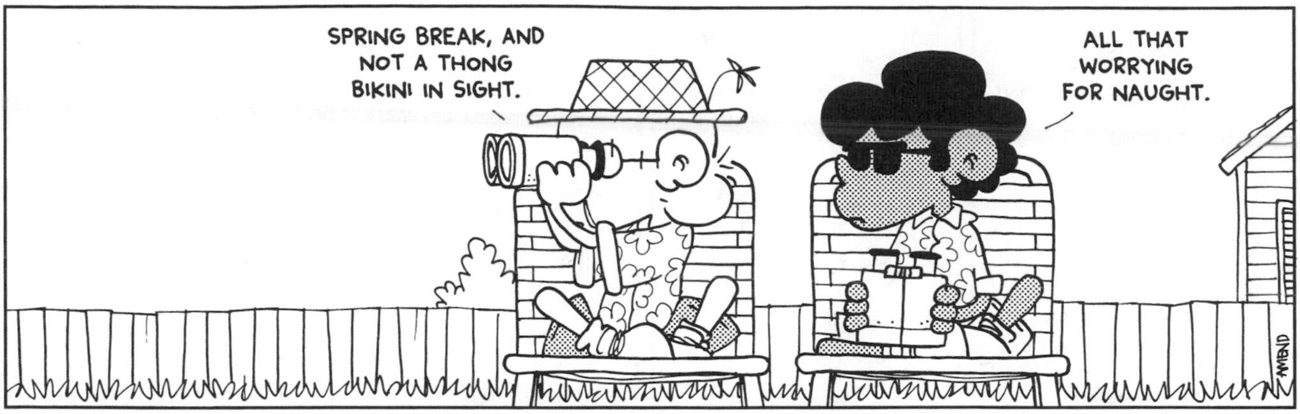
SPRING BREAK, AND NOT A THONG BIKINI IN SIGHT.
ALL THAT WORRYING FOR NAUGHT.
AMEND

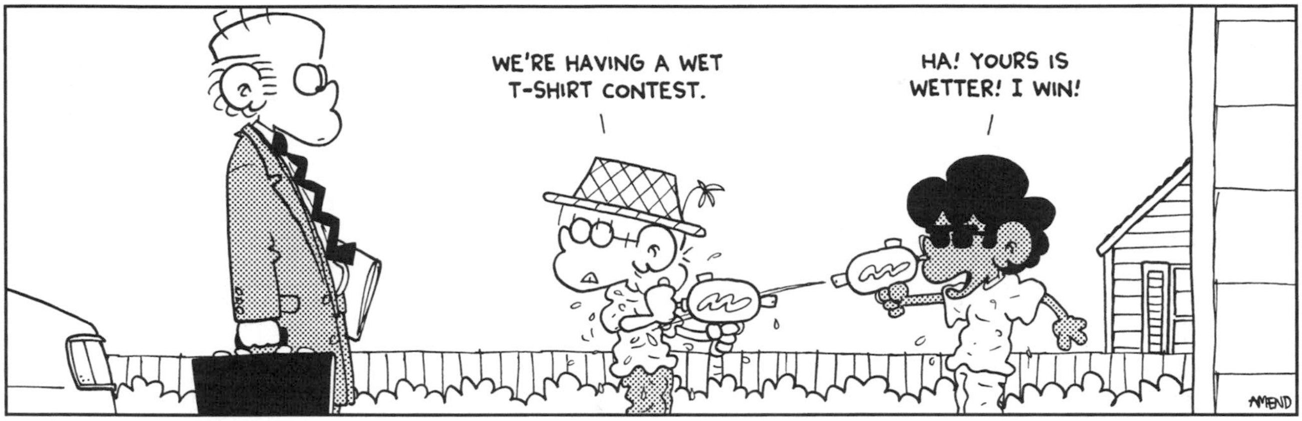
WE'RE HAVING A WET T-SHIRT CONTEST.
HA! YOURS IS WETTER! I WIN!
AMEND

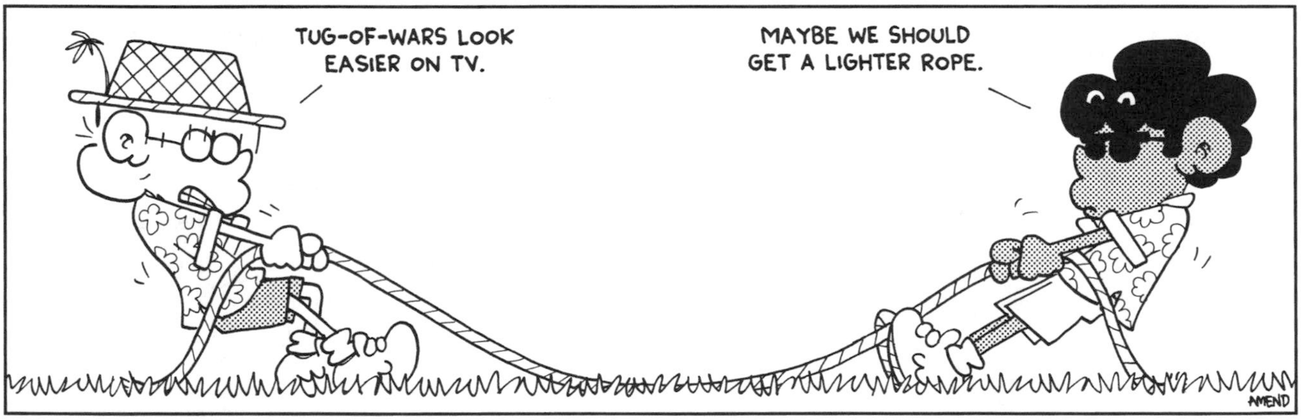
TUG-OF-WARS LOOK EASIER ON TV.
MAYBE WE SHOULD GET A LIGHTER ROPE.
AMEND

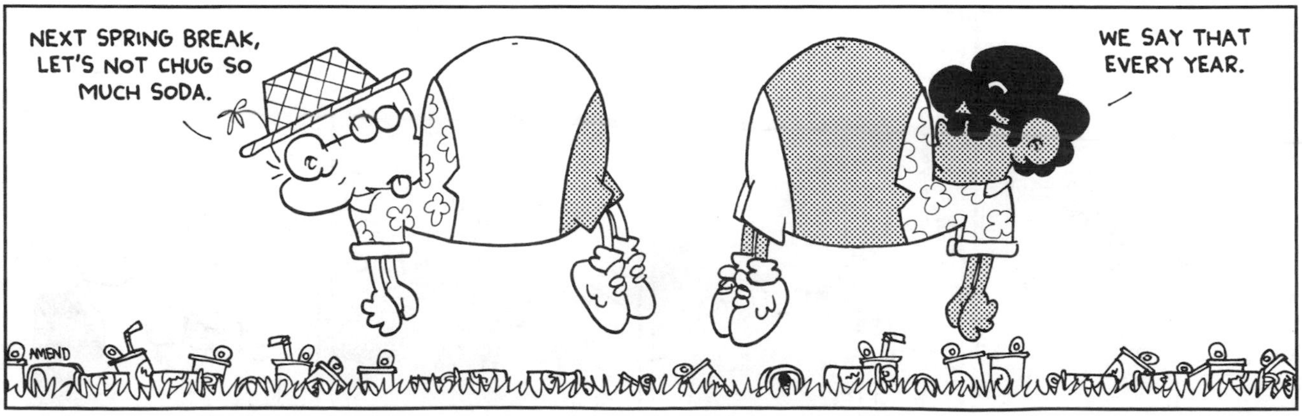
NEXT SPRING BREAK, LET'S NOT CHUG SO MUCH SODA.
WE SAY THAT EVERY YEAR.
AMEND

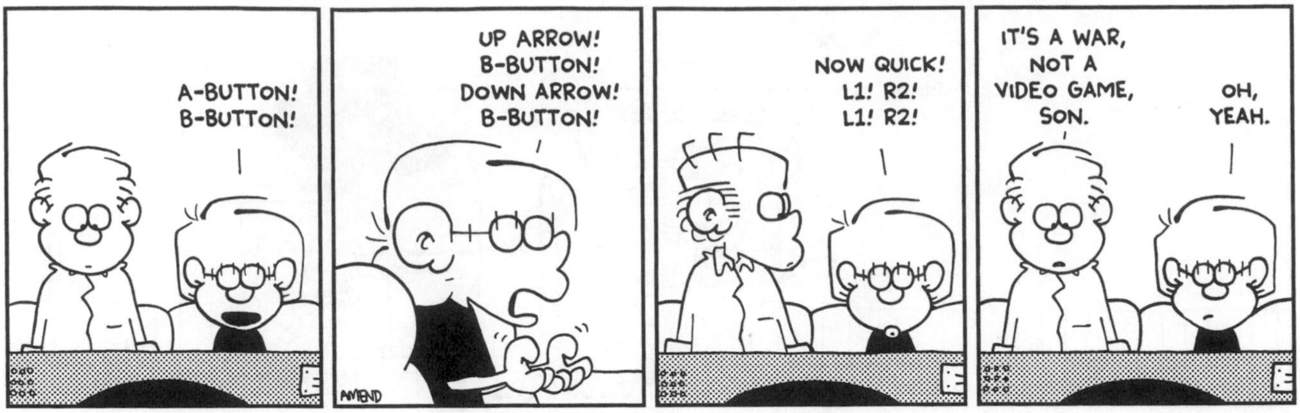
A-BUTTON! B-BUTTON!
UP ARROW! B-BUTTON! DOWN ARROW! B-BUTTON!
AMEND
NOW QUICK! L1! R2! L1! R2!
IT'S A WAR, NOT A VIDEO GAME, SON.
OH, YEAH.

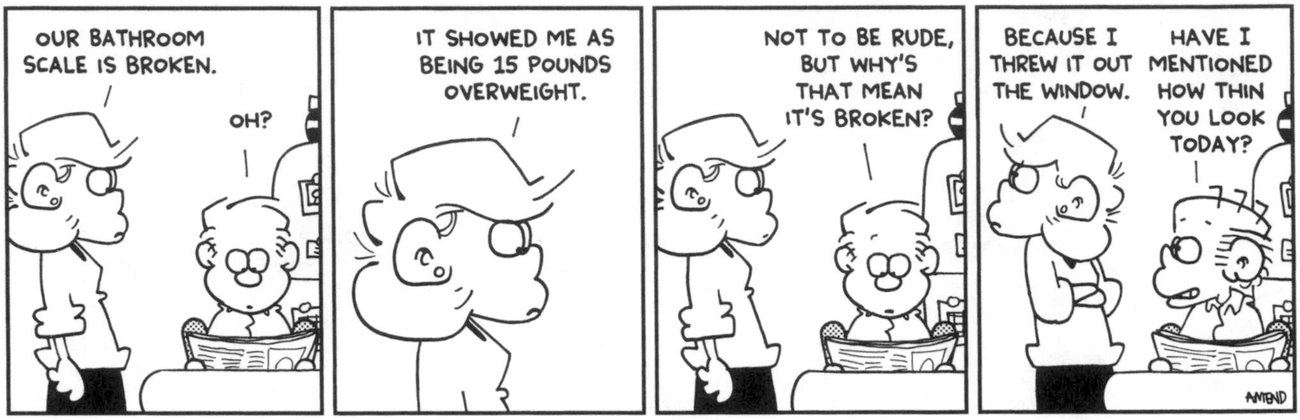
OUR BATHROOM SCALE IS BROKEN.
OH?
IT SHOWED ME AS BEING 15 POUNDS OVERWEIGHT.
NOT TO BE RUDE, BUT WHY'S THAT MEAN IT'S BROKEN?
BECAUSE I THREW IT OUT THE WINDOW.
HAVE I MENTIONED HOW THIN YOU LOOK TODAY?
AMEND

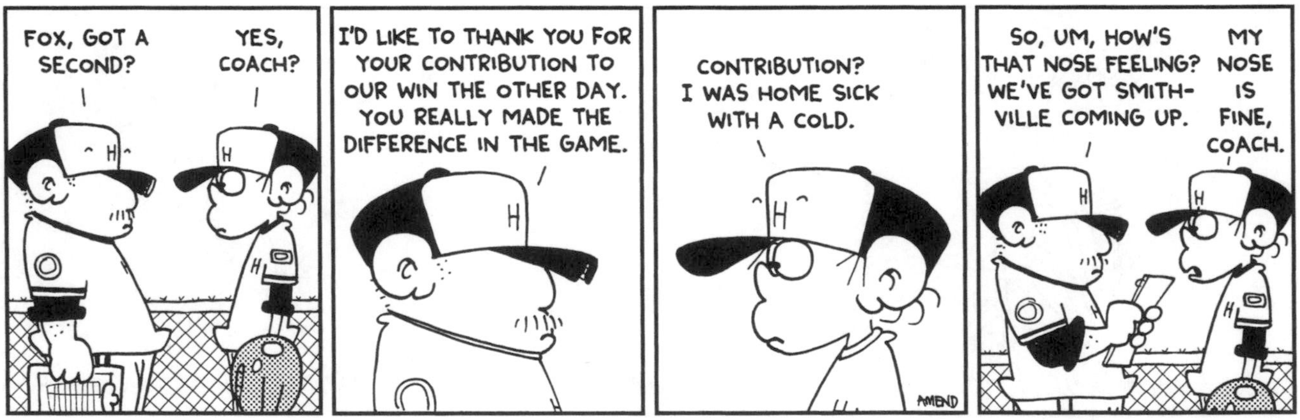
FOX, GOT A SECOND?
YES, COACH?
I'D LIKE TO THANK YOU FOR YOUR CONTRIBUTION TO OUR WIN THE OTHER DAY. YOU REALLY MADE THE DIFFERENCE IN THE GAME.
CONTRIBUTION? I WAS HOME SICK WITH A COLD.
AMEND
SO, UM, HOW'S THAT NOSE FEELING? WE'VE GOT SMITH-VILLE COMING UP.
MY NOSE IS FINE, COACH.

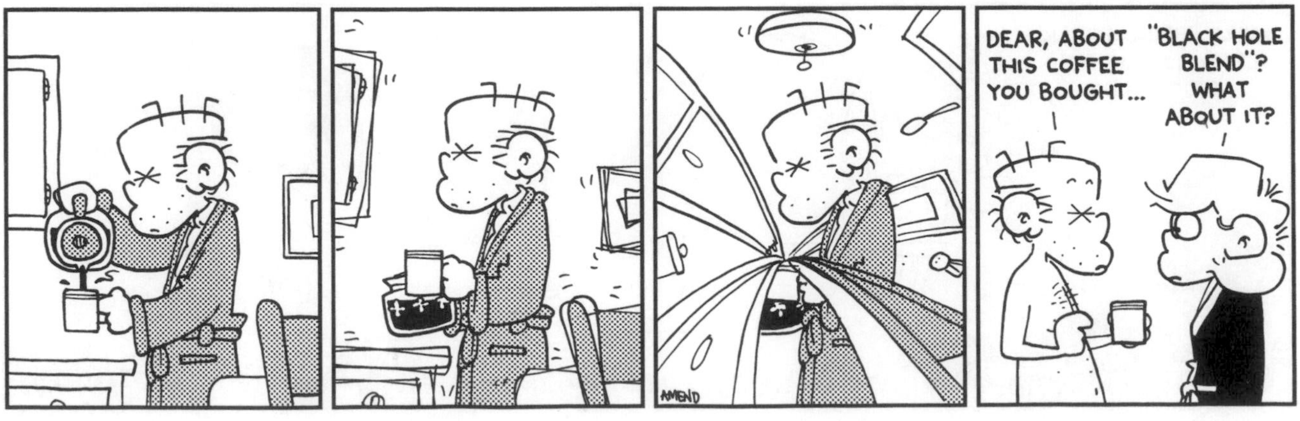
AMEND
DEAR, ABOUT THIS COFFEE YOU BOUGHT...
"BLACK HOLE BLEND"? WHAT ABOUT IT?

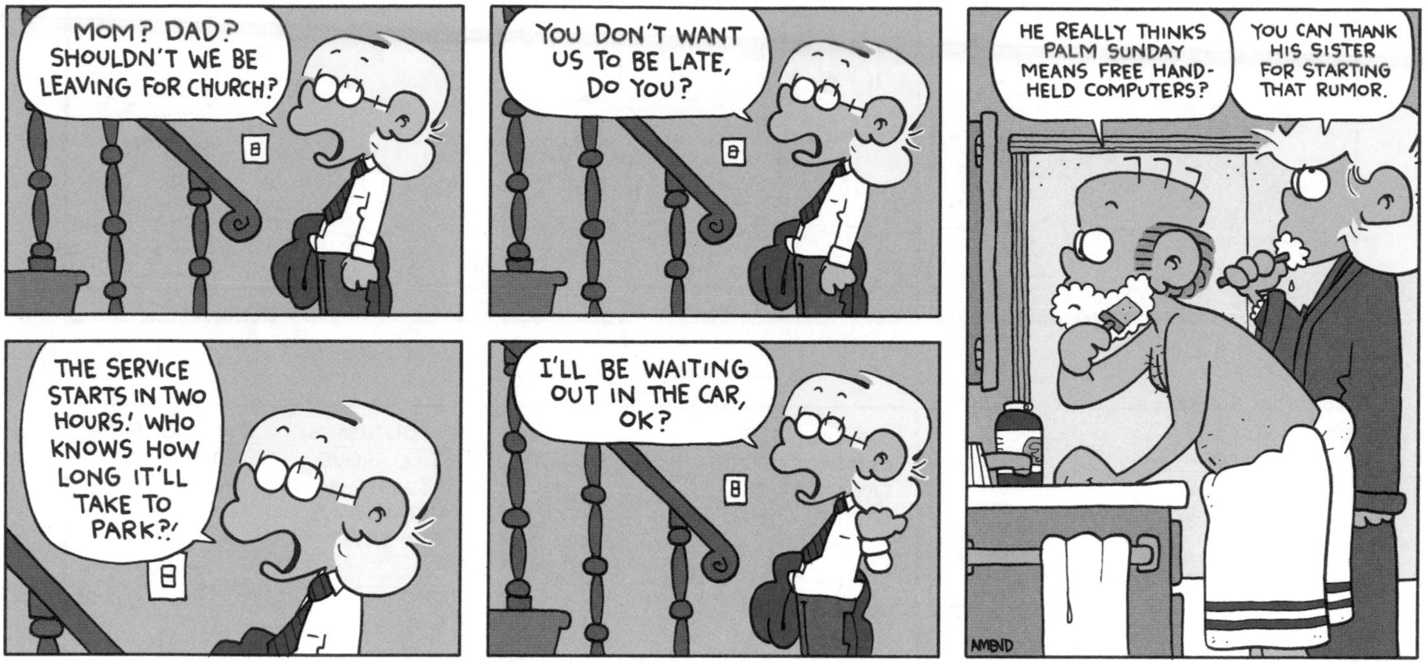
MOM? DAD? SHOULDN'T WE BE LEAVING FOR CHURCH?
YOU DON'T WANT US TO BE LATE, DO YOU?
THE SERVICE STARTS IN TWO HOURS! WHO KNOWS HOW LONG IT'LL TAKE TO PARK?!
I'LL BE WAITING OUT IN THE CAR, OK?
HE REALLY THINKS PALM SUNDAY MEANS FREE HAND-HELD COMPUTERS?
YOU CAN THANK HIS SISTER FOR STARTING THAT RUMOR.
AMEND

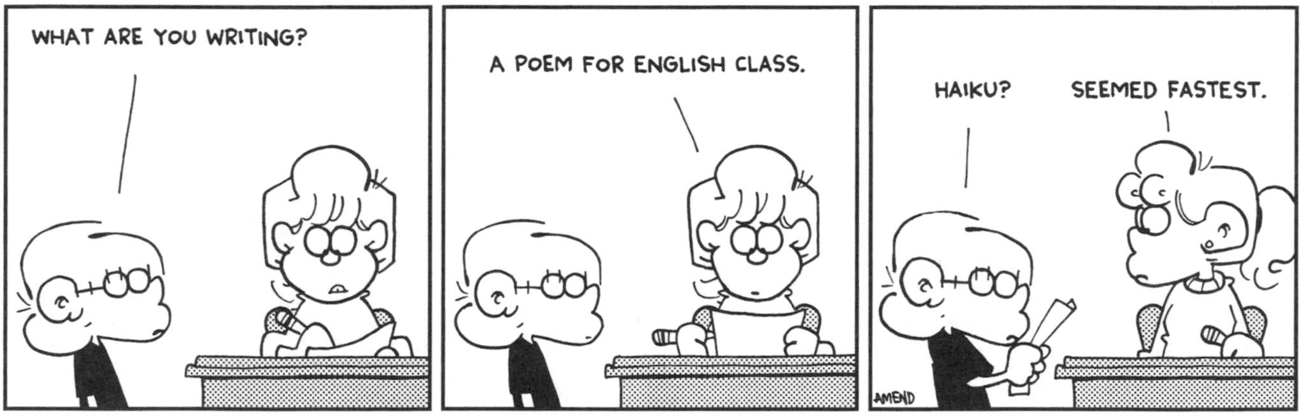
WHAT ARE YOU WRITING?
A POEM FOR ENGLISH CLASS.
HAIKU?
SEEMED FASTEST.
AMEND

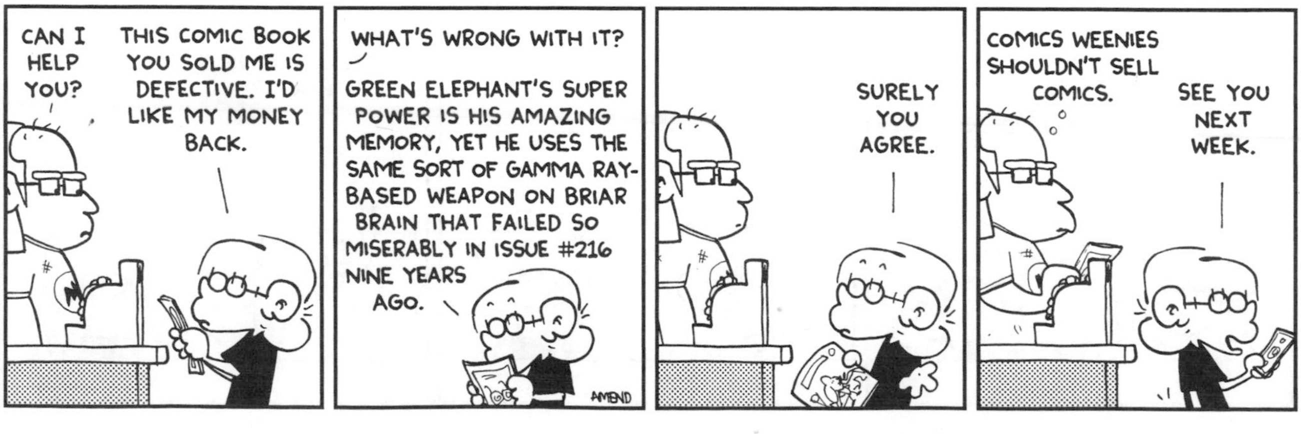
CAN I HELP YOU?
THIS COMIC BOOK YOU SOLD ME IS DEFECTIVE. I'D LIKE MY MONEY BACK.
WHAT'S WRONG WITH IT?
GREEN ELEPHANT'S SUPER POWER IS HIS AMAZING MEMORY, YET HE USES THE SAME SORT OF GAMMA RAY-BASED WEAPON ON BRIAR BRAIN THAT FAILED SO MISERABLY IN ISSUE #216 NINE YEARS AGO.
AMEND
SURELY YOU AGREE.
COMICS WEENIES SHOULDN'T SELL COMICS.
SEE YOU NEXT WEEK.

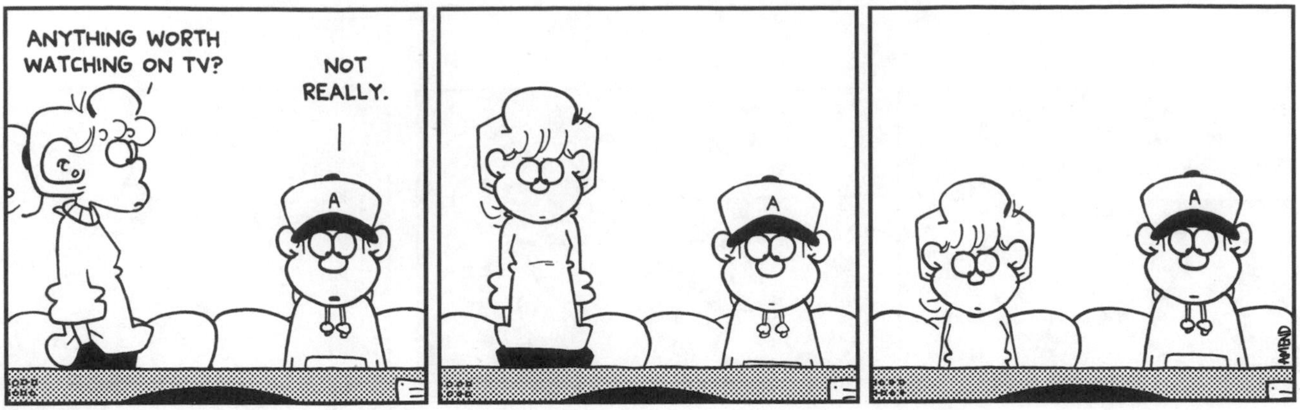
ANYTHING WORTH WATCHING ON TV?
NOT REALLY.
AMEND

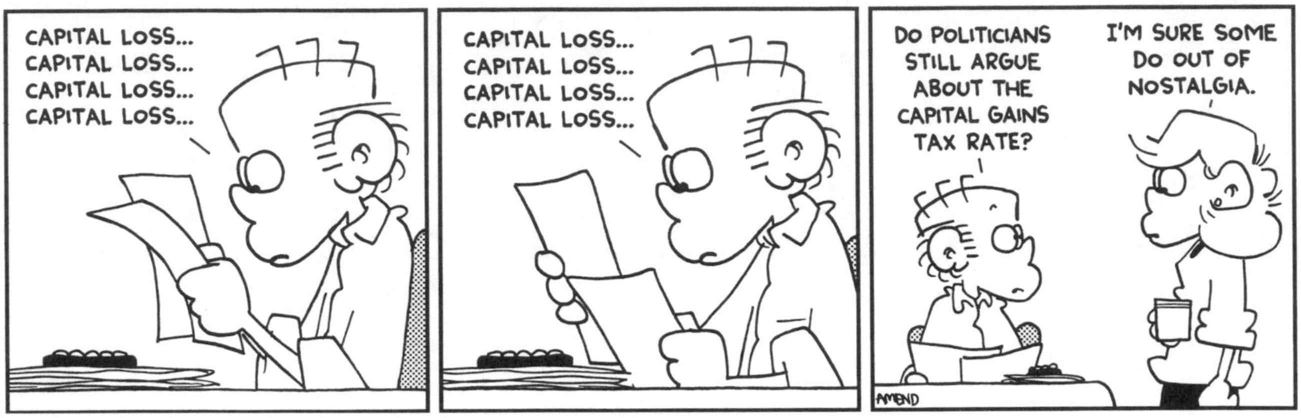
CAPITAL LOSS... CAPITAL LOSS... CAPITAL LOSS... CAPITAL LOSS...
CAPITAL LOSS... CAPITAL LOSS... CAPITAL LOSS... CAPITAL LOSS...
DO POLITICIANS STILL ARGUE ABOUT THE CAPITAL GAINS TAX RATE?
I'M SURE SOME DO OUT OF NOSTALGIA.
AMEND

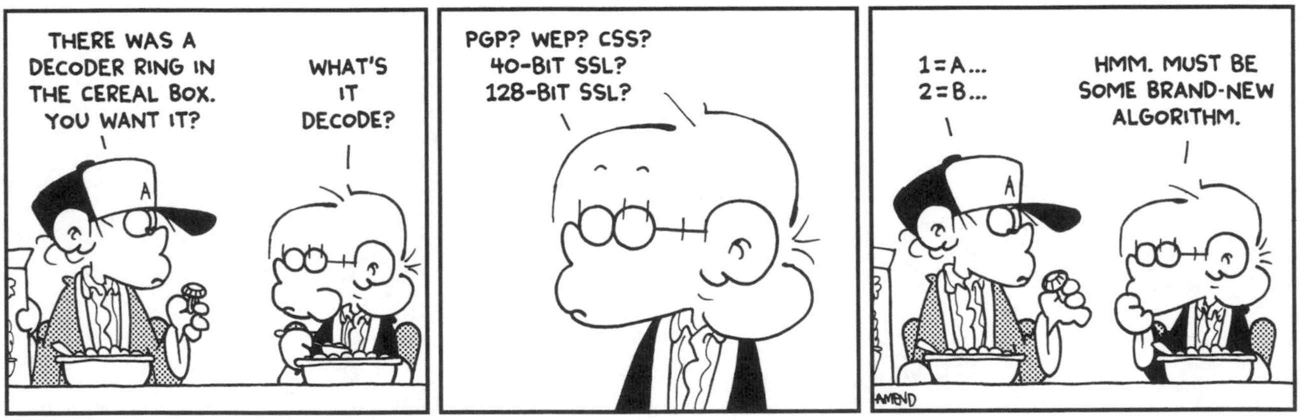
THERE WAS A DECODER RING IN THE CEREAL BOX. YOU WANT IT?
WHAT'S IT DECODE?
PGP? WEP? CSS? 40-BIT SSL? 128-BIT SSL?
1=A... 2=B...
HMM. MUST BE SOME BRAND-NEW ALGORITHM.
AMEND

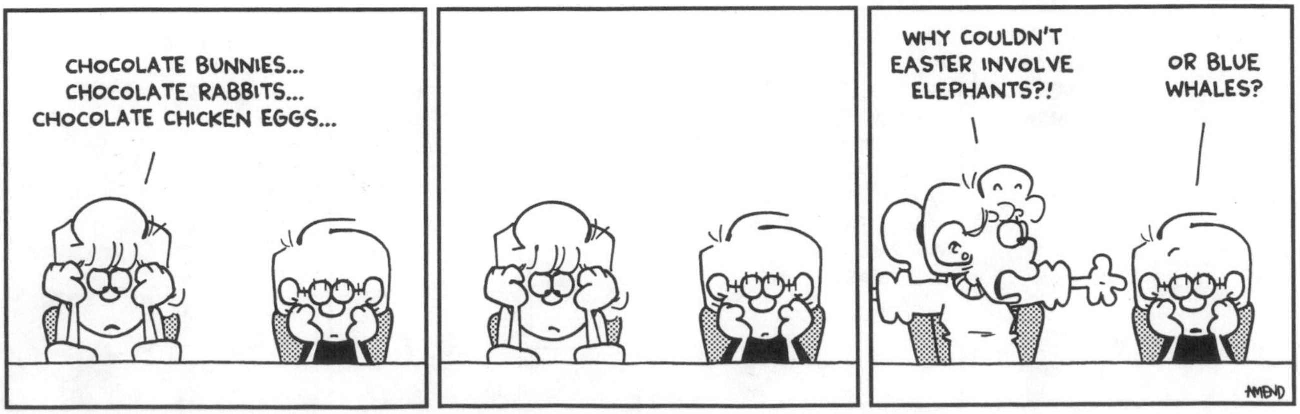
CHOCOLATE BUNNIES... CHOCOLATE RABBITS... CHOCOLATE CHICKEN EGGS...
WHY COULDN'T EASTER INVOLVE ELEPHANTS?!
OR BLUE WHALES?
AMEND

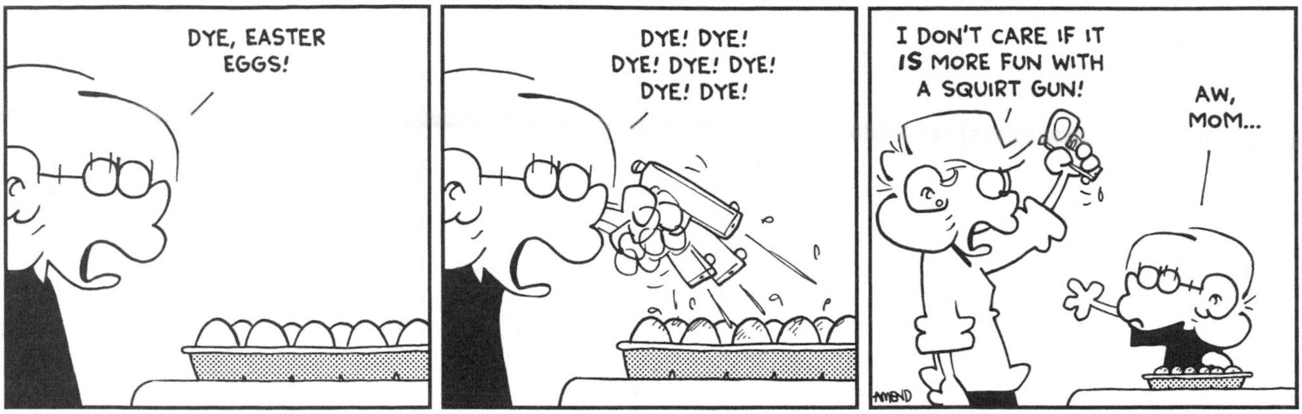
DYE, EASTER EGGS!
DYE! DYE! DYE! DYE! DYE! DYE! DYE!
I DON'T CARE IF IT **IS** MORE FUN WITH A SQUIRT GUN!
AW, MOM...
AMEND

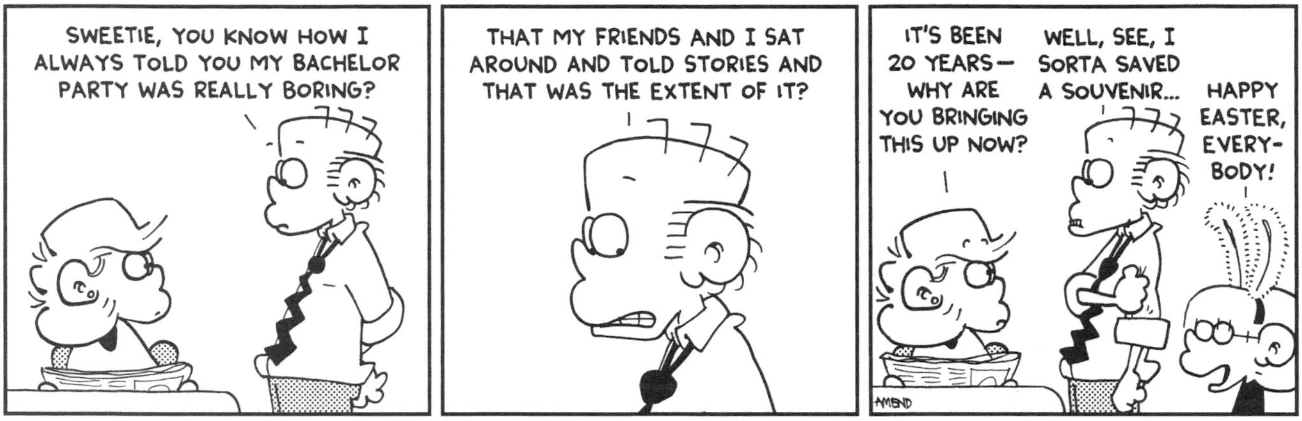
SWEETIE, YOU KNOW HOW I ALWAYS TOLD YOU MY BACHELOR PARTY WAS REALLY BORING?
THAT MY FRIENDS AND I SAT AROUND AND TOLD STORIES AND THAT WAS THE EXTENT OF IT?
IT'S BEEN 20 YEARS— WHY ARE YOU BRINGING THIS UP NOW?
WELL, SEE, I SORTA SAVED A SOUVENIR...
HAPPY EASTER, EVERY-BODY!
AMEND

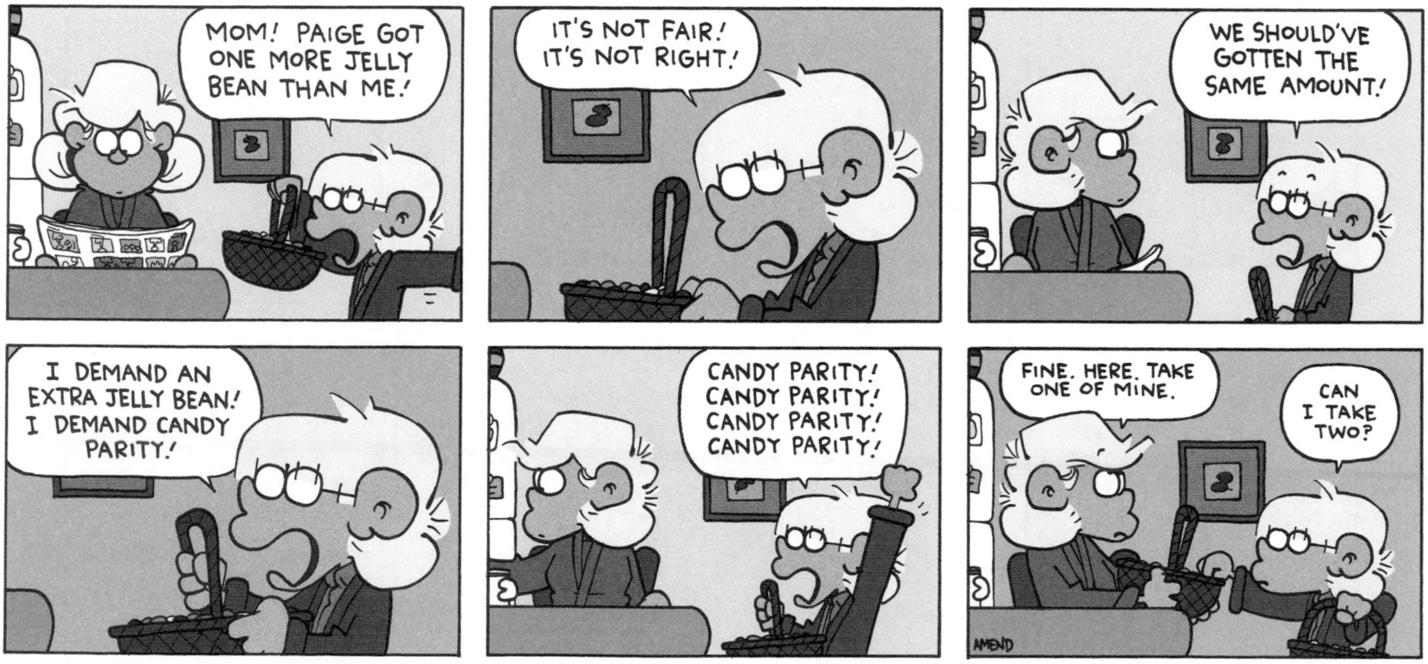
MOM! PAIGE GOT ONE MORE JELLY BEAN THAN ME!
IT'S NOT FAIR! IT'S NOT RIGHT!
WE SHOULD'VE GOTTEN THE SAME AMOUNT!
I DEMAND AN EXTRA JELLY BEAN! I DEMAND CANDY PARITY!
CANDY PARITY! CANDY PARITY! CANDY PARITY! CANDY PARITY!
FINE. HERE. TAKE ONE OF MINE.
CAN I TAKE TWO?
AMEND

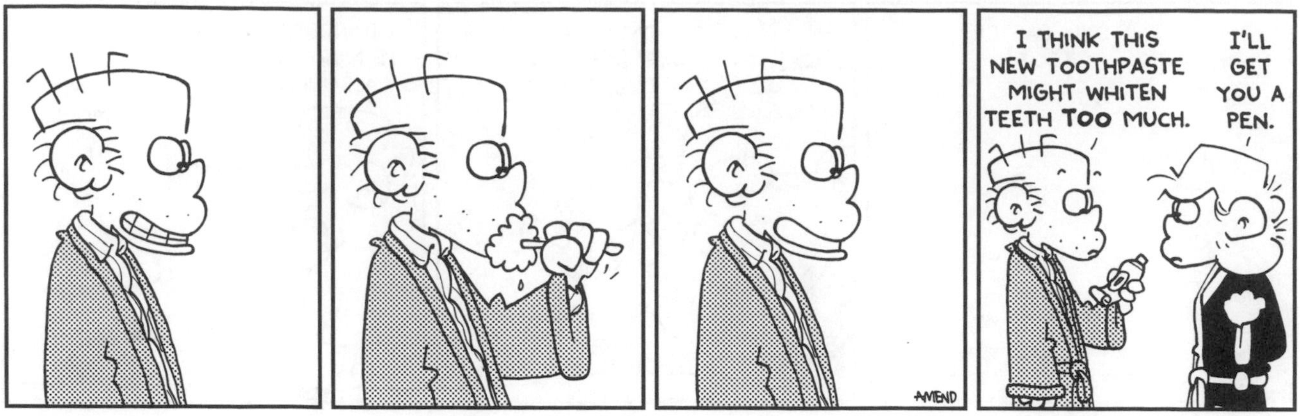
AMEND
I THINK THIS NEW TOOTHPASTE MIGHT WHITEN TEETH **TOO** MUCH.
I'LL GET YOU A PEN.

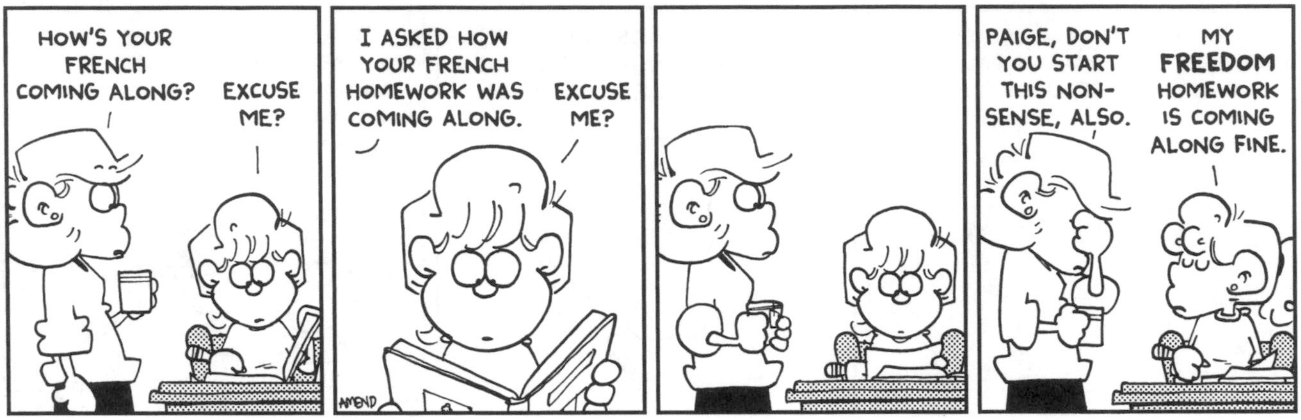
HOW'S YOUR FRENCH COMING ALONG?
EXCUSE ME?
I ASKED HOW YOUR FRENCH HOMEWORK WAS COMING ALONG.
EXCUSE ME?
AMEND
PAIGE, DON'T YOU START THIS NON-SENSE, ALSO.
MY **FREEDOM** HOMEWORK IS COMING ALONG FINE.

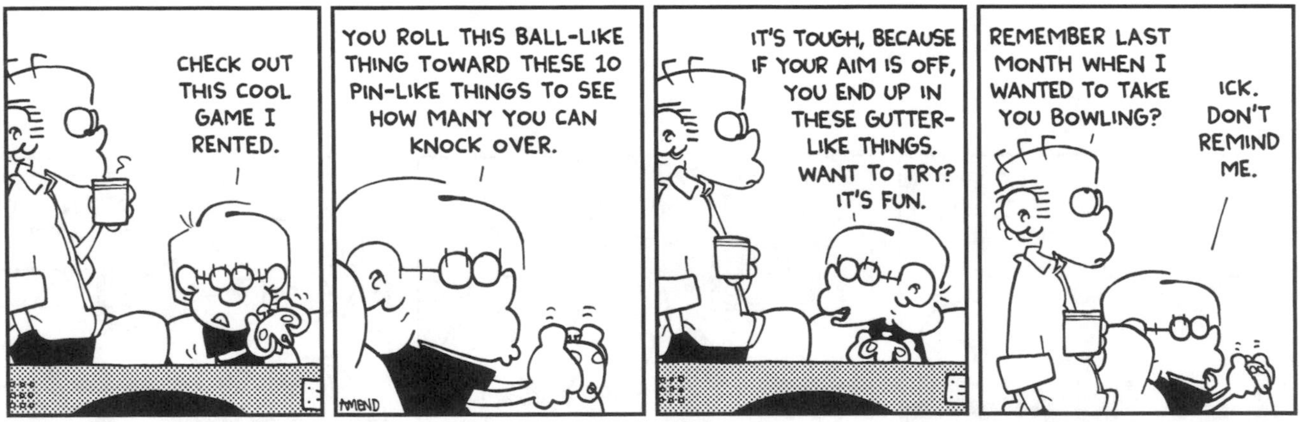
CHECK OUT THIS COOL GAME I RENTED.
YOU ROLL THIS BALL-LIKE THING TOWARD THESE 10 PIN-LIKE THINGS TO SEE HOW MANY YOU CAN KNOCK OVER.
AMEND
IT'S TOUGH, BECAUSE IF YOUR AIM IS OFF, YOU END UP IN THESE GUTTER-LIKE THINGS. WANT TO TRY? IT'S FUN.
REMEMBER LAST MONTH WHEN I WANTED TO TAKE YOU BOWLING?
ICK. DON'T REMIND ME.

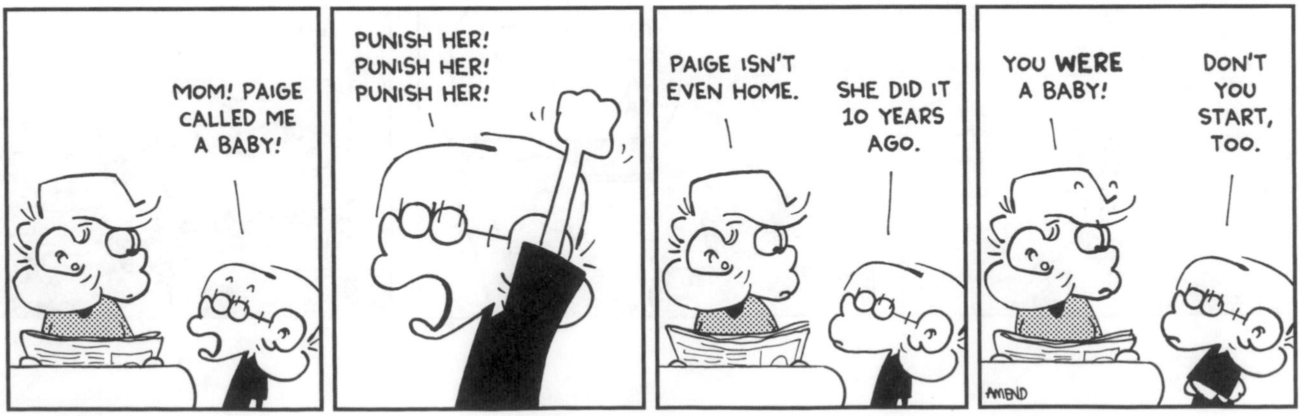
MOM! PAIGE CALLED ME A BABY!
PUNISH HER! PUNISH HER! PUNISH HER!
PAIGE ISN'T EVEN HOME.
SHE DID IT 10 YEARS AGO.
YOU **WERE** A BABY!
DON'T YOU START, TOO.
AMEND

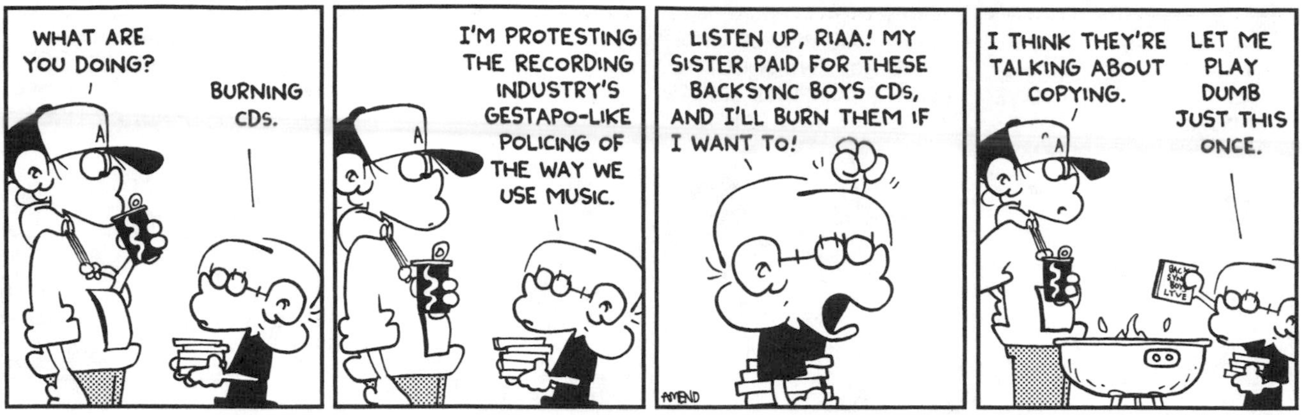
WHAT ARE YOU DOING?
BURNING CDs.
I'M PROTESTING THE RECORDING INDUSTRY'S GESTAPO-LIKE POLICING OF THE WAY WE USE MUSIC.
LISTEN UP, RIAA! MY SISTER PAID FOR THESE BACKSYNC BOYS CDs, AND I'LL BURN THEM IF I WANT TO!
AMEND
I THINK THEY'RE TALKING ABOUT COPYING.
LET ME PLAY DUMB JUST THIS ONCE.

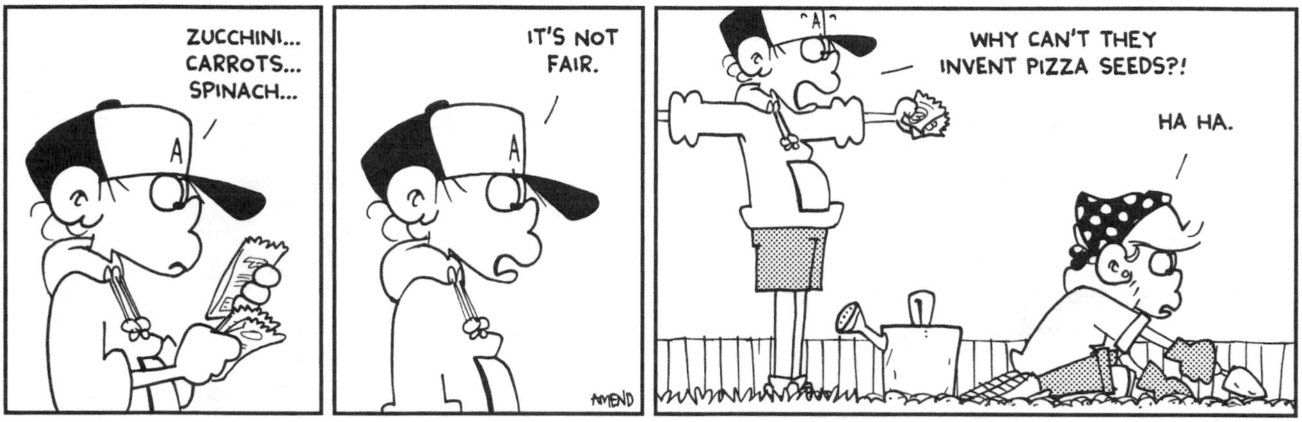
ZUCCHINI... CARROTS... SPINACH...
IT'S NOT FAIR.
AMEND
WHY CAN'T THEY INVENT PIZZA SEEDS?!
HA HA.

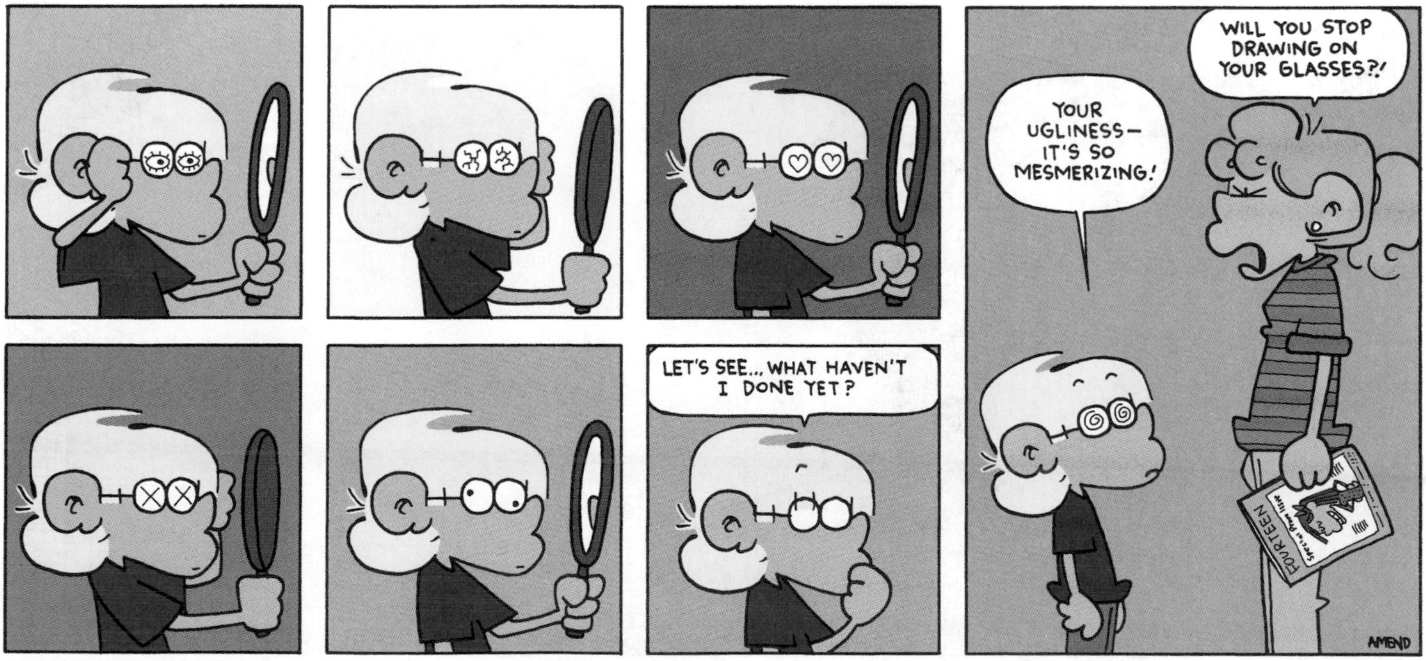
LET'S SEE... WHAT HAVEN'T I DONE YET?
YOUR UGLINESS— IT'S SO MESMERIZING!
WILL YOU STOP DRAWING ON YOUR GLASSES?!
FOURTEEN
AMEND

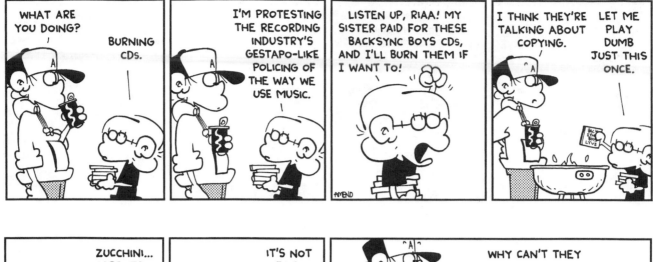

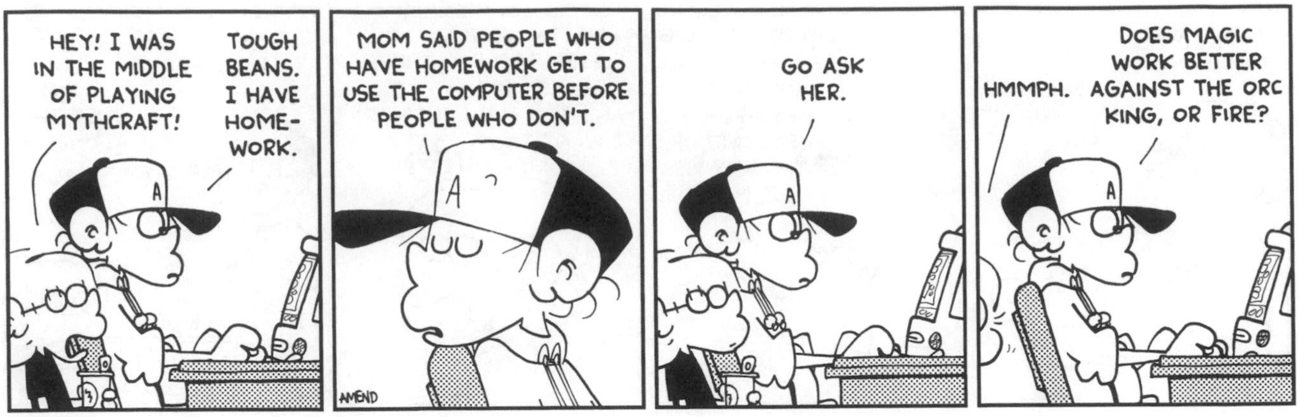
HEY! I WAS IN THE MIDDLE OF PLAYING MYTHCRAFT!
TOUGH BEANS. I HAVE HOME-WORK.
MOM SAID PEOPLE WHO HAVE HOMEWORK GET TO USE THE COMPUTER BEFORE PEOPLE WHO DON'T.
GO ASK HER.
HMMPH.
DOES MAGIC WORK BETTER AGAINST THE ORC KING, OR FIRE?
AMEND

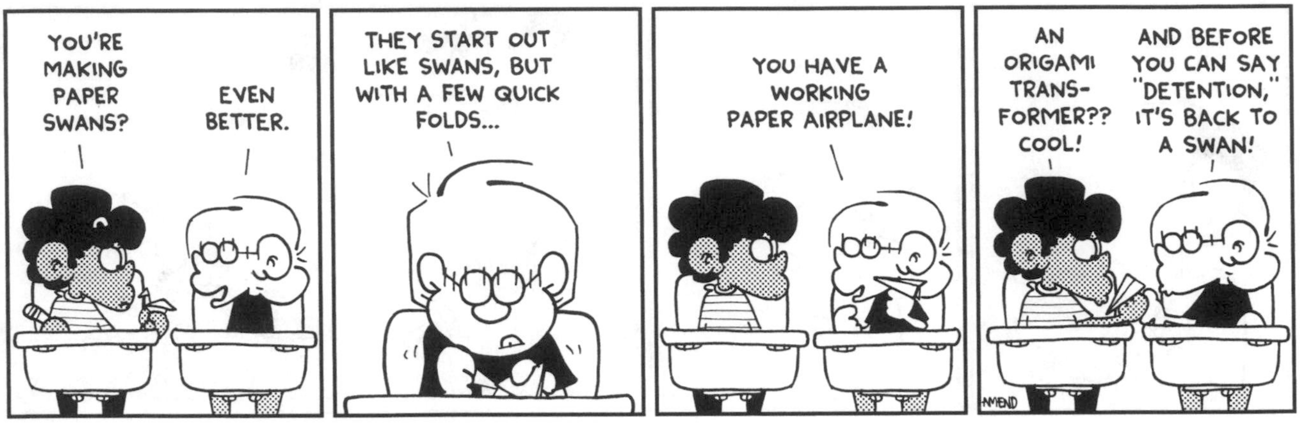
YOU'RE MAKING PAPER SWANS?
EVEN BETTER.
THEY START OUT LIKE SWANS, BUT WITH A FEW QUICK FOLDS...
YOU HAVE A WORKING PAPER AIRPLANE!
AN ORIGAMI TRANS-FORMER?? COOL!
AND BEFORE YOU CAN SAY "DETENTION," IT'S BACK TO A SWAN!
AMEND

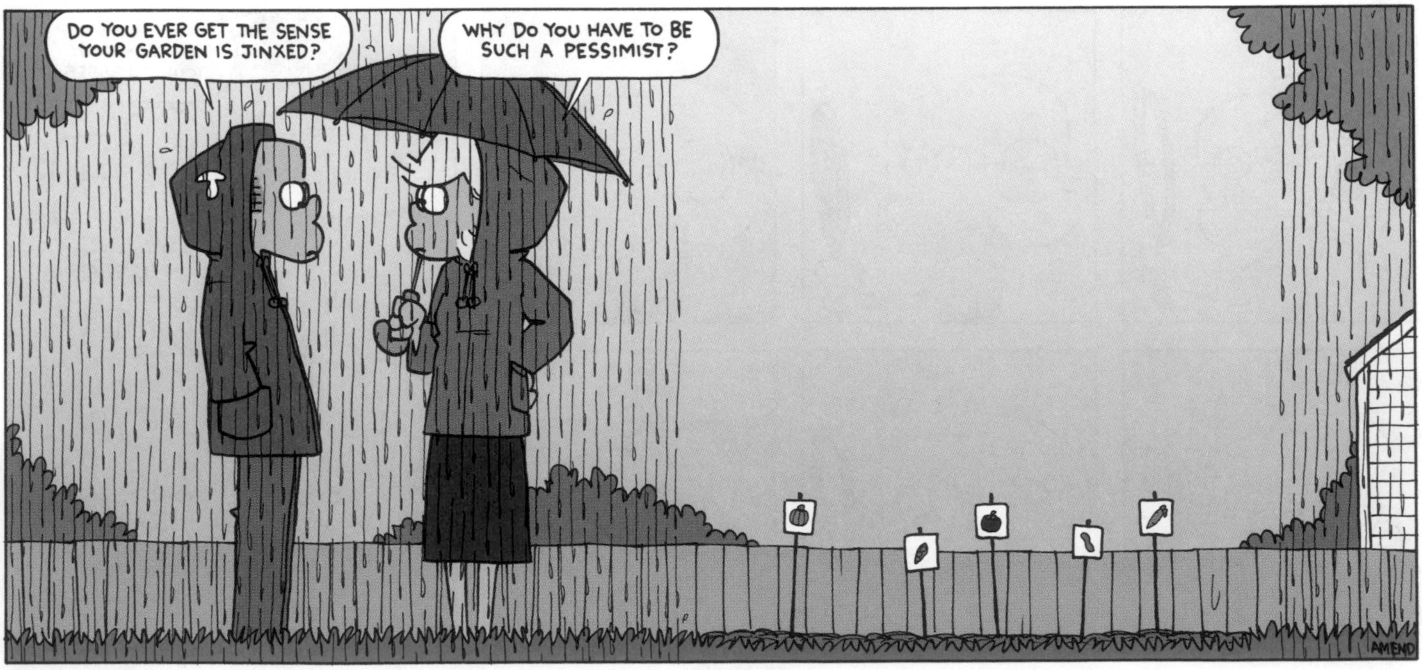
DO YOU EVER GET THE SENSE YOUR GARDEN IS JINXED?
WHY DO YOU HAVE TO BE SUCH A PESSIMIST?
AMEND

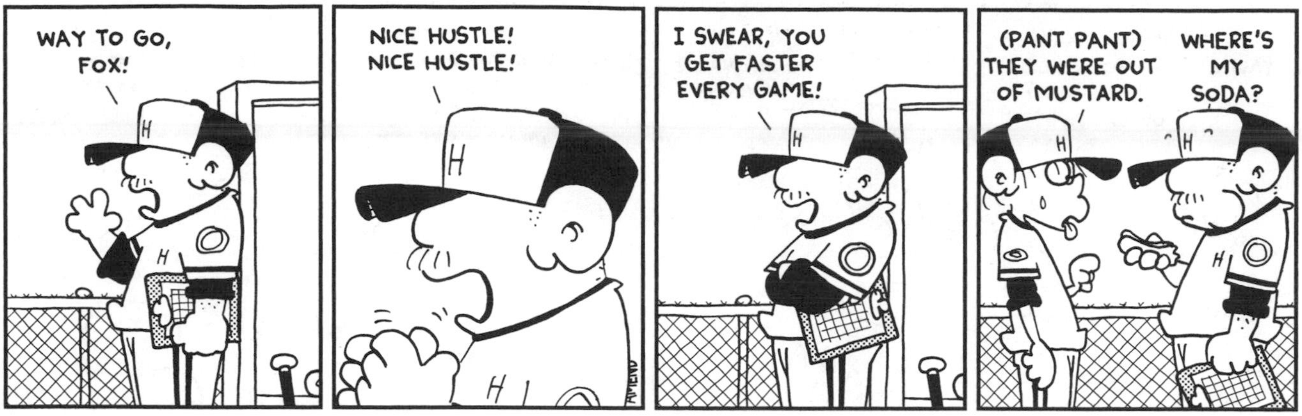
WAY TO GO, FOX!
NICE HUSTLE! NICE HUSTLE!
I SWEAR, YOU GET FASTER EVERY GAME!
(PANT PANT) THEY WERE OUT OF MUSTARD.
WHERE'S MY SODA?
AMEND

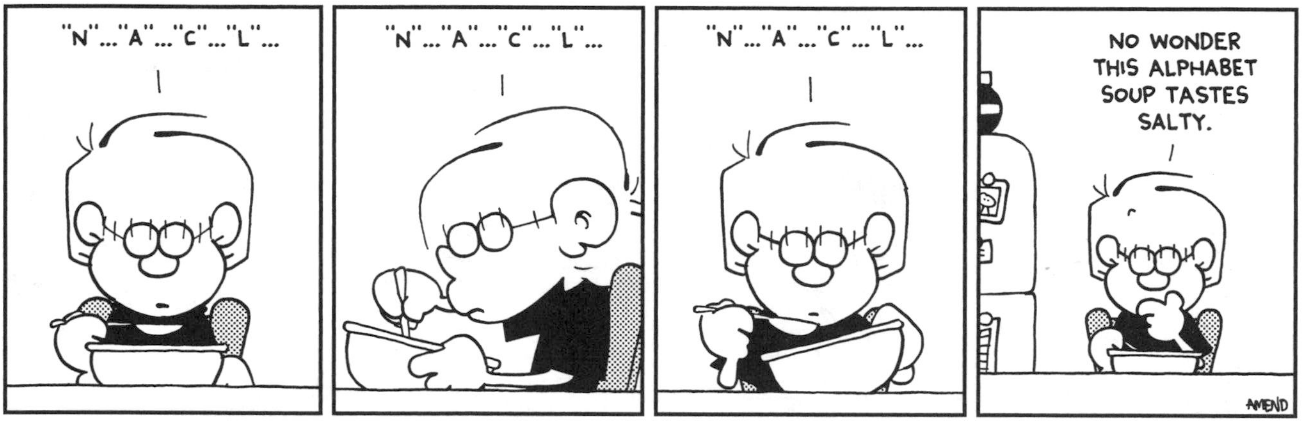
"N"..."A"..."C"..."L"...
"N"..."A"..."C"..."L"...
"N"..."A"..."C"..."L"...
NO WONDER THIS ALPHABET SOUP TASTES SALTY.
AMEND

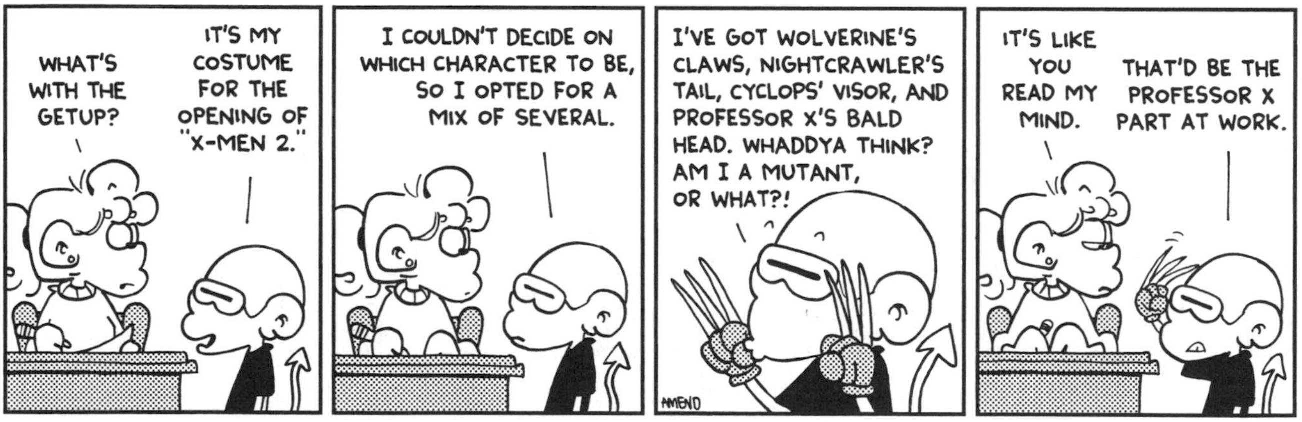
WHAT'S WITH THE GETUP?
IT'S MY COSTUME FOR THE OPENING OF "X-MEN 2."
I COULDN'T DECIDE ON WHICH CHARACTER TO BE, SO I OPTED FOR A MIX OF SEVERAL.
I'VE GOT WOLVERINE'S CLAWS, NIGHTCRAWLER'S TAIL, CYCLOPS' VISOR, AND PROFESSOR X'S BALD HEAD. WHADDYA THINK? AM I A MUTANT, OR WHAT?!
AMEND
IT'S LIKE YOU READ MY MIND.
THAT'D BE THE PROFESSOR X PART AT WORK.

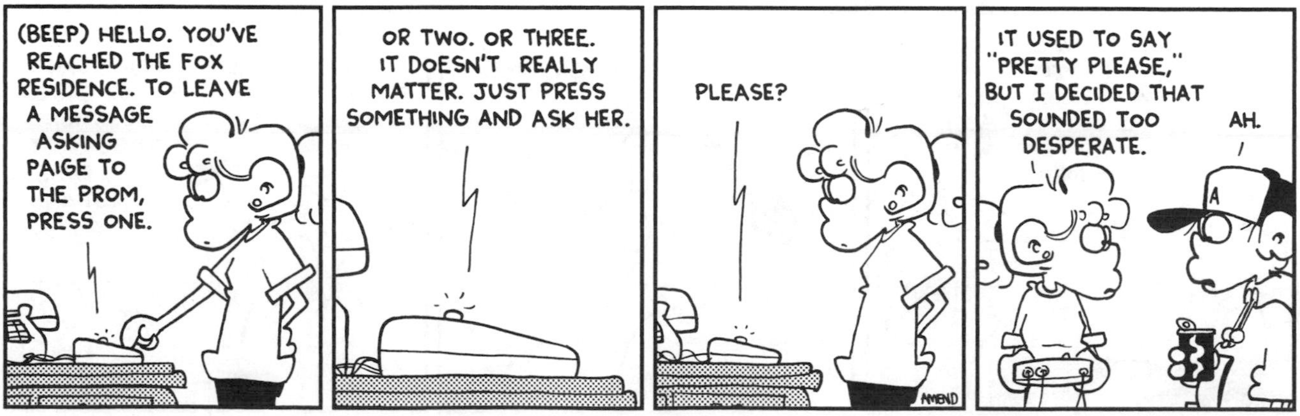
(BEEP) HELLO. YOU'VE REACHED THE FOX RESIDENCE. TO LEAVE A MESSAGE ASKING PAIGE TO THE PROM, PRESS ONE.
OR TWO. OR THREE. IT DOESN'T REALLY MATTER. JUST PRESS SOMETHING AND ASK HER.
PLEASE?
AMEND
IT USED TO SAY "PRETTY PLEASE," BUT I DECIDED THAT SOUNDED TOO DESPERATE.
AH.

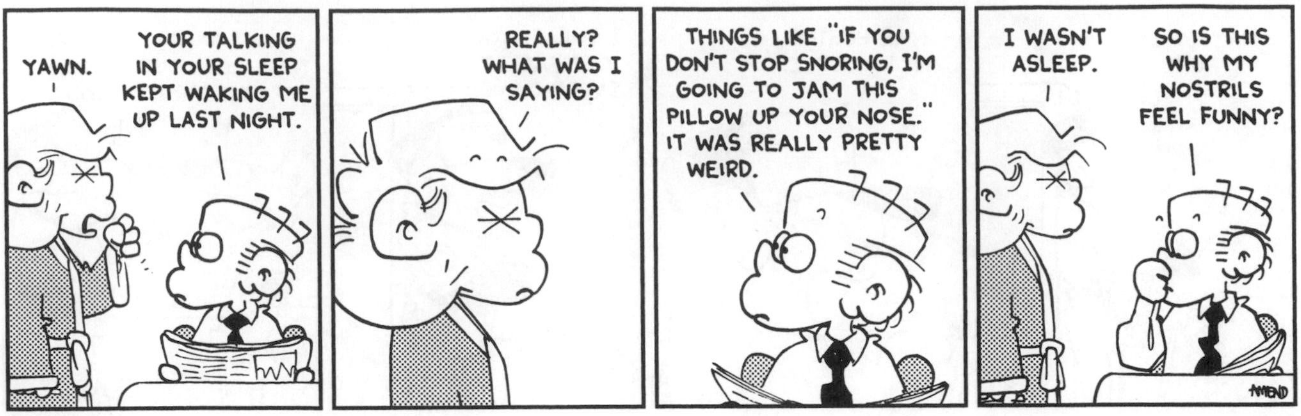
YAWN.
YOUR TALKING IN YOUR SLEEP KEPT WAKING ME UP LAST NIGHT.
REALLY? WHAT WAS I SAYING?
THINGS LIKE "IF YOU DON'T STOP SNORING, I'M GOING TO JAM THIS PILLOW UP YOUR NOSE." IT WAS REALLY PRETTY WEIRD.
I WASN'T ASLEEP.
SO IS THIS WHY MY NOSTRILS FEEL FUNNY?
AMEND

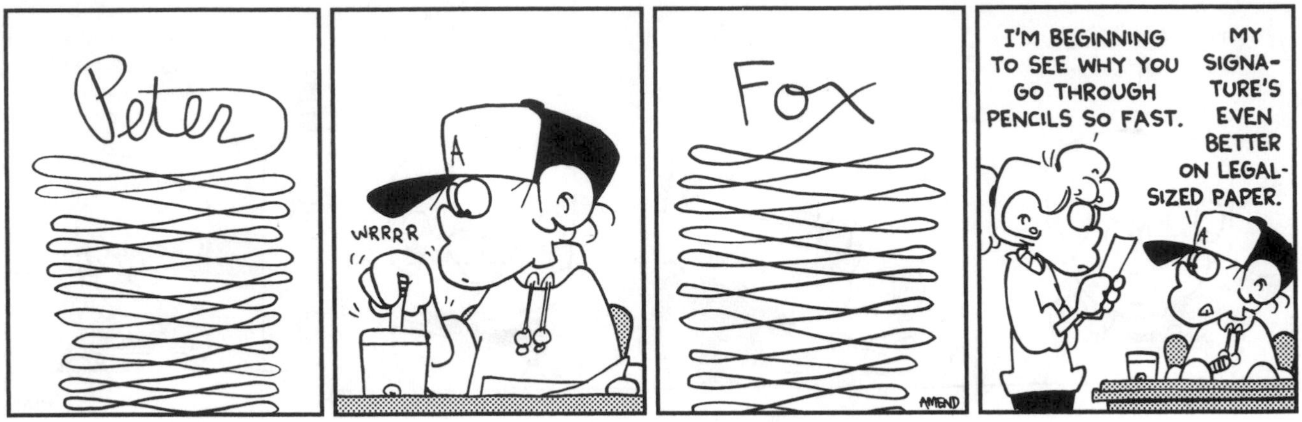
Peter
WRRRR
Fox
AMEND
I'M BEGINNING TO SEE WHY YOU GO THROUGH PENCILS SO FAST.
MY SIGNATURE'S EVEN BETTER ON LEGAL-SIZED PAPER.

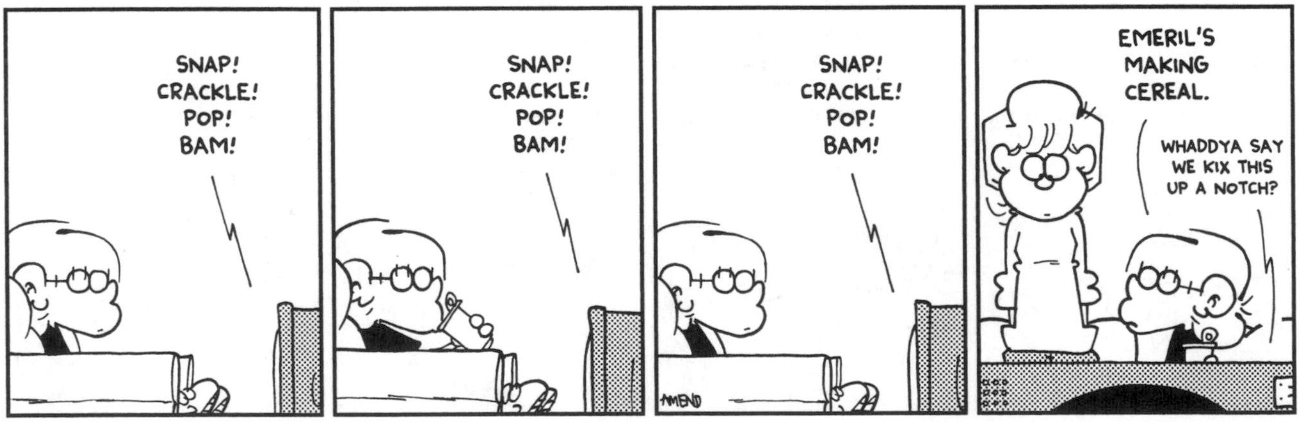
SNAP! CRACKLE! POP! BAM!
SNAP! CRACKLE! POP! BAM!
SNAP! CRACKLE! POP! BAM!
AMEND
EMERIL'S MAKING CEREAL.
WHADDYA SAY WE KIX THIS UP A NOTCH?

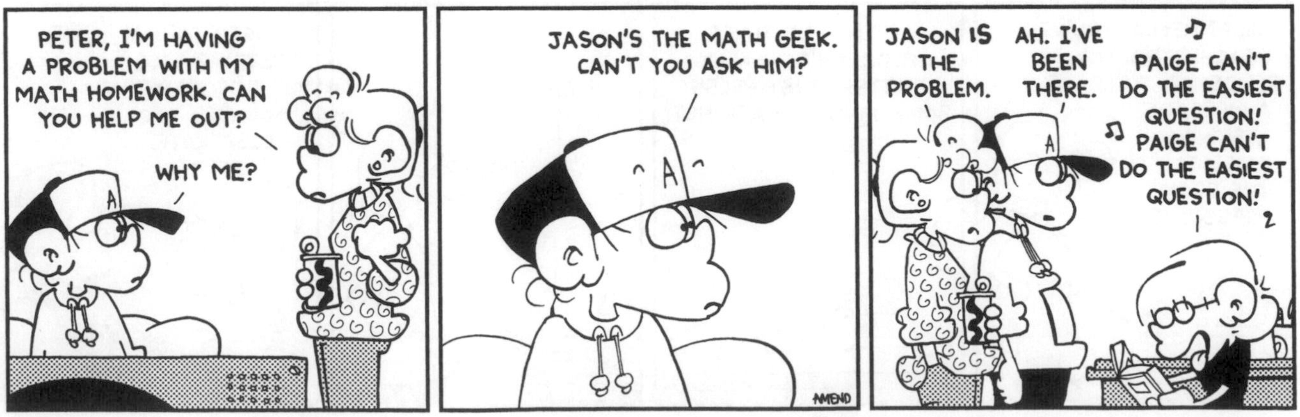
PETER, I'M HAVING A PROBLEM WITH MY MATH HOMEWORK. CAN YOU HELP ME OUT?
WHY ME?
JASON'S THE MATH GEEK. CAN'T YOU ASK HIM?
AMEND
JASON IS THE PROBLEM.
AH. I'VE BEEN THERE.
PAIGE CAN'T DO THE EASIEST QUESTION! PAIGE CAN'T DO THE EASIEST QUESTION!

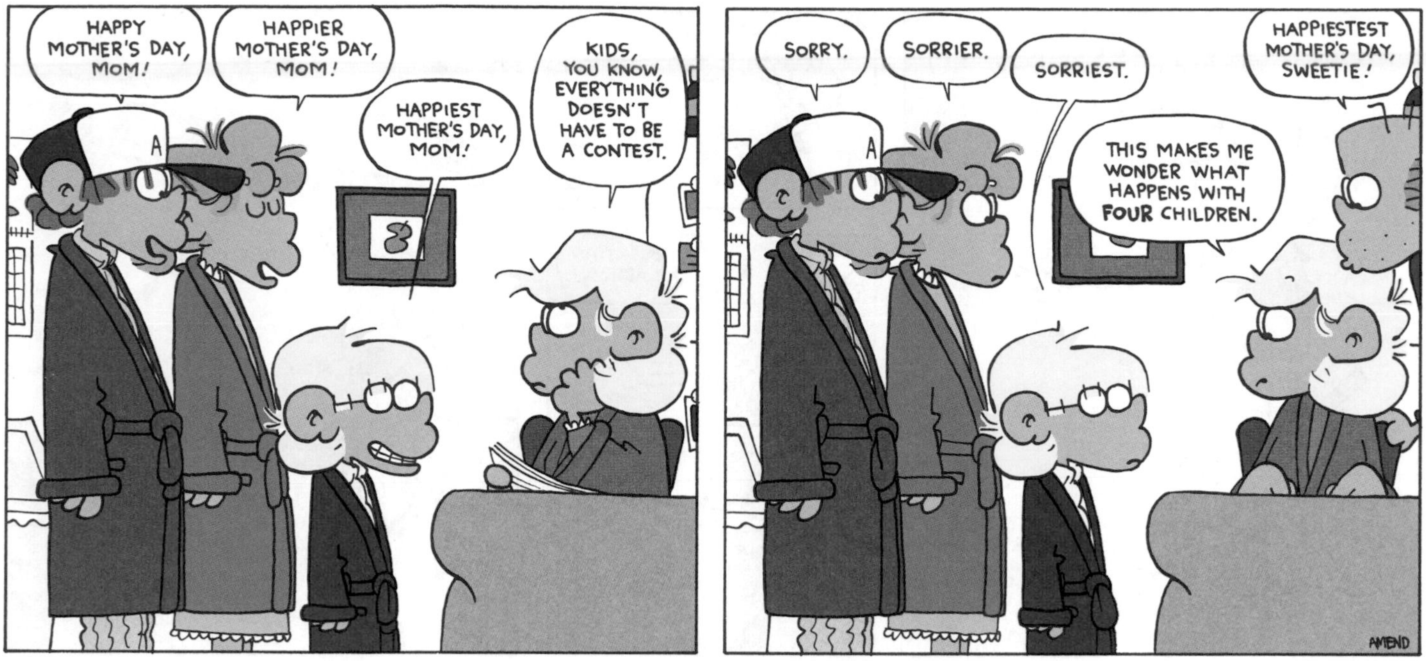
HAPPY MOTHER'S DAY, MOM!
HAPPIER MOTHER'S DAY, MOM!
HAPPIEST MOTHER'S DAY, MOM!
KIDS, YOU KNOW, EVERYTHING DOESN'T HAVE TO BE A CONTEST.
SORRY.
SORRIER.
SORRIEST.
HAPPIESTEST MOTHER'S DAY, SWEETIE!
THIS MAKES ME WONDER WHAT HAPPENS WITH **FOUR** CHILDREN.
AMEND

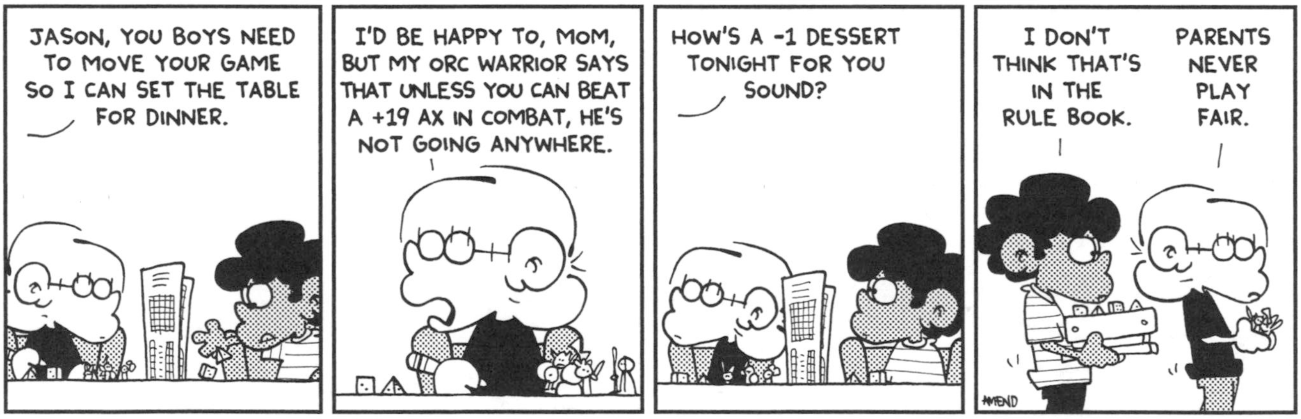
JASON, YOU BOYS NEED TO MOVE YOUR GAME SO I CAN SET THE TABLE FOR DINNER.
I'D BE HAPPY TO, MOM, BUT MY ORC WARRIOR SAYS THAT UNLESS YOU CAN BEAT A +19 AX IN COMBAT, HE'S NOT GOING ANYWHERE.
HOW'S A -1 DESSERT TONIGHT FOR YOU SOUND?
I DON'T THINK THAT'S IN THE RULE BOOK.
PARENTS NEVER PLAY FAIR.
AMEND

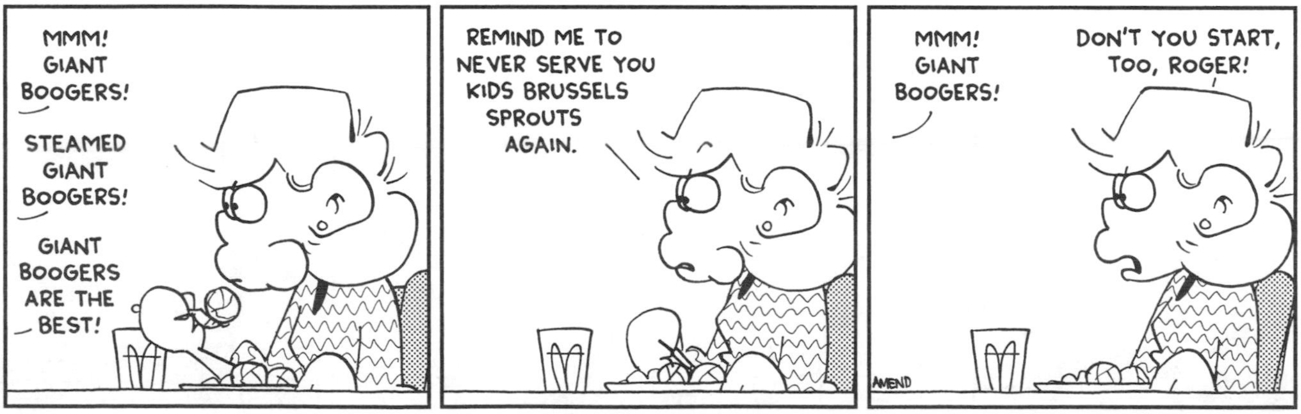
MMM! GIANT BOOGERS!
STEAMED GIANT BOOGERS!
GIANT BOOGERS ARE THE BEST!
REMIND ME TO NEVER SERVE YOU KIDS BRUSSELS SPROUTS AGAIN.
MMM! GIANT BOOGERS!
DON'T YOU START, TOO, ROGER!
AMEND

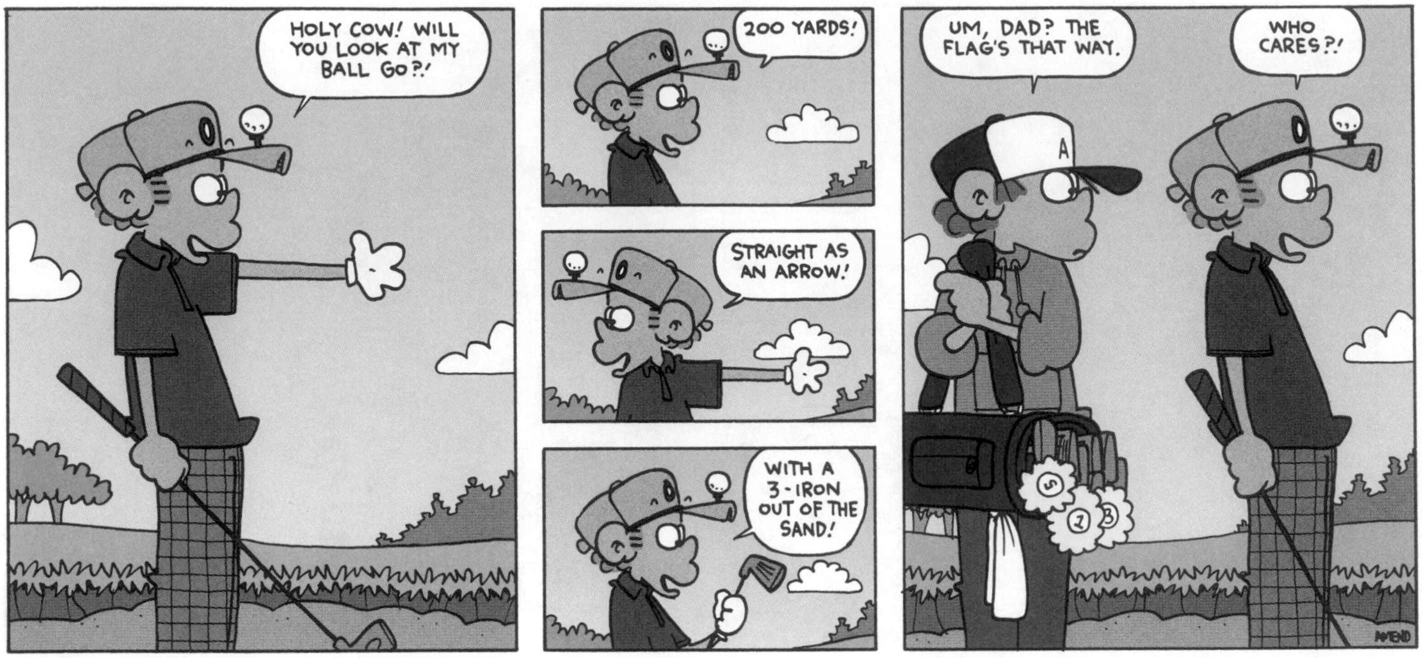
HOLY COW! WILL YOU LOOK AT MY BALL GO?!
200 YARDS!
STRAIGHT AS AN ARROW!
WITH A 3-IRON OUT OF THE SAND!
UM, DAD? THE FLAG'S THAT WAY.
WHO CARES?!
AMEND

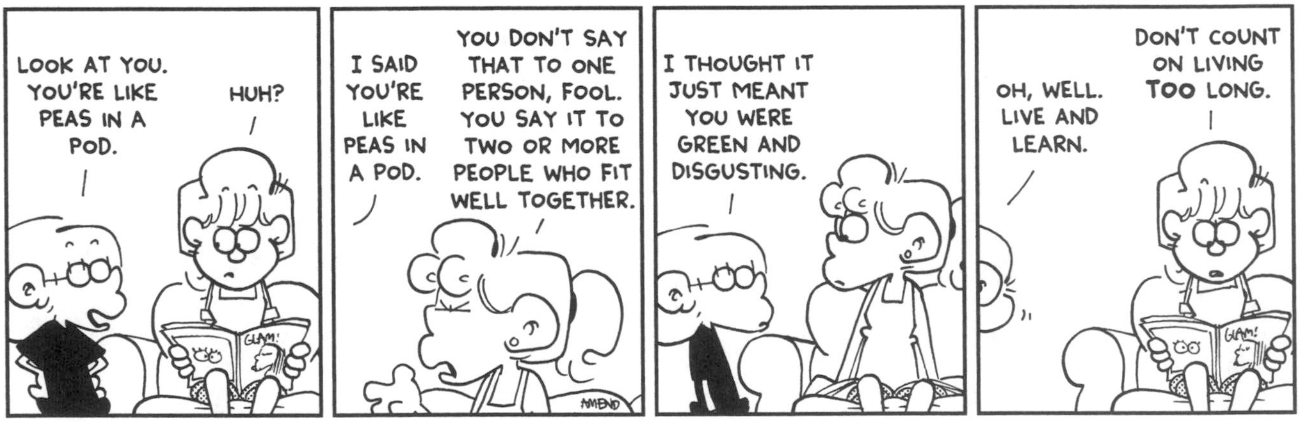
LOOK AT YOU. YOU'RE LIKE PEAS IN A POD.
HUH?
I SAID YOU'RE LIKE PEAS IN A POD.
YOU DON'T SAY THAT TO ONE PERSON, FOOL. YOU SAY IT TO TWO OR MORE PEOPLE WHO FIT WELL TOGETHER.
AMEND
I THOUGHT IT JUST MEANT YOU WERE GREEN AND DISGUSTING.
OH, WELL. LIVE AND LEARN.
DON'T COUNT ON LIVING TOO LONG.

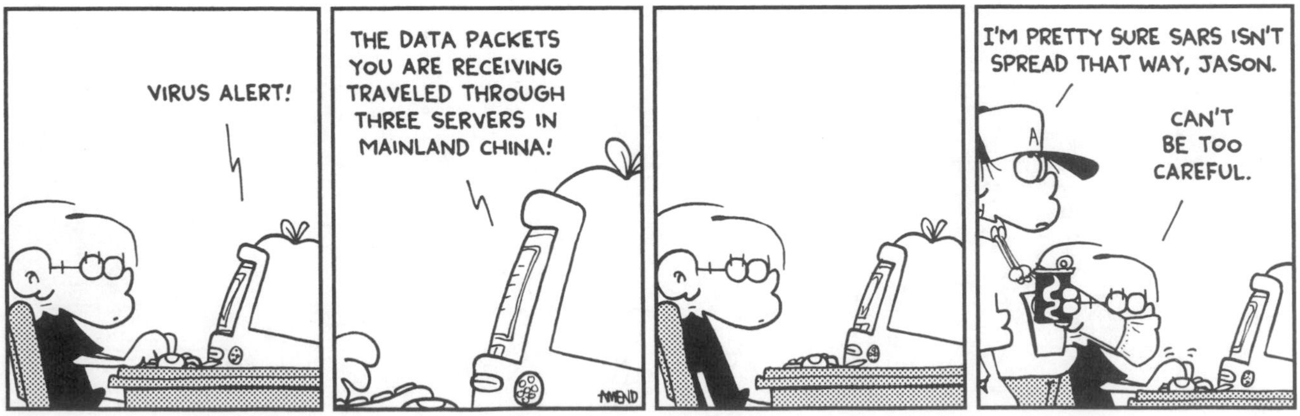
VIRUS ALERT!
THE DATA PACKETS YOU ARE RECEIVING TRAVELED THROUGH THREE SERVERS IN MAINLAND CHINA!
AMEND
I'M PRETTY SURE SARS ISN'T SPREAD THAT WAY, JASON.
CAN'T BE TOO CAREFUL.

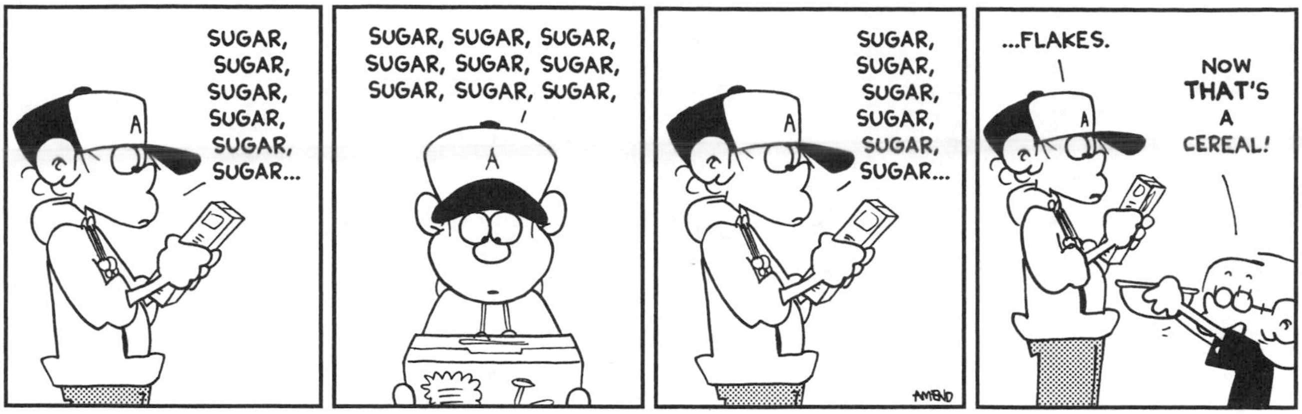
SUGAR, SUGAR, SUGAR, SUGAR, SUGAR, SUGAR...
SUGAR, SUGAR, SUGAR, SUGAR, SUGAR, SUGAR, SUGAR, SUGAR, SUGAR,
SUGAR, SUGAR, SUGAR, SUGAR, SUGAR, SUGAR...
...FLAKES.
NOW THAT'S A CEREAL!

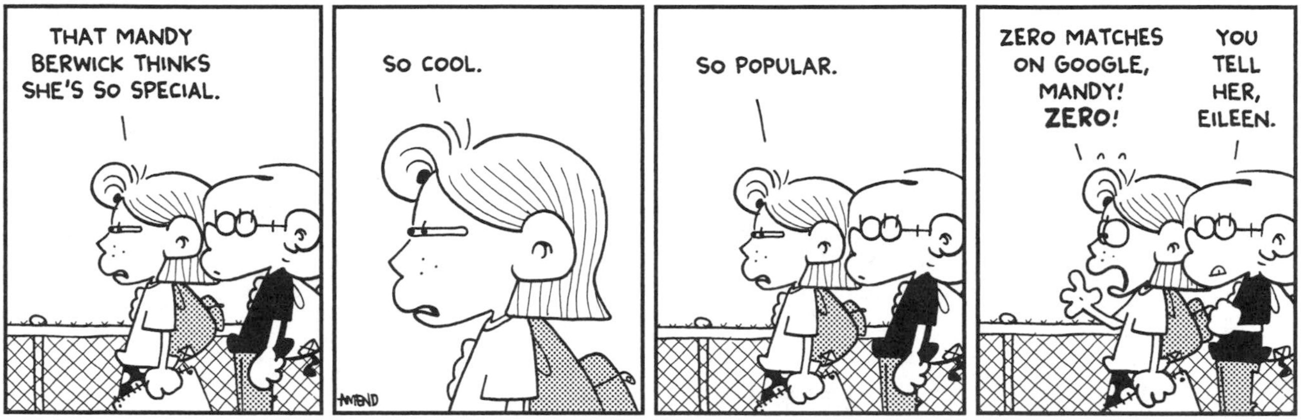
THAT MANDY BERWICK THINKS SHE'S SO SPECIAL.
SO COOL.
SO POPULAR.
ZERO MATCHES ON GOOGLE, MANDY! ZERO!
YOU TELL HER, EILEEN.

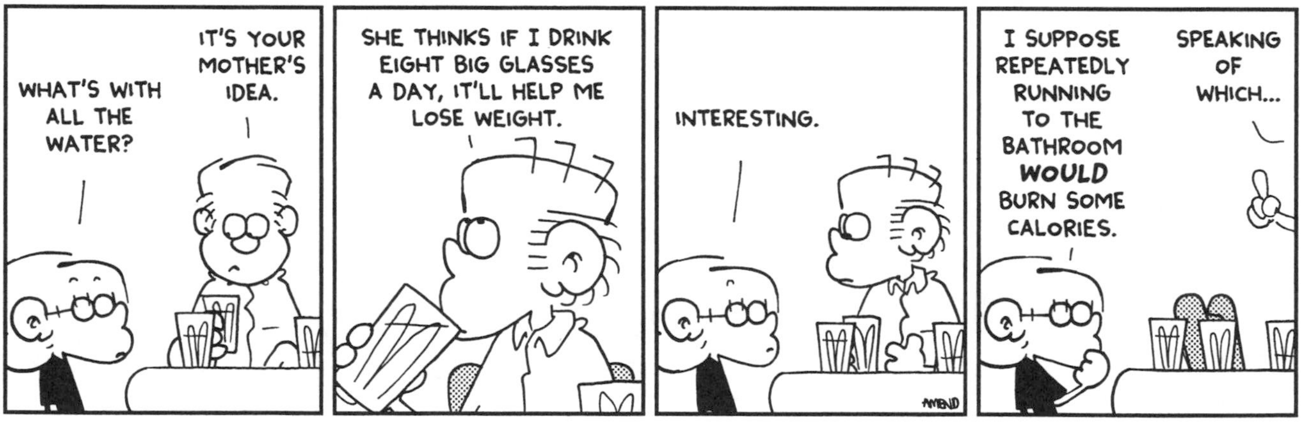
WHAT'S WITH ALL THE WATER?
IT'S YOUR MOTHER'S IDEA.
SHE THINKS IF I DRINK EIGHT BIG GLASSES A DAY, IT'LL HELP ME LOSE WEIGHT.
INTERESTING.
I SUPPOSE REPEATEDLY RUNNING TO THE BATHROOM WOULD BURN SOME CALORIES.
SPEAKING OF WHICH...

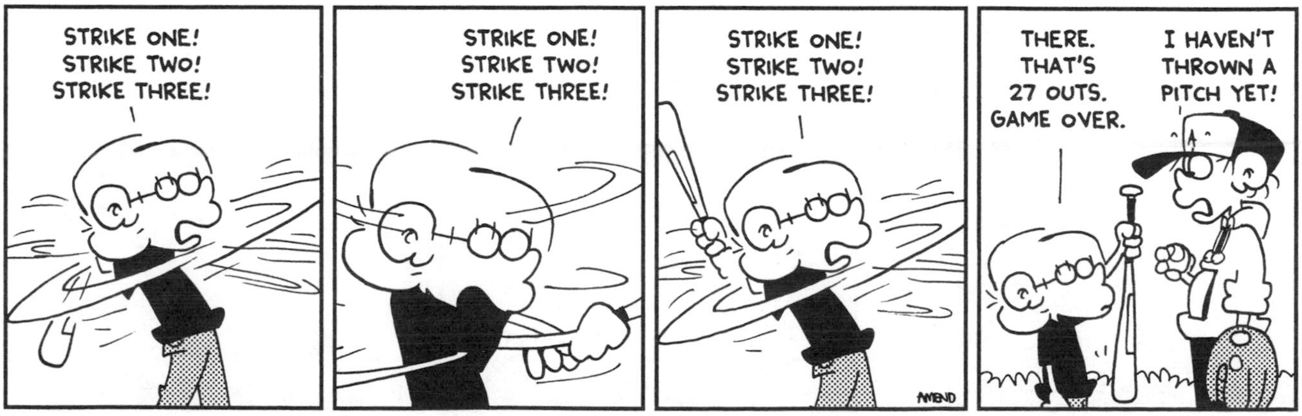
STRIKE ONE! STRIKE TWO! STRIKE THREE!
STRIKE ONE! STRIKE TWO! STRIKE THREE!
STRIKE ONE! STRIKE TWO! STRIKE THREE!
THERE. THAT'S 27 OUTS. GAME OVER.
I HAVEN'T THROWN A PITCH YET!

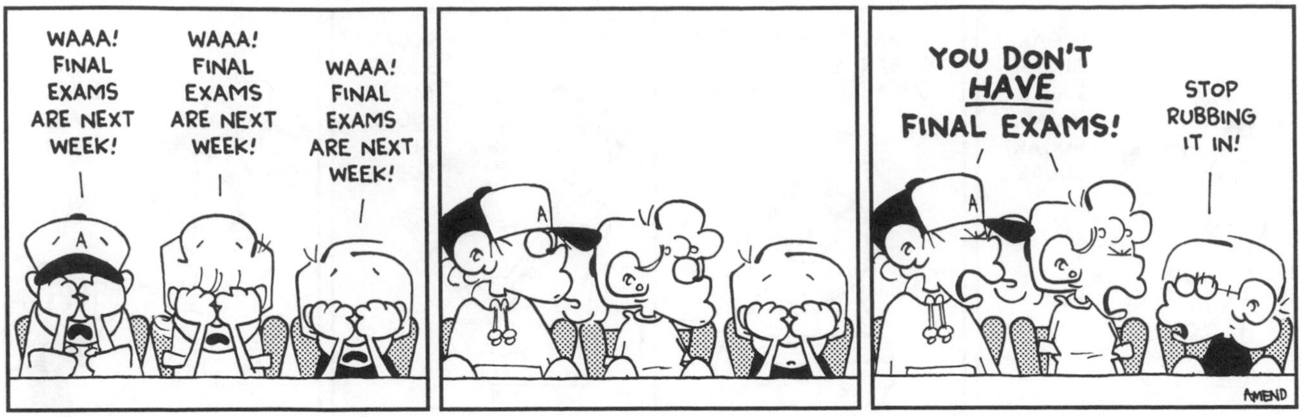
WAAA! FINAL EXAMS ARE NEXT WEEK!
WAAA! FINAL EXAMS ARE NEXT WEEK!
WAAA! FINAL EXAMS ARE NEXT WEEK!
YOU DON'T HAVE FINAL EXAMS!
STOP RUBBING IT IN!
AMEND

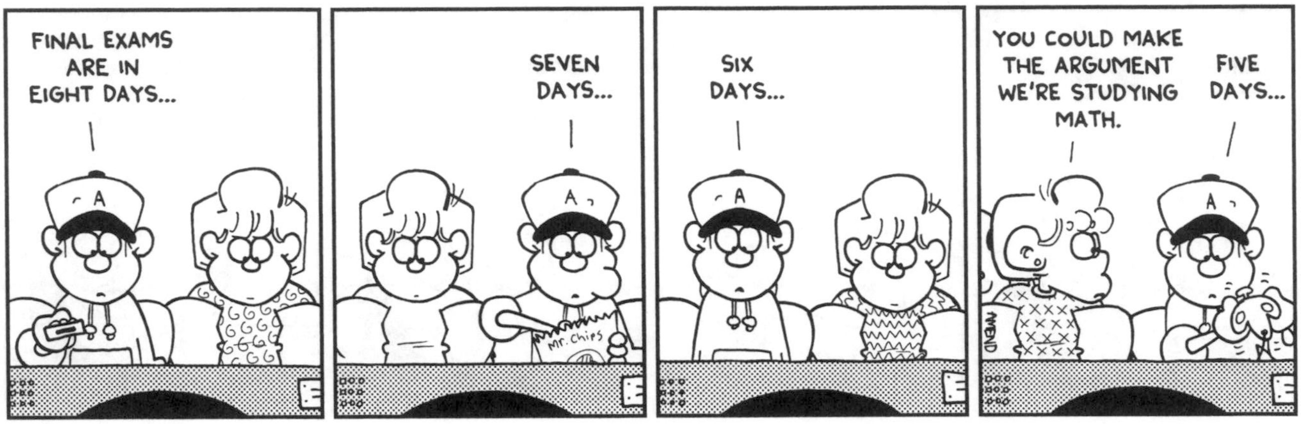
FINAL EXAMS ARE IN EIGHT DAYS...
SEVEN DAYS...
Mr. Chips
SIX DAYS...
YOU COULD MAKE THE ARGUMENT WE'RE STUDYING MATH.
FIVE DAYS...
AMEND

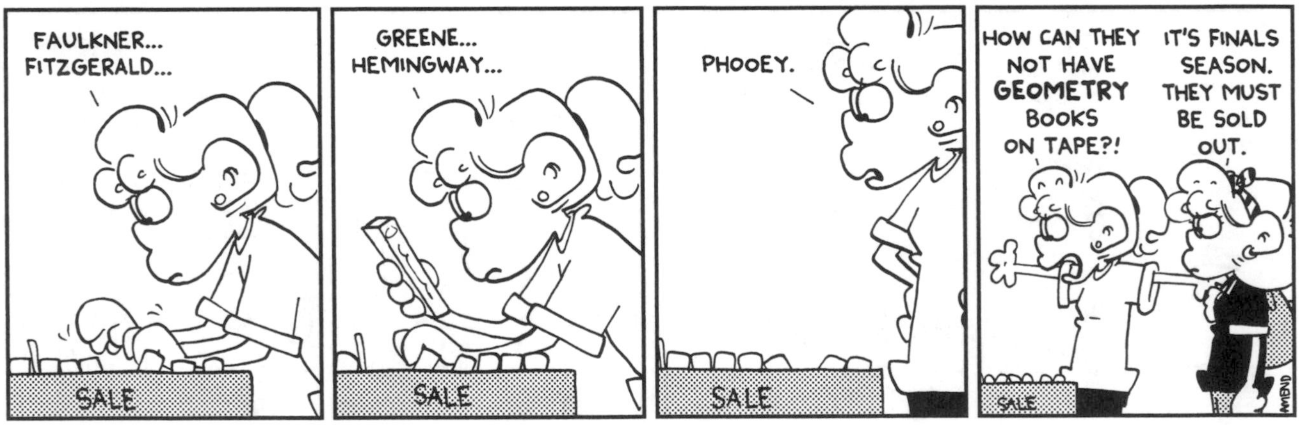
FAULKNER... FITZGERALD...
SALE
GREENE... HEMINGWAY...
SALE
PHOOEY.
SALE
HOW CAN THEY NOT HAVE GEOMETRY BOOKS ON TAPE?!
IT'S FINALS SEASON. THEY MUST BE SOLD OUT.
SALE
AMEND

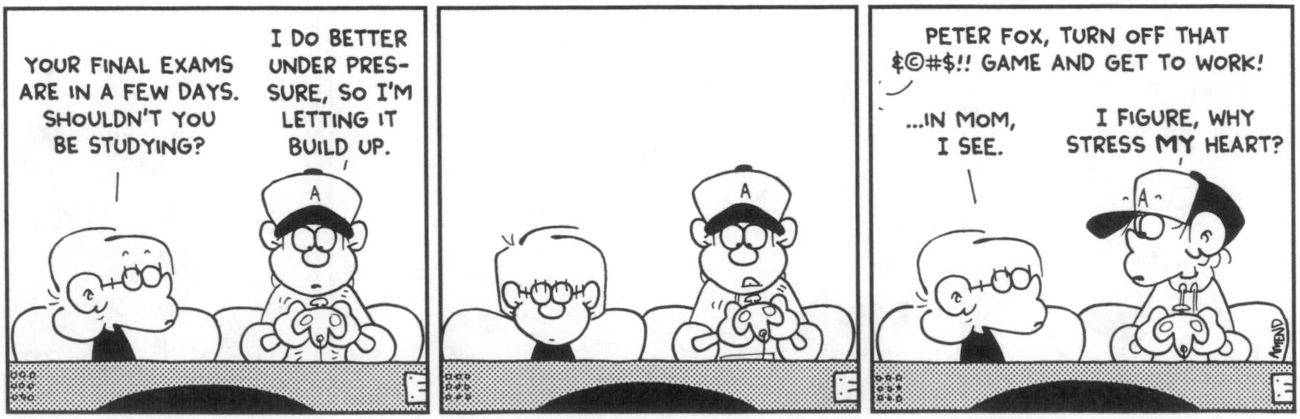
YOUR FINAL EXAMS ARE IN A FEW DAYS. SHOULDN'T YOU BE STUDYING?
I DO BETTER UNDER PRES-SURE, SO I'M LETTING IT BUILD UP.
PETER FOX, TURN OFF THAT $©#$!! GAME AND GET TO WORK!
...IN MOM, I SEE.
I FIGURE, WHY STRESS MY HEART?
AMEND

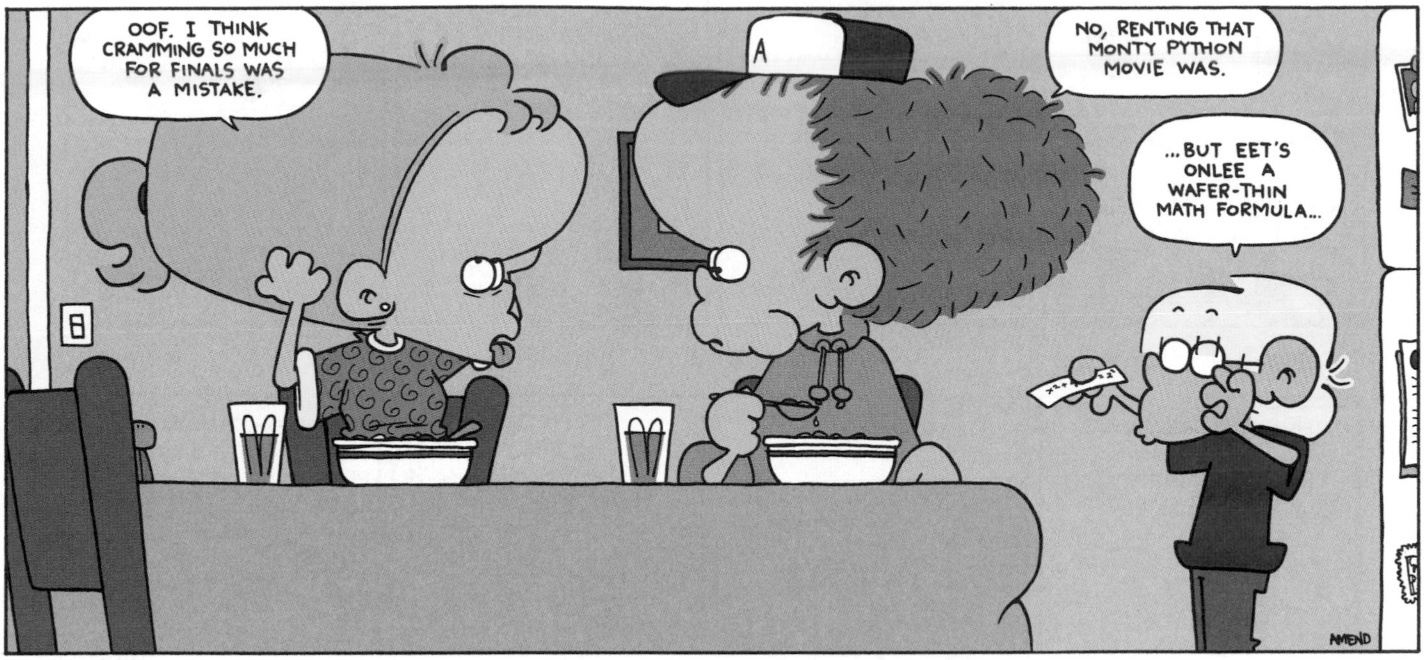
OOF. I THINK CRAMMING SO MUCH FOR FINALS WAS A MISTAKE.
NO, RENTING THAT MONTY PYTHON MOVIE WAS.
...BUT EET'S ONLEE A WAFER-THIN MATH FORMULA...
AMEND

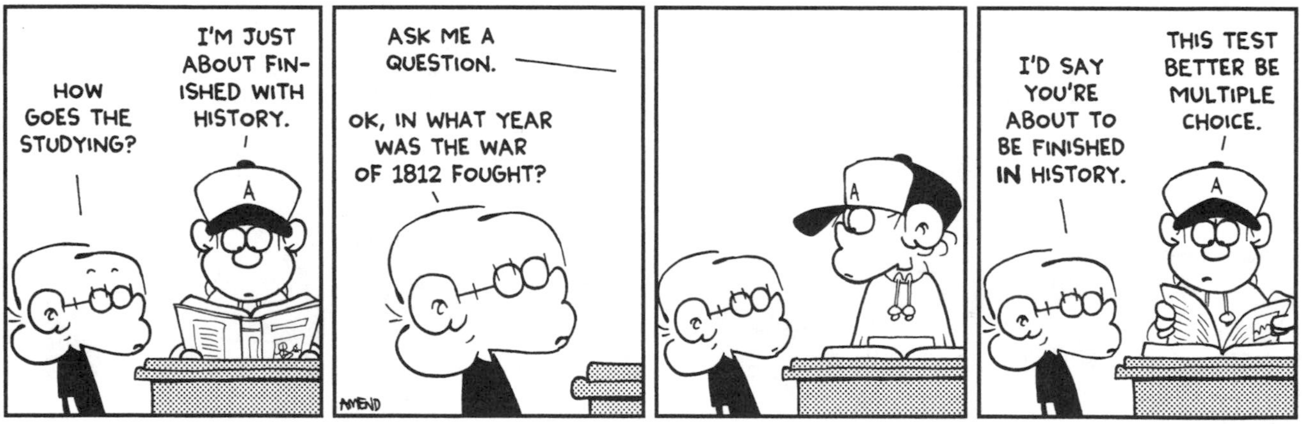
HOW GOES THE STUDYING?
I'M JUST ABOUT FIN-ISHED WITH HISTORY.
ASK ME A QUESTION.
OK, IN WHAT YEAR WAS THE WAR OF 1812 FOUGHT?
AMEND
I'D SAY YOU'RE ABOUT TO BE FINISHED IN HISTORY.
THIS TEST BETTER BE MULTIPLE CHOICE.

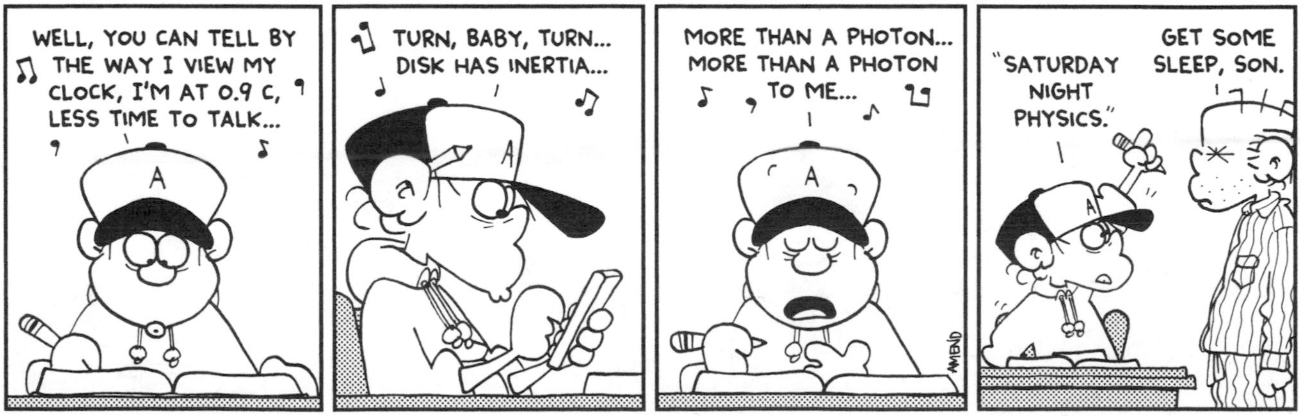
WELL, YOU CAN TELL BY THE WAY I VIEW MY CLOCK, I'M AT 0.9 C, LESS TIME TO TALK...
TURN, BABY, TURN... DISK HAS INERTIA...
MORE THAN A PHOTON... MORE THAN A PHOTON TO ME...
AMEND
"SATURDAY NIGHT PHYSICS."
GET SOME SLEEP, SON.

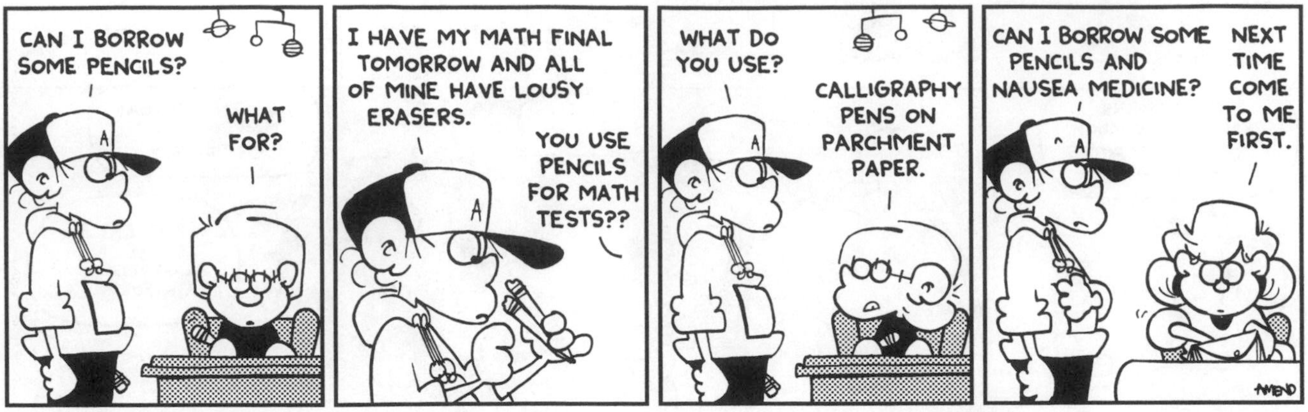
CAN I BORROW SOME PENCILS?
WHAT FOR?
I HAVE MY MATH FINAL TOMORROW AND ALL OF MINE HAVE LOUSY ERASERS.
YOU USE PENCILS FOR MATH TESTS??
WHAT DO YOU USE?
CALLIGRAPHY PENS ON PARCHMENT PAPER.
CAN I BORROW SOME PENCILS AND NAUSEA MEDICINE?
NEXT TIME COME TO ME FIRST.

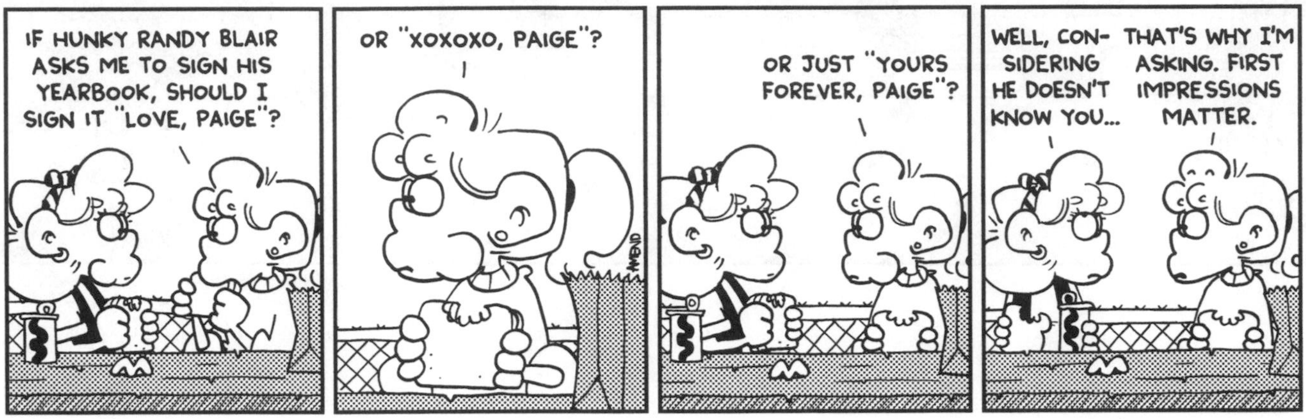
IF HUNKY RANDY BLAIR ASKS ME TO SIGN HIS YEARBOOK, SHOULD I SIGN IT "LOVE, PAIGE"?
OR "XOXOXO, PAIGE"?
OR JUST "YOURS FOREVER, PAIGE"?
WELL, CONSIDERING HE DOESN'T KNOW YOU...
THAT'S WHY I'M ASKING. FIRST IMPRESSIONS MATTER.

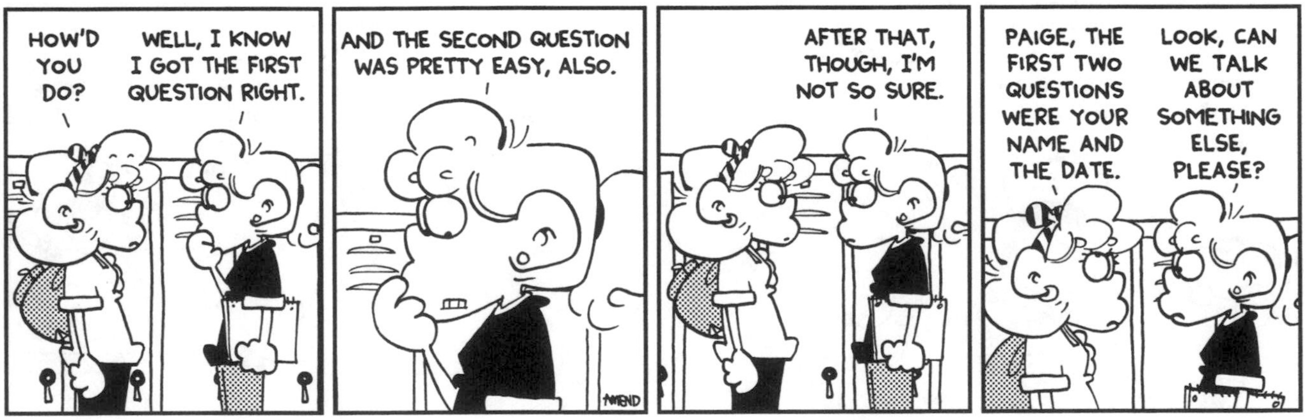
HOW'D YOU DO?
WELL, I KNOW I GOT THE FIRST QUESTION RIGHT.
AND THE SECOND QUESTION WAS PRETTY EASY, ALSO.
AFTER THAT, THOUGH, I'M NOT SO SURE.
PAIGE, THE FIRST TWO QUESTIONS WERE YOUR NAME AND THE DATE.
LOOK, CAN WE TALK ABOUT SOMETHING ELSE, PLEASE?

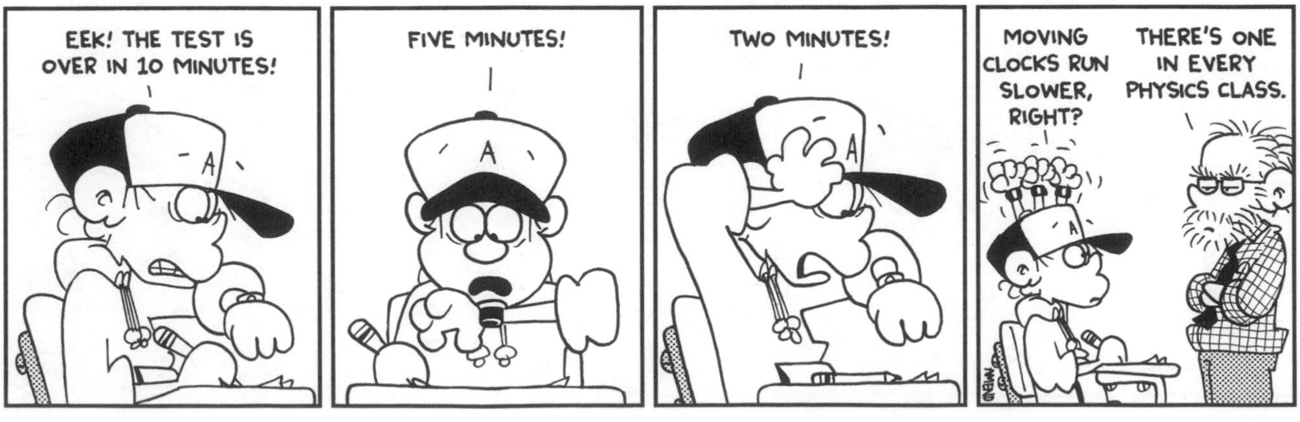
EEK! THE TEST IS OVER IN 10 MINUTES!
FIVE MINUTES!
TWO MINUTES!
MOVING CLOCKS RUN SLOWER, RIGHT?
THERE'S ONE IN EVERY PHYSICS CLASS.

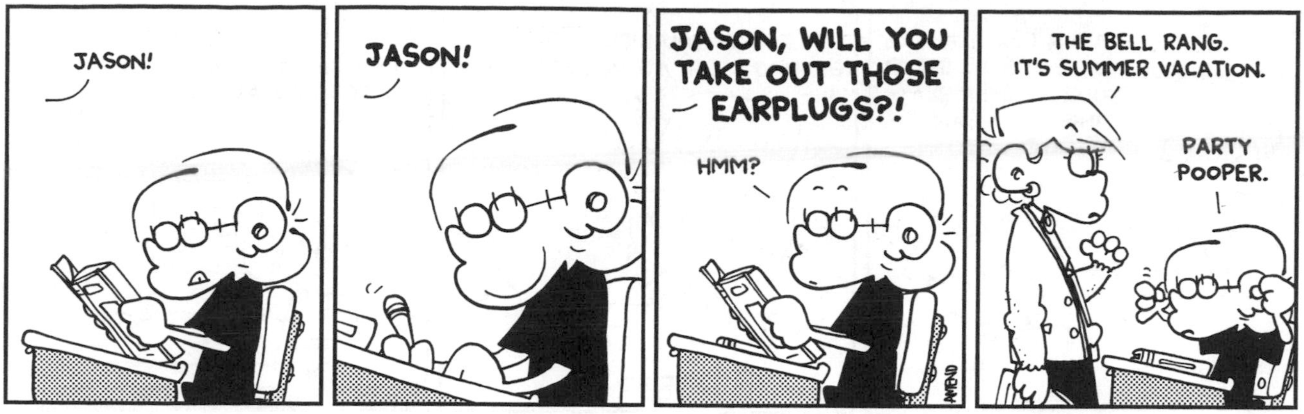
JASON!
JASON!
JASON, WILL YOU TAKE OUT THOSE EARPLUGS?!
HMM?
THE BELL RANG. IT'S SUMMER VACATION.
PARTY POOPER.

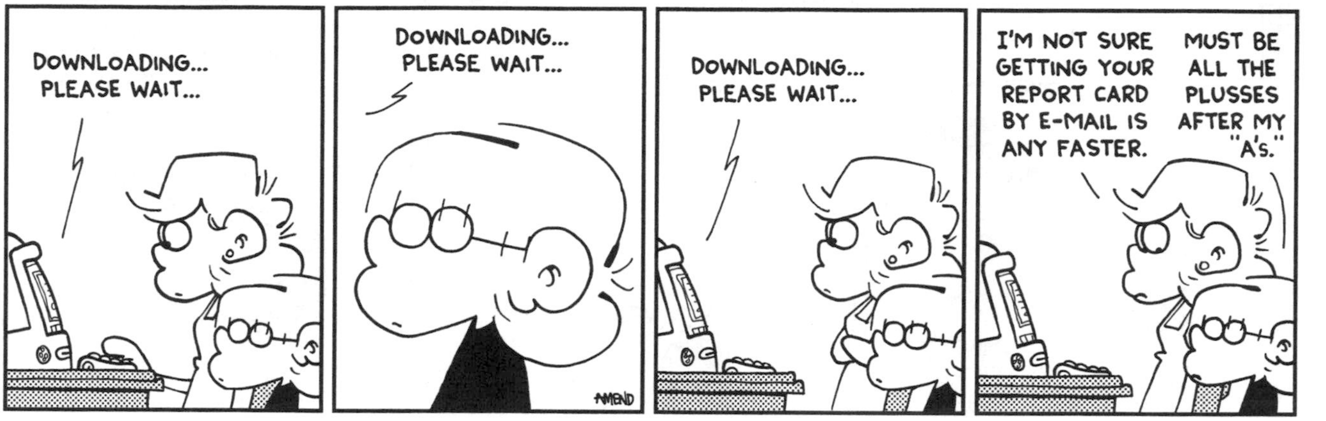
DOWNLOADING... PLEASE WAIT...
DOWNLOADING... PLEASE WAIT...
DOWNLOADING... PLEASE WAIT...
I'M NOT SURE GETTING YOUR REPORT CARD BY E-MAIL IS ANY FASTER.
MUST BE ALL THE PLUSSES AFTER MY "A's."

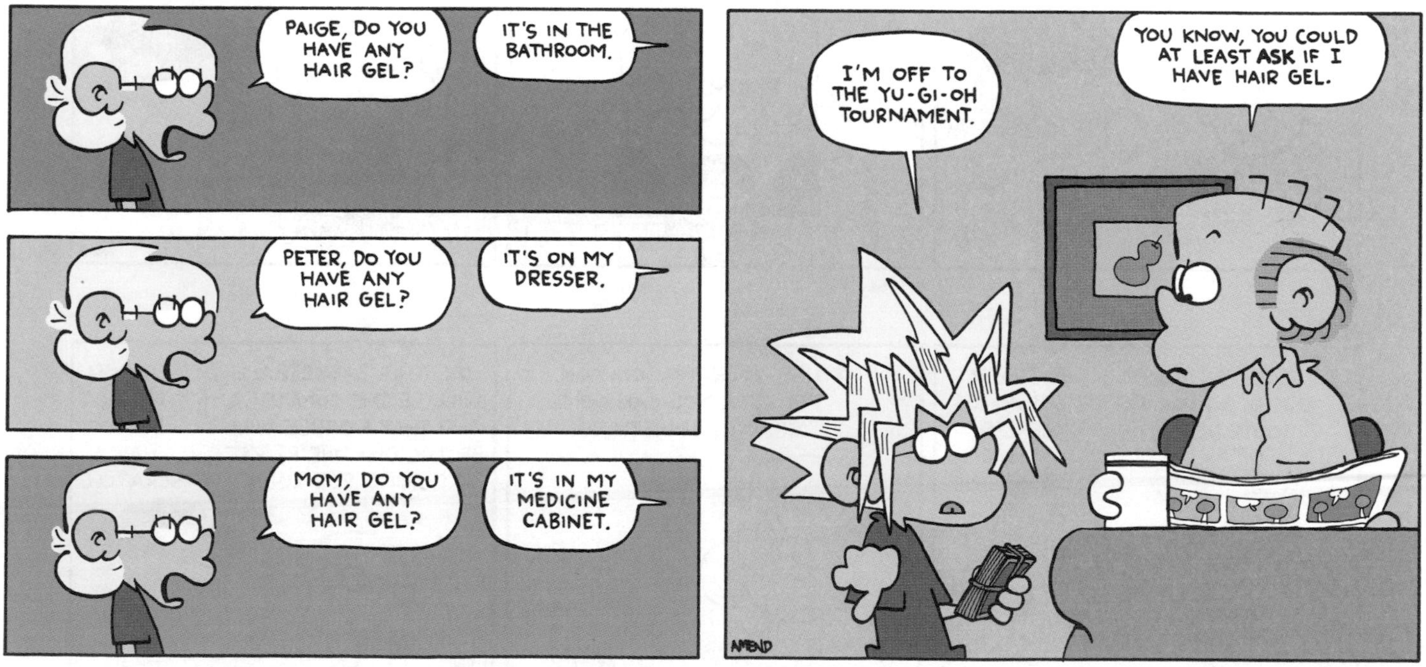
PAIGE, DO YOU HAVE ANY HAIR GEL?
IT'S IN THE BATHROOM.
PETER, DO YOU HAVE ANY HAIR GEL?
IT'S ON MY DRESSER.
MOM, DO YOU HAVE ANY HAIR GEL?
IT'S IN MY MEDICINE CABINET.
I'M OFF TO THE YU-GI-OH TOURNAMENT.
YOU KNOW, YOU COULD AT LEAST ASK IF I HAVE HAIR GEL.

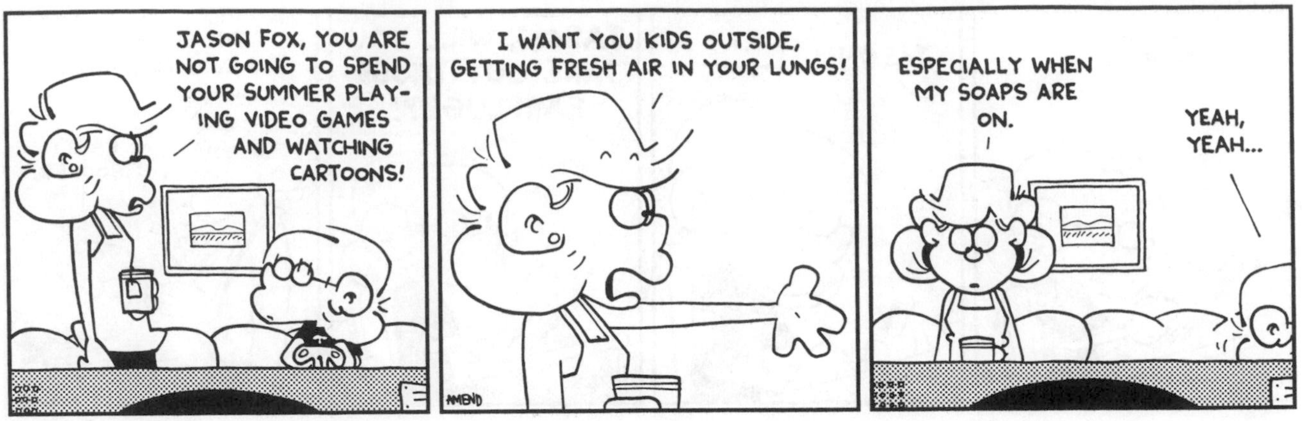
JASON FOX, YOU ARE NOT GOING TO SPEND YOUR SUMMER PLAYING VIDEO GAMES AND WATCHING CARTOONS!
I WANT YOU KIDS OUTSIDE, GETTING FRESH AIR IN YOUR LUNGS!
ESPECIALLY WHEN MY SOAPS ARE ON.
YEAH, YEAH...
AMEND

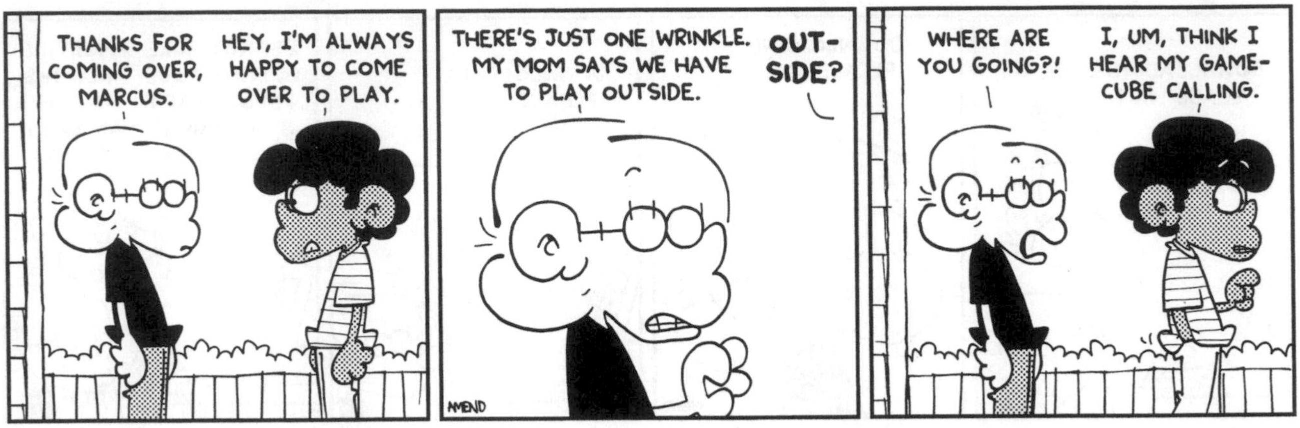
THANKS FOR COMING OVER, MARCUS.
HEY, I'M ALWAYS HAPPY TO COME OVER TO PLAY.
THERE'S JUST ONE WRINKLE. MY MOM SAYS WE HAVE TO PLAY OUTSIDE.
OUT-SIDE?
WHERE ARE YOU GOING?!
I, UM, THINK I HEAR MY GAMECUBE CALLING.
AMEND

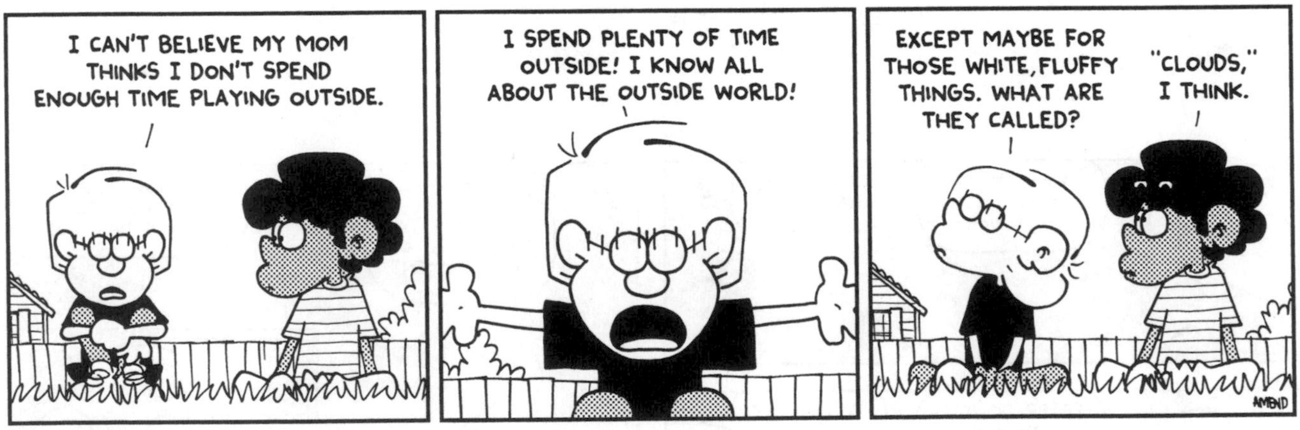
I CAN'T BELIEVE MY MOM THINKS I DON'T SPEND ENOUGH TIME PLAYING OUTSIDE.
I SPEND PLENTY OF TIME OUTSIDE! I KNOW ALL ABOUT THE OUTSIDE WORLD!
EXCEPT MAYBE FOR THOSE WHITE, FLUFFY THINGS. WHAT ARE THEY CALLED?
"CLOUDS," I THINK.
AMEND

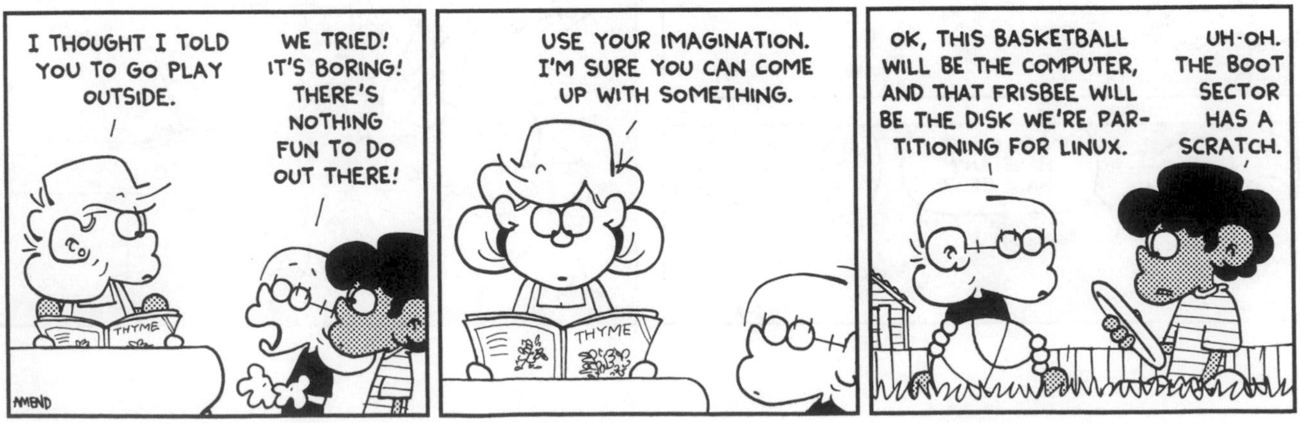
I THOUGHT I TOLD YOU TO GO PLAY OUTSIDE.
WE TRIED! IT'S BORING! THERE'S NOTHING FUN TO DO OUT THERE!
THYME
USE YOUR IMAGINATION. I'M SURE YOU CAN COME UP WITH SOMETHING.
THYME
OK, THIS BASKETBALL WILL BE THE COMPUTER, AND THAT FRISBEE WILL BE THE DISK WE'RE PARTITIONING FOR LINUX.
UH-OH. THE BOOT SECTOR HAS A SCRATCH.
AMEND

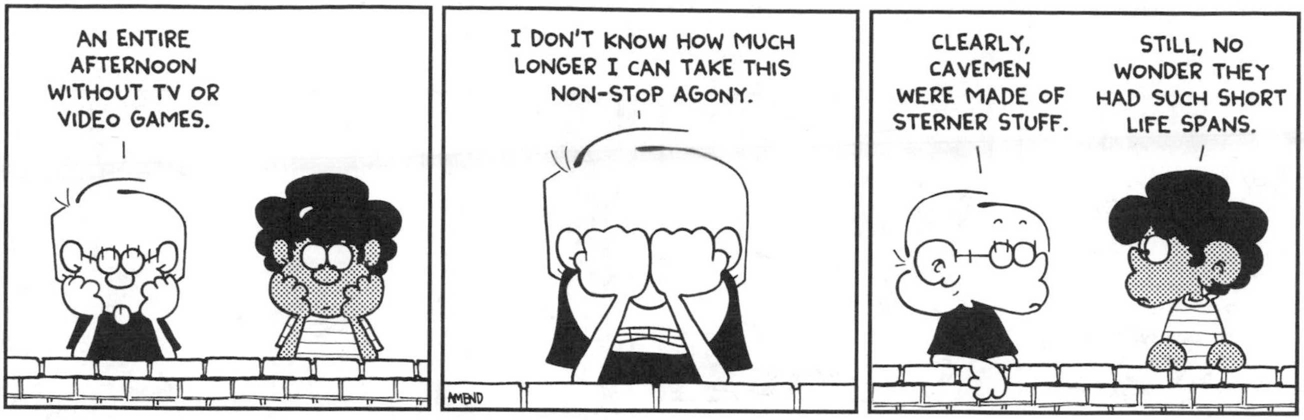
AN ENTIRE AFTERNOON WITHOUT TV OR VIDEO GAMES.
I DON'T KNOW HOW MUCH LONGER I CAN TAKE THIS NON-STOP AGONY.
CLEARLY, CAVEMEN WERE MADE OF STERNER STUFF.
STILL, NO WONDER THEY HAD SUCH SHORT LIFE SPANS.
AMEND

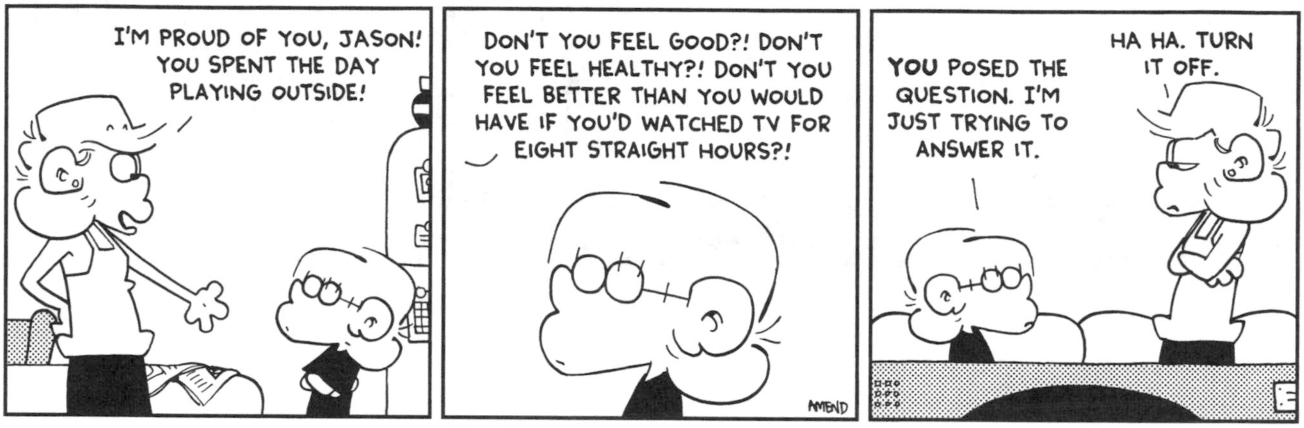
I'M PROUD OF YOU, JASON! YOU SPENT THE DAY PLAYING OUTSIDE!
DON'T YOU FEEL GOOD?! DON'T YOU FEEL HEALTHY?! DON'T YOU FEEL BETTER THAN YOU WOULD HAVE IF YOU'D WATCHED TV FOR EIGHT STRAIGHT HOURS?!
AMEND
YOU POSED THE QUESTION. I'M JUST TRYING TO ANSWER IT.
HA HA. TURN IT OFF.

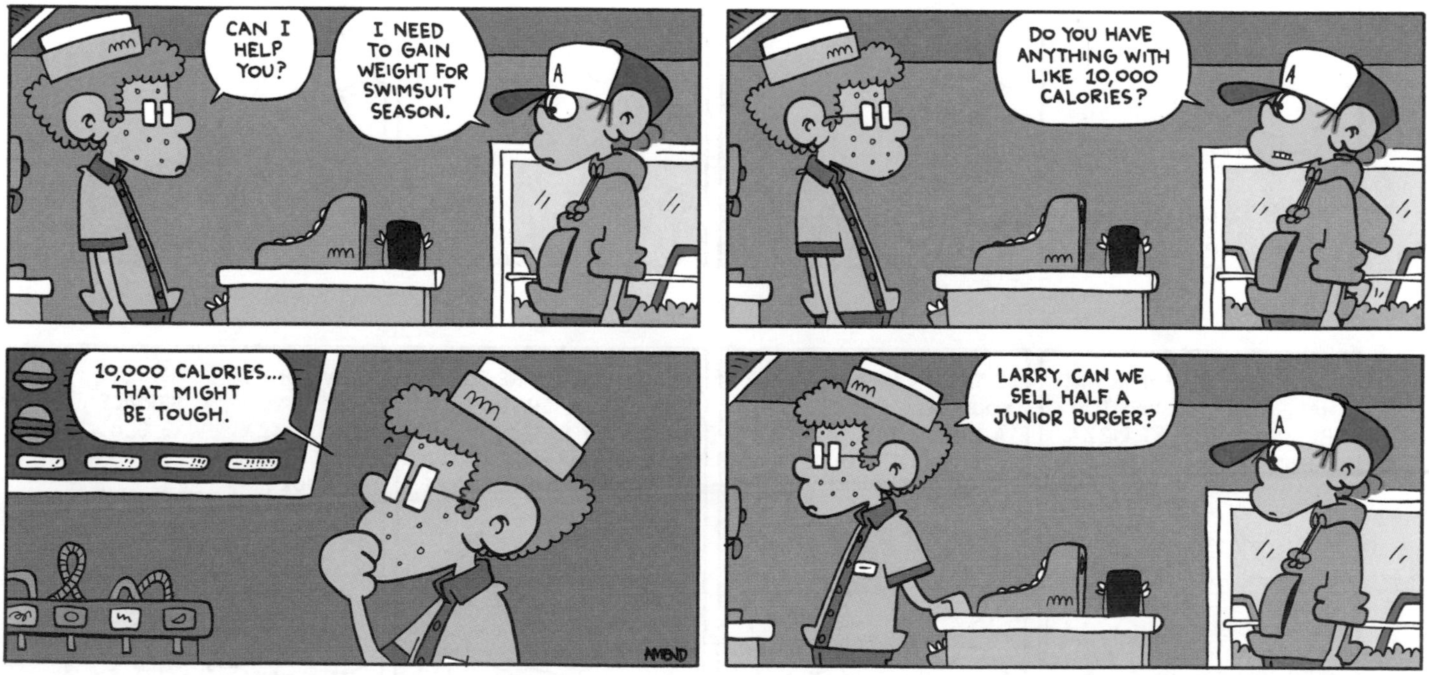
CAN I HELP YOU?
I NEED TO GAIN WEIGHT FOR SWIMSUIT SEASON.
DO YOU HAVE ANYTHING WITH LIKE 10,000 CALORIES?
10,000 CALORIES... THAT MIGHT BE TOUGH.
AMEND
LARRY, CAN WE SELL HALF A JUNIOR BURGER?

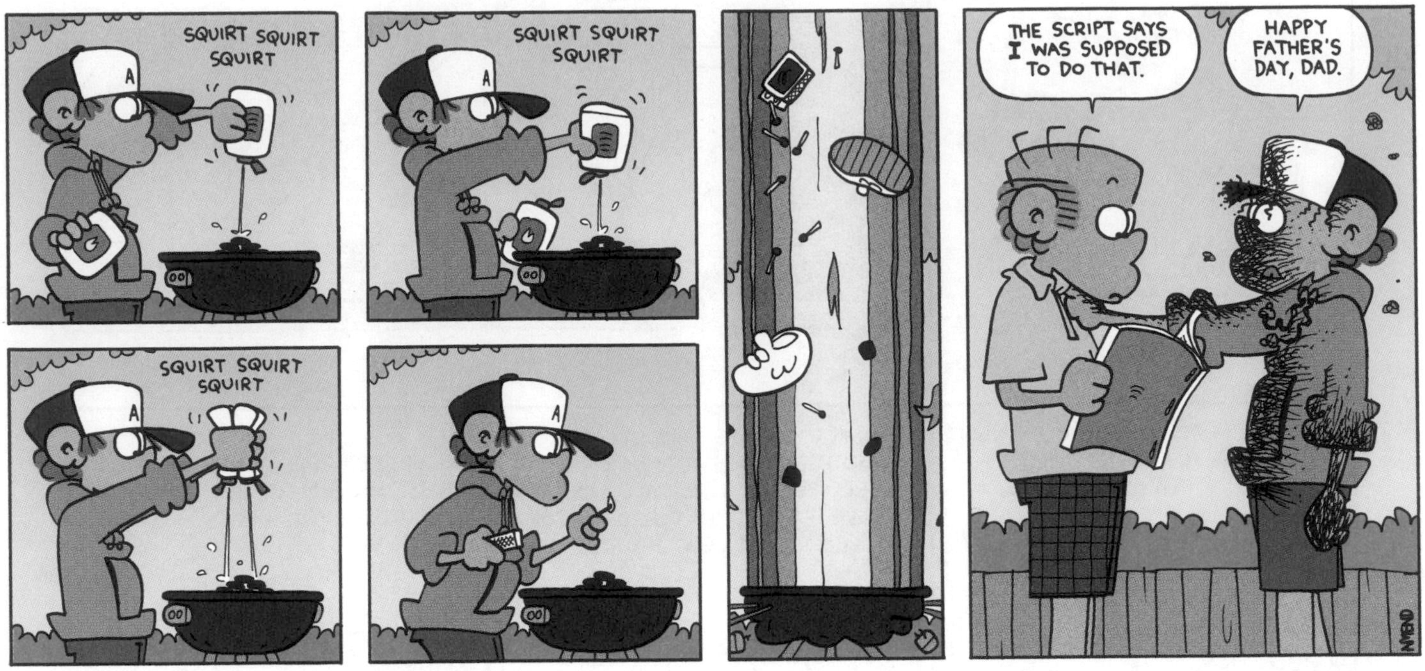
SQUIRT SQUIRT SQUIRT
SQUIRT SQUIRT SQUIRT
SQUIRT SQUIRT SQUIRT
THE SCRIPT SAYS I WAS SUPPOSED TO DO THAT.
HAPPY FATHER'S DAY, DAD.
AMEND

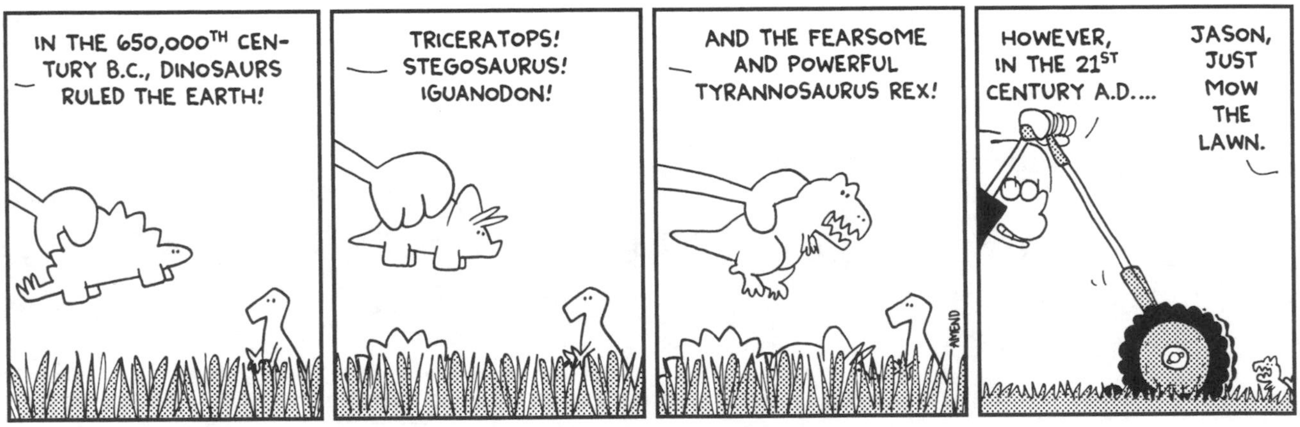
IN THE 650,000TH CENTURY B.C., DINOSAURS RULED THE EARTH!
TRICERATOPS! STEGOSAURUS! IGUANODON!
AND THE FEARSOME AND POWERFUL TYRANNOSAURUS REX!
AMEND
HOWEVER, IN THE 21ST CENTURY A.D....
JASON, JUST MOW THE LAWN.

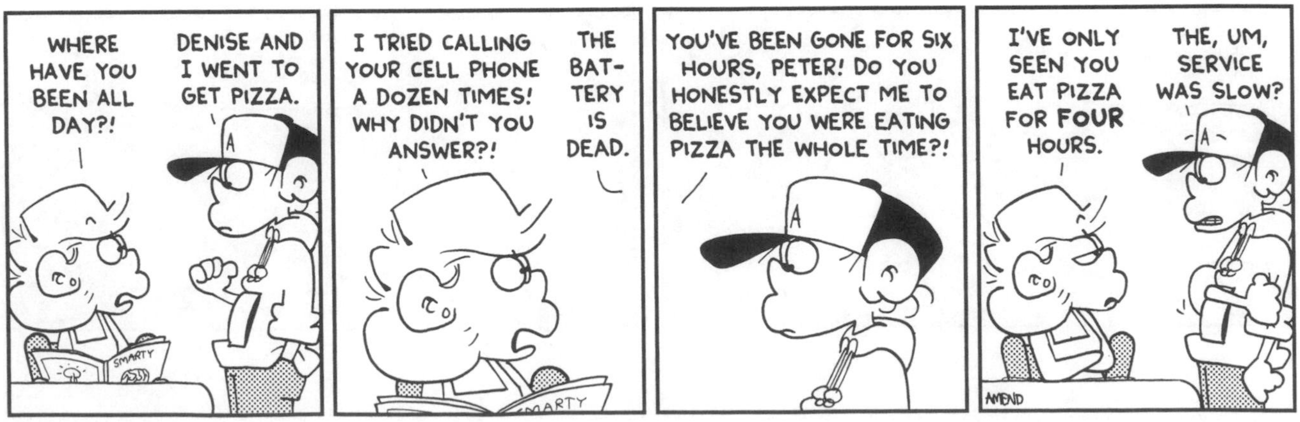
WHERE HAVE YOU BEEN ALL DAY?!
DENISE AND I WENT TO GET PIZZA.
SMARTY
I TRIED CALLING YOUR CELL PHONE A DOZEN TIMES! WHY DIDN'T YOU ANSWER?!
THE BATTERY IS DEAD.
SMARTY
YOU'VE BEEN GONE FOR SIX HOURS, PETER! DO YOU HONESTLY EXPECT ME TO BELIEVE YOU WERE EATING PIZZA THE WHOLE TIME?!
I'VE ONLY SEEN YOU EAT PIZZA FOR FOUR HOURS.
THE, UM, SERVICE WAS SLOW?
AMEND

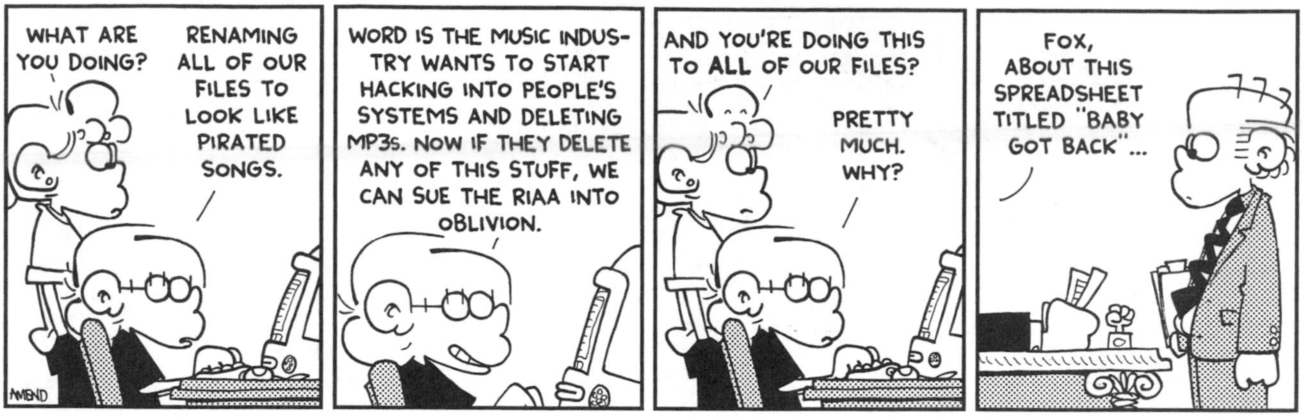
WHAT ARE YOU DOING?
RENAMING ALL OF OUR FILES TO LOOK LIKE PIRATED SONGS.
WORD IS THE MUSIC INDUSTRY WANTS TO START HACKING INTO PEOPLE'S SYSTEMS AND DELETING MP3s. NOW IF THEY DELETE ANY OF THIS STUFF, WE CAN SUE THE RIAA INTO OBLIVION.
AND YOU'RE DOING THIS TO ALL OF OUR FILES?
PRETTY MUCH. WHY?
FOX, ABOUT THIS SPREADSHEET TITLED "BABY GOT BACK"...
AMEND

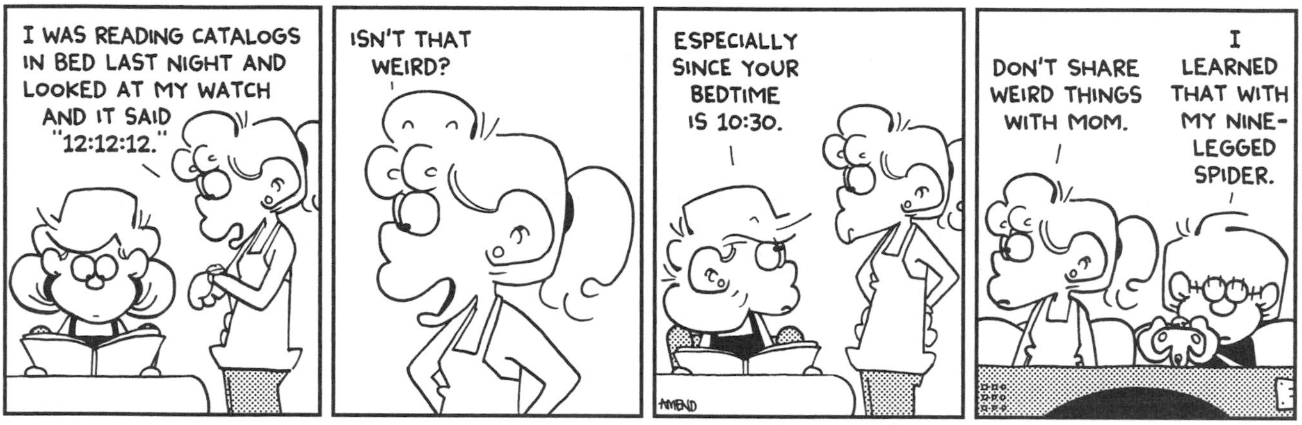
I WAS READING CATALOGS IN BED LAST NIGHT AND LOOKED AT MY WATCH AND IT SAID "12:12:12."
ISN'T THAT WEIRD?
ESPECIALLY SINCE YOUR BEDTIME IS 10:30.
AMEND
DON'T SHARE WEIRD THINGS WITH MOM.
I LEARNED THAT WITH MY NINE-LEGGED SPIDER.

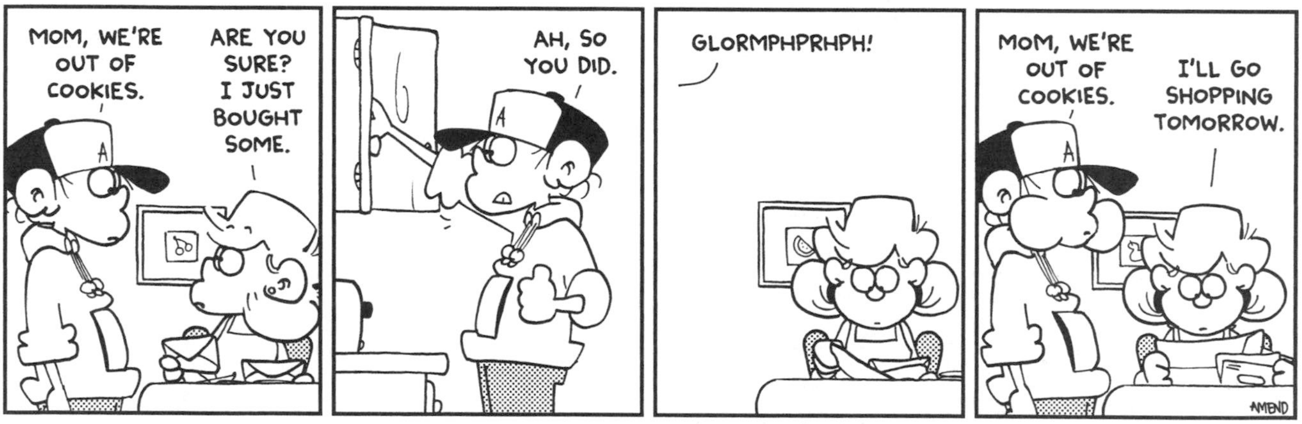
MOM, WE'RE OUT OF COOKIES.
ARE YOU SURE? I JUST BOUGHT SOME.
AH, SO YOU DID.
GLORMPHPRHPH!
MOM, WE'RE OUT OF COOKIES.
I'LL GO SHOPPING TOMORROW.
AMEND

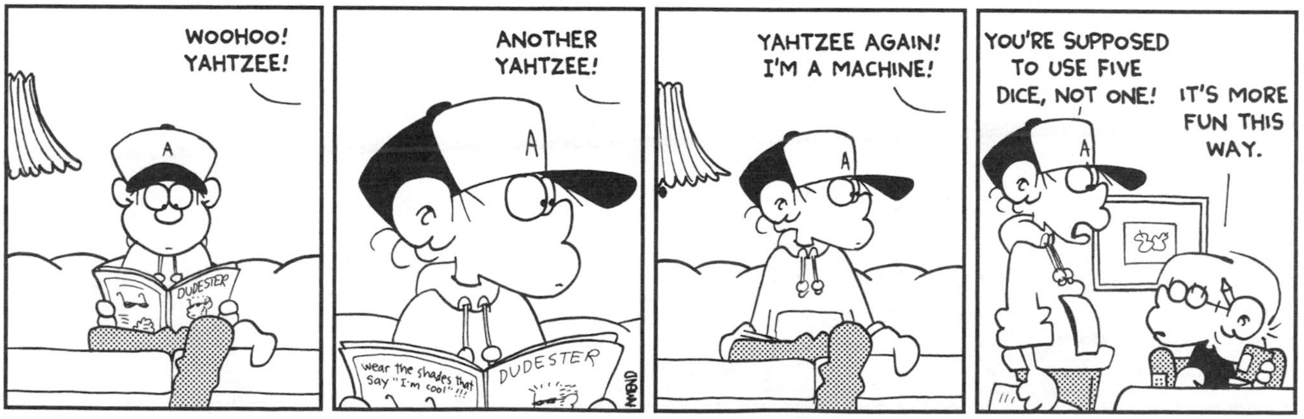
WOOHOO! YAHTZEE!
DUDESTER
ANOTHER YAHTZEE!
wear the shades that say "I'm cool"!!!
DUDESTER
AMEND
YAHTZEE AGAIN! I'M A MACHINE!
YOU'RE SUPPOSED TO USE FIVE DICE, NOT ONE!
IT'S MORE FUN THIS WAY.

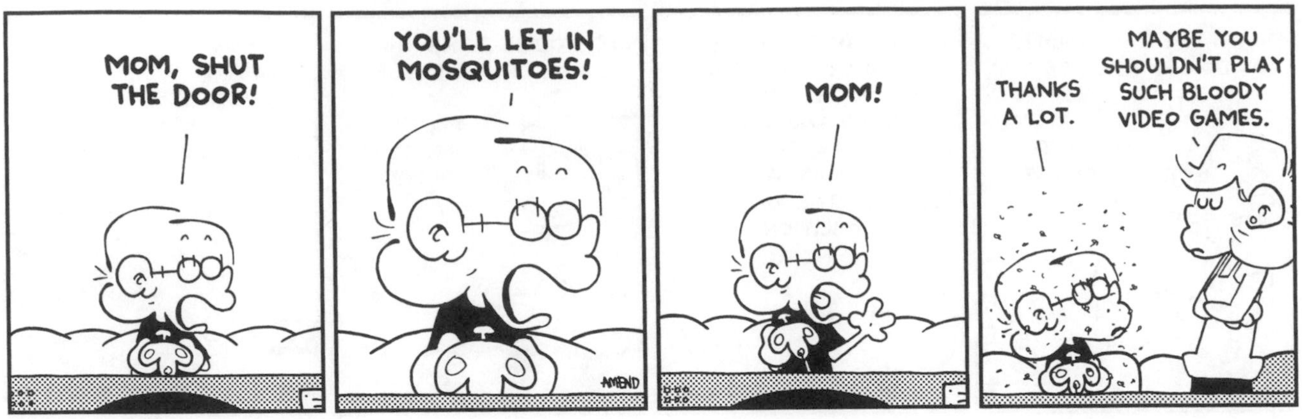
MOM, SHUT THE DOOR!
YOU'LL LET IN MOSQUITOES!
MOM!
THANKS A LOT.
MAYBE YOU SHOULDN'T PLAY SUCH BLOODY VIDEO GAMES.
AMEND

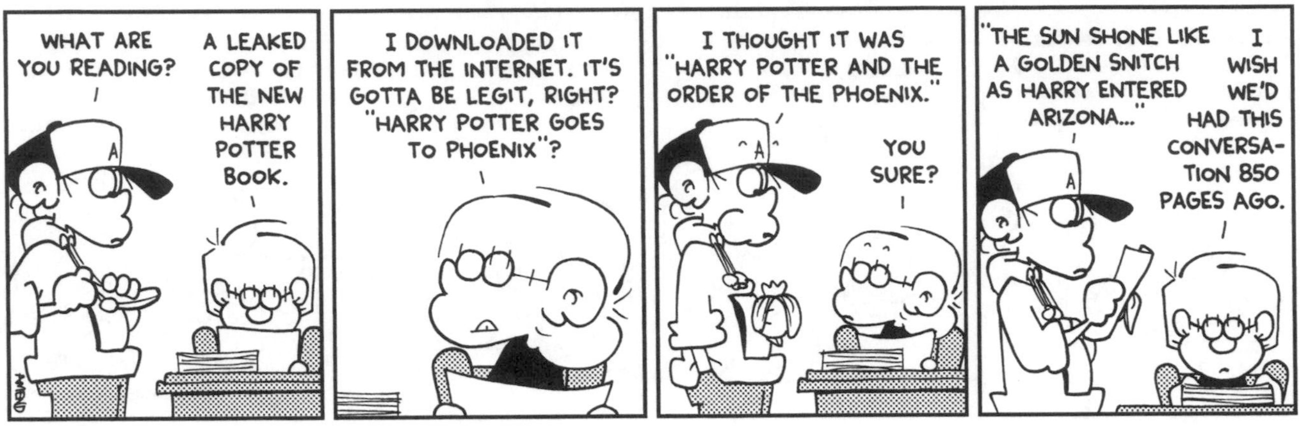
WHAT ARE YOU READING?
A LEAKED COPY OF THE NEW HARRY POTTER BOOK.
I DOWNLOADED IT FROM THE INTERNET. IT'S GOTTA BE LEGIT, RIGHT? "HARRY POTTER GOES TO PHOENIX"?
I THOUGHT IT WAS "HARRY POTTER AND THE ORDER OF THE PHOENIX."
YOU SURE?
"THE SUN SHONE LIKE A GOLDEN SNITCH AS HARRY ENTERED ARIZONA..."
I WISH WE'D HAD THIS CONVERSATION 850 PAGES AGO.
AMEND

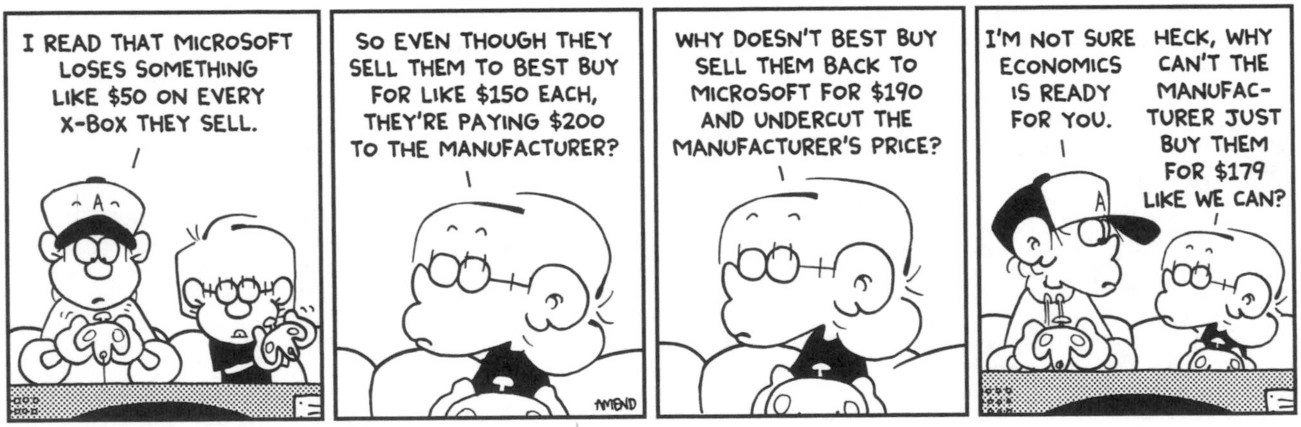
I READ THAT MICROSOFT LOSES SOMETHING LIKE $50 ON EVERY X-BOX THEY SELL.
SO EVEN THOUGH THEY SELL THEM TO BEST BUY FOR LIKE $150 EACH, THEY'RE PAYING $200 TO THE MANUFACTURER?
WHY DOESN'T BEST BUY SELL THEM BACK TO MICROSOFT FOR $190 AND UNDERCUT THE MANUFACTURER'S PRICE?
I'M NOT SURE ECONOMICS IS READY FOR YOU.
HECK, WHY CAN'T THE MANUFACTURER JUST BUY THEM FOR $179 LIKE WE CAN?
AMEND

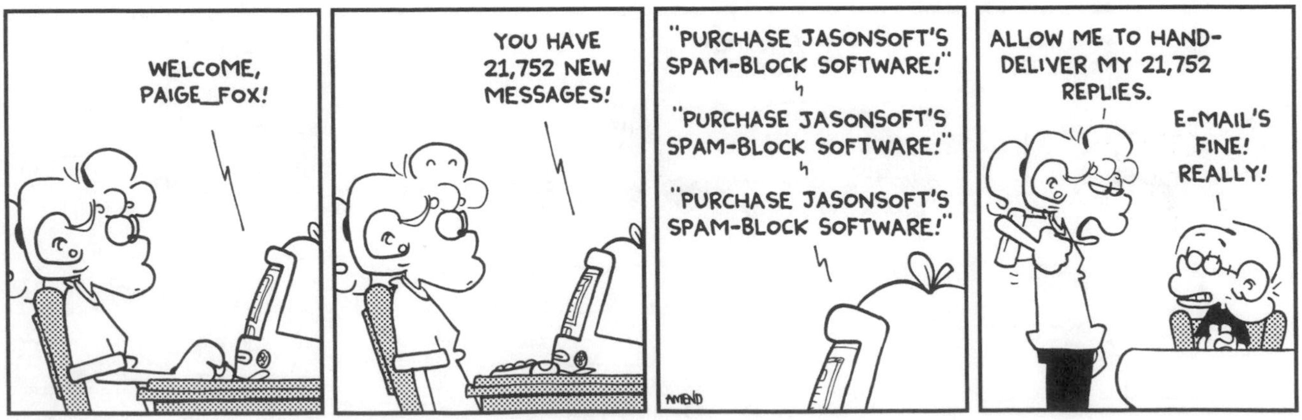
WELCOME, PAIGE_FOX!
YOU HAVE 21,752 NEW MESSAGES!
"PURCHASE JASONSOFT'S SPAM-BLOCK SOFTWARE!"
"PURCHASE JASONSOFT'S SPAM-BLOCK SOFTWARE!"
"PURCHASE JASONSOFT'S SPAM-BLOCK SOFTWARE!"
ALLOW ME TO HAND-DELIVER MY 21,752 REPLIES.
E-MAIL'S FINE! REALLY!
AMEND

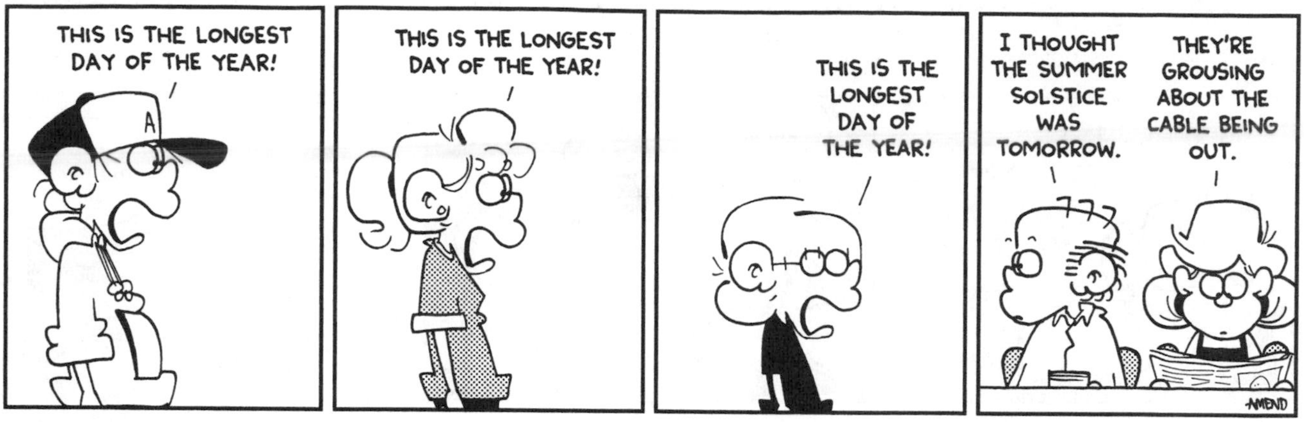
THIS IS THE LONGEST DAY OF THE YEAR!
THIS IS THE LONGEST DAY OF THE YEAR!
THIS IS THE LONGEST DAY OF THE YEAR!
I THOUGHT THE SUMMER SOLSTICE WAS TOMORROW.
THEY'RE GROUSING ABOUT THE CABLE BEING OUT.
AMEND

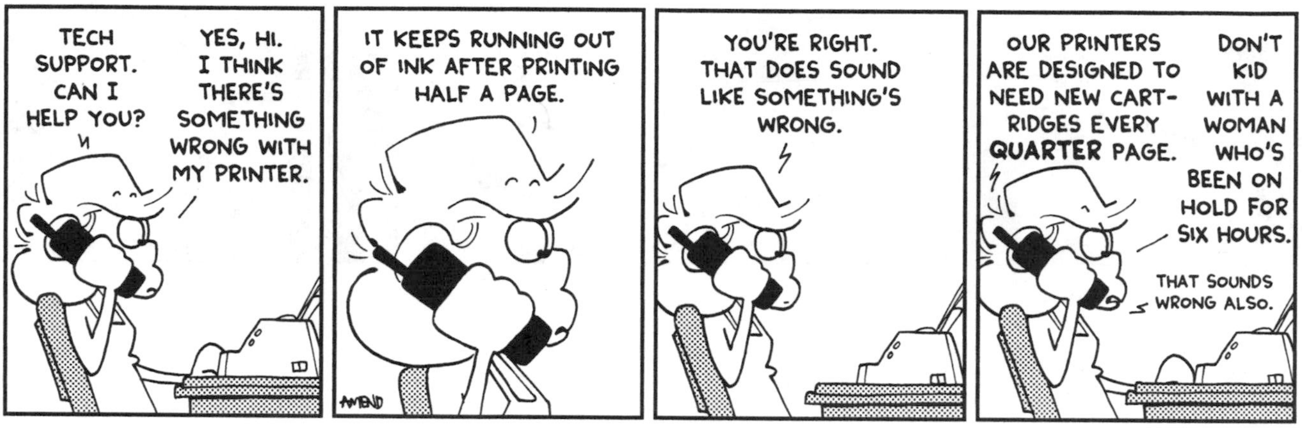
TECH SUPPORT. CAN I HELP YOU?
YES, HI. I THINK THERE'S SOMETHING WRONG WITH MY PRINTER.
IT KEEPS RUNNING OUT OF INK AFTER PRINTING HALF A PAGE.
AMEND
YOU'RE RIGHT. THAT DOES SOUND LIKE SOMETHING'S WRONG.
OUR PRINTERS ARE DESIGNED TO NEED NEW CARTRIDGES EVERY **QUARTER** PAGE.
DON'T KID WITH A WOMAN WHO'S BEEN ON HOLD FOR SIX HOURS.
THAT SOUNDS WRONG ALSO.

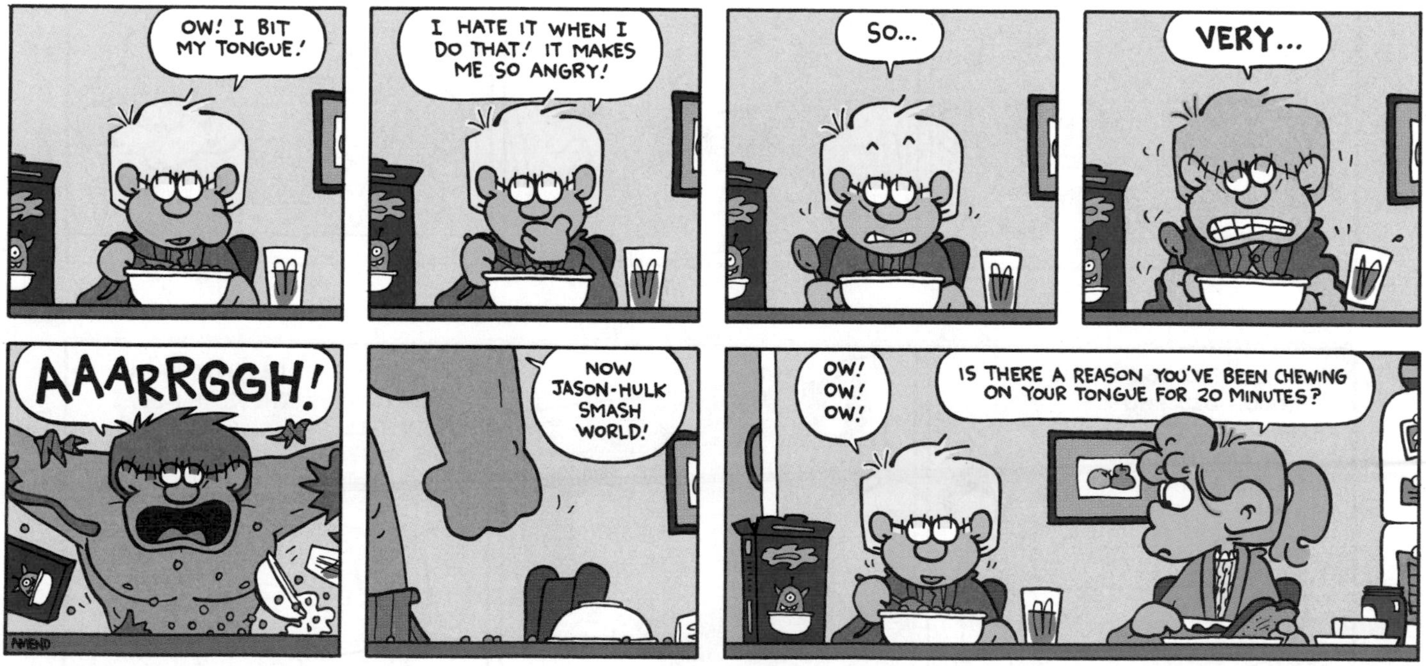
OW! I BIT MY TONGUE!
I HATE IT WHEN I DO THAT! IT MAKES ME SO ANGRY!
SO...
VERY...
AAARRGGH!
AMEND
NOW JASON-HULK SMASH WORLD!
OW! OW! OW!
IS THERE A REASON YOU'VE BEEN CHEWING ON YOUR TONGUE FOR 20 MINUTES?

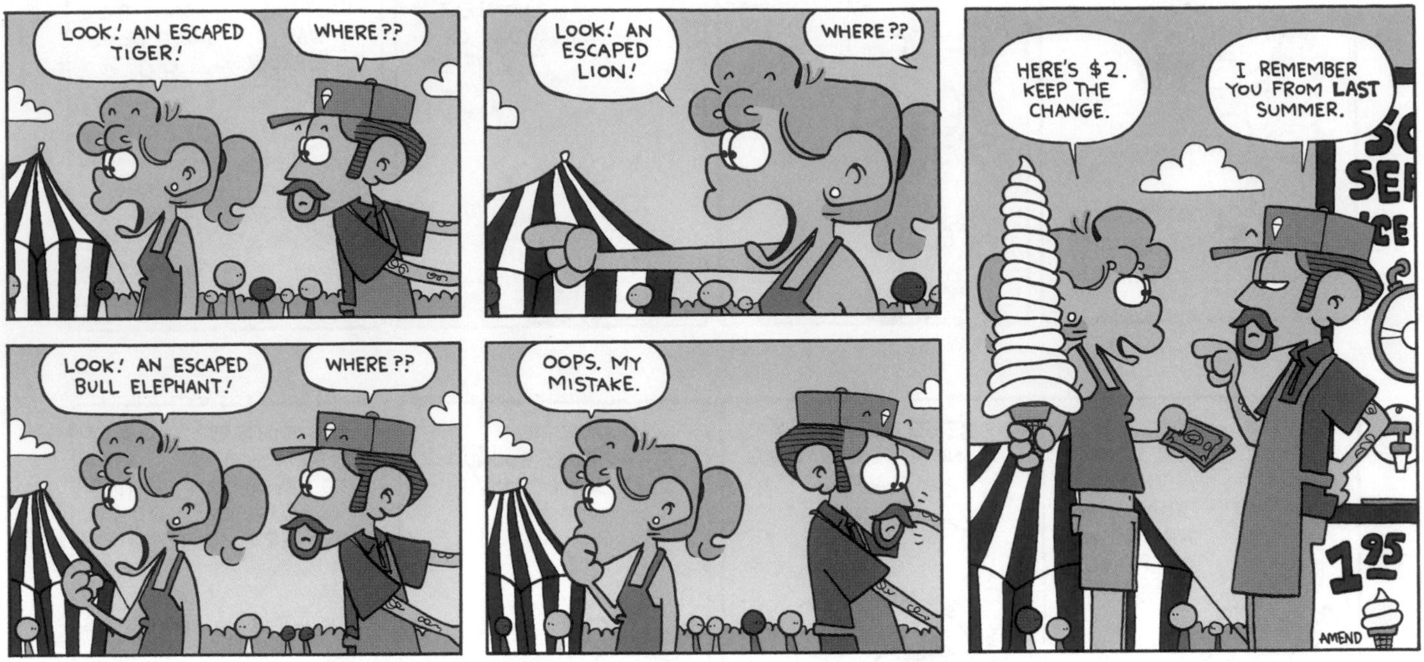
LOOK! AN ESCAPED TIGER!
WHERE??
LOOK! AN ESCAPED LION!
WHERE??
HERE'S $2. KEEP THE CHANGE.
I REMEMBER YOU FROM LAST SUMMER.
LOOK! AN ESCAPED BULL ELEPHANT!
WHERE??
OOPS. MY MISTAKE.
1.95
AMEND

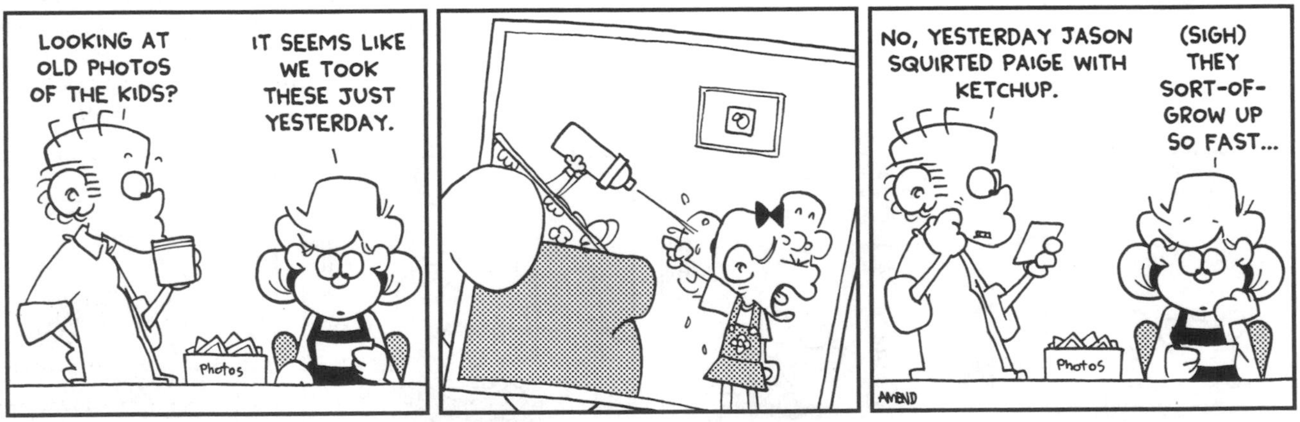
LOOKING AT OLD PHOTOS OF THE KIDS?
IT SEEMS LIKE WE TOOK THESE JUST YESTERDAY.
Photos
NO, YESTERDAY JASON SQUIRTED PAIGE WITH KETCHUP.
(SIGH) THEY SORT-OF-GROW UP SO FAST...
Photos
AMEND

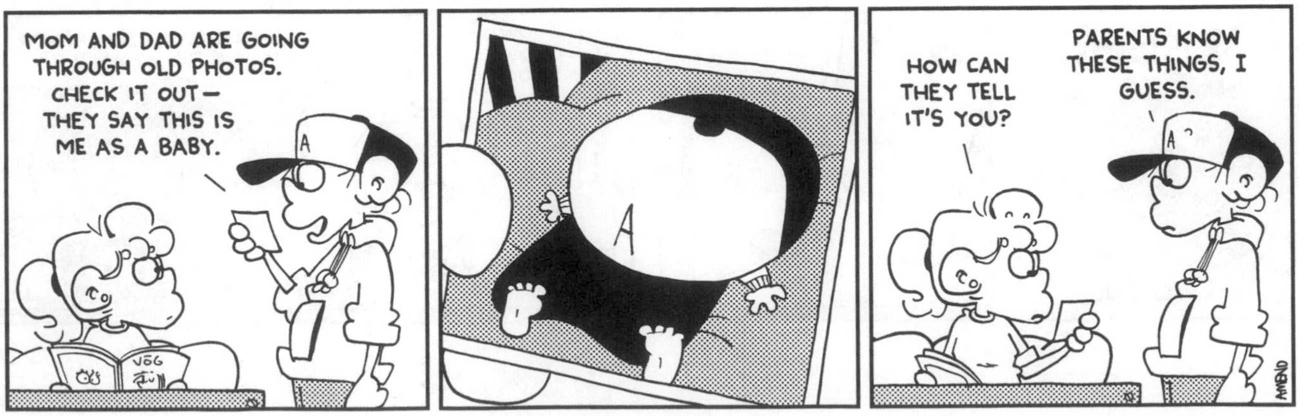
MOM AND DAD ARE GOING THROUGH OLD PHOTOS. CHECK IT OUT— THEY SAY THIS IS ME AS A BABY.
HOW CAN THEY TELL IT'S YOU?
PARENTS KNOW THESE THINGS, I GUESS.
AMEND

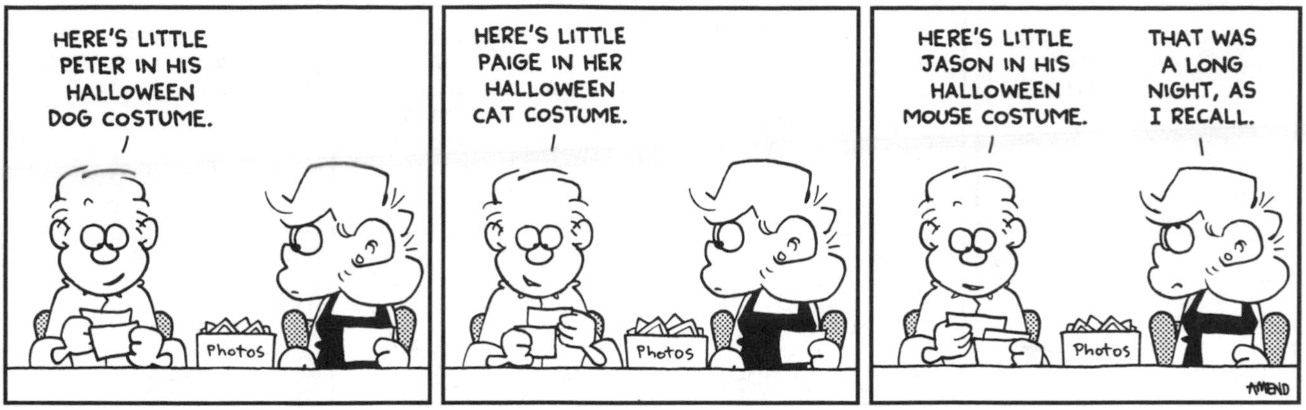
HERE'S LITTLE PETER IN HIS HALLOWEEN DOG COSTUME.
Photos
HERE'S LITTLE PAIGE IN HER HALLOWEEN CAT COSTUME.
Photos
HERE'S LITTLE JASON IN HIS HALLOWEEN MOUSE COSTUME.
THAT WAS A LONG NIGHT, AS I RECALL.
Photos
AMEND

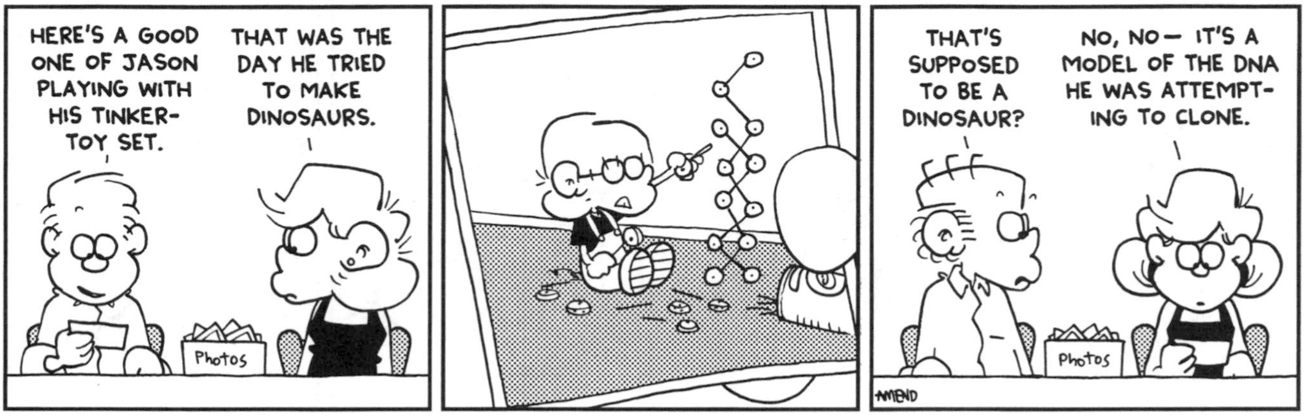
HERE'S A GOOD ONE OF JASON PLAYING WITH HIS TINKER-TOY SET.
THAT WAS THE DAY HE TRIED TO MAKE DINOSAURS.
Photos
THAT'S SUPPOSED TO BE A DINOSAUR?
NO, NO— IT'S A MODEL OF THE DNA HE WAS ATTEMPTING TO CLONE.
Photos
AMEND

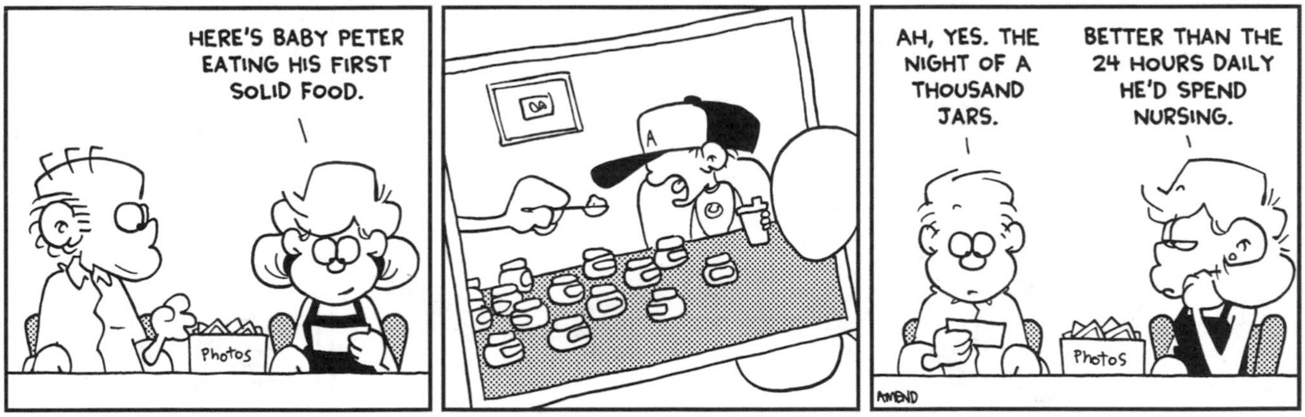
HERE'S BABY PETER EATING HIS FIRST SOLID FOOD.
Photos
AH, YES. THE NIGHT OF A THOUSAND JARS.
BETTER THAN THE 24 HOURS DAILY HE'D SPEND NURSING.
Photos
AMEND

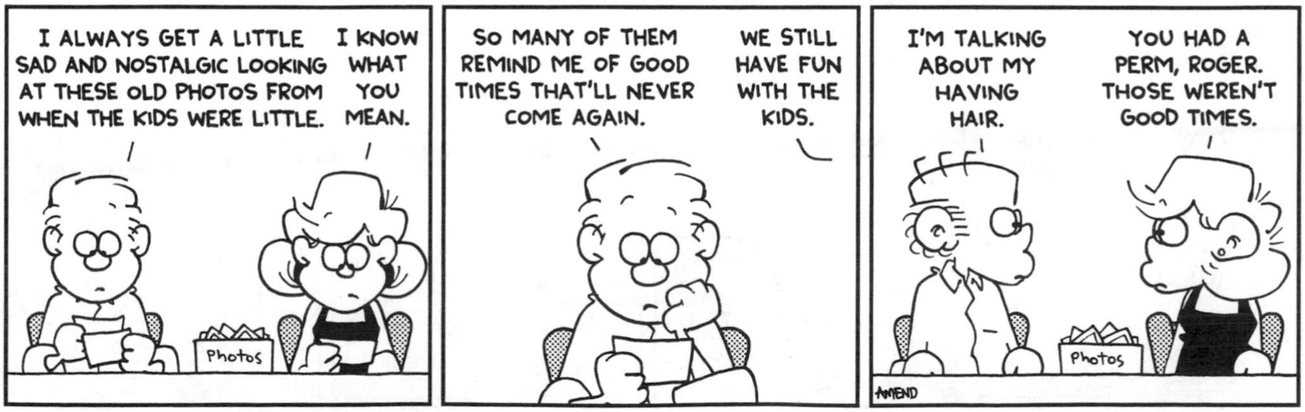
I ALWAYS GET A LITTLE SAD AND NOSTALGIC LOOKING AT THESE OLD PHOTOS FROM WHEN THE KIDS WERE LITTLE.
I KNOW WHAT YOU MEAN.
Photos
SO MANY OF THEM REMIND ME OF GOOD TIMES THAT'LL NEVER COME AGAIN.
WE STILL HAVE FUN WITH THE KIDS.
I'M TALKING ABOUT MY HAVING HAIR.
YOU HAD A PERM, ROGER. THOSE WEREN'T GOOD TIMES.
Photos
AMEND

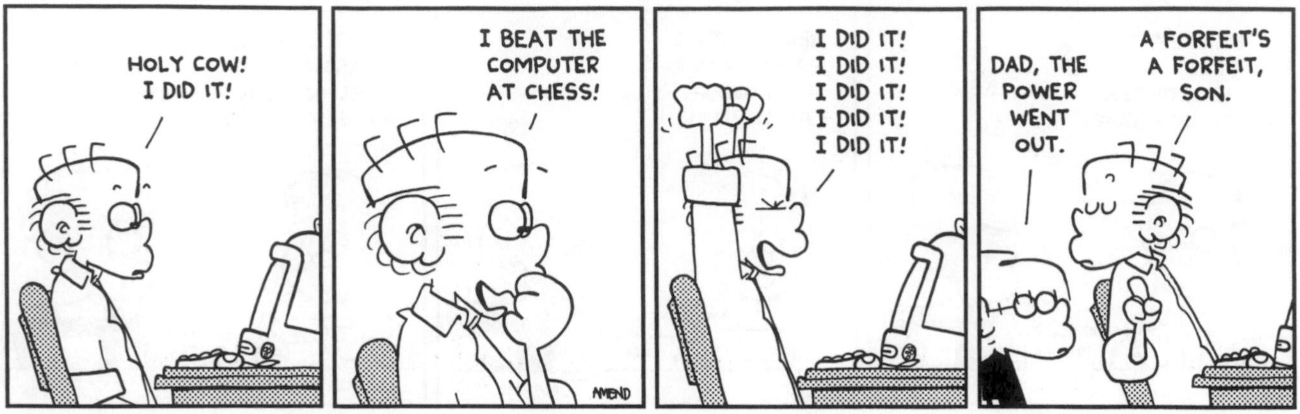
HOLY COW! I DID IT!
I BEAT THE COMPUTER AT CHESS!
I DID IT! I DID IT! I DID IT! I DID IT! I DID IT!
DAD, THE POWER WENT OUT.
A FORFEIT'S A FORFEIT, SON.
AMEND

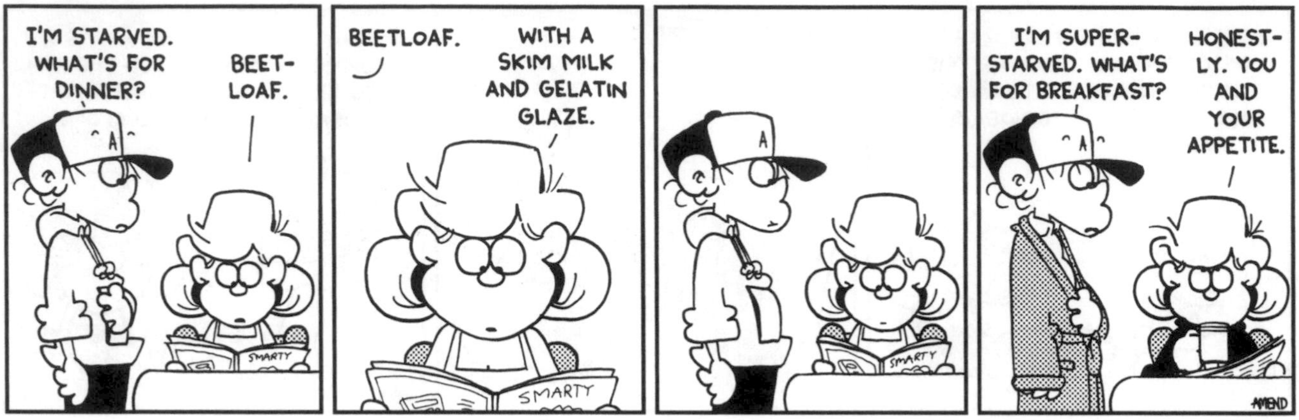
I'M STARVED. WHAT'S FOR DINNER?
BEET-LOAF.
SMARTY
BEETLOAF.
WITH A SKIM MILK AND GELATIN GLAZE.
SMARTY
SMARTY
I'M SUPER-STARVED. WHAT'S FOR BREAKFAST?
HONEST-LY. YOU AND YOUR APPETITE.
AMEND

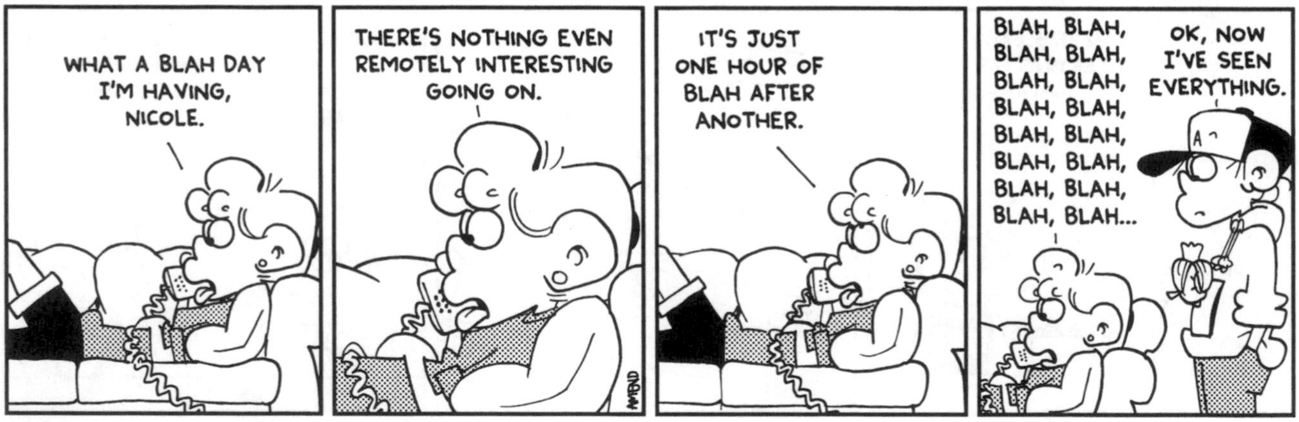
WHAT A BLAH DAY I'M HAVING, NICOLE.
THERE'S NOTHING EVEN REMOTELY INTERESTING GOING ON.
AMEND
IT'S JUST ONE HOUR OF BLAH AFTER ANOTHER.
BLAH, BLAH, BLAH, BLAH, BLAH, BLAH, BLAH, BLAH, BLAH, BLAH, BLAH, BLAH, BLAH, BLAH, BLAH, BLAH...
OK, NOW I'VE SEEN EVERYTHING.

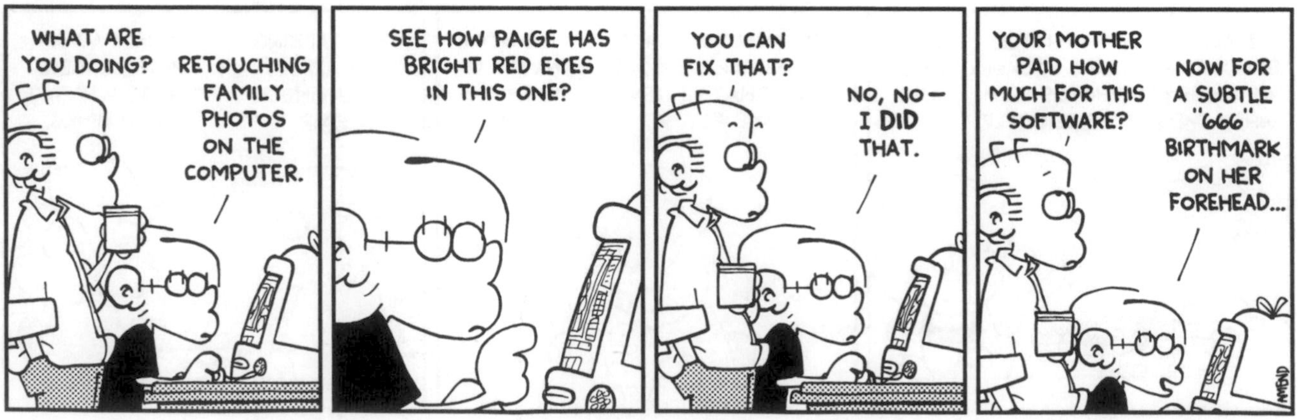
WHAT ARE YOU DOING?
RETOUCHING FAMILY PHOTOS ON THE COMPUTER.
SEE HOW PAIGE HAS BRIGHT RED EYES IN THIS ONE?
YOU CAN FIX THAT?
NO, NO— I DID THAT.
YOUR MOTHER PAID HOW MUCH FOR THIS SOFTWARE?
NOW FOR A SUBTLE "666" BIRTHMARK ON HER FOREHEAD...
AMEND

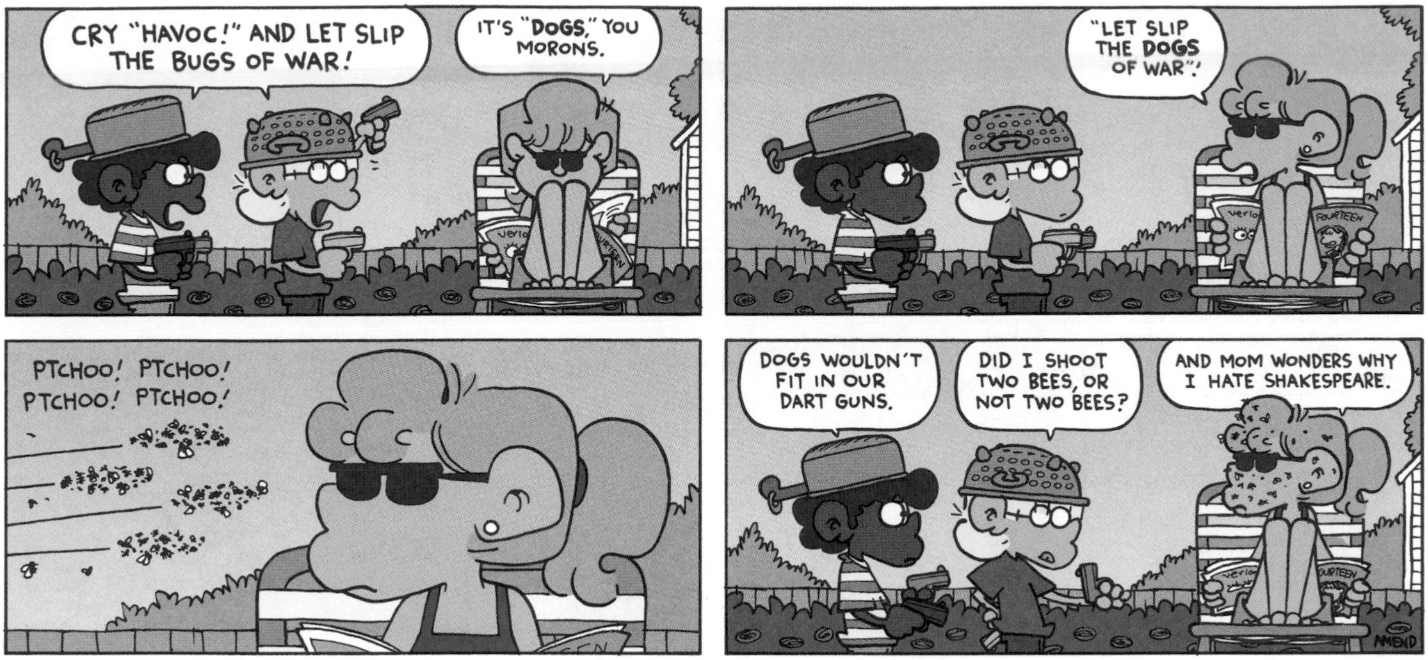
CRY "HAVOC!" AND LET SLIP THE BUGS OF WAR!
IT'S "DOGS," YOU MORONS.
"LET SLIP THE DOGS OF WAR"!
PTCHOO! PTCHOO! PTCHOO! PTCHOO!
DOGS WOULDN'T FIT IN OUR DART GUNS.
DID I SHOOT TWO BEES, OR NOT TWO BEES?
AND MOM WONDERS WHY I HATE SHAKESPEARE.
AMEND

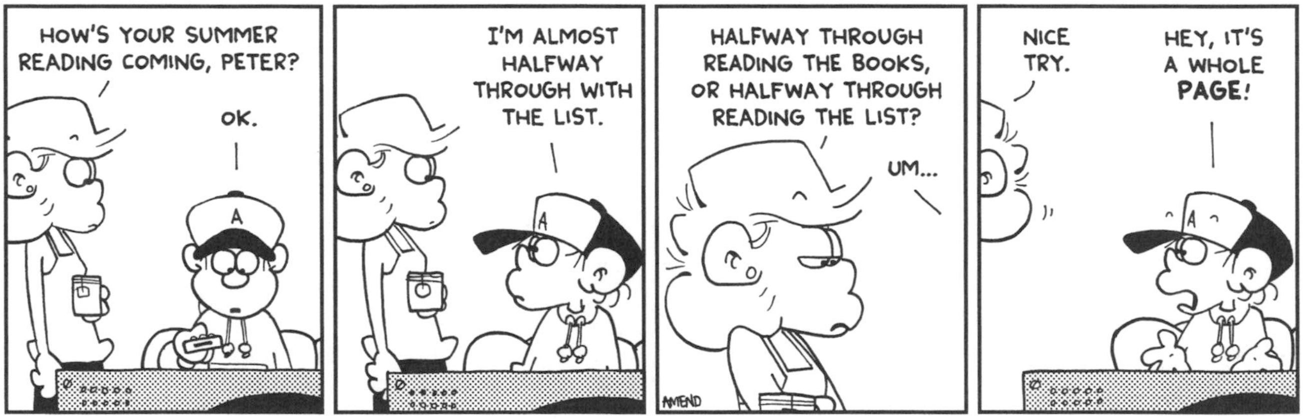
HOW'S YOUR SUMMER READING COMING, PETER?
OK.
I'M ALMOST HALFWAY THROUGH WITH THE LIST.
HALFWAY THROUGH READING THE BOOKS, OR HALFWAY THROUGH READING THE LIST?
UM...
AMEND
NICE TRY.
HEY, IT'S A WHOLE PAGE!

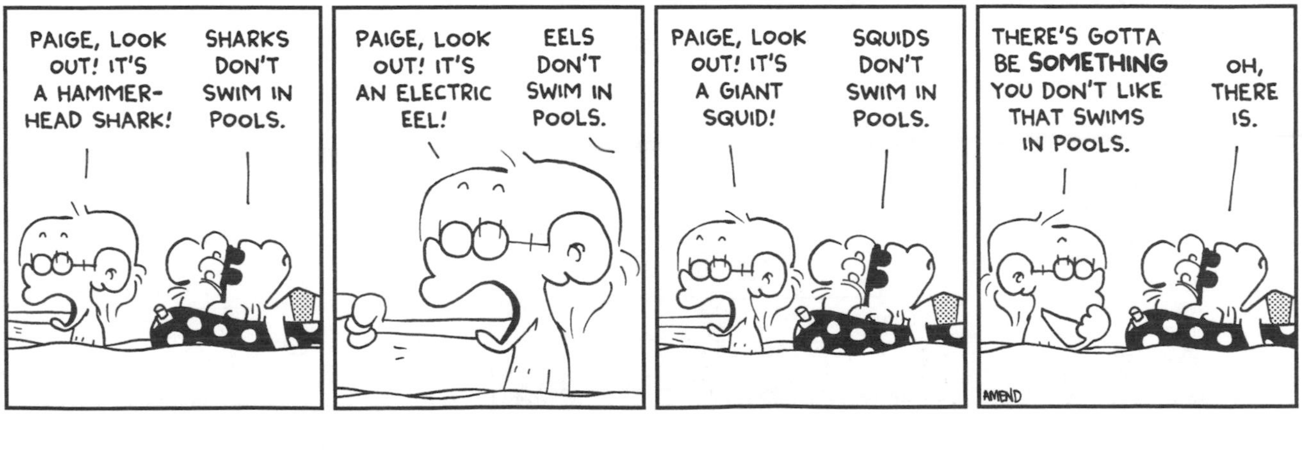
PAIGE, LOOK OUT! IT'S A HAMMER-HEAD SHARK!
SHARKS DON'T SWIM IN POOLS.
PAIGE, LOOK OUT! IT'S AN ELECTRIC EEL!
EELS DON'T SWIM IN POOLS.
PAIGE, LOOK OUT! IT'S A GIANT SQUID!
SQUIDS DON'T SWIM IN POOLS.
THERE'S GOTTA BE SOMETHING YOU DON'T LIKE THAT SWIMS IN POOLS.
OH, THERE IS.
AMEND

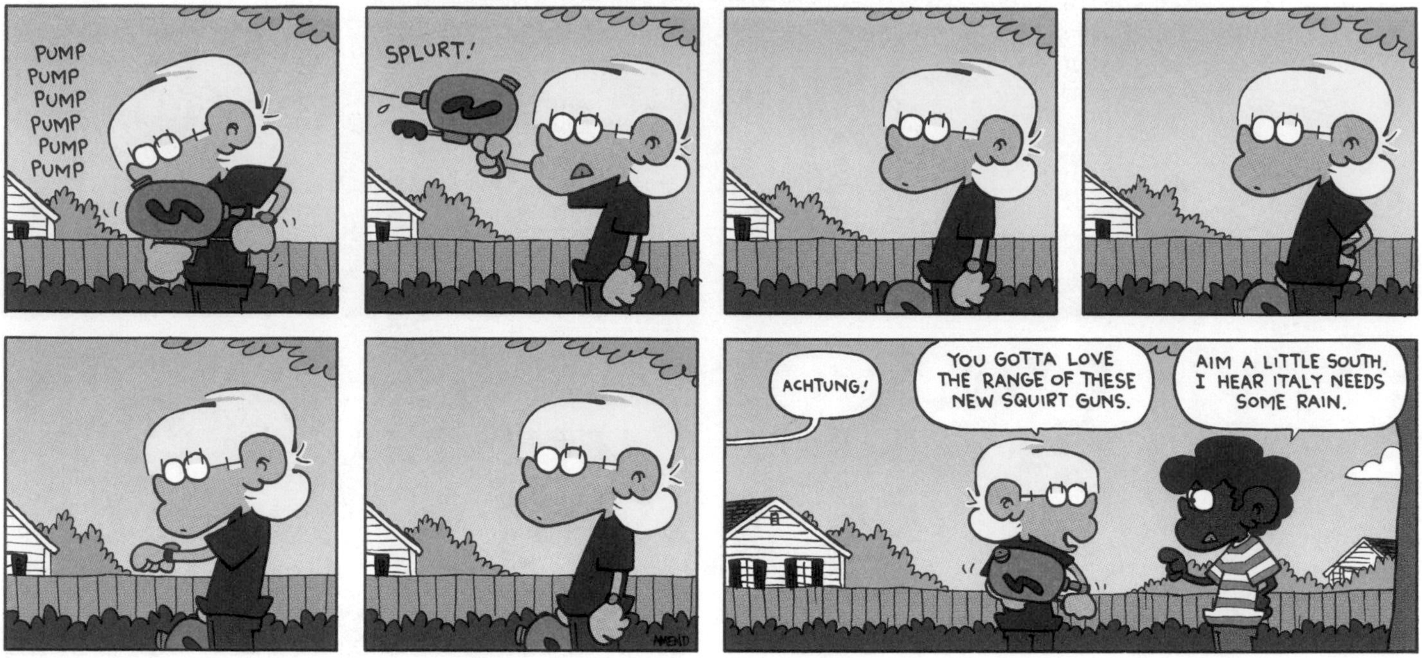
PUMP
PUMP
PUMP
PUMP
PUMP
PUMP
SPLURT!
AMEND
ACHTUNG!
YOU GOTTA LOVE THE RANGE OF THESE NEW SQUIRT GUNS.
AIM A LITTLE SOUTH. I HEAR ITALY NEEDS SOME RAIN.

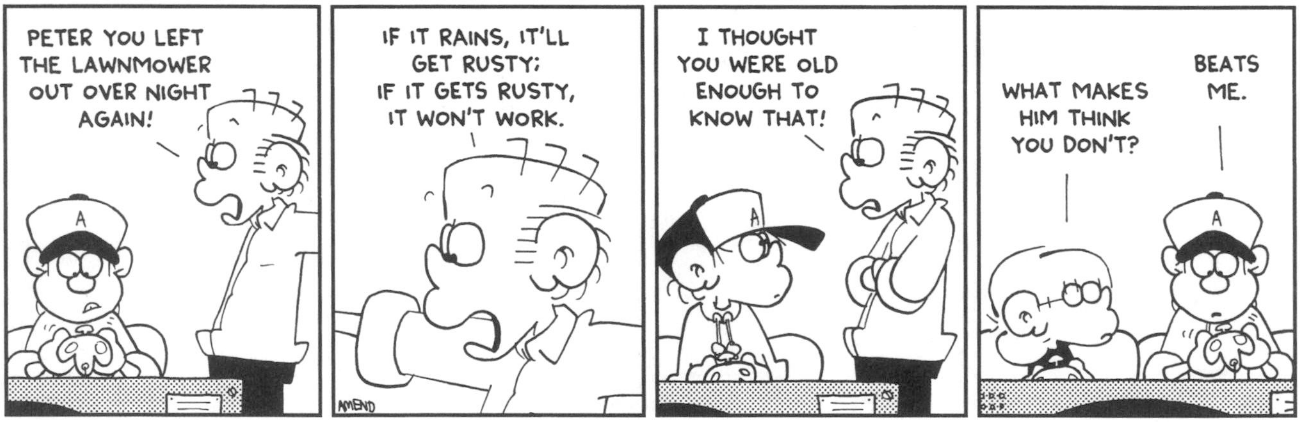
PETER YOU LEFT THE LAWNMOWER OUT OVER NIGHT AGAIN!
IF IT RAINS, IT'LL GET RUSTY; IF IT GETS RUSTY, IT WON'T WORK.
AMEND
I THOUGHT YOU WERE OLD ENOUGH TO KNOW THAT!
WHAT MAKES HIM THINK YOU DON'T?
BEATS ME.

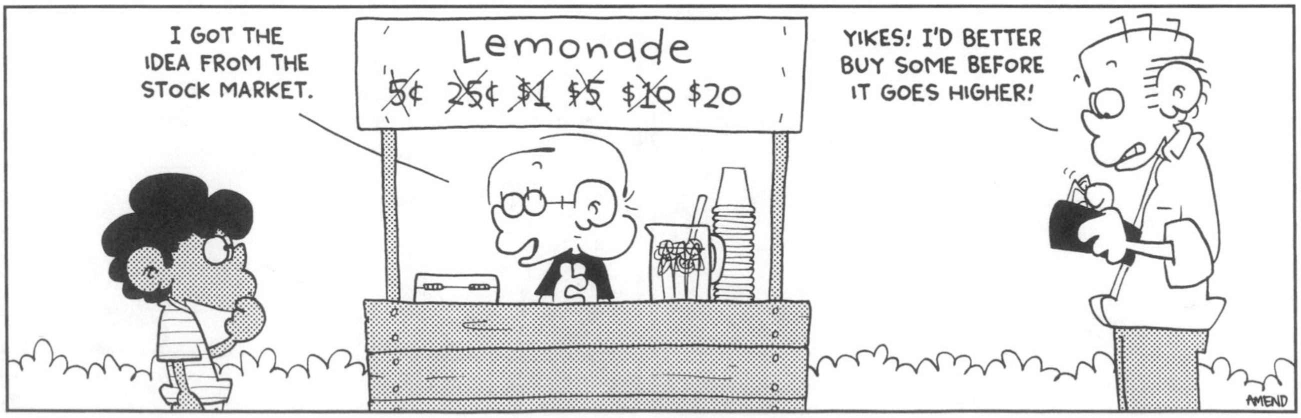
I GOT THE IDEA FROM THE STOCK MARKET.
Lemonade
~~5¢~~ ~~25¢~~ ~~$1~~ ~~$5~~ ~~$10~~ $20
YIKES! I'D BETTER BUY SOME BEFORE IT GOES HIGHER!
AMEND

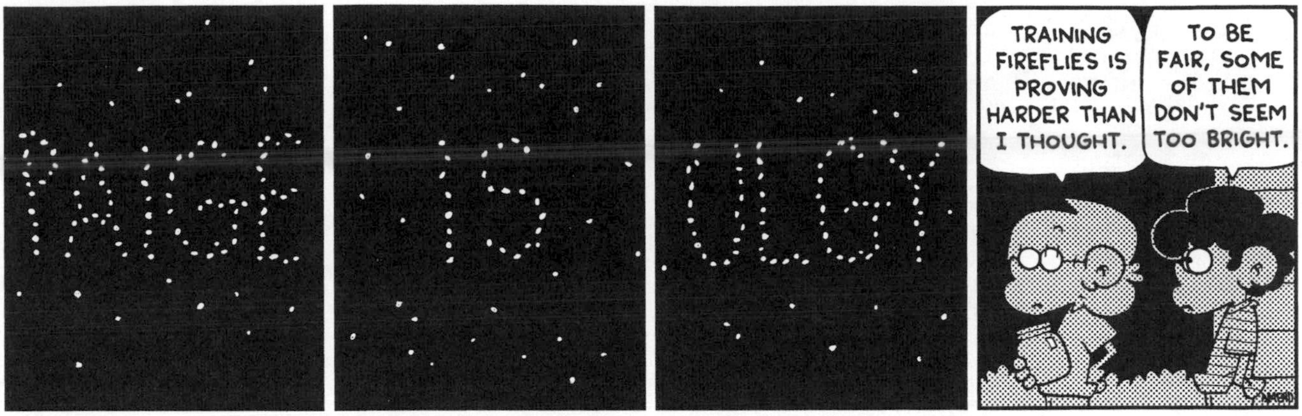
PAIGE
IS
UGLY
TRAINING FIREFLIES IS PROVING HARDER THAN I THOUGHT.
TO BE FAIR, SOME OF THEM DON'T SEEM TOO BRIGHT.

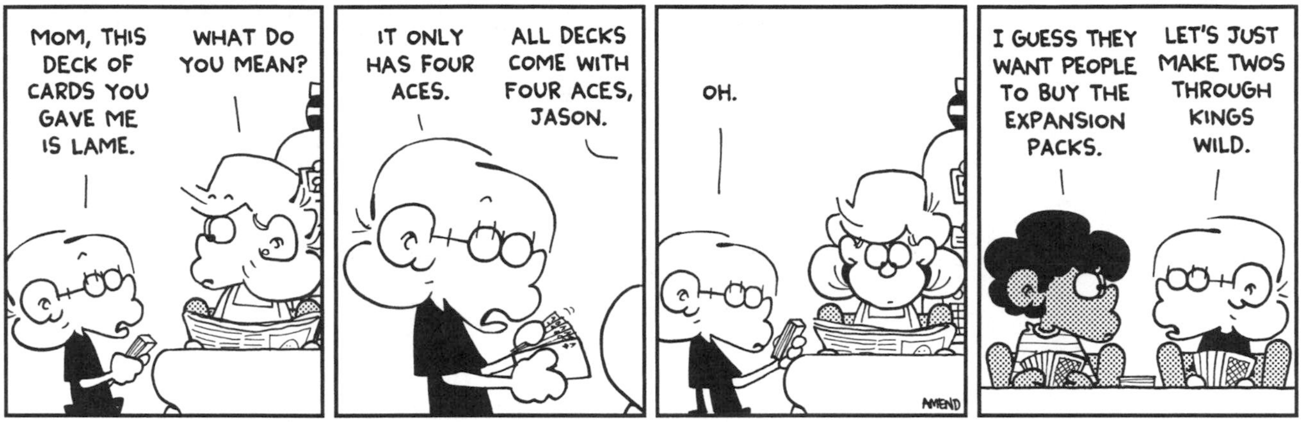
MOM, THIS DECK OF CARDS YOU GAVE ME IS LAME.
WHAT DO YOU MEAN?
IT ONLY HAS FOUR ACES.
ALL DECKS COME WITH FOUR ACES, JASON.
OH.
I GUESS THEY WANT PEOPLE TO BUY THE EXPANSION PACKS.
LET'S JUST MAKE TWOS THROUGH KINGS WILD.

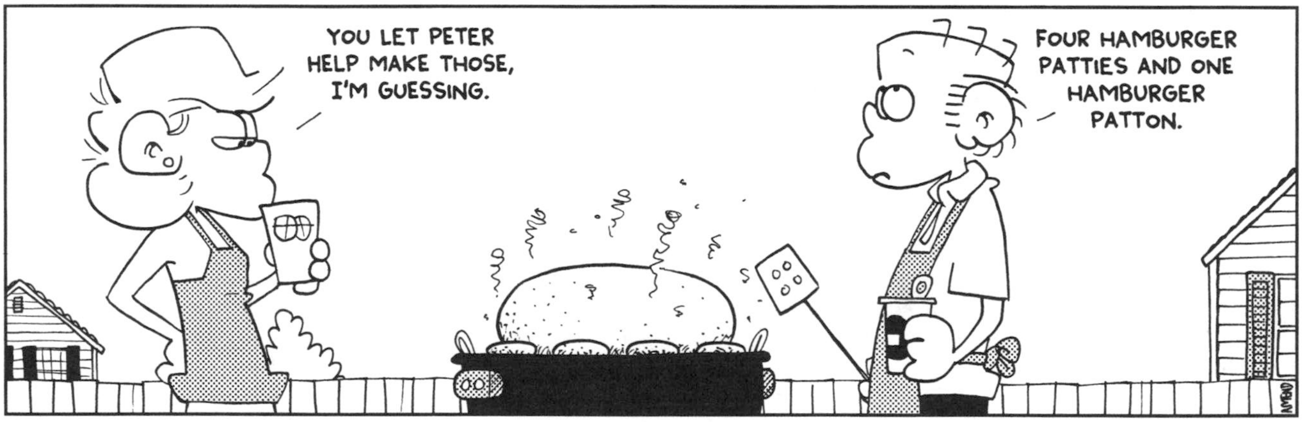
YOU LET PETER HELP MAKE THOSE, I'M GUESSING.
FOUR HAMBURGER PATTIES AND ONE HAMBURGER PATTON.

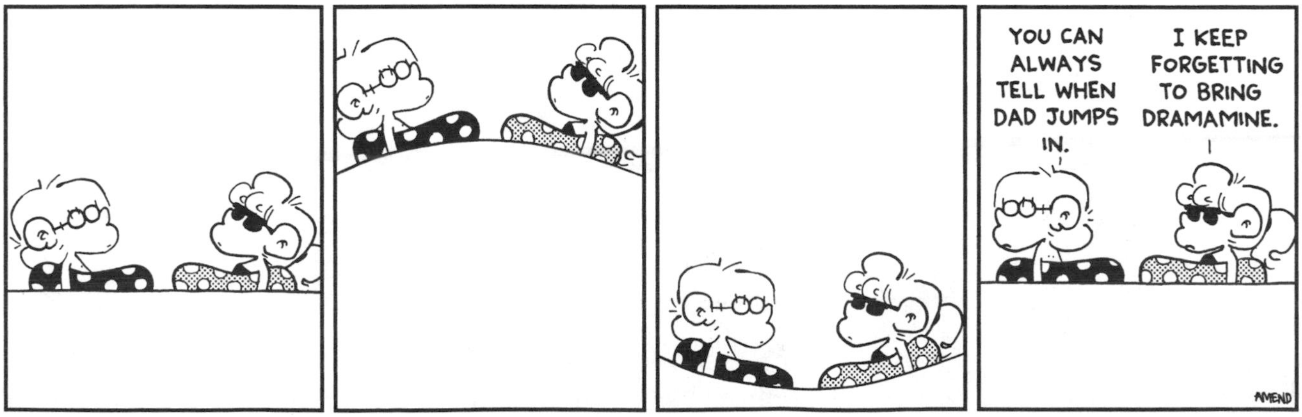
YOU CAN ALWAYS TELL WHEN DAD JUMPS IN.
I KEEP FORGETTING TO BRING DRAMAMINE.

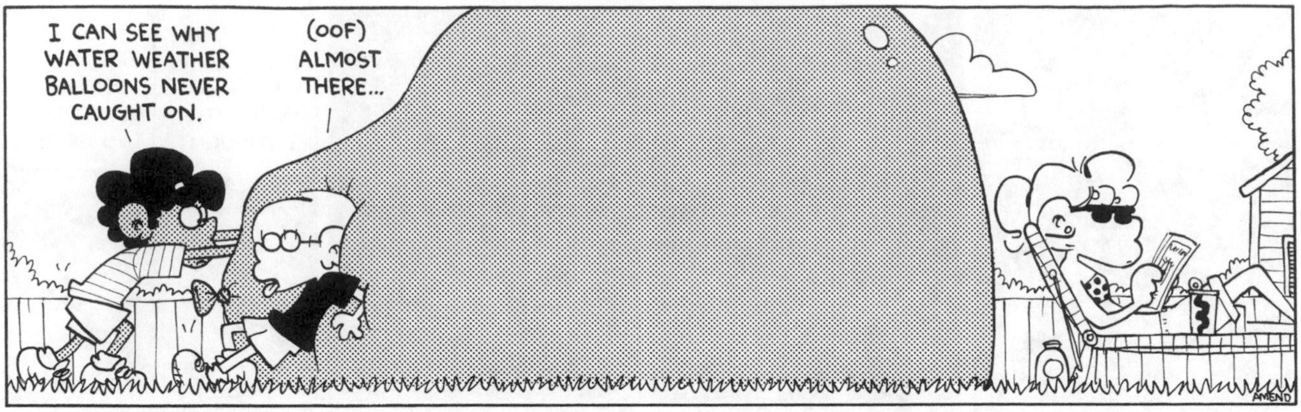
I CAN SEE WHY WATER WEATHER BALLOONS NEVER CAUGHT ON.
(OOF) ALMOST THERE...
AMEND

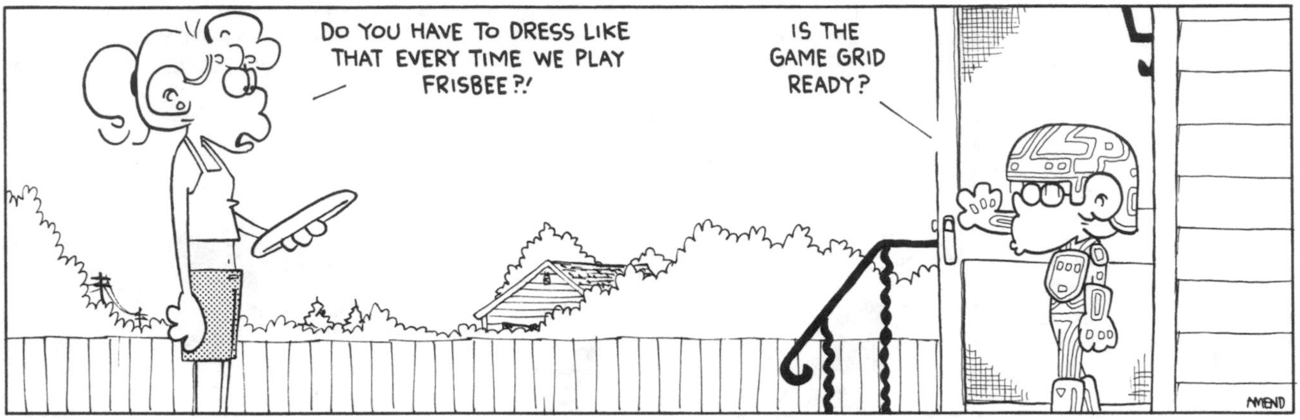
DO YOU HAVE TO DRESS LIKE THAT EVERY TIME WE PLAY FRISBEE?!
IS THE GAME GRID READY?
AMEND

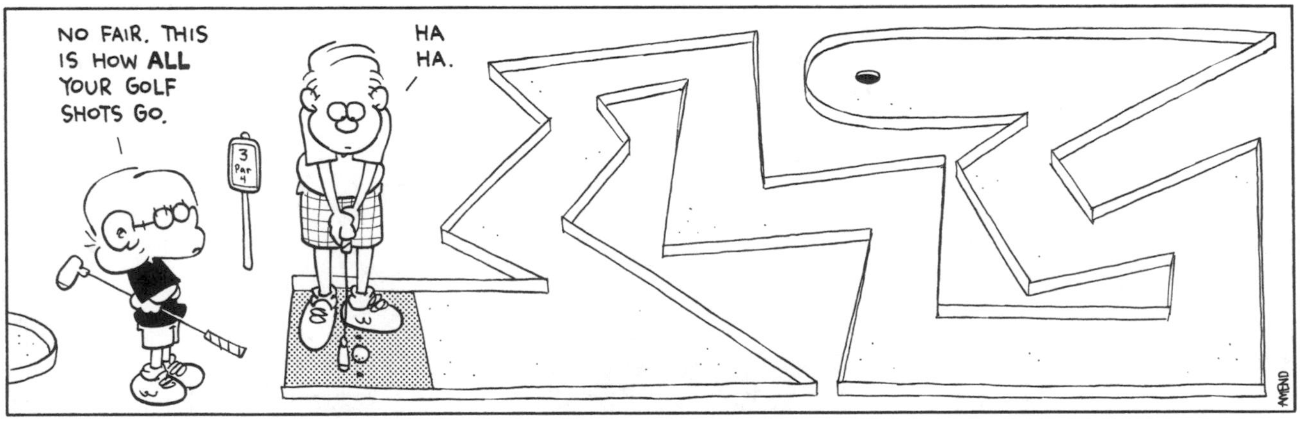
NO FAIR. THIS IS HOW ALL YOUR GOLF SHOTS GO.
HA HA.
3 Par 4
AMEND

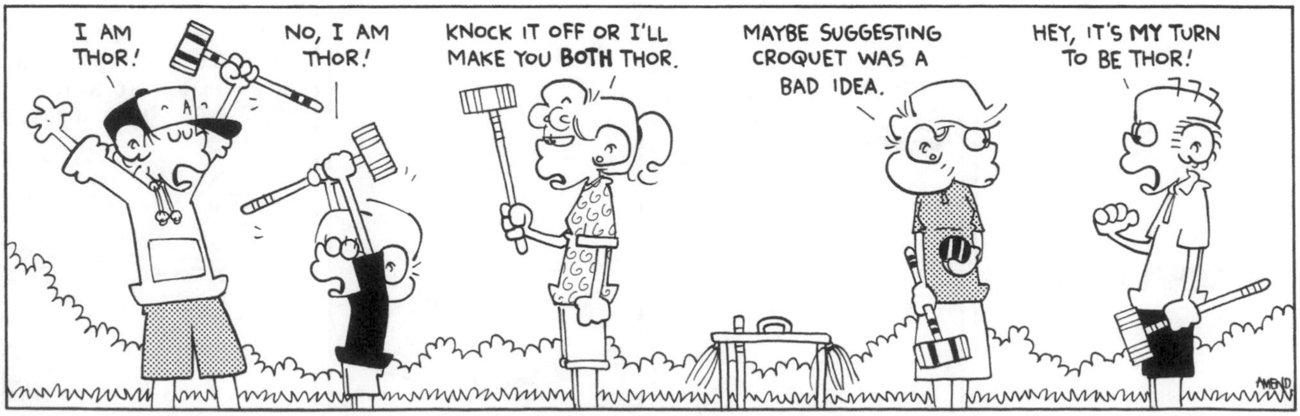
I AM THOR!
NO, I AM THOR!
KNOCK IT OFF OR I'LL MAKE YOU BOTH THOR.
MAYBE SUGGESTING CROQUET WAS A BAD IDEA.
HEY, IT'S MY TURN TO BE THOR!
AMEND

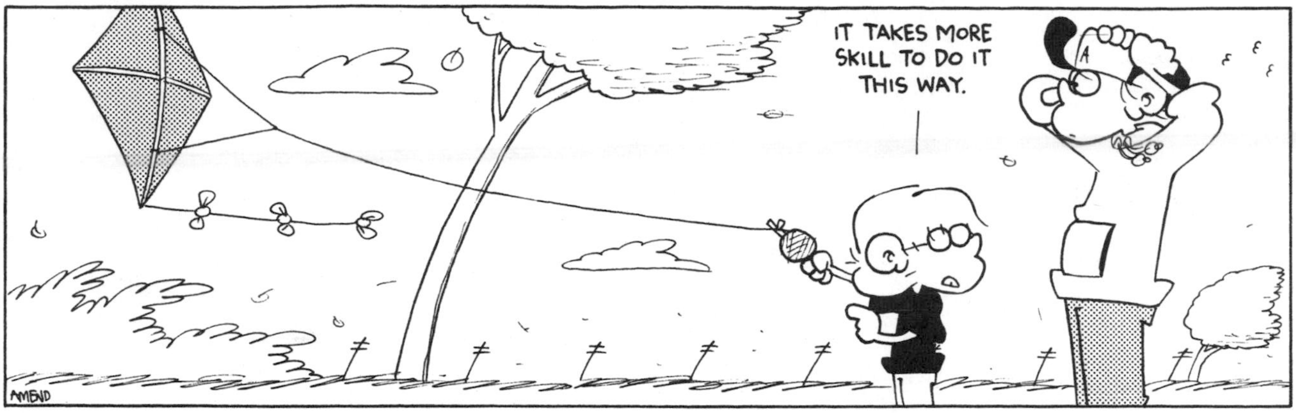
IT TAKES MORE SKILL TO DO IT THIS WAY.

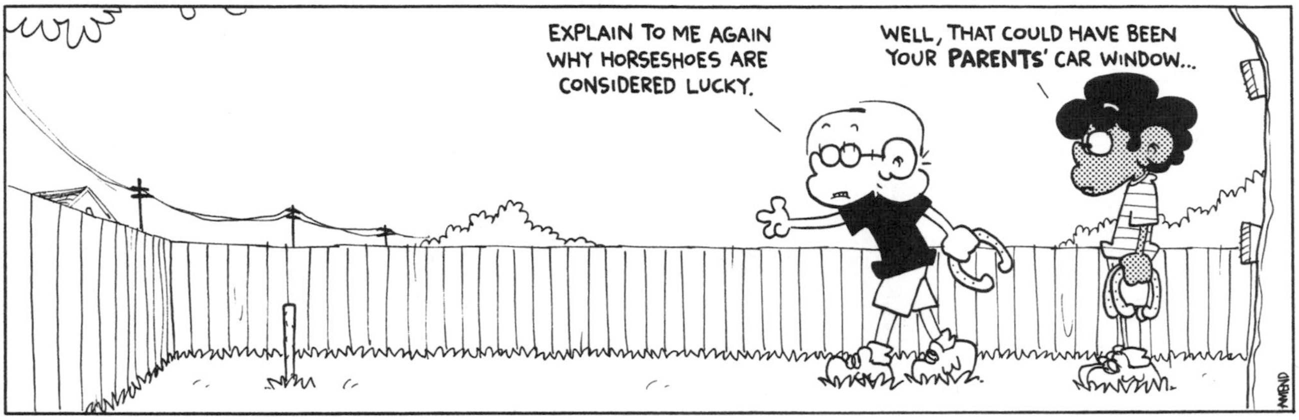
EXPLAIN TO ME AGAIN WHY HORSESHOES ARE CONSIDERED LUCKY.
WELL, THAT COULD HAVE BEEN YOUR **PARENTS'** CAR WINDOW...

One book not enough FoxTrot for you?

Visit foxtrot.com on the World Wide Web for the latest cartoons, news, merchandise, and more!

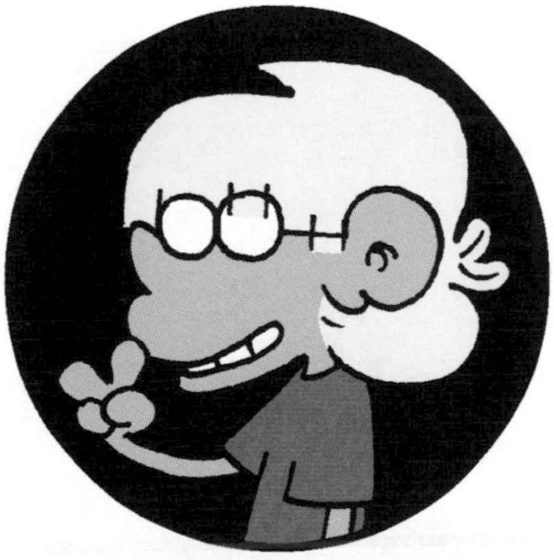

www.foxtrot.com